P9-AGG-076

COMMUNICATING WITH STRANGERS

AN APPROACH TO INTERCULTURAL COMMUNICATION

FOURTH EDITION

William B. Gudykunst

California State University, Fullerton

Young Yun Kim

University of Oklahoma

Mc
Graw
Hill

Boston   Burr Ridge, IL   Dubuque, IA   Madison, WI   New York
San Francisco   St. Louis   Bangkok   Bogotá   Caracas   Kuala Lumpur
Lisbon   London   Madrid   Mexico City   Milan   Montreal   New Delhi
Santiago   Seoul   Singapore   Sydney   Taipei   Toronto

McGraw-Hill Higher Education

A Division of The **McGraw-Hill** Companies

COMMUNICATING WITH STRANGERS:
An Approach to Intercultural Communication
Published by McGraw-Hill, a business unit of The McGraw-Hill Companies, Inc., 1221 Avenue of the Americas, New York, NY, 10020. Copyright © 2003, 1997, 1992, 1984, by The McGraw-Hill Companies, Inc. All rights reserved. No part of this publication may be reproduced or distributed in any form or by any means, or stored in a database or retrieval system, without the prior written consent of The McGraw-Hill Companies, Inc., including, but not limited to, in any network or other electronic storage or transmission, or broadcast for distance learning. Some ancillaries, including electronic and print components, may not be available to customers outside the United States.

This book is printed on acid-free paper.

4 5 6 7 8 9 0 QSR/QSR 0 9 8 7

ISBN-13: 978-0-07-232124-1
ISBN-10: 0-07-232124-5 (student edition)

Sponsoring editor: *Nannette Kauffman*
Developmental editor II: *Jennie Katsaros*
Senior marketing manager: *Daniel M. Loch*
Producer, Media technology: *Jessica Bodie*
Senior project manager: *Jean Hamilton*
Lead production supervisor: *Lori Koetters*
Freelance design coordinator: *Mary Kazak*
Supplement producer: *Nathan Perry*
Cover art: *"Wonderous Strange Adventure" by Jules Hiller (used with permission)*
Typeface: *10/12 Times Roman*
Compositor: *Shepherd Incorporated*
Printer: *Quebecor World Fairfield Inc.*

Library of Congress Cataloging-in-Publication Data
Gudykunst, William B.
    Communicating with strangers : an approach to intercultural communication / William B. Gudykunst and Young Yun Kim.—4th ed.
        p. cm.
    Includes bibliographical references (p.) and index.
    ISBN: 0-07-232124-5 (softcover: alk. paper)
    1. Intercultural communication. 2. Intergroup relations. I Kim, Young Yun. II. Title.
HM1211.G83 2003
303.48'2—dc21   2002070288

Copyright © 2003. Exclusive rights by The McGraw-Hill Companies, Inc. for manufacture and export. This book cannot be re-exported from the country to which it is sold by McGraw-Hill. The International Edition is not available in North America.

www.mhhe.com

ABOUT THE AUTHORS

WILLIAM B. GUDYKUNST is a professor of speech communication and a member of the Asian American Studies Program Council at California State University, Fullerton. He received his B.S. and M.A. degrees in sociology from Arizona State University. After completing his M.A., Bill spent three years in the U.S. Navy, serving in Yokosuka, Japan. He became interested in intercultural communication while working as an Intercultural Relations Specialist in the Navy. Bill helped develop the intercultural relations seminar in Japan, which was designed to help naval personnel and their families adjust to living in Japan. After his service in the Navy, Bill completed his Ph.D. at the University of Minnesota.

Bill's work focuses on developing a theory of interpersonal and intergroup effectiveness that can be applied to improving the quality of communication, and explaining cross-cultural differences in communication. Bill is the author of *Bridging Differences* and *Asian American Ethnicity and Communication,* as well as coauthor of *Culture and Interpersonal Communication, Bridging Japanese/North American Differences,* and *Ibunkakan Komyunikeishon: Beyondo Ansahtenti* (Intercultural Communication: Beyond Uncertainty), among others. He has edited or coedited numerous books, including *Communication in Japan and the United States, Handbook of International and Intercultural Communication, Theories of Intercultural Communication, Intergroup Communication,* and *Communication in Personal Relationships across Cultures,* among others. *Communicating with Strangers* and *Culture and Interpersonal Communication* received the "Outstanding Book" award from the International and Intercultural Division of the National Communication Association. Bill served as editor of the *International and Intercultural Communication Annual* (Vols. VII–IX) and *Communication Yearbook 24–26.* He is a Fellow of the International Communication Association.

YOUNG YUN KIM is a professor of communication at the University of Oklahoma, Norman, and formerly taught at Governors State University in Illinois. Young was born and raised in Seoul, South Korea, where she received her B.A. degree from Seoul National University. In 1970, she moved to the United States and completed her M.A. degree at the University of Hawaii in conjunction with the East-West Center. She continued her graduate study at Northwestern University in Evanston, Illinois, where she received her Ph.D. degree in 1976. Young teaches courses and directs doctoral theses in the area of intercultural and interethnic/interracial communication. Her research has been aimed primarily at explaining the role of communication in the cross-cultural adaptation process of immigrants, sojourners, and native-born ethnic minorities, as well as employees of multinational organizations. Her current research extends this research interest to examining the associative and dissociative interethnic communication behaviors among citizens of the United States. Young has published her work in journals such as *Communication Yearbook, Human Communication Research,* and *International Journal of Intercultural Relations.* She is the author or editor of a number of books, including *Interethnic Communication* (Sage, 1986), *Theories in Intercultural Communication* (Sage, 1988, with W. Gudykunst), *Communication and Cross-Cultural Adaptation* (Multilingual Matters, 1988), and *Becoming intercultural* (Sage, 2001). Young has served on the board of directors of the International Communication Association, the Speech Communication Association, and the International Academy for Intercultural Research. Currently, she is a member of the editorial boards of *Communication Research* and *International Journal of Intercultural Relations.*

CONTENTS

PREFACE

This book is designed to be a text for upper division undergraduate and graduate courses in intercultural or intergroup communication. We focus on theoretical issues more than authors of other texts on intercultural communication, especially in this edition (see below). We believe that to understand the process of intercultural communication and to improve our intercultural effectiveness, it is necessary to have the conceptual and theoretical tools to understand what is happening. Following Kurt Lewin, we believe that "there is nothing so practical as a good theory." Throughout the book, we apply the theories we have been developing over the years. Gudykunst's (1988, 1993, 1995) theory of effective interpersonal and intergroup communication provides the conceptual foundation for much of the book. Kim's (1988, 1995, 2001) theory of cross-cultural adaptation and intercultural growth is used to organize Chapters 13 and 14.

In writing the fourth edition, we have maintained the basic structure of the book from the previous three editions. We argue that to understand intercultural communication (e.g., communication between people from different cultures), we must understand cross-cultural differences in communication (e.g., how communication is similar or different across cultures). We take the position that intercultural communication is one "type" of intergroup communication. We discuss other "types" of intergroup communication (e.g., interethnic communication, communication between people who are disabled and people who are not disabled) but focus on intercultural communication. We also believe that the process of communication is the same no matter whether the people with whom we are communicating come from our own culture (or group) or from a different culture (or group). We use the metaphor of communicating with "strangers" to refer to this common underlying process.

Part One provides an introduction to the study of intercultural communication. We present our views of communication and culture in Chapter 1 and outline our approach to studying intercultural communication in Chapter 2. In Part Two, we examine the major influences on the process of intercultural communication. We discuss culture and how cultures vary in Chapter 3 and look at the sociocultural factors (e.g., our memberships in social groups, our social identities, such as our ethnic identities) that influence our communication in Chapter 4. We examine how psychocultural factors (e.g., stereotypes, prejudice, ethnocentrism) influence our communication in Chapter 5. We conclude Part Two by discussing environmental influences (e.g., situations, norms/rules, patterns of time) on our intercultural communication in Chapter 6.

Part Three is devoted to analyzing the exchange of messages between people from different groups. We examine how we interpret strangers' messages in Chapter 7. We discuss how we exchange verbal messages in Chapter 8 and nonverbal messages in Chapter 9.

In Part Four, we look at what is involved in communicating effectively with strangers in Chapter 10 and how we manage conflict and negotiate face (e.g., our public images) in Chapter 11. In Chapter 12, we look at how we develop friendships and romantic relationships with strangers. We explain the process of cross-cultural adaptation in Chapter 13 and the accompanying process of becoming intercultural in Chapter 14. In Chapter 15, we conclude the book by presenting some principles for building community with strangers.

We have thoroughly updated the third edition. We added research that has been conducted in the years that have passed since the third edition was published. We expanded our discussion of several areas of research (e.g., interethnic dating, ingroup biases, ethnic identities, prejudiced communication, face and facework, cultural and ethnic differences in conflict, changing our expectations for strangers' behavior). We also added new material in several chapters (e.g., cultural communication, stereotype content and processes, civic engagement, interaction involvement, politeness rules, apologies, self-ingroup relationships in collectivistic cultures, implicit theories of social groups, power in intergroup interactions).

The major change in this edition involves incorporating the principal theories of intercultural communication. The theories have been incorporated in the chapters throughout the book where appropriate. Chapter 4, for example, focuses on the social identities that influence our communication with strangers. We, therefore, added theories that focus on identity negotiation or identity management at the end of this chapter. We added theories of overt and covert prejudice in Chapter 5 on intergroup attitudes. Theories focusing on verbal messages (e.g., conversational constraint theory, communication accommodation theory) were incorporated in Chapter 8. The chapter on conflict (Chapter 11) was reorganized to examine managing conflict and negotiating face. We added face-negotiation theory to explain cross-cultural variability in these processes. We also added theories of intergroup conflict at the end of this chapter. We added a discussion of cultural communication theory at the end of Chapter 3 to present an alternative perspective to the one we use throughout the book. Other theories were incorporated where we discuss material most closely related to the theories.

We have not included all theories of intercultural communication, but we have included those theories that we believe have had major influences on research in the field. The vast majority of the theories included are compatible with each other. Many of the theories are different simply because they focus on different aspects of intercultural communication. This is especially true for cross-cultural theories. This edition of

Communicating with Strangers is the only text to incorporate the major theories in the field. The addition of the theories should increase the utility of the book, especially in courses for majors.

Several people have influenced our approach to the study of intercultural communication, and we want to take this opportunity to recognize them. Harry C. Triandis and Edward T. Hall are cited in virtually every chapter of the book. These two scholars have had a profound effect on our work. We also want to recognize the influence of Georg Simmel, whose concept of the stranger provides the foundation for our approach. Chuck Berger's work on uncertainty and Walter Stephan and Cookie Stephan's work on intergroup anxiety serve as intellectual roots of the approach we use throughout most of the book.

Before concluding, we want to express our gratitude to friends, students, and colleagues who contributed their time and expertise in reviewing various versions of the book. We cannot name all the people individually, but we want them to know that we appreciate their feedback. San Rao initially encouraged us to write the book, and Linda Fisher, our editor at Addison-Wesley for the first edition, was a constant source of support throughout the completion of the original version of the book. Hilary Jackson, our editor at McGraw-Hill for the second and third editions, encouraged us to improve the book and make it more useful to students. Nanette Kauffman and Jennie Katsaros, our editors for the fourth edition, coordinated our revision of the third edition. Peggy Henderson provided invaluable assistance in getting the third and fourth editions written.

Bill Gudykunst

Young Yun Kim

PART ONE

CONCEPTUAL FOUNDATIONS

On April 8, 1960, the world entered a new era. On that date, the first attempt was made to "communicate" with extraterrestrial life as part of Project Ozma organized by Frank Drake of the National Radio Astronomy Observatory in Green Bank, West Virginia. *Pioneer 10,* launched on March 3, 1972, included a six by nine-inch gold-plated aluminum plaque with a message for any extraterrestrial being coming across it. The plaque on *Pioneer 10* was designed by the astronomer Carl Sagan. The left side of the plaque contained a representation of the periods of pulsars to indicate the solar system of origin, while across the bottom the planets of the solar system were drawn with an indication that *Pioneer 10* originated on the third planet. The right side of the plaque contained drawings of unclothed male and female figures, the man having his right arm raised with the palm extending outward. Pictures of the plaque appeared in newspapers around the world when *Pioneer 10* was launched.

What does the plaque on *Pioneer 10* have to do with the study of intercultural communication? Think about it for a moment. Does the plaque have anything in common with your attempts to communicate with people from other cultures? The plaque illustrates what often happens when two people who do not have a common language try to communicate: They try to get their ideas across nonverbally. Reactions to the plaque when it appeared in newspapers around the world further illustrate what can happen when we use this method in our everyday encounters with people from other cultures. People in some cultures interpreted the man's gesture to be a universal gesture of friendliness, while people in other cultures interpreted it as one of hostility. We can only imagine how extraterrestrial beings will interpret the gesture; they might take it to mean that one arm of one of the sexes is permanently angled at the elbow while that of the other sex is not. The point is that gestures used by people in one culture often do not mean the same thing in another culture. Trying to communicate through nonverbal means, therefore, may lead to misunderstandings.

To minimize misunderstandings when we communicate with people from other cultures, we need to understand the process of intercultural communication. The importance of understanding this process is called to our attention by two former presidents of the United States:

> So let us not be blind to our differences, but let us direct our attention to our common interests and to the means by which those differences can be resolved. And if we cannot end now our differences, at least we can make the world safe for diversity.
>
> John F. Kennedy

> It is . . . in our interest—and the interest of other nations—that Americans have the opportunity to understand the histories, cultures and problems of others, so that we can understand their hopes, perceptions and aspirations. [These efforts] will contribute to our capacity as a people and a government to manage our foreign affairs with sensitivity, in an effective and responsible way.
>
> Jimmy Carter

These two former presidents imply that understanding people of other cultures and their patterns of communication is important not only to decrease misunderstandings but also to make the world a safer place in which to live.

Throughout the book we focus on the concepts necessary to understand people from other cultures, their patterns of communication, and our interactions with them. More specifically, our intent is to present a framework for understanding your encounters with people from other cultures and subcultures, for determining when misunderstandings occur, and for improving the effectiveness of your intercultural communication.

The purpose of Part One is to outline our perspective on communication in general and intercultural communication in particular. In Chapter 1, we specify the assumptions we make about the process of communication and define the two major terms—communication and culture—used in the book. Our approach to intercultural communication is presented in Chapter 2, where we examine the concept of the stranger and outline the model we use to organize the elements in the process of communication.

1

INTRODUCTION

Greetings. I am pleased to see that we are different.
May we together become greater than the sum of both of us.

Vulcan Greeting (*Star Trek*)

In the past most human beings were born, lived, and died within a limited geographical area, never encountering people of other races and/or cultural backgrounds. Such an existence, however, no longer prevails in the world. Even members of once isolated groups of people like the Tasadays in the Philippines now frequently have contact with members of other cultural groups. McLuhan (1962) characterizes today's world as a "global village" because of the rapid expansion of worldwide transportation and communication networks (e.g., airplanes, communication satellites, telephones, the Internet). It is now possible for any person from an industrialized country to communicate with any person in another industrialized country within minutes by phone, fax, and video conference and within hours face-to-face. In fact, when important or interesting events such as wars, presidential debates in the United States, major sporting events, and royal weddings in one country often are transmitted simultaneously to more than 100 different countries.

The expansion of worldwide communication networks, combined with increases in travel for pleasure or business and the international migration of refugees, heightens our awareness of the need for understanding other cultures and their people. The work of the Presidential Commission on Foreign Language and International Studies (1979) illustrates this increased awareness. In its final report to the president of the United States, the commission points out that

> nothing less is at issue than the nation's security. At a time when the resurgent forces of nationalism and of ethnic and linguistic consciousness so directly affect global realities, the United States requires far more reliable capacities to communicate with its allies, analyze the behavior of potential adversaries, and earn the trust and sympathies of the uncommitted. Yet there is a widening gap between these needs and the [U.S.] American competence to understand and deal successfully with other peoples in a world in a flux. (pp. 1–2)

The problems isolated by the presidential commission in 1979 are even more important today. The commission set forth a number of recommendations so that the people of the United States could understand and deal successfully with other peoples of the world, including increased foreign language instruction, more international educational exchanges, citizen education in international affairs, and increases in international training for business and government personnel. Central to most of the commission's recommendations is the need for increased awareness and understanding of communication between people from different cultures.

3

In a world of international interdependence, the ability to understand and communicate effectively with people from other cultures takes on extreme urgency. The need for intercultural understanding, however, does not begin or end with national boundaries. Within any nation a multitude of racial and ethnic groups exist, and their members interact daily. Legislation and legal rulings in the United States on affirmative action, school busing, and desegregation underscore the importance of nondiscriminatory contact between members of different groups. The importance of good intergroup relations also is apparent when current demographic trends are examined. It is projected, for example, that in the near future the workplace will change from a place dominated by European American (i.e., white) males to a place dominated by women, immigrants, and non-European American (i.e., nonwhite) ethnics (Hudson Institute, 1987). For work to be accomplished effectively in the multicultural/multiethnic organization, people of different groups need to be able to understand one another's patterns of communication.

It is recognized widely that one of the characteristics separating humans from other animals is our development of culture. The development of human culture is made possible through communication, and it is through communication that culture is transmitted from one generation to another. Culture and communication are intertwined so closely that Hall (1959) maintains that "culture is communication" and "communication is culture." In other words, we communicate the way we do because we are raised in a particular culture and learn its language, rules, and norms. Because we learn the languages, rules, and norms of our cultures by a very early age (between 5 and 10 years old), however, we generally are unaware of how culture influences our behavior in general and our communication in particular.

When we communicate with people from other cultures, we often are confronted with languages, rules, and norms different from our own. Confronting these differences can be a source of insight into the rules and norms of our own cultures, as well as being a source of frustration or gratification. Although the presence of cultural differences may suggest the need for accommodation in our communication, it cannot be taken automatically as either a barrier to or a facilitator of effective communication (Ellingsworth, 1977). Communication between people from different cultures can be as effective as communication between people from the same culture (Taylor & Simard, 1975). Stated in another way, communicating with people from other cultures may be either easier or more difficult than communicating with people from our own cultures.

One of the major factors influencing our effectiveness in communicating with people from other cultures is our ability to understand their cultures. It is impossible to understand the communication of people from other cultures if we are highly ethnocentric. Sumner (1940) characterizes ethnocentrism as the "view of things in which one's own group is the center of everything, and all others are scaled and rated with reference to it" (p. 27). Ethnocentrism leads us to see our own culture's ways of doing things as "right" and all others as "wrong." The tendency to make judgments according to our own cultural standards is natural, but it hinders our understanding of other cultures and the patterns of communication used in those cultures. Becoming more culturally relativistic, in contrast, can be conducive to understanding.

Cultural relativism suggests that the only way we can understand the behavior of others is in the context of their cultures. Herskovits (1973) says behaviors must be understood "relative to the cultural background out of which they arise" (p. 14). This is not to say we must never make value judgments of people in other cultures. Making them is often necessary. Postponing these value judgments, or recognizing their tentative nature, until adequate information is gathered and we understand the people from the other culture, however, greatly facilitates effective communication.

The purpose of this book is to provide the conceptual tools needed to understand culture, communication, how culture influences communication, and the process of communication between people from different cultures. Such knowledge is extremely important. In fact, it is necessary if we are to comprehend fully the daily events in today's multicultural world. The concepts discussed should help you understand better your communication with people from other cultures and international situations such as the holding of United States diplomats in Iran. Understanding the material presented also should help you not only to analyze your intercultural encounters in order to determine where misunderstandings occur but also to determine how these misunderstandings can be minimized in future interactions. Given this brief introduction, we will define what we mean when we use the terms communication, culture, and intercultural communication. In the next section, we outline the assumptions we make about the nature of communication. Following this, we examine the concept of culture and develop a working definition for intercultural communication.

CONCEPTUALIZING COMMUNICATION

Everyone communicates and has a preconceived notion of what communication is and how it takes place. Our purpose here is to specify our preconceived notions about the nature of communication. It is not necessary for you to agree with our conceptualization; however, while reading the remainder of the book, remember that we take the ideas expressed here for granted. Because we take these ideas for granted, we present them as assumptions.

Assumption 1: Communication is a Symbolic Activity

Communication involves the use of symbols. *Symbols* are things used to stand for, or represent, something else. Symbols are not limited to words; they also include nonverbal displays and other objects (e.g., the flag). Virtually anything can be a symbol—written words, spoken words, gestures, facial expressions, flags, and so forth. Symbols have referents, or things they symbolize. A red light at an intersection, for example, symbolizes "stop." Red lights may have other meanings in different contexts. The important thing to remember is that symbols are symbols only because a group of people agree to consider them as such. There is not a natural connection between symbols and their referents; the relationships are arbitrary and vary from culture to culture. Bram (1955) points out that

> the relationship between symbols and the "things" which they symbolize is not a self-evident or natural one. . . . Symbols derive their specific function from group consensus or social convention and have no effect whatever (outside their rather trivial physical characteristics) on any person not acquainted with such consensus or convention. (p. 2)

Symbols are symbols because a group of people have agreed on their common usage.

One of the defining characteristics of culture is the agreement among the people who share a culture on the general meaning of symbols. This does not imply, however, that all members of a culture share a common meaning for any given symbol. The meanings we attach to symbols are a function of our cultures, our ethnic groups, our families, and our unique individual experiences, to name only a few of the factors influencing meanings. Two people *never* attach exactly the same meaning to a specific symbol. Within a culture, nevertheless, there is sufficient agreement that people can communicate with relative clarity on most topics of communication.

It is the human ability to utilize symbols that makes possible the development of speech and language and the capacity to deal with relationships among people and objects in the absence of those people and objects. The meanings of symbols are learned through the process of socialization, the process of learning to be a member of our culture. Symbols may take on different meanings in different situations. In this respect, symbols differ from signs. Signs are concrete and fixed regardless of context (Dance, 1982). When we show a dog the palm of the hand, for example, it means "down" regardless of where we use this gesture.

Assumption 2: Communication Is a Process Involving the Transmitting and Interpreting of Messages

Since it is impossible to transmit electrical impulses directly from one person's brain to that of another person, it is necessary for us to put our ideas into codes that can be transmitted, either verbally or nonverbally. *Transmitting messages* refers to the process of putting our thoughts, feelings, emotions, or attitudes, for example, into a form recognizable by others. The symbols used may be written, verbal, nonverbal, mathematical, or musical, to cite only a few possibilities. We refer to the transmitted set of symbols as a message. *Interpreting messages* is the process of perceiving and making sense of incoming messages and stimuli from the environment.

The way we transmit and interpret messages is influenced by our background—our culture, our ethnicity, our family upbringing—and our unique individual experiences (including our experiences with others and the emotions we have felt). Since no two people have exactly the same background or individual experiences, no two people transmit or interpret messages in the same way.

Messages can be transmitted from one person to another, but *meanings cannot.* Since meanings are not determined solely by the message, the net result of any communication is a partial difference between the meanings held by the communicators. In other words, the meaning of the message one person transmits is never exactly the same as the meaning another person interprets. Fisher (1978) argues that "to say that meaning in communication is never totally the same for all communicators is not to say that communication is impossible or even difficult—only that it is imperfect" (p. 257).

Transmission and interpretation of messages are not static activities. We transmit and interpret messages at the same time. We interpret other people's messages at the same time we transmit messages to them. We may change what we are saying because of our interpretation of other people's messages while we are talking.

The fact that we transmit and interpret messages at the same time suggests that communication is a process. Berlo (1960) points out if we conceptualize communication as a *process,* "we view events and relationships as dynamic, on-going, ever-changing, continuous. . . . we also mean that it does not have a beginning, an end, a fixed sequence of events. It is not static, at rest. It is moving. The ingredients within a process interact: each affects all of the others" (p. 24). Viewing communication as a process, therefore, allows for recognition of its continuity, complexity, unrepeatability, and irreversibility.

Assumption 3: Communication Involves the Creation of Meaning

As indicated earlier, messages can be transmitted from one person to another but meanings cannot. One of the reasons we cannot transmit meanings is the ambiguity inherent in the language we speak. Ortega y Gasset (1957) points out that

> man [or woman] when he [or she] sets himself [or herself] to speak, does so because he [or she] believes that he [or she] will be able to say what he [or she] thinks. Now, this is an illusion. Language is not up to that. It says more or less, a part of what we think, and raises an impenetrable obstacle to the transmission of the rest. It serves quite well for mathematical statements and proofs. . . . But in proportion as conversation treats of more important, more human, more "real" subjects than these, its vagueness, clumsiness, and confusion steadily increases. Obedient to the inveterate prejudice that "talking leads to understanding," we speak and listen in such good faith that we end by misunderstanding one another far more than if we remained mute and set ourselves to divine each other. Nay, more: since our thought is in large measure dependent on our language. (p. 245)

We also cannot transmit meanings because the meanings we attach to messages are a transaction among the message itself (e.g., what is said and how it is said), the channel used (e.g., whether the message was spoken or written), the situation in which the message is transmitted (e.g., an office or a home), the people who transmit and interpret it, and the specific interaction that is taking place between the individuals.

The channel used to transmit a message influences how we interpret the message. A message transmitted face-to-face using the spoken word may be interpreted differently if it is said exactly the same way on a telephone answering machine. An order from our bosses written in memo form is interpreted differently than are the same words said in person with a pleasant tone of voice. Similarly, messages transmitted over computer-mediated networks may be expressed differently than messages in a handwritten letter or those transmitted face-to-face. Computer-mediated messages, for example, make it easier to express anger. To illustrate, one manager reports that "before [computers], if I was really angry, it took time to find the person and vent my anger. A lot of the times I cooled down. . . . Now, I can just hit a button and in a matter of 30 seconds, send hate mail to dozens of people" (Scott, 1993, p. A33).

The situation in which a message is transmitted also influences its interpretation. The same message transmitted in two different locations may be interpreted very differently. If we have friends who are physicians and they say "How are you?" we interpret the message one way at a party and another way in the physicians' offices.

The situation also influences the degree to which we must elaborate our messages in order to be understood. Sometimes we must use concrete language and complete sentences to be understood. At other times this type of elaboration is not necessary. In communicating with close friends in an informal situation, for example, we may use shorthand speech and slang. We would not, however, use the same speech patterns in our places of work when talking to our supervisors. At work we would use formal language.

The people involved in any particular encounter also influence the interpretation of the messages exchanged. If we know other people, we use our knowledge of them in interpreting their messages. If we do not know others, we use our stereotypes of their group memberships (our mental image of the groups) in interpreting their messages. The cultural, ethnic, social class, and age of the people involved influence how we interpret their messages.

Meanings also emerge out of the interaction that occurs. We interpret other people's messages in terms of the messages they have transmitted to us during the same encounter and in terms of the messages we have transmitted to them during the same encounter. If it appears that we are attaching different meanings to messages than are the people with whom we are communicating, we can negotiate a new meaning with them. Suppose we are having a conversation with a friend, for example, and we say something like, "My partner thinks that we should take a short trip over the weekend." The word partner is used to refer to a romantic partner. If the friend says, "I didn't know you had a business," it is clear that there is a misunderstanding, and the problem can be corrected by telling the friend that "partner" refers to a romantic partner.

To decrease our chance of misinterpreting other people's messages, we must be aware of how misinterpretations occur. Beck (1988) argues that misinterpretations occur because:

1. We can never know the state of mind—the attitudes, thoughts, and feelings—of other people.
2. We depend on [messages], which are frequently ambiguous, to inform us about the attitudes and wishes of other people.
3. We use our own coding system, which may be defective, to decipher these [messages].
4. Depending on our state of mind at a particular time, we may be biased in our method of interpreting other people's behavior. . . .
5. The degree to which we believe that we are correct in divining another person's motives and attitudes is not related to the actual accuracy of our belief. (p. 18)

Many of the ideas discussed throughout this book are designed to help you improve the accuracy of your interpretations and, in turn, improve the quality of your communication.

When we communicate, we present ourselves as we want others to see us and respond to how others present themselves to us. We modify how we see ourselves on the basis of the feedback we receive from others. If others consistently tell us we are incompetent, for example, we begin to see ourselves as incompetent. Through communication we can facilitate others' personal growth or destroy them. Gerbner (1978) refers to the latter possibility as "symbolic annihilation."

Assumption 4: Communication Takes Place at Varying Levels of Awareness

As we are socialized into our culture, we learn much of our behavior unconsciously. Learning to walk is a good illustration. No one told us how to walk. We just did it and, through trial and error, eventually mastered it. Much of our communication behavior was learned the same way. Because we learned much of it unconsciously, we usually are not aware of our behavior when we communicate.

A large amount of our social interaction occurs at very low levels of awareness (e.g., Abelson, 1976; Berger & Bradac, 1982; Langer, 1978, 1989). We behave with low levels of awareness in situations we consider "normal," or routine.

When our communication is routine, our communication is based on our implicit theories of communication. Our *implicit personal theories of communication* are our unconscious, taken-for-granted assumptions about communication. As human beings, we "construct theories about social reality. [Our] theories have all of the features of the formal theories constructed by scientists. They employ concepts and relationships derived from observation; they provide a structure through which social reality is observed; they enable [us] to make predictions" about how other people will communicate with us (Wegner & Vallacher, 1977, p. 21). We are not, however, highly aware of the theories we use to guide our behavior.

Since we are not aware that we are using implicit, unconscious theories to guide our behavior, we do not question our theories or think about how they can be modified. Not questioning our implicit theories leads us to assume that the predictions we make about other people's behavior (based on our implicit theories) are accurate. The predictions we make based on our implicit theories, however, are not always accurate. To be able to improve our accuracy in predicting other people's behavior, we must become aware of the implicit theories we use to guide our behavior and think about how they can be improved.

Our implicit theories tell us with whom we should communicate, when we should communicate with others, what we should communicate, how we should communicate with others, how we should present ourselves when we communicate, what effective communication is, and how to interpret other people's communication behavior. Because we learned our implicit personal theories of communication as we were growing up, they are based on the cultures in which we were raised, our ethnic backgrounds, our genders, our social classes, and the regions of the country in which we were raised, as well as on our unique individual experiences.

When we encounter new or novel situations, we become aware of our behavior (our behavior is enacted consciously). One difference to be expected between our communication with people from our own cultures and with people from other cultures, therefore, is the level of awareness we have of our behavior. We are more aware of our behavior with people who are from other cultures than we are with people from our own cultures. This is the case because interaction with people from other cultures is less routine and involves new and novel situations compared with interaction with people from our own cultures.

Assumption 5: Communicators Make Predictions about the Outcomes of Their Communication Behavior

Miller and Steinberg (1975) argue that "when people communicate, they make predictions about the effects, or outcomes, of their communication behaviors; that is, they choose among various communicative strategies on the basis of how the person receiving the message will respond" (p. 7). Our communication behaviors, including our predictions, are not always conscious. Miller and Steinberg suggest that our awareness of making predictions varies with the degree to which we are aware of alternative outcomes for the situations in which we find ourselves. The more aware we are of alternative outcomes, the more aware we are of making predictions. When our behavior is unconscious (outside of our awareness), generally we are not aware of making predictions. When we are conscious of our behavior, we are more aware of the predictions we make.

When we feel that others' behavior is predictable, we feel that there is rhythm to our interactions with them. We need to feel that there is a rhythm to our interactions with others to feel comfortable interacting with them (Turner, 1988). The rhythm we expect to take place varies with the context of our interaction. We expect one kind of predictability when we interact with a server in a restaurant and another kind when we are talking with a close friend. When other people's behavior is not predictable, we feel anxiety.

If we do not feel a part of the interaction taking place, we will have a difficult time seeing other people's behavior as predictable. Our cultural, ethnic, and gender identities provide us with implicit predictions about other people's behavior. The categories in which we place others (e.g., based on their culture, ethnicity, age) also provide us with implicit predictions of their behaviors. When we categorize others, our stereotypes of the groups (the traits we associate with the groups) in which we categorize them are activated. Our stereotypes provide predictions of other people's behavior, and our interactions will appear to have rhythm if other people conform to our stereotypes. If other people do not follow our stereotypes, our interaction with them will seem to lack rhythm.

Predictability tends to increase as relationships become more intimate (we have more predictability about friends than about acquaintances), but within a specific relationship predictability fluctuates over time. There is a dialectic between predictability and novelty. We need both predictability *and* novelty to maintain our relationships. Predictability is necessary to know how to expect other people to behave, but novelty is needed to keep our relationships interesting and to facilitate effective communication. When we are not conscious of our communication behavior, however, we may focus exclusively on our need for predictability and ignore our need for novelty.

Assumption 6: Intention Is Not a Necessary Condition for Communication

Intentions are instructions we give ourselves about how to communicate (Triandis, 1977). When we think about what we want to do in a particular situation (i.e., engage in cognitive activity), we form intentions. Intention, therefore, is a cognitive construct—it is part of our thought processes. We may not be able to accomplish our intentions, however. Our intention, for example, may be to be nonjudgmental in our interactions with others, but in actuality we may be very judgmental.

Our assumption is derived from Watzlawick, Beavin, and Jackson's (1967) first axiom of communication: "one cannot not communicate" (p. 51, emphasis deleted). The basis for this axiom is that any behavior, or the absence of any behavior, communicates something if there is someone in the environment to notice the behavior or its absence. In making this assumption, we are not contending that all behavior is communication; rather, communication occurs any time one person attributes meaning to his or her own or another person's behavior. Taking this view implies that it is not necessary for a person to transmit a message intentionally in order to communicate. Many intercultural misunderstandings, in fact, are due to the unintentional behavior of a person from one culture being perceived, interpreted, and reacted to by a person from another culture. In other words, behavior that was not meant to communicate was interpreted by another person and influenced the messages that person sent.

It is important to recognize that intentions are only one source of our communication behavior. Our communication behavior also can be based on two other sources: habits and emotions (Triandis, 1977). We engage in much of our communication behavior out of habit. We have learned scripts which we enact in particular situations. *Scripts* are predetermined courses of action we have learned. The greeting ritual is one example. The ritual for greeting others reduces the vast amount of uncertainty and anxiety present in initial interactions to manageable proportions and allows us to interact with others as though there were relatively little uncertainty or anxiety. The norms and rules for the ritual provide us with predictions about how others will respond in the situation. When someone deviates from a script or we enter a new situation, we cannot fall back on the rituals' implicit predictions. Under these circumstances, we have to reduce our uncertainty and anxiety actively before we can make accurate predictions and communicate effectively.

Our communication behavior also can be based on our affect (our feelings or emotions). We often react to others on a strictly emotional basis. If we feel we were criticized, for example, we may become defensive and strike out at others without thinking. We can, however, cognitively manage our emotional reactions. Our communication behavior can be based on any one of these three sources (i.e., habits/scripts, intentions, emotions) or some combination.

Assumption 7: Every Communication Message Has a Content Dimension and a Relationship Dimension

Watzlawick, Beavin, and Jackson (1967) argue that every communication message can be interpreted on two levels: what is said (the content level) and how it is said (the relationship level). The content level specifies the substance of the message, and the relationship level indicates how the substance is to be interpreted. The relationship dimension is "only rarely defined deliberately or with full awareness" (p. 52); it is, therefore, usually transmitted and interpreted unconsciously. The content level usually is transmitted verbally, while the relationship level tends to be transmitted nonverbally. A student, for example, can say "I want to discuss my grade" to a professor, but the tone of voice will tell the professor whether it is going to be a friendly discussion or a hostile encounter.

The way we communicate offers a definition of the relationship between us. The children's saying "Sticks and stones may break my bones, but words will never hurt me" is not accurate. The words we choose and the way we say them to others can and do hurt others and our relationships with them. As we show later, cultures vary with respect to the emphasis they place on these two levels.

Assumption 8: Communicators Impose Structure on Their Interactions

Watzlawick, Beavin, and Jackson's (1967) third axiom states that "the nature of a relationship is contingent upon the punctuation of the communicational sequences between the communicants" (p. 59, emphasis deleted). *Punctuation of the sequence of events* refers to the grouping of elements into a recognizable pattern, or the imposition of structure on the communication process. Without this grouping of elements, or imposition of structure, interaction would be uninterpretable. People not only impose a beginning and an ending on a sequence of events but also interpret a particular event as being a "cause" or an "effect" of their behavior. A husband, for example, may say he drinks (an effect) because his wife always works late (a cause). The wife, in contrast, may say she works late (an effect) because her husband drinks (a cause).

Every time we communicate, we impose structure on the process. Watzlawick et al. (1967) argue that "culturally, we share many conventions of punctuation which, while no more or less accurate than other views of the same events, serve to organize common and important interactional sequences" (p. 56). When communicating with people from our own cultures, we usually are safe in assuming that the structure we impose is roughly the same as the one they impose. When communicating with people from other cultures, however, we must determine how they impose structure on the process of communication if we are to interpret and predict their behavior accurately.

To summarize, the assumptions outlined above present a relatively clear picture of how we view communication. We elaborate on our conceptualization in the next chapter, but the above specification of our assumptions is sufficient to demonstrate what we mean by communication. To review, those aspects of our assumptions necessary for delimiting communication are as follows: (1) it is a symbolic activity, (2) it is a process, (3) it involves the transmitting and interpreting of messages, (4) it involves creating meaning, (5) it takes place at varying levels of conscious awareness, and (6) intention is not necessary for it to take place.

Uncertainty and Anxiety

There are many reasons why we communicate. We communicate to inform someone about something, to entertain another person, to change another person's attitudes or behavior, and to reinforce our view of ourselves, to name only a few of the possibilities. No matter what the reason is, we always experience some degree of uncertainty (a cognitive response, or a response involving our thoughts) and anxiety (an affective, or emotional, response). High levels of uncertainty and anxiety inhibit effective communication.

Interacting with people from other cultures and/or ethnic groups is a novel situation for most of us. Novel situations are characterized by high levels of uncertainty and anxiety. Herman and Schield (1960) point out that "the immediate psychological result of being in a new situation is lack of security. Ignorance of the potentialities inherent in the situation, of the means to reach a goal, and of the probable outcomes of an intended action causes insecurity" (p. 165). Attempts to deal with the ambiguity of new situations involve a pattern of information seeking (uncertainty reduction) and tension (anxiety) reduction (Ball-Rokeach, 1973).

Uncertainty refers to our inability to predict or explain others' behavior, feelings, attitudes, or values (Berger & Calabrese, 1975). When we reduce uncertainty about others and ourselves, understanding is possible. Understanding involves obtaining information, knowing, comprehending, and interpreting. Three levels of understanding can be differentiated: description, prediction, and explanation (Berger et al., 1976). Description involves specifying what is observed in terms of its physical attributes (i.e., drawing a picture in words). Prediction involves projecting what will happen in a particular situation, and explanation involves stating why something occurred.

We make predictions and create explanations all the time when we communicate. We rarely describe others' behavior, however. When we communicate with others, we typically interpret messages by attaching meaning directly to them. We do not stop to describe what we saw or heard before we interpret it. Rather, we interpret messages as we perceive them. The problem is that we base our interpretations on our life experiences, cultures, or ethnic group memberships. Since our life experiences differ from the other person's, our interpretations of that person's behavior may be incorrect. This often leads to misunderstandings.

Anxiety refers to the feeling of being uneasy, tense, worried, or apprehensive about what might happen. It is an affective (emotional) response, not a cognitive response like uncertainty. Uncertainty results from our inability to predict others' behavior, and "anxiety stems from the anticipation of negative consequences. People fear at least four types of negative consequences: psychological or behavioral consequences for the self, and negative evaluations by members of the outgroup and the ingroup" (Stephan & Stephan, 1985, p. 159).

Our ingroups are groups with which we identify that are important to us and for which we will make sacrifices (Triandis, 1988). If we define our religious group as important and identify with being members of our religion, for example, it is one of our ingroups. Other religious groups then become outgroups for us. We may, however, identify with many ingroups. When we interact with another person, we categorize or place that person into an ingroup or an outgroup. We experience more uncertainty and anxiety when we communicate with members of outgroups than we do when we communicate with members of ingroups.

There are many other factors that affect the amount of uncertainty and anxiety we experience in a particular situation. The degree to which we are familiar with the situation and know how to behave, the expectations we have for our own and others' behavior, and the degree to which we perceive ourselves to be similar to others, for example, influence our level of uncertainty and anxiety. Our ability to reduce our uncertainty and anxiety, in turn, influences the degree to which we can communicate effectively.

We do not mean to imply that we want to reduce our uncertainty and anxiety totally when we communicate with strangers. Low levels of uncertainty and anxiety are not functional. If anxiety is too low, we do not care enough to perform well. If uncertainty is too low, there is little "mystery" and we get bored. Moderate levels of uncertainty and anxiety are desirable for effective communication and adaptation to new environments (Gudykunst, 1995). We examine uncertainty and anxiety in more detail in Chapter 2.

CONCEPTUALIZING CULTURE

Culture is a term that means many different things to different people. Some writers discuss culture in terms that suggest it is the same as society, while others define it in such a way that they can talk about male and female cultures. To clarify our conceptualization of culture, we will take a brief digression into the more general study of social organization. Through an understanding of social organization we will generate a working definition for culture.

The Process of Social Organization

The study of social organization is concerned with the way in which human activity is coordinated or organized. Olsen (1978) contends that social life is "a process that is continually being created and recreated as individuals bring order and meaning to their collective social life" (p. 4). In other words, like communication, social life is a dynamic, ongoing process without a beginning or an end.

Social organization cannot come about unless some degree of "order" exists. Olsen (1978) differentiates three levels of ordering involved in social life: personal, social, and cultural. *Personal ordering* refers to the process that "gives coherence and stability to the various cognitive and affective psychological processes occurring within an individual" (p. 7). This level of ordering takes place within us as our minds bring together our feelings, attitudes, and needs into a coherent whole, which we call a personality.

For *social ordering* to exist, two or more individuals must interact with each other over time. Social interaction occurs whenever the behavior of one person influences another person's thoughts and/or behavior (Olsen, 1978). As individuals interact over time, ongoing social relationships are formed among them. When these patterns of behavior become stable, we can say social ordering takes place. Stated differently, social ordering "grows out of the interactions and relationships of individuals as these activities become patterned and recurrent through time" (Olsen, 1978, p. 7).

Obviously, different levels of social ordering occur. When two people interact for an extended period of time and their behavior becomes patterned, for example, one form of social ordering takes place (a friendship is formed). Similarly, when a man and a woman get married and have children and interact on a daily basis, their behavior becomes patterned and another type of social ordering occurs (a family). Furthermore, when people within some geographical area interact over time and their behavior becomes patterned, we again can say that social ordering develops (a society is "born"). If a group of people interact together over time and their behavior becomes patterned (i.e., social ordering has taken place), they develop shared agreements about how to interpret the world they inhabit. Stated differently, patterned and recurrent social interactions "give rise to shared sets of cultural ideas that symbolize, reflect and give meaning to the social order" (Olsen, 1978, p. 163).

Cultural ordering involves the development of a set of shared symbolic ideas associated with patterns of social ordering (Olsen, 1978). Any group that develops social ordering also displays cultural ordering. Cultural ordering is associated not only with large collectivities (such as nations) but also with smaller collectivities (such as ethnic groups and families) that interact on an ongoing basis. To the extent that collectivities are interrelated or overlap with each other, they share cultural ideas (Olsen, 1978).

A Working Definition for Culture

Olsen's (1978) analysis of the process of social organization specifies how cultural ordering emerges, but it does not define culture adequately. Over 100 definitions of culture have been proposed (e.g., see Krober & Kluckhohn, 1952). Culture can be seen as everything that is human-made (e.g., Herskovits, 1955) or as a system of shared meaning (e.g., Geertz, 1973), to name only two possible definitions. As indicated earlier, Hall (1959) argues that "culture is communication and communication is culture" (p. 159). Birdwhistell (1970) takes a slightly different position. He suggests that culture and communication are interconnected highly, but "as 'culture' the focus is on structure; as 'communication' it is on process" (p. 318).

We use Keesing's (1974) conceptualization of culture because it is compatible with the notion that we have implicit theories of communication:

> Culture, conceived as a system of competence shared in its broad design and deeper principles, and varying between individuals in its specificities, is then not all of what an individual knows and thinks and feels about his [or her] world. It is his [or her] theory of what his [or her] fellows know, believe, and mean, his [or her] theory of the code being followed, the game being played, in the society into which he [or she] was born. . . . It is this theory to which a native actor [or actress] refers in interpreting the unfamiliar or the ambiguous, in interacting with strangers (or supernaturals), and in other settings peripheral to the familiarity of mundane everyday life space; and with which he [or she] creates the stage on which the games of life are played. . . . But note that the actor's [or actress'] "theory" of his [or her] culture, like his [or her] theory of his [or her] language may be in large measure unconscious. Actors [or actresses] follow rules of which they are not consciously aware, and assume a world to be "out there" that they have in fact created with culturally shaped and shaded patterns of mind. We can recognize that not every individual shares precisely the same theory of the cultural code, that not every individual knows all the sectors of the culture . . . no one native actor [or actress] knows all the culture, and each has a variant version of the code. Culture in this view is ordered not simply as a collection of symbols fitted together by the analyst but as a system of knowledge, shaped and constrained by the way the human brain acquires, organizes, and processes information and creates "internal models of reality." (p. 89)

This conceptualization suggests that our cultures provide us with implicit theories of the "games being played" in our societies.

We use our theories of the games being played in interacting with the people we encounter. Our theories tell us how to communicate with others and how to interpret their behavior. We use our theories to interpret unfamiliar things we come across. We generally are not highly aware of the rules of the games being played, but we behave as though there were general agreement on the rules.

We learn our theories of the games being played and how to be members of our cultures from our parents, from our teachers in schools, from our religious institutions, from our peers, and from the mass media. Originally, we learn about our culture from our parents. Our parents begin to teach us the norms and communication rules that guide behavior in our cultures. Norms are guidelines for how we should behave or how we should not behave that have a basis in morality. Rules, in contrast, are guidelines for the ways we are expected to communicate. Rules are not based in morality (Olsen, 1978). Our parents do not explicitly tell us the norms and rules of our cultures. They do not, for example, tell us that when we meet someone for the first time, we should stick out our right hands and shake three times. Rather, they teach us the norms and rules by modeling how to behave and correcting us when we violate a norm or rule.

Once we are old enough to interact with other children, they reinforce the norms and rules we learned from our parents. We also learn additional norms and rules of our cultures from them. We learn, for example, how to be cooperative and how to compete with others from our peers. When we attend religious services or school, we learn other norms and rules of our cultures. The other way we learn about our cultures is through the mass media, especially television. Television teaches us many of the day-to-day norms of our cultures and provides us with views of reality. Television has become the medium through which most of us learn what others' expectations are for our behavior. It appears that the more television we watch, the more our views of reality overlap with those of others (Gerbner, Gross, Morgan, & Signorielli, 1980).

Members of a culture do not all share exactly the same view of their culture (Keesing, 1974). No one member of a culture knows all aspects of the culture, and all the members of a culture have a unique view of the culture. The theories that members of a culture share, however, overlap sufficiently so that the members can coordinate their behavior in everyday life. Olsen (1978) points out that

> as people communicate the meanings of their actions to each other and work out shared interpretations of activities and definitions of situations, they develop a common culture that is shared by all the participants. Shared culture in turn influences and guides—but does not fully determine—these people's collective activities by providing them with interpretations of social life, role expectations, common definitions of situations, and social norms. (p. 107)

Since we developed our individual implicit theories of communication while learning to be members of our cultures, there is overlap in the implicit personal theories of communication members of the same culture use to guide their communication.

Our cultures influence our behavior directly through the norms and rules we use to guide our behavior when we interact with others. Our cultures also indirectly affect our communication through the individual characteristics we learn when we are socialized into our cultures. To illustrate, as we are socialized into our cultures, we learn how we are expected to view ourselves (e.g., in the United States people learn to think of themselves as unique individuals). The way we view ourselves, in turn, influences

FIGURE 1.1
Cultural influences on communication.

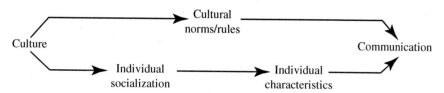

the way we communicate. Figure 1.1 provides a visual summary of how culture influences our communication. We discuss this model in detail in Chapter 3 when we focus on culture.

Our culture provides us with a system of knowledge that generally allows us to know how to communicate with other members of our cultures and how to interpret their behavior (Keesing, 1974). The term *culture* usually is reserved to refer to the systems of knowledge used by relatively large numbers of people (i.e., cultural ordering at the societal level). The boundaries between cultures usually, but not always, coincide with political, or national, boundaries between countries. To illustrate, we can speak of the culture of the United States, the Mexican culture, the Japanese culture, and so forth.

If the term *culture* is reserved for cultural ordering at the societal level, we need a term to use to refer to cultural ordering at lower levels of social ordering. The term traditionally used for this purpose is *subculture*. A *subculture,* therefore, involves a set of shared symbolic ideas held by a collectivity within a larger society. A subculture's set of cultural ideas generally is derived from the larger (societal) culture but differs in some respect. Although the term *subculture* often is used to refer to racial and/or ethnic groups, there obviously are other types of subcultures. We can, for example, talk about a student subculture, a Deaf subculture, a medical subculture (people who work in medicine), a lower-class subculture, a middle-class subculture, or a business subculture, to name only a few subcultures. Each of these groups shares many common cultural ideas with a larger culture but has some that are unique.

Before proceeding, it is necessary to point out that we believe that our cultures influence our communication and that our communication influences our cultures. We focus throughout the remainder of the book, however, on the influence of culture on communication. This influence is mostly out of our awareness. To communicate effectively with people from other cultures and/or ethnic groups, we must be aware of culture's influence on our communication.

DIFFERENTIATING TERMINOLOGY

Given the preceding conceptualizations of communication and culture, we are now ready to present a working definition for intercultural communication. Putting the two conceptualizations together, we stipulate that *intercultural communication is a transactional, symbolic process involving the attribution of meaning between people from different cultures.* It should be noted this definition does not suggest that communication must be effective in order to be labeled intercultural. When we use the term *intercultural communication,* we are not implying that the communication is either effective or ineffective. Effectiveness is a separate dimension, but to say that two people engaged in intercultural communication is not to say that they understood each other. (In Chapter 10 we examine intercultural communication effectiveness, which is defined as minimizing misunderstandings when people from different cultures communicate.)

Many terms are used to refer to related aspects of communication. So that there is no confusion concerning how we use these terms and how they are used in the intercultural literature, we must introduce these terms. If intercultural communication refers to communication between people from different cultures, then *intracultural* communication refers to communication between people from the same culture. It should be remembered that we reserve the term *culture* for cultural ordering at the societal level. If we examine communication between two Japanese *or* between two Germans, for example, we are looking at intracultural communication. If we observe communication *between* a Japanese *and* a German, in contrast, we are looking at intercultural communication.

It should be noted here that we see the underlying communication processes in intracultural and intercultural communication as being essentially the same. The two forms of communication are not different in kind, only in degree. Stated differently, the variables influencing intracultural and intercultural communication are the same, but some variables have more influence on our communication in one situation than in another. Our ethnocentric attitudes, for example, influence our intercultural communication more than our intracultural communication, but our ethnocentric attitudes also influence our intracultural communication. We differentiate between intracultural and intercultural only for the sake of clarity in communicating with you, not to suggest they are different types of communication.

Another term that needs to be clarified is cross-cultural. While this term often is used as a synonym for intercultural, the term *cross-cultural* traditionally implies a comparison of some phenomena across cultures. If we examine the use of self-disclosure in Japan *and* Germany, for example, we are making a cross-cultural comparison. If we look at how Japanese use self-disclosure when communicating *with* Germans and how Germans use self-disclosure when communicating *with* Japanese, in contrast, we are looking at intercultural communication.

If the term *culture* refers to societal cultures, then, as indicated earlier, a subculture is a subset of a culture having some different values, norms, and/or symbols that are not shared by all members of the larger culture. In other words, a subculture involves a set of ideas that arise from the larger culture but differ in some respects. With respect to our differentiation of terminology, the most important subcultures are races and ethnic groups. The labels *race* and *ethnic group* often are used interchangeably. This is incorrect. A *race* is a group of people who are biologically similar. An *ethnic group,* in contrast, is a group of people who share a common cultural heritage usually based on a common national origin or language. Both race and ethnic group are socially constructed categories (we discuss this idea in detail in Chapter 4). Jews, therefore, are an ethnic group, not a race. An ethnic group may be made up of many races, and, similarly, a race may consist of more than one ethnic group.

Even though the process of communication between people from different subcultures is essentially the same as the process of communication between people from different cultures, different terms often are used. The terms used to designate communication between people from different subcultures are not as clear as we would like, but at times it is useful to be able to differentiate the type of communication being discussed by using specific terms. We, therefore, stipulate that *interracial communication* refers to communication between people from different races and *interethnic communication* refers to communication between people from different ethnic groups. It is not that simple, however. One culture may include several races and/or ethnic groups, and one race or ethnic group may exist in different cultures. This leads to problems in labeling some forms of communication. If we look at communication between a white person from the United States and a black person from Ghana, for example, are we observing interracial communication or intercultural communication? The answer, obviously, is both. As another example, what if a Jew from the United States is communicating with a Jew from Israel? Such communication is both intraethnic and intercultural. Such situations lead to conceptual confusion when we try to apply these terms.

Since the underlying processes in intracultural, intercultural, interracial, and interethnic communication are essentially the same and there is confusion about when some of the terms are applicable, we need a way to refer to the common underlying process without differentiating among the different "types" of communication. The term intercultural communication is the most general; however, it is not adequate because it has specific connotations. The title of this book, *Communicating with Strangers,* hints at our solution to this problem. Anytime we communicate with people who are different and unknown and those people are in an environment unfamiliar to them, we are communicating with strangers. The people generally viewed as the most unknown and unfamiliar are those from different societal cultures, but people from different races or ethnic groups are also unknown and unfamiliar. In addition, people from our own culture can be unknown and unfamiliar in the same sense; for example, a new groom approaching his bride's family for the first time is a stranger, according to our use of the term. In Chapter 2 we elaborate on our conceptualization of strangers; for now it is sufficient to say that when we talk about communicating with strangers, we are referring to the underlying process shared in common by intracultural, intercultural, intraracial, interracial, intraethnic, and interethnic communication.

PLAN FOR THE BOOK

In the next chapter, we elaborate on our conceptualization of strangers and give an overview of the process of communicating with strangers. Also in Chapter 2, we present a model of communication used to organize the material covered in Part Two and Part Three of the book.

In Part Two (Chapters 3 to 6) we examine the conceptual filters influencing our communication with strangers. The strategy employed in this part is to introduce the relevant concepts, examine how they vary across cultures, and apply them where feasible to our communication with strangers. Specifically, in Chapter 3 we examine the cultural influences on our communication with strangers. Chapter 4 focuses on the sociocultural influences on our communication with strangers, including our memberships in social groups and our social identities. In Chapter 5 we look at social cognitive factors that create expectations when we communicate with strangers, our stereotypes and intergroup attitudes (e.g., ethnocentrism and prejudice)—the psychocultural influences. Chapter 6, the final chapter in Part Two, focuses on the environmental influences on our communication with strangers, including climate, geography, architecture, the situation, privacy regulation, and temporality.

In Part Three (Chapters 7 to 9), we look at the transmitting and interpreting processes. Our strategy in this part is to introduce the concepts, to examine their variation across cultures, and to apply them to our communication with strangers. We begin by examining cultural variations in interpreting, focusing on perception, attributional processes, cognitive styles, and patterns of thought in Chapter 7. In Chapter 8, we look at cultural variations in verbal behavior, including language and patterns of thought. Cultural variations in nonverbal behaviors are examined in Chapter 9.

The final part of the book, Part Four (Chapters 10 to 15), considers selected aspects of intercultural interaction. The issues of intercultural communication effectiveness and perceived communication competence are discussed in Chapter 10. In Chapter 11, managing conflict and negotiating face (our public images) are examined. Chapter 12 focuses on relationships between people from different subcultures or cultures, including friendships and marital relationships. In Chapter 13, we examine strangers' adaptation to new cultural environments. We examine both short-term adjustment and long-term acculturation of strangers in that chapter. Chapter 14 contains a discussion of the process of becoming intercultural, which is one outcome that occurs as a result of our communication with strangers. We conclude in Chapter 15 by discussing how cultural and ethnic differences can be used as resources in building community.

SUMMARY

The purpose of this chapter was to introduce the two major concepts—communication and culture—used throughout the remainder of this book. In light of the eight assumptions we make about the nature of communication, we stipulate that communication is a symbolic process involving the attribution of meaning. We reserve the term *culture* for the cultural ordering process associated with the societal level of social ordering. Intercultural communication, therefore, is stipulated to be communication between people from different societal cultures.

We take the position that the underlying process of communication between people from different cultures or subcultures is the same as the underlying process of communication between people from the same culture or subculture. Given the similarity of the underlying process and the confusion of existing terminology, we argue what is needed is a way to refer to the underlying process that all types of communication (i.e., intracultural, interracial, interethnic, and intercultural) have in common. Since none of the present terms are adequate, we introduce our notion of communicating with strangers. By communicating with strangers we mean communicating with people who are unknown and unfamiliar, including people from another culture and people from our own cultures or subcultures who are in an environment new to them.

STUDY QUESTIONS

1. Why do different people attach different meanings to symbols?
2. What factors influence the meanings we attach to messages?
3. Why can messages be transmitted from one person to another, while meanings cannot?
4. How do our implicit theories of communication influence the way we communicate?
5. How does predictability provide rhythm to our interactions?
6. Why are intentions not necessary for communication to take place?
7. What is the difference between the content and relationship dimensions of messages?
8. How do we impose structure on our communication?
9. Why are uncertainty and anxiety important aspects of communication?
10. What is meant by saying that "culture is our theory of the game being played"?
11. How do cross-cultural and intercultural communication differ?

SUGGESTED READINGS

Fisher, B. A. (1978). *Perspectives on human communication.* New York: Macmillan.

Gudykunst, W. B., & Mody, B. (Eds.). (2001). *Handbook of international and intercultural communication.* Thousand Oaks, CA: Sage.

Olsen, M. (1978). *The process of social organization* (2nd ed.). New York: Holt, Rinehart, and Winston.

Triandis, H. C. (1994). *Culture and social behavior.* New York: McGraw-Hill.

Watzlawick, P., Beavin, J., & Jackson, D. (1967). *The pragmatics of human communication.* New York: Norton.

2

AN APPROACH TO THE
STUDY OF INTERCULTURAL
COMMUNICATION

See at a distance an undesirable person;
See close at hand a desirable person;
Come closer to the undesirable person;
Move away from the desirable person.
Coming close and moving apart,
how interesting life is.

Gensho Ogura

Cultural variability in people's backgrounds influences their communication behavior. This cultural variability in communication leads many scholars studying intercultural communication to view it as a unique form of communication, differing in kind from other forms of communication (e.g., intracultural communication, communication between people from the same culture). This point of view, however, is not accepted widely. Sarbaugh (1979) points out that

> there appears to be a temptation among scholars and practitioners of communication to approach intercultural communication as though it were a different process than intracultural communication. As one begins to identify the variables that operate in the communication being studied, however, it becomes apparent that they are the same for both intracultural and intercultural settings. (p. 5)

We agree with Sarbaugh. The variables are the same, and the underlying communication processes also are the same.

We believe that any approach to the study of intercultural communication must be consistent with the study of intracultural communication. In this chapter, and in the remainder of this book, we present a perspective for the study of communication that is useful not only for understanding our communication with people from other cultures or subcultures but also for understanding our communication with people from our own cultures or subcultures. We begin by looking at the linking concept in our view of communication, the concept of the stranger.

THE CONCEPT OF THE STRANGER

When we are confronted with cultural differences (and other forms of group differences, such as gender, ethnic, or class differences), we tend to view people from other cultures (or groups) as strangers. The term *stranger* is somewhat ambiguous in that it often is used to refer to aliens, intruders, foreigners, outsiders, newcomers, and immigrants, as well as any person who is unknown and unfamiliar. Despite this ambiguity, "the concept of the stranger remains one of the most powerful sociological tools for analyzing social processes of individuals and groups confronting new social orders" (Shack, 1979, p. 2).

Simmel (1950/1908) views strangers as possessing the contradictory qualities of being both near and far at the same time:

> The unity of nearness and remoteness in every human relation is organized, in the phenomenon of the stranger, in a way which may be most briefly formulated by saying that in the relationship to him [or her], distance means that he [or she], who is also far, is actually near. . . . The stranger . . . is an element of the group itself. His [or her] position as a full-fledged member involves being both outside it and confronting it. (p. 402)

Strangers represent the idea of nearness because they are physically close and the idea of remoteness because they have different values and ways of doing things. Strangers are physically present and participating in a situation and, at the same time, are outside the situation because they are not members of the ingroup.

Wood's (1934) view of strangers is broader than Simmel's. She adds a new dimension to describing strangers meeting for the first time:

> We shall describe the stranger as one who has come into face-to-face contact with the group for the first time. . . . For us the stranger may be, as with Simmel, a potential wanderer who comes today and goes tomorrow, or he [or she] may come today and remain with us permanently. The condition of being a stranger is not . . . dependent upon the future duration of the contact, but it is determined by the fact that it was the first face-to-face meeting of individuals who have not known one another before. (pp. 43–44)

Wood, therefore, sees strangers as newly arrived outsiders.

Like Wood, Schuetz (1944) takes a broader view of the concept of the stranger than Simmel. For Schuetz, the term *stranger* means "an adult individual . . . who tries to be permanently accepted or at least partially tolerated by the group which he [or she] approaches" (p. 499). This conceptualization includes not only the obvious cases of immigrants and sojourners to other cultures but also people trying to join a closed club, grooms attempting to be accepted by the brides' families, recruits entering the army, or any person coming into a new and unfamiliar group. Schuetz argues that strangers do not understand the social world inhabited by the members of the group they approach. Parrillo (1980) succinctly summarizes Schuetz's perspective:

> Because this is a shared world, it is an intersubjective one. For the native, then, every social situation is a coming together not only of roles and identities, but also of shared realities— the intersubjective structure of consciousness. What is taken for granted by the native is problematic for the stranger. In a familiar world, people live through the day by responding to daily routine without questioning or reflection. To strangers, however, every situation is new and is therefore experienced as a crisis. (p. 3)

One of the defining characteristics of this view is that strangers may perceive their interactions in their new surroundings as a series of crises.

Herman and Schield (1960) take a similar position when they argue that the major problem strangers face in their new surroundings is "lack of security." Strangers do not have the knowledge necessary to fully understand their new environment or the communication of the people who live in it. Further, members of the host group do not possess information regarding individual strangers, even though they may have some information about the groups or cultures from which the strangers come. Since we do not have information regarding individual strangers, our initial impression of them must, therefore, be an abstract or categoric one (i.e., a stereotypic one). Strangers are classified on the basis of whatever information we can obtain. If the only information we have is their cultures, we base our initial impression on this information. If we have additional information (their ethnicities, genders, classes), we use that as well.

Strangers, as we conceive of them, are people who are members of different groups and are unknown to us. It should be obvious that strangerhood is a figure-ground phenomenon—a stranger's status is always defined in relation to a host, a native, or some existing group. A person from the United States visiting another country and a person from another country visiting the United States are both strangers. A European American teacher in a predominantly African American school, a Native American working in a predominantly European American organization, a Vietnamese refugee in the United States, a new bride visiting the groom's family, and a Chicano or Chicana moving into a predominantly European American neighborhood are all examples of strangers. In general, we include anyone entering a relatively unknown or unfamiliar environment under the rubric of *stranger*. This conceptualization, therefore, subsumes Simmel's, Wood's, and Schuetz's views of strangers.

Obviously, not everyone we meet for the first time is truly unknown and unfamiliar. Sometimes we are familiar with or know something about people we meet for the first time. Cohen (1972) argues that we can say our social interactions, not just our interactions with people we meet for the first time, vary with respect to the degree of strangeness and/or familiarity present in the interaction. Our interactions with close friends and relatives involve a high degree of familiarity, but our interactions with acquaintances and coworkers involve less familiarity and more strangeness. When we meet people for the first time, there may be any degree of strangeness and/or familiarity. When we meet a close friend of our best friend for the first time, for example, we may be somewhat familiar with that person already because of what our close friend has told us about the person. When we meet a person from another subculture of our cultures (e.g., a person from another ethnic group), in contrast, our interaction with that person usually involves more strangeness than familiarity. Because those people do not share the same culture, our interactions with people from other cultures often involve the highest degree of strangeness and the lowest degree of familiarity.

Our use of the term *stranger* throughout this book refers to those relationships where there is a relatively high degree of strangeness and a relatively low degree of familiarity. Since our interactions with people from other cultures tend to involve the highest degree of strangeness and the lowest degree of familiarity, we focus on these interactions, but we also examine other interactions involving a relatively high degree of strangeness (e.g., those with members of different ethnic groups, social classes, ages).

As indicated earlier, strangerhood is a figure-ground phenomenon. When members of other groups approach our groups in our environments, they are the strangers. When we approach other groups in their environments, we are the strangers. Harman (1987) points out that "in the dominant mode of social organization in western society—the metropolis—the stranger is not the exception but the rule . . . strangeness is no longer a temporary condition to be overcome, but a way of life" (p. 44). She contends that we are all strangers trying to become members of different groups or maintain our group memberships. Harman argues that "the defining characteristics of the modern stranger are cultural fluency and membership orientation. The expert navigator of the cultural world is one who may 'fit in' anywhere by being acutely aware of the cultural nuances" (p. 159). Kristeva (1991) also suggests that when we see others as strangers, we come to recognize the strangeness in ourselves; "By recognizing *our* uncanny strangeness we shall neither suffer from it nor enjoy it from the outside. The [stranger] is within me, hence we are all [strangers]" (p. 192).

In looking at the general process of communication with strangers, we are able to overcome one of the major conceptual problems of many analyses of intercultural communication: drawing artificial distinctions among intracultural, intercultural, interracial, and interethnic communication. Some variables may take on more importance in one situation than in another (e.g., our ethnic prejudices may be more important in interethnic encounters than in intraethnic encounters), but each of the situations is influenced by the same variables (e.g., our prejudices also influence our intraethnic communication, but they may be other prejudices, for example, sexism). If the variables influencing each situation and the underlying process of communication are the same, it does not make sense to draw artificial distinctions among them. By using the stranger as a linking concept, we can examine general processes, communicating with strangers, which subsume intracultural, intercultural, interracial, and interethnic communication into one general framework. Before moving on, however, it is worth reiterating some of the qualities of the stranger concept that help us understand our communication with people from different groups.

Levine (1979) points out that it is the dialectic between closeness and remoteness

> that makes the position of strangers socially problematic in all times and places. When those who would be close, in any sense of the term, are actually close, and those who should be distant are distant, everyone is "in his [or her] place." When those who should be distant are close, however, the inevitable result is a degree of tension and anxiety which necessitates some special kind of response. (p. 29)

Levine goes on to argue that

> group members derive security from relating in familiar ways to fellow group members and from maintaining their distance from nonmembers through established insulating mechanisms. In situations where an outsider comes into the social space normally occupied by group members only, one can presume an initial response of anxiety and at least latent antagonism. (p. 30)

As we indicated in Chapter 1, reducing anxiety is one of the major functions of communication when we interact with strangers. The anxiety we experience when interacting with strangers is a critical factor influencing our communication and one of the factors that differentiate communication with strangers from communication with people who are familiar. We discuss this concept in more detail later in this chapter.

Prior to presenting our organizing model of communication, we overview the process of communicating with strangers. Our focus in the next section is on differentiating how communication with strangers (i.e., intergroup communication) differs from communication with people who are familiar (i.e., interpersonal communication).

INTERGROUP AND INTERPERSONAL BEHAVIOR

The communication processes underlying interpersonal and intergroup communication are the same. Different factors, nevertheless, are given different weights in the two types of communication. In this section, we present two different but complementary ways of differentiating interpersonal and intergroup behavior.

Types of Data Used in Making Predictions

Miller and Steinberg (1975) argue that we use three types of data when we make predictions about other people's behavior. The first type of data we use is *cultural.* The people in any culture generally behave in a regular fashion because of their cultural norms, rules, and values. It is this regularity that allows us to make predictions on the basis of cultural data. Miller and Sunnafrank (1982) point out that

> knowledge about another person's culture—its language, dominant values, beliefs, and prevailing ideology—often permits predictions of the person's probable responses to certain messages. . . . Upon first encountering a stranger, cultural information provides the only grounds for communicative predictions. This fact explains the uneasiness and perceived lack of control most people experience when thrust into an alien culture: they not only lack information about the individuals with whom they must communicate, they are bereft of information concerning shared cultural norms and values. (pp. 226–227)

Cultural data are used to predict the behavior of people from our own cultures and that of people from other cultures.

Two major factors influence the accuracy of our predictions when we use cultural data. First, the more experiences at the cultural level we have, the better our predictive accuracy is. When we are confronting people from our own cultures, the experiences to which we refer are in our cultures. When we are communicating with strangers, in contrast, our accuracy depends on our experiences with their cultures. If we know little or nothing about strangers' cultures, our predictions will be more inaccurate than they are if we know a lot about their cultures. Second, errors in predictions are made either because we are not aware of the strangers' cultural experiences or because we try to predict the behavior of strangers on the basis of cultural experiences different from the ones they have had, for example, when we make ethnocentric predictions on the basis of our own cultural experiences (Miller & Steinberg, 1975).

The second type of data used in making predictions is sociological. *Sociological predictions* are based on strangers' memberships in or aspirations to particular social groups. Miller and Sunnafrank (1982) argue that "knowledge of an individual's membership groups, as well as the reference groups to which he or she aspires, permits numerous predictions about responses to various messages" (p. 227). Membership in social groups may be voluntary, or strangers may be classified as members of groups because of certain characteristics they possess. Our predictions at the sociological level, for example, include those based on strangers' memberships in political or other social groups, the roles they fill, their genders, or their ethnicities. Miller and Sunnafrank contend that sociological-level data are the principal kind used to predict the behavior of people from the same culture. The major error in making predictions using sociological level data stems from the fact that strangers are members of many groups, and when we communicate with strangers, it is not always possible to be sure which group's norms and values are influencing their behavior (Miller & Steinberg, 1975).

The final type of data used in making predictions about the outcomes of our communication behavior is psychological. *Psychological predictions* are based on the specific strangers with whom we are communicating. When using this type of data, we are concerned with how these strangers are different from and similar to other members of their cultures and the groups to which they belong. When predictions are based on psychological data, "each participant relates to the other in terms of what sets the other apart from most people. They take into consideration each other's individual differences in terms of the subject and the occasion" (Dance & Larson, 1972, p. 56).

It is important to keep in mind that our predictions rarely are made using only one type of data. Once we have some psychological information about strangers with whom we are communicating, we use this information and combine it with our cultural and sociological data to make predictions about their behavior. Most of our predictions are some combination of the three levels of data, but one level of data tends to predominate.

For the purpose of the present analysis, we modify the labels for the three levels of data used in making predictions. Since all three levels are highly interrelated, we use labels reflecting the interrelations: *cultural, sociocultural,* and *psychocultural.* Our modification of the last two labels is intended only to emphasize that the three levels of data are interrelated, not to reflect a disagreement with Miller and Steinberg (1975).

Our Identities Influence Our Behavior

We think about ourselves differently in different situations. The different ways we think about ourselves are our *identities.* In any particular situation, we may or may not be conscious of the identities influencing our behavior. Even though we may not be aware of the identities influencing our behavior, we act as a though there were a clear identity guiding our behavior (R. H. Turner, 1987).

Our identities can be grouped under three broad categories: human, social, and personal (J. C. Turner, 1987). Our *human identities* involve those views of ourselves that we believe we share with all other humans. It is important to recognize that "people and their cultures perish in isolation, but they are born or reborn in contact with other men and women, with men and women of another culture, another creed, another race. If we do not recognize our humanity in others, we shall not recognize it in ourselves" (Fuentes, 1992, back cover). To understand our human identities, we have to look for those things we have in common with all other humans.

Our *social identities* involve those views of ourselves that we assume we share with other members of our ingroups. Ingroups are "groups of people about whose welfare [we are] concerned, with whom [we are] willing to cooperate without demanding equitable returns, and separation from whom leads to discomfort or even pain" (Triandis, 1988, p. 75). Our social identities may be based on the roles we play, such as student, professor, or parent; the demographic categories in which we are categorized, such as our nationality, ethnicity, gender, or age; and our membership in formal/informal organizations, such as a political party, organization, or social club. Social identities are discussed in detail in Chapter 4.

Our *personal identities* involve those views of ourselves that differentiate us from other members of our ingroups—those characteristics that define us as unique individuals. Our personality characteristics, for example, are part of our personal identities. Our personal identities may involve viewing ourselves as intelligent, attractive, caring, and so forth.

Our different identities influence our behavior in different situations. Tajfel's (1978) distinction between intergroup and interpersonal behavior is based on which identity is guiding our behavior:

> These differences can be conceived as lying on a continuum, one extreme of which can be described as being "purely" interpersonal and the other as being "purely" intergroup. What is meant by "purely" interpersonal is any social encounter between two or more people in which all interaction that takes place is determined by the personal relationship between the individuals and by their respective individual characteristics [e.g., personal identities generate behavior]. The "intergroup" extreme is that in which all of the behavior of two or more individuals towards each other is determined by their membership in different social groups or categories [e.g., social identities generate behavior]. (p. 41)

Tajfel's distinction is similar to Miller and Steinberg's (1975) discussion of making predictions based on cultural, sociological, or psychological data. Pure interpersonal behavior occurs when all predictions are made using psychological data. Pure intergroup behavior, in contrast, takes place when all predictions are made on the basis of sociological and/or cultural data. Pure intergroup behavior takes place when no individual differences are recognized. The source of intergroup behavior is our social identities, and the source of interpersonal behavior is our personal identities.

Tajfel (1978) argues that it is impossible to conceive of pure interpersonal behavior, that no instance of it can be found: "it is impossible to imagine a social encounter between two people which will not be affected, at least to some minimal degree, by their mutual assignments of one another to a variety of social categories about which some general expectations concerning their characteristics and behavior exist in the mind of the interactants" (p. 41). Tajfel contends this is true even for husbands and wives and close friends. It is possible, in contrast, to conceive of at least one example of pure intergroup behavior. Tajfel (1978) cites an example of a bomber crew on a mission against an enemy population. In this case the bomber crew is involved in pure intergroup behavior if its members are viewing the enemy as all alike.

If you watch the television program *M*A*S*H*, you may recall the episode "Dear Sigmund," in which a U.S. bombardier limps into the 4077th for medical aid. While Hawkeye is administering to his wounds, the flyer talks about how the war does not inconvenience him much. All he does is strap himself into his seat in the plane, fly over the enemy, push a button, and drop his bombs, returning to his wife in Tokyo every weekend. Hawkeye then asks the bombardier if he has ever seen the enemy, and the flyer says he has not. The bombardier is engaged in a pure form of intergroup behavior because he sees all of the enemy as the same. During his stay at the 4077th the bombardier is put to work carrying the wounded into the operating room. During one trip into the operating room, he notices a young Korean child who is about to undergo surgery. He asks Hawkeye what happened to the child. Hawkeye tells him that a bomb exploded in the child's village. The bombardier then asks whether it was one of "ours" or one of "theirs." Colonel Potter responds by saying that it doesn't make any difference whose bomb it was. The bombardier declares that it makes a difference to him. Hawkeye counters by saying it doesn't make any difference to the child. At this point the bombardier begins to see the Koreans, on whom he has been dropping bombs, as individuals. Since he now recognizes individual differences, however slight, in the members of the other group, the bombardier's future behavior will not be pure intergroup behavior.

Other conceptualizations suggest that the interpersonal-intergroup continuum oversimplifies the nature of communication involved (Giles & Hewstone, 1982; Gudykunst & Lim, 1986; Stephenson, 1981). Stephenson (1981), for example, argues that

> it is difficult to think of any social situation which may not have both intergroup and interpersonal significance. Making love, for example, may seem unambiguously interpersonal, yet a consideration of the objectives achieved by James Bond's sexual exploits should prevent our being overly sentimental about performance, even in that sphere. In any interaction with another, our apparent membership in different social groups—be it male, female, young, English, black, or European—is at least a potential allegiance which may be exploited by the other, such that we act in some sense as *representatives* of fellow members of those groups. When our nationality, sex, or occupation becomes salient in the interaction, this does not necessarily obliterate the interpersonal significance of the encounter; indeed, it may enhance it. (p. 195)

This suggests that both interpersonal and intergroup factors operate in every situation.

Stephenson (1981) distinguishes between encounters that involve both high interpersonal and high intergroup salience and those that involve low interpersonal and high intergroup salience in terms of how negotiations take place. If they are conducted face-to-face, then they involve high interpersonal and high intergroup salience. When negotiations take place over the phone, by contrast, they involve high intergroup and low interpersonal salience. Stephenson believes the difference is that in the face-to-face situation negotiators are aware of the interpersonal significance of their behavior, while they are much less aware of it when they negotiate over the phone. Situations that involve high interpersonal and low intergroup salience include most encounters between friends, lovers, mates, and so forth. Situations that involve low interpersonal and low intergroup salience encompass a large percentage of encounters between strangers, including strangers on public transportation, interaction between clerk and customer, and other encounters of this nature.

Interpersonal salience and intergroup salience can and do change within specific encounters (Coupland, 1980). Stated differently, personal and social identities can both serve as generative mechanisms for behavior in the same encounter. This suggests that explanations of communication in social relationships must take both interpersonal and intergroup factors into consideration.

ANXIETY/UNCERTAINTY MANAGEMENT

When we interact with strangers, our ability to communicate effectively is based, at least in part, on our ability to manage our anxiety and uncertainty (Gudykunst, 1995). In this section, we examine the nature of uncertainty, anxiety, and mindfulness (the cognitive process that allows us to manage our uncertainty and anxiety). We begin with uncertainty.

Uncertainty in Interactions with Strangers

Marris (1996) contends that "what constitutes uncertainty depends on what we want to be able to predict, what we can predict, and what we might be able to do about it" (p. 16). We perceive uncertainty "in situations which lie between the two extremes of determinacy. At one extreme, we are so confident of our predictions that we no longer experience doubt at all; at the other, what will happen is so absolutely unpredictable it can only be treated fatalistically" (p. 18). Between the two extremes, we have to deal with our uncertainties. We do not just perceive uncertainties and try to manage them, Marris points out that "the way we understand the world, our purpose in it and our power to control our daily destiny leads us to [uncertainties]. The structure of meaning which make the world orderly and predictable also define significant uncertainties" (p. 18).

Often when we meet people from our own cultures, the norms and rules guiding our behavior in the situation provide sufficient information for us to be comfortable interacting with them. This, however, is not always the case. When the situation does not reduce our uncertainty, we must reduce it ourselves. Berger (1979) argues that we try to reduce uncertainty when strangers we meet will be encountered in the future, provide rewards to us (e.g., affection, prestige, status), or behave in a deviant fashion.

The Nature of Uncertainty   Berger and Calabrese (1975) point out there are at least two distinct types of uncertainty present in our interactions with strangers. First, there is the uncertainty we have about strangers' attitudes, feelings, beliefs, values, and behavior. We need to be able, for example, to predict which of several alternative behavior patterns strangers will choose to employ. An illustration is the situation when we meet people we find attractive at a party. Assuming we want to see the people we find attractive again after the party, we try to think about different ways we can approach them in order to persuade them to see us again. The different approaches we think about are the predictions of alternative behaviors that reduce our uncertainty. The second type of uncertainty Berger and Calabrese (1975) isolate involves explanations of strangers' behavior. Whenever we try to figure out why strangers behaved the way they did, we are engaging in explanatory uncertainty reduction. The problem we are addressing is one of reducing the number of possible explanations for strangers' behavior. This is necessary if we are to understand their behavior and, thus, be able to increase our ability to predict their behavior in the future.

We have greater uncertainty in our initial interactions with strangers than in those with members of our ingroups (Gudykunst & Shapiro, 1996). This does not, however, mean that we will be motivated to reduce uncertainty actively more when we communicate with strangers than when we communicate with members of our ingroups. Strangers may behave in a deviant fashion (e.g., not follow *our* norms or communication rules), but they rarely are seen as sources of rewards and we may not anticipate seeing them again in the future. When we do not try actively to reduce our uncertainty regarding strangers' behavior, we rely on our categorizations of strangers to reduce our uncertainty and guide our predictions. As indicated earlier, this often leads to misunderstandings.

Minimum and Maximum Thresholds Some degree of uncertainty exists in all relationships. We can never totally predict or explain strangers' behavior. We also may not always want to minimize our uncertainty. Weick (1979), for example, contends that equivocality can lead to creativity. We also may not be able to minimize our uncertainty because "ambiguous modes of expression are rooted in the very nature of language and thought" (Levine, 1985, p. 20), or strangers transmit equivocal messages (e.g., Bavelas et al., 1990). When communicating with strangers we may be ambiguous on purpose. To illustrate, Levine contends that ambiguity allows us to protect ourselves through "opaqueness." Eisenberg (1984) also believes that ambiguity has benefits in some situations (e.g., it allows us to maintain power over strangers).

We all have maximum and minimum thresholds for uncertainty (Gudykunst, 1993). If our uncertainty is above our maximum thresholds or below our minimum thresholds, we feel uncomfortable and will have difficulty communicating effectively. If our uncertainty is above our maximum thresholds, we do not think we have enough information to predict or explain strangers' behavior. When uncertainty is above our maximum thresholds, we do not have confidence in our predictions and explanations of strangers' behavior. When there are norms or rules guiding behavior in a particular situation, the norms or rules allow us to predict unconsciously how strangers will behave, and our uncertainty, therefore, will be below our maximum thresholds. Also, when we have some information about strangers so that we feel comfortable predicting how they will behave in the situation, our uncertainty will be below our maximum thresholds. When our uncertainty is below our maximum thresholds, we have sufficient confidence in the information we have to predict and explain strangers' behavior.

If our uncertainty is below our minimum thresholds, we think strangers' behavior is highly predictable; we have a high level of confidence in our ability to predict strangers' behavior. High levels of predictability, however, often are associated with boredom. When this occurs, there may not be sufficient novelty in our relationships for us to sustain interest in interacting with strangers, and we may not be motivated to communicate. It also is important to remember that confidence in our predictions does not mean that our predictions are accurate. When we see strangers' behavior as highly predictable, we also are likely to misinterpret their messages because we do not consider the possibility that our interpretations of their messages are wrong. In other words, overconfidence can breed misinterpretations.

Communicating effectively requires that our uncertainty be between our minimum and maximum thresholds (Gudykunst, 1995). If our uncertainty is above our maximum thresholds or below our minimum thresholds, we need to manage our uncertainty consciously to improve the effectiveness of our communication.

Uncertainty over Time Generally, as we get to know strangers, our uncertainty regarding their behavior tends to decrease (Hubbert, Gudykunst, & Guerrero, 1999). Uncertainty, however, does not always decrease as relationships change over time. It also can increase. When we first meet strangers, our uncertainty tends to be above our maximum thresholds since we do not feel comfortable predicting their behavior. Once we meet strangers and see that they follow the rules of interacting, our uncertainty will drop below our maximum thresholds. We assume that we can use cultural norms to predict their behavior. As we get to know strangers in the United States, we use their attitudes, values, and beliefs to predict and explain their behavior (cultural differences in uncertainty reduction are discussed below).

Uncertainty tends to decrease as we get to know strangers, but events may occur in our established relationships or strangers may do something we do not expect that increases our uncertainty. To illustrate, when we lose closeness in a relationship or when we find out that strangers have deceived or betrayed us, our uncertainty may increase (Planalp, Rutherford, & Honeycutt, 1988). The more surprised we are, the more our uncertainty is likely to increase. It is possible that our uncertainty may increase so much that it rises above our maximum thresholds. If this occurs, we must reduce our uncertainty to feel comfortable interacting with strangers. We can do this by seeking information, such as asking them why they behaved the way they did.

Depending on the nature of the event that increases our uncertainty and how we manage the uncertainty, increases in uncertainty can have positive or negative consequences for our relationships with strangers. If we find out that a romantic partner is seeing someone else, for example, it probably will increase our uncertainty above our maximum thresholds. Depending on the partner's explanation, we may or may not be able to reduce our uncertainty below our maximum thresholds. If we cannot reduce our uncertainty, it may signal the end of the relationship. If we can reduce our uncertainty and we are confident that the romantic partner will not see others in the future, in contrast, our uncertainty probably will return to our comfort ranges.

To summarize, our uncertainty regarding strangers' behavior fluctuates over time. If our uncertainty is above our maximum threshold or below our minimum threshold, we need to manage it consciously to increase the effectiveness of our communication. Figure 2.1 provides a visual summary of how uncertainty may change over time. The specific patterns that emerge depend on the two people involved in the relationship, what happens between them, and events external to the relationship (e.g., changes in the relationship between the two groups of which the participants are members).

Uncertainty in Intergroup Encounters Many factors influence the amount of uncertainty we experience when we communicate with strangers (Gudykunst, 1988b, 1995). These factors include, but are not limited to, our expectations, our social identities, the perception of similarity between our group and the strangers' groups, the degree to which we share communication networks with strangers, and the interpersonal salience of our contact with strangers.

Well-defined expectations (e.g., complex images of strangers and their groups) help us reduce uncertainty. The more well defined our expectations are, the more confident we will be regarding predicting strangers' behavior. We can have well-defined posi-

FIGURE 2.1
Hypothetical form of uncertainty over time.

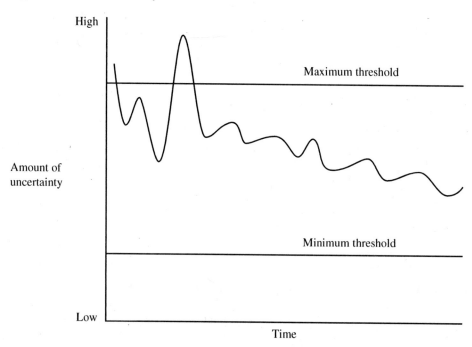

tive or negative expectations. Well-defined expectations alone, however, do not necessarily help us explain strangers' behavior. To explain strangers' behavior accurately, we need to have accurate information regarding strangers' cultures, their group memberships, and the individual strangers with whom we are communicating. We discuss several strategies for acquiring this information in Chapter 12.

Gudykunst (1988b) argues that the stronger our social identities are (e.g., the more important our group memberships are to how we define ourselves), the greater our predictive certainty regarding strangers' behavior. This claim, however, has to be qualified. Gudykunst and Hammer (1988b) report that strength of social identity reduces uncertainty only when we recognize that the strangers are from another group and when the strangers with whom we are communicating are perceived to be typical members of their groups. When the strangers are perceived to be atypical members of their groups, we do not treat them on the basis of their group membership; for example, we see them as "an exception to the rule." In this case, our communication is influenced by our personal identities, not our social identities. When communication is based on our personal identities, we need information about the individual stranger with whom we are communicating to reduce uncertainty.

The degree to which our group is similar to strangers' groups also influences our ability to reduce uncertainty (Gudykunst, 1988b). If we perceive that the strangers' groups are similar to our own ingroups, we have more confidence in our ability to predict strangers' behavior. Perceived similarity, however, may not increase our ability to explain strangers' behavior accurately because we may perceive similarities when we are actually different or perceive differences when we are actually similar. Knowledge of the actual similarities or dissimilarities between our group and the strangers' groups is necessary to reduce our explanatory uncertainty.

The degree to which we share communication networks with the strangers also influences the amount of uncertainty we experience when we communicate with strangers (Gudykunst, 1988b). The more we know the same people that the strangers with whom we are communicating know, the more we can reduce uncertainty. Further, the degree to which we want to establish an interpersonal relationship with the specific strangers contributes to the reduction of uncertainty. The more we are physically or socially attracted to the strangers with whom we are communicating, the more our confidence in our ability to predict strangers' behavior will increase. In addition, our cultural and linguistic knowledge of strangers' cultures helps us predict their behavior. The more we understand and can speak the strangers' languages and the more knowledge we have of their cultures, the more our uncertainty will be reduced. We will discuss the role of linguistic knowledge in more detail in Chapter 8.

Anxiety in Interactions with Strangers

When we communicate with strangers, we not only have a high level of uncertainty, we also have a high level of anxiety. Anxiety refers to the feelings of being uneasy, tense, worried, and apprehensive about what might happen (Stephan & Stephan, 1985). It is an affective (i.e., emotional) response to strangers, not a cognitive response like uncertainty. Anxiety is one of the fundamental problems with which all humans must cope (Lazarus, 1991; May, 1977). The amount of diffuse anxiety we experience influences our motivation to communicate with strangers (J. H. Turner, 1988). If our diffuse anxiety is too high or too low, we are not motivated to communicate.

Our anxiety tends to be higher in intergroup encounters than in interpersonal encounters (e.g., Ickes, 1984; Word, Zanna, & Cooper, 1974). Interactions with strangers tends to lead to fear across cultures (Walbott & Scherer, 1986). Experiencing anxiety causes us to engage in social categorizations (i.e., create ingroups and outgroups; Greenland & Brown, 1999). Our explanations for why we experience anxiety, however, can vary widely (e.g., because we do not want to appear prejudiced, because we have hostile feelings toward an outgroup; see data reported in Greenland & Brown, 2000).

Minimum and Maximum Thresholds We have maximum and minimum thresholds for anxiety (Gudykunst, 1993). If our anxiety is above our maximum thresholds, we are so uneasy that we do not want to communicate with strangers. If our anxiety is below our minimum thresholds, there is not enough adrenaline running through our systems to motivate us to communicate with strangers. For us to be motivated to communicate with strangers, our anxiety has to be below our maximum thresholds and above our minimum thresholds. The role of anxiety in interpersonal communication is similar to its role in our performance on tests. If we are too anxious, we do not perform well on tests. Similarly, if we are not at all anxious, we do not perform well. This argument also is consistent with Janis' (1971) theory of anticipatory fear. He contends that moderate levels of fear lead to adaptive processes, while low and high levels do not. There is an optimal level of anxiety that facilitates our experiencing flow or having optimal experiences (Csikszentmihalyi, 1990).

To communicate effectively with strangers, our anxiety needs to be below our maximum thresholds and above our minimum thresholds. When anxiety is above our maximum or below our minimum thresholds, we tend to process information in a very simplistic fashion. To illustrate, when our anxiety is too high, we use only our stereotypes to predict strangers' behavior. Since stereotypes are never accurate when applied to individuals, our predictions are inaccurate and our communication, therefore, is likely to be ineffective.

Individuals' minimum and maximum thresholds differ. One way we can tell if our anxiety is above our maximum thresholds is by paying attention to our "gut reactions." If we feel a few butterflies in our stomachs, our anxiety probably is not above our maximum thresholds. A few butterflies probably indicate a normal amount of anxiety, an amount between our minimum and maximum thresholds. When we do not feel any butterflies or nervousness, our anxiety is probably below our minimum thresholds. If, however, we have stomachaches or the palms of our hands are sweating, our anxiety is probably above our maximum thresholds. The physical indicators each of us can use will differ. By paying attention to our reactions, we can figure out when our anxiety is so high that we do not feel comfortable communicating and when it is so low that we do not care what happens. Once we know where these points are, we can manage our anxiety cognitively.

Anxiety over Time   Generally, as we get to know strangers, the anxiety we experience in interacting with them tends to decrease (Hubbert et al., 1999). We do not mean to imply, however, that anxiety continually decreases. While there is a general trend for our anxiety to decrease the more we get to know strangers, our anxiety can increase or decrease at any particular point in a relationship depending on what is going on in the relationship and how we interpret it.

When we first meet strangers, our anxiety may be above our maximum thresholds, especially if we see strangers as attractive in some way or as a member of different groups. After we talk with strangers, our anxiety probably decreases somewhat, assuming that we see that the strangers are not a threat to us. As our relationship with strangers becomes more intimate, our overall level of anxiety tends to decrease. As we get to know strangers, however, our anxiety fluctuates depending on the specific circumstances of our interactions. The first time we kiss a date, for example, our anxiety may be high.

If we become extremely comfortable with strangers, our anxiety may drop below our minimum thresholds. If this occurs, our motivation to communicate with strangers is low and we may not make the effort to communicate. It is also possible, however, that something will occur in our relationships and our anxiety will increase dramatically, possibly rising above our maximum thresholds. If we are involved in romantic relationships, think that the relationships are going well, and want them to continue, our anxiety may increase dramatically if our partners tell us that they want to break off the relationships.

To summarize, our anxiety about communicating with strangers fluctuates over time. If our anxiety is above our maximum thresholds or below our minimum thresholds, we need to manage it consciously to communicate effectively. Figure 2.2 provides a visual summary of how anxiety may change over time. The specific pattern

FIGURE 2.2
Hypothetical form of anxiety over time.

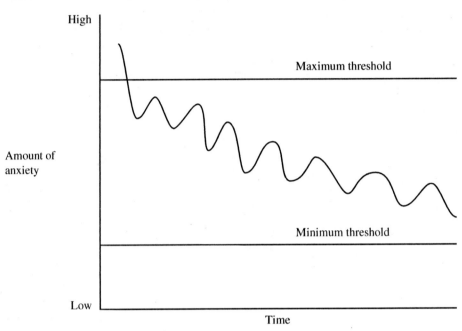

that emerges is a function of the two people involved, what happens in the relationships, and external events (e.g., the relationships between the groups of which individuals are members).

Anxiety in Intergroup Interactions   Stephan and Stephan (1985) argue that we fear four types of negative consequences when interacting with strangers. First, we fear negative consequences for our self-concepts. In interacting with strangers, we worry "about feeling incompetent, confused, and not in control. . . . [We] anticipate discomfort, frustration, and irritation due to the awkwardness of intergroup interactions" (p. 159). We also may fear the loss of self-esteem, that our social identities will be threatened, and that we will feel guilty if we behave in ways that offend strangers.

Second, we may fear that negative behavioral consequences will result from our communication with strangers (Stephan & Stephan, 1985). We may feel that strangers will exploit us, take advantage of us, or try to dominate us. We also may worry about performing poorly in the presence of strangers or worry that physical harm or verbal conflict will occur.

Third, we fear negative evaluations by strangers (Stephan & Stephan, 1985). We fear rejection, ridicule, disapproval, and being stereotyped negatively. These negative evaluations, in turn, can be seen as threats to our social identities. Hoyle, Pinkley, and Insko (1989) report that we perceive communication with people who are familiar as more agreeable and less abrasive than communication with strangers. Crocker, Major, and Steele (1998) point out that our anxiety may make us appear prejudiced to strangers. They suggest that "discomfort resulting from the desire to be nonprejudiced combined with the lack of confidence in one's ability to act appropriately may be misinterpreted [by strangers] as stemming from hostility and prejudice" (p. 515).

Fourth, we may fear negative evaluations by members of our ingroups (Stephan & Stephan, 1985). If we interact with strangers, members of our ingroups may disapprove. We may fear that "ingroup members will reject" us, "apply other sanctions," or identify us "with the outgroup" (Stephan & Stephan, 1985, p. 160).

Several factors are associated with the amount of anxiety we experience when we communicate with strangers. Thinking about the behavior in which we need to engage when communicating with strangers, for example, can reduce our anxiety about interacting with them (Janis & Mann, 1977). Further, if we focus on finding out as much as we can and forming accurate impressions of strangers, the biases we have, based on our anxiety and negative expectations, will be reduced (Leary, Kowalski, & Bergen, 1988; Neuberg, 1989). Stephan and Stephan (1989) also report that the less the intergroup contact we have experienced, the less ethnocentric we are, and the more positive our stereotypes are, the less the intergroup anxiety we experience.

Fiske and Morling (1996) point out that the amount of anxiety we experience in intergroup interactions is partly a function of the degree to which we feel in control. The less powerful we feel in a situation, the more anxious we will be. The greater the anxiety we experience, the more intrusive thoughts we experience. These intrusive thoughts decrease our cognitive capacity (e.g., we tend to think in a simplistic fashion). When we are anxious, we see strangers as easier to control than ourselves, and we, therefore, often try to control strangers when we are highly anxious.

Stephan and Stephan (1985) isolate three broad categories of antecedents to intergroup anxiety: prior intergroup relations, intergroup cognitions (e.g., stereotypes and intergroup attitudes), and situational factors. The important aspects of prior intergroup relations that influence the amount of intergroup anxiety we experience when communicating with strangers are the amount of contact we have had with the strangers' groups and the conditions under which that contact occurred. Stephan and Stephan argue that the more contact we have had and the clearer the norms are for intergroup relations, the less intergroup anxiety we will experience. If, however, there has been prior conflict between our group and the strangers' groups or if our economic and political interests do not coincide, we are likely to experience intergroup anxiety.

The way we think about strangers influences our affective reactions toward them. The important intergroup cognitions are our knowledge of strangers' cultures, our stereotypes, our prejudice, our ethnocentrism, and our perceptions of ingroup-outgroup differences (Stephan & Stephan, 1985). The less knowledge we have of strangers' groups, the more anxiety we will experience. Negative cognitive expectations (e.g., negative stereotypes and prejudice) lead to intergroup anxiety. The greater the differences (real or imagined) we perceive between our groups and strangers' groups, the more intergroup anxiety we will experience.

The situational factors that contribute to intergroup anxiety include the amount of structure in the situation in which contact occurs, the type of interdependence, the group composition, and the relative status of the participants. Stephan and Stephan point out that in structured situations, the norms provide guides for our behavior and reduce our anxiety. The more unstructured the situation is, therefore, the greater our intergroup anxiety. Situations in which we cooperate with strangers involve less anxiety than situations in which we compete with them. Further, we will experience less anxiety when we find ourselves in situations where our ingroup is in the majority than we will in situations where our ingroup is in the minority. Finally, we will experience less anxiety in situations where our ingroup has higher status than the strangers' groups than we will in situations where our ingroup has lower status.

Stephan and Stephan (1985) isolate cognitive, behavioral, and affective consequences of intergroup anxiety. While their focus is on the negative consequences, positive consequences also can occur. One of the behavioral consequences of anxiety is avoidance. We avoid strangers because doing so reduces our anxiety. When we are experiencing anxiety and cannot avoid strangers, we will terminate the interaction as soon as we can. Cognitively, intergroup anxiety leads to biases in information processing. The more anxious we are, the more likely it is we will attune to the behaviors we expected to see (e.g., those based on our stereotypes; see Chapter 5) and the more likely we are to confirm these expectations (e.g., we will not attune to behavior that is inconsistent with our expectations). The greater our anxiety is, the more we will be self-aware and concerned with our self-esteem. When we are highly anxious, we, therefore, try to make our own groups look good in comparison to strangers' groups.

As indicated above, experiencing anxiety influences the way we process information. Wilder and Shapiro (1989) point out that when anxiety is high (e.g., above our maximum thresholds), we tend to process information in a simplistic fashion. Wilder (1993) points out that high levels of anxiety generate arousal which leads to self-focused attention that distracts us from what is happening and decreases our ability to make differentiations regarding strangers. This line of reasoning suggests that we are not able to gather new or accurate information about strangers when our anxiety is high and, therefore, we are not be able to make accurate predictions or explanations of strangers' behavior. Wilder and Shapiro (1996), however, point out that "integral anxiety" (e.g., anxiety attributed to strangers' groups) can facilitate information processing, but intense anxiety (e.g., anxiety from unknown sources) inhibits it.

Greenland and Brown (2000) also propose that our strategies for coping with anxiety may depend on our explanations for why we experience anxiety. They contend that having a "positive" reason for experiencing anxiety (e.g., we do not want to appear to be prejudiced) should lead to processing information systematically and not engaging in stereotyping. Having a "negative" reason for experiencing anxiety (e.g., because we have hostile feelings toward an outgroup), in contrast, should lead to simplistic information processing.

Mindfulness

To manage our uncertainty and anxiety, we must be conscious (i.e., mindful) of our communication. We do not, however, generally think much about our behavior. Much of our communication behavior, for example, is habitual. When we are communicating habitually, we are following scripts—"a coherent sequence of events expected by the individual involving him [or her] either as a participant or an observer" (Abelson,

1976, p. 33). Langer (1978) argues that when we first encounter a new situation, we consciously seek cues to guide our behavior. As we have repeated experiences with the same event, we have less need to think consciously about our behavior. Langer (1978) points out that "the more often we engage in the activity, the more likely it is that we rely on scripts for the completion of the activity and the less likely there will be any correspondence between our actions and those thoughts of ours that occur simultaneously" (p. 39).

As indicated earlier, when we are engaging in habitual or scripted behavior, we are not highly aware of what we are doing or saying. To borrow an analogy from flying a plane, we are on automatic pilot. In Langer's (1978) terminology, we are mindless. We do not, however, communicate totally on automatic pilot. Rather, we pay sufficient attention that we can recall key words in the conversations we have (Kitayama & Burnstein, 1988).

Langer (1989) isolates three characteristics of mindfulness: (1) creating new categories, (2) being open to new information, and (3) awareness of more than one perspective. One condition that contributes to being mindless is the *use of broad categories.* Categorization often is based on physical (e.g., gender, race) or cultural (e.g., ethnic background) characteristics, but we also can categorize others in terms of their attitudes (e.g., liberal-conservative) or approaches to life (e.g., Christian or Buddhist; Trungpa, 1973). Langer (1989) points out that "categorizing is a fundamental and natural human activity. It is the way we come to know the world. Any attempt to eliminate bias by attempting to eliminate the perception of differences is doomed to failure" (p. 154). Being mindful involves making more, not fewer, distinctions. To illustrate, when we are on automatic pilot, we tend to use broad categories to predict strangers' behavior, for example, strangers' cultures, ethnicities, genders, or the roles they are playing. When we are mindful, we can create new categories that are more specific. Rather than using the broad category *professor,* for example, students can subcategorize professors into males/females, professors who are formal/professors who are informal, professors who call me by my name/professors who do not call me by my name, and so forth. The more subcategories we use, the more personalized the information we use to make predictions will be.

Mindfulness involves being *open to new information* (Langer, 1989). When we behave on automatic pilot in a particular situation, we tend to see the same thing occurring in the situation that we saw the previous time we were in the same situation. If we are consciously open to new information, we see the subtle differences in our own and strangers' behavior that may take place. The more we think about how to behave in situations, the more appropriate and effective our behavior tends to be (Cegala & Waldron, 1992).

Being open to new information involves focusing on the process of communication that is taking place, not the outcome of our interactions with others. Langer (1989) argues that

> an outcome orientation in social situations can induce mindlessness. If we think we know how to handle a situation, we don't feel a need to pay attention. If we respond to the situation as very familiar (as a result, for example, of overlearning), we notice only minimal cues necessary to carry out the proper scenarios. If, on the other hand, the situation is strange, we might be so preoccupied with the thought of failure ("what if I make a fool of myself?") that we miss nuances of our own and others' behavior. In this sense, we are mindless with respect to the immediate situation, although we may be thinking quite actively about outcome related issues. (p. 34)

When we focus on the outcome, we miss subtle cues in our interactions with others, and this often leads to misunderstandings. Focusing on the process of communication forces us to be mindful of our behavior and pay attention to the situations in which we find ourselves (Langer, 1989).

To be mindful, we must also recognize that there is *more than one perspective* that can be used to understand or explain our interactions with strangers (Langer, 1989). Suppose a friend sprained her or his ankle and asked you to go to the local pharmacy for an Ace bandage. What would you do if the local pharmacy was out of Ace bandages (and there was only the one pharmacy available)? Most of us probably would return and tell our friend that the pharmacy was out of Ace bandages if we were acting on automatic pilot (Langer, 1989). If we were mindful, however, we might think to ask the pharmacist if there are alternatives to using an Ace bandage on a sprained ankle.

When we communicate on automatic pilot, we do not recognize alternative perspectives. The mindset we bring to communication situations limits our ability to see the choices we actually have about how to behave in most situations (Langer, 1989). When we communicate mindfully, however, we can look for the options that are available to us and not be limited to only those that come to mind in the situation. When we are communicating mindfully, we can use all the communication resources available to us rather than limiting ourselves to those in our implicit personal theories of communication.

Recognizing alternative perspectives is critical to effective communication. Effective communication requires recognizing that strangers use their own perspectives to interpret our messages and that they may not interpret our messages the way we intended them. The problem is that when we communicate on automatic pilot, we assume everyone uses the same perspective we do. It is only when we are mindful of the process of our communication that we can determine how our interpretations of messages differ from strangers' interpretations of those messages.

We often become conscious of our behavior when we enter new situations such as communicating with strangers. Berger and Douglas (1982) isolate five conditions under which we are highly cognizant of our behavior:

> (1) in novel situations where, by definition, no appropriate script exists, (2) where external factors prevent completion of a script, (3) when scripted behavior becomes effortful because substantially more of the behavior is required than is usual, (4) when a discrepant outcome is experienced, or (5) where multiple scripts come into conflict so that involvement in any one script is suspended. In short, individuals will enact scripted sequences whenever those sequences are available and will continue to do so until events unusual to the script are encountered. (pp. 46–47)

It can be inferred that we are more aware of our behavior when communicating with strangers than we are when communicating with members of our ingroups. The problem, however, is that we tend to be aware of outcomes, not the process of communication. Our mindfulness, therefore, does not increase our effectiveness.

Uncertainty, Anxiety, Mindfulness, and Effective Communication

In general, our uncertainty and anxiety decrease the better we get to know strangers. Uncertainty and anxiety, however, do not increase or decrease consistently over time. Uncertainty, for example, is not reduced every time we communicate with strangers.

We may reduce our uncertainty the first time we communicate, but something may occur the second time we communicate (e.g., the stranger does something we did not expect) and our uncertainty might increase. Once we have established relationships with strangers, we can expect that our uncertainty and anxiety regarding strangers will fluctuate over time. As our relationships become more intimate, nevertheless, there should be a general pattern for uncertainty and anxiety to decrease. To illustrate, there tends to be less uncertainty and anxiety in acquaintance relationships than in relationships with people we do not know, and there is less uncertainty and anxiety in friendships than in acquaintance relationships. At the same time, within any stage (e.g., acquaintance, friend) of a particular relationship, uncertainty and anxiety will fluctuate over time.

We do not want to try to reduce our anxiety and uncertainty totally. At the same time, we cannot communicate effectively if our uncertainty and anxiety are too high. If uncertainty and anxiety are too high, we cannot interpret strangers' messages accurately or make accurate predictions about strangers' behavior. If anxiety is above our maximum thresholds, as it often is when we first meet strangers, we are too anxious to communicate effectively. When anxiety is above our maximum thresholds, the way we process information becomes very simple, thereby decreasing our ability to predict strangers' behavior (Wilder & Shapiro, 1989). When uncertainty is above our maximum thresholds, we do not think we can predict strangers' behavior. In most situations, however, there are sufficiently clear norms and rules for communication that our uncertainty and anxiety are reduced below our maximum thresholds. Even if our uncertainty and anxiety are below the maximum thresholds, either or both still may be too high for us to communicate effectively. For us to communicate effectively, our anxiety needs to be sufficiently low that we can interpret and predict strangers' behavior accurately. When anxiety is too high, we communicate on automatic pilot and interpret strangers' behavior using our own cultural frames of reference.

If uncertainty and anxiety are low, we may not be motivated to communicate. If both uncertainty and anxiety are consistently below our minimum thresholds in a particular relationship, for example, the relationship will become boring. Kruglanski (1989) points out that we all have a need to avoid closure on topics or people to allow for mystery to be maintained. When uncertainty is below our minimum thresholds, we also become overconfident that we understand strangers' behavior and do not question whether our predictions are accurate. For us to communicate effectively, our uncertainty and anxiety both must be above our minimum thresholds.

Uncertainty and anxiety do not necessarily increase and decrease at the same time. We may reduce our uncertainty and be highly anxious. Consider, for example, a situation in which we predict very confidently that something negative is going to happen. We also may reduce our anxiety and have high uncertainty. To communicate effectively, our anxiety must be sufficiently low (i.e., well below our maximum thresholds but above our minimum thresholds) that we can reduce our explanatory uncertainty. If our anxiety is high, we must manage our anxiety cognitively (i.e., become mindful) if we are to communicate effectively (we discuss this process in detail in Chapter 10, on effectiveness).

When we have managed our anxiety, we need to try to develop accurate predictions and explanations for strangers' behavior. This also requires that we be mindful of our communication. When we communicate on automatic pilot, we predict and interpret strangers' behavior by using our frames of reference. When we are mindful, in contrast, we are open to new information and aware of alternative perspectives (e.g., strangers' perspectives; Langer, 1989). If we focus on the process of our communication with strangers and try to understand how they are interpreting our messages, we can increase the accuracy of our predictions and explanations for strangers' behavior. This inevitably will increase the effectiveness of our communication with strangers (effectiveness is discussed in more detail in Chapter 10).

Strangers tend to be more mindful in intergroup interactions than ingroup members. Frable, Blackstone, and Sherbaum (1990) argue that strangers pay attention to how their interactions with ingroup members are going and are aware of alternative ways the interactions may develop. Often, strangers' mindfulness is a defensive strategy because they are unsure how ingroup members will respond to them (Frable et al., 1990). Further, strangers tend to be aware of ingroup members' perspectives more than ingroup members are aware of strangers' perspectives. Devine, Evett, and Vasquez-Suson (1996) suggest that this results in strangers being able to "negotiate potentially problematic social interactions more effectively" than ingroup members (p. 444).

Devine et al. (1996) argue that the extent that ingroup members' mindfulness leads to effective interactions depends on strangers' biases and objectivity. They contend that "socially stimatized members of society [e.g., many, but not all, strangers] are generally mistrusting and suspicious of majority group members' intentions and motives" (p. 445). Strangers responses to ingroup members also is affected by strangers' "attributional ambiguity" (i.e., strangers may attribute ingroup members' behavior to ingroup members' personal qualities or ingroup members' stereotypes of strangers' groups; Crocker et al., 1991). Devine et al. suggest that strangers who expect to be treated negatively "may misperceive social anxiety as antipathy" (p. 449) even for ingroup members who are low in prejudice. There is no research on how strangers respond when ingroup members are mindful. We think that strangers' responses to ingroup members mindfulness will lead to smooth interactions if strangers perceive that ingroup members are not highly prejudiced and ingroup members' intentions are positive. This should be the case if ingroup members are mindful of the process of communication, rather than mindful of the outcome of their interactions.

The preceding discussion of anxiety, uncertainty, mindfulness, and effective communication outlined the primary components of anxiety/uncertainty management theory (e.g., Gudykunst, 1988, 1993, 1995). Following Lieberson (1985), Gudykunst argues that mindful anxiety and uncertainty management are the "primary causes" of effective communication. Other factors that influence effective communication (e.g., social identities, intergroup expectations, prior intergroup contact) are considered "secondary causes" because their influence on effective communication is mediated through anxiety and uncertainty (see Figure 2.3). We use anxiety/uncertainty management theory to guide our discussion of effective communication throughout the book. Where appropriate, we link the secondary causes of effective communication to anxiety and uncertainty management.

FIGURE 2.3
A diagram of anxiety/uncertainty management theory.

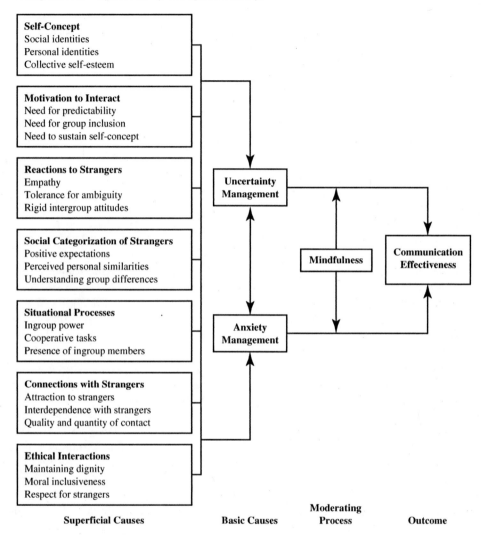

Source: Gudykunst (forthcoming).

AN ORGANIZING MODEL FOR STUDYING COMMUNICATION WITH STRANGERS

The model presented in this section is designed to serve as a guide to the organization of the material presented in Parts Two and Three of the book. Our purpose in presenting the model is not to describe the process of communication with strangers (we use anxiety/uncertainty management theory to do this) but rather to organize the elements influencing the process so that they can be discussed systematically. The model is diagramed in Figure 2.4. In constructing the model, we attempted to find a workable compromise between complexity and simplicity. As it stands, the model contains all the major elements yet is simple enough to be interpreted easily. The elements included in the model are transmitting and interpreting messages, as well as the cultural, sociocultural, psychocultural, and environmental influences on the communication process.

In examining the model it is necessary to keep in mind that any model, of necessity, excludes certain elements. The problem of premature closure, as the exclusion of elements is called, is unavoidable in constructing a model. Since each of the elements of the model is discussed in detail in Parts Two and Three of the book, the following is intended only as an introduction. Our purpose here, therefore, is to put the material presented in the next two parts of the book into context.

An Overview of the Model

Given our view of communication, we see encoding and decoding of communication messages to be an interactive process influenced by conceptual filters, which we categorize into cultural, sociocultural, psychocultural, and environmental factors. This is illustrated in Figure 2.4 by the way the center circle, which contains the interaction between encoding and decoding of messages, is surrounded by three other circles representing cultural, sociocultural, and psychocultural influences. The circles are drawn with dashed lines to indicate that the elements affect, and are affected by, the other elements. The two persons represented in the model are surrounded by a dashed box representing the environmental influences. This box is drawn with dashed rather than solid lines because the immediate environment in which the communication takes place is not an isolated, or "closed," system. Most communication between people takes place in a social environment that includes other people who also are engaging in communication and is influenced by factors outside the immediate communication situation (i.e., it is an "open system").

The message/feedback between the two communicators is represented by the lines from one person's transmitting to the other person's interpreting and from the second person's transmitting to the first person's interpreting. Two message/feedback lines are shown to indicate that anytime we communicate, we are simultaneously engaged in transmitting and interpreting messages. In other words, communication is not static; we do not transmit a message and do nothing until we receive feedback. Rather, we interpret incoming stimuli at the same time we are transmitting messages.

The cultural, sociocultural, and psychocultural influences serve as conceptual filters for our transmitting and interpreting of messages. By *filters*, we mean mechanisms that delimit the number of alternatives from which we choose when we transmit and interpret messages. More specifically, the filters limit the predictions we make about how strangers may respond to our communication behavior. The nature of the predictions we make, in turn, influences the way we choose to transmit our messages. Further, the filters delimit what stimuli we pay attention to and how we choose to interpret incoming messages.

FIGURE 2.4
An organizing model for studying communication with strangers.

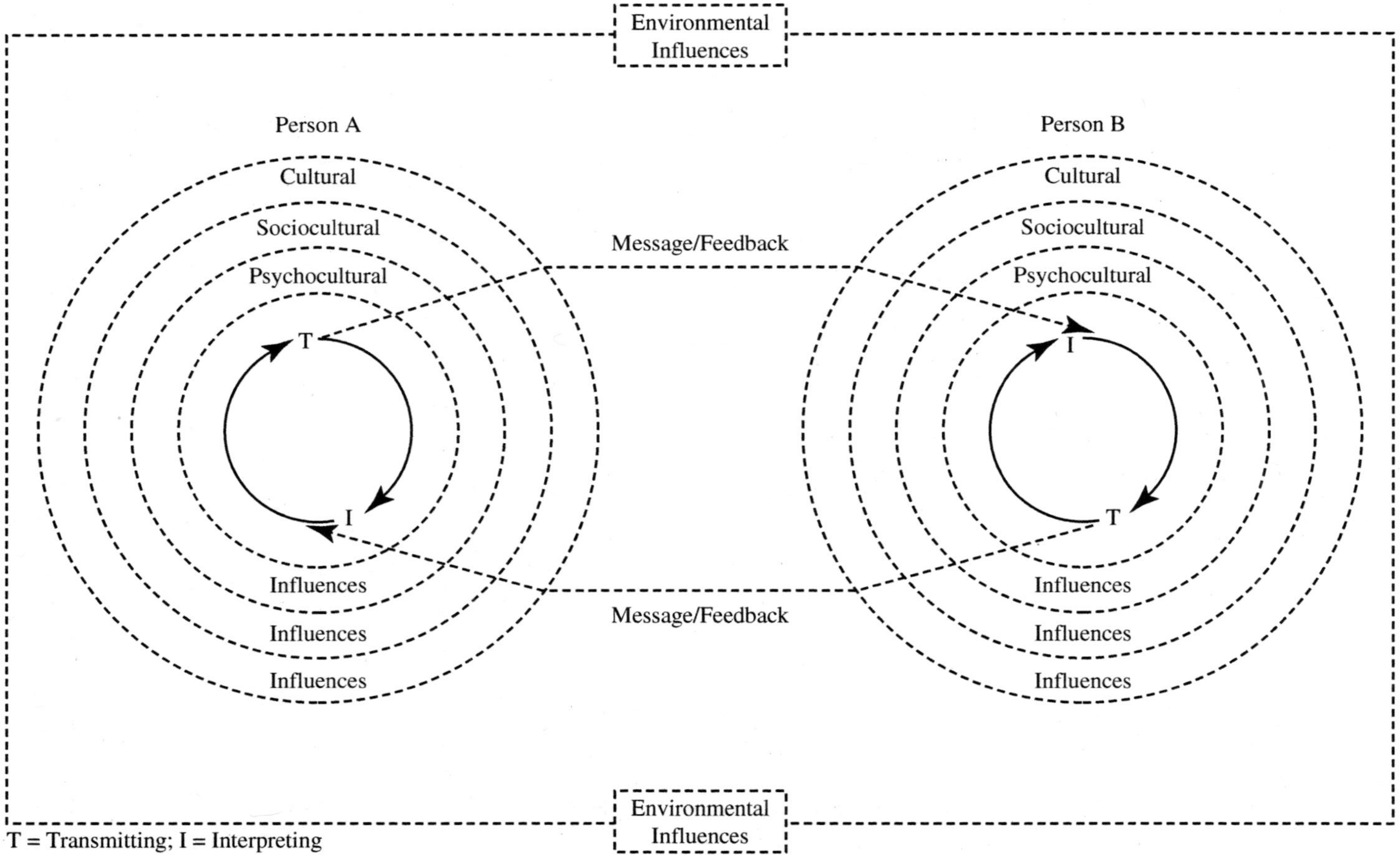

Person B

Cultural
Sociocultural
Psychocultural

T

I

Influences
Influences
Influences

Environmental
Influences

Message/Feedback

Message/Feedback

Person A

Cultural
Sociocultural
Psychocultural

T

I

Influences
Influences
Influences

Environmental
Influences

T = Transmitting; I = Interpreting

45

Transmitting Messages

Since it is impossible to transmit electrical impulses directly from one's brain to that of another person, it is necessary for us to put messages into codes that can be transmitted. Messages can be transmitted in many forms, but for the purpose of our analysis two are most relevant: language (verbal codes) and nonverbal behaviors (we exclude codes such as mathematics and music). As indicated earlier, the process of transmitting messages is accomplished at varying levels of consciousness.

Language is one of the major vehicles through which we encode messages. Obviously, languages can differ from culture to culture. Culture and language are closely intertwined, with each influencing the other. Our language is a product of our culture, and our culture is a product of our language. The language we speak influences what we see and think, and what we see and think, in part, influences our culture.

Not only are messages transmitted verbally, they also are encoded nonverbally. Nonverbal messages, like language, vary from culture to culture. Language is mostly a conscious activity, while nonverbal behavior is mostly an unconscious activity. That is, we generally are not aware of the messages we are encoding nonverbally through our gestures, facial expressions, or tones of voice, to name only a few ways we encode. When we encounter nonverbal behaviors greatly different from our own (e.g., when communicating with strangers), however, we may become unusually conscious of those behaviors. We discuss the transmitting of messages in detail in Chapters 8 and 9.

Interpreting Messages

To a certain extent interpreting messages is the opposite of transmitting messages. When we interpret a message, our perceptions depend on what the other person says verbally, what nonverbal behavior the other person exhibits, our own messages, our conceptual filters, and the context in which the message is received. In other words, how we interpret the messages encoded by strangers is a function of what they have transmitted, what we transmitted to them previously, the context in which we are communicating, and our conceptual filters.

As indicated earlier, the way in which we process the incoming stimuli is partially a function of our conceptual filters. More specifically, the filters delimit the stimuli we observe and tell us how specific stimuli are to be interpreted. Consider strangers who are visiting Japan and are invited into a Japanese home, where it is expected that shoes will be removed before people enter the house. The strangers may see the Japanese family's shoes by the door but, because of their conceptual filters, not attribute any meaning to the stimuli and, therefore, walk into the house with shoes still on their feet. When the Japanese hosts become upset, the strangers will have no idea what they did wrong. The strangers' conceptual filters have delimited the stimuli to which they attribute meaning, thereby influencing the interpretations they make about the situation. We discuss interpreting messages in detail in Chapter 7.

Cultural Influences

The cultural influences include those factors involved in the cultural ordering process described in Chapter 1. For the purpose of our analysis, we focus on dimensions that explain similarities and differences across cultures. Is our culture dominated by concerns for the individual (i.e., individualism) or for the collectivity (i.e., collectivism)? These dimensions affect the values and the norms and rules that influence our communication behavior. *Values* are shared conceptions of the desired ends of social life and the means to reach those goals. They express a collective view of what is important and unimportant, good and bad. The norms and rules of a culture specify the acceptable and unacceptable behavior in our interactions with others. It is the norms and rules of a culture that allow its members to engage spontaneously in everyday social behavior without continually having to "guess" what other people are going to do. More formally, we can say that norms and rules are sets of expected behaviors for particular situations.

The dimensions of cultural variability (e.g., individualism-collectivism), values, and communication norms/rules that predominate in our culture influence how we transmit messages and interpret incoming stimuli when we communicate with strangers. To illustrate, consider a visit to the United States by strangers from a culture with a communication rule requiring that direct eye contact always be avoided. When interacting with these strangers, U.S. Americans will try to establish direct eye contact. If the strangers do not look them in the eye when talking, the U.S. Americans will assume that the strangers either have something to hide or are not telling the truth, since the communication rule in the United States requires direct eye contact to establish one's sincerity. A rule of the U.S. American culture, therefore, has influenced the way in which U.S. Americans interpret the strangers' behavior. It should be noted, however, that there are some subcultures in the United States (e.g., the lower-class black subculture) where this rule may not be applicable. We discuss cultural influences in detail in Chapter 3.

Sociocultural Influences

The sociocultural influences are those involved in the social ordering process. As indicated in Chapter 1, social ordering develops out of our interactions with others when the patterns of behavior become consistent over time (Olsen, 1978). We are members of groups either because we are born into them or because we join them. Groups we are born into include, but are not limited to, racial and ethnic groups, families, age groups, and gender groups. Groups we join include service groups (e.g., the Lions Club), occupational groups, religious groups, and ideological groups (e.g., the Democratic and Republican parties, the Ku Klux Klan), to name only a few. The various groups of which we are members enforce sets of expected behaviors (norms and rules) and have shared values and, therefore, have an impact on how we communicate with strangers.

Our memberships in social groups influence the way we see ourselves. Our self-concepts are composed of at least two components: social and personal identities.

Our social identities are derived from our membership in our social groups. Our personal identities are based on our unique individual experiences. The degree to which we identify with our groups and feel comfortable about ourselves as individuals influences our communication with strangers.

When we communicate with another person and make our predictions on the basis of a position that person holds in a group, we are engaging in a role relationship. The idea of position can be illustrated best by examples; positions include clerk, judge, father, mother, boss, physician, professor, student, and so forth. People filling one of these positions are expected to perform certain behaviors. The sets of behaviors they are expected to perform are referred to as their roles. Our role expectations influence how we interpret behavior and what predictions we make about people in a given role. Role expectations vary within any culture, but there is a tendency for them to vary more across cultures. If we do not know strangers' role expectations, we inevitably will make inaccurate interpretations of and predictions about their behavior.

Psychocultural Influences

The variables included under the psychocultural influences are those involved in the personal ordering process. Personal ordering, you will recall, is the process that gives stability to psychological processes. The variables influencing our communication with strangers include our stereotypes of and attitudes toward (e.g., ethnocentrism and prejudice) strangers' groups. Our stereotypes and attitudes create expectations of how strangers will behave. Our expectations, in turn, influence the way in which we interpret incoming stimuli and the predictions we make about strangers' behavior. Being highly ethnocentric, for example, leads us to interpret strangers' behavior from our own cultural frame of reference and to expect strangers to behave the same way we do. This invariably leads to misinterpretations of the strangers' messages, as well as inaccurate predictions about their future behavior.

The influence of our expectations on our interpretation of strangers' behavior is mediated through the uncertainty and anxiety we are experiencing. If we are highly uncertain and/or anxious, we cannot interpret strangers' behavior accurately. To communicate effectively, our anxiety needs to be sufficiently low that we can make accurate predictions of strangers' behavior. We discuss psychocultural influences in detail in Chapter 5.

Environmental Influences

The environment in which we communicate influences our transmitting and interpreting of messages. The geographical location, climate, and architectural setting, as well as our perceptions of the environment, influence how we interpret incoming stimuli and the predictions we make about strangers' behavior. Since strangers may have different perceptions of and orientations toward the environment, they may interpret behavior differently in the same setting. As an illustration, a U.S. American visiting a Colombian family would expect to engage in informal interaction in the living room. The Colombian host, in contrast, probably would define the living room as a place for formal behavior. Each, therefore, would interpret the other's behavior in light of his or her own expectations and make predictions about the other's behavior on the basis of those expectations. Such a situation, in all likelihood, would lead to misunderstanding. We discuss environmental influences in Chapter 6.

SUMMARY

Communication with people from our own cultures, with people from other races or ethnic groups, and with people from other cultures has the same underlying process. While communication in these different situations differs in degree, it does not differ in kind. Various names are available to label communication in these different situations, but ambiguity exists as to which label is appropriate for certain situations. Communication between a white person from South Africa and a black person from the United States, for example, can be labeled as either intercultural or interracial communication.

Given the similarity of the underlying process of communication and the confusion in applying the various labels, we believe what is needed is a way to refer to the underlying process without referring to a particular situation. Talking about communication with strangers is a way to accomplish this end. Strangers can be conceived of as people who are unknown and unfamiliar and are confronting a group for the first time. An African American student in a mainly white school, a Mexican student studying at a university in the United States, a groom meeting the bride's family for the first time, and a manager from the United States working in Thailand are all examples of strangers.

Intergroup communication is guided by our social identities and involves predicting strangers' behavior by using cultural and sociocultural data. Interpersonal communication, in contrast, is guided by our personal identities and involves predicting others' behavior by using psychological data. Both interpersonal and intergroup factors are present in virtually any encounter we have with another person. To communicate effectively in interpersonal or intergroup situations, we have to manage our anxiety and uncertainty. To accomplish this, we must be mindful. Being mindful involves creating new categories, being open to new information, and being aware of alternative perspectives.

Our communication with strangers is influenced by our conceptual filters, just as their communication with us is influenced by their filters. Our conceptual filters can be placed into four categories: cultural, sociocultural, psychocultural, and environmental. Each of these filters influences how we interpret messages encoded by strangers and what predictions we make about strangers' behavior. Without understanding strangers' filters, we cannot interpret or predict their behavior accurately.

STUDY QUESTIONS

1. How does the concept of the stranger help link interpersonal and intergroup communication?
2. Why is anxiety a typical reaction to encountering strangers?

3. Why is there greater uncertainty when we encounter strangers than when we encounter people who are familiar?
4. Why do misunderstandings occur when our uncertainty is below our minimum thresholds?
5. How does uncertainty change over time as we communicate with others?
6. What factors influence the amount of uncertainty we have when we communicate with strangers?
7. Why do we have anxiety when we communicate with strangers?
8. Why do we make inaccurate predictions of strangers' behavior when our anxiety is above our maximum thresholds?
9. How does anxiety change over time when we communicate with strangers?
10. What factors increase our anxiety when we communicate with strangers?
11. What are the consequences of high levels of anxiety?
12. What are the characteristics of mindfulness?
13. Why do we need to focus on being mindful of the process of communication (as opposed to the outcome) to communicate effectively with strangers?

SUGGESTED READINGS

Berger, C. R., & Bradac, J. (1982). *Language and social knowledge.* London: Edward Arnold.

Harman, L. (1987). *The modern stranger.* New York: Mouton de Gruyter.

Langer, E. (1989). *Mindfulness.* Reading, MA: Addison-Wesley.

Langer, E. (1997). *The power of mindful learning.* Reading, MA: Addison-Wesley.

Tajfel, H. (1982). *Human groups and social categories.* Cambridge, UK: Cambridge University Press.

Turner, J. (1987). *Rediscovering the social group.* London: Blackwell.

PART TWO

INFLUENCES ON THE PROCESS OF COMMUNICATING WITH STRANGERS

In Part One we defined communication and culture and overviewed the process of communicating with strangers. In this part we examine, in depth, the major influences on our communication with strangers.

As indicated in Chapter 2, there are four major groups of influences on our communication with strangers: cultural, sociocultural, psychocultural, and environmental. Cultural influences include the dimensions on which cultures differ (e.g., individualism-collectivism). Sociocultural influences include those stemming from our membership in social groups and our social identities. Psychocultural influences involve our expectations for strangers based on our stereotypes and the intergroup attitudes we hold, particularly ethnocentrism and prejudice. Environmental influences consist of the physical environment, geography, climate, and architecture; the situation in which communication occurs; the situational norms and rules guiding behavior; and our perceptions of the environment. Each of these groups of influences affects the way we interpret incoming stimuli and the predictions we make about strangers' behavior.

The focus of Part Two is on examining the variables making up each group of influences and looking at how they vary across cultures. We believe knowledge of how these influences vary across cultures is a prerequisite to effective communication with strangers. Without an understanding of the cultural variation in the variables, it is impossible to make accurate predictions about strangers' behavior or to interpret incoming messages from them correctly.

The four groups of influences examined in this part do not operate independently of one another; rather, each one is intertwined highly with each of the others. The cultures in which we are raised, for example, have an influence on the groups to which we belong and our group memberships and social identities (the sociocultural influences), as well as on the way we categorize things (e.g., stereotypes) and the intergroup attitudes we hold (e.g., prejudice, ethnocentrism; the psychocultural influences). Further, our cultures are influenced by the environment in which they exist and are affected by both the sociocultural and the psychocultural factors as well. Even though we separate the four groups of influences in the four chapters in this part, you should keep in mind as you read that they are interrelated highly.

3

CULTURAL INFLUENCES ON THE PROCESS

Human beings draw close to one another
by their common nature, but habits
and customs keep them apart.

Confucian saying

We examine the cultural influences on our communication with strangers in this chapter. There are two general approaches to examining cultural processes. One approach is to look at how a particular culture works from the inside. When using this approach, we are concerned with trying to understand the behavior of people in a culture from their point of view. Another approach to understanding culture is to compare one culture with another. With this approach, we use predetermined categories to examine selected aspects of the cultures being studied. In other words, the objective is to understand how the cultures compare with respect to some particular quality. These approaches are referred to as emic and etic, respectively (Pike, 1966). Our approach throughout most of this chapter is etic in nature, but we present emic research where applicable. We also summarize one emic approach used in communication (cultural communication theory) at the end of the chapter to illustrate an alternative perspective.

In order to understand similarities and differences in communication across cultures, it is necessary to have a way of talking about how cultures differ and how they are similar. It does not explain cultural differences to say that "Yuko communicates indirectly because she is Japanese" or that "Kim communicates directly because she is from the United States." This only tells us *how* people in Japan and the United States communicate; it does not tell us *why* there are differences between the ways people communicate in the United States and Japan. There has to be some aspect of the cultures in Japan and the United States that is different, and this difference, in turn, explains why Japanese communicate indirectly and people from the United States communicate directly. In other words, there are dimensions on which cultures can be different or similar that can be used to explain communication across cultures. We refer to these variables as dimensions of cultural variability.

It is important to recognize that communication is unique within each culture and, at the same time, that there are systematic similarities and differences across cultures. These similarities and differences can be explained and predicted theoretically by using dimensions of cultural variability (e.g., individualism-collectivism). In individualistic cultures, for example, individuals take precedence over groups, while in collectivistic cultures, groups take precedence over individuals (Triandis, 1988). There are systematic variations in communication that can be explained by cultural differences in individualism and collectivism. To illustrate, members of individualistic cultures emphasize person-based information to predict each other's behavior, and members of collectivistic cultures emphasize group-based information to predict each other's behavior (Gudykunst & Nishida, 1986a).

There are general patterns of behavior that are consistent in individualistic cultures, and there are general patterns of behavior that are consistent in collectivistic cultures. Individualism and collectivism, however, are manifested in unique ways in each culture. In the Japanese culture, for example, collectivism involves a focus on the concepts of *wa* (roughly translated as "harmony"), *amae* (roughly translated as "dependency"), and *enryo* (roughly translated as "reserve" or "restraint") (Gudykunst & Nishida, 1994). Other collectivistic cultures emphasize different cultural constructs as part of their collectivistic tendencies. Understanding communication in any culture, therefore, requires culture general information (e.g., where the culture falls on the various dimensions of cultural variability) and culture-specific information (e.g., the specific cultural constructs associated with the dimension of cultural variability). Our purpose in this chapter is to focus on the general patterns and illustrate how the dimensions of cultural variability can be used to explain communication across cultures.

There are many dimensions on which cultures differ. We begin by focusing on individualism-collectivism, the dimension that is used most frequently throughout the remainder of the book. We then discuss Hofstede's (1980) dimensions of cultural variability, Kluckhohn and Strodtbeck's (1960) value orientations, Parsons' pattern variables, and structural tightness. These dimensions of cultural variability provide ways to understand how communication differs across cultures even if we do not have information about specific cultures. To illustrate, if we meet people from another culture and do not know their cultural background (or we know the culture but do not have any information about it), we can make reasonable interpretations of their behavior if we understand the dimensions of cultural variability discussed in this chapter.

Before proceeding, we need to draw a distinction between the two different levels of analysis: cultural and individual. There are general tendencies in every culture on each of the dimensions of cultural variability. These general tendencies within a culture are at the cultural level of analysis. As indicated in Chapter 1, however, not all members of a culture share the general tendencies of their culture. To illustrate, Figure 3.1 diagrams how individualistic and collectivistic tendencies might differ in Japan and the United States. Most people in the United States have individualistic tendencies, but there are people with collectivistic tendencies. Similarly, most people in Japan have collectivistic tendencies, but there are people with individualistic tendencies. Cultural-level tendencies, therefore, do not predict the behavior of all individual members of a culture. To understand individuals' behavior, it is necessary to understand the individual characteristics that mediate the influence of cultural-level tendencies on individual communication. To date, most research has been on isolating individual characteristics that mediate the influence of cultural individualism-collectivism on communication. These factors are discussed in the next section.

FIGURE 3.1
Hypothetical distribution of individualistic (a) and collectivistic (b) tendencies in two cultures.

(a) Individualistic Tendencies

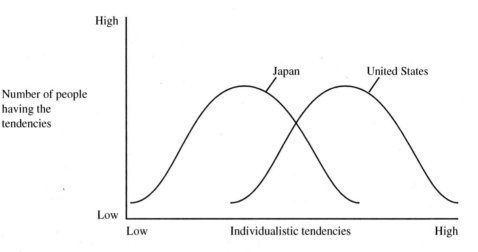

(b) Collectivistic Tendencies

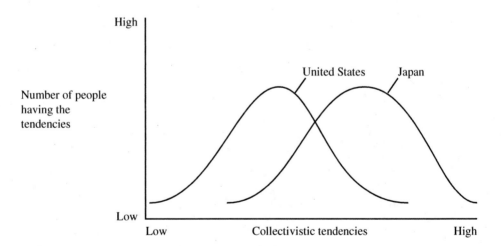

INDIVIDUALISM-COLLECTIVISM

Individualism-collectivism is the major dimension of cultural variability used to explain cross-cultural differences and similarities in communication across cultures. It also is the dimension with the clearest individual-level equivalents of the cultural-level tendencies. We begin our discussion of individualism-collectivism by looking at cultural-level tendencies.

Cultural-Level Individualism-Collectivism

Individuals' goals are emphasized more than the ingroup's goals in individualistic cultures. The ingroup's goals, in contrast, take precedence over individuals' goals in collectivistic cultures. Hofstede and Bond (1984) point out that "people are supposed to look after themselves and their immediate family only" in individualistic cultures, and "people belong to ingroups or collectivities which are supposed to look after them in exchange for loyalty" in collectivistic cultures (p. 419).

The emphasis in individualistic cultures is on individuals' initiative and achievement, and emphasis is placed on belonging to ingroups in collectivistic societies. Individualistic cultures, for example, promote self-realization. Waterman (1984) states that

chief among the virtues claimed by individualist philosophers is self-realization. Each person is viewed as having a unique set of talents and potentials. The translation of these potentials into actuality is considered the highest purpose to which one can devote one's life. The striving for self-realization is accompanied by a subjective sense of rightness and personal well-being. (pp. 4–5)

Collectivistic cultures, in contrast, require that individuals fit into their ingroups. This is illustrated by the Kenyan culture. Saleh and Gufwoli (1982) argue that

in Kenyan tribes nobody is an isolated individual. Rather, his [or her] uniqueness is a secondary fact. . . . First, and foremost, he [or she] is several people's contemporary. His [or her] life is founded on these facts economically, socially and physically. In this system group activities are dominant, responsibility is shared and accountability is collective. . . . Because of the emphasis on collectivity, harmony and cooperation among the group tend to be emphasized more than individual function and responsibility. (p. 327)

These descriptions clearly illustrate the focus on the individual in individualistic cultures and the focus on ingroups in collectivistic cultures.

Importance of Ingroups   Triandis (1988, 1995) argues that the relative importance of ingroups is one of the major factors that differentiate individualistic and collectivistic cultures. Ingroups are groups that are important to their members and for which members will make sacrifices (Triandis, 1988). Members of individualistic cultures belong to many specific ingroups (e.g., family, religion, social clubs, profession, to name only a few) that might influence their behavior in any particular social situation. Since there are many ingroups, individual ingroups exert relatively little influence on behavior. Members of collectivistic cultures belong to a few general ingroups (e.g., work group, university, family, to name the major ingroups that influence behavior in collectivistic cultures) which have a strong influence on individuals' behavior across situations. People in individualistic cultures tend to be universalistic and apply the same value standards to all people. People in collectivistic cultures, in contrast, tend to be particularistic and apply different value standards for members of their ingroups and outgroups.

The ingroup may be the same in individualistic and collectivistic cultures, but the sphere of its influence is different. The sphere of influence in an individualistic culture is very specific (e.g., the ingroup affects behavior in very specific circumstances), and the sphere of influence in a collectivistic culture is very general (e.g., the ingroup affects behavior in many different aspects of a person's life). To illustrate, in the individualistic culture of the United States the university people attend generally influences their behavior only when they are at the university or at an alumni event. In collectivistic cultures like Japan and Korea, in contrast, the university people attend influences their behavior throughout their adult lives.

Collectivistic cultures emphasize goals, needs, and views of ingroups over those of the individual; the social norms of ingroups, rather than individual pleasure; shared ingroup beliefs, rather than unique individual beliefs; and a value on cooperation with ingroup members, rather than maximizing individual outcomes. Ingroups have different rank-orders of importance in collectivistic cultures; some, for example, put family ahead of all other ingroups, and others put their companies ahead of other ingroups (Triandis, 1988). To illustrate, the company often is considered the primary ingroup in Japan (Nakane, 1970), the family is the primary ingroup in many other collectivistic cultures (e.g., Latin America), and the community is the primary ingroup in most of Africa.

Individualism-collectivism is expected to affect communication mainly through its influence on group identities and the differentiation between ingroup and outgroup communication. Cultures tend to be predominantly either individualistic or collectivistic, but both cultural tendencies exist in all cultures. Parsons (1951), for example, suggests that a self-orientation involves the "pursuit of private interests" (p. 60), and a collectivity-orientation involves the "pursuit of the common interests of the collectivity" (p. 60). He points out that the same behavior can be simultaneously self and collectivity oriented. To illustrate this position, Parsons points to department heads in organizations whose actions may be aimed toward their own welfare, the department's welfare, the firm's welfare, and even society's welfare at the same time.

Self-Ingroup Relationships in Collectivistic Cultures   In most writing on collectivism, the self-ingroup relationship is portrayed one way. U. Kim (1994) argues, however, that there are three types of self-ingroup relationships that operate in collectivistic cultures: undifferentiated, relational, and coexistence.

The *undifferentiated facet* of collectivism "is defined by firm and explicit group boundaries, coupled with undifferentiated self-group boundaries" (U. Kim, 1994, p. 33). This form of self-ingroup relationship develops in one of two ways. First, some individuals have not developed separation from their ingroups and view themselves as "enmeshed" with their ingroups. Second, some individuals choose to give up their self-identities and immerse themselves in their ingroups (e.g., cult members). In this form of collectivism, individuals are "governed and defined" by their ingroups. U. Kim contends that most discussions of collectivism (e.g., Triandis, 1995) are based on this type of collectivism. U. Kim suggests that this form of collectivism is relatively rare and often is confused with the other two forms of self-ingroup relationships.

The *relational facet* of collectivism "is depicted by porous boundaries between ingroup members that allow thoughts, ideas, and emotions to flow freely. It focuses on the relationship shared by in-group members" (U. Kim, 1994, p. 34). U. Kim suggests that this form of collectivism requires "the willingness and ability to feel and think what others are feeling and thinking, to absorb this information without being told, and to help others satisfy their wishes and realize their goals" (Markus & Kitayama, 1991, p. 229). The qualities of this type of collectivism have been discussed in terms of *amae* ("dependence") in Japan and *chong* ("affection") in Korea.

The *coexistence facet* of collectivism separates the public self and the private self (U. Kim, 1994). The public self is "enmeshed with collectivist values" (e.g., ingroup solidarity, family loyalty) and "coexists with the private self, which maintains individualist values" (e.g., personal striving) (U. Kim, 1994, p. 36). In this form of collectivism, individuals follow group norms and fulfill their roles because collective actions "need to be orchestrated cooperatively and harmoniously" (p. 37). If individuals' goals are not compatible with the ingroup's goals, those individuals are expected to make sacrifices for the harmony of the group. U. Kim points out, however, that this does not mean that individuals agree with the social norms or rules. This form of collectivism relates to the notion of *tatemae* ("conventions") and *honne* ("true intentions") in Japan. In Japan, individuals are expected to behave on the basis of *tatemae* (e.g., what is expected of them), not *honne* (e.g., what they want to do).

As indicated earlier, most analyses of collectivism focus on the undifferentiated facet of collectivism. U. Kim (1994) contends that the relational and coexistence facets of collectivism are used in Southeast Asian cultures. The relational facet is used in the Mexican culture, traditional African cultures, and Pacific Island cultures. The coexistence facet is used in the Bedouin Arab culture and Moroccan culture. Yuki and Brewer's (1999) research suggests that the undifferentiated facet of collectivism is used in the United States more than it is in Japan. They report that interdependent and distinct individuals (e.g., relational facet of collectivism) is used in Japan.

Is Distinctiveness Universal? Brewer (1991) argues that individuals have needs for inclusion in social groups as well as for distinctiveness from others. Optimal distinctiveness occurs at the point of equilibrium between the two needs, and this involves moderate distinctiveness. Brewer points out that "being highly individuated leaves one vulnerable to isolation. . . . However, total deindividuation provides no basis for comparative appraisal and self-definition" (p. 478). Brewer and Pickett (1999) suggest that inclusion and differentiation are "universal human motives," not cultural values (p. 85).

Vignoles, Chryssochoou, and Breakwell (2000) argue that distinctiveness and similarity play important roles in the construction of identities across cultures. They conclude that

> the distinctiveness principle has a fundamental role in establishing meaning in identity, which does not appear to be specific to individualistic cultures. . . . distinctiveness can be achieved in terms of position, difference, or separateness. These constructs coexist within cultures and individuals, but they will be emphasized differently according to culture and context, and they have different implications for identity processes and behavior. (p. 350)

There is, however, a need to test these conclusions in a variety of contexts and cultures.

Individualism-Collectivism and Self-Enhancement Kitayama et al. (1997) argue that there is a "cultural force in the direction of self-enhancement—namely, in the direction of attending, elaborating, and emphasizing positively valenced aspects of the self" in the United States (p. 1260). The Japanese, in contrast, must "identify consensual standards of excellence shared in a relationship (or in the society in general) and to engage in the process of self-criticism by identifying those shortcomings, deficits, or problems that prevent one from meeting such standards" in order to fit in with their ingroups (p. 1260). The Japanese, therefore, tend to engage in self-criticism rather than self-enhancement.

Heine and Lehman (1999) contend that Japanese engage in more self-criticism than U.S. Americans because Japanese have to adapt themselves to others' expectations. They report that Japanese are more dissatisfied with themselves than European Canadians, and that Japanese are distressed by self-critical attitudes less than European Canadians. Heine, Takata, and Lehman (2000) conclude that the "cultural practice of self-criticism appears to serve Japanese in their quest to achieve connection and interpersonal harmony with others" (p. 77).

Yik, Bond, and Paulhus (1998) note that the Chinese in Hong Kong engage in self-enhancement to a lesser degree than U.S. Americans. Chinese demonstrate a tendency to engage in self-effacement on communal dimensions (e.g., sociability). Individual Chinese view their self-enhancement as related to adjustment (e.g., self-esteem, emotional stability), but their peers view their self-enhancement as reflecting lack of adjustment.

Differences in self-effacing behavior appear to apply to individualistic and collectivistic ethnic groups in the United States. Akimoto and Sanbonmatsu (1999) argue that self-effacement helps maintain group harmony. They point out that "modesty may allow one to avoid offense and thereby maintain a sense of social or collective harmony. For example, if one behaves modestly by playing down one's performance, no one can be threatened or offended" (p. 160). They report that European Americans perceive Japanese Americans who engage in self-effacing behaviors as low in competence. Japanese Americans, however, do not perceive their self-effacing behaviors as reflecting negative self-evaluations. Rather, when Japanese Americans describe their behavior modestly, they may be behaving in ways they perceive to be appropriate.

Tafarodi and Swann (1996) draw a distinction between two components of self-esteem: self-competence and self-liking. They point out that "an individual's generalized attitude of self-liking is founded on others' appraisals of the individual's personal worth" (p. 653). Self-competence, in contrast, is "derived from a personal history of successful goal-directed behavior" (p. 653). These are distinct, but interrelated aspects of self-esteem. Tafarodi and Swann argue that the need to be sensitive to others and emphasizing group goals over individual goals in collectivistic cultures are conducive to self-liking because "social acceptance is promoted by adjusting one's private intentions to better fit with the perceived wishes of those in one's social milieu" (p. 654). The sense of being in control of what individuals do and who they are in individualistic cultures leads to an emphasis on self-competence. Tafarodi and Swann, therefore, propose the *cultural trade-off hypothesis:* "self-liking should be higher and self-competence lower in a highly collectivistic society than in a highly individualistic society" (p. 655). Self-liking also should be lower and self-competence higher in highly individualistic cultures than in highly collectivistic cultures. Their research in the United States and China supports this hypothesis. Tafarodi, Lang, and Smith (1999) report that individual-level measures of individualism-collectivism (e.g., idiocentrism-allocentrism; see below) also support the hypothesis.

Individualistic and Collectivistic Cultural Values   Rokeach (1972) contends that values "have to do with modes of conduct and end-states of existence. To say that a person 'has a value' is to say that he [or she] has an enduring belief that a specific mode of conduct or end-state of existence is personally and socially preferable to alternative modes of conduct or end-states of existence" (pp. 159–160).

To illustrate individualistic and collectivistic values, we compare the values that predominate in the individualistic culture of the United States with those that predominate in collectivistic Arabic cultures. Vander Zanden (1965) argues that seven principal values guide behavior in the United States:

1. *Materialism.* [U.S.] Americans are prone to evaluate things in material and monetary terms. . . . [U.S. Americans] tend to get quite excited about things as opposed to ideas, people, and aesthetic creations.
2. *Success.* Part of the [U.S.] American faith is that "There is always another chance" and that "If at first you do not succeed, try, try again." If we ourselves cannot succeed, then we have the prospect for vicarious achievement through our children.
3. *Work and Activity.* Work and activity are exalted in their own right; they are not merely means by which success may be realized; in and of themselves they are valued as worthwhile.
4. *Progress.* A belief in the perfectibility of society, man and [woman], and the world has been a kind of driving force in [U.S.] American history. . . . [U.S.] Americans tend to equate "the new" with "the best."
5. *Rationality.* [U.S.] Americans almost universally place faith in the rational approach to life. We continuously search out "reasonable," "time-saving," and "effort-saving" ways of doing things.
6. *Democracy.* "Democracy" has become almost synonymous with "the [North] American way of life." . . . We extol the Declaration of Independence with its insistence that "all men are created equal" and "governments (derive) their just power from the consent of the governed."
7. *Humanitarianism.* Philanthropy and voluntary charity have been a characteristic note of [the United States]. More recently, more attention has been given to numerous programs for social welfare, with government playing an active role. (pp. 67–69)

Obviously, all these values are not held by every person living in the United States. They are, however, values which tend to be held by a majority of the people, especially in the middle-class subculture, and, therefore, can be considered characteristic of the U.S. culture. The first five values in this list are individualistic values.

As a contrast to the U.S. American values, consider Arab values derived from the Bedouin culture (desert dwellers). Only a small percentage (about 10 percent) of present-day Arabs are Bedouins, but contemporary Arab culture holds the "Bedouin ethos as an ideal to which, in theory at least, it would like to measure up" (Patai, 1976, p. 73). Patai isolates five values predominating in the Bedouin culture:

1. *Hospitality.* The value of hospitality is aimed at meeting a more general goal of strengthening the group. This value requires a family to receive and give asylum to anyone who comes and requests it. The actual practice of hospitality varies in villages and urbanized areas, but it is still a value held by the vast majority of Arabs (Patai, 1976).
2. *Generosity.* Generosity is tied very closely with the rules of Islam and the Muslim duty of *zakat* (paying a part of one's wealth to the poor). Patai (1976) points out that "lavish generosity in traditional Arab society counterbalances

the accumulation of wealth and the development of extreme riches and poverty" (p. 87).

3. *Courage.* Courage "means essentially the ability to stand physical pain or emotional strain with such self-control that no sound or facial expression betrays the trial one is undergoing" (Patai, 1976, p. 89). It is sometimes difficult to distinguish this value from the concept of bravery, which requires that Arabs be willing to give their lives for the group.

4. *Honor.* In the Arab world honorable behavior is that "which is conducive to group cohesion and group survival, that which strengthens the group and serves its interest; while shameful behavior is that which tends to disrupt, endanger, impair, or weaken the social aggregate" (Patai, 1976, p. 90).

5. *Self-respect.* Patai (1976) argues that "Arab ethics revolve around a single focal point, that of self-esteem or self-respect. The most important factor on which the preservation of this self-esteem depends is the sexual behavior of the women for whom the Arab is responsible: his daughters and sisters" (p. 96). This value is group-based because self-respect depends on other group members' behavior.

These five values clearly are collectivistic, and they are very different from the individualistic values in the United States. (Note: Schwartz, 1994b, argues that individualistic and collectivistic values are not the only cultural values that systematically vary across cultures.)

Horizontal versus Vertical Cultures   Triandis (1995) argues that individualistic and collectivistic cultures can differ with respect to whether relations among people in the culture are horizontal or vertical. People are not expected to stand out from others in horizontal cultures. In horizontal cultures, people tend to see themselves as the same as others and there is an emphasis on valuing equality. People are expected to try to stand out from others in vertical cultures. In vertical cultures, people tend to see themselves as different from others and equality is not valued highly.

In horizontal, collectivistic cultures people highly value equality but not freedom (Triandis, 1995). To illustrate, in Japan there is a saying, "The nail that sticks out gets hammered down," which illustrates that members of the culture are not expected to stand out. In vertical, collectivistic cultures (e.g., India) individuals are expected to fit into the ingroup and, at the same time, are allowed or expected to try to stand out in the ingroup. People in vertical, collectivistic cultures do not value equality or freedom. In vertical, individualistic cultures (e.g., United States, Britain, France, Germany), people are expected to act as individuals and try to stand out from others. People in these cultures highly value freedom but not equality. In horizontal, individualistic cultures (e.g., Sweden, Norway), people are expected to act as individuals but, at the same time, not stand out from others. People in these cultures highly value equality and freedom.

To summarize, individualism-collectivism has been used widely to explain cultural differences in different types of behavior (see Triandis, 1990, for a summary). Individualism and collectivism exist in all cultures, but one tendency predominates in each culture. Table 3.1 contains a summary of the characteristics of individualistic and collectivistic cultures and presents example cultures.

TABLE 3.1

INDIVIDUALISTIC AND COLLECTIVISTIC CULTURES*

Individualism	Collectivism
Major characteristics	
Focus on individuals' goals	Focus on ingroup's goals
Emphasis on self-realization	Emphasis on fitting into ingroups
Many ingroups affect behavior	Few ingroups affect behavior
Little difference between ingroup and outgroup communication (except ethnicity)	Large difference between ingroup and outgroup communication
"I" identity emphasized	"We" identity emphasized
Universalistic	Particularistic
Individual level	
Idiocentrism	Allocentrism
Value stimulation, hedonism, power, self-direction	Value traditions, conformity, benevolence
Independent self construals	Interdependent self construals
Communication	
Low-context messages: direct, precise, clear, and absolute	High-context messages: indirect, often ambiguous, implicit, and probabilistic
*Example cultures**	
Australia	Brazil
Belgium	China
Canada	Colombia
Denmark	Egypt
Finland	Greece
France	India
Germany	Japan
Great Britain	Kenya
Ireland	Korea
Israel	Mexico
Italy	Nigeria
Netherlands	Panama
New Zealand	Pakistan
Norway	Peru
South Africa	Saudi Arabia
Sweden	Thailand
Switzerland	Venezuela
United States	Vietnam

*Example cultures are based on the predominate tendencies in each culture and Hofstede's (1980, 2001) scores.

Kashima (1989) points out that there are problems with using dimensions of cultural variability to explain individual-level behavior. One area where there are problems is that of developing causal explanations; it is impossible to test causal explanations of behavior on the basis of cultural-level explanations (e.g., culture cannot be controlled in an experiment). The second area where there are problems is in mapping individualistic and collectivistic cultures. Hofstede (1980) and the Chinese Culture Connection (1987) present cultural-level scores regarding various dimensions of cultural variability, including individualism-collectivism. (Note: These scores do not recognize that both individualism and collectivism exist in all cultures. Rather, the scores are based on the predominate tendencies in each culture.) When specific samples are collected, however, they do not necessarily correspond with the cultural-level scores. To illustrate, when college students are sampled in Japan and the United States, the Japanese college students often are more individualistic than the college students in the United States (Gudykunst et al., 1992; Triandis et al., 1988). To overcome these problems, ways to study individualism-collectivism at the individual level are needed.

Individual Factors That Mediate the Influence of Cultural Individualism-Collectivism on Individual Behavior

At least three different individual characteristics mediate the influence of individualism-collectivism on individuals' communication: our personalities, our individual values, and our self construals. Figure 3.2 schematically illustrates how the influence of cultural individualism-collectivism on communication is mediated by these factors. This relationship should be kept in mind as you read the remainder of this section. We begin with personality orientations.

FIGURE 3.2
The influence of individualism-collectivism on communication.

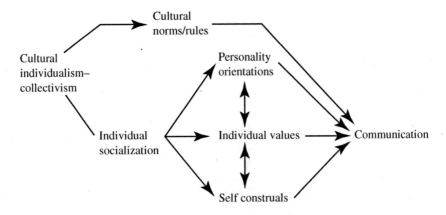

Personality Orientations The effect of cultural individualism-collectivism on communication is mediated by our personalities. Triandis, Leung, Villareal, and Clack (1985), for example, propose idiocentrism and allocentrism as the personality orientations we learn as a function of individualism and collectivism, respectively. They report that allocentrism is correlated positively with social support and negatively with alienation and anomie in the United States. Idiocentrism, in contrast, is correlated positively with an emphasis on achievement and perceived loneliness in the United States.

Gudykunst, Gao, Nishida, Nadamitsu, and Sakai (1992) report that the more idiocentric people are in the United States, the less sensitive they are to others' behavior. The more idiocentric Japanese are, the less sensitive they are to others' behavior, the less they pay attention to others' status characteristics, and the less concern they have for behaving in a socially appropriate fashion. Gudykunst, Gao, and Frankly-Stokes (1996) note that the more idiocentric Chinese and English are, the less they pay attention to others' status characteristics and the less concerned they are with behaving in a socially appropriate fashion.

Idiocentric individuals in individualistic cultures see it as natural to "do their own thing" and disregard the needs of their ingroups, and allocentric individuals in individualistic cultures are concerned about their ingroups (Triandis et al., 1988). Allocentric individuals in collectivistic cultures "feel positive about accepting ingroup norms and do not even raise the question of whether or not to accept them," and idiocentric individuals in collectivistic cultures "feel ambivalent and even bitter about acceptance of ingroup norms" (Triandis et al., 1988, p. 325).

Yamaguchi (1994) argues that collectivism at the individual level involves the tendency to give priority to the collective self over the private self, especially when the two are in conflict. He finds that the more collectivistic Japanese are, the more sensitive they are to others and the less they have a tendency to want to be unique. Yamaguchi, Kuhlman, and Sugimori (1995) report that these tendencies extend to people in Korea and the United States.

Chatman and Barsade (1995) contend that our idiocentrism-allocentrism interacts with situational demands to influence our behavior. They report that people engage in lower degrees of cooperation in individualistic situations than in collectivistic situations. Allocentrics in collectivistic situations are highly cooperative, and idiocentrics are only moderately cooperative in those situations. Ybarra and Trafimow (1998) demonstrate that activating idiocentric personalities leads people to base their behavior on their individual attitudes. Activating allocentric personalities, in contrast, leads people to base their behavior on subjective norms (i.e., what the people think their "most important others" think they should do).

Individual Values The second way that the influence of cultural individualism-collectivism on communication is mediated is through the values we hold (see Schwartz, 1994a, and Schwartz & Sagiv, 1995, for discussions of individual values). Ball-Rokeach, Rokeach, and Grube (1984) argue that our values are the central core of our personalities. They contend that our values serve as the major component of our personalities that help us maintain and enhance our self-esteem. Feather (1995) reports that the types of values we hold influence the valences (positiveness/negativeness) we attach to different behaviors. Feather (1990) points out that our values influence the way we define situations but are not tied to specific situations.

Schwartz (1992) isolates 11 motivational domains of values. Value domains specify the structure of values and consist of specific values. Specific values fall in each of the domains (example values are given in brackets):

1. *Self-direction.* "Independent thought and action—choosing, creating, and exploring" (p. 5). [independent, freedom, curious]
2. *Stimulation.* "Excitement, novelty, and challenge in life" (p. 8). [exciting life, daring]
3. *Hedonism.* "Pleasure or sensuous gratification for oneself" (p. 8). [pleasure, enjoy life]
4. *Achievement.* "Personal success through demonstrated competence" (p. 8). [social recognition, capable, ambitious]
5. *Power.* "Attainment of social status and prestige, and control or dominance over people" (p. 9). [authority, wealth, social recognition]
6. *Security.* "Safety, harmony, and stability of society, of relationships, and of self" (p. 9). [family security, social order, healthy]
7. *Conformity.* "Restraint of actions, inclinations, and impulses likely to upset or harm others and to violate social expectations or norms" (p. 9). [obedient, politeness, self-discipline]
8. *Tradition.* "Respect, commitment and acceptance of the customs and ideas that one's culture or religion imposes on the individual" (p. 10). [respect for tradition, humble, moderate]
9. *Spirituality.* "Endow life with meaning and coherence in the face of seeming meaninglessness of everyday existence" (p. 10). [meaning in life, inner harmony, devout]
10. *Benevolence.* "Preservation and enhancement of the welfare of people with whom one is in frequent social contact" (p. 11). [helpful, loyal, responsible]
11. *Universalism.* "Understanding, appreciation, tolerance, and protection for the welfare of *all* people and for nature" (p. 12). [equality, world at peace, social justice]

Stimulation, hedonism, power, achievement, and self-direction serve individual interests; tradition, conformity, and benevolence serve collective interests; and security, universalism, and spirituality serves mixed interests.

Schwartz (1990) contends that individualistic and collectivistic values do not necessarily conflict. With respect to individualistic values, he points out that

> hedonism (enjoyment), achievement, self-direction, social power, and stimulation values all serve self interests of the individual, but not necessarily at the expense of any collectivity. . . . These same values might be promoted by leaders or members of collectivities as goals for their ingroup. (p. 143)

With respect to collectivistic tendencies, Schwartz indicates that

> prosocial, restrictive conformity, security, and tradition values all focus on promoting the interests of others. It is other people, constituting a collective, who benefit from the actor's [or actress'] concern for them, self-restraint, care for their security, and respect for shared traditions. But this does not necessarily occur at the expense of the actor [or actress]. (p. 143)

Individuals, therefore, can have both individualistic and collectivistic tendencies. We can hold both individualistic and collectivistic values, but one set of values tends to predominate (e.g., guide our behavior more than the other). In the United States, for example, there are collective tendencies and some subcultures tend to be collectivistic, but most people hold individualistic values.

Schwartz and Bardi (2001) examine pancultural value hierarchies across cultures. They report that data from 13 representative samples provide a pattern of value hierarchies that is similar to those attained in student samples in 54 countries and teacher samples in 56 countries. They note that "benevolence, self-direction, and universalism values are consistently most important; power, tradition, and stimulation values are least important; and security, conformity, achievement, and hedonism [are] in between" (p. 268). Schwartz and Bardi point out that when we focus on differences, we find systematic variations at the cultural and individual levels. The differences are related to variations in individuals' behavior. When we focus on similarities, however, we find common value priorities. These similarities "can be understood as reflecting adaptive functions of values in meeting three basic requirements of successful societal functioning, ordered by importance: cooperative and supportive primary relations, productive and innovative task performance, and gratification of self-oriented needs and desires" (p. 287).

Self Construals The third way the influence of cultural individualism-collectivism on communication is mediated is through the way we conceive of ourselves (e.g., Kashima, 1989; Markus & Kitayama, 1991, 1994a, 1994b; Triandis, 1989). Triandis, for example, argues that cultural variations in individualism-collectivism can be linked directly to the ways members of cultures conceive of themselves. The focus on self construal is important because how individuals conceive of the self is one of the major determinants of their behavior. The most widely used conceptualization of self construal is Markus and Kitayama's (1991) distinction between independent and interdependent self construals. The independent self construal *predominates* in individualistic cultures, and the interdependent self construal *predominates* in collectivistic cultures.

The independent construal of self involves the view that an individual's self is a unique, independent entity (see Figure 3.3). Geertz (1975), for example, describes the self "as a bounded, unique, more or less integrated motivational and cognitive universe, a dynamic center of awareness, emotion, judgment, and action organized into a distinctive whole and set contrastively both against other such wholes and against a social and natural background" (p. 48). Individualists' cultural "goal of independence requires construing oneself as an individual whose behavior is organized and made meaningful primarily by reference to one's own internal repertoire of thoughts, feelings, and action, rather than by reference to the thoughts, feelings, and actions of others" (Markus & Kitayama, 1991, p. 226).

The important tasks for people emphasizing an independent self construal are to be unique, strive for their own goals, express themselves, and be direct (e.g., "say what you mean"; Markus & Kitayama, 1991). Individuals' self-esteem is based on their ability to express themselves and their ability to validate their internal attributes (Markus & Kitayama, 1991).

Markus and Kitayama (1991) point out that "experiencing interdependence entails seeing oneself as part of an encompassing social relationship and recognizing that

FIGURE 3.3
Independent self construals in the family.

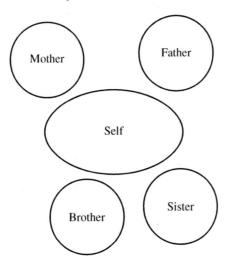

FIGURE 3.4
Interdependent self construals in the family.

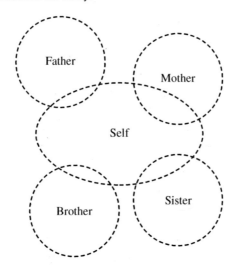

one's behavior is determined, contingent on, and, to a large extent, organized by what the actor [or actress] perceives to be the thoughts, feelings, and actions of *others* in the relationship" (p. 227; see Figure 3.4). The self-in-relation to specific others guides behavior in specific social situations. Depending on the situation, different aspects of the interdependent self will guide people's behavior. If the behavior is taking place at home, the family interdependent self guides behavior; if the behavior is taking place on the job, the coworker interdependent self guides behavior.

The important tasks for people emphasizing an interdependent self construal are to fit in with the ingroup, act in an appropriate fashion, promote the ingroup's goals, occupy their proper place, be indirect, and read other people's minds (Markus & Kitayama, 1991). Markus and Kitayama also point out that "giving in is not a sign of weakness; rather it reflects tolerance, self-control, flexibility, and maturity" (p. 229). Self-esteem is based on people's ability to adjust to others and their ability to maintain harmony in the social context when interdependent self construals predominate (Markus & Kitayama, 1991).

Gardner, Gabriel, and Lee (1999) argue that situations prime individuals to think or behave in individualistic or collectivistic ways. They had respondents in the United States and Hong Kong read a story about a trip to a city and circle either collective pronouns (e.g., "we," "they"; the interdependent prime) or independent pronouns (e.g., "I," "me"; the independent prime). The self construal that was primed by circling pronouns influenced the values the respondents endorsed (e.g., respondents in the independent prime condition in both cultures endorsed individualistic values more than those in the interdependent prime in both cultures, and vice versa). This research suggests that situational factors influence the self construals individuals use to guide their behavior.

Kanagawa, Cross, and Markus (2001) also contend that self construals are situationally based. They point out that "the content of the working self-concept is determined by the social situation at a given time and by the person's current goals, affect, and motivational states. Once activated, the working self-concept orients and directs an individual's behavior so as to facilitate adaptation to a given social context" (p. 91). Kanagawa et al. report that Japanese self-descriptions vary across situations more than U.S. Americans' self-descriptions. The reason for this is that because Japanese use an interdependent self construal, they must identify how they have to adapt to situations and relationships.

Gudykunst and Nishida (2002) examine the effect of general and family-specific self construals on family communication styles. They report that general self construals do not predict family communication styles in Japan or the United States. Family-specific self construals, in contrast, are good predictors of family communication styles in both Japan and the United States. This research suggests that self construals need to be conceptualized and measured specifically in relation to ingroups when ingroup communication is being studied.

In recent years, some researchers have questioned whether there are only two self construals. Kashima et al. (1995) and Kashima and Hardie (2000), for example, argue there are at least three self construals: individual self, relational self, and collective self (see Sedikides & Brewer, 2001, for descriptions of the three components). The individual self and the collective self are compatible with Markus and Kitayama's (1991) independent and interdependent self construals, respectively. The relational self is not based on memberships in groups, but rather on ties with specific individuals with whom people have relationships. To date, however, virtually all communication research has used Markus and Kitayama's independent and interdependent self construals.

To conclude, independent construals of the self *predominate* in individualistic cultures and interdependent construals of the self *predominate* in collectivistic cultures. It is important to recognize, however, that everyone has both an independent and an interdependent construal of the self. Further, people with predominately interdependent construals of the self exist in individualistic cultures like the United States and Australia and people with predominately independent construals of the self exist in collectivistic cultures like Japan and Korea. The critical issue is which self construal predominates to influence individuals' behavior and which self construal individuals use in guiding their behavior in a particular situation.

Low- and High-Context Communication

Individualism-collectivism provides a powerful explanatory framework for understanding cultural similarities and differences in communication in ingroups and outgroups. There are cultural differences in the communication processes that predominate in individualistic and collectivistic cultures.

Characteristics of Low-Context and High-Context Communication   Hall (1976) differentiates between low- and high-context communication. A high-context message is one in which "most of the information is either in the physical context or internalized in the person, while very little is in the coded, explicit, transmitted part of the message" (Hall, 1976, p. 79). A low-context message, in contrast, is one in which "the mass of information is vested in the explicit code" (p. 70). Hall points out that

> people raised in high-context systems expect more of others than do the participants in low-context systems. When talking about something that they have on their minds, a high-context individual will expect his [or her] interlocutor to know what's bothering him [or her], so that he [or she] doesn't have to be specific. The result is that he [or she] will talk around and around the point, in effect putting all the pieces in place except the crucial one. Placing it properly—this keystone—is the role of his [or her] interlocutor. (p. 98)

These expectations clearly are different from those used in low-context communication, where information is embedded mainly in the messages transmitted.

Members of individualistic cultures predominately use low-context communication and tend to communicate in a direct fashion, and members of collectivistic cultures predominately use high-context messages when ingroup harmony is important and tend to communicate in an indirect fashion. Levine (1985) describes communication in the collectivistic Amhara culture in Ethiopia:

> The Amhara's basic manner of communicating is indirect, often secretive. Amharic conversation abounds with general, evasive remarks, like *Min yeshallal?* ("What is better?") when the speaker has failed to indicate what issue he [or she] is referring to, or *Setagn!* ("Give me!") when the speaker fails to specify what it is he [or she] wants. When the speaker then is quizzed about the issue at hand or the object he [or she] desires, his [or her] reply still may not reveal what is really on his [or her] mind; and if it does, his [or her] interlocutor will likely as not interpret that response as a disguise. (p. 25)

Levine goes on to describe communication in the individualistic culture of the United States:

> The [U.S.] American way of life, by contrast, affords little room for the cultivation of ambiguity. The dominant [U.S.] American temper calls for clear and direct communication. It expresses itself in such common injunctions as "Say what you mean," "Don't beat around the bush," and "Get to the point." (p. 28)

These descriptions suggest that high-context communication is ambiguous and indirect and that low-context communication is direct and relatively clear.

People who generally use low-context communication often view high-context communication as ineffective. This, however, is not necessarily the case. When members of collectivistic cultures use high-context communication with ingroup members, it often (but not always) is very effective. One reason for this is that listeners use their knowledge of the context and the speaker to interpret the speaker's intent. Examples of when high-context communication is not effective are discussed below.

Conversational Maxims   Grice (1975) isolates four assumptions regarding coordinated social interaction that are characteristic of low-context communication. First, individuals should not give others more or less information than necessary (the quantity maxim). Second, people should state only that which they believe to be true with sufficient evidence (the quality maxim). Third, individuals' contributions should be pertinent to the context of conversations (the relevancy maxim). Fourth, people should avoid obscure expressions, ambiguity, excessive verbosity, and disorganization (the manner maxim). These conversational maxims are not characteristic of high-context communication.

Direct communication (Grice's, 1975, manner maxim) involves transmitting verbal messages that "embody and invoke speakers' true intentions," and indirect communication involves transmitting verbal messages that "camouflage and conceal speakers' true intentions" (Gudykunst & Ting-Toomey, 1988, p. 100). Indirect communication emphasizes listeners' abilities to infer speakers' intentions, and direct communication emphasizes speakers' ability to express their intentions (K. Okabe, 1987; R. Okabe, 1983; Yum, 1988). To illustrate, K. Okabe (1987) points out that someone being direct might say "The door is open" when asking someone to close the door, and someone being indirect might say "It is somewhat cold today."

R. Okabe (1983) suggests that low-context communication involves the use of categorical words such as "certainly," "absolutely," and "positively." High-context communication, in contrast, is expressed through the use of qualifiers such as "maybe," "perhaps," and "probably" (R. Okabe, 1983, p. 34) in conversation. Qualifier words are used to avoid leaving an assertive impression with the listener.

High-context communication involves the use of indirect, implicit, ambiguous messages when speaking. When individuals' responses to others' messages are indirect and ambiguous, the responses may not appear to be relevant to what the others said (e.g., they appear to violate Grice's, 1975, relevancy maxim). In order to communicate successfully using high-context communication, listeners must infer how what speakers say is relevant to what they said. Listeners also must infer speakers' intentions accurately to understand utterances correctly. Yum (1988b) contends that to be a competent high-context communicator, people must "hear one and understand ten" (p. 384). This saying emphasizes the importance of receivers' sensitivities and abilities to capture the nonverbal aspect of indirect communication.

Consistent with Grice's (1975) quality maxim, speaking one's mind and telling the truth are "characteristic of a sincere and honest person" using low-context communication (Hofstede, 1991). People using low-context communication are expected to communicate in ways that are consistent with their feelings (Hall, 1976). People using high-context communication, in contrast, are expected to communicate in ways that maintain harmony in their ingroups. This may involve people transmitting messages that are inconsistent with their true feelings (Hall, 1976).

Speaking their minds and telling the truth in low-context communication require that individuals be open with others. Openness involves revealing "personal information about the self in communicative interactions" (Norton, 1978, p. 101). Personal information is necessary to predict behavior when low-context communication is being used (Gudykunst & Ting-Toomey, 1988). When individuals are open, they are not reserved and are approachable. Open communicators also are not secretive and are relatively frank with others (Norton, 1978).

Openness is not characteristic of high-context communication. In high-context communication, individuals do not reveal large amounts of personal information about themselves. Personal information is not used to predict behavior in high-context communication. Rather, group-based information (e.g., background, group memberships, status, age) is needed (Gudykunst & Nishida, 1986a). Communicators perceived as competent high-context communicators are not open but tend to be reserved (R. Okabe, 1983). Being reserved is considered active, not passive, behavior in collectivistic cultures.

Low-context communication also involves being precise (Grice's, 1975, quantity maxim), and high-context communication involves the use of understatement. As indicated earlier, Grice's (1975) quantity maxim states that individuals' contributions to conversations should provide neither more nor less information than is required. High-context communication, in contrast, is not precise. Rather, high-context communication involves using understatement, or providing the least amount of information possible that allows listeners' to infer speakers' intentions, and using pauses and silences in everyday conversation. R. Okabe (1983) argues that high-context communication requires transmitting messages through understatement and hesitation rather than through superlative expression (the opposite of Grice's, 1975, quantity maxim). In high-context communication, there is a negative association between the number of spoken words people use and the images other people have of them, especially in terms of their trustworthiness. People who use few words are viewed as more trustworthy than people who use many words (Lebra, 1987).

Closely related to the lack of emphasis on spoken words is the use of silence. In low-context communication, silence is space to be filled (Mare, 1990). People using low-context communication tend to experience a general discomfort with silence because it interrupts the flow of conversations. Silence often is interpreted by people using low-context communication as violating the quantity maxim. Silence also can be viewed as violating the relevancy maxim when individuals are using low-context communication. In high-context communication, in contrast, "silence is a communicative act rather than a mere void in communicational space" (Lebra, 1987, p. 343). Lebra argues that silence can be used to indicate truthfulness, disapproval, embarrassment, and disagreement.

Individualism-Collectivism and Low-Context and High-Context Communication

High-context communication can be characterized as being indirect, ambiguous, and understated, with speakers being reserved and sensitive to listeners. Low-context communication, in contrast, can be characterized as being direct, explicit, open, and precise and being consistent with one's feelings. As indicated earlier, these patterns of communication are compatible with collectivism and individualism, respectively.

Cultural-Level Individualism-Collectivism   One of the major differences between individualistic and collectivistic cultures is that members of collectivistic cultures draw a sharper distinction between ingroups and outgroups than members of individualistic cultures (Triandis, 1988). Consistent with this view, Japanese and Koreans report greater differences in personalization, synchronization, and difficulty of communication between ingroup (classmate) and outgroup (stranger) relationships than U.S. Americans (Gudykunst & Nishida, 1986b; Gudykunst, Yoon, & Nishida, 1987). The more collectivistic the culture, the greater the difference between ingroup and outgroup communication. Similarly, there are greater differences in uncertainty management (e.g., uncertainty, self-disclosure) in ingroup and outgroup relationships in Japan than in the United States (Gudykunst & Nishida, 1986a; Gudykunst, Nishida, & Schmidt, 1989; Gudykunst, Gao, Nishida, Bond, Leung, Wang, & Barraclough, 1992).

There is further support for the argument outlined here in two studies replicating Asch's (1956) classic studies of conformity in Japan. Frager (1970) notes that levels of conformity are low in Japan (in fact, the conformity was lower than in Asch's study in the United States) when the confederates in the study are strangers (i.e., not members of an ingroup). More recently, Williams and Sogon (1984) report that when confederates are members of the respondents' ingroup, conformity is much higher than in Asch's original study. Bond and Smith (1996) report that conformity is higher in collectivistic cultures than in individualistic cultures.

Individuals use low- and high-context messages depending on their relationship with the person with whom they are communicating. To illustrate, people in the individualistic culture of the United States use low-context communication in the vast majority of their relationships (Hall, 1976). They may, however, use high-context messages when communicating with a twin or a spouse of 20 years. In these relationships, it is unnecessary to be direct and precise to be clearly understood. People in Asian, African, and Latin collectivistic cultures, in contrast, tend to use high-context messages most of the time when they communicate. They, nevertheless, also use low-context messages in some relationships (e.g., close friendships).

Research on cultural differences in communication supports Gudykunst and Ting-Toomey's (1988) argument that low-context communication and high-context communication are a function of individualism-collectivism. Members of individualistic cultures, for example, are more affect-oriented (i.e., base their behavior on their feelings; Frymier, Klopf, & Ishii, 1990) and more inclined to talk (Gaetz, Klopf, & Ishii, 1990) than are members of collectivistic cultures. Members of individualistic cultures are more motivated to communicate interpersonally to achieve affection, pleasure, and inclusion than members of collectivistic cultures (Fernandez-Collado, Rubin, & Hernandez-Sampieri, 1991). Members of collectivistic cultures pay more attention to others' behavior and more attention to others' status characteristics than members of individualistic cultures (Gudykunst, Gao, Nishida, Nadamitsu, & Sakai, 1992).

Individual-Level Individualism-Collectivism   As indicated earlier, not all members of individualistic cultures are individualists and not all members of collectivistic cultures are collectivists (Triandis et al., 1985). Individuals' communication styles are dependent on the degree to which they have internalized the values of the culture in which they are socialized and the way their culture socializes people to see themselves (e.g., as independent, unique individuals or individuals embedded in social groups). It, therefore, is necessary also to examine the way the influence of cultural individualism-collectivism is mediated by individual factors.

At the individual level, Markus and Kitayama (1991) argue that emphasizing independent self construals (one individual-level aspect of individualism) is associated with being unique, expressing the self, realizing internal attributes, and being direct. They suggest that emphasizing interdependent self construals (one individual-level component of collectivism), in contrast, is associated with belonging (fitting in), occupying one's proper place, engaging in appropriate action, and being indirect. Individuals emphasize independent and interdependent self construals in different situations, and depending on their cultures/ethnicities, they tend to use one more than the other.

Gudykunst and Nishida (1994) point out that "when a person's goal is to assert him or herself as a unique person (individualism), he or she must be direct so that others will know where he or she stands" (p. 40). Singelis and Brown (1995) report that interdependent self construals are related to using high-context communication styles, while independent self construals are not related to using high-context communication styles. Ellis and Wittenbaum (2000) note that independent self construals are correlated positively with self-promotion (i.e., "extolling one's own attributes," p. 704) and negatively with other-promotion (i.e., "extolling significant others' contributions to self-success," p. 704). Interdependent self construals are correlated positively with other promotion and negatively with self-promotion.

Gudykunst, Matsumoto, Ting-Toomey, Nishida, Kim, and Heyman (1996) report that independent self construals and individualistic values positively influence the use of dramatic communication, the use of feelings to guide behavior, openness of communication, and preciseness of communication. Interdependent self construals and collectivistic values positively influence the tendency to use indirect communication and be interpersonally sensitive. They also note that self construals are better predictors of communication styles than are cultural-level individualism-collectivism and individual-level values.

Singelis and Sharkey (1995) note that independent self construals are correlated negatively with embarrassability. Singelis, Bond, Sharkey, and Lai (1999) report that interdependent self construals correlate positively with embarrassability and that independent self construals correlate negatively with embarrassability.

Given the overview of individualism-collectivism, we turn our attention to other dimensions of cultural variability. Our emphasis in the following discussion is on the cultural level of analysis because individual-level equivalents of these dimensions have not been isolated. We begin with Hofstede's (1980, 1991, 2001) dimensions of cultural variability.

HOFSTEDE'S DIMENSIONS OF CULTURAL VARIABILITY

Hofstede (1980, 1983) empirically derived four dimensions of cultural variability in his large-scale study of a multinational corporation. The first dimension isolated in his study—individualism—already has been discussed. The other three dimensions are uncertainty avoidance, power distance, and masculinity-femininity.

Uncertainty Avoidance

Uncertainty avoidance deals with the degree to which members of a culture try to avoid uncertainty. In comparison to members of cultures low in uncertainty avoidance, members of cultures high in uncertainty avoidance have a lower tolerance "for uncertainty and ambiguity, which expresses itself in higher levels of anxiety and energy release, greater need for formal rules and absolute truth, and less tolerance for people or groups with deviant ideas or behavior" (Hofstede, 1979, p. 395). In high uncertainty avoidance cultures, aggressive behavior of self and others is acceptable; however, individuals prefer to contain aggression by avoiding conflict and competition. Since there is a strong desire for consensus in cultures high in uncertainty avoidance, deviant behavior is not acceptable. Members of high uncertainty avoidance cultures also tend to display emotions more than members of low uncertainty avoidance cultures. Members of low uncertainty avoidance cultures have lower stress levels and weaker superegos and accept dissent and taking risks more than members of high uncertainty avoidance cultures.

Hofstede (1991) points out that uncertainty avoidance should not be equated with risk avoidance.

> People in uncertainty avoiding cultures shun ambiguous situations. People in such cultures look for a structure in their organizations, institutions, and relationships which makes events clearly interpretable and predictable. Paradoxically, they are often prepared to engage in risky behavior to reduce ambiguities, like starting a fight with a potential opponent rather than sitting back and waiting. (p. 116)

Hofstede summarizes the view of people in high uncertainty avoidance cultures as "what is different, is dangerous," (p. 119) and the credo of people in low uncertainty avoidance cultures as "what is different, is curious" (p. 119).

Hofstede (1980) reports that in comparison to members of low uncertainty avoidance cultures, members of high uncertainty avoidance cultures resist change more, have higher levels of anxiety, have higher levels of intolerance for ambiguity, worry about the future more, see loyalty to their employers as more of a virtue, have a lower motivation for achievement, and take fewer risks. In organizations, workers in high uncertainty avoidance cultures prefer a specialist career, prefer clear instructions, avoid conflict, and disapprove of competition between employees more than workers in low uncertainty avoidance cultures.

Hofstede (2001) isolates several implications of cultural uncertainty avoidance for intergroup relations. He points out that there are more "critical attitudes toward younger people" and a "larger generation gap" in high uncertainty avoidance cultures than in low uncertainty avoidance cultures (p. 160). There is a "suspicion of foreigners as managers" in high uncertainty avoidance cultures and an "acceptance of foreigners as managers" in low uncertainty avoidance cultures (p. 160). Members of high uncertainty avoidance cultures reject members of other races as neighbors, believe "immigrants should be sent back" home, and are not prepared to live abroad. Members of low uncertainty avoidance cultures, in contrast, accept members of other races as neighbors, tolerate immigrants, and are prepared to live abroad.

Uncertainty avoidance is useful in understanding differences in how strangers are treated. People in high uncertainty avoidance cultures try to avoid ambiguity and, therefore, develop rules and rituals for virtually every possible situation in which they might find themselves, including interacting with strangers. Interaction with strangers in cultures high in uncertainty avoidance may be highly ritualistic and/or very polite. If people from high uncertainty avoidance cultures interact with strangers in a situation where there are not clear rules, they may ignore the strangers—treat them as though they did not exist.

Different degrees of uncertainty avoidance exist in every culture, but one tends to predominate. One individual-level factor that mediates the influence of cultural uncertainty avoidance on communication is certainty/uncertainty orientation (Gudykunst, 1995). A certainty orientation predominates in high uncertainty avoidance cultures, and an uncertainty orientation predominates in low uncertainty avoidance cultures (certainty/uncertainty orientation is discussed in Chapter 7). Another individual-level factor is tolerance for ambiguity. People in low uncertainty avoidance cultures have greater tolerance for ambiguity than members of high uncertainty avoidance cultures (tolerance for ambiguity is discussed in Chapter 10). Table 3.2 contains a summary of the characteristics of low and high uncertainty avoidance cultures and provides example cultures.

Power Distance

Power distance is "the extent to which the less powerful members of institutions and organizations accept that power is distributed unequally" (Hofstede & Bond, 1984, p. 419). Individuals from high power distance cultures accept power as part of society. As a result, superiors consider their subordinates to be different from themselves and vice versa. Members of high power distance cultures see power as a basic fact in society and stress coercive or referent power, while members of low power distance cultures believe power should be used only when it is legitimate and prefer expert or legitimate power.

In summarizing the differences between cultures low in power distance and cultures high in power distance, Hofstede (1991) points out that

> in small power distance countries there is limited dependence of subordinates on bosses, and a preference for consultation, that is, *interdependence* between boss and subordinate. The emotional distance between them is relatively small: subordinates will quite readily approach and contradict their bosses. In large power distance countries there is considerable dependence of subordinates on bosses. Subordinates respond by either *preferring* such dependence (in the form of an autocratic or paternalistic boss), or rejecting it entirely, which in psychology is known as *counterdependence:* that is dependence, but with a negative sign. (p. 27)

TABLE 3.2

LOW AND HIGH UNCERTAINTY AVOIDANCE CULTURES

Low uncertainty avoidance	High uncertainty avoidance
Major characteristics	
Low stress and anxiety	High stress and anxiety
Dissent accepted	Strong desire for consensus
Comfortable in ambiguous situations	Fear of ambiguous situations
High level of risk taking	Low level of risk taking
Deviant behavior tolerated	Deviant behavior suppressed
Few rituals	Many rituals
"What is different is curious"	"What is different is dangerous"
Workers accept ambiguous instructions	Workers want clear instructions
Small generation gap	Large generation gap
Acceptance of foreign managers	Suspicion of foreign managers
Members of other races accepted as neighbors	Members of other races rejected as neighbors
Individual level	
Uncertainty orientation	Certainty orientation
High tolerance of ambiguity	Low tolerance of ambiguity
*Example cultures**	
Canada	Egypt
Denmark	Argentina
England	Belgium
Hong Kong	Chile
India	France
Jamaica	Greece
Philippines	Japan
South Africa	Korea
Sweden	Mexico
United States	Spain

* Example cultures are based on the predominate tendencies in each culture and Hofstede's (1980, 2001) scores.

The power distance dimension focuses on the relationships between people with different statuses (e.g., superiors and subordinates in organization).

Hofstede (1980) reports that parents in high power distance cultures value obedience in their children and that students value conformity and display authoritarian attitudes more than those in low power distance cultures. In organizations, close supervision, fear of disagreement with the supervisor, lack of trust among coworkers, and directed supervision are all manifested more in high power distance cultures than in low power distance cultures. Further, Hofstede notes that members of low power distance cultures see respect for the individual and equality as antecedents to "freedom," while members of high power distance cultures view tact, servitude, and money as antecedents to "freedom." Antecedents to "wealth" in low power distance cultures include happiness, knowledge, and love. Inheritance, ancestral property, stinginess, deceit, and theft, in contrast, are viewed as antecedents to "wealth" in high power distance cultures.

Hofstede (2001) isolates implications of cultural power distance for intergroup relations. He reports that there is "latent conflict between the powerful and the powerless" and that "older people are respected and feared" in high power distance cultures (p. 98). In low power distance cultures, in contrast, there is "latent harmony between the powerful and the powerless" and "older people [are] neither respected nor feared" (p. 98).

Power distance is useful in understanding strangers' behavior in role relationships, particularly those involving different degrees of power or authority. People from high power distance cultures, for example, do not question their superiors' orders. They expect to be told what to do. People in low power distance cultures, in contrast, do not necessarily accept superiors' orders at face value; they want to know why they should follow them. When people from the two different systems interact, misunderstanding is likely unless one or both understand the other person's system.

Low and high power distance tendencies exist in all cultures, but one tends to predominate. The individual-level factor that mediates the influence of cultural power distance on communication is egalitarianism (Gudykunst, 1995). High egalitarianism predominates in low power distance cultures, and low egalitarianism predominates in high power distance cultures. Table 3.3 presents a summary of the characteristics of low and high power distance cultures and provides example cultures.

Masculinity-Femininity

The major differentiation between masculine and feminine cultures is how gender roles are distributed in cultures. Hofstede (1991) points out that

> *masculinity* pertains to societies in which social gender roles are clearly distinct (i.e., men are supposed to be assertive, tough, and focused on material success whereas women are supposed to be more modest, tender and concerned with the quality of life); *femininity* pertains to societies in which social gender roles overlap (i.e., both men and women are supposed to be modest, tender, and concerned with the quality of life). (pp. 82–83)

High masculinity involves a high value placed on things, power, and assertiveness, while systems in which people, quality of life, and nurturance prevail are low on masculinity or high on femininity (Hofstede, 1980). Cultural systems high in masculinity emphasize performance and ambition, and cultures high in femininity (low in masculinity) value quality of life and service.

Hofstede (1980) reports that in comparison to people in feminine cultures, people in masculine cultures have stronger motivation for achievement, view work as more central to their lives, accept the company's "interference" in their private lives, have higher job stress, have greater value differences between men and women in the same position, and view recognition, advancement, or challenge as more important to their satisfaction with their work.

TABLE 3.3

LOW AND HIGH POWER DISTANCE CULTURES

Low power distance	High power distance
Major characteristics	
Individuals viewed as equals	Individuals viewed as unequal
Emphasis on legitimate power	Emphasis on coercive/referent power
Superiors and subordinates are interdependent	Subordinates are dependent on superiors
Subordinates do not accept superiors' orders at face value	Subordinates do not question superiors' orders
Obedience of children to parents is not valued highly	Obedience of children to parents is valued highly
Old people not respected or feared	Old people respected and feared
Latent harmony between powerless and powerful	Latent conflict between powerless and powerful
Individual level	
High egalitarianism	Low egalitarianism
Example cultures*	
Australia	Egypt
Canada	Ethiopia
Denmark	Ghana
Germany	Guatemala
Ireland	India
Israel	Malaysia
New Zealand	Nigeria
Sweden	Panama
United States	Saudi Arabia
	Venezuela

*Example cultures are based on the predominate tendencies in each culture and Hofstede's (1980, 2001) scores.

Hofstede (1998) points out that in masculine cultures women are assigned the role of being tender and taking care of relationships. In feminine cultures, in contrast, both men and women engage in these behaviors. Fathers are expected to deal with facts with children and mothers are expected to deal with children's feelings in masculine cultures. Both parents deal with facts and feelings in feminine cultures. Employees in organizations "live in order to work" in masculine cultures" and "work in order to live" in feminine cultures (p. 16). Members of masculine cultures focus on ego enhancement, and members of feminine cultures focus on relationship enhancement, regardless of group ties.

Masculinity-femininity is useful in understanding cultural differences and similarities in opposite-sex and same-sex relationships. People from highly masculine cultures, for example, tend to have little contact with members of the opposite-sex when they are growing up. They tend to see same-sex relationships as more intimate than

TABLE 3.4

MASCULINE AND FEMININE CULTURES

Masculine	Feminine
Major characteristics	
Differentiated gender roles	Overlapping gender roles
Assertiveness, performance, things, and power are valued	Quality of life, service, being nurturing, and caring for others are valued
Sympathy for the strong	Sympathy for the weak
"Live in order to work"	"Work in order to live"
Ego enhancement	Relationship enhancement
Emphasis on performance and ambition	Emphasis on quality of life and service
Women are tender and take care of relationships	Both men and women can be tender and take care of relationships
Fathers deal with facts with children, and mothers deal with feelings	Both parents deal with facts and feelings
Individual level	
Masculine/feminine gender roles	Androgyny/undifferentiated gender roles
*Example cultures**	
Arab cultures	Chile
Austria	Costa Rica
Germany	Denmark
Italy	East African cultures
Jamaica	Finland
Japan	Netherlands
Mexico	Norway
Switzerland	Sweden
Venezuela	Thailand

*Example cultures are based on the predominate tendencies in each culture and Hofstede's (1980, 2001) scores.

opposite-sex relationships. For people from a feminine culture to communicate effectively with strangers from a masculine culture, especially if they are male and female, they must understand each other's orientation toward sex-roles.

As with the other dimensions of cultural variability, both masculinity and femininity tendencies exist in all cultures. One tendency, however, tends to predominate. One individual-level factor that mediates the influence of cultural masculinity-femininity on communication is psychological gender roles (Gudykunst, 1995). Masculine and feminine gender roles predominate in masculine cultures, and undifferentiated and androgynous gender roles predominate in feminine cultures (see Chapter 4 for a discussion of gender roles). Table 3.4 contains a summary of the characteristics of masculinity-femininity and provides example cultures.

Confucian Work Dynamism

Hofstede (1980, 1983) observed the four dimensions discussed in this section (individualism-collectivism, power distance, uncertainty avoidance, and masculinity-femininity) in his study of a large multinational company. The dimensions may have a western bias because of the methodology used in collecting the data. The Chinese Culture Connection (1987; the Chinese Culture Connection is a group of researchers organized by Michael Bond at the Chinese University of Hong Kong) tested Hofstede's conclusions by using a methodology with a Chinese bias. They isolate four dimensions of cultural variability: Confucian work dynamism, integration, human-heartedness, and moral discipline. Three of the these dimensions correlate with dimensions observed in Hofstede's study: Integration correlates with individualism, moral discipline correlates with power distance, and human-heartedness correlates with masculinity-femininity. The only dimension that does not correlate with one of Hofstede's dimensions is Confucian work dynamism (Hofstede, 2001, refers to this dimension as long-term orientation; see below for the rationale).

The Confucianism work dynamism dimension involves eight values. Four values are associated positively with the dimension: "ordering relationships by status and observing this order," "thrift," "persistence," and "having a sense of shame." Four values are associated negatively with the dimension: "protecting your face"; "personal steadiness and stability"; "respect for tradition"; and "reciprocation of greetings, favors, and gifts." The Chinese Culture Connection (1987) argues that the four positively loaded items reflect a hierarchical dynamism present in Chinese society and the four negatively loaded items reflect "checks and distractions" to this dynamism.

The Confucian work dynamism dimension is consistent with Confucianism. Hofstede (1991) summarizes the tenets of Confucianism as follows:

1. The stability of society is based on unequal relationships between people. . . .
2. The family is the prototype for all social organizations. . . .
3. Virtuous behavior towards others consists of not treating others as one would not like to be treated oneself. . . .
4. Virtue with regard to one's task in life consists of trying to acquire skills and education, working hard, not spending more than necessary, being patient, and persevering. (p. 165, italics omitted)

Confucianism influences behavior in most Asian cultures and influences the behavior of Asians living in non-Asian cultures.

Yum (1988b) suggests that in Confucianism "right conduct" emerges from "*jen* (humanism), *i* (faithfulness), [and] *li* (propriety)" (p. 377). *Jen* ("humanism") "means warm human feelings between people" (p. 377). The practice of *jen* involves engaging in virtuous behavior toward others (see tenet 3). Central to *jen* ("humanism") is *shu* ("reciprocity" or "like-heartedness") (McNaughton, 1974). The second principle, *i* ("faithfulness"), suggests that "human relationships are not based on individual profit, but rather on betterment of the common good" (Yum, 1988b, p. 377). *Li* ("ritual propriety") is the "fundamental regulatory etiquette of human behavior" (p. 378), or behaving in ways that demonstrate respect for the proper social forms.

Confucianism directly influences several different aspects of behavior in most Asian cultures. Confucianism, for example, leads Asians to see themselves in webs of reciprocal obligation; individuals are obligated to others, who in turn are obligated to them (Yum, 1988b). The obligations exist in the *wu lun* (the five basic relationships; see tenet 1 above) and other ingroup relationships. *Li* ("ritual propriety") requires that individuals meet these obligations in the proper ways. The principle of *i* ("faithfulness") is limited to ingroups. Yum (1988b) argues that "Confucianism provides an elaborate moral code for relationships among known members, but it does not provide any universal rules for others because Confucianism is a situation- and context-centered philosophy" (pp. 379–380). The primary function of communication in Confucianism is to develop and maintain social relationships.

As indicated earlier, Hofstede (2001) labels this dimension long-term orientation. (Note: A long-term orientation is associated with the values loading positively on the dimension; a short-term orientation is associated with the values loading negatively.) He changes the label because people in most cultures are not familiar with Confucius' teachings. Hofstede describes key differences between short- and long-term orientation cultures. Long-term orientation cultures are characterized by "differentiation between older and younger brothers and sisters," "shared tastes and interests not a requirement for marriages," and "old age seen as coming sooner but as a satisfying life period" (p. 366). A long-term orientation influences the ways members of cultures think: "either full or no confidence," "what is good and evil depends on the circumstances," "opposites complement each other," and "synthetic thinking" (p. 366). Short-term orientation cultures are characterized by "all siblings are equal," "couples should share tastes and interests," and "old age seen as coming later" (p. 366). Short-term orientations also influence members' of cultures thinking: "probabilistic thinking," "belief in absolute guidelines about good and evil," "need for cognitive consistency," and "analytic thinking" (p. 366).

Short- and long-term orientations exist in all cultures, but one tends to predominate. Cultures which tend to have long-term orientations include China, Hong Kong, Taiwan, Japan, South Korea, Brazil, India, Thailand, Singapore, the Netherlands, and Bangladesh (Hofstede, 2001). Cultures which tend to have short-term orientations include: Pakistan, Nigeria, the Philippines, Canada, Zimbabwe, Great Britain, United States, New Zealand, Australia, Germany, Poland, and Sweden.

Replications of Hofstede's Dimensions

The data Hofstede (1980) used to create his dimensions of cultural variability were collected over 30 years ago. Some researchers have questioned whether those scores for the four dimensions still describe where various cultures fall on each of the dimensions. Dorfman and Howell (1988), for example, created new measures for the four dimensions. Fernandez et al. (1997) used those measures to compare Hofstede's scores with scores obtained in their study in several cultures. Their data suggest that there have been some changes in country scores. Unfortunately, since they used different measures and did not use comparable samples, their conclusions must be questioned.

Merritt (2000) examines Hofstede's scores for 19 countries by using commercial airline pilots. This study suggests that recent scores correlate moderately to highly at the cultural level with Hofstede's original scores. Similarly, Oudenhoven's (2001) analysis of organizations in 10 cultures supports Hofstede's original scores. Hofstede's scores, therefore, still appear to provide reasonable descriptions of the predominate tendencies in the cultures studied.

KLUCKHOHN AND STRODTBECK'S VALUE ORIENTATIONS

Value orientations are "complex but definitely patterned . . . principles . . . which give order and direction to the ever-flowing stream of human acts and thoughts as these relate to the solution of 'common human problems' " (Kluckhohn & Strodtbeck, 1961, p. 4). The theory of value orientations is based on three assumptions: (1) People in all cultures must find solutions to a limited number of common human problems; (2) the available solutions to these problems are not unlimited but vary within a range of potential solutions; and (3) while one solution tends to be preferred by the members of any given culture, all potential solutions are present in every culture.

Kluckhohn and Strodtbeck (1961) posit five problems for which all cultures must find solutions. Posed as questions, these problems are as follows: (1) What is the innate character of human nature (human nature orientation)? (2) What is the relationship of people to nature (person-nature orientation)? (3) What is the focus of human life with respect to time (time orientation)? (4) What is the focus of human activity (activity orientation)? and (5) What is the relationship of one person to another (relational orientation)? As indicated above, every culture must find a solution to each of these problems. The solutions available, however, are limited for each of the problems.

Human Nature Orientation

The human nature orientation deals with the innate character of human nature (Kluckhohn & Strodtbeck, 1961). The potential solutions to this problem are relatively straight-forward: Humans can be seen as innately good, innately evil, or a mixture of good and evil. It is not quite that simple, however. Humans not only can be viewed as either good or evil but also can be seen as either able to change (mutable) or not able to change (immutable). In addition, we must recognize that viewing human nature as a mixture of good and evil is not the same as viewing human nature as neutral. If we combine these various aspects, we find that there are six potential solutions to this problem: (1) Humans are evil but mutable, (2) humans are evil and immutable, (3) humans are neutral with respect to good and evil, (4) humans are a mixture of good and evil, (5) humans are good but mutable, and (6) humans are good and immutable.

In applying this orientation to the United States, it is not always easy to decide which solution predominates. People in the United States inherited a view of human nature as evil but mutable from their Puritan predecessors. In this view discipline and self-control are seen as necessary if humans are to change. Some subcultures within the United States definitely adopt this solution (e.g., the Hutterites), but the predominant view in the middle-class subculture of the United States is probably the view of human nature as a mixture of good and evil.

Person-Nature Orientation

There are three potential types of relations between humans and nature: mastery over nature, harmony with nature, and subjugation to nature (Kluckhohn & Strodtbeck, 1961). These solutions are relatively straight-forward and are illustrated best by examples.

In industrialized societies like the United States, the mastery-over-nature view tends to predominate (Kluckhohn & Strodtbeck, 1961). This orientation involves the view that all natural forces can and should be overcome and/or put to use by humans; examples are damming rivers, moving mountains, and controlling illness through medicine.

The harmony-with-nature orientation draws no distinctions among human life, nature, and the supernatural—any one is just an extension of another (Kluckhohn & Strodtbeck, 1961). The Cheyenne Indians of North America, for example, see themselves as living in harmony with nature. In their view, "human aspirations are realizable not so much through the appeasement of whimsical spirit beings and gods as through action that fits the conditions of environmental organization and functioning" (Hoebel, 1960, p. 85). This orientation also predominates in other Native American groups, such as the Navajo, as well as in many Asian cultures, including those of China and Japan.

The final solution to this problem, subjugation to nature, predominates in cultures like those of the Spanish Americans of the southwestern United States (Kluckhohn & Strodtbeck, 1961). One example is sheep herders who believe nothing can be done to control nature if it threatens—neither land nor flock can be protected from storms.

Time Orientation

The temporal focus of human life can be directed on the past, the present, or the future (Kluckhohn & Strodtbeck, 1961). The concern here is not with hours, days, weeks, months, or even years but rather with a broader concept of time. People in any culture must, of course, come to terms with all three solutions, but, as pointed out above, one solution tends to predominate in a particular culture.

The past orientation predominates in cultures placing a high value on tradition (Kluckhohn & Strodtbeck, 1961). This orientation predominates in cultures worshiping ancestors (e.g., the Shinto religion in Japan) or emphasizing strong family ties. Also included here are cultures where there is some degree of traditionalism and aristocracy (e.g., England).

The present orientation predominates where people pay relatively little attention to what has gone on in the past and what might happen in the future (Kluckhohn & Strodtbeck, 1961). In this orientation, the past is seen as unimportant and the future is seen as vague and unpredictable. The Navajo Indians of northern Arizona, for example, have this orientation. To them only the here and now is real; the future and the past have little reality (Hall, 1959).

The future orientation predominates where change is valued highly. In this orientation the future generally is viewed as "bigger and better," while being "old-fashioned" (the past) is scorned. Both Kluckhohn and Strodtbeck (1961) and Hall (1959) see this orientation as predominating in the United States.

This dimension is one way to differentiate the United States and England. In the United States the future orientation tends to predominate, and in England the past orientation does. Kluckhohn and Strodtbeck (1961) argue that "some of the chief differences between the peoples of the United States and England derive from their somewhat varying attitudes toward time. [U.S.] Americans have difficulty understanding the respect the English have for tradition, and the English do not appreciate the typical [U.S.] American's disregard for it" (p. 15).

Activity Orientation

Human activity can be handled in three ways: doing, being, and being-in-becoming (Kluckhohn & Strodtbeck, 1961). The predominant orientation in the United States is doing. A doing orientation involves a focus on those types of activities which have outcomes external to the individual that can be measured by someone else. Activities must be tangible. In appraising a person, people in the United States tend to ask questions like "What did he or she do?" and "What has she or he accomplished?" If you are sitting at your desk thinking, you are not doing anything because your thoughts cannot be measured externally.

The being orientation is almost the extreme opposite of the doing orientation. This orientation involves "a spontaneous expression of what is conceived to be 'given' in the human personality" (Kluckhohn & Strodtbeck, 1961, p. 16). An example of this is the Mexican fiesta, which reveals pure impulse gratification.

The final activity orientation, being-in-becoming, is concerned with who we are, not what we have accomplished (Kluckhohn & Strodtbeck, 1961). The focus of human activity is on striving for an integrated whole in the development of the self. The best example of this orientation may be Zen Buddhist monks, who spend their lives in contemplation and meditation to develop the self fully. This view also was manifested in the self-improvement movement of the 1960s and 1970s in the United States, for example, in Maslow's (1970) self-actualized person, who is in a constant state of being-in-becoming.

Relational Orientation

This value orientation is consistent with the broad dimension of cultural variability—individualism-collectivism—discussed earlier, but there are sufficient differences that it needs to be discussed here. Kluckhohn and Strodtbeck (1961) isolate three potential ways in which humans can define their relationships to other humans: individualism, lineality, and collaterality. As we might expect, individualism is the predominant orientation in the United States. This orientation is characterized by the autonomy of the individual; in other words, individuals are seen as unique, separate entities. In this orientation individual goals and objectives take priority over group goals and objectives.

The lineality orientation focuses on the group, with group goals taking precedence over individual goals (Kluckhohn & Strodtbeck, 1961). The crucial issue in the lineality orientation is the continuity of the group through time. Specific individuals are important only for their group memberships. One example of this orientation is the aristocracy of many European countries.

Collaterality, the third relational orientation, also focuses on the group, but not the group extended through time (Kluckhohn & Strodtbeck, 1961). Rather, the focus is on the laterally extended group (an individual's most immediate group memberships in time and space). The goals of the group take precedence over those of the individual. In fact, in this orientation people are not considered except vis-à-vis their group memberships. One example of this orientation is the identification of Japanese people with the company for which they work or the university from which they graduated.

PARSONS' PATTERN VARIABLES

Another view of cultural variability is Parsons' (1951) concept of pattern variables. A *pattern variable* is "a dichotomy, one side of which must be chosen by an actor [or actress] before the meaning of a situation is determinate for him [or her], and thus before he [or she] can act with respect to that situation" (Parsons & Shils, 1951, p. 77). In other words, pattern variables are mutually exclusive choices individuals make before engaging in action. These choices are made both consciously and unconsciously; however, they generally are made unconsciously since they are learned during the socialization process at an early age. Parsons' first pattern variable is self-orientation; collective-orientation is identical to individualism-collectivism and, therefore, is omitted here.

Affectivity–Affective Neutrality

The affectivity–affective neutrality orientation is concerned with the nature of the gratification we seek (Parsons, 1951). Do we look for immediate gratification from the situation at hand (affectivity), or do we delay gratification into the future by expressing self-restraint (affective neutrality)? Affectivity is associated with emotional responses throughout Parsons' writings. Affective neutrality, in contrast, is associated with people responding from a more cognitive (nonemotional) level. The United States typically is characterized as having an affective neutrality orientation, and Latin American cultures usually are characterized as showing an affectivity orientation. People from the United States, therefore, are more likely to base decisions on cognitive information, and people from cultures with an affectivity orientation are more likely to base decisions on emotional responses.

Universalism-Particularism

This orientation is concerned with modes of categorizing people or objects (Parsons, 1951). The categorization of people or objects in terms of some universal or general frame of reference is a universalistic orientation. The categorization of people or objects in specific categories is a particularistic orientation. Universalistic interaction generally follows a standardized pattern, and particularistic interaction is unique to the situation. Given this, we expect individualistic cultures like the United States to be characterized by a universalistic orientation, while a particularistic orientation tends to predominate in collectivistic cultures like those in Asia. People from cultures in which a universalistic orientation predominates communicate with strangers in the same way in a variety of situations, and people from cultures in which a particularistic orientation predominates communicate with strangers differently in different situations.

Diffuseness-Specificity

The universalism-particularism orientation as a pattern variable is concerned with how we categorize people or objects (Parsons, 1951). The diffuseness-specificity orientation is concerned with how we respond to people or objects. If a person or an object is responded to in a holistic manner, a diffuseness orientation is displayed. If a particular aspect of a person or an object is responded to, in contrast, a specificity orientation is used. In collectivistic cultures there is a tendency for a diffuseness orientation to predominate, and the specificity orientation tends to prevail in individualistic cultures like the United States. When people from a culture in which a diffuseness orientation predominates interact with a waiter or waitress, for example, they respond to the waiter or waitress as a whole person, not just as a person filling a role. People from cultures in which the specificity orientation predominates, in contrast, respond to the waiter or waitress only in a more role-specific way.

Ascription-Achievement

Are objects or people treated in terms of qualities ascribed to them or in terms of qualities they have achieved (Parsons, 1951)? With an ascription orientation people are judged on qualities inherent in them (e.g., gender or family heritage). The prevalent orientation in the United States is achievement, while that in many other cultures (e.g., India) is ascription. People from cultures in which an ascription orientation predominates base their sociocultural predictions about others' behavior on the groups into which the others were born (gender, age, race, ethnic group, caste, etc.). People from cultures in which an achievement orientation predominates, in contrast, base their sociocultural predictions on group memberships others have achieved through their own efforts (occupational group, social class, etc.).

Instrumental-Expressive Orientation

What is the nature of the goals we seek in our interactions with others (Parsons, 1951)? Are our interactions a means to another goal (instrumental), or are our interactions an end in and of themselves (expressive)? In the expressive orientation interactions are valued because they are important, not because they will lead to anything else. Instrumental interactions, in contrast, are valued only because they help the person reach another goal. The instrumental orientation is the predominant pattern in the United States, while the expressive orientation predominates in many other cultures (e.g., Arab and Latin American cultures). People from cultures in which an expressive orientation predominates tend to value friendships for their own sake more than do people from cultures in which an instrumental orientation predominates.

To conclude, the pattern variables presented above can be used to analyze cultural differences. One specific illustration of such use is Lipset's (1963) comparison of

Great Britain, Canada, Australia, and the United States. The results of his study indicate "the United States emphasizes achievement, egalitarianism, universalism, and specificity. Canada is lower than the United States on all of these dimensions. Great Britain in turn ranks lower than Canada. Australia was found more egalitarian but less achievement-oriented, universalistic, and specific" (Zavalloni, 1980, p. 89). Thus, although these cultures appear very similar on the surface, their underlying orientations toward action are significantly different.

STRUCTURAL TIGHTNESS

Structural tightness focuses on the norms, rules, and constraints cultures place on individuals' behavior. Norms and rules are discussed in depth in Chapter 6, but for our present purpose we can define norms as guidelines for behavior based on the moral code and rules as guidelines for behavior that are not based on the moral code (Olsen, 1978). Tight cultures impose many rules and constraints on behavior, while loose cultures place few rules and constraints on behavior (Triandis, 1994). This dimension shares many similarities with Hofstede's uncertainty avoidance dimension of cultural variability (i.e., low uncertainty avoidance cultures are "loose," and high uncertainty avoidance cultures are "tight").

In tight cultures, the norms and rules of the culture tend to be clear and people are expected to follow the norms and rules of the culture (Pelto, 1968). If members violate the norms or rules of the culture, sanctions are imposed on them (e.g., they are punished in some way; this may vary from a disapproving glance to being ostracized from the group). In loose cultures, the norms and rules may not be very clear and people are allowed to deviate from the norms and rules to some degree (Pelto, 1968). The norms and rules in loose cultures tend to rather elastic, rather than rigid as they are in tight cultures. When norms and rules are violated in loose cultures, the sanctions are not as severe as they are in tight cultures.

Triandis (1994) argues that cultural homogeneity (people are similar) tends to lead to structural tightness. One reason for this is that similarity among members of a culture tends to lead to agreement about behavior that is correct in specific situations. Cultural heterogeneity (people are different) tends to lead to cultural looseness. One reason for this is that it is difficult to get people who are different to agree on what behavior is correct in a particular situation. The degree to which there is a need for coordinated action also influences the degree of structural tightness. The greater the need for coordinated action, the more tight the culture.

Mosel (1973) points out a relationship between the looseness or tightness of the social structure and the predictability of behavior. He believes behavior is much more predictable in a tight social structure than in a loose social structure. The degree of certainty we have about how another person will behave, therefore, decreases as we go from a culture with a tight social structure to one with a loose social structure.

The United States tends to be a loose culture, but it is not as loose as Thailand. To illustrate, Phillips (1965) reports that behavior in Thailand is not highly disciplined or regimented and lacks regularity. In companies, he observes that there may not be clear hours employees are expected to work. Phillips also notes that employees may decide to quit a job and just stop coming to work rather than formally resigning. The reasons for leaving may vary from being bored to wanting to take a trip, wanting to go home (e.g., the home village of a person working in a city). In general, Thais see behavior as unpredictable and view life as a series of accidents.

To illustrate the problems of intercultural communication in a highly loose social structure, we can look at a U.S. American businessman working in Thailand (this example is drawn from *The Bridge,* Summer, 1979, p. 19). After spending some time in Thailand, the U.S. American businessman discovers that the deadlines he imposed for his Thai subordinates are not being met. The employees verbally agree to complete the work on time; in other words, they agree to meet the supervisor's role expectation. When it is time to turn in their work, however, they fail to do so, and the U.S. American becomes increasingly upset with this behavior. In order to understand the problem, the businessman talks about it with several Thai supervisors. Each of the Thai supervisors tells the U.S. American the same thing, *Mai pen rai,* a Thai saying meaning roughly, "Don't worry about it; it doesn't really matter." This example suggests that a tremendous amount of variation from the ideal role is tolerated in Thai culture.

Japan is an example of a tight culture (Embree, 1950). Hearn (1956), an early observer of Japanese society, notes that "the only safe rule of conduct in a Japanese settlement is to act in all things according to local custom; for the slightest divergence from the rule will be observed with disfavor" (p. 100). Benedict (1946) also observes that Japan is a "rigidly chartered world" where the value of a person is measured by his or her ability to carry out "all the rules of good behavior" (p. 225). While the rules are rigid, there are groups of people who are not expected to follow the rules (Edgerton, 1985). Drunks, mentally ill people, and foreigners, for example, can violate rules without harsh penalties because they are not responsible for their behavior (drunks and the mentally ill) or are not expected to know the rules (foreigners).

The tightness of the Japanese culture is seen in the concepts of *on* and its reciprocal, *ongaeshi*. *On* and *ongaeshi* involve a reciprocal set of obligations between a superior and a subordinate. Beardsley (1965) explains that "*on* is a beneficence handed down from one's superior. It institutes an obligation (*ongaeshi*) to the superior on the part of the person who receives its benefit. By its very nature, *on* always connotes a hierarchical relation between two specific [people]" (p. 94). Although the superior-inferior aspect of the *on-ongaeshi* relationship is not stated explicitly, it is accepted by all parties. Beardsley (1965) points out that the person filling the superior role may be one of four types: (1) "a class superior," for example, an employer; (2) "a kin superior," for example, a person's grandparent or parent; (3) "an age-status superior," for example, a teacher; and (4) "a superior in a limited situation," for example, the person who arranges one's marriage. Once an *on-ongaeshi* relationship is begun, the inferior has an obligation for loyalty to the superior for as long as the relationship lasts, with little deviation being permitted.

CULTURAL COMMUNICATION

The preceding material in this chapter has focused on etic approaches to studying the influence of culture on communication (i.e., using constructs developed by researchers such as individualism-collectivism to look at how communication varies across cultures). As indicated in the introduction to the chapter, the other approach to studying culture and communication is emic (i.e., trying to understand communication in a culture from insiders' perspectives). The major emic approach used to study communication and culture is cultural communication.

Philipsen (1981) lays out the groundwork for the study of cultural communication. He argues that

> the function of communication in cultural communication is to maintain a healthy balance between the forces of individualism and community, to provide a sense of shared identity which nonetheless preserves individual dignity, freedom, and creativity. This function is performed through maintaining a balance or equilibrium between the two sub-processes of cultural communication, (1) the creation, and (2) the affirmation, of shared identity. (p. 5)

Cultural communication, therefore, involves the negotiation of cultural codes through communal conversations. Communal conversations are communicative processes through which individuals negotiate how they will "conduct their lives together."

Philipsen (1981) isolates three characteristic forms of cultural communication we use to create and affirm shared identities: rituals, myths, and social dramas. *Rituals* involve a "structured sequence of symbolic acts" (p. 6). One example of a ritual is the "call-response" used in African American churches. Philipsen argues that rituals help us maintain the consensus "necessary for social equilibrium" (p. 7). A *myth* is a "great symbolic narrative which holds together the imagination of a people and provides bases of harmonious thought and action" (p. 7). *Social dramas* "consist of a dramatic sequence in which social actors [or actresses] manifest concern with, and negotiate the legitimacy and scope of, the group's rules of living" (p. 8). Social dramas provide ways to define a group's boundaries. Philipsen suggests that different rituals, myths, and social dramas exist in different groups. In individualistic cultures, for example, we would expect to see social dramas in which individuals are reintegrated into their communities.

Philipsen (1992) draws on ethnographic research in numerous cultures to propose speech code theory, a theory of "culturally distinctive codes of communication conduct" (p. 56). Speech code theory posits that communal conversations imply distinctive codes of communication. He suggests that "a speech code refers to a historically enacted, socially constructed system of terms, meanings, premises, and rules pertaining to communicative conduct" (p. 56).

Philipsen (2001) isolates two principles of cultural communication. Principle 1 states that "every communal conversation bears traces of culturally distinctive means and meanings of communicative conduct" (p. 53). Philipsen believes that the notion that members of groups engage in communal conversations is a universal of human life but that each communal conversation has culture-specific aspects. He goes on to point out that communal conversations take place through particular means and have particular meanings:

> *Means* refer to particular languages, dialects, styles, routines, organizing principles, interpretive conventions, ways of speaking, and genres of communication. The *meanings* of these means refer to the significance that people experience in relation to them, that is, what they take them to be and whether they judge them to be appropriate, intelligible, efficacious, pleasing, and so forth. (p. 55)

The means and meanings are culture-specific resources for communication.

Philipsen's (2001) second principle of cultural communication is that "communication is a heuristic and performative resource for performing the cultural function in the lives of individuals and communities" (p. 59). The communal function involves "how individuals are to live as members of a community" (p. 59). Communication is "heuristic" because it is through communication that babies and newcomers to the community learn the specific means and meanings in the community. Communication is "performative" because it allows individuals to participate in the communal conversation.

There has been extensive cultural communication research in a variety of communities (e.g., *dugri* speech in Israel, Colombian address terms, pronouns of personal address in Mexico and Germany; see Philipsen, 2001, for a listing of research). Some of this research is cited where appropriate in the remainder of the book.

SUMMARY

In this chapter we examined dimensions of cultural variability which allow us to understand why patterns of communication are similar or different across cultures. Individualism-collectivism is the dimension of cultural variability most widely used to explain communication across cultures. Low-context communication is the predominant mode of communication in individualistic cultures, and high-context communication is the predominant mode of communication in collectivistic cultures. The influence of cultural individualism-collectivism on communication is mediated by our personalities, our values, and our self construals.

Hofstede's dimensions of cultural variability, Kluckhohn and Strodtbeck's value orientations, Parsons' pattern variables, and structural tightness also can be used to explain variations in communication behavior across cultures. By understanding where strangers' cultures fall on the various dimensions of cultural variability guiding their behavior, we can increase our ability to interpret and predict their behavior accurately, thereby decreasing the likelihood of misunderstandings. The study of cultural communication provides a way to describe culture-specific components of communication.

STUDY QUESTIONS

1. What are the differences between the emic and etic approaches to the study of culture?
2. Why do we use dimensions of cultural variability to explain similarities and differences in behavior across cultures?
3. Why do ingroups have more influence on behavior in collectivistic cultures than in individualistic cultures?
4. Why is there an emphasis on independent self construals in individualistic cultures and on interdependent self construals in collectivistic cultures?
5. Why does low-context communication predominate in individualistic cultures and high-context communication predominate in collectivistic cultures?
6. Why is ambiguity a major problem in high uncertainty avoidance cultures but not in low uncertainty avoidance cultures?

7. How can we use power distance to understand cultural variation in communication behavior?
8. What differences would you expect in same-sex and opposite-sex communication in masculine and feminine cultures?
9. How does the activity orientation explain cultural variability in communication?
10. How does the structural tightness of a culture influence the predictability of its members' behavior?
11. How does cultural communication explain the relationship between communication and culture?

SUGGESTED READINGS

Edgerton, R. (1985). *Rules, exceptions, and social order.* Berkeley: University of California Press.

Hall, E. T. (1976). *Beyond culture.* New York: Doubleday.

Hofstede, G. (1997). *Culture and organizations* (2nd ed.). London: McGraw-Hill.

Hofstede, G. (2001). *Culture's consequences* (2nd ed.). Thousand Oaks, CA: Sage.

Kim, U., Triandis, H. C., Kagitcibasi, C., Choi, S. C., & Yoon, G. (Eds.). (1994). *Individualism-collectivism: Theory, method, and application.* Thousand Oaks, CA: Sage.

Kluckhohn, F., & Strodtbeck, F. (1961). *Variations in value orientations.* New York: Row, Petersen.

Philipsen, G. (1992). *Speaking culturally.* Albany: State University of New York Press.

Sedikides, C., & Brewer, M. (Eds.). (2001). *Individual self, relational self, collective self.* Philadelphia: Psychology Press.

Triandis, H. C. (1995). *Individualism & collectivism.* Boulder, CO: Westview.

4

SOCIOCULTURAL INFLUENCES ON THE PROCESS

In every situation the person seems to know what group he [or she] belongs to and to what group he [or she] does not belong. He [or she] knows more or less clearly where he [or she] stands, and this position largely determines his [or her] behavior.

Kurt Lewin

Our communication with strangers is influenced by our cultures and by the group memberships we form within our cultures. Our group memberships provide us with social identities that guide our communication. We have numerous social identities that influence our communication with strangers including our cultural identities, our ethnic identities, our gender identities, our age identities, and our social class identities, as well as our identities based on whether we have a disability and our identities based on the roles we fill.

Our purpose in this chapter is to examine the sociocultural influences on our communication with strangers. More specifically, we examine the influence of our memberships in social groups, our social identities, and our role relationships on our communication with strangers. Each of these factors is influenced by our cultures, and each, in turn, influences the others. Our memberships in social groups, for example, influence our social identities and how we look at our role relationships. We conclude by presenting theories of identity negotiation in intergroup encounters.

MEMBERSHIPS IN SOCIAL GROUPS

A *social group* is "two or more individuals who share a common social identification of themselves or . . . perceive themselves to be members of the same social category" (Turner, 1982, p. 15). There are many different aspects of our group memberships that influence our communication with strangers. We begin by looking at membership and reference groups.

Membership and Reference Groups

We are members of many different social groups, such as our families, social classes, racial groups, ethnic groups, sexes, occupational groups, and nationalities. If we are conscious of belonging to groups or social categories, those groups are *membership groups.* Janis and Smith (1965) isolate several factors that lead us to maintain our associations with our membership groups. First, we obtain positive rewards from our membership in groups, including affection, prestige, status, and friendship. Second, we desire to avoid the social isolation that can take place without close group ties. Finally, there are restraints that act upon us to keep us in certain groups even if we prefer to leave. We cannot, for example, choose our races or ethnic groups.

There is a difference between those groups to which we actually belong and those groups to which we would like to belong. When we look to another group for guidance in determining our behavior, that group is a *reference group.* Sarbin and Allen (1968) define a reference group as

> a group which a person values. It is often used to explain behavior oriented toward audiences not physically present. A reference group may be a membership or nonmembership group, a single other person . . . a category of people, or even nonexistent groups or categories of people, for example, the future generation, God, ancestors. (p. 532)

In other words, reference groups are groups to which we look for guidance in how to behave. The closer our values coincide with those held by particular groups, the greater is the likelihood that we view those groups as reference groups (Sarbin & Allen, 1968).

One of the largest membership groups to which we belong is our nation. Nations usually are defined in terms of historical, political, social, and economic events shared by groups of people. Such a conceptualization, however, ignores the degree of consensus people have about their membership in their groups or nations. Emerson (1960) proposes that "the simplest statement that can be made about a nation is that it is a body of people who feel they are a nation; and it may be that when all the fine-spun analysis is concluded this will be the ultimate statement as well" (p. 102).

All of us are members of majority groups and minority groups. Schaefer (1979) isolates five characteristics of minority group membership. First, members of minority groups are treated differently from members of a majority group by the members of the majority group. This inequality usually takes the form of segregation, prejudice, and discrimination. Second, members of minority groups have either physical or cultural characteristics that make them stand out from the majority group. Third, because members of minority groups stand out, membership in them is not voluntary. Fourth, members of minority groups tend to associate with and marry other members of their groups. Finally, "members of a minority group are aware of their subordinate status, which leads to strong group solidarity" (Schaefer, 1979, p. 8). The term *minority group* is not viewed positively by many non-European Americans in the United States today. Also, given the demographic changes taking place in the United States, there will not be a "majority group" sometime in this century. We avoid the use of this classification whenever possible, but there are a few points where it is necessary to use it.

Wirth (1945) distinguishes between two types of minority groups. *Racial groups* possess "racial marks, . . . the most visible and permanent marks with which we are afflicted" (p. 347). *Ethnic groups,* in contrast, possess distinctive linguistic, religious, cultural, or national characteristics. The distinction between racial and ethnic groups often is not clear, and this is often a difficult distinction to make. It is important, however, to keep in mind that both race and ethnicity are socially constructed categories. Jacobson, for example, refers to race as a "fabricated" social category. Many groups considered races 100 years ago are no longer considered separate races today.

Several writers argue that the concept of race should be dropped from both popular and scientific usage. Montagu (1952), for example, suggests a broad definition of ethnic group, which encompasses the concept of race:

> An ethnic group represents one of a number of populations, which together comprise the species *Homo sapiens,* but individually maintain their differences, physical or cultural, by means of isolating mechanisms such as geographic and social barriers. These differences will vary as the power of the geographic and social boundaries vary. Where these boundaries are of low power, neighboring ethnic groups will integrate or hybridize one another. Where the barriers are of high power, such ethnic groups will tend to remain distinct from each other or replace each other geographically or ecologically. (pp. 87–88)

Montagu (1972) contends that substituting the term ethnic group for race would help avoid the negative connotations associated with racial terms.

There also is another reason to focus on ethnicity rather than race. Our "biological race" does not influence our communication. Our ethnicity, in contrast, does influence our communication. Ethnicity influences our communication because it is based on a shared cultural heritage in our ethnic groups. We use the term ethnicity rather than race whenever possible. Race, however, cannot be ignored because European Americans often categorize non-European Americans on the basis of their races.

In addition to nation, minority-majority, race, and ethnicity, there are other group categorizations that influence our communication with strangers. These include, but are not limited to, female-male, social class, able-bodied–disabled, and young-old. Like nation, social class, minority-majority, race, and ethnicity, other group categories are the basis for classifying people as members of ingroups or outgroups. We discuss social identities based on these group memberships later in this chapter.

Ingroups and Outgroups

As part of our socialization into our membership groups, we are taught to interact with members of certain groups of people because of their ethnic heritage, religion, or social class, to name only a few of the characteristics. The groups with which we are taught to associate are referred to as ingroups. More formally, *ingroups* are "groups of people about whose welfare [we are] concerned, with whom [we are] willing to cooperate without demanding equitable returns, and separation from whom leads to discomfort or even pain" (Triandis, 1988, p. 75). The groups of people with whom we are taught *not* to associate, in contrast, are referred to as outgroups. *Outgroups* are groups of people about whose welfare we are not concerned and with which we require an equitable return in order to cooperate. The tendency to draw a distinction between ingroups and outgroups is universal among humans (Brewer & Campbell, 1976).

Members of collectivistic cultures draw a firmer distinction between ingroups and outgroups than members of individualistic cultures (Triandis, 1995). When collectivists encounter strangers who are members of one of their ingroups, they are "inclined to help, support, cooperate, and even self-sacrifice" (Triandis & Trafinow, 2001, p. 372). When collectivists encounter strangers who are members of outgroups, in contrast, "distrust, competition, and hostility can be typical responses. Individualists do not show such strong differences in behavior when they deal with ingroup and outgroup members" (p. 372). There also is a greater difference in ingroup-outgroup communication in collectivistic cultures than in individualistic cultures (e.g., Gudykunst et al., 1992; Gudykunst et al., 1987).

There are several consequences of the formation of ingroups and outgroups. First, there is a tendency for us to expect other members of our ingroups to behave and think similarly to the way we do (Tajfel, 1969a). Second, individualists tend to perceive outgroups as highly homogeneous and see more variability in ingroups than in outgroups (Tajfel, 1969a). Collectivists, however, tend to see both ingroups and outgroups as relatively homogeneous (Triandis, McCusker, & Hui, 1990). Third, we have a tendency to put our own groups in a favorable light when they are compared to outgroups (i.e., there is an *ingroup bias;* Brewer, 1979). Triandis and Trafinow (2001) argue that the ingroup bias is greater in collectivistic cultures than in individualistic cultures. The first three consequences influence the way we categorize and use information about strangers, who are, by definition, members of outgroups. Fourth, we have less anxiety about interacting with members of our ingroups than about interacting with members of outgroups (Stephan & Stephan, 1985). Fifth, we tend to be more accurate in predicting the behavior of members of our ingroups than we are in predicting the behavior of members of outgroups (Gudykunst, 1995).

As indicated in the preceding paragraph, the ingroup bias is one of the major consequences of drawing a distinction between ingroups and outgroups. Social identity theory (e.g., Tajfel & Turner, 1979) suggests that we maintain positive social identities by evaluating our ingroups positively when we compare them to outgroups. Rubin and Hewstone (1998) report that intergroup discrimination elevates ingroup members' self-esteem, but this does not always happen. Aberson, Healy, and Romero (2000) note that individuals with high self-esteem consistently exhibit an ingroup bias. The ingroup bias exhibited by people with low self-esteem, however, is constrained by situational factors. Individuals with low self-esteem do not tend to use direct strategies (e.g., rating their ingroups higher than outgroups) to exhibit ingroup bias. Rather, they use indirect strategies (e.g., "favoring groups to which the individual did not contribute," p. 170) to exhibit ingroup bias.

Ingroup bias does not always occur at high levels in intergroup encounters. Crisp, Hewstone, and Rubin (2001), for example, report that categorizing outgroup members in more than one category can reduce ingroup bias. To illustrate, if African Americans are interacting with European Americans, the African Americans may use ethnicity and religion to categorize the European Americans. When ingroup members use more than one category, they treat outgroup members "more like individuals than group members" (p. 85), and this reduces the ingroup members' tendency to exhibit the ingroup bias. Multiple categorization and cross-cutting categories are discussed in more detail in the final section of Chapter 5.

Mummendey and Wenzel (1999) argue that how we view the way the outgroups are different from our ingroups influences how we respond. They point out that "if the outgroup's difference is judged to be nonnormative and inferior, devaluation, discrimination, and hostility are likely responses to the outgroup. Judging the outgroup's difference to be normative or positive leads to acceptance and appreciation of this group" (p. 158, italics omitted).

Grieve and Hogg (1999) also contend that categorization is not sufficient to lead to discrimination against outgroups. They report that outgroup discrimination occurs when individuals categorize themselves as members of ingroups in order to reduce subjective uncertainty about members of outgroups. They point out that "people strive to feel certain that they are correct so they may ascribe meaning to their world and their place within it" (p. 927). Correctness, however, emerges from "perceived agreement with others who are considered to be similar to self on conceptually relevant dimensions" (p. 927). This research suggests that if we are not trying to reduce subjective uncertainty about strangers, discrimination against strangers does not necessarily occur.

The images ingroup members have of outgroups are passed to children by adults. Levine (1965) argues that

> the images of an out-group that adults pass on to children are affected by the amount of direct experience the adults have had with members of the out-group and by the amount of conspicuous difference (in physical features, dress, language, and occupational specialization) between the in-groups and the out-groups. (p. 49)

Not only are images of outgroups passed to children by adults, they also are reinforced by peer group interactions within a culture.

As would be expected given our discussion of individualism-collectivism in Chapter 3, there are cultural differences in communication with members of ingroups and outgroups. Wetherall (1982), for example, notes that both Europeans (individualistic) and Polynesians (collectivistic) in New Zealand display bias when interacting with people from other groups, but Polynesians moderate their discrimination and show greater generosity to outgroup members compared with Europeans. Wetherall's findings are compatible with Feldman's (1968) field study in Paris, Boston, and Athens. Feldman observes that outgroup members were "treated better" in Athens (the most collectivistic) than in Boston and Paris (both individualistic). Feldman's results, however, may be unique to Greece, where foreigners and guests are perceived as potential members of the ingroup. Strangers in other collectivistic cultures generally are not viewed as potential members of the ingroup (Triandis, 1988).

THE NATURE OF SOCIAL IDENTITIES

The most important component of our self-concepts influencing our communication with strangers is our social identities. Tajfel (1972) contends that we constantly strive to define ourselves regarding the world in which we live. One of the major cognitive "tools" we use in this process is social categorization. *Social categorization* is "the ordering of social environment in terms of groupings of persons in a manner which makes sense to the individual" (Tajfel, 1978, p. 61), for example, men and women, students and professors, Vietnamese Americans and African Americans. Grieve and Hogg (1999) argue that "people apply social categorizations to themselves and others to clarify their perception of the social world and their place in it and thus render it more meaningful and predictable—identification reduces subjective uncertainty" (p. 936). Members of collectivistic cultures define the self in terms of social categories more than members of individualistic cultures (Altouchi & Altouchi, 1995; Traindis, McCusker, & Hui, 1990).

The strategies we use in social categorization are learned through socialization into the various social groups to which we belong. Once we become aware of belonging to one or more social groups, our social identities begin to form. *Social identities* are those parts of an "individual's self-concept which derive from his [or her] knowledge of his [or her] membership in a social group (or groups) together with the value and emotional significance attached to that membership" (Tajfel, 1978, p. 63). Our social identities can be based on membership in demographic categories (e.g., nationality, ethnicity, gender, age, social class), the roles we play (e.g., student, professor, parent), membership in formal or informal organizations (e.g., political parties, social clubs), associations or vocations (e.g., scientist, artist, gardener), or membership in stigmatized groups (e.g., homeless person, person with AIDS; see Deaux et al., 1995, for a study of the parameters of social identities).

Deaux and Perkins (2001) argue that our self-representations (including our social identities) are relatively consistent and enduring. Our identities provide a "set of meanings" that influence our interpretations of strangers' behavior and influence our behavior. The various aspects of our self-concepts (e.g., our personal and social identities) combine to provide a coherent sense of self. Even though our identities are relatively stable, they can change over time. The identities we use to guide our behavior are independent of any particular social setting (Deaux & Perkins, 2001), but situations influence the identities we activate to guide our behavior.

Characteristics of Social Identities

Brewer (1991) argues that our social identities emerge from the tension between our need to be seen as similar to and fit in with others and our need to be seen as unique. The need to be seen as similar allows us to identify with different groups and involves the general process of *inclusion.* Stevens and Fiske (1995) view belonging to groups as an important motive for our behavior because it removes ambiguity about ourselves and others, and helps us plan our actions. The need to be seen as unique is based on the general process of *differentiation,* or making ourselves stand out from others (Brewer, 1991). In individualistic cultures like the United States, balancing these two tensions usually involves emphasizing differentiation more than inclusion. In collectivistic cultures, in contrast, balancing the tensions usually involves emphasizing inclusion more than differentiation.

Brewer and Roccas (2001) point out that people with individualistic value orientations identify with "larger and more inclusive social groups" than people with collectivistic value orientations (p. 232). They go on to argue that whether we see our ingroups as distinct or overlapping influences how we view our social identities. Brewer and Roccas contend that

> to the extent that individuals see their multiple group identities as different or nonoverlapping, they will have complex, differentiated social identities and will conceptualize their ingroups as heterogeneous and inclusive. To the extent that individuals perceive their ingroups as highly similar and overlapping, their conceptualization of in-groups will be simple, homogeneous, and exclusive. (p. 233)

They conclude that identity complexity (e.g., heterogeneous and nonoverlapping ingroups) is higher among individualists than among collectivists.

Smith and Bond (1993) point out that some social identities, such as ethnicity and gender, are important in most situations. Other social identities, in contrast, are important only when they are distinctive, when there are only a few people holding the social identity present in the situation. To illustrate, if a lower-class person is alone in a group of upper-middle-class people, the lower-class person's social class identity will be activated. If there are an equal number of lower-class and upper-middle-class people present, in contrast, social class identities may not be activated.

The degree to which we perceive strangers to be typical members of their groups also influences whether we activate our social identities (Smith & Bond, 1993). If we are interacting with members of other ethnic groups and perceive them to be typical members of their groups, for example, we activate our ethnic identities. If we do not perceive others to be typical members of their ethnic groups, in contrast, we do not activate our ethnic identities. Rather, we use other social identities or our personal identities to guide our behavior.

The social relations between groups also affect whether social identities are activated (Smith & Bond, 1993). If there are good relations between ethnic groups, for instance, ethnic identities may not be activated when members of different ethnic groups interact. If there are hostile relations between ethnic groups, in contrast, ethnic identities are activated when members of different ethnic groups interact.

Dimensions of Social Identities

Deaux (1991) argues that social identities differ on two dimensions: voluntary-involuntary and desirable-undesirable. A *voluntary identity* is one that we can choose, while an *involuntary identity* is one where we do not necessarily have free choice (others may categorize us in an involuntary identity). *Desirable identities* are those we think are positive, and *undesirable identities* are those we think are negative. The voluntary nature of identities influences the amount of effort we need to maintain the identities; voluntary identities require more effort and work than do involuntary identities. The desirability dimension influences the degree to which we express our identities or hide them (Deaux, 1991). This dimension, therefore, influences the degree to which we feel pride or shame when expressing our identities. We feel pride when expressing identities we perceive to be desirable and shame when expressing identities we perceive to be undesirable.

Table 4.1 displays *one group* of people's perceptions of various social identities on these dimensions. Your perceptions of the identities in Table 4.1 may be different from those listed. There is not widespread agreement on the desirability of some social identities. Gay and lesbian, for example, are social identities listed as undesirable in Table 4.1. Obviously, not everyone would agree that gay and lesbian are undesirable social identities. One consequence of viewing gay/lesbian as an undesirable social identity, however, is that gay bashing has become widespread in the United States in recent years.

People who can hear often view deafness as an undesirable identity. Deaf people do not necessarily agree with this assessment. Lane (1993), for example, points out:

> If the birth of a Deaf child is a priceless gift, then there is only cause for rejoicing, as at the birth of a black child, or an Indian one. Medical intervention is inappropriate, even if a per-

TABLE 4.1

ONE GROUP'S PERCEPTIONS OF SOCIAL IDENTITIES*

Voluntary, desirable identities	*Voluntary undesirable identities*
Catholic	Alcoholic
Club member	[Drug addict]
Democrat/Republican	Gay/lesbian
Feminist	Smoker
Friend	[Transgender]
Husband/wife	
Mother/father	
Student	
Involuntary, desirable identities	*Involuntary, undesirable identities*
African American	[Blind]
Daughter/son	Deaf
Hispanic	[Disabled]
Jew	Old person
Man	
Woman	

*Adapted from Deaux and Ethier (1990) as reported in Deaux (1991). The perceptions presented here are those of one group of people. Your perceptions of the identities may be different. The identities in brackets have been added to illustrate further how other identities tend to be perceived.

fect "cure" were available. Invasive surgery on healthy children is morally wrong. We know that, as members of a stigmatized minority, these children's lives will be full of challenge but, by the same token, they have a general contribution to make to their own community and the larger society. (pp. 490–491)

Viewing strangers' social identities as undesirable is communicated to them in the way we transmit our messages (recall the discussion of the content and relationship dimensions of messages in Chapter 1). To communicate effectively or to develop intimate relationships with strangers, we must be aware of our biases and mindfully manage them when we transmit messages and interpret strangers' messages.

There often is a difference between our subjective social identities (those we use to define ourselves) and our objective characteristics (the groups into which others might categorize us based on our physical traits; Deaux, 1991). We, therefore, need to keep in mind that strangers may not see the groups into which we categorize them as important aspects of their identities, and strangers may categorize us in ways we do not consider important.

Our social identities are relatively consistent over time (Deaux, 1991). In any given interaction and at any given time, one social identity tends to predominate to influence our behavior. The importance of our identities, our background, and the situational characteristics influence which identity guides our behavior. Deaux (1991), for example, points out that "the individual entering a classroom brings out the professor or student identity; the individual moving into an operating room takes on the identity of surgeon, nurse, or patient" (p. 85).

As indicated earlier, the characteristics of the situation influence the importance we place on our social identities. If we find ourselves in a situation where people sharing our identities are in a numerical minority, that identity becomes important to us. Most European Americans, for example, do not think much about their ethnicity. When they find themselves in an area dominated by other ethnic groups, however, this identity becomes important. Finally, strangers' actions can influence the identities we choose to guide our behavior. To illustrate, if strangers communicate with us on the basis of their ethnic identities, we probably will use our ethnic identities to guide our behavior.

Collective Self-Esteem

Social identity theory (e.g., Tajfel, 1978) suggests that we try to achieve positive social identities in our interactions with strangers. Luthanen and Crocker (1992) contend that there are individual differences in the degree to which we have positive social identities. *Collective self-esteem* is the degree to which we generally evaluate our social groups positively. Crocker and Luthanen (1990) argue that our level of collective self-esteem moderates the degree to which we try to protect or enhance our social identities when they are threatened. When our social identities are threatened and we derogate the outgroup threatening our social identities, our collective self-esteem increases (Branscombe & Wann, 1994).

There are four components to our collective self-esteem (Luthanen & Crocker, 1992). First, private collective self-esteem involves the degree to which we evaluate our social groups positively. Second, membership esteem involves the degree to which we evaluate ourselves as good members of the social groups to which we belong. Third, public collective self-esteem involves our perceptions about how others evaluate our social groups. Fourth, the importance of our group memberships involves the degree to which our group memberships are central to how we define ourselves.

We can have different levels of collective self-esteem for the different social identities we have. We may, for example, have high collective self-esteem for our ethnic identities and low collective self-esteem for our gender identities.

Cross-Cultural Variability in Social Identities

In the United States and most other western cultures, the self is viewed in individualistic terms. Geertz (1975), for example, illustrates this view when he describes the "western" self "as a bounded, unique, more or less integrated motivational and cognitive universe, a dynamic center of awareness, emotion, judgment, and action organized into a distinctive whole and set contrastively both against other such wholes and against a social and natural background" (p. 48). Self-actualization and/or self-realization are viewed as important goals in individualistic cultures. Self-esteem in individualistic cultures is based on how well individuals can stand on their own feet.

Members of collectivistic cultures view the self differently. In collectivistic cultures, the self is defined in relation to others. People, for example, might define themselves on the basis of the company for which they work, the university they attended, and so forth. In some collectivistic cultures, individuals may deny their own self-importance. This occurs in Japan, especially when individuals are communicating with someone of higher social status (Doi, 1986). In some collectivistic cultures, there is not an ethical category for the person. To illustrate, Read (1955) describes the self-concept in the Gahuku-Gana culture of New Guinea. He points out that in this culture people do not "separate the individual from the social context and, ethically speaking, grant him [or her] an intrinsic moral value apart from that which attaches to him [or her] as the occupant of a particular status" (p. 257). Read goes on to argue that the value of people "does not reside in themselves as individuals or persons; it is dependent on the position they occupy within a system of inter-personal and inter-group relationships" (p. 250).

Overall, it appears that members of collectivistic cultures emphasize social identities more than members of individualistic cultures. Gabrenya and Wang (1983), for example, observe that the Chinese utilize more group-oriented self-conceptions than people in the United States. Cousins (1989) obtains similar results when comparing the United States and Japan. Bond and Chueng's (1983) research, however, suggests that individualism-collectivism may not explain all of the variability in social identities. They note that Hong Kong Chinese and U.S. Americans emphasize family roles more than Japanese, while Japanese mention sex and age more than the other two groups. These differences may be due to masculinity-femininity; highly masculine cultures like Japan emphasize gender and age more and family less than feminine cultures. Further, social roles based on hierarchical group memberships (e.g., caste, social class) should be influenced by cultural variations in power distance.

Given this overview of social identity, we turn our attention to specific social identities (i.e., cultural, ethnic, gender, disability, age, social class) that influence our communication with strangers. Following this, we summarize theories of identity negotiation.

SOCIAL IDENTITIES INFLUENCING OUR COMMUNICATION WITH STRANGERS

There are many social identities that could influence our communication with strangers. In this section, we discuss identities based on our cultures, our ethnic groups, our genders, our disability statuses, our ages, our social classes, and our roles. We begin with cultural identities.

Cultural Identities

Our cultural identities involve the degree to which we identify with our cultures. To illustrate, if people are born and raised in the United States, their cultural identities involve the degree to which they identify with being "Americans." Billig (1995) argues that our national cultural identities are "flagged" in the media through the use of symbols and habits of language. Symbols and language usage remind us of our cultures, but they operate mindlessly, beyond our conscious awareness. Baker (2001), for example, says: "I'm an American. I don't *feel* like an American, I don't think about it, it's not an identity I'm attached to, I don't carry it around as a description of myself. . . . But it is something that I *express,* and any expression is something I'm one with—I'm not necessarily aware of it, it's just there" (p. 60).

There are two dimensions of our cultural identities that affect our communication with strangers from other cultures: the strength of our identification and the content of our identities. Members of cultures vary in the strength of their identifications with their cultures. Some people strongly identify with being members of their cultures, and others weakly identify with their cultures. The strength of our identification with our cultures varies from situation to situation. U.S. Americans, for example, may not identify strongly with their cultures when they are in the United States, but when they visit another country and there are very few other U.S. Americans around, the strength of their identification will increase. Kosmitzki (1996) reports that individuals who have lived in other cultures see themselves as more similar to others sharing their cultural identities than individuals who have not lived in other cultures. People who have lived in other cultures also rate the content of their cultural identities more positively than individuals who have not lived in other cultures. Ting-Toomey et al. (2000) report that African Americans have weaker cultural identities than European Americans, Asian Americans, and Latino(a) Americans.

The content of our cultural identities involves the things we associate with being members of our cultures. One way to define the content of our cultural identities is by looking at the values we hold. Our identities, for example, can be either individualistic or collectivistic. The content of cultural identities for U.S. Americans who strongly identify with their culture generally involves holding individualistic values. Gudykunst (2001) reports that Asian Americans who strongly identify with the U.S. culture emphasize independent self construals and hold individualistic values more than Asian Americans who weakly identify with the U.S. culture. The content of the cultural identities for U.S. Americans who do not strongly identify with their culture, in contrast, does not necessarily involve holding individualistic values and *may* involve holding collectivistic values.

Gudykunst and Nishida (1999) argue that it is necessary to take the strength of cultural identities into consideration when comparing values across cultures. Their study suggests that when the strength of cultural identities is ignored, individuals' values may not be consistent with cultural-level values (e.g., U.S. Americans do not value being independent more than the Japanese). When members of cultures who strongly identify with their cultures are compared, however, individuals' values tend to be consistent with cultural-level values. Gudykunst and Nishida report that U.S. Americans who strongly identify with their culture value freedom, pleasure, social recognition, and being independent more than U.S. Americans who weakly identify with their culture and more than Japanese who strongly identify with their culture. Japanese who strongly identify with their culture value self-sacrifice, harmony, and accepting traditions more than Japanese who weakly identify with their culture and more than U.S. Americans who strongly identify with their culture. These findings are consistent with cultural-level values.

Ethnic Identities

Another important social identity that influences our communication with strangers is our ethnic identities. The way we react toward strangers often is based on our assumptions about their ethnicities; for example, we categorize strangers and impose ethnic labels on them. When we impose labels on strangers, however, we may not impose the labels the strangers would use to describe themselves (Barth, 1969). DeVos (1975) suggests that ethnicity involves the use of some aspect of a group's cultural background to separate group members from others. Giles and Johnson (1981), in contrast, see an ethnic group as "those individuals who identify themselves as belonging to the same ethnic category" (p. 202).

In actuality, we impose ethnic categories on strangers *and* strangers claim memberships in ethnic groups when they interact with us. A European American interacting with a Chinese American, for example, may view the other person as an "Asian American" while the Chinese American may see the relevant category as being "American." The use of different categories will affect the communication that occurs between the two people. Anytime we categorize ourselves as members of ethnic groups, we also categorize strangers as not being members of our ethnic groups and, therefore, being members of other ethnic groups (Turner, 1987). Categorization of ethnicity may be based on cultural, social, psychological, or biological characteristics. Gorden (1964) points out that ethnicity may be based on race, national origin, religion, or some combination of these.

Yinger (1994) isolates three primary ingredients used in defining ethnic groups:

> (1) The group is perceived by others in the society to be different in some combination of the following traits: language, religion, race, or ancestral homeland with its related culture; (2) the members also perceive themselves to be different; and (3) they participate in shared activities built around their (real or mythical) common origin and culture. (pp. 3–4)

Yinger argues that if any one of these three ingredients are present in our interactions, ethnicity is influencing what is happening.

Assimilation versus Pluralism   There have been changes in recent years in the way people in the United States view ethnicity. In the past, an assimilationist view of ethnicity predominated and was not questioned. *Assimilation* refers to the process of giving up one culture and taking on the characteristics of another. Park (1950) argues that the "cycle of contact, competition, accommodation, and eventual assimilation [among ethnic groups] is apparently progressive and unreversible" (p. 13). Park (1930), however, points out that "the chief obstacle to assimilation [of African Americans] seems to be not cultural differences, but physical traits" (p. 282). Glazer (1993) argues that virtually all discussions of assimilation in the United States before World War II focused on immigrants of European ancestry. Perceptions of immigrants of European ancestry today are more positive than perceptions of immigrants of non-European ancestry (see Simon, 1993, for summaries of national polls).

The assimilationist view often leads to the use of race as a metaphor, where "Americanness" is defined as "white" (Morrison, 1992, p. 42). Explaining the culture of the United States by using this metaphor will not work, however, when European Americans become a numerical minority in the country sometime in this century. (Note: By the time you read this, European Americans may be a numerical minority in California.) The changes in the ethnic composition of the United States are redefining what it means to be "American." Henry (1990) points out that "the deeper significance of America's becoming a majority nonwhite society is what it means to the national psyche, to individuals' sense of themselves and their nation—their idea of what it is to be an American" (p. 30).

A pluralistic view of ethnicity has predominated in recent years. In the *pluralistic* view, ethnicity "is an internal attitude which predisposes, but does not make compulsory, the display of ethnic identification in interaction. When it facilitates self-interest, ethnic identity will be made self-evident; it is left latent when it would hinder" (Hraba & Hoiberg, 1983, p. 385). When members of a group decide to exert their ethnicity depends on the particular circumstances in which they find themselves (Glazer & Moynihan, 1975).

Some writers are concerned with pluralism and the tendency for non-European Americans to identify with their ethnic groups. Schlesinger (1992), for example, argues that "watching ethnic conflict tear one nation after another apart, one cannot look with complacency at proposals to divide the United States into distinct and immutable ethnic and racial communities, each taught to cherish its own separateness from the rest" (p. 15). These concerns are not likely to come from pluralistic tendencies.

Wolfe (1998) reports that a large majority of middle-class U.S. Americans from all ethnic groups strongly disagree or disagree with the statement "There are times when loyalty to an ethnic group or to a race should be valued over loyalty to the country as a whole" (p. 158). There also is evidence that identifying with ethnic groups does not take away from identifying with the U.S. culture (e.g., Gaertner & Dovidio, 2000). Also, it is important to keep in mind that

> [U.S.] Americans have never thought of themselves as a single people as the Germans do. Although white, English-speaking Christians of European ancestry have set most of the norms for [U.S.] American society, there is still no sense of *Volk* (a group that shares a common ancestry and culture that embodies the national identity). Ideas, not biology, are what generate oneness and homogeneity in the United States, and so long as faith in these ideas has remained strong, the country has remained strong, the country has shown an extraordinary capacity to absorb people of many nationalities. (Suro, 1998, pp. 303–304)

Etzioni (2001) presents extensive evidence that there are *not* large differences among members of different ethnic groups in the United States with respect to values and aspirations (e.g., "the American dream"). He points out that there is more variability in values within ethnic groups than across ethnic groups.

Ethnic Identity and Behavior   Alba (1990) defines *ethnic identity* as "a person's subjective orientation toward his or her ethnic origins" (p. 25). Roosens (1989) points out that asserting our ethnic identities helps us define who we are; it offers

> commonality in language, a series of customs and symbols, a style, rituals, and appearance, and so forth, which can penetrate life in many ways. These trappings of ethnicity are particularly attractive when one is continually confronted by others who live differently. . . . If I see and experience myself as a member of an ethnic category or group, and others—fellow

members and outsiders—recognize me as such, "ways of being" become possible for me that set me apart from the outsiders. These ways of being contribute to the *content* of my self-perceptions. In this sense, I *become* my ethnic allegiance; I experience any attack on the symbols, emblems, or values (cultural elements) that define my ethnicity as an attack on myself. (pp. 17–18)

Our ethnicities, therefore, influence all aspects of our lives.

Alba (1990) argues that there has been a transformation regarding how ethnic identity is manifested for whites in the United States. He concludes that ethnic distinctions based on ancestry from specific European countries are fading and that these identities are being replaced by a "new" ethnic group, "one based on ancestry from *anywhere* on the European continent" (p. 3). As evidence for this change, Alba points to the tremendous rate of intermarriage among whites from different European countries—three of every four marriages between whites involves crossing country-of-origin boundaries. Alba notes that partners in marriages where the two trace their origins to different European countries do not perceive their partners to be from different ethnic groups. We refer to this group as European Americans.

European Americans often do not recognize their ethnicity or do not strongly identify with their ethnic groups (Kleg, 1993). One reason for this is that European Americans are members of the dominant ethnic group in the United States. Kleg points out that

the popular notion that ethnics are somewhat different or exotic, along with the fact that members of the national ethnos do not perceive anything special about their own culture, probably contribute to the lack of identification. The cliché of not being able to see the forest for the trees is quite appropriate in this case. (p. 52)

European Americans also may feel disassociated from their ethnic groups because non-European Americans' ethnicity is stressed and romanticized (Kleg, 1993).

Jen (1997) argues that the way non-European Americans identify themselves involves identity politics. European Americans often use non-European Americans' races to categorize them. When this happens, non-European Americans' ethnicity cannot be separated from race. Omi and Winant (1994) refer to this as "racialized ethnicity."

Tuan (1998) points out that racial identities are more important than ethnic identities for Asian Americans raised in predominately European American neighborhoods. Asian Americans raised in European neighborhoods are "made aware to varying degrees of being racially different and [are] reminded in both inadvertent and meanspirited forms" (p. 104). She goes on to argue that as racialized ethnics, Asian Americans

maneuver between a maze of choices and constraints in constructing an identity for themselves. On the one hand, they feel constrained to identify in ethnic or racial terms because others continue to define, respond to, and treat them as separate from the American mainstream. . . . On the other hand, there are signs of resistance . . . as they struggle to work within imposed limitations and fashion an identity that resonates for them. (p. 151)

Tuan's description of identity politics for Asian Americans probably applies to other non-European Americans as well.

Identity politics does not necessarily carry over to individuals' attitudes toward public issues and policies. Hunter and Bowman (1996) report some differences on specific issues but note that there is more agreement than disagreement across ethnic groups. They point out that "the majority of [U.S.] Americans do not . . . engage in identity politics—a politics that insists that opinion is mainly a function of racial, ethnic, or gender identity, or identities rooted in sexual preference" (p. 34).

Symbolic Ethnicity   Alba (1990) points out that European Americans can choose whether to express ethnic identities. Gans (1979) argues that the notion of symbolic ethnicity accurately describes the manifestation of ethnicity among European Americans today. *Symbolic ethnicity* refers to "the desire to retain a sense of being ethnic, but without any deep commitment to the ethnic social ties and behavior" (Alba, 1990, p. 306). Similarly, Waters (1990) points out that

> the reality is that [European American] ethnics have a lot more choice and room for maneuver than they themselves think they do. The situation is very different for members of racial minorities, whose lives are strongly influenced by their race or national origin regardless of how much they choose not to identify themselves in ethnic or racial terms. (p. 157)

Waters points out that symbolic ethnicity does not apply to non-European Americans.

European Americans generally do not recognize the differences between their experiences of ethnicity and the ways non-European Americans experience it (Waters, 1990). The voluntary aspect of European Americans asserting their ethnicity and the enjoyment they receive from expressing it when they do (e.g., it is asserted at ethnic celebrations such as weddings) make it difficult for them to understand the way ethnicity affects non-European Americans. Since non-European Americans usually stand out when they are interacting with European Americans, European Americans tend to view non-European Americans in ethnic terms. When European Americans categorize non-European Americans in terms of ethnicity, non-European Americans tend not to have a choice about activating their ethnic identities.

The influence of ethnic identity for non-European Americans is illustrated by the way Gotanda (1991), a Japanese American playwright, describes his experiences. Gotanda was raised in the United States but lived in Japan. His time in Japan helped him understand his ethnicity:

> After I'd been living in Japan for about a year, I had an extraordinary experience. . . . I was walking down the streets and I looked over to my left and I saw a bank of televisions all lined up, and they were filled with a Japanese newscaster. I looked up at the billboard and there was a Japanese face, I looked at the magazines on display and they were filled with Asian faces; I looked ahead and I saw a sea of people coming toward me, all about my same height, with black hair, with skin that looked exactly like mine. . . . What I experienced for the first time was this extraordinary thing called anonymity—the sense of being able to be part of a group, of everything around me reinforcing what I was. I didn't have to second guess my obviousness, to be constantly aware that I was different. . . . in that instant in Tokyo something lifted from me, and I was able to move freely. . . . Of course, the longer I was in Japan the more I became aware of the fact that I wasn't strictly Japanese either, that I would never be Japanese Japanese—that I was Japanese-American. (pp. 9–10)

Gotanda's experience clearly illustrates that ethnicity is not "symbolic" for non-European Americans in the United States.

Language and Ethnic Identity   Our skin colors and national origins are only two of the markers used to define ethnicity. The languages we speak also mark boundaries between our ethnic groups and others. This is true in informal conversations with acquaintances and friends as well as in formal communication situations (e.g., when we talk to our supervisors at work).

There are at least four reasons why language is an important aspect of ethnicity (Giles & Coupland, 1991). First, language is one of the major criteria for ethnic group membership. Some researchers argue that ethnic groups cannot survive without their ethnic languages (see Edwards, 1985). Some members of ethnic groups may consider ethnic linguistic abilities as necessary for "full and 'legitimate' membership" in their ethnic groups (Giles & Coupland, 1991, p. 96).

The second reason language is important to ethnicity is that language often is used by outgroup members to categorize individuals as members of ethnic groups (Giles & Coupland, 1991). If members of non-European American ethnic groups speak their ethnic languages, others probably will make the inference that they identify with their ethnic groups. Use of ethnic languages, however, may not be as important as having those languages available. DeVos (1975) claims that "ethnicity is frequently related more to the symbol of a separate language than to its actual use by all members of a group" (p. 15).

The third reason language is an important aspect of ethnicity is that language provides an emotional component to ethnic identities (e.g., members of ethnic groups feel closer to each other when speaking ethnic languages than when speaking English; see below) (Giles & Coupland, 1991). If members of ethnic groups make the effort to learn the languages of their heritages, other members of their ethnic groups perceive them positively.

The fourth reason language is an important aspect of ethnicity is that it facilitates ingroup cohesion (Giles & Coupland, 1991). Speaking ethnic languages, for example, clearly separates members of different ethnic groups from European Americans. Separating themselves from European Americans promotes feelings of solidarity within non-European American ethnic groups.

Rodriguez (1982) illustrates the importance of language in describing the effect of hearing his father speak English to a European American gas station attendant when he was growing up:

> I cannot forget the sounds my father made as he spoke. At one point his words slid together to form one word—sounds as confused as the threads of blue and green oil in the puddle next to my shoes. His voice rushed through what he had left to say. And, toward the end, reached falsetto notes, appealing to his listeners' understanding. I looked away to the lights of passing automobiles. I tried not to hear anymore. (p. 15)

In contrast to the alienation he felt when he heard his father speaking English, he felt comfort when members of his family spoke to him in Spanish:

> A family member would say something to me and I would feel specially recognized. My parents would say something to me and I would feel embraced by the sounds of their words.

> Those words said: I am speaking with ease in Spanish. I am addressing you in words I never use with los gringos. I recognize you as someone special, close, like no one outside. You belong with us. In the family. (p. 15, italics omitted)

Speaking their native languages creates solidarity among members of different ethnic groups.

Ethnic Labels   Another way language affects our ethnic identities is through the labels we use to define ourselves and others. The labels strangers use regarding their ethnic group memberships can tell us a lot about their orientations. People who label themselves Chicano(a), for example, define themselves differently than people who use the label Mexican American (see Gimienez et al., 1992). The people who define themselves as Chicano(a) probably have political goals (e.g., promoting "La Raza") that the people who define themselves as Mexican American do not. To communicate effectively with members of either group, it would be important to know why they prefer one label or the other.

It appears that the vast majority of blacks prefer to use the label African American when they refer to themselves. Two individuals provide the reasons for the use of this term:

> I grew up in a time when "black" was the accepted term. It was used on application forms and among family and friends. I changed to African American because it seemed more accurate and more enduring to our culture.
>
> [In the past] I didn't prefer "black," it was just used. However, when I began to realize that the term "black" was just making us be seen in terms of skin color (and not including our ethnic heritage), I embraced the term African American. After all, a "white, American, Irish person" is Irish American. We've done just as much for the country, and we have a heritage from *our* mother land, so why not express it! (Larkey et al., 1993, p. 19)

There is *not* a hyphen in the label African American. In fact, most non-European Americans no longer use a hyphen for their ethnicities (e.g., Japanese American, Mexican American). It may seem like a minor point, but omitting or including a hyphen may be interpreted as providing self-concept support (omitting) or denying a self-concept (including it). We, therefore, need to pay attention to the labels strangers use to refer to themselves.

Concern over the use of ethnic labels is not limited to African Americans. Many people born in Mexico, Puerto Rico, and Cuba find the panethnic term (i.e., a term used for all these cultures combined) Hispanic archaic and offensive (e.g., see Gonzalez, 1992). Participants in a Latino Political Survey report that they prefer the term Latino over Hispanic (summarized in Gonzalez, 1992). Even the pronunciation of the term can be a statement of identity (the preferred pronunciation is lah-TEEN-oh). Sandra Cisneros (the author of *Woman Hollering Creek*) points out that "to say Latino is to say you came to my culture in a manner of respect" (quoted by Gonzalez). Cisneros believes that people who prefer the term Hispanic want to fit into the mainstream U.S. culture (that is, give up their original culture), and people who use Latino(a) want to maintain their ethnicities.

Martin, Krizek, Nakayama, and Bradford (1996) examine the labels European Americans use for themselves. The preferred labels for the respondents in their study are (from most to least preferred): "White," "Caucasian," "White American," "European American," "Euro American," "Anglo," and "WASP" (White Anglo Saxon Protestant). It is important to note that the first three preferred labels focus on race, not ethnicity. Since our focus in this book is on ethnicity, not race, we use European American throughout unless it is necessary to refer to race.

All panethnic terms (e.g., Latino American, Native American, Asian American) are misleading to some extent since they imply homogeneity across the groups included under a term. People who come from Mexico, Cuba, and Puerto Rico, for example, share some similarities based on a common language, but there are many cultural differences among the three groups which cannot be ignored. Respondents in the Latino Political Survey clearly indicate that they prefer labels based on their country of origin (e.g., Mexican American, Cuban American) rather than panethnic terms (e.g., Latino) (Gonzalez, 1992). Similarly, first-generation Asian Americans may share a collectivistic upbringing, but there are many differences among Chinese Americans, Japanese Americans, Korean Americans, and Vietnamese Americans, to name only a few of the Asian groups that often are lumped together.

The term "Asian American" emerged from European Americans categorizing Asian Americans into one group (Espiritu, 1992). Asian American panethnicity, therefore, emerged from a political process. This does not mean, however, that there is not a common Asian American culture. Once panethnic groups are established, interaction among the members of the various groups can create a panethnic culture. Espiritu claims that as Asian Americans of "diverse backgrounds came together to discuss their problems and experiences, they began to develop common views of themselves and of one another and common interpretations of their experiences" (p. 12). She goes on to say that "the construction of pan-Asian ethnicity involves the creation of a common Asian American heritage out of our diverse histories. Part of the heritage being created hinges on what Asian Americans share: a history of exploitation, oppression, and discrimination" (p. 17).

Tuan (1998) reports that one of the factors that has contributed to the development of panethnic identities among Japanese Americans and Chinese Americans is the fact that distinct cultural patterns associated with specific ethnic groups are "watered down" the later the Asian Americans' generation in the United States. She contends that Asian Americans tend not to focus on ethnic differences among Asian Americans and "instead recognize the similarities linking their experiences. While the impetus for the boundary expansion may not have originated from group members, the resulting identity has taken on a life and meaning of its own as those members have taken to constructing a culture base reflecting their common experiences" (pp. 166–167). Espiritu and Tuan both argue that interethnic marriages between members of different Asian American groups are related to the development of panethnic identities.

The labels strangers use regarding their ethnic group memberships can tell us a lot about them. To communicate effectively with strangers, it is important to know which labels they prefer. This is important because effective communication requires that we support strangers' self-concepts, including their preferred ethnic and/or panethnic identities.

Strength and Content of Ethnic Identity   The labels we use for our ethnicities influence our communication. To fully understand how our ethnicities influence our communication, however, we also must take into consideration the strength and content of our ethnic identities. As with our cultural identities, we vary in the degree to which we identify with our ethnic groups (see Root, 1995, for how people with multiple identities act). Some of us strongly identify with our ethnic groups, and some of us weakly identify with our ethnic groups. Recognizing this difference is critical to effective communication with strangers.

Ethnic identity appears to be more important to how Asian Americans view themselves than to how European Americans view themselves (e.g., Chin, 1983). Similarly, Larkey and Hecht (1995) note that ethnic identities are more important for African Americans than for European Americans. Gaines et al. (1997) report that African Americans, Asian Americans, and Latino(a) Americans have stronger ethnic identities than European Americans. Ting-Toomey et al. (2000) also observe that African Americans have stronger ethnic identities than Asian Americans, Latino(a) Americans, and European Americans and that European Americans have weaker ethnic identities than members of the other groups.

Ethnic identities are more important to Asian Americans who are geographically or psychologically close to other Asian Americans than to those who are not close to other Asian Americans (Hayano, 1981). Sinclair, Sidanius, and Levin (1998) report that attachment to the U.S. culture and ethnic attachment are associated negatively for Asian Americans. Similarly, Gudykunst (2001) notes that strength of ethnic and cultural identities is correlated negatively for Asian Americans. Larkey and Hecht (1995) observe that the more importance European Americans place on their ethnic identities, the less satisfied they are with interactions with African Americans, especially in relationships low in intimacy. Importance of ethnic identity is not related to interethnic communication satisfaction for African Americans.

Often someone will say that we should ignore ethnic differences and strive for a "color-blind" society. If all people weakly identified with their ethnic groups, this might make sense. We may be able to ignore ethnic group differences when interacting with strangers who weakly identify with their ethnic groups. If strangers strongly identify with their ethnic groups, in contrast, we cannot ignore group differences. When strangers strongly identify with their ethnic groups and we ignore their ethnicities when we interact with them, we are *not* supporting their self-concepts and will not be able to understand their behavior. This is a problem because self-concept support is necessary for strangers to be satisfied with their communication with us (Hecht, Ribeau, & Alberts, 1989).

The content of our ethnic identities can be described similarly to the content of our cultural identities. The content of our ethnic identities, for example, may be highly individualistic or highly collectivistic. The content of our ethnic identities depends on our national heritages and the strength of our identities. To illustrate, if individuals' national heritages can be traced to collectivistic cultures and they strongly identify with their ethnic identities, the content of their identities will tend to be collectivistic values. If they do not strongly identify with their ethnic groups, in contrast, the content of their identities will not tend to involve strongly collectivistic values. Whether these people will hold individualistic values depends on their cultural identities. If they are "Americans" who strongly identify with their culture, their values probably will be individualistic.

There have been several studies that compare individualistic and collectivistic tendencies in European Americans and members of other ethnic groups. Gaines et al. (1997), for example, report that African Americans, Asian Americans, and Latino(a) Americans are more collectivistic than European Americans but that there is no difference in individualism across the four groups. Other studies indicate that Asian Americans (e.g., Coon & Kemmelmeir, 2001; Hetts, Sakuna, & Pelham, 1999; Kim & Kitani, 1998; Rhea et al., 1996; Singelis, 1994; Singelis & Sharkey, 1995; Singelis et al., 1995), African Americans (Coon & Kemmelmeir, 2001; Oyserman et al., 1995), and Mexican Americans (Freeberg & Stein, 1996) are more collectivistic than European Americans. The results for individualism in these studies, however, do not fit a clear pattern. Some studies find that European Americans are more individualistic than members of other ethnic groups (e.g., Doherty et al., 1994; Hetts et al., 1999; Rhea et al., 1996; Singelis, 1994), and other studies report no differences between European Americans and non-European Americans (e.g., Freeberg & Stein, 1996; Gaines et al., 1997; Singelis & Sharkey, 1995). One reason for this is that the non-European Americans in these studies were born in the United States or have lived in the United States long enough to adopt individualistic values. Also, these studies do not assess strength of ethnic identity. It may be that those who weakly identify with their ethnic groups hold individualistic values.

Gudykunst (2001) reports that Asian Americans who strongly identify with their ethnic groups emphasize interdependent self construals, hold collectivistic values, speak the languages of their ethnic heritages, and share networks with other Asian Americans more than Asian Americans who weakly identify with their ethnic groups. He also notes that Asian Americans who strongly identify with their ethnic groups expect interactions with other members of their ethnic groups to be more intimate and trusting than those who weakly identify with their ethnic group.

The preceding suggests that in order to understand strangers' communication, we must understand their cultural and ethnic identities (see Table 4.2). Strangers who weakly identify with their cultures and strongly identify with their ethnic groups tend to base their communication on their ethnic identities across situations. Strangers who strongly identify with their cultures and weakly identify with their ethnic groups, in

TABLE 4.2

INTERACTION BETWEEN CULTURAL AND ETHNIC IDENTITIES

		Cultural identity	
		Weak	*Strong*
Ethnic Identity	*Weak*	Neither cultural nor ethnic identity has strong influence on behavior	Behavior generally is based on cultural identity
	Strong	Behavior generally is based on ethnic identity	Behavior is based on cultural or ethnic identity, depending on the situation

contrast, tend to base their communication on their cultural identities across situations. Strangers who strongly identify with both their cultural identities and their ethnic identities will choose which identity to use to guide their behavior in specific situations. To illustrate, they may choose to base their communication at work on their cultural identities and base their communication at home on their ethnic identities. Strangers who weakly identify with both their cultural identities and their ethnic identities tend to base their communication on other social identities or their personal identities. These people, however, may base their communication on their cultural or ethnic identities if others categorize them on the basis of those identities and act on the basis of that categorization.

To summarize, the way we define ourselves and the way others define us with respect to our ethnicities influence our communication. To communicate effectively with strangers, we need to understand how they define their ethnic identities. Our supporting the ethnic identities strangers prefer and strangers supporting the way we want to be viewed will help us communicate effectively.

Gender Identities

One of the major social identities affecting our communication is the way we define our gender roles. There are differences in the way men and women relate to the world that affect their social identities. Tajfel (1978) argues that social identity involves a cognitive process of differentiation and comparison. Men tend to engage in differentiation more than women. Women's social identities, in contrast, tend to be based more on communal processes than on differentiation processes (e.g., Williams, 1984). These differences have implications for intergroup behavior; "women are more inclined [than men] to value relationships with other people from groups other than their own" (Skevington, 1989, p. 56).

It is not our biological sex that influences our communication, but rather our gender roles. *Gender roles* are "the psychological traits and the social responsibilities that individuals have and feel are appropriate for them because they are male or female" (Pleck, 1977, p. 182). Bem (1974) isolates four gender roles: feminine, masculine, undifferentiated, and androgynous. *Feminine gender roles* involve exhibiting a high degree of stereotypical feminine traits and behaviors (e.g., compassionate, gentle, sensitive to others' needs, understanding, warm). *Masculine gender roles* involve exhibiting a high degree of stereotypical masculine traits and behaviors (e.g., aggressive, competitive, forceful, self-reliant). *Undifferentiated gender roles* exist when individuals do not exhibit high degrees of either masculine or feminine traits or behaviors. *Androgynous gender roles* involve exhibiting high degrees of *both* masculine and feminine traits and behaviors. Bem (1993) argues that gender roles provide a lens that influences the way we look at the world. She goes on to point out that traditionally gender-oriented individuals (i.e., highly masculine men and highly feminine women) tend to organize and recall information on the basis of gender.

There are cultural differences in gender roles. Hofstede (1980) argues that in highly masculine cultures, there are clearly differentiated gender roles. In these cultures, there is a tendency for masculine and feminine gender roles to predominate. Hofstede points out that in highly feminine cultures there are not clearly differentiated gender roles. In these cultures, undifferentiated and androgynous gender roles tend to predominate. Research on gender role ideology (e.g., Best & Williams, 1984) and family gender role development (e.g., Salamon, 1977) supports Hofstede's claims (see Best & Williams, 1997, for a review of cross-cultural studies).

There are important differences in the ways men and women communicate in the United States. Beck (1988), for example, points out that women tend to see questions as a way of keeping a conversation going, and men see questions as requests for information. Women tend to make connections between what their partners said and what they have to say. Men, in contrast, do not use conversational bridges as much and may appear to ignore what their partners just said in a conversation. Men tend to view aggressiveness as a way of communicating, while women tend to interpret aggressiveness as an attack. Women may discuss problems and only be looking for reassurances. Men, on the other hand, interpret the discussion of a problem as a request for a solution. These differences can be viewed in terms of subcultural differences. In this view, men and women are seen as being socialized into different subcultures with different beliefs about the nature of communication and different rules for communication (Maltz & Borker, 1982; Tannen, 1990). Men and women come from different "subcultures which have different conceptions of what constitutes friendly conversation, different rules for engaging in such conversations and different rules for interpreting interaction behavior" (Henley & Kramarae, 1991, p. 24). Mulac, Bradac, and Gibbons (2001) report research that supports the view that gender differences reflect cultural or subcultural differences in communication.

Women tend to be socialized to develop close relationships with others (Maltz & Borker, 1982) and to be involved with others (Tannen, 1990). Women also tend to be socialized to view talk as important for developing and maintaining relationships (Tannen, 1990). Men, in contrast, tend to learn to assert their dominance (Maltz & Borker, 1982) and to be independent (Tannen, 1990). Men also tend to learn to see talk as a way to establish their dominance and, therefore, as not central to intimate relationships, where dominance is not important. Men tend to see talk as weakening intimate relationships (Tannen, 1990). Misunderstandings that occur between women and men in the cultural differences perspective are due to interpreting cues from the other group by using their own group's rules (Maltz & Borker, 1982).

Identities Based on Disabilities

Another social category that affects our communication is whether one of the people is perceived as disabled (see Braithwaite & Thompson, 2000, for reviews of research). We categorize others on the basis of their physical appearance and evaluate novel appearances negatively (McArthur, 1982). When nondisabled people communicate with people who are visibly disabled in some way, they tend to experience uncertainty and anxiety and avoid interaction when possible (e.g., there is a bias toward the ingroup). Nondisabled people communicating with people in a wheelchair, for example, predict more negative outcomes and are less aware of the person in the wheelchair than they do when communicating with other nondisabled individuals (Grove & Werkman, 1991). Similar observations can be made about interactions with other people who are viewed as stigmatized (e.g., the blind, the deaf, AIDS victims, the mentally ill; see Goffman, 1963). The bias toward the ingroup is a two-way street. To illustrate, there is a sign in the American Sign Language with the right index finger circling forward in front of the forehead which indicates a deaf person who thinks like a hearing person. This sign is *not* meant as a compliment, and its use demonstrates a bias toward the Deaf ingroup (Barringer, 1993).

Members of groups with disabilities can be seen as sharing a common culture. Reagan (1995), for example, contends that there is a Deaf cultural community in the United States. Members of this group share a common language (the American Sign Language) and an awareness of their deaf identities. Hearing-impaired people who are acculturated into the hearing world, however, do not share this common identity. Members of the Deaf culture also share communication rules (e.g., eye contact, use of facial expressions) and cultural artifacts (e.g., the technological devices that help them live in a hearing society).

Coleman and DePaulo (1991) point out that the visibility of disabilities influences whether others see people as disabled:

> External markers of a disability, such as the use of sign language by the deaf, canes and guide dogs by the blind, and wheelchairs by amputees and paraplegics, render those special conditions even more salient. However, even conditions almost completely invisible can be perceived as disabling and can engender miscommunications if they are known to others. . . . For example, women who have recently had mastectomies may find themselves to be the object of unusual regard in their initial interactions with others immediately following the surgery. (p. 64)

They also suggest that conditions that are not physically disabling (e.g., facial scars) may be psychologically disabling.

Coleman and DePaulo (1991) argue that both nondisabled and disabled people contribute to miscommunications when they interact. Nondisabled people, for example, have negative stereotypes of disabled people. Disabled people are seen as "dependent, socially introverted, emotionally unstable, or depressed, hypersensitive, and easily offended, especially with regard to their disability" (p. 69). Nondisabled people may expect that disabled people will view them as prejudiced against the disabled. When nondisabled people interact with disabled people, they may experience anxiety, fear, and surprise. These reactions often are displayed nonverbally (e.g., in the voice or on the face), even though nondisabled people may try to control their reactions.

Disabled people also contribute negative expectations to their interactions with nondisabled individuals. Coleman and DePaulo (1991) point out that disabled people may be "bitter and resentful about their disability" (p. 75). Disabled people also may expect to be perceived negatively by nondisabled individuals; "for example, blind people think that sighted persons perceive them as slightly retarded and hard of hearing" (p. 75). It is important to recognize that disabled people's disabilities may affect their communication with nondisabled people. To illustrate, blind people cannot make eye contact and hearing-impaired people who read lips cannot pick up nuances of communication in tone of voice.

There are idioms in English such as "the blind leading the blind" and "that's a lame excuse" to which disabled individuals react negatively (Pogrebin, 1987). Also, the labels that nondisabled people use to refer to disabled can cause problems in communication. Pogrebin (1987), for example, reports that "a man who wears leg braces says the issue is accuracy. I'm not handicapped, people's attitudes about me handicap me" (p. 218). "Differently abled" and physically challenged" do not appear to be accepted widely by disabled people either. Pogrebin quotes Harilyn Rousso, a psychotherapist with cerebral palsy, as saying:

> Friends who care most sometimes think they're doing you a favor by using euphemisms or saying "I never think of you as disabled." The reason they don't want to acknowledge my disability is that they think it is so negative. Meanwhile, I'm trying to recognize it as a valued part of me. I'm more complex than my disability and I don't want my friends to be obsessed by it. But its clearly there, like my eye color, and I want my friends to appreciate and accept me with it. (p. 219)

Some disabled people prefer the label "cripple" or "gimp" because they are not euphemisms and force others to recognize the realities facing disabled people. As with members of different ethnic groups, it is important that we know what the individuals with whom we are communicating want their groups to be called.

Age Identities

Members of other groups do not have to be visually disabled for us to experience uncertainty and anxiety and want to avoid communicating with them; for example, young people often avoid communicating with old people (see Williams & Nussbaum, 2001, for a summary of research). We categorize others on the basis of age when we guess their ages from their physical appearances, when others disclose their ages, when others make references to age categories (e.g., indicating they are retired), and when others talk about experiences in the past that suggest their ages. Age-based identities can take place at the beginning of interactions with others or emerge out of our communication with others (Coupland, Nussbaum, & Coupland, 1991).

Rose (1965) argues that several factors have contributed to the development of age-based identities in the United States: (1) the growing number of old people; (2) the development of retirement communities which segregate old people; (3) the increase in retirement, which decreases interaction between young and old on the job; (4) the amount of money available to older people; and (5) the emergence of groups and organizations exclusively for old people. Older people demonstrate

> all of the signs of group identification. There is a desire to associate with fellow-agers, especially in formal associations, and to exclude younger adults from these associations. There are expressions of group pride. . . . There are manifestations of a feeling of resentment at "the way older people are being mistreated," and indications of their taking social action to remove the sources of their resentment. (p. 14)

Intergeneration interaction, therefore, is clearly a form of intergroup communication.

Young people view elderly people as less desirable interaction partners than other young people or middle-aged people (Tamir, 1984). When young people are communicating with the elderly, they use several different strategies to adapt their behavior (Coupland, Coupland, Giles, & Henwood, 1988). First, young people adapt their behavior by over accommodating to the elderly because they assume the elderly are handicapped (e.g., hard of hearing). Second, young people communicate with the elderly in ways that reflect the attitude that the elderly are dependent on the young. This allows young people to control the elderly. Third, young people may speak differently than elderly people speak to establish their identity as young people (e.g., using slang the elderly do not understand). Fourth, young people may over accommodate to the elderly to nurture them (e.g., young people may use baby talk when talking to the elderly). Fifth, young people may not adapt their behavior to the elderly. The elderly, in turn, may perceive this as lack of interest in them.

The elderly also use strategies in adapting their behavior to the young (Coupland et al., 1988). First, the elderly may not accommodate their behavior to the young. One reason for this is that they may have little contact with young people and not know how to adapt their behavior. Second, the elderly may use self-protecting strategies because they anticipate negative interactions with young people. Third, the elderly may anticipate that they will not perform well when they communicate with young people. Fourth, the elderly may engage in self-stereotyping (e.g., they may have negative stereotypes of being old). Fifth, the elderly may speak differently from the way young people do because they want to establish their social identity.

Self-concept support is necessary for effective intergenerational communication. One of the major concerns of older people is maintaining healthy self-concepts. Older people's self-concepts are threatened by the process of aging and by young people's attitudes toward old people (Tamir, 1984). Tamir argues that "lack of self-affirmation by others can lead to a vicious circle of decreasing self-worth and continued negative and self-effacing encounters" (p. 36). Older people will find interactions with younger people who support the older people's self-concepts more satisfying than interactions with younger people who do not support their self-concepts.

There are cross-cultural differences in intergenerational communication. In collectivistic cultures, for example, old people have high status, and, therefore, young people tend to show respect to them. Age, however, does not tend to provide status in individualistic cultures. Williams et al. (1997) report that perceptions of interactions with older adults are more negative in Asian cultures than in western cultures. This may be due to young people in Asian cultures having to take status differences between themselves and older people into consideration more than young people in western cultures.

Social Class Identities

We identify with a social class whether we are aware of it or not. Social class

> is much more than a convenient pigeonhole or merely arbitrary divisional unit—like minutes, ounces, I.Q. points or inches—along a linear continuum. It is a distinct reality which embraces the fact that people live, eat, play, mate, dress, work, and think at contrasting and dissimilar levels. These levels—social classes—are the blended product of shared and analogous occupational orientations, educational backgrounds, economic wherewithal, and life experiences. Persons occupying a given level need not be conscious of their class identity. But because of their approximately uniform backgrounds and experiences and because they grew up perceiving or "looking at things" in similar ways, they will share comparable values, attitudes, and lifestyles. (Hodges, 1964, p. 13)

The social class to which we belong may be the class with which we identify if we are satisfied with our position in society. Alternatively, if we are seeking upward mobility, our class identity may be based on the social class to which we aspire.

Sociologists tend to divide the social classes in the United States into upper class, upper middle class, middle class, lower middle class, and lower class. No matter how the class structure is divided, we sort ourselves and others into social classes when we interact. The criteria we use for sorting ourselves and others usually is based on income, occupation, education, beliefs/attitudes, styles of life, or kind of family (Jackman & Jackman, 1983). Fussell (1983) points out that we also can tell others' social classes by their hometowns, their houses, their yards, and the decorations in their houses, as well as the clothes they wear and the cars they drive.

Our class identities influence the way we communicate. We can tell strangers' class backgrounds from the way they speak. Using the standard dialect (e.g., the dialect used by newscasters on national broadcasts) is attributed higher social status than using a nonstandard dialect. Fussell (1983), for example, points out that the use of double negatives (e.g., "I can't get no satisfaction") and ungrammatical numbers (e.g., "He don't," "I wants it") clearly distinguishes lower-class speakers from middle-class speakers. The way people pronounce words and the vocabulary they use distinguish between middle-class and upper-middle/upper-class speakers.

Role Identities

As indicated earlier, we have social identities based on the roles we play. Sarbin and Allen (1968) point out that role is "a term borrowed directly from the theater, is a metaphor intended to denote that conduct adheres to certain 'parts' (or positions) rather than the players who read or recite them" (p. 489). In other words, a *role* is a set of behavioral expectations associated with a particular position in a group. Examples of positions include, but are not limited to, professor, student, father, mother, physician, lawyer, judge, police officer, clerk, and customer. The behaviors we expect professors to perform, for example, are considered their roles.

Role Expectations   Once we learn the role expectations associated with the positions we hold, we tend to conform to those expectations when we communicate on automatic pilot. Our tendency to conform to our roles is a function of how clearly the roles are defined and how much consensus there is on how people are expected to behave in those roles. The greater the clarity of the role definition and the greater the consensus on the role expectations, the more we tend to conform to role expectations (Stryker & Statham, 1985). Our tendency to conform is due to the fact that role expectations are taken for granted (Bem, 1970). Since we take the behavioral expectations for granted, we often assume that our roles cannot be redefined. We can, however, choose to redefine our roles when we are mindful of our communication.

Other people do not always share our role expectations and may have different expectations for our roles than we do. We may fulfill our own role expectations and not fulfill the expectations other people have for us, or we may fulfill other people's expectations and not our own. Failure to live up to role expectations is traumatic to some degree. The trauma we experience when we do not meet role expectations is partly due to other people's responses to our performances (Stryker & Statham, 1985). We want to perform our roles adequately so that other people will view us as competent. It is important, however, to recognize that cooperation from other people is necessary for us to perform our roles adequately. To illustrate, for instructors to perform their roles adequately, the students in their classes must cooperate and meet student role expectations. If instructors try to hold a discussion in class and the students do not participate, the instructors will not be able to meet their role expectations.

Cross-Cultural Variability in Role Identities   One area where there are often different behavioral expectations across cultures is the *degree of personalness* expected in a role relationship. In the United States, when interpersonal relationships do not exist between people filling positions, role relationships tend to be impersonal. In many other cultures, people are expected to treat others in role relationships in a personal way. To illustrate, consider a Kenyan student's reaction to waiters in the United States: "Waiters extend courtesy to get a bigger tip or because the manager is around. They are very impersonal; it's just a job to them" (Feig & Blair, 1975, p. 31). In Kenya waiters and waitresses are expected to see customers as people and treat them in a personal way.

To further illustrate expectations of personalness in role relationships consider U.S. Americans in Athens and their Greek coworkers. Triandis (1967) found that Greeks perceive U.S. Americans' behavior in organizations as " 'inhumanly' legalistic, rigid, cold, and over concerned with efficiency" (p. 21). Even though Greek organizations are highly complex bureaucracies, "decisions are often taken on the basis of friendship and following strictly personal norms. . . . Greeks cannot understand the distinction between 'work behavior' and 'friendship behavior' " (p. 21). Thus, Greeks tend to place a high degree of importance on personalness in role relationships. A similar tendency occurs among Mexican bank employees (Zurcher, 1968).

The dimension of the degree of personalness expected in role relationships is related directly to Parsons' (1951) pattern variable of diffuseness or specificity. Specifically, an expectation of impersonalness stems from a specificity orientation, the tendency to respond to specific aspects (e.g., the role) of another person. An expectation of personalness, in contrast, stems from a diffuse orientation, the tendency to respond to others as total persons.

Role relationships also differ across cultures with respect to the degree of formality expected in the relationship. In the United States, interaction between people in a role relationship may be informal (e.g., students may call professors by their first names). Role relationships in many others cultures, however, tend to be highly formal. A Turkish woman talking about the student-teacher relationship illustrates this pattern; she says, "You're supposed to fear the teacher like you fear Allah. When he [or she] comes into the class, all stand up. When you meet him [or her] on the street, you bow" (Feig & Blair, 1975, p. 39). Iranians display a similar attitude: "a professor who allows himself [or herself] to be treated without the utmost respect or one who confesses ignorance on a subject is not generally taken seriously by Iranian students. 'The average student,' said one man, 'loses respect for a teacher when he [or she] is too friendly and common with his [or her] pupils' " (Feig & Blair, 1975, p. 83).

Another area where there are cultural differences in the nature of role relationships is the degree of hierarchy present in the relationship. In the United States, role relationships may be hierarchical, but this generally is not stressed. In other cultures, the hierarchical nature of the relationship is critical. To illustrate, role relationships in Vietnam involve high degrees of hierarchy. Social relations, including role relationships, between Vietnamese are influenced by Confucianism. Liem (1980) points out that Confucianism is a doctrine of social hierarchies that "defines, by rigid rules, the attitudes which each member of the society should have" (p. 15). With respect to the employer-employee relationship, Liem points out that

> the Vietnamese employee considers his [or her] employer as his [or her] mentor. As such, the latter is expected to give guidance, advice, and encouragement, and the former is supposed to execute orders, to perform his task quietly, and not to ask questions or have doubt about the orders. Because of his [or her] concept of the relationship, the Vietnamese employee does not voice his [or her] opinion to the boss, he [or she] just listens to his [or her] orders. (p. 16)

Obviously, such an expectation differs from the employer-employee relationship in western cultures.

Asian cultures are not the only cultures that have hierarchical role relationships; many African cultures also have similar role expectations. The clientship relationship of the Kanuri culture in the Bornu province of Nigeria, for example, involves a wide-ranging hierarchical relation between a patron and a client. Tessler, O'Ban, and Spain (1973) describe the relationship, indicating that

> the term clientship refers to the diffuse relationship between two individuals (adult males), one of whom is considered the superior or patron and the other the subordinate or client. It is a diffuse relationship because the patron may demand a wide range of services from the client, while the client may expect a wide range of considerations from his patron. . . . In general two types of client relationships may be distinguished: the apprentice-master relationship and the "simple" dependence relationship. For both, the relationship is entered into on a voluntary basis after initiation by the subordinate and with the agreement of the superior. . . . they both "agree with" or are satisfied with the behavior of the other. The stress on behavior in such agreements reflects their mutual trust in the willingness and ability of each to meet the role expectations of the other. (pp. 144–146)

The clientship relationship clearly involves a high degree of hierarchy.

The hierarchical nature of social relations in general, and role relationships in particular, often is reflected in the language of the culture. In Japanese, for example, different verb endings are used depending on whether a person is talking to people of equal status, higher status, or lower status. Thus, any time people speak in Japan, they are placing themselves into the social hierarchy.

IDENTITY NEGOTIATION IN INTERGROUP ENCOUNTERS

For effective communication to take place, the identities we use and the identities strangers use in intergroup encounters must be coordinated. There are two major theories that address identity negotiation: Cupach and Imahori's (1993a) identity management theory and Ting-Toomey's (1993) identity negotiation theory. Orbe's (1998a,

1998b) co-cultural theory also deals with the identities "minority" group members use when interacting with "majority" group members (i.e., European Americans). We begin with identity management theory.

Identity Management Theory

Cupach and Imahori's (1993a) identity management theory (IMT) is based in interpersonal communication competence, and the authors believe it generalizes to intercultural competence (see Menigan, 2000, for an application of the theory to able-bodied–disabled communication). IMT is based on the work of Goffman (1967) on self-presentation and facework.

Cupach and Imahori (1993a) view identity as providing "an interpretive frame for experience" (p. 113). Identities provide expectations for behavior and motivate individuals' behavior. Individuals have multiple identities, but Cupach and Imahori view cultural identities (based on Collier & Thomas, 1988) and relational identities (identities within specific relationships) as central to identity management. Following Collier and Thomas, Cupach and Imahori view identities as varying as a function of scope (the number of individuals who share an identity), salience (the importance of identity), and intensity (the strength with which identity is communicated to others). They differentiate intercultural communication (interlocutors have different cultural identities) and intracultural communication (interlocutors share cultural identities).

Cupach and Imahori (1993a) argue that aspects of individuals' identities are revealed through the presentation of face (situated identities that individuals claim). They contend that "the maintenance of face is a natural and inevitable *condition* of human interaction" (p. 116). In IMT, "interpersonal communication competence should include the ability of an individual to successfully negotiate mutually acceptable identities in interaction" (p. 118, italic omitted). The ability to maintain face in interactions is one indicator of individuals' interpersonal communication competence. Cupach and Imahori believe this extends to intercultural communication competence as well.

Cupach and Imahori (1993a) argue that since individuals often do not know much about strangers' cultures, they manage face in intercultural encounters by using stereotypes. Stereotyping, however, is face-threatening because it is based on externally imposed identities. The result is a dialectical tension regarding three aspects of face: (1) fellowship face versus autonomy face, (2) competence face versus autonomy face, and (3) autonomy face versus fellowship or competence face. Intercultural communication competence involves successfully managing face, which involves managing these three dialectical tensions.

Cupach and Imahori (1993a) contend that competence in developing intercultural relationships goes through three phases. The first phase involves "trial-and-error" processes of finding identities on which communicators share some similarities. The second phase involves enmeshment of the identities of the participants into "a mutually acceptable and convergent relational identity, in spite of the fact that their cultural identities are still divergent" (p. 125). The third phase involves renegotiating identities. "Competent intercultural interlocutors use their narrowly defined but emerging relational identity from the second phase as the basis for renegotiating their separate cultural identities" (p. 127). Cupach and Imahori argue that the three phases are "cyclical" and that individuals in intercultural relationships may go through the three phases for each aspect of their identities that are relevant to their relationships.

Identity Negotiation Theory

Ting-Toomey (1993) argues that intercultural communication competence is "the effective identity negotiation process between two interactants in a novel communication episode" (p. 73). She makes eight assumptions: (1) everyone has multiple images concerning a sense of self; (2) cultural variability influences the sense of self; (3) self identification involves security and vulnerability; (4) identity boundary regulation motivates behavior; (5) identity boundary regulation involves a tension between inclusion and differentiation; (6) individuals try to balance self, other, and group memberships; (7) managing the inclusion-differentiation dialectic influences the coherent sense of self; and (8) a coherent sense of self influences individuals' communication resourcefulness (i.e., "the knowledge and ability to apply cognitive, affective, and behavioral resources appropriately, effectively, and creatively in diverse interaction situations," p. 74).

Ting-Toomey (1993) includes 20 propositions in identity negotiation theory (INT). She argues that the more secure individuals' self-identifications are, the more they are open to interacting with members of other cultures (proposition [P]1). The more vulnerable individuals feel, the more anxiety they experience in these interactions (P2). Individuals' vulnerability is affected by their need for security (P3). The more individuals need inclusion, the more they value ingroup and relational boundaries (P4). The more individuals need differentiation, the more distance they place between themselves and others (P5).

Individuals' resourcefulness in negotiating identities is affected by effectively managing the security-vulnerability (P6) and inclusion-differentiation (P7) dialectics. The more secure individuals' self-identifications, the greater their identity coherence (P8) and global self-esteem (P9). The greater individuals' self-esteem (P10) and the greater their membership collective esteem (P11), the more resourceful they are when interacting with strangers.

Individuals' motivation to communicate with strangers influences the degree to which they seek out communication resources (cognitive, affective, and behavioral resources for communication; P12). The greater individuals' cognitive (mindfulness; P13), affective (ability to manage reactive emotions; P14), and behavioral (behavioral adaptation; P15) resourcefulness are, the more effective they are in identity negotiation. The more diverse individuals' communication resources are, the more effective they are in interactive identity confirmation (positive views of self and others; P16), coordination (synchronizing meanings; P17), and attunement (a coherent understanding of self and others; P18). Finally, the more diverse individuals' communication resources are, the more flexible they are in "co-creating interactive goals" (P19) and "developing mutual identity meanings and comprehensibility" (P20) (Ting-Toomey, 1993, p. 110).

Co-Cultural Theory

Orbe's (1998a, 1998b) co-cultural theory is based in muted group theory (e.g., social hierarchies in society privilege some groups over others; Ardener, 1975; Kramarae, 1981) and standpoint theory (e.g., specific positions in society provide subjective ways in which individuals look at the world; Smith, 1987). Co-cultures include, but are not limited, to nonwhites, women, people with disabilities, homosexuals, and those in the lower social classes.

Orbe (1998b) points out that "in its most general form, co-cultural communication refers to interactions among underrepresented and dominant group members" (p. 3). The focus of co-cultural theory is providing a framework "by which co-cultural group members negotiate attempts by others to render their voices muted within dominant societal structures" (p. 4). Two premises guide co-cultural theory: (1) co-cultural group members are marginalized in the dominant societal structures, and (2) co-cultural group members use certain communication styles to achieve success when confronting the "oppressive dominant structures."

Orbe (1998b) argues that co-cultural group members generally have one of three goals for their interactions with dominant group members: (1) assimilation (e.g., become part of the mainstream culture; in this case cultural identities predominate), (2) accommodation (e.g., try to get the dominant group members to accept co-cultural group members), and (3) separation (e.g., rejecting the possibility of common bonds with dominant group members; in this case ethnic identities predominate). Other factors that influence co-cultural group members, communication are "field of experience" (e.g., past experiences), "abilities" (e.g., individuals' abilities to enact different practices), the "situational context" (e.g., where are they communicating with dominant group members), "perceived costs and rewards" (e.g., the pros and cons of certain practices), and the "communication approach" (i.e., being aggressive, assertive, or nonassertive).

Orbe (1998a, 1998b) isolates practices (e.g., ways members of "marginalized groups negotiate their muted group status," 1998b, p. 8) co-cultural group members use in their interactions with dominant group members. The practices used are a function of the co-cultural group members' goals and communication approaches. The combination of these yield nine communication orientations in which different practices tend to be used: (1) Nonassertive separation involves practices of "avoiding" and "maintaining interpersonal barriers"; (2) nonassertive accommodation involves practices of "increasing visibility" and "dispelling stereotypes"; (3) nonassertive assimilation involves practices of "emphasizing commonalities," "developing positive face," "censoring self," and "averting controversy"; (4) assertive separation involves practices of "communicating self," "intragroup networking," "exemplying strengths," and "embracing stereotypes"; (5) assertive accommodation involves practices of "communicating self," "intragroup networking," "utilizing liaisons," and "educating others"; (6) assertive assimilation involves practices of "extensive preparation," "overcompensating," "manipulating stereotypes," and "bargaining"; (7) aggressive separation involves practices of "attacking" and "sabotaging others"; (8) aggressive accommodation involves practices of "confronting" and "gaining advantage"; and (9) aggressive assimilation involves practices of "dissociating," "mirroring," "strategic distancing," and "ridiculing self."

SUMMARY

Our communication with strangers is influenced by the groups to which we belong, the roles we fill, and how we define interpersonal relationships. Our membership groups and our reference groups influence the values, as well as the norms and rules, we learn. As part of our socialization into these groups, we are taught to avoid people from certain other groups (our outgroups). The orientation we learn toward outgroups causes us unconsciously to try to put our ingroup in a more favorable light when it is compared to them. This tendency in turn often leads us to make inaccurate attributions and predictions about the behavior of strangers from the outgroup.

Our social identities influence our communication more than our personal identities when we communicate with strangers. Depending on how we categorize strangers, the social identity guiding our behavior may be our cultural identities, ethnic identities, gender identities, social class identities, age group identities, and so forth. Supporting strangers' identities is critical if we want to form an ongoing relationship with them. If we interact with strangers from other ethic groups who do not strongly identify with their ethnic groups and focus on their ethnicity, we are not supporting their self-concepts. Also, if we interact with strangers who strongly identify with their ethnic groups and act as though their ethnicity did not matter, we are not supporting their self-concepts.

Our role identities also influence our communication with strangers. We learn what behavior is expected in different roles as we are socialized into our culture and membership groups. Since roles tend to vary across cultures, it is necessary to know strangers' role expectations if we are to understand and predict their behavior accurately.

STUDY QUESTIONS

1. How does distinguishing between membership and reference groups help us understand our own and strangers' communication?
2. Why is it more useful to focus on ethnicity than on race in understanding communication behavior?
3. How does drawing a distinction between ingroups and outgroups affect our communication with strangers?
4. What is the relationship between social categorization and social identities?
5. How does collective self-esteem influence our social identities?
6. What is the difference between cultural and ethnic identities? Why is it important to consider the strength and content of cultural and ethnic identities to understand strangers' communication?
7. How do European Americans and non-European Americans experience ethnicity differently?
8. How does language influence ethnic identity?
9. Why is it important to recognize the labels strangers use to define their ethnicities?
10. How can gender differences in communication be explained?
11. How do disabled and nondisabled people contribute to misunderstandings in communication?
12. How is intergenerational communication a form of intergroup communication?
13. Why is our communication with members of other social classes a form of intergroup communication?

14. How does identity management theory suggest that we negotiate identities with strangers?

15. How does identity negotiation theory suggest that we negotiate identities with strangers?

SUGGESTED READINGS

Abrams, D., & Hogg, M. (Eds.). (1990). *Social identity theory: Constructive and critical advances.* New York: Springer-Verlag.

Alba, R. (1990). *Ethnic identity.* New Haven, CT: Yale University Press.

Billig, M. (1995). *Beyond nationalism.* London: Sage.

Braithwaite, D., & Thompson, T. (Eds.). (2000). *Handbook of communication and people with disabilities.* Mahwah, NJ: Erlbaum.

Hogg, M., & Abrams, D. (1988). *Social identifications.* London: Routledge.

Root, M. (Ed.). (1995). *The multiracial experience.* Thousand Oaks, CA: Sage.

Tajfel, H. (Ed.). (1982). *Social identity and intergroup relations.* Cambridge, UK: Cambridge University Press.

Waters, M. (1990). *Ethnic options.* Berkeley: University of California Press.

Williams, A., & Nussbaum, J. (2001). *Intergenerational communication across the lifespan.* Mahwah, NJ: Erlbaum.

5

PSYCHOCULTURAL
INFLUENCES ON
THE PROCESS

*Most of the business of life can go on with
less effort if we stick together with our own
kind. Foreigners are a strain. . . .*

Gordon Allport

In the preceding two chapters, we examined how our socialization within our cultures
and our group memberships within our cultures influence our communication with
strangers. Our analysis must go one step further and examine the processes occurring
within individuals. The psychological processes occurring within individuals make intergroup interactions feel like a strain, as the Allport quote above suggests. The focus
of this chapter is, therefore, on those influences we have labeled psychocultural.

The psychocultural factors that influence our communication with strangers include
our stereotypes of strangers' groups and our intergroup attitudes toward strangers'
groups. The intergroup attitudes we discuss include ethnocentrism, prejudice, sexism,
and ageism. Our stereotypes of strangers' groups and our intergroup attitudes create
expectations for strangers' behavior (i.e., how we think strangers will behave). We
begin by looking at the nature of expectations and how they are created.

THE NATURE OF EXPECTATIONS

Berger, Wagner, and Zelditch (1985) define *expectation states* as "self-other relational
structures that organize behavior among interactants" (p. 32). *Expectations,* therefore,
involve our anticipations of and predictions about how others will communicate with
us. Our expectations are derived in large part from the social norms and communication rules we learned as children. They also emerge from our experiences with others,
observations of our own behavior, the mass media, and our ingroups. Other factors,
however, also create expectations. When we communicate with strangers, for example, expectations emerge from our intergroup attitudes and the stereotypes we hold. In
addition to these social cognitive factors, expectations are created by our affect or
emotional responses to others. The expectations we have for strangers' behavior influences the uncertainty and anxiety we experience when we communicate with them.
Generally, the more positive our expectations are, the more our uncertainty and anxiety are reduced (Hubbert, Gudykunst, & Guerrero, 1999).

Jackson (1964) argues that "people who interact develop expectations about each others' behavior, not only in the sense that they are able to predict the regularities, but also in the sense that they develop preferences about how others *should* behave under certain circumstances" (p. 225). Our cultures and ethnicities provide guidelines for appropriate behavior and the expectations we use in judging competent communication. Burgoon and Hale (1988), for example, point out that in the European American middle-class subculture in the United States

> one expects normal speakers to be reasonably fluent and coherent in their discourse, to refrain from erratic movements or emotional outbursts, and to adhere to politeness norms. Generally, normative behaviors are positively valued. If one keeps a polite distance and shows an appropriate level of interest in one's conversational partner, for instance, such behavior should be favorably received. (p. 61)

The rules for what is a polite distance and what constitutes an emotional outburst vary across cultures and subcultures within a culture.

If strangers violate our expectations to a sufficient degree that we recognize the violation, we become aroused and have to assess the situation (Burgoon & Hale, 1988). In other words, the violation of our expectations leads to some degree of mindfulness. We may, however, become mindful of the outcome of the interaction and *not* the process of the interaction. If we become mindful of the outcome, it will *not* facilitate effective communication. Mindfulness of the process, in contrast, will facilitate effective communication.

Burgoon and Hale (1988) argue that the degree to which others provide us with rewards affects how we evaluate the violations and the people committing the acts. As used here, rewards do not refer to money (although money might be a consideration if the other person is a boss or a client). Rather, *rewards* include the benefits we obtain from our interactions with others (e.g., prestige, affection). If others provide us with rewards, we choose the most positive of the possible interpretations of violations that have multiple possible interpretations; "for example, increased proximity during conversation may be taken as a sign of affiliation if committed by a high reward person but as a sign of aggressiveness if committed by a low reward person" (Burgoon & Hale, 1988, p. 63).

Burgoon and Hale (1988) suggest that positively evaluated violations of our expectations should have positive consequences for our communication with violators (e.g., not lead to misinterpretations, increase intimacy). Negatively evaluated violations, in contrast, generally lead to negative outcomes (e.g., misinterpretations, decreases in intimacy). There are, however, exceptions for negative violations. Burgoon and Hale point out that if others provide rewards and commit extreme violations of our expectations, positive outcomes (e.g., higher credibility and/or interpersonal attraction) are possible.

Stephan (1985) contends that we often believe our expectations have been fulfilled when we communicate with strangers, regardless of how the strangers behave. Stephan suggests that we tend not to change our behavior when strangers disconfirm our expectations. He goes on to argue that the

> affective consequences of confirmation or disconfirmation depend to a great degree on whether the expectancy is positive or negative. Confirmation of positive expectancies and disconfirmation of negative expectancies would be expected to elicit favorable affective responses to the behavior, such as pride and happiness. Disconfirmation of positive expectancies and confirmation of negative expectancies may lead to negative affect, such as sadness

or low self-esteem or resentment and hostility directed toward the self or the holder of the expectancy. (p. 637)

Burgoon and Hale (1988), however, point out that whether strangers provide rewards influences how we interpret the confirmation or disconfirmation of our expectations.

Our expectations have major consequences for our communication with strangers. Allport (1954), for example, believes that "in all human relations—familial, ethnic, international—the engendering power of expectancy is enormous. If we foresee evil in our fellow man [or woman], we tend to provoke it; if good, we elicit it" (p. 160). In the next two sections of this chapter, we focus on two social cognitive factors: intergroup attitudes (i.e., ethnocentrism, prejudice, sexism, ageism) and the stereotypes we have of strangers that create expectations when we communicate with strangers. We begin by looking at stereotypes.

STEREOTYPES

Lippman (1922) refers to stereotypes as "pictures in our heads." He points out that stereotypes have both a cognitive component and an affective component:

> [Stereotyping] is not merely a way of substituting order for the great blooming, buzzing confusion of reality. It is not merely a shortcut. It is all these things and more. It is a guarantee of our self-respect; it is the projection upon the world of our own sense of value, our own position and our own rights. The stereotypes are, therefore, highly charged with feelings that are attached to them. (pp. 63–64)

Stereotypes, therefore, are cognitive representations of another group that influence our feelings toward members of that group.

Hewstone and Brown (1986) isolate three aspects of *stereotypes* as mental representations:

1. Often individuals are categorized, usually on the basis of easily identifiable characteristics such as sex or ethnicity.
2. A set of attributes is ascribed to all (or most) members of that category. Individuals belonging to the stereotyped group are assumed to be similar to each other, and different from other groups, on this set of attributes.
3. The set of attributes is ascribed to any individual member of that category. (p. 29)

Hewstone and Brown's view of stereotypes is consistent with that of most writers who see stereotypes as mental representations of other groups.

We stereotype strangers immediately upon meeting them, and this occurs "within milliseconds after first encounters" (Operario & Fiske, 2001b, p. 33). We tend to categorize strangers by using visual cues such as skin color, body size, and social roles. We often are not aware of our categorization of strangers.

One problem with conceiving stereotypes as mental representations is the assumption that we ascribe traits to all or most members of a group. We often ascribe traits to a small percentage of a group. Stagnor and Lange (1994), for example, report that on average we associate positive traits with about 60 percent of a group and negative traits with about 50 percent of a group. They, therefore, suggest that we conceive of stereotypes as the extent to which a characteristic is associated strongly with the relevant category in our memory.

Tajfel (1981) draws a distinction between stereotypes and *social stereotypes:*

> "stereotypes" are certain generalizations reached by individuals. They derive in large mea-
> sure from, or are an instance of, the general cognitive process of categorizing. The main
> function of the process is to simplify or systematize, for purposes of cognitive and behav-
> ioral adaptation, the abundance and complexity of the information received from its environ-
> ment by the human organism. . . . But such stereotypes can become *social* only when they
> are shared by large numbers of people within social groups. (pp. 146–147)

Some of our stereotypes are unique and are based on our individual experiences, but
some are shared with other members of our ingroups. The stereotypes we share with
others are our social stereotypes. We may know what the social stereotype of a group
is but still hold a different view of that group (Devine, 1989).

Social stereotypes often are used in the media, and we learn many of our stereotypes from the media. Anyone who watches Saturday morning cartoons, for example,
knows that villains are non-Europeans. With respect to aging, the "dirty old man" is
used frequently in the media, and aging is depicted as involving evil, failures, and unhappiness in television dramas (Arnoff, 1974). Similarly, disabled people often are
presented as bitter, self-pitying, and maladjusted, while nondisabled people are portrayed as not having trouble accepting the disabled people's identities (Longmore,
1987). A large percentage of the stereotypes of the old, the disabled, and non-Europeans
presented in the media are negative and inaccurate.

Stereotypes also are used in advertising. An advertisement for a cleaning service one
of the authors received in the mail, for example, indicated that the company had "German
thoroughness, Swedish spotlessness, Polish flexibility, Discreet as a Swiss bank, Cheap as
Russian promises." Some of these are positive stereotypes, but others are negative and are
offensive to members of those groups. Ruscher (2001) points out that current stereotypes
in advertisements "may not be blatantly stereotypic as the black mammy Aunt Jemima,
the Chinese laundryman in the Calgon ad, and the devilishly thieving Frito Bandito. Still,
the continual pairing of older adults primarily with products that link declining health
with age may reinforce the view that elders are weak and sickly" (p. 181).

Our stereotypes are multidimensional images. Vassiliou, Triandis, Vassiliou, and
McGuire (1972) contend that stereotypes vary along six dimensions:

1. *Complexity.* The number of traits assigned to the other group.
2. *Clarity.* (a) *Polarization* of the judgments on each trait dimension, that is, the extent to which
   people from one group assign non-neutral values of the trait to people from another group.
   (b) *Consensus,* that is, agreement among people in assigning the trait to another group.
3. *Specificity-Vagueness.* The extent to which the traits are specific or vague (abstract).
4. *Validity.* The extent to which the stereotypes correspond to substantially realistic assignment of traits.
5. *Value.* The favorability of the assigned traits.
6. *Comparability.* The extent to which the framework of the perceiver is involved in the
   stereotyping so that a comparison is made between autostereotype (group looking at self)
   and heterostereotype (one group looking at another). (pp. 90–91)

All stereotypes vary along each of these dimensions. When stereotypes involve substantially realistic assignments of traits to a group of people (i.e., are valid), Bogardus
(1959) refers to them as "sociotypes."

Vassiliou et al. (1972) differentiate between normative and nonnormative stereotypes formed by members of ingroups prior to contact with members of outgroups. A *normative stereotype* is a "cognitive norm for thinking about a group of people" (p. 112) based on information gained from education, the mass media, and/or historical events. A *nonnormative stereotype,* in contrast, is not formed on the basis of information from such sources. When one group does not have a normative stereotype about another group with whom friendly relations exist, the members of the group begin thinking about the other group as being "like us." Nonnormative stereotypes, in other words, are purely projective in nature. U.S. Americans, for example, tend to have little information about Greeks. If they have had no previous contact with Greeks, they are likely to project their image of themselves and see Greeks as very similar to themselves. If friendly relations do not exist, the stereotype of the outgroup formed by the ingroup will be a normative one.

Vassiliou et al. (1972) argue that "contact has the effect of changing the stereotypes to match the sociotypes; that is, it increases the validity of the stereotypes" (p. 114). It should be noted, however, that although contact has a tremendous influence on nonnormative stereotypes, it has a lesser influence on normative stereotypes. More specifically, contact increases the clarity of nonnormative stereotypes but has little or no effect on the clarity of normative stereotypes. Further, contact with members of the outgroup increases the complexity and specificity of the ingroup's stereotype of them.

Stereotype Content

The content of stereotypes tells us individuals' "constellation of beliefs about members of social groups," or what individuals think about other groups (Operario & Fiske, 2001b, p. 23). Operario and Fiske (2001b) argue that three basic principles underlie stereotype content: "(a) stereotypes contain ambivalent beliefs reflecting relationships between groups, (b) stereotypes augment perceptions of negative and extreme behavior, and (c) stereotypes maintain division between ingroup ('us') and outgroups ('them')" (p. 24).

Fiske, Xu, Cuddy, and Glick (1999) contend that competence and niceness are core dimensions of the content of stereotypes. The relative status of the group being stereotyped determines whether its members are perceived as competent. The interdependence (cooperation versus competition) of our group and the group being stereotyped influences whether we see outgroup members as nice. Fiske et al. report that blind people, disabled people, the elderly, retarded people, and housewives are perceived as "nice, but incompetent." African American professionals, Jews, Asians, feminists, and businesswomen, in contrast, are perceived to be "competent, but not nice." Operario and Fiske (2001b) argue that "the beliefs associated with these two clusters reflect the relationship with the dominant majority (white, male, middle-class, able-bodied). The first group [nice, but incompetent] presents no threat to the majority, whereas the second group [competent, but not nice] presents a significant threat" (p. 25).

As indicated earlier, Operario and Fiske (2001b) contend that stereotypes "augment perceptions of negative and extreme behavior." They point out that our attention is drawn to "negative and extreme stimuli" because we generally expect our perceptions of others to be slightly positive. We tend to associate other ethnic groups with negative and extreme behavior because we do not have much experience with other ethnic groups; "when encountering both an unusual group and a rare group, perceivers assume the two are directly associated" (p. 26).

The third principle underlying stereotype content is that it helps maintain the distinction between "us" and "them." Social identity theory (e.g., Tajfel & Turner, 1979) suggests that we tend to advantage our ingroups over outgroups when we compare the two groups (i.e., there is an ingroup bias; see Chapter 4).

Bar-Tal (1997) takes a slightly different position regarding the content of stereotypes. He isolates three groups of factors that influence the content of our stereotypes: background factors, transmitting factors, and personal mediating factors. The background factors include the history of relations between the groups involved (e.g., European American–African American relations in the United States), the political and social climate in which we live (e.g., does the political climate support positive intergroup relations?), economic conditions (e.g., are the groups competing for resources?), and the behavior of the members of the groups. The transmitting factors include direct contact with members of the other group and our families, as well as the political, cultural (e.g., media), social (e.g., religion), and educational institutions. Finally, our attitudes, personalities, motivation, and cognitive styles mediate how these factors influence the formation of our stereotypes.

Since 1933, a series of studies has examined the content of individuals' stereotypes for 10 national and ethnic groups (i.e., "American," African Americans, Chinese, English, Germans, Irish, Italians, Jewish, Japanese, Turkish) (Devine & Elliot, 1995; Dovidio & Gaertner, 1986; Gilbert, 1951; Katz & Braly, 1933; Karlins, Coffman, & Walters, 1969; Madon et al., 2001). These studies analyze the content of individuals' stereotypes (i.e., the attributes associated with each of the groups) and the degree of consensus (i.e., the agreement on the content) on the stereotypes. In most of the studies, respondents selected 5 attributes for each group from a list of 84 attributes. Some of the studies also looked at the favorableness of the stereotypes, and some looked only at stereotypes of "Americans" and African Americans.

The first three studies were conducted at Princeton University. Katz and Braly's (1933) original study discovered that European American college students associated distinct attributes with each group and that there was a high degree of consensus on the attributes. Gilbert (1951) found that European American college students' stereotypes were similar to those held in 1933 but that the consensus was lower. Karlins et al. (1969) observed that the content of stereotypes had changed and that the level of consensus was similar to the level in 1951. Dovidio and Gaertner (1986) and Devine and Elliot (1995) reported that the content of European Americans' stereotypes of African Americans had changed a lot over time and that the consensus had decreased. Madon et al. (2001) argue that one reason for these results may be that the attributes used to stereotype African Americans are different from those included in the 84 attributes used in the studies (Note: Devine & Elliot added nine attributes and found consensus on those attributes.)

Madon et al.'s (2001) first study replicated the original 1933 study using the same 84 attributes and 10 groups, but they included non-European Americans in their study. They report that there are generally high levels of agreement in the attributes used to stereotype the various groups between European Americans and non-European Americans. Madon et al. note that the stereotype that involved the greatest change over the years is the African American stereotype. The results of this study suggest that the stereotypes of eight of the remaining nine groups remained relatively constant over the years. The Japanese stereotype, however, was significantly different in 2001 than it was in 1933. Madon et al. also contend that the degree of consensus for the various stereotypes remained relatively stable over the years. They argue that these results may be due to the list of attributes used.

Madon et al.'s (2001) second study included about 400 attributes and each attribute was rated on a scale indicating how characteristic it is of the group (as opposed to selecting five attributes in other studies). They conclude that

> the European American sample most often perceived Germans as liking to drink beer, Italians as loyal to family ties, African Americans as listening to a lot of music and noisy, Irish as liking to drink beer, English as competitive, Jews as very religious and wealthy, Americans as diverse, Chinese as disciplined, Japanese as scientifically minded and disciplined, and Turks as very religious. The non-European American sample most often perceived Germans as liking to drink beer; Italians as macho; African Americans as musical and tough; Irish as liking to drink beer; English as egotistical, proud, and liberal; Jews as proud; Americans as diverse; Chinese and Japanese as loyal to family ties; and Turks as cultural. (p. 1003)

These results suggest there is some agreement and some disagreement in European Americans' and non-European Americans' stereotypes today but that there is general agreement overall. The results also suggest that there is more change in stereotypes over time than indicated in their first study, where only 84 attributes were used.

Madon et al. (2001) report that there is greater consensus among non-European Americans in the stereotypes of eight groups ("Americans" and Turks not included) than among European Americans. Overall, however, consensus tends to be higher today than in previous years. Madon et al. also note that stereotypes today tend to be more favorable than those held in the 1930s, the 1950s, and the 1960s. There are, nevertheless, some stereotypes that have not become more favorable (e.g., there is no increase in the favorableness of the African American stereotype between 1969 and 2001).

Stereotyping Processes

As indicated earlier, stereotypes provide the content of our social categories. We have social categories in which we place people, and it is our stereotype that tells us what people in that category are like. Stereotypes, therefore, reduce our uncertainty and increase our confidence in predicting strangers' behavior. Stereotypes, however, do not necessarily increase the accuracy of our predictions (see below for more details). Stereotyping is the result of our tendency to overestimate the degree of association between group membership and psychological attributes. There may be some association between group membership and the psychological characteristics of group members, but it is much smaller than we assume when we communicate on automatic pilot. Only 28 to 37 percent of the people in a culture, for example, have the traits attributed to them (Wallace, 1952). In some cases, there is more similarity between people in the same occupation across cultures than there is between people in different occupations within a culture (Inkeles, 1974).

Our stereotypes tend to be activated automatically when we categorize strangers and are not communicating mindfully (see von Hippel et al., 1995). We, therefore, cannot not stereotype when we communicate on automatic pilot. Our tendency to stereotype automatically is enhanced when we are highly anxious. Wilder (1994) points out that "when anxiety distracts persons from careful attention to the environment, they rely more on cognitive structures such as social stereotypes in making judgments of others" (pp. 87–88). Islam and Hewstone (1993) report that the greater our anxiety is, the less variability we see in outgroups (i.e., the more we assume members of outgroups are alike).

Our stereotypes influence the way we process information. We remember more favorable information about our ingroups and more unfavorable information about outgroups (Hewstone & Giles, 1986). This, in turn, affects the way we interpret incoming messages from members of ingroups and outgroups. Our processing of information is "biased in the direction of maintaining the preexisting belief systems. . . . These processes, then, can produce the *cognitive confirmation* of one's stereotypic beliefs" (Hamilton et al., 1992, p. 138).

Our stereotypes also create expectations regarding how members of other groups will behave. Unconsciously, we assume that our expectations are correct and behave as though they are. Hamilton et al. (1992) point out that

> stereotypes operate as a source of expectancies about what a group as a whole is like (e.g., Hispanics) as well as about what attributes individual group members are likely to possess (e.g., Juan Garcia). Their influence can be pervasive, affecting the perceiver's attention to, encoding of, inferences about, and judgments based on that information. And the resulting interpretations, inferences, and judgments typically are made so as to be consistent with preexisting beliefs that guided them. (p. 142)

We, therefore, unconsciously try to confirm our expectations when we communicate with strangers.

Snyder and Haugen (1995) suggest that our tendency to engage in confirming behaviors depends on our goal in the interaction. If our goal is to adjust to the other person and have smooth interactions, we tend to engage in confirming behaviors. If our goal is to gather information about the other person, in contrast, we do not necessarily engage in confirming behaviors. Operario and Fiske (2001b) argue that we tend to find information inconsistent with our stereotypes under very limited conditions; "for example, when expectancies are weak, when incongruencies are strong, and when perceivers have explicit impression formation goals" (p. 34). When we are motivated highly and have enough information, we can modify our existing stereotypes by incorporating the new information.

Our stereotypes constrain strangers' patterns of communication and engender stereotype-confirming communication. Stated differently, stereotypes create self-fulfilling prophecies. We tend to see behavior that confirms our expectations even when it is absent. We ignore disconfirming evidence when communicating on automatic pilot. Hamilton et al. (1992) point out that

> perceivers can influence a person with whom they interact by constraining the person's behavior. However, perceivers typically do not recognize this influence or take it into consider-

ation when interpreting the target's behavior. Although a target person's behavior may be affected by perceiver-induced constraints, it is often interpreted by the perceiver as a manifestation of the target's personality. (p. 149)

In other words, if we create self-fulfilling prophecies, we generally are not aware that strangers behave the way they do because of how we behave.

Steele (cited in Watters, 1995) proposes an explanation for stereotype-confirming behaviors. He argues that confirming others' stereotypes may be due to stereotype vulnerability. *Stereotype vulnerability* does not involve consciously or unconsciously accepting a stereotype; rather, it emerges from having to contend with the stereotype when mental abilities are already taxed. Steele argues that stereotype vulnerability has broad implications:

> I think much of what is mistaken for racial animosity in America today is really stereotype
> vulnerability. Imagine [an African American] man and [a European American] man meeting
> for the first time. Because the [African American] person knows the stereotype of his group,
> he attempts to deflect those negative traits, finding ways of trying to communicate, in effect,
> "Don't think of me as incompetent." The [European American], for his part, is busy deflect-
> ing the stereotype of his group: "Don't think of me as a racist.") Every action becomes
> loaded with the potential of confirming the stereotype, and you end up with two people
> struggling with the phantoms they're only half aware of. The discomfort and tension is often
> mistaken as racial animosity. (p. 47)

The problem is that the two people are being mindful of the outcome (i.e., "Don't think of me as incompetent" and "Don't think of me as a racist") rather than being mindful of the communication process that is taking place between them.

We are likely to stereotype strangers when we have power over them (Operario & Fiske, 2001b). One reason for this is that we tend not to pay attention to individuating information when we have power over strangers. Operario and Fiske (2001b) point out that "not only does power perpetuate beliefs associated with social subordinates and minority groups, it also enables people to act upon stereotypic beliefs through legislation, economic policies, and institutional practices" (p. 37). Members of low-power groups, however, may recognize their groups' disadvantaged status but tend to "minimize perceptions of personal vulnerability to discrimination" so that they can maintain their self-esteem and sense of control (p. 37).

When we communicate on automatic pilot, we do not cognitively process all the information about others that is available to us (Johnston & Macrae, 1994). As indicated earlier, we tend to process information that is consistent with our stereotypes, and our stereotypes do not change. We can process most of the information available to us if we are mindful of our communication. (Note: We believe it is impossible to process all the information from our interactions even if we are mindful.) When we process most of the information available to us, our stereotypes of strangers can change (see the final section of this chapter for more details). Also, when we are involved highly in interactions and receive information inconsistent with our stereotypes from highly credible sources, we tend to change our stereotypes (Johnston & Coolen, 1995).

One way we may try to stop stereotyping from influencing our behavior is by suppressing our stereotypes. This approach, however, usually does not work and frequently results in more stereotyping than occurs when we do not try to suppress our stereotypes (Bodenhausen & Macrae, 1996). When we try to suppress our stereotypes, the rebound effect (i.e., more, not less, stereotyping) occurs most frequently for those of us who are highly prejudiced. It also occurs, however, for those of us who *want* to be low in prejudice but still react negatively to strangers. The rebound effect occurs least in those of us who are low in prejudice (Monteith, Shermnan, & Devine, 1998). The extent to which we are able to process complex information also influences the extent to which the rebound effect will occur. When something inhibits our abilities to process complex information (e.g., high levels of anxiety, cognitive overload), the rebound effect tends to take place (Monteith et al., 1998).

Richards and Hewstone (2001) argue that there are two ways we deal with members of other groups who do not fit our stereotypes. One way we deal with strangers who do not fit our stereotypes is to put them in a "subtype" which includes members of other groups who are "exceptions to the rule." This process allows us to maintain our stereotypes because the original stereotype remains the same when we put exceptions in a separate subtype. Another way we can deal with strangers who do not fit our stereotypes is to create "subgroups" in our stereotypes. When we do this, we put members of the other group who are alike in some ways and different in others into subgroups. We can create subgroups with members of the other group who fit the stereotype well too. Richards and Hewstone point out that "different subgroups could all manifest the stereotype, but in different ways" (p. 57). Subgrouping tends to lead us to see greater variability in the outgroup than subtyping does and, therefore, may facilitate stereotype change. (Note: Creating subgroups is similar to Langer's, 1989, notion of creating new categories.)

Devine (1989) argues that conscious control of our reactions when our stereotypes are activated is necessary to control our prejudice:

> Nonprejudiced responses are . . . a function of intentional controlled processes and require a conscious decision to behave in a nonprejudiced fashion. In addition, new responses must be learned and well practiced before they can serve as competitive responses to the automatically activated stereotype-congruent response. (p. 15)

Von Hippel et al. (1995) argue that people who are not highly prejudiced do not act on their "automatically activated stereotypes" (p. 224). This position is consistent with Langer's notion that mindfulness is necessary to reduce prejudice.

Accuracy of Predictions Based on Stereotypes

Stereotypes, in and of themselves, do not lead to miscommunication and/or communication breakdown. If, however, inaccurate or negative stereotypes are held rigidly, they lead to inaccurate predictions of strangers' behavior and misunderstandings. In addition to inaccurate stereotypes, simple stereotypes of other groups can lead to misunderstandings. To increase our effectiveness in communicating with strangers, we need to increase the complexity of our stereotypes (e.g., include a large number of traits in the stereotype and differentiate subgroups within the group being stereotyped) and question our unconscious assumption that most, if not all, members of a group fit a single stereotype (Stephan & Rosenfield, 1982).

Individual members of a group may or may not fit a stereotype we have of that group. Ting-Toomey (1989) isolates four possible options between how individuals identify with a group and the way they behave: (1) Individuals may see themselves as typical group members and behave typically, (2) individuals may see themselves as typical group members and behave atypically, (3) individuals may see themselves as atypical group members and behave atypically, and (4) individuals may see themselves as atypical group members and behave typically. It is actually more complicated than this, however, because our perceptions of others as typical or atypical members of their groups may not be the same as theirs.

The accuracy of our predictions depends on whether the traits we include in our stereotypes of another group are similar to the ones in the other group's stereotype of its own group (e.g., are our stereotypes valid?). If the traits we apply to another group agree with the traits members of that group apply to themselves, our stereotype should lead to accurate interpretations of the behavior of members of the group who are typical. Valid stereotypes, however, will lead to misinterpretations of the behavior of atypical members of the group.

When we place strangers in a category, our stereotypes of strangers' groups help us predict their behavior if we perceive that strangers are typical members of their groups. We are able to reduce our uncertainty because we assume that our stereotypes tell us how typical group members communicate (Krauss & Fussell, 1991). If strangers have informed us of their group memberships, our predictions may be accurate. To illustrate, if we are communicating with a woman from Mexico and she tells us she is a Chicana, not a Mexican American, we can make some accurate predictions of her behavior if our stereotypes of people from Mexico differentiate Chicanos/Chicanas from Mexican Americans. If our stereotypes do not include this differentiation, our predictions probably will not be accurate. It is rare, however, for strangers to tell us their group memberships directly (Kellermann, 1993).

Rather than using strangers' self-categorizations (the group memberships they announce), we tend to base our categorizations on their skin color, their dress, their accents, the cars they drive, and so forth (Clark & Marshall, 1981). The cues we use, however, are not always accurate ways to categorize strangers (e.g., an inaccurate categorization occurs when we put strangers in categories in which they would not place themselves). This is true for all social categories, including ethnicity. To illustrate, recall from Chapter 4 that we vary in the degree to which we identify with our ethnic groups and cultures. If we categorize strangers who do not identify strongly with their ethnic groups and who do strongly identify with their cultures on the basis of their ethnicities, our predictions in all likelihood will be inaccurate. Predictions based on ethnicity probably will be accurate only for strangers who identify strongly with their ethnic groups and do not identify strongly with their cultures.

Another source of inaccuracy in our predictions based on our stereotypes is that the boundaries between many social groups are fuzzy (Clark & Marshall, 1981). What, for example, is the boundary between educated and uneducated people or between young and old people? Even skin color may not be a good predictor of category membership. To illustrate, there are light-skinned African Americans who look like European Americans. These individuals may be categorized as European American solely on the basis of skin color. They may, however, identify strongly with being African Americans. Similarly, dark-skinned African Americans may not identify strongly with their ethnic groups. Obviously, predictions about their behavior based on skin color will be inaccurate.

Even if strangers are typical members of the groups in which we categorize them, the inferences we make about them on the basis of their group memberships may not be accurate. One reason for this is that our stereotypes are not valid (i.e., our stereotypes of strangers' groups are different from their stereotypes of their groups). Another reason our predictions may not be accurate is that the group memberships we are using to categorize strangers may not be affecting their behavior in this situation. We are all members of many social groups that influence our behavior and provide us with different social identities. When communicating with strangers, we might categorize them based on one group membership (e.g., ethnicity) and assume that their social identities based on this category are influencing their behavior. The strangers, however, may be basing their behavior on a different social identity (e.g., social class, gender, role). To increase our accuracy in making predictions, we must try to understand which social identity is guiding strangers' behavior in a particular situation.

To summarize, stereotypes are the content of the categories when we are categorizing people. The stereotypes we hold have a direct influence on our communication with strangers. Our initial predictions about strangers' behavior must, of necessity, be based on the stereotypes we have about the strangers' cultures, races, or ethnic groups. To the degree that our stereotypes are accurate, we can make accurate cultural-level or sociocultural-level predictions about strangers' behavior. If our stereotypes are inaccurate, we cannot make correct attributions about strangers' behavior. Further, if we rigidly hold our stereotypes and are not willing to question them, we can never reach the point where we know strangers as individuals (e.g., we can never make psychocultural predictions about their behavior), and our attributions about an individual stranger's behavior will continue to be incorrect.

INTERGROUP ATTITUDES

An *attitude* "is a learned predisposition to respond in an evaluative (from extremely favorable to extremely unfavorable) manner toward some attitude object" (Davidson & Thompson, 1980, p. 27). Attitudes predispose us to behave in a positive or negative manner toward various objects or people.

Attitudes generally are conceptualized as having three components: cognitive, affective, and conative (McGuire, 1969). The cognitive component involves our beliefs about the attitude object (e.g., a group of people). Rokeach (1972) defines a *belief* as "any simple proposition, conscious or unconscious, inferred from what a person says or does, capable of being preceded by the phrase 'I believe that' " (p. 113). Examples of beliefs include "blacks are musical," "the Irish are heavy drinkers," and "the Japanese are ambitious." The affective component of an attitude involves our emotional or evaluative reactions to the attitude object. Thus, the affective component refers to our subjective evaluation of the positive or negative aspects of the attitude object. The conative component of an attitude involves our behavioral intentions toward the attitude object. This may involve, for example, an intention to avoid members of outgroups.

Intergroup attitudes serve several functions for the people who hold them. By functions, we mean what the attitudes do for people who hold them or, in other words, the uses of attitudes. Katz (1960) proposes four general functions any attitude can serve:

1. *The utilitarian or adjustment function.* We hold some attitudes because they are useful in our cultures; they lead to the attainment of rewards.
2. *The ego-defensive function.* We hold some attitudes because they allow us to protect our self-images (egos). These attitudes allow us to avoid admitting uncomfortable things about ourselves.
3. *The value-expressive function.* We hold some attitudes because we want to express those parts of our lives that are important to us.
4. *The knowledge function.* We hold some attitudes because they allow us to structure or organize incoming stimuli in a way that makes sense to us.

These functions can have positive and negative consequences. Negative intergroup attitudes, for example, increase our confidence in predicting strangers' behavior, but they also decrease the accuracy of our predictions (Gudykunst, 1988b). Negative intergroup attitudes also lead to anxiety in interacting with strangers (Stephan & Stephan, 1985).

Research on children's development suggests that they develop prejudices as young as three years old (see Cameron et al., 2001). Camron et al., however, question this conclusion. They argue that prior studies have not differentiated between "ingroup positivity" and "outgroup negativity." Cameron et al. contend that young children mainly learn "ingroup positivity." Depending on their experiences, what they learn from those in their environments (e.g., parents, teachers, peers), and social structural conditions, ingroup positivity can turn into outgroup negativity.

Ethnocentrism

The word *ethnocentrism* is derived from two Greek words: *ethnos,* or "nation," and *kentron,* or "center." This suggests that ethnocentrism occurs when our nation is seen as the center of the world. In common usage, however, the concept is applied more broadly. Sumner (1940) defines *ethnocentrism* as

> the technical name for the view of things in which one's own group is the center of everything, and all others are scaled and rated with reference to it. . . . the most important fact is that ethnocentrism leads people to exaggerate and intensify everything in their own folkways which is peculiar and which differentiates them from others. It therefore strengthens the folkways. (p. 13)

In other words, ethnocentrism refers to our tendency to identify with our ingroup (e.g., ethnic or racial group, culture) and to evaluate outgroups and their members according to our ingroups' standards.

Everyone is ethnocentric to some degree. Because we are ethnocentric, we tend to view our own cultural values and ways of doing things as more real, or as the "right" and natural values and ways of doing things. One major consequence of ethnocentrism is that we see our ingroups' values and ways of doing things as superior to outgroups' values and ways of doing things. Another consequence of ethnocentrism is that it leads us to be anxious about interacting with strangers (Stephan & Stephan, 1992). Ethnocentrism exists in all cultures (Triandis, 1984), but collectivists tend to be more ethnocentric than individualists (Lee & Ward, 1998).

Ethnocentrism is not the same as xenophobia. *Xenophobia* is a "fear of strangers" (Kleg, 1993, p. 153). Kleg points out that this fear is natural and that we all have "some degree of fear of others who seen strange and different" (p. 153). One reason for xenophobia is that people who are strange are perceived as threats to the predictability and stability of our social worlds.

Ethnocentrism is not usually deliberate. Often the expression of ethnocentrism is a function of how we are socialized. People born and raised in the United States, for example, are taught many subtle cues that suggest that the United States is the center of the world. Consider the major league baseball championship series played between the winners of the two leagues. Is it called the United States Series? No, obviously not; it is called the World Series, implying that no other nation has baseball teams (granted, there have been Canadian teams in the World Series, but no Japanese, Korean, or Mexican teams). Another example of the tendency for people in the United States to view their country as the center of the world is the use of the term "American." Citizens of the other members of the Organization of American States (OAS) from North, Central, and South America are also "Americans." This is why we use "U.S. Americans" throughout the book to refer to people from the United States.

The existence of ethnocentrism is not limited to recent historical times or to the United States. The early Greeks used the term *barbarikos* ("barbarians") to refer to those people living around them who did not speak Greek. Because they did not speak Greek, the ancient Persians and Egyptians were considered inferior by the Greeks. In current times, many languages have a word with very similar meaning. The Japanese word *gaijin*, for example, means "foreigner," a person who is not Japanese, and may be used with a condescending overtone.

Klass and Heliman (1971) point out that ethnocentrism often is expressed in the way people draw their maps:

> There is nothing unusual about this type of thinking: the Chinese, who called their country the Middle Kingdom, were convinced that China was the center of the world, and similar beliefs were held by other nations—and still are held. The British drew the Prime Meridian of longitude to run through Greenwich, near London. Europeans drew maps of the world with Europe at the center, [North] Americans with the New World at the center. (p. 61)

The way we draw maps clearly reflects ethnocentrism involving seeing our country as the center of the world.

The opposite of ethnocentrism is cultural relativism. *Cultural relativism* involves trying to understand others' behavior in the context of the cultures or groups of the people engaging in the behavior (Herskovits, 1973). We cannot understand others' behavior if we use our own cultural or ethnic frames of reference to interpret their behavior. Kurt Vonnegut, Jr., says

> I didn't learn until I was in college about all other cultures, and I should have learned that in first grade. A first grader should understand that his or her culture isn't a rational invention; that there are thousands of other cultures and they all work pretty well; that all cultures function on faith rather than truth; that there are lots of alternatives to our own society. Cultural relativity is defensible and attractive. It also is a source of hope. It means we don't have to continue this way if we do not like it. [Note: This quote is from the afterword of a book for elementary school teachers published in the 1970s, but the exact reference has been lost.]

Some degree of cultural relativism is necessary to understand strangers' behavior. Cultural relativism, however, should not be extended to moral relativism (this issue is discussed in more detail in Chapter 15).

Functions and Dysfunctions of Ethnocentrism   Ethnocentrism is related closely to the attitude of nationalism. Rosenblatt (1964) believes both attitudes arise from a comparison of ingroups with outgroups. The attitudes differ, however, in that ethnocentrism focuses on cultural patterns of behavior, while nationalism focuses on a nation's political ideology. Rosenblatt argues that high levels of nationalism and ethnocentrism both serve several functions that maintain the integrity of the ingroup, including:

1. GROUP SURVIVAL—Groups with high ethnocentrism and high nationalism are more likely to survive the threats of external forces.
2. TANGIBLE PAYOFFS—Administrative efficacy is promoted (e.g., power in policy making decisions, division of labor, promotion of group welfare).
3. INCREASED HOMOGENEITY—Groups will have more homogeneous attitudes, greater cohesiveness, and increased conformity.
4. GREATER VIGOR AND PERSISTENCE—Problems affecting the group are addressed with persistence and energy.
5. GREATER EASE OF STRIVING AGAINST OUTSIDERS—Relations against outgroups are executed with greater ease because of strong commitments to group maintenance.
6. DECREASED SOCIAL DISORGANIZATION—Intragroup organization increases.
7. INCREASED TENURE OF LEADERS—Leaders are more likely to remain in the leadership position.
8. NEW DISSENSION—Intragroup conflicts arise frequently amid the strain toward homogeneity.
9. MISPERCEPTION OF OUTGROUPS—Attributions to out-group members are not accurate because of misperceptions.
10. FACILITATION OF LEARNING—Learning correct in-group behavior is easier when the pressures to conform are pervasive. (Rosenblatt, 1964, summarized in Burk, 1976, pp. 21–22)

Ethnocentrism, therefore, can have positive functions for the ingroup, but its consequences for outgroups tend to be negative.

High levels of ethnocentrism and nationalism are functional when they satisfy needs in the lives of group members and when the ingroup is strengthened or becomes more cohesive (Burk, 1976). Ethnocentric attitudes serve all four of the functions Katz (1960) isolates. The utilitarian function involves the notion that if we are highly ethnocentric, we tend to conform to our culture and, thus, be in a better position to obtain its rewards. Ethnocentrism also helps us protect ourselves from uncomfortable things about ourselves (e.g., we can put down parts of another culture, thereby elevating the qualities of our own). An ethnocentric attitude also serves a value-expressive function. Specifically, this attitude allows us to express our values as the true and correct ones to hold. Finally, ethnocentrism serves the knowledge function; it allows us to structure a set of beliefs about people in other cultures based on our own culture.

High levels of ethnocentrism and nationalism are also dysfunctional. Burk (1976) argues that the extremes of these attitudes are dysfunctional when they lead to hostility and conflict with outgroup members. Holmes (1965) argues that "when the in-group feeling develops to the extent that the members of a particular society feel their way of life is so superior to all others that it is their duty to change other people to their way of thinking and doing (if necessary by force), then this attitude becomes a menace" (p. 347). High levels of ethnocentrism and nationalism, therefore, are causes of wars. Catton (1961) hypothesizes that "ethnocentrism is a factor which enables homo sapiens to engage in war despite rational considerations to the contrary" (p. 205).

High levels of ethnocentrism are also dysfunctional with respect to effective communication with strangers. Specifically, high levels of ethnocentrism lead to misperceptions of members of outgroups; this misperception causes us to make inaccurate attributions about strangers' behavior. In other words, a high level of ethnocentrism leads us to interpret strangers' behavior using our own cultural frames of reference, thereby distorting the meaning of the strangers' behavior. If we do not understand strangers' behavior, effective communication is impossible.

A Consequence of Ethnocentrism: Communicative Distance   Our intergroup attitudes influence the way we speak to strangers. The speed with which we talk or the accent we use may be varied in order to generate different feelings of distance between us and the strangers with whom we communicate (i.e., to make the distance seem smaller or greater). Peng (1974) uses the concept of "communicative distance" to explain this linguistic diversity:

> A communicative distance cannot be measured directly. It is not even visible. But we can be sure of its presence when we hear certain words or expressions. In other words, our awareness of a communicative distance in the midst of a conversation depends to a large extent on certain linguistic devices which serve, from the speaker's point of view, to set up the communicative distance, or from the hearer's point of view, to let the hearer know that it has already been set up by the speaker. (p. 33)

We, therefore, establish communicative distances between ourselves and strangers when we speak with them.

Lukens (1978) expands Peng's conceptualization of communicative distance to cover *ethnocentric speech,* which is reflected in three communicative distances: (1) the distance of indifference, (2) the distance of avoidance, and (3) the distance of disparagement. Lukens goes on:

> In essence, speech in accordance with the three communicative distances may be used: (1) to demonstrate lack of concern for persons of other cultures and reflect an insensitivity to cultural differences (the distance of indifference), (2) to avoid or limit the amount of interaction with out-groups (the distance of avoidance), and (3) to demonstrate feelings of hostility towards out-groups and to deride or belittle them (the distance of disparagement). (p. 41)

Lukens associates each of the three distances with a different level of ethnocentrism (low, moderate, and high, respectively).

The *distance of disparagement* reflects the animosity of the ingroup toward the outgroup (Lukens, 1978). It arises when the two groups are in competition for the same resources and involves attacking strangers' self-concepts. Lukens indicates that at this distance imitation and mockery of speech styles are characteristic. The use of "baby talk" with the elderly is an example of language perceived as mockery by the group toward which it is directed.

The distance of disparagement is characterized by the use of pejorative expressions and ethnophaulisms. Ehrlich (1973) specifies three types of ethnophaulisms: (1) ethnic names used as an disparagement (e.g., "Irish confetti," "Jewbird"); (2) explicit group devaluations (e.g., "luck of the Irish," "Jew them down"); and (3) disparaging nicknames (e.g., "Polack," "jungle bunny," "honky"). If you are familiar with the television program *All in the Family,* you will recognize that Archie Bunker uses these three types of ethnophaulisms. Palmore (1962) notes that all racial and ethnic groups use ethnophaulisms and that they usually express unfavorable stereotypes. His study also reveals that when ethnophaulisms are directed toward other races, physical characteristics generally are highlighted. When ethnophaulisms are directed toward people from the same racial group, in contrast, highly visible cultural differences usually are highlighted. Further, the number of ethnophaulisms we use is related to the degree of our ethnocentrism, and our use of ethnophaulisms can intensify our ethnocentrism. Palmore concludes that "we may discover that ethnophaulisms are essential for the existence of such forms of ethnocentrism as chauvinism, pejorative stereotypes, scapegoats, segregation, and discrimination" (p. 445).

The *distance of avoidance* is established in order to avoid or minimize contact with members of outgroups (Lukens, 1978). One technique commonly used to accomplish this is the use of ingroup dialects. Lukens (1978) argues that emphasizing "an ethnic dialect and other linguistic differences between the in-group and outsiders may be purposefully used by in-group members to make themselves appear esoteric to the outgroup thus lessening the likelihood for interaction" (p. 45). At this distance, members of ingroups also may use terms of solidarity. Feelings of cultural pride and solidarity are increased through the use of such terms as "black power," "black is beautiful," and "red power." In establishing this distance, jargon common to ingroups is used extensively.

The *distance of indifference* is the speech form used to "reflect the view that one's own culture is the center of everything" (Lukens, 1978, p. 42). This distance, therefore, reflects insensitivity to strangers' perspectives. One example of the speech used at this distance is "foreigner talk," the form of speech used when talking to people who are not native speakers of a language. It usually takes the form of loud and slow speech patterns, exaggerated pronunciation, and simplification (e.g., deletion of articles). Downs (1971) points out that "we tend to believe that, if we speak slowly enough or loudly enough, anyone can understand us. I have done this myself quite without realizing it, and others have tried to reach me in the same way in Japanese, Chinese, Thai, Punjabi, Navajo, Spanish, Tibetan, and Singhalese" (p. 19). The use of idiomatic expressions such as "black sheep," "black list," "black magic," "low person on the totem pole," "Indian giver," "Mexican standoff," and "the blind leading the blind" suggests indifference to other groups' points of view.

We agree that Lukens' (1978) three levels of communicative distance are manifested in speech patterns and are based on differing levels of ethnocentrism, but we also believe the trichotomy is incomplete as it stands. As indicated earlier, ethnocentrism is only one side of the coin, with the other side being cultural relativism. Cultural relativism, as indicated earlier, involves the view that the values and behavior of people in a culture can be understood only by using that culture as a frame of reference. Often ethnocentrism and cultural relativism are discussed separately; that is, they are seen as two distinct attitudes. We believe, however, that ethnocentrism and cultural relativism are opposite sides of the same coin. If we adopt this view, a high level of ethnocentrism and a high level of cultural relativism can be seen as opposite ends of an attitudinal continuum. We can label at least five different points on the continuum: high ethnocentrism, moderate ethnocentrism, low ethnocentrism/low cultural relativism, moderate cultural relativism, and high cultural relativism. Each of these five points should be reflected in a different level of communicative distance. Lukens' (1978) analysis addresses the first three but not the last two.

The level of moderate cultural relativism reflects none of the characteristics of Lukens' three distances. Rather, this level reveals a sensitivity to cultural differences. The speech at this level reflects our desire to decrease the communicative distance between ourselves and strangers. This distance is labeled the *distance of sensitivity*. Speech at this distance reflects a sensitivity to group differences, but the groups are not necessarily viewed as equal. When speaking at this distance, for example, we would use the terms for strangers' ethnic groups that they prefer rather than the terms we usually use.

The level of high cultural relativism reflects our desire to minimize the distance between ourselves and strangers. This distance involves an attitude of equality, one where we demonstrate that we are interpreting the language and behavior of strangers in terms of their culture. This distance is labeled the *distance of equality*. Speech at this distance avoids evaluating other groups. The use of nonsexist language (e.g., "he or she") instead of sexist language (e.g., using "he" as a generic pronoun to include "she"), for example, illustrates equality between males and females.

Ethnic Prejudice

The term *prejudice* stems from the Latin word *praejudicium,* which means a "precedent", or "a judgment based on previous decisions and experiences" (Allport, 1954, p. 7). Prejudice can be positive or negative, but most of us think of it as negative. Consistent with this view, Allport defines *negative ethnic prejudice* as "an antipathy based on a faulty and unflexible generalization. It may be felt or expressed. It may be directed toward a group as a whole, or toward an individual because he [or she] is a member of that group" (p. 10).

Prejudice typically is conceived as an attitude. Smith (1994, p. 299) points out that this view usually takes the following form:

Negative Stereotype: *Members of Group A are dirty, hostile, lazy.* . . .
leads to
Prejudiced attitude: *I don't like As*
leads to
Discrimination: *I prefer to avoid As, exclude them from good jobs.* . . .

Smith, however, argues that prejudice can be viewed as an emotion. He defines prejudice as a "social emotion experienced with respect to one's social identity as a group member, with an outgroup member as a target" (p. 304). When prejudice is seen as an emotion, the logic takes the following form:

Appraisals: *A member of Group A is receiving benefits that are undeserved and paid for by my tax dollars*
leads to
Prejudiced emotion: *I feel anger and resentment at As*
leads to
Discrimination: *I want to harm As by reducing food stamps and welfare benefits. . . .* (p. 305)

Prejudice can be manifested in emotions such as fear, disgust, contempt (dislike), anger, and jealousy. Most research on prejudice, however, views it as an attitude.

Dimensions of Prejudice   We tend to think of prejudice in terms of a dichotomy; either we are prejudiced or we are not. It is more accurate, however, to think of the strength of our prejudice as varying along a continuum from low to high. This suggests that *we all are prejudiced to some degree*. We also are all racist, sexist, ageist, and so forth to some degree. As with ethnocentrism, this is natural and unavoidable. It is the result of our being socialized as members of our ingroups. Even people with low levels of prejudice prefer to interact with people who are similar to themselves because such interactions are more comfortable and less stressful than interactions with strangers.

As indicated earlier, racism is one form of prejudice. There are two levels of racism: individual and institutional. Everyone exhibits individual-level racism to some degree. European Americans, for example, exhibit racist attitudes toward African Americans, Latino(a) Americans, Asian Americans, and so forth, to some degree. Similarly, African Americans exhibit individual-level racism toward European Americans and members of other ethnic groups to some degree. Institutional racism, in contrast, is directed at non-European Americans only. Institutional racism involves racism in social policies, housing, access to medical treatment, and so forth. Members of "dominant groups" make the policies that lead to institutional racism directed at members of "subordinate groups." Institutional racism may be intentional or unintentional. Antiblack individual-level racism is the most widely studied form of racism in the United States. There is a need for more research on other forms of racism (e.g., African American racism directed at whites).

The second most widely studied form of prejudice in the United States is anti-Semitism. Anti-Semitism was evident when Jews immigrated to the United States in large numbers around 1870 and peaked in the 1920s and 1930s (Schaeffer, 1979). After World War II, concern about anti-Semitism was low until the late 1960s and early 1970s. The rise in anti-Semitism at that time is associated with major wars in the Middle East. Anti-Semitism continues to be a major form of prejudice operating today.

Devine, Evett, and Vasquez-Suson (1996) argue that the degree of our prejudice is related to our personal standards for how to treat strangers. People who are low in prejudice want to behave in ways that are consistent with their standards for treating strangers. Those standards are an important part of the self-concepts of people low in prejudice. People who are low in prejudice, therefore, are motivated to interact with strangers in nonprejudiced ways. People who are low in prejudice, however, sometimes respond in more prejudiced ways than they find acceptable. When this occurs, they feel guilty and criticize themselves. People who are high in prejudice do not have well-defined standards for treating strangers, and those standards are not particularly important to them. They, therefore, do not feel guilty when their behavior does not meet their standards for treating strangers.

We also can think of prejudice as varying along a second continuum ranging from very positive to very negative. We tend to be positively prejudiced toward our ingroups and negatively prejudiced toward outgroups. It is possible, however, to be positively prejudiced toward outgroups and negatively prejudiced toward our ingroups. The valence (positive or negative) of our prejudice must be taken into consideration in trying to understand our reactions to violations of our expectations. The tendency over the years has been for younger European Americans to have a more positive view of African Americans than older European Americans. More recent research, however, suggests that this trend may have come to an end. An Anti-Defamation League survey indicates that 35 percent of European Americans over age 50 are highly prejudiced against African Americans, while 23 percent of those between 30 and 49 and 31 percent of those between 18 and 29 are highly prejudiced (*Los Angeles Times,* June 12, 1993, p. A25).

Brewer and Brown (1998) contend that intergroup prejudice may not be as simple as positive versus negative attitudes. They believe that there may be two different types of intergroup prejudice: one based on negative affect toward outgroups and one based on the absence of positive feelings for outgroups. They argue that "ultimately, many forms of discrimination and bias may develop not because outgroups are hated, but because positive emotions such as admiration, sympathy, and trust are reserved for the ingroup and withheld from the outgroup" (p. 575). Brewer (1999) also points out that

> many discriminatory perceptions and behaviors are motivated primarily by the desire to promote and maintain positive relations within the ingroup rather than any direct antagonism toward outgroups. Ingroup love is not a necessary precursor of outgroup hate. However, the very factors that make ingroup attachment and allegiance important to individuals also provide a fertile ground for antagonism and distrust of those outside the ingroup boundaries. (pp. 441–442)

Threats, distrust, power politics, and social comparison processes all contribute to transforming ingroup identification into outgroup hostility.

Another issue that needs to be taken into consideration is that expressing our prejudices may be related to the identity we activate in specific situations (Verkuytent & Hagendorn, 1998). If we are prejudiced toward members of other ethnic groups, for example, we tend to express our prejudice when our ethnic identities are activated. If we interact with members of other ethnic groups on the basis of our personal identities or other social identities (i.e., not our ethnic identities), in contrast, we tend not to express our prejudices toward members of other ethnic groups.

Functions of Prejudice   Prejudice, like ethnocentrism, is functional for people who hold that attitude. People who are highly prejudiced, for example, tend to ignore information not consistent with their faulty and inflexible generalizations. Allport (1954) presents an example of the process used by a highly prejudiced person when confronted with contradictory information:

Mr. X: The trouble with Jews is that they only take care of their own group.

Mr. Y: But the record of the Community Chest campaign shows that they give more generously, in proportion to their numbers, to the charities of the community, than do non-Jews.

Mr. X: That shows they are always trying to buy favor and intrude into Christian affairs. They think of nothing but money; that is why there are so many Jewish bankers.

Mr. Y: But a recent study shows that the percentage of Jews in the banking business is negligible, far smaller than the percentage of non-Jews.

Mr. X: That's just it; they don't go in for respectable business; they are only in the movie business or run night clubs. (pp. 13–14)

Thus, highly prejudiced people tend to alter their beliefs to justify their attitudes when confronted with contradictory information. Allport refers to this process as "rationalization."

What if people changed their minds after being confronted with accurate information? Allport (1954) argues that "errors of prejudgment" are different from prejudice. If people do not change a prejudgment when given new information, they are prejudiced; however, if they rectify an erroneous prejudgment on the basis of the new information, they are not highly prejudiced.

Brislin (1979) examines the functions of prejudice by using Katz's (1960) scheme (see the introduction to our discussion of intergroup attitudes). The first function prejudice performs is to help us either avoid punishment or obtain rewards in our culture (utilitarian function). Brislin (1979) points out "people want to be well liked by others in their culture. If such esteem is dependent upon rejecting members of a certain group, then it is likely that people will indeed reject members of the outgroup" (p. 29).

The second function prejudice performs is to protect us from information that might damage our self-images (ego-defensive function). Brislin (1979) argues that people who are not successful in their chosen occupations can blame their lack of success on members of outgroups (who may be seen as a bunch of cheaters) rather than admit to any personal inadequacies if they are highly prejudiced.

Another function that prejudice performs is to allow us to express important aspects of our lives (value-expressive function). Brislin (1979) points out that people of one religion may react negatively toward members of another religion "because they see themselves as standing up for the one true God (as defined by their religion)" (p. 30).

The final function that prejudice serves is to assist us in organizing the world around us (knowledge function). Prejudice allows us to behave in accordance with the categories we have constructed rather than on the basis of the actual incoming stimuli. Aronson (1972) provides an example of how highly prejudiced people interpret incoming stimuli so that they are consistent with their attitudes:

Prejudiced people see the world in ways that are consistent with their prejudice. If Mr. Bigot sees a well dressed, [European American] Protestant sitting on a park bench sunning himself [or herself] at three o'clock on a Wednesday afternoon, he thinks nothing of it. If he sees a well-dressed [African American] man doing the same thing, he is liable to leap to the conclusion that the person is unemployed—and he becomes infuriated, because he assumes that his hard-earned taxes are paying that shiftless good-for-nothing enough in welfare subsidies to keep him in good clothes. If Mr. Bigot passes Mr. [European American's] house and notices that a trash can is overturned and some garbage is strewn about, he is apt to conclude that a stray dog has been searching for food. If he passes Mr. Garcia's house and notices the same thing, he is inclined to become annoyed, and to assert that "those people live like pigs." Not only does prejudice influence his conclusions, his erroneous conclusions justify and intensify his negative feelings. (p. 174)

The attributions we make about strangers are influenced by the attitudes we hold about the groups to which they belong.

Prejudice and Discrimination   Prejudice should not be confused with its behavioral counterpart, discrimination. Williams (1947) defines *discrimination* as "the degree that individuals of a given group who are otherwise formally qualified are not treated in conformity with these nominally universal institutionalized codes" (p. 39). In other words, discrimination involves behaving in such a way that members of outgroups are treated disadvantageously.

What is the relationship between prejudice and discrimination? Do highly prejudiced people always discriminate? Do people with a relatively low level of prejudice always engage in nondiscriminatory behavior? If attitudes always guided behavior, the answer to these two questions would be a simple yes; however, attitudes are not the only factor influencing behavior. A simple yes, therefore, is not sufficient.

Merton (1957) presents a model of the possible relationships between prejudice and discrimination. His model suggests it is conceivable for people who have low levels of prejudice to discriminate under certain circumstances:

1. *The prejudiced discriminator, or "active bigot."* For this group of people there is consistency between attitudes and behavior. Prejudiced discriminators openly express their beliefs about outgroups and openly practice discriminatory behavior.
2. *The prejudiced nondiscriminator, or "timid bigot."* The behavior of members of this group is not consistent with their attitudes. Timid bigots believe many of the stereotypes about outgroups and also feel hostility toward them but do not express their beliefs. Timid bigots do not express their beliefs because of their desire to conform and not to violate social norms or laws. If there are no laws or social pressure, timid bigots will discriminate.
3. *The nonprejudiced discriminator, or "fair-weather liberal."* Like timid bigots, fair-weather liberals do not behave in accordance with their attitudes. Probably the key word for this group of people is expediency. When people around them discriminate or talk in a prejudicial manner, fair-weather liberals will take the expedient course of action and keep quiet. The major reason for the inconsistency in attitudes and behavior is the social norms of the situation.
4. *The nonprejudiced nondiscriminator, or "all-weather liberal."* There is no inconsistency between attitudes and behavior for all-weather liberals. Merton argues that people in this group are likely to discuss the issues of prejudice and discrimination with others and will not keep quiet when faced with people who discriminate or talk in a prejudicial manner.

Obviously, these four types of people will communicate with strangers differently.

As Merton's typology suggests, there are individual differences in discrimination. Well-intentioned European Americans, for example, do not discriminate against African Americans, but European Americans who are not well-intentioned do (Dovido et al., 1989). The degree to which we discriminate also is a function of the norms/rules guiding behavior in the situation. When there are clear situational norms/rules for appropriate intergroup behavior, we tend not to engage in discrimination (Gaertner & Dovidio, 1986). We do engage in discrimination, however, when the situational norms/rules suggest that it is justifiable or is not inappropriate (Frey & Gaertner, 1986).

Taylor, Wright, and Porter (1994) point out that when strangers experience discrimination, they tend to perceive that the discrimination is directed toward their group rather than toward them as individuals. They conclude that this is related to the identity guiding the behavior. Since social identities guide intergroup behavior where discrimination occurs, the focus is on group memberships, not personal characteristics. With a focus on group memberships in these situations, it would be expected that strangers would perceive others' behavior as directed toward the group.

Operario and Fiske (2001a) report that non-European Americans' ethnic identities influence how they respond to European Americans' expressions of prejudice. Non-European Americans who strongly identify with their ethnic groups perceive themselves as more vulnerable to discrimination than those who weakly identify with their ethnic groups. Also, non-European Americans who strongly identify with their ethnic groups have stronger reactions to European Americans' subtle prejudiced expressions than those who weakly identify with their ethnic groups.

An Explanation for Overt Prejudice   There are numerous explanations for overt prejudice (e.g., exploitation theory, scapegoat theory, authoritarian personality). Our focus here is on integrated threat theory (e.g., Stephan & Stephan, 1996; see Stephan, Stephan, & Gudykunst, 1999, for a summary). Stephan and Stephan's work on integrated threat theory (ITT) emerged out their research on intergroup anxiety (e.g., Stephan & Stephan, 1985, 1992). They see intergroup anxiety as one of the four threats that we perceive that influence our degree of prejudice. Anxiety leads to "amplified cognitive, affective, and behavioral responses, most of which are negative in intergroup contexts" (Stephan et al., 1999, p. 619).

The second threat that we perceive is "realistic threats." Realistic threats include threats to the existence of our ingroups and threats to our well-being or the well-being of our ingroups. Stephan et al. (1999) argue that "realistic threats encompass an perceived threat to the welfare of the group or its members. . . . the perception of threat can lead to prejudice, regardless of whether or not the threat is 'real' " (p. 619).

The third threat is "symbolic threats." Symbolic threats involve perceived differences between our ingroups and strangers' outgroups (Stephan et al., 1999). These may be differences in values, customs, attitudes, morals, and so forth. Symbolic threats are threats because we tend to see our ingroups' ways of doing things as the "right" ways to do things, especially when we are on automatic pilot (i.e., behaving mindlessly).

The final threat that influences our degree of prejudice is our negative stereotypes of strangers' outgroups. Negative stereotypes are threats because they create negative expectations for interactions with strangers and negative expectations often lead to negative experiences when interacting with strangers (Stephan et al., 1999). Our overall level of prejudice in ITT is based on these four threats. The more anxiety we experience when interacting with strangers, the more realistic and symbolic threats we perceive from strangers' groups, and the more negative our stereotypes of strangers' groups, the more we are prejudiced against strangers' outgroups.

Stephan et al. (1999) isolate several factors that influence our perceptions of the four threats. The amount of prior contact we have had with strangers' groups heightens our perceptions of the four threats. The more positive our contact with strangers (relative to negative contact), the less we perceive strangers' groups as threatening. Status inequality between our ingroups and strangers' groups also heighten our expectations for threats. The less knowledge we have about strangers' groups, the more likely we are to see strangers' groups as threatening. Finally, Stephan and Stephan argue that the stronger our identifications with our ingroups, the more we perceive strangers' groups as threatening. We believe, however, that the effect of our ingroup identification is moderated by how secure we are in our ingroup identities. If we are very secure, our identifying with our ingroups will not lead us to perceive strangers' groups as threatening.

Explanations for Covert Prejudice   Not all prejudice is expressed overtly, and several researchers argue that there has been a decrease in the expression of overt prejudice in recent years. Crosby, Bromley, and Saxe (1980), for example, contend that European Americans in the United States generally try to express nonbigoted ideologies and behave in nondiscriminatory ways but, at the same time, have not internalized the feelings that correspond to the attitudes they express.

Sears (1988) argues that covert prejudice is due to the symbolic racism existing in the United States today. Sears suggests that *symbolic racism* is "not racism composed of derogations of and antagonism toward blacks *per se,* or of support for formal inequality." Rather, it blends "some antiblack feeling with the first and proudest of traditional [U.S.] American values, particularly individualism" (p. 54). Symbolic racists believe that African Americans are not discriminated against today and that African Americans are receiving special favors and are still making demands for equity. The individualist values that European Americans who are symbolic racists hold lead them to expect individual African Americans to better their lives through individual effort. Sears reports that symbolic racists tend to be well-educated European Americans who are politically conservative. They, therefore, expect African Americans to be self-reliant.

An alternative explanation for covert prejudice is Gaertner and Dovidio's (1986) aversive racism theory. They argue that *aversive racists* hold egalitarian values and, at the same time, have negative feelings toward African Americans of which they are unaware. Aversive racists disavow racism, but they are uncomfortable around African Americans. Aversive racists try to maintain nonprejudiced self-images when they interact with African Americans. This, however, can create problems. Gaertner and Dovidio (1986) argue that

> the attempt to maintain a nonprejudiced self-image can, in itself, also increase disaffection for African Americans because interracial interactions become characterized by anxiety and uneasiness. Rather than being relaxed and spontaneous, Aversive racists may have to guard vigilantly against even an unwitting transgression that could be attributed by themselves or by others to racial antipathy. Thus, interracial interactions may arouse negative affect that can become associated directly with African Americans. (p. 64)

In other words, aversive racists are mindful of the outcomes of their interactions with African Americans, not mindful of the process of communication.

A third explanation for covert prejudice is Katz, Hass, and Wackenhut's (1986) response amplification theory (RAT). Katz et al. argue that European Americans have positive and negative feelings toward non-European Americans. They point out that "there is ample documentation of almost unanimous public support for a national policy against racial discrimination. . . . Nevertheless, certain antiblack stereotypes and aversion to close interracial contacts are still prevalent in the majority" (p. 35). European Americans hold egalitarian values which lead them to be sympathetic toward African Americans and their struggle for equality. European Americans, however, also hold individualistic values which predispose them to think that African Americans should be self-reliant and achieve economic advancement through their own hard work. When European Americans are aware of these incompatible beliefs, they experience psychological discomfort and anxiety.

Myrdall (1944) argues that people in the United States have a dilemma regarding interethnic relations. The "American Dilemma"

> is the ever-raging conflict between, on the one hand, the valuations preserved on the general plane which we shall call the American Creed, where the American thinks, talks, and acts under the influence of high national and Christian percepts, and on the other hand, the valuations on specific planes of individual and group living where . . . group prejudices against particular persons or types of people; and all sorts of miscellaneous wants, impulses, and habits dominate his [or her] outlook. (p. lxxi)

People in the United States, therefore, experience inner conflict regarding members of other ethnic groups. We have both favorable and unfavorable attitudes that are not necessarily related to each other.

Prejudice and Communication   Ruscher (2001) summarizes research on prejudiced communication. She points out that

> communication that is prejudiced or stereotypic specifically involves the explicit or implicit conveyance of stereotypic beliefs, prejudiced attitudes or discriminatory intentions. Although prejudiced communication includes blatant forms such as hate speech, written discriminatory policies, and extreme symbolism (e.g., swastikas), a good portion of prejudiced communication is subtle. . . . Communicators may not always be consciously aware that these behaviors transmit beliefs that the outgroup is unworthy of greater consideration or is simply inferior, or even that they are conveying feelings of disdain or distrust. Indeed, without a direct comparison between how individuals treat ingroup and outgroup members, onlookers may fail to recognize subtle behaviors as reflecting prejudice. (pp. 2–3)

Ruscher also points out that prejudiced communication also occurs at the institutional or societal level (e.g., people demand that members of outgroups use the ingroup's language).

Billig et al. (1988) suggest that there is an ambivalence inherent in our racial discourse (talk). They point out that even individuals who are highly authoritarian (and, therefore, are expected to hold negative views of other groups) tend to verbally qualify the views of other groups they express so that they appear reasonable. Billig et al. also note that people who appear very liberal "introduce innuendos and . . . cast aspersions in the most polite and outwardly 'reasonable' ways" (p. 107). If people are going to make a negative comment about strangers, for example, they preface their comment with a claim of not being prejudiced. To illustrate, one interviewee in van Dijk's (1984) study responds in this way:

> *[Interviewer]:* Did you ever have any unpleasant experiences [with foreigners]?
> *[Interviewee]:* I have nothing against foreigners. But their attitude, their aggression is scaring. We are no longer free here. You have to be careful. (p. 65)

Nayo (1995), an African American law professor, reports that a European American woman approached her after a meeting saying that "the media have made such monsters of black men that I find myself afraid when I meet two black men on the street" (p. B7). Here the blame is placed on the media.

Another strategy we use in expressing prejudiced views is to explain our personal experiences. Verkuyten et al. (1994) point out that personal "examples and stories make events factual, give firm ground to one's statements, making them independent of the speaker's own (prejudicial) concerns. In this way, the credibility, the rationality, and the expertise of the speaker is established" (p. 296). This strategy allows moderately prejudiced communicators to "excuse themselves for not being more racist" (p. 296).

Billig et al. (1988) claim that the ambivalence inherent in qualified prejudiced discourse does not simply reflect an inconsistency between attitudes and impression management. Rather, they suggest that it indicates that we have "dilemmatic" or dialectical thoughts—we may be prejudiced and tolerant at the same time. We believe that the prejudiced pole of the dialectic is manifested when we communicate on automatic pilot and that the tolerance pole of the dialectic is manifested when we communicate "mindfully."

Van Dijk (1984) observes that prejudiced talk clusters in four categories: (1) "they are different (culture, mentality)"; (2) "they do not adapt themselves"; (3) "they are involved in negative acts (nuisance, crime)"; and (4) "they threaten our (social, economic) interests" (p. 70).

The way we talk about strangers is, in part, a function of how we want to be seen by our ingroups. Wilder and Shapiro (1991) report that the presence of ingroup members leads us to identify strongly with the ingroup and see outgroup members as typical members of their groups. Van Dijk (1984) points out that

> people "adapt" their discourse to the rules and constraints of interaction and communication social settings. Especially when delicate topics, such as "foreigners," are concerned, social members will strategically try to realize both the aims of positive self-presentation and those of effective persuasion. Both aims, however, derive from the position of social members within their group. Positive self-presentation is not just a defense mechanism of individuals as persons, but also as respected, accepted, and integrated social members of ingroups. And the same holds for the persuasive nature of prejudiced talk; people do not merely lodge personal complaints or uneasiness about people of other groups, but intend to have their experiences, their evaluations, their opinions, their attitudes, and their actions shared by other members of the ingroup. (p. 154)

Everyone engages in prejudiced talk to some degree. It is inevitable. We can, however, reduce the degree to which we engage in prejudiced talk if we are mindful of our communication.

Ruscher (2001) argues that the "manner in which people talk to outgroup members reflects their lowered expectations for them" (p. 91). When communicating with strangers from other ethnic groups, for example, prejudiced communication may take the form of using controlling talk (e.g., controlling the conversation by interrupting strangers), being impolite, or being pedantic. When communicating with elderly adults, prejudiced communication may involve "secondary baby talk" (e.g., "overaccommodating for the listeners' perceived lack of competence with a variety of babyish qualities such as simplistic lexical choices and high pitch," p. 92). Rusher argues that controlling talk occurs most frequently when speakers think that strangers want "equal status." To illustrate, elderly adults are spoken to using baby talk more than controlling talk when they do not "assert their independence."

Ruscher (2001) contends that prejudiced communication often occurs in the news media. She points out that

> the news media's video and audio depictions of less powerful groups, namely, women and minorities, seem largely consistent with cultural stereotypes. Women subtly are portrayed as weak objects compared to their male counterparts; blacks often are portrayed as criminals. . . . Which visual depictions are recorded or published may reflect a subtle but insidious form of bias. Media consumers who strive to avoid a prejudiced self-image may quickly take umbrage at explicit verbal expressions of prejudice and try mentally to counteract the effects of such messages. They may not, however, recognize subtle but consistent differences in visual images or audio selections. Without realizing it, even the most well-intentioned media consumer may be processing prejudiced images. (pp. 143–144)

This clearly suggests that we need to be mindful not only when interacting with strangers but also when we see or hear messages about strangers in the media.

There is one additional aspect of prejudice and communication that needs to be addressed; namely, hate speech. *Hate speech* can range from "speech attacks based on race, religion or sexual orientation to any offensive expression directed toward women, discrete minorities, and ethnic, religious, and racial groups" (Ruscher, 2001, p. 194). Allen (1990) points out that "nearly every ethnic group—majority and minority alike—has slurred nearly every other group in the country. . . . Words are weapons and hurling epithets is a universal trait of hostile intergroup relations" (p. vii). One survey in California reveals that 68 percent of the men and 46 percent of the women in non-European American ethnic groups have experienced racially based hate speech (Cowan & Hodge, 1996). Matsuda et al. (1993) argue that the predominant response to hate speech is withdrawing from the situation rather than retaliating.

Being a victim of hate speech can be devastating to the people involved. Thomas (1999), for example, reports his experience: "We were riding home from school and were fighting with boys on the bus who were seated in front of us. The argument became heated, and one of the boys called me a [the "N" word] while the other spit on my sister. . . . The affective experience associated with the name-calling incident did wane over time, but this encounter had a strong impact on my self-concept and racial identity" (p. 36).

Leets and Giles (1997) examine the implications of hate speech in a legal situation. They report that the more severe the hate speech, the more harmful it is perceived to be by European Americans and Asian Americans. European Americans, however, perceive hate speech directed at Asian Americans to be more harmful than Asian Americans. European Americans perceive direct messages aimed at Asian Americans to be more harmful than Asian Americans, and Asian Americans perceive indirect messages aimed at them to be more harmful than European Americans. Leets, Giles, and Noels (1999) look at the exchange of messages between European Americans and Asian Americans. In this study, European Americans also perceive racist messages as more harmful than Asian Americans. Leets et al. expected Asian Americans to perceive hate speech as more harmful than European Americans. We believe that one potential explanation for these findings is that the Asian American respondents in the studies do not identify strongly with their ethnic groups. This explanation could not be tested, however, because strength of ethnic identity was not measured.

Responding to Ethnocentrism and Prejudice

We can influence the amount of ethnocentric speech or prejudiced talk in which others engage. When we express culturally relative or antiprejudiced sentiments, others are less likely to make ethnocentric or prejudiced comments in our presence (Blanchard, Lilly, & Vaughn, 1991). When European Americans who hold negative stereotypes of non-European American ethnic groups receive feedback that other European Americans have different beliefs about the ethnic groups, this can lead them to change their beliefs about the ethnic groups (Stangor, Sechrist, & Jost, 2001). Telling European Americans that other European Americans have beliefs about non-European American ethnic groups that are similar to theirs, however, bolsters their beliefs and inhibits stereotype change.

When we are bystanders, we "can define the meaning of events and move others toward empathy and indifference. [We] can promote values and norms of caring, or by passivity or participation in the system, [we] can affirm the perpetrators" (Staub, 1989, p. 87). If we find other people are making prejudiced remarks in our presence, we can point out that this type of speech is not acceptable to us. If we do not, we are being morally exclusive (see below). We could say something like "I'd prefer you did not put down members of other ethnic groups in my presence." By simply stating our opinion in this way, we decrease the likelihood that others will continue to make prejudiced remarks in our presence. If we do not speak out when other people make prejudiced comments or behave in a discriminatory manner, we are partly responsible for the consequences of the remarks or behavior.

Another way to respond to others' ethnocentric speech or expressions of prejudice is to create cognitive dissonance (Shea, 1997). Individualists want to see themselves as holding consistent sets of beliefs and behave in ways that are consistent with those beliefs. (Note: Collectivists do not necessarily have the same need for consistency.) When individualists recognize inconsistencies, they become uncomfortable and try to modify their thoughts or behaviors to restore consistency. If we know individualists view themselves as "unprejudiced" and hear them express prejudice, we can point out the inconsistencies to them. If individualists recognize the inconsistencies, they probably will strive to make their behaviors consistent with their views of themselves (stop expressing prejudice).

Dignity and Integrity   Dignity and integrity play a large role in ethical behavior and help explain why it is necessary to say something when others engage in prejudicial behavior or make prejudiced comments. *Dignity* involves a minimal level of self-respect (Pritchard, 1991). It refers to feeling worthy, honored, or respected as a person. *Being moral* involves maintaining our own sense of dignity and maintaining others' sense of dignity as well.

Pritchard (1991) contends that personal integrity reflects our view of what is important. Personal integrity is linked closely to moral integrity. *Moral integrity* requires "a somewhat unified moral stance. . . . Those with moral integrity can be expected to refuse to compromise moral standards for the sake of personal expediency" (Pritchard, 1991, p. 90). The "Aspen Declaration on Character Education" isolates six core values that make up a unified moral stance: (1) respect, (2) responsibility, (3) trustworthiness, (4) caring, (5) justice and fairness, and (6) civic virtue and citizenship. With respect to moral integrity, Pritchard (1991) argues it is important to recognize that

> when morality conflicts with other considerations, morality should prevail. Contemporary philosophers refer to this as the *overridingness* of morality. . . . The overridingness of morality need require only that one's conduct be limited to what is morally acceptable. That is, one should not choose immoral or morally objectionable courses of action over those that are morally acceptable. (pp. 225–226)

The overridingness of morality must be a major concern any time we communicate with strangers, see others communicate with strangers, or overhear others talking about strangers.

Behaving in a moral fashion requires that we respect strangers and their moral views (Gutmann, 1992). We do not have to agree with strangers' views of morality to respect them; we only have to see their views as based on a moral system. Gutmann (1992) contends that if people disregard the views of strangers, they are not worthy of respect. This view has clear implications for hate speech (speech that puts down others because of their membership in a group). Gutmann argues that there is "no virtue in misogyny, racial or ethnic hatred" (p. 22). She goes on to point out that racist and anti-Semitic remarks (hate speech) are not defensible on moral grounds: "Hate speech violates the most elementary moral injunction, to respect the dignity of all human beings" (p. 23). Galston (1991) takes a similar position when he says that

> the language of rights is morally incomplete. To say that "I have a right to do X" [e.g., engage in hate speech] is not to conclude that "X is the right thing for me to do." . . . Rights give reasons to others not to interfere with me in the performance of the protected acts; however, they do not in and of themselves give me sufficient reason to perform the acts. There is a gap between rights and rightness that cannot be closed without a richer moral vocabulary—one that involves principles of decency, duty, responsibility, and the common good, among others. (p. 8)

Etzioni (1993) suggests that our rights are limited by the rights of others; we can do what we want only if it does not harm others.

Gutmann (1992) contends that we have a moral obligation to respond when we hear others engage in hate speech. Etzioni (1993) concurs, arguing that "if we care about attaining a higher level of moral conduct than we now experience, we must be ready to express our moral sense" (p. 36, italics omitted). This does not mean that we should not disagree with members of other groups. We can and should articulate our disagreements with others in a respectful fashion.

Moral Inclusion-Exclusion   Optow (1990) points out that "moral exclusion occurs when individuals or groups are perceived as outside the boundary in which moral values, rules, and considerations of fairness apply. Those who are morally excluded are perceived as nonentities, expendable, or undeserving; consequently, harming them appears acceptable, appropriate, or just" (p. 1, italics omitted). Optow argues that three attitudes are associated with being morally inclusive. First, people who are morally inclusive assume that considerations of fairness apply to other people. Second, people who are morally inclusive are willing to provide a share of community resources to others who need them. Third, people who are morally inclusive are willing to make sacrifices to help others.

Optow (1990) isolates two major factors that lead us to behave in a morally exclusive fashion. When we are engaged in group conflict, for example, ingroup cohesiveness is high, but at the same time concern for fairness for members of outgroups is low. Another factor that contributes to moral exclusiveness is feeling unconnected to the other person or group. When we feel connected to others in any way, in contrast, we feel attraction and empathy and engage in helpful behavior toward them. These behaviors are morally inclusive. When we see someone within our moral community (i.e., those we believe should be treated morally) harmed, we perceive an injustice to have taken place. If we harm others in our moral community, we will feel shame, guilt, remorse, or self-blame. When we see someone outside our moral community harmed, in contrast, we may not perceive that that person's rights are violated and may not be concerned. When this occurs, we are being morally exclusive.

The Reverend Martin Niemoeller, a Protestant minister who was imprisoned in Dachau, a concentration camp in Germany, in 1938, illustrates one of the problems with being morally exclusive when he said:

> In Germany, the Nazis first came for the communists, and I didn't speak up because I wasn't a communist. Then they came for the Jews, and I didn't speak up because I wasn't a Jew. Then they came for the trade unionists, and I didn't speak up because I wasn't a trade unionist. Then they came for the Catholics, but I didn't speak up because I was a Protestant. Then they came for me, and by that time there was no one left to speak for me. (from a wall at the Holocaust Museum in Washington, DC)

Clearly, if we are morally exclusive toward strangers, they will be morally exclusive toward us.

Moral exclusion can take many forms. It can range from slavery, genocide, political repression, and violations of human rights to failing to recognize undeserved suffering in others. The Holocaust during World War II and the My Lai massacre during the Vietnam War are examples of severe moral exclusion. Moral exclusion, however, occurs in everyday interactions too. If we distance ourselves from strangers psychologically, ignore our responsibility to strangers, glorify violence, behave in a prejudicial fashion, or allow others to behave in a prejudicial fashion, we are being morally exclusive.

Other Forms of Prejudice: Sexism and Ageism

Negative ethnic prejudice is not the only type of prejudice affecting our communication with strangers. Prejudice against any group influences communication with the members of that group. Space does not permit us to discuss all other forms of prejudice. We briefly examine sexism and ageism.

Sexism *Sexism* occurs when we assign characteristics to others based on their sex (Nilsen, Bosdmajian, Gershuny, & Stanley, 1977). We can be sexist toward either males or females, but sexism usually is viewed as prejudice against women. Sexism is manifested by viewing women as genetically inferior, supporting discriminatory practices against women, engaging in hostility toward women who do not fulfill traditional sex roles, not supporting the women's movement, using derogatory names to refer to women or negatively stereotyping women, and treating women as sexual objects (Benson & Vincent, 1980). Both men and women are sexist. Men, however, tend to be more sexist than women. If we look at individual gender roles, it appears that masculine men and feminine women are more sexist than men and women who are androgynous or have undifferentiated gender roles (Faulkender, 1985).

Sexism is manifested mainly in the language we use. There are three major forms of sexism in language: (1) ignoring women, (2) the way women are defined, and (3) deprecation of women (Henley, Hamilton, & Thorne, 1985). The first way that language usage is sexist is in how *women are ignored.* Probably the main way our language usage ignores women is through the use of masculine words to include both males and females (Schmidt, 1991). There are many words in the English language, for example, that include the word "man" that traditionally have been meant to include women. Examples of these words include, but are not limited to "chairman," "mailman," "spokesman," and "mankind." Another way women are ignored in language usage is through using "he" or other male pronouns as generic pronouns. Many of us learned that when we write or talk, pronouns for males can be used to refer to both males and females. This, however, is not how we actually process the information. When we use male pronouns, it elicits a vision of a male for the reader or listener (Schneider & Hacker, 1973).

The second way our language usage can be sexist is in *how women are defined.* One way women are defined is in our tendency to address women by their first names in situations where we would not address a man by his first name (McConnell-Ginet, 1978). Also "women, much more than men, are addressed through terms of endearment such as honey, cutie, and sweetie, which function to devalue women by depriving them of their name while renaming them with trivial terms" (Schmidt, 1991, p. 30).

The third way our language is sexist is in *deprecating women.* In English, for example, there are over 200 terms used to call women sexually promiscuous but fewer than 25 used to call men sexually promiscuous (Stanley, 1977). There are more masculine terms (more than 350) in the English language than feminine terms (fewer than 150), but there are more negative feminine terms than negative masculine terms (Nilsen, 1977).

Swim et al. (2001) report that college women experience one to two sexist incidents per week. These incidents involve demeaning or degrading comments or behavior, sexual objectification, and/or prejudice based on traditional sex role stereotypes. The sexist encounters decrease women's psychological well-being (e.g., make them feel uncomfortable, angry, depressed).

Swim and Campbell (2001) point out that positive and negative attitudes toward women coexist. They believe this coexistence provides an explanation for why some people like women but do not respect them. Glick and Fiske (1996) argue that some men's attitudes reflect "ambivalent sexism." They isolate two types of ambivalent sexism: "benevolent" and "hostile." *Benevolent sexism* occurs when men's behavior toward women reflects a desire to care for women (e.g., paternalism), a desire to have heterosexual intimacy, and a desire for gender differentiation. *Hostile sexism,* in contrast, involves men's behavior that reflects viewing women as conflictual and a desire to stop women from gaining equality with men. Benevolent sexism generally does not involve hostility toward women, but there may be implicit hostility (e.g., "paternalism leads to perceiving women as incompetent adults," Swim & Campbell, p. 231).

Swim and Campbell (2001) argue that individuals "who attribute gender differences primarily to biological factors may be more likely to prescribe differences in behavior [e.g., endorse traditional gender roles] than those who attribute the same gender differences to socialization or discrimination" (pp. 223–224). They also contend that individuals' beliefs about women may appear to be benign, but they are sexist if they are associated with thinking that men or women should behave in a way that maintains gender inequality.

Jackson, Esses, and Burris (2001) argue that contemporary sexism involves a greater respect for men than for women. This bias has consequences for hiring decisions in organizations. Jackson et al. report that higher respect for men than women influences hiring decisions more than sex-role stereotyping. Rudman and Kilianski (2000) also note that "prejudice against female authority may be due more to associations linking men to power and influence than to role or trait expectancies" (p. 1326). They also find that women demonstrate less explicit prejudice against women than men but that women's implicit attitudes toward female authorities are as negative as men's.

Ageism   Palmore (1982) argues that "many, if not most, of the 'problems of aging' stem from or are exacerbated by prejudice and discrimination against the aged" (p. 333). *Ageism* involves negative attitudes toward people who are older than we are (usually people we consider "old"). Teenagers, for example, may be prejudiced against people over 30, and people who are middle-aged may be prejudiced against people who are retired. Ageism is based on "a deep-seated uneasiness on the part of the young and middle-aged—a personal revulsion to and distaste for growing older" (Butler, 1969, p. 243). It also can emerge from competition between the groups (young and old) over scarce resources and jobs (Levin & Levin, 1980). Overall, attitudes toward aging tend to be negative (Palmore, 1982).

Ageism is manifested in our language usage. The term "old" has connotations of experience, skill, and wisdom, but it also is used in derogatory terms used for others (e.g., "old hag," "old foggy"; Covey, 1988). There are a wide variety of terms in the English language referring to old people with negative overtones (e.g., "battleaxe," "geezer") and the attributes used to talk about the elderly (e.g., "cantankerous," "grumpy") often have negative connotations (Nuessel, 1984). More than half the jokes in English about aging reflect negative views of old people, with a greater proportion of jokes about women than about men being negative. Terms such as "aged" and "elderly" are perceived to be negative, and terms such as "senior citizen" and "retired person" are evaluated more positively by people of all age groups (Barbato & Feezel, 1987).

CHANGING OUR EXPECTATIONS OF STRANGERS

In the preceding sections, we discussed the major attitudes influencing our communication with strangers. The next issue that needs to be addressed involves the question of whether the attitudes of ethnocentrism and prejudice and our stereotypes, once developed, are set for life or can be changed.

Brewer and Miller (1988) argue that when we communicate with strangers, there are three ways that our experiences with individual strangers can generalize to change our attitudes toward and stereotypes of their groups: (1) "Change in attitudes toward the group as a whole," (2) "increased complexity of intergroup perceptions," and (3) "decategorization" (p. 316). Miller and Gaertner (2001) add two additional ways to change intergroup expectations: (4) "recategorization" and (5) "mutual differentiation."

Change in Attitudes toward the Group as a Whole

Many people assume that if we have contact with strangers, our attitudes toward their groups will become more positive. This, however, is not necessarily the case. Contact can promote better relations between groups *or* increase hostility between groups. The question that needs to be answered is, When does contact lead to better relations between groups?

Stephan (1985) isolates 13 characteristics of the contact situation that are necessary for positive attitude change toward strangers' groups to occur as a result of our individual contact with specific strangers:

1. Cooperation within groups should be maximized and competition between groups should be minimized.
2. Members of the in-group and the out-group should be of equal status both within and outside the contact situation.
3. Similarity of group members on nonstatus dimensions (beliefs, values, etc.) appears to be desirable.
4. Differences in competence should be avoided.
5. The outcomes should be positive.
6. Strong normative and institutional support for the contact should be provided.
7. The intergroup contact should have the potential to extend beyond the immediate situation.
8. Individuation of group members should be promoted.
9. Nonsuperficial contact (e.g., mutual disclosure of information) should be encouraged.
10. The contact should be voluntary.
11. Positive effects are likely to correlate with the duration of the contact.
12. The contact should occur in a variety of contexts with a variety of in-group and out-group members.
13. Equal numbers of in-group and out-group members should be used. (p. 643)

While this list is long, Stephan points out that it is incomplete. If we want to design a program to reduce prejudice or ethnocentrism, we should make sure that the contact we arrange meets as many of these conditions as possible.

Increased Complexity of Intergroup Perceptions

Increasing the complexity of our intergroup perceptions involves seeing social categories as heterogeneous (i.e., different), rather than homogeneous (i.e., alike). Stated differently, we can increase the complexity of our intergroup perceptions by recognizing how members of social categories are different. Think of the social groups males and females. Are all males and all females the same? Obviously, the answer is no. We see differences among males and females and place them in subcategories. Females, for example, may categorize males into "male chauvinists" and "feminists." The more subcategories we create, the more complex our intergroup perceptions.

Increasing the complexity of our intergroup perceptions is consistent with Langer's notion of mindfulness. As you may recall from Chapter 2, one aspect of becoming mindful of our communication is the creation of new categories. Creating new categories means differentiating among the individuals within the broad social categories we use. This mean increasing the number of "discriminations" we make—using specific rather than global labels (e.g., a person with a lame leg rather than a "cripple"). When we are mindful of differences among the members of the various outgroups with which we communicate, our expectations are based on the subcategories, not the broader social category.

Decategorization

Decategorization occurs when we communicate with strangers on the basis of their individual characteristics rather than the categories in which we place them (i.e., communication is mainly interpersonal, not mainly intergroup). To accomplish this, we must differentiate individual strangers from their groups. Differentiation alone, however, is not sufficient for decategorization or personalization to occur.

When we personalize or decategorize our interactions with strangers, personal identity takes on more importance than social identity. Brewer and Miller (1988) explain it this way:

> To illustrate this distinction, consider the statement "Janet is a nurse." This description can be psychologically represented in one of two ways. It could mean that Janet is subordinate to (i.e., a specific instance of) the general category of nurses. Or it could mean that being a nurse is subordinate to (i.e., a particular characteristic of) the concept of Janet. The former interpretation is an example of category-based individuation, and the later is an example of personalization. (p. 318)

The difference lies in how we process the information. If we focus on the strangers' personal identities, we can decrease the degree to which their social identities affect our expectations.

Recategorization

Brewer and Gaertner (2001) argue that the goal of recategorization is "to structure a definition of group categorization at a higher level of category inclusiveness in ways that reduce intergroup bias and conflict" (p. 459). The common ingroup identity model (e.g., Gaertner & Dovidio, 2001; also see Dovidio et al., 2001), for example, suggests that ingroup bias can be reduced when individuals' identities are transformed from two separate identities to a common, inclusive identity. To illustrate, an African American woman and a European American woman may discover that they are both mothers of children attending the same school, members of the same religious congregation, or employees of the same company (all common ingroup identities).

Brewer and Gaertner (2001) point out that the cognitive processes that lead to ingroup favoritism when individuals perceive that they are members of different groups is "redirected to benefit the former outgroup members" (p. 459). When a common ingroup identity is discovered, "cooperative interaction, for example, enhances positive evaluations of outgroup members, at least in part, because cooperation transforms members' representations of the membership from 'Us' and 'Them' to a more inclusive 'We' " (p. 459).

Mutual Differentiation

Hewstone and Brown (1986) contend that ingroup bias can be reduced when members of different groups engage in cooperative interactions without changing the original ingroup and outgroup distinction. Bewer and Gaertner (2001) point out that "this model favors encouraging groups working together to perceive complementarity by recognizing and valuing mutual superiorities and inferiorities within the context of an interdependent cooperative task or common superordinate goals" (p. 461).

Hewstone and Brown (1986) suggest that contact situations be set up in ways that allow members of different groups to have complementary roles that need to be performed to achieve a common goal. The cooperative interdependence between the groups is assumed to override the typical ingroup bias.

Hybrid Models

Brewer and Gaertner (2001) suggest that various approaches to reducing prejudice can be combined to increase their effectiveness. They point out that most researchers tend to assume that social identities are mutually exclusive and that only one social identity guides behavior at a particular time. When members of ingroups "simultaneously perceive themselves as members of different groups but also part of the same team or superordinate entity, intergroup relations between these subgroups are more positive than if members only considered themselves as separate groups" (p. 462). To illustrate, individuals who perceive themselves as members of ethnic groups and as "Americans" would have less ingroup bias than individuals who perceive themselves only as members of ethnic groups. Brewer and Gaertner conclude that "identification with a more inclusive social group does not require individuals deny their ethnic identity" (p. 463).

Hornsey and Hogg (2000) argue that threats to our subgroup (e.g., ethnic) identities play an important role in intergroup relations. They point out that

> subgroup identity threat is the greatest obstacle to social harmony; social arrangements that threaten social identity produce defensive reactions that result in conflict. Social harmony is best achieved by maintaining, not weakening, subgroup identities, and locating them within the context of a binding superordinate identity. (p. 143, italics omitted)

The superordinate identity can involve either nested subgroups or cross-cutting subgroups.

Another alternative is for individuals to have cross-cutting identities. Brewer and Gaertner (2001) point out that

> many bases of social category differentiation—gender, age, religion, ethnicity, occupation—represent cross-cutting cleavages. From the standpoint of a particular person, other individuals may be fellow ingroup members on one dimension of category differentiation but outgroup members on another. . . . It is possible that such orthogonal social identities are kept isolated from each other so that only one ingroup-outgroup distinction is activated in a particular social context. But there are reasons to expect simultaneous activation of multiple ingroup identities both is possible and has potential for reducing prejudice and discrimination based on any one category distinction. (p. 463)

One explanation for why this may work is that the cross-cutting identities reduce the weight of each specific identity in guiding behavior.

SUMMARY

The stereotypes we develop and the intergroup attitudes we hold are learned as part of our socialization into our culture and the various groups of which we are members. In turn, the intergroup attitudes and the stereotypes we develop create expectations for how strangers will behave.

The stereotypes we hold provide the initial predictions we make about strangers' behavior at both the cultural and sociocultural levels. To the degree that our stereotypes are valid, we will be able to make accurate predictions about strangers' behavior. Also, if we are not willing to question our stereotypes, we will never be able to make accurate psychocultural predictions about strangers. In other words, if our stereotypes are rigidly held, we will never get to know strangers as individuals.

The two major attitudes influencing our communication with strangers are prejudice and ethnocentrism. High levels of either of these attitudes lead us to misinterpret strangers' behavior. Being very ethnocentric, for example, impels us to interpret strangers' behavior by using our own cultural standards. This tendency inevitably causes us to misinterpret strangers' behavior and make inaccurate predictions about their behavior, thereby increasing the likelihood of misunderstandings. Since it is natural for everyone to be prejudiced and ethnocentric to some degree, we must control our attitudinal responses consciously if we want to communicate effectively with strangers.

STUDY QUESTIONS

1. How do expectations influence our communication with strangers?
2. Why are stereotypes a natural product of the communication process?
3. How do stereotypes influence our communication?
4. How does the use of stereotypes lead to inaccurate predictions?
5. How does ethnocentrism have positive consequences? negative consequences?
6. How does ethnocentrism influence the distances we create from strangers?

7. How is prejudice different from ethnocentrism? How are the two similar?
8. How does prejudice influence the way we communicate with strangers?
9. How do we adapt the way we talk about strangers?
10. How is sexism manifested in our language usage?
11. How is ageism manifested in our language usage?.
12. Why is it important that we respond to others when they engage in prejudiced behavior or speak in a prejudiced manner?
13. How can we change our expectations for strangers behavior?

SUGGESTED READINGS

Brown, R., & Gaertner, S. (Eds.). (2001). *Intergroup processes.* Oxford, UK: Blackwell.

Essed, P. (1991). *Understanding everyday racism.* Thousand Oaks, CA: Sage.

Kleg, M. (1993). *Hate, prejudice and racism.* Albany: State University of New York Press.

Leyens, J., Yzerbyt, V., & Schadron, G. (1994). *Stereotypes and social cognition.* Thousand Oaks, CA: Sage.

Mackie, D., & Hamilton, D. (Eds.). (1994). *Affect, cognition, and stereotyping.* New York: Academic Press.

Ruscher, J. (2001). *Prejudiced communication.* New York: Guilford.

Van Dijk, T. (1984). *Prejudice in discourse.* Amsterdam: Benjamins.

Whilock, R., & Slayden, D. (Eds.). (1995). *Hate speech.* Thousand Oaks, CA: Sage.

Zanna, M., & Olsen, J. (Eds.). (1994). *The psychology of prejudice.* Hillsdale, NJ: Erlbaum.

6

ENVIRONMENTAL INFLUENCES ON THE PROCESS

Physical concepts are free creations of the human mind,
and are not, however it may seem,
uniquely determined by the external world.

Albert Einstein

The purpose of this chapter is to complete our examination of the major influences on our communication behavior. In the preceding three chapters, we looked at the cultural, sociocultural, and psychocultural influences on our communication with strangers. In this chapter, we examine the environmental influences on our communication behavior.

The environment in which interaction occurs influences the communication taking place. These influences, however, are generally outside our awareness. The environmental influence on behavior is so strong that Lewin (1936) includes it as one of the two factors in his definition of behavior: $B = f(P,E)$, where B = behavior, P = person, and E = environment. Lewin believes the behavior in which we engage is a function of us and the person with whom we are communicating as well as of the environment within which the interaction takes place.

In Lewin's (1936) analysis, the environment is divided into the physical environment and the psychological environment, or what people think about the physical environment. Both aspects of the environment influence communication. To illustrate the influence of the psychological environment, we need only look at the research on the influence of different types of rooms on behavior. When we enter a room, we rarely feel indifferent about it (Saarinen, 1948). Mintz (1956) reports that prolonged exposure to an "ugly" room brings about such reactions "as monotony, fatigue, headache, sleep, discontent, irritability, hostility, and avoidance of the room" (p. 466). Exposure to a "beautiful" room, in contrast, brings about "feelings of comfort, pleasure, enjoyment, importance, energy, and a desire to continue [the] activity" (p. 466).

The physical setting and the situation in which communication occurs define what is proper. Obviously, such settings as an office behind closed doors, an elevator, a living room, a bedroom, and a formal dining room suggest different forms of communication within specific cultures. People in a culture are taught during the socialization process what it is appropriate to talk about in each of these different settings. Deutsch (1954) observes that "it is evident that behavior settings are 'coercive' primarily because there exist shared frames of reference of collective action as to what is appropriate behavior in a given behavior setting or with a given behavior-object" (p. 194).

(Note: The preceding should not be taken to suggest that the same communication cannot occur in different settings, because it can and does.) The setting in which the communication occurs also performs the function of telling us how to interpret messages. The same message transmitted in different settings can have two entirely different meanings. Physicians asking members of the opposite sex to remove their clothes means one thing in physicians' offices but an entirely different thing in bedrooms; only the context tells receivers how to interpret the message. Deutsch (1961) suggests that a "social act is always interpreted in relation to some normative context" (p. 398).

The physical setting is important when we communicate with strangers for at least two reasons. First, what is appropriate behavior in a particular setting can differ across cultures. In some cultures (e.g., the United States), for example, being in the living room of a home calls for informal conversation, and in other cultures (e.g., Colombia), being in the living room calls for formal behavior. Second, when we communicate with strangers, the strangers are often in a physical setting unfamiliar to them. Strangers, therefore, may not know what behavior is expected in that setting. The strangers also may not have the "sense of place" necessary to understand what is going on in their lives (Downs & Stea, 1977).

We divide our discussion of the environmental influences on our communication with strangers into four sections: the physical environment, the situation, situational norms and rules, and the psychological environment. The *physical environment,* as we are using the term, involves geography, climate, landscape, and architecture. The *situation* includes the setting in which communication occurs. The norms and rules guiding our behavior are a function of the situations in which our communication takes place. The *psychological environment* includes our perceptions of the physical environment and the situation, our perceptual and cognitive beliefs about the environment, and how we use the environment when we interact with strangers.

PHYSICAL ENVIRONMENT

The physical environment in which our communication occurs influences how we communicate. If you are sitting on the deck of your house in shorts looking at the Pacific Ocean in January, you will be in a different frame of mind than you will be in if you are in the middle of a blizzard in the midwest. In addition to the climate, the geographical location and the built environment in our cultures influence the way we communicate. We begin our discussion of the physical environment by looking at geography and climate.

Geography and Climate

Meggers (1954) argues that the "environment is an important conditioner of culture" (p. 801). Meggers goes on to point out that "the primary point of interaction between a culture and its environment is in terms of subsistence, and the most vital aspect of environment from the point of view of culture is its suitability for food production" (p. 802). In other words, the geography in which cultures exist influences how the people obtain food. Since food can be imported, people in cultures are not limited to the food they can produce. The geographical location of a culture also has other influences. Barnlund (1968) suggests that "it would seem almost obvious that mountains or flat terrain, barren or fertile land, and the availability of resources, particularly of water, would affect human institutions and thereby alter the forms of social behavior" (p. 512).

Another factor in the physical environment closely associated with geography is climate, including temperature and humidity. Climatic factors have subtle influences on behavior. Hippocrates observed that

> Asia (Minor) differs widely from Europe in the nature of all its inhabitants and its vegetation . . . the one region is less wild than the other, the character of its inhabitants is milder and more gentle. The cause of this is the temperate climate, because it lies toward the east midway between risings of the sun, further away than is Europe from the cold. (cited by Biswas, 1984, p. 6)

Huntington (1945) argues that living in the midlatitudes produces the greatest productivity and efficiency. McClelland (1961) concurs, arguing that climate affects the achievement of people in different societies. Further, it often is pointed out that murder rates in the United States increase during the summer months, when the temperature and humidity rise.

There also are climatic variations within cultures. Andersen, Lustig, and Andersen (1990) examine the influence of climate in the United States on interpersonal communication. They report that "the southern culture is more verbally dominant, opinionated, intolerant, and authoritarian than are relatively more northern US cultures" (p. 305). Their data also suggest that northerners are more touch avoidant, open, and confirming than southerners. Andersen et al. suggest that in the United States individuals may proactively choose their place of residence to match their communication needs. To illustrate,

> sun lovers and outdoor recreationists might be more attracted to the sunbelt and the corresponding arousal, esteem, social independence, and isolation that it provides. Other individuals, who prefer closer social networks, more interpersonal dependence, and less arousal might be happier in the social climates that the more northern latitudes create. (p. 306)

This view may explain individuals' locations in highly mobile cultures like the United States, but it does not explain the effect of climatic differences on behavior around the world. People in the vast majority of the cultures in the world are not as geographically mobile as people in the United States and cannot choose the climate in which they want to live.

Architecture and Landscape

Those aspects of the environment constructed by members of cultures also influence our communication behavior. To borrow an analogy from the theater, the architecture and landscape, combined with the geography and climate, provide the stage for the human players. Barnlund (1968) points out that "the streets of Calcutta, the avenues of Brasilia, the Left Bank of Paris, the gardens of Kyoto, the slums of Chicago, and the canyons of lower Manhattan provide dramatically different backgrounds for human interaction" (p. 512). The physical structure of buildings, as well as the way they are decorated, is influenced by the cultures in which they exist and also influences the interaction occurring within cultures. Winston Churchill often is quoted as saying, "We shape our buildings, and afterwards our buildings shape us." A conversation on the same topic held in an adobe house in New Mexico and a Japanese house in Kyoto in all likelihood will not be the same. Many aspects of architecture and landscape vary across cultures; however, we focus here on the aspect most central to people's lives: housing.

Rapoport (1969) argues that the physical environment influences the way houses are designed and constructed and that the design of houses also is influenced by the cultures in which they are built. Human shelter varies from buildings with one room to structures with several hundred. Not only do the physical aspects of houses (e.g., construction material, size, shape, layout of rooms) differ across cultures, but how houses and their parts are defined and perceived also varies. Are houses, for example, places where visitors are entertained, or are they reserved for only close friends and family? Do certain rooms in houses have a single function (e.g., sleeping), or is the same room used for several different functions (e.g., sleeping, eating, and entertaining guests)? There is obviously tremendous variation in the construction and perception of houses within any one culture; however, there are many similarities that remain relatively constant. These similarities may not be obvious until houses based on other cultural assumptions are examined. To illustrate cross-cultural variations in housing, we look at Japanese, Arab, German, and Latin American homes.

Most houses in the United States distinguish particular rooms to fill specific functions (e.g., eating in the dining room, sleeping in the bedroom). These distinctions, however, are not made in traditional Japanese homes. (Note: The distinctions are made in many contemporary Japanese homes.) The same room often is used for dining, entertaining, and sleeping. This is accomplished through the use of very little furniture in traditional Japanese homes (and traditional rooms in contemporary houses). Rooms are separated by sliding walls (those made with rice paper are called *shoji*) rather than by fixed walls as in the United States. In traditional Japanese homes, therefore, people cannot go into their own rooms and lock the door to be alone. Floors in traditional Japanese homes are covered with straw mats (*tatami*), and people remove their shoes upon entering houses.

What furniture there is in traditional Japanese homes usually is found in the center of the room rather than around the edges, as in the United States. The multipurpose room usually has one low table, which is used for many purposes (e.g., studying, eating). Rather than sitting in chairs by the table, Japanese sit on cushions that can be moved easily when it is time for the room to change its function. When it is time to sleep, the table and cushions are removed, thick sleeping mats (*futons*) are laid out, and the room becomes a bedroom.

Japanese do not tend to make the distinctions made in the United States among dining room, living room, and bedroom, but they do draw a distinction between the bath and the toilet. In the United States the bath and toilet are found in the same room. In Japan, however, the two rooms are separate. The bath (*ofuro*) is only for bathing (becoming clean), not for the "dirty" function of using the toilet (*otearai*).

In contrast to Japanese homes, Arab homes tend to have a lot of space, very high ceilings, and unobstructed views (Hall, 1966). The desire for an unobstructed view is so strong that one way to "get even" with neighbors is to obstruct the view from their homes. Hall (1966) points to a structure built by a person in Beirut that is several stories high but only four feet wide. The house is referred to as the "spite house" by local residents because it was built for the purpose of punishing neighbors by blocking their view of the Mediterranean.

Like people in the United States, but unlike the Japanese, Arabs tend to entertain guests in their homes. The amount and type of contact guests have in a house, however, are determined by their relationship with the family. In a typical Arab home all rooms look alike, with the function of each room decided by the family, but one room usually is set aside for entertaining guests. In this room, the family displays heirlooms, souvenirs, and the best furnishings (Condon & Yousef, 1975). Guests who are not longtime friends usually are entertained in this room and may never see any other part of the house. Because guests are entertained in the most formal part of the home and introduced only to selected family members, "the guest is honored and the family status is reflected" (Condon & Yousef, 1975, p. 160). As guests become accepted by the family, they may see other parts of the house. Indicators of this change in status are increases in the length of visits and meeting family members of the opposite sex. (Note: Arabs may be friends for years without meeting family members of the opposite sex.)

German homes tend to be surrounded by hedges and fences to ensure privacy, a pervasive value in German life (Condon & Yousef, 1975). Condon and Yousef (1975) point out that "the ideal German home has a foyer or entryway that leads visitors into the house without exposing them to specific rooms and a resultant loss of privacy for the family members" (p. 165). The most formal room in the house is the living room (*wohnzimmer*), which is used for entertaining guests. Unlike children in the United States, German children who are old enough to greet guests are expected to come into the living room when guest arrive and remain for the length of the visit, speaking only when someone speaks to them.

A typical German home, like a typical German office, is characterized by large furniture and heavy doors (Hall, 1966). The large furniture is used so that guests will not be tempted to move the furniture and change the order of the room. A heavy door performs two functions. First, because of its weight, the door serves a soundproofing function when closed, thus fulfilling the German desire for privacy. Second, since the door typically is closed in both homes and offices, it preserves the "integrity of the room and provides a protective boundary between people" (Hall, 1966, p. 136).

The typical middle-class Colombian home is built much closer to the street than is the typical U.S. American home (Gorden, 1974). Generally, the front yard is very small, and the backyard is large, enclosed with a high fence. Each house abuts the houses on both sides of it. There is no yard space between houses; only double walls separate houses. This pattern of constructing houses is different from the common one in the United States, but the two patterns appear to be aimed at the same goal, privacy. Gorden observes that "privacy in the United States is obtained by increasing the open space between a person and his [or her] neighbor, while in Bogota it is achieved by abutting walls with no doors or windows" (p. 16).

Colombians tend to invite kinfolk into their homes, but not coworkers or neighbors. People may work side by side for years and live near each other but never see the inside of each other's homes. Gorden (1974) points out that the house "is more strictly a family thing in the sense of a tendency to exclude nonrelatives and to include relatives beyond the nuclear family" (pp. 22–23).

The various rooms in Colombian homes have different functions than do the same rooms in U.S. American homes. The living room, for example, in a Colombian home is a formal room not used for family gatherings. A bedroom, in contrast, may be used for family gatherings and entertaining friends. In discussing problems U.S. exchange students have when living with Colombian host families, Gorden (1974) points out that

> some misunderstandings between the [U.S.] American guest and the Colombian host hinge upon the basic difference in their assumptions regarding the function of a bedroom. Both cultures accept the bedroom as a place to sleep, to make conjugal love, and to read, but beyond that there is little agreement. The [U.S.] American thinks of it (particularly when he [or she] is in a foreign country) as a place to retreat, to find privacy, to study, to listen to records. The Colombian host families did not agree on all these things. The señora thinks of her bedroom as being a place to socialize with her friends, to watch television with members of the family and with friends. (p. 51)

U.S. Americans taking refuge in the bedroom, therefore, often are perceived as "aloof" by the Colombian host family.

In trying to make sense of cultural differences in housing, Altman and Gauvain (1981) proposed dialectical relationships among culture, behavior, and the home environment. They contend that the home environment that predominates in cultures reflects the degree to which members of cultures try to cope with two sets of dialectical opposites: identity-communality and accessibility-inaccessibility.

The *identity-communality dialectic* involves the degree to which houses reflect the uniqueness and individuality of the occupants (i.e., the personal or family identity of the occupants) or the ties of the occupants (i.e., their communality) with the larger culture (Altman & Gauvain, 1981). The *accessibility-inaccessibility dialectic* reflects the degree to which the home environment emphasizes the openness or closedness of the occupants to outsiders. The differences Altman and Gauvain observe can be related to individualism-collectivism. It appears that middle-class homes in individualistic cultures are separated from the community at large through the use of front yards, backyards, gates, and lawns. The furniture and decor of homes in individualistic cultures illustrate the desire of the occupants to differentiate themselves from others. In middle-class homes in collectivistic cultures, in contrast, the architectural design of the home is integrated with central plazas, a community center, or other neighborhood dwellings. The furniture and decor in these homes express the group identity and the communal desire of get together.

THE SITUATION

One approach we could use to understand how situations influence our communication is to examine the objective characteristics of situations, such as physical locations (whether it is a classroom or a living room in a home) and their characteristics. The objective characteristics of situations, however, are not good predictors of behavior (Cody & McLaughlin, 1985). A better predictor of how people behave in particular situations is how they perceive the situations. Understanding what is required of us in particular situations helps us manage our uncertainty and anxiety.

Situations can be divided into two broad components: the scene and the participants (Brown & Fraser, 1979). The *scene* tells us the setting and the purpose of the interaction. The *setting* includes the locale of the interaction, the time of the interaction, and the bystanders observing the interaction. The *purpose* of the interaction focuses on the type of activity in which we are engaged and the subject matter of the conversation. The type of activity involves our goals for the interaction and the roles we are filling, such as professor or student, clerk or customer, and friend. The subject matter includes the task being completed and the specific topic of conversation.

The *participants* are divided into two components: the individual participants and the relationships between the participants (Brown & Fraser, 1979). There are two aspects of the *individual participants* that are relevant. We act as individuals based on our personalities, physical appearances, moods, or attitudes and also as members of social groups, such as members of our cultures, ethnicities, classes, genders, and ages. There also are two aspects of the *relationship between participants* that influence our behavior: the interpersonal relations between the people communicating (such as whether they like each other or whether they know each other) and the roles/categories they are filling (such as the relative difference in power and status between the people).

Our perceptions of the situation are critical to understanding our behavior in any situation (Brown & Fraser, 1979). Understanding how perceptions of situations influence our communication behavior is important in improving the quality of our communication.

Setting

The setting for communication involves the locale of our interactions with others, the time of our interactions, and the bystanders who observe our interactions. The physical space in which our interactions occur and the "props" that are present influence the way we communicate. Large spaces provide different opportunities for communication than small spaces. Space divided into many regions, such as offices or hallways, leads to different types of communication than open spaces. The physical appearance of the locale also affects our communication. Where interactions take place "offers a host of cues that tell people how to orient themselves" (Turner, 1988, p. 156). The cues provided by the locale of our interactions make coordination of our behavior easier and allow for smoother interactions. Without the cues that are provided by the locale, we would have to seek information to know how to expect others to act in different situations.

Who is present (bystanders) in situations also influences our communication. The status of the people who are observing our behavior influences how we present ourselves (Goffman, 1959). We tend to be more concerned with how we present ourselves if there are high-status bystanders than we are if the bystanders are low in status. We try to gain other people's favor and use self-enhancing statements more when there are high-status bystanders than when low-status bystanders are present (Ralston, 1985).

The degree to which we are familiar with bystanders also influences how we present ourselves in particular situations. Since people with whom we are familiar already have an impression of us, we tend to be more concerned about the impression we make on unfamiliar bystanders than the impression we make on familiar bystanders. The familiarity of the bystanders also influences the way we explain our behavior in situations. The more familiar the people are, the more likely we are to provide justifications for our behavior (try to explain our internal states and how they affected our behavior; Cody & McLaughlin, 1985). Justifications of our behavior, however, do not appear to work well with people we do not know (e.g., strangers).

Purpose

The purpose of our interaction with others is based on the types of activities in which we are engaged and the subject matter we are discussing. The types of activities in which we are engaged influence the scripts we use to guide our behavior. The more we engage in particular activities, the more likely we are to learn scripts for the activities. A script is "a coherent sequence of events expected by the individual, involving him [or her] either as a participant or an observer" (Abelson, 1976, p. 33). Scripts are cognitive structures that help us understand the situations in which we find ourselves. Scripts, therefore, help us reduce the uncertainty we have about various situations (Berger & Bradac, 1982). We learn scripts by participating in situations or by observing others participate (Abelson, 1976). We have learned both task-oriented and non-task-oriented scripts. We have to figure out whether we have scripts for the situations and what our roles in the script are. This process, however, takes place at relatively low levels of awareness. Once we recognize the scripts, we know basically how we are expected to behave in situations and can communicate on automatic pilot. Scripts provide guides for the conversations we have in different scenes. It is important to keep in mind that people in different cultures learn different scripts for behavior.

The task on which we are working and the topic being discussed affect our communication in any situation. Whether we define situations as cooperative or competitive influences our perceptions of the tasks, and whether we define situations as intimate or superficial influences how we approach the topics. Cooperation involves "acting together, in a coordinated way at work, leisure, or in social relationships, in the pursuit of shared goals, the enjoyment of the joint activity, or simply furthering the relationship" (Argyle, 1991, p. 4). Defining a task as cooperative involves recognizing that the efforts of at least two people are needed and that there is a need for complementary skills and knowledge to accomplish the task. Defining tasks as cooperative has at least two major effects on our communication with others (Argyle, 1991). First, cooperation leads to positive feelings for others participating on the task. Second, cooperation leads to interpersonal attraction toward the people with whom we are cooperating.

Our individualistic and collectivistic cultural identities influence the degree to which we perceive situations as cooperative or competitive. Collectivists in Hong Kong, for example, perceive situations as more cooperative than individualists in Australia. Individualists in Australia, in contrast, perceive the same situations as more competitive than collectivists in Hong Kong (Forgas & Bond, 1985).

We perceive the *topics of conversations* to vary on the intimate-superficial dimension of situations. Some topics are perceived to be more intimate than others. In the United States, for example, telling others where we were born, what we do for a living, our political party affiliations, and so forth, is considered relatively superficial. Telling others about our love lives, in contrast, is considered intimate. There appears to be consistency in the topics considered intimate and superficial across cultures. To illustrate, tastes and opinions are viewed as the most appropriate topics for conversation and physical attributes and personality traits are the least preferred topics in Japan and the United States (Barnlund, 1975).

Individual Participants

We perceive the people with whom we interact as members of social groups and as individuals. Stable characteristics of individuals such as their personalities, physical appearances, and interests influence how they respond to us and how we respond to them in specific situations (Brown & Fraser, 1979). In addition to stable characteristics such as our personalities, our moods and emotions influence how we respond and how others respond in specific situations (Brown & Fraser, 1979). These characteristics differ from our personalities in that our moods and emotions are temporary.

Our moods and emotions are not the only temporary aspects of our behavior that influence how others respond to us in different situations. Our speech patterns also influence the impressions others form of us and the ways they respond to us. Haslett (1990) argues that "standard [dialect] speakers are more positively perceived and judged than nonstandard [dialect] speakers" (p. 332; this issue is discussed in more detail in Chapter 8).

Our group memberships and strangers' group memberships influence how we define various situations. The ways we are socialized into the various groups of which we are members tell us how to define situations and how to expect others to behave in those situations. Strangers' group memberships influence whether we define situations as interpersonal or intergroup in nature. When we define situations as interpersonal in nature, our personal identities influence our behavior more than our social identities, and our predictions of strangers' behavior are based mainly on their unique characteristics (psychocultural data). When we define situations as mainly intergroup in nature, our social identities influence our behavior more than our personal identities, and our predictions of strangers' behavior are based on their group memberships or the roles they fill (cultural or sociocultural data).

Some of the groups into which we categorize strangers involve some degree of stigmatization. Stigmatization involves discounting strangers because they are different (Goffman, 1963). Our expectations for how strangers we perceive to be stigmatized will behave in situations are different from our expectations for those we do not perceive to be stigmatized. Strangers who are disabled, for example, often are perceived to be stigmatized by nondisabled people. Whether we perceive strangers to be disabled influences how we communicate with them. A blind person describes how a taxi driver's communication changed when the taxi driver found out that he was blind:

> I could tell at first that the taxi driver didn't know that I was blind because for a while there he was quite a conversationalist. Then he asked me what these sticks were for (a collapsible

cane). I told him it was a cane, and then he got so different. . . . He didn't talk about the same things as he did at first. (Davis, 1977, p. 85)

It appears that the taxi driver initially defined the situation as interpersonal in nature, but when he discovered that the passenger was blind, he redefined the situation as intergroup in nature.

Relationships between Participants

The relationships between the participants in situations influence their communication. Both the interpersonal relations and the role the individuals are filling and the ways individuals are categorized affect the way people behave in situations. One of the major factors influencing the interpersonal relations between participants as individuals is the degree to which they are attracted to each other. Probably the most important factors influencing the attraction between participants as individuals is the degree to which they perceive themselves to be similar. When we are free to choose the people with whom we communicate, we tend to select people like us (Rogers & Bhowmik, 1971). It often is assumed that communication between people who are similar is more effective than communication between dissimilar people. *Moderate dissimilarities* between communicators who are generally similar, however, lead to the most effective communication (Simons, Berkowitz, & Moyer, 1970; see Chapter 12 for more on similarity). The similarities facilitate attributing similar meanings to messages, and the dissimilarities keep the communicators from assuming that others interpret their messages the same way they intended them (they do not become overconfident).

The roles we are filling influence our communication in terms of the degree to which we define situations as formal or informal. In the United States, for example, if we perceive that we are interacting with our bosses in work situations, we probably define the situations as formal. If we are interacting with our bosses at parties, in contrast, we may define the situations as informal. At parties, people in the United States may assume that their bosses are not filling the roles of bosses and, therefore, define the situations as informal rather than formal.

The extent to which we define situations as formal or informal influences many aspects of our behavior. When we define situations as formal, we tend to use standard speech patterns (Furnham, 1986). When we view the situation as informal, in contrast, we may use nonstandard dialects, such as a speech dialect based on our ethnicities or the region of the country in which we live. When talking in formal situations we also speak slowly and attempt to use correct grammar. In informal situations we may speak rapidly and not worry as much about our grammar.

How we categorize strangers influences our communication in terms of the degree to which we define situations as between people who are equal or unequal. When the participants in social situations are not equal in status, the higher-status people can define the situations by the speech patterns they use (Giles & Hewstone, 1982). Respect and authority often are established by using standard, formal speech patterns rather than using nonstandard dialects (such as regional or ethnic dialects) and informal speech patterns. Once status is established using formal language, for example, people can switch to using informal language to develop a relaxed atmosphere. If higher-status people begin using speech patterns designed to define situations as informal and their authority is questioned, they are likely to switch to more formal speech patterns. If lower-status people perceive that they are being treated unfairly in particular situations, they can choose to redefine the situations with the speech patterns they use. To illustrate, the lower-status people might use their ingroup speech patterns to change the definition of the situation from being based on status factors to defining the situations in terms of demonstrating solidarity with members of their ingroups.

The situation influences the power members of our ingroups and strangers have. Power is the ability to influence others (e.g., French & Raven, 1959). Lack of power leads to anxiety and attempts to cope with the anxiety (Fiske, Morling, & Stevens, 1996). Strangers tend to have less power that ingroup members. Strangers also tend to be more aware of power differences between groups than ingroup members (e.g., Gurin et al., 1999). The nature of the stranger-ingroup relationship influences strangers' and ingroups' power and the potential for conflict between them. The more power our ingroups have over strangers, the less anxiety we have about interacting with strangers. Power also leads to cognitive and evaluative biases (Goodwin, Operario, & Fiske, 1998) and, therefore, to inaccurate predictions of strangers' behavior.

SITUATIONAL NORMS AND RULES

Norms and rules specify the acceptable means to achieving the ends of social life in our cultures. The means consist of the prescriptions (what should be done) and pro-scriptions (what should not be done) for acceptable behavior. When the standards of acceptable behavior have moral or ethical connotations, we refer to them as norms, and when there are no moral or ethical connotations in the standards, we refer to them as rules (Olsen, 1978).

Differentiating Norms and Rules

Norms can be defined as "rules of conduct," "blueprints for behavior," and "cultural expectations." Gibbs (1965) isolates three attributes of a *norm:* "(1) a collective evalu-ation of behavior in terms of what ought to be; (2) a collective expectation as to what behavior will be; [and] (3) particular reactions to behavior including attempts to apply sanctions or otherwise induce a particular kind of behavior" (p. 590). *Norms,* there-fore, can be defined as socially shared guidelines for expected and accepted behaviors, violation of which leads to some form of sanctions. The sanctions can vary from a dis-approving look, to ostracism from the group, to death.

Social life is possible to the extent we take into account the existence of others and their expected responses to our behavior. When the expectations are shared by a group of people, we can say a norm exists. Once norms are formed and we have internalized them, we tend to follow them unconsciously. Birenbaum and Sagarin (1976) point out that

> most people are aware that rules exist in all areas of life and take them into account when en-gaged in or anticipating interaction with other people. This awareness is part of the organized character of social life . . . even when people dislike or reject a rule, it may be extremely

difficult for them not to obey it, for much everyday life involves opportunities to demonstrate social competency, a factor that may override the will to disobey. Often obedience to the rule is simply reflexive, whereas transgression is effortful. (p. 4)

Two aspects of Birenbaum and Sagarin's position deserve brief elaboration. First, they are using the terms *rules* and *norms* interchangeably. This is consistent with some people's writing on norms, but there are many who use the terms differently. Olsen (1978), for example, believes norms have an ethical or moral connotation that is lacking in rules. Rules, in contrast, are developed for reasons of expediency, because they allow people to coordinate their activities more easily. (As noted earlier, we distinguish between norms and rules.)

Second, the other aspect of the above quotation requiring comment is Birenbaum and Sagarin's argument that obedience to norms and rules is reflexive. Obedience to norms or rules can be reflexive, however, only if we grow up in the cultures where the rule exists and internalize them from a very early age. If a person socialized into one culture is living in or visiting another culture, obedience to the norms and rules of the host culture is effortful, and transgression may be reflexive. This suggests that following norms and rules in cultures other than those in which we were raised requires that we be mindful of our behavior.

Sumner (1940) divides norms into three categories: folkways, mores, and laws. Sumner views *folkways* as those pervasive everyday activities widely accepted by members of cultures. Folkways include, but are not limited to, such actions as the way we greet others, the way we dress, the way we eat, the way we smell, the way we say good-bye, and other such actions that are widely accepted. Since folkways do not have moral or ethical connotations, they can be considered rules (which are defined below) rather than norms in our terminology. *Mores* are those norms expressing strong moral demands on individuals' behavior. Examples of mores include the commandments derived from religious doctrine, incest taboos, and rules about what is acceptable to eat (e.g., in the United States it is unacceptable to eat the meat of dogs, cats, and people). The final category of norms is laws. *Laws* are norms codified by political entities such as nations, states, and cities. Laws may be derived from either the folkways or the mores of a culture.

As indicated earlier, *rules* differ from norms in that rules do not have moral or ethical connotations. Noesjirwan (1978) points out that

rules provide a statement of expected or intended behaviour and its outcome. As such, rules provide a number of related functions that serve to order social life and render it meaningful. Rules provide a set of mutual expectations, thus rendering the behaviour of each person predictable and understandable to the other. . . . The rules partly serve to define the meaning a situation has, and to define the meaning that any given action has within a situation. (pp. 305–306)

Rules, therefore, perform many of the same functions that norms do in establishing coordinated activities among individuals.

Violations of norms or rules bring some form of sanctions on the people committing the violations. The sanctions vary from a disapproving glance to the loss of life. The sanctions imposed for violations of folkways are through interpersonal channels. If, for example, you were to "slurp" your soup in public in the United States, you probably would receive only disapproving glances from the people who heard you (of course, they also may make comments to their friends about your impolite behavior). If, in contrast, you do not slurp your soup in some cultures, you may receive disapproving glances. Similarly, if you were to wear informal clothes (e.g., your best jeans) to a black-tie dinner, people would look at you disapprovingly, make comments about your lack of appropriate attire, and probably not invite you to a formal dinner again, but they would not use more severe sanctions.

Violations of mores bring about more severe sanctions than violations of folkways. An extreme example of a mos (singular of mores) in the United States is that we do not eat dogs or cats (there is a prohibition on eating dogs and cats). If people find out that you ate dog or cat meat, in all likelihood they will avoid you (you will be ostracized).

Violations of laws obviously bring about legal sanctions. These sanctions, of course, can vary from a verbal reprimand from a judge to the death penalty.

Members of cultures are aware of some of the norms and rules guiding their behavior and unaware of many others. Even if people are aware that the norms and rules exists, however, they probably cannot articulate all the specific behavioral expectations associated with the norms and rules. This lack of awareness is illustrated by something as simple as a handshake. Shaking hands is a communication rule when greeting people for the first time in the United States, but what are the rules for shaking hands? Can you tell people who have never shaken hands before (e.g., someone from Mars) all the rules necessary for them to shake hands "correctly"? Many people would say that you grip the other person's extended hand and pump up and down. But is it that simple? What would you do if you met people for the first time and they extended the left hand? That obviously is not appropriate because U.S. Americans shake hands with the right hand. What if others extend the right hand but do not hold on to your hand (e.g., use a "limp" grip)? Is this acceptable? No, probably not. What if they use the "correct" grip with the right hand and when you shake hands don't stop but continue to pump up and down, up and down? How would you feel? Comfortable? Uncomfortable? Probably uncomfortable because the rule is that U.S. Americans pump their hands a few (one or two) times and stop. We could go on, but by now you get the point that shaking hands is not as simple as it initially seems. It is a complex process with many subtle expectations. U.S. Americans may not be able to explain all the expectations, but they know when they are violated.

One way to become aware of the norms and communication rules guiding our behavior is to have them violated. When we interact with people from our cultures, our expectations generally are not violated often because people of the same culture share similar expectations. When we communicate with strangers, however, our behavioral expectations may be violated because strangers learned different sets of norms and rules in their cultures. When our expectations are violated, we may react to strangers negatively; this is a "normal" reaction. There is also the possibility of positive outcomes, however. When our expectations are violated, for example, we can gain tremendous insight into the norms and rules of our cultures and how they influence our behavior. In addition, we come to see alternative behavioral patterns, which we might prefer. In other words, confronting cultural differences offers the possibility of personal growth and/or cultural change.

Cultural Differences in Norms and Rules

There are patterned cultural differences in norms and rules. We begin by looking at how the dimensions of norms and rules vary across cultures. Next, we examine cultural variations in the justice and reciprocity norms. We conclude by examining representative cross-cultural studies of rules.

Dimensions of Norms and Rules   Rules (and norms) vary along four dimensions: (1) level of understanding, (2) clarity, (3) range, and (4) homogeneity or consensus (Cushman & Whiting, 1972). Both rules and norms can vary with respect to level of understanding. Cushman and Whiting argue that the greater the need for coordination in human activities, the greater is the degree of accuracy in understanding of the rules (and norms). Given our discussion of uncertainty avoidance in Chapter 3, it can be argued that there is greater coordination of activities in high uncertainty avoidance cultures than in low uncertainty avoidance cultures. This should lead to a correspondingly greater degree of accuracy in the understanding of rules (and norms) in high uncertainty avoidance cultures than in low uncertainty avoidance cultures.

In addition to varying with respect to level of understanding, rules (and norms) vary with respect to the specificity of the actions required or permitted in situations in which rules apply and in terms of the span of situations in which particular actions are permitted or required (the range of rules). When rules have a large range and a low degree of specificity, habitual communication behavior emerges (Cushman & Whiting, 1972). Given the conceptualizations of cultural uncertainty avoidance, it can be inferred that rules (and norms) are more specific and have more range in high uncertainty avoidance cultures than in low uncertainty avoidance cultures. Stated differently, rules (and norms) are more specific with respect to the behaviors permitted or required in a situation in high uncertainty avoidance cultures than in low uncertainty avoidance cultures.

As indicated earlier, rules (and norms) also vary with respect to the degree of consensus there is about them. Cushman and Whiting (1972) argue that "the homogeneity of a rule system refers to the degree to which accurate understandings of standard usage are evenly distributed among participants in a communication system" (p. 233). Given the nature of collectivistic cultures, they tend to be more homogeneous than are individualistic cultures like the United States. Because of the homogeneity of their cultures, members of collectivistic cultures are more likely to exhibit coordinated activities than are members of individualistic cultures.

Justice Norms   There are two main orientations toward justice: the equity norm and the equality norm. The *equity norm* involves rewarding or punishing people on the basis of their effort. It is tied closely to the notion of "deservingness." The *equality norm*, in contrast, is based on rewarding or punishing people equally regardless of their input.

People in individualistic cultures tend to subscribe to the equity norm, and people in collectivistic cultures tend to subscribe to the equality norm with ingroup members. Mahler, Greenberg, and Hayashi (1981), for example, report that Japanese students prefer the equality norm for distributing rewards and students in the United States prefer the equity norm. Leung and Bond (1982, 1984) note that students in the United States prefer the equity norm and Chinese students prefer the equality norm. When students are asked to allocate rewards to ingroup and outgroup members, the Chinese use the equality norm with ingroup members more than with outgroup members.

Reciprocity Norm   The *reciprocity norm* involves two conditions: "(1) people should help those who have helped them, and (2) people should not injure those who have helped them" (Gouldner, 1960, p. 171). The reciprocity norm is an implicit contract that binds people together.

Ting-Toomey (1986) argues that members of individualistic cultures follow voluntary reciprocity norms and members of collectivistic cultures use obligatory reciprocity norms. Voluntary reciprocity norms are based on individuals' free will and free choices. Obligatory reciprocity norms are based on requirements necessary to maintain membership in groups. Ting-Toomey also contends that members of individualistic cultures engage in short-term reciprocity (i.e., reciprocate shortly after others engage in behavior). Members of collectivistic cultures, in contrast, engage in long-term reciprocity (i.e., engage in reciprocity over the course of relationships, not necessarily immediately following others' behavior).

Cultural Variability in Communication Rules   Noesjirwan (1978) demonstrates how rules can be seen to vary systematically across cultures. In her study of Indonesia (collectivistic) and Australia (individualistic), she finds little systematic variation in 69 different rules or value statements within cultures, and there are many between-culture variations in the same statements. To illustrate, her study reveals different rules for dealing with people in waiting rooms and at bus stops. The rule in both situations in Indonesia requires one to talk to others who are present. The rule for Australians in both situations, in contrast, requires one to ignore others who are present.

Argyle and Henderson (1984) argue that there are six "universal" rules in personal relationships: (1) One should respect others' privacy, (2) one should look the other person in the eye during conversations, (3) one should or should not discuss that which is said in confidence with the other person, (4) one should or should not indulge in sexual activity with the other person, (5) one should not criticize the other person in public, and (6) one should repay debts, favors, or compliments no matter how small. Argyle et al. (1986) report that the respect privacy rule receives the strongest endorsement across cultures. The keeping confidence rule receives strong support in all cultures except Japan. The public criticism rule is endorsed more strongly in Japan and Hong Kong than in Italy and Britain. This finding is to be expected given that Japan and Hong Kong are collectivistic cultures and Italy and Britain are individualistic cultures. Harmony is maintained in collectivistic cultures by avoiding criticism.

Ogawa and Gudykunst (1999) examine politeness rules in Japan and the United States. They report that cultural individualism-collectivism influences 23 politeness rules. Twelve of the rules are associated with cultural individualism (e.g., "Treat others as I want to be treated"), and 11 are associated with cultural collectivism (e.g., "Avoid direct confrontations"). Seventeen rules appear to be common politeness rules in the two cultures (e.g., "Use polite language," "Make the conversation smooth").

Ogawa and Gudykunst (1999) also report that self construals influence the politeness rules Japanese and U.S. Americans perceive to be operating in their cultures. Nineteen rules are associated with emphasizing independent self construals (e.g., "Avoid obscure language," "Respect others' privacy"). Most of these rules are associated with polite low-context messages. Twenty-one rules are associated with emphasizing interdependent self construals (e.g., "Behave modestly," "Compliment others"). Most of these rules are associated with polite high-context communication.

This brief overview of rules should suffice to demonstrate that to communicate effectively with strangers we must attempt to understand their rules. Noesjirwan (1978) illustrates the importance of understanding strangers' rules when she points out that "given a knowledge of the rule/value structure of the two cultures it becomes possible to predict, among other things, the likely sources of misunderstanding and conflict between those cultures, and the likely difficulties in adjustment faced by a person of one culture moving to the other" (p. 314).

PSYCHOLOGICAL ENVIRONMENT

As we indicated earlier, the psychological environment refers to our perceptual and cognitive beliefs about the physical environment and how we use the physical environment where we interact with others. Ittelson (1973) argues that there are at least five levels at which we relate to the surrounding environment: (1) We have feelings about the environment, (2) we are oriented spatially within the environment, (3) we categorize phenomena in the environment, (4) we organize the environment in terms of relationships among its features, and (5) we manipulate the environment. Each of these levels can influence our behavior. Some writers, in fact, believe the psychological environment is more important than the physical environment in influencing behavior. Dubos (1981) observes that

> in addition to the influences that reach us from the outside—the world external to us—there are other influences that exist in the individual mind of each of us and that constitute our private conceptual environment. Whether primitive or poorly informed, or sophisticated and learned, each one of us lives as it were in a private world of his [or her] own. In fact, the conceptual environment may be more important than the external environment because it affects all aspects of our lives. (p. 31)

This suggests that we must understand strangers' perceptions of the psychological environment to communicate effectively with them.

Although there is very little cross-cultural research on differences in psychological environments, there is some relevant work that can be examined. In this section, we look at three aspects of the psychological environment: perceptions of privacy, the use of time, and the "interaction potential" of the environment.

Privacy

The concept of privacy is intertwined closely with our perceptions of the environment. Altman (1975) defines *privacy* as the "selective control of access to the self or to one's group" (p. 18). Privacy, therefore, is a mechanism that allows us to control our interactions with others. Altman differentiates between *desired privacy*, "how much or how little contact is desired at some moment in time," and *achieved privacy,* "the actual degree of contact that results from interaction with others" (p. 10). To the extent that desired privacy and achieved privacy match, we have controlled the interactions.

Altman (1975) views privacy as a dialectical process. He argues that the oppositional qualities of being closed and being open to social interaction vary over time. Our desire for privacy shifts depending on our moods and the circumstances in which we find ourselves. At the core of Altman's conceptualization is that when we regulate our privacy, we are regulating our interpersonal boundaries—the dividing lines between ourselves and others.

Altman (1975) and Altman and Chemers (1980a) argue that the specific mechanisms for privacy vary across cultures but that every culture has some method for regulating privacy. Privacy regulation, therefore, can be considered a cultural universal.

Westin (1970) outlines four types of privacy: solitude, intimacy, anonymity, and reserve. Solitude occurs when we are alone and cannot be observed by others, and intimacy occurs when a dyad or small group of people separate themselves from others to be alone. When we are "lost in a crowd," not expecting to be recognized by others, we are anonymous. The final type of privacy—reserve—involves "the creation of a psychological barrier against unwanted intrusion" (Westin, 1970, p. 32).

In the United States, privacy often is regulated through the use of closed doors. A closed door—whether it leads to a bedroom, den, office, or bathroom—sends the message "leave me alone!" (Altman, 1975). People in the United States tend to use other physical barriers (e.g., fences, hedges) in addition to doors as ways to achieve privacy. This is not necessarily the case in some other cultures. Hall (1966) observes that people in England do not tend to have private offices; instead, they conduct their business in open spaces. Privacy in England is achieved by speaking softly and directing voices carefully, not by closing doors.

Privacy in many cultures is regulated psychologically rather than through the use of environmental barriers. Geertz, for example, argues that in Java it is impossible to regulate privacy through manipulation of the environment because the people do not put up physical barriers between themselves and outsiders. To [U.S.] Americans, therefore, it often appears that there is no privacy at all in a Javanese household. This is not the case, however. Geertz points out that

> people speak softly, hide their feelings and even in the bosom of a Javanese family you have the feeling that you are in a public square and must behave with appropriate decorum. Javanese people shut people out with a wall of decorum, . . . with emotional restraint, and with a general lack of candor in both speech and behavior. It is not, in short, that the Javanese do not wish or value privacy, but merely that because they put up no physical or social barriers against the physical ingress of outsiders into their household life they must put up psychological ones and surround themselves with barriers of a different sort. (Cited in Westin, 1970, p. 16)

Thus, Javanese privacy regulation can be described as "reserve," using Westin's four categories.

Privacy also is regulated through the use of territory (territory is discussed in detail in Chapter 9). The concept of territory in the social sciences is very similar to its everyday usage (e.g., "my turf"). Altman (1975) suggests that "territorial behavior is a self/other boundary-regulation mechanism that involves personalization of or marking of a place or object and communication that it is 'owned' by a person or group" (p. 107). In other words, territorial behavior is the personalizing of an area in order to regulate communication. Perception of what constitutes "owned" territory obviously can vary across cultures. Hall (1966) illustrates this by comparing the use of territorial boundaries in Germany and the United States. If you are standing on the porch of a house with the screen door closed, for example, you are considered to be "outside" the house in the United States. Similarly, if you "poke" your head into the door of an office, you still are considered to be outside the office. In Germany the person in both of these situations is considered to be "inside," or within the other person's territory. Germans consider people to be inside their territory if they can see inside; if you can see, you are intruding.

Gudykunst and Ting-Toomey (1988) argue that privacy regulation is influenced by individualism-collectivism and that the way privacy is regulated affects the amount people self-disclose. They suggest that in individualistic cultures people use physical space to assert their privacy and provide a boundary between themselves and others. Because privacy is controlled through the use of physical space, individualists can allow themselves to be accessible through verbal self-disclosure. In collectivistic cultures, in contrast, people do not use physical space to control privacy or set up a boundary between themselves and others. Rather, they use psychological mechanisms to control their privacy. Since psychological mechanisms are used, collectivists must be careful about how they allow themselves to be accessible through the use verbal self-disclosure.

Baker and Gudykunst (1990) isolate differences in how individualists from the United States and collectivists from Japan indicate to others that they want privacy on a particular topic of conversation. The predominate way the individualists indicate a desire for privacy is to not be attentive to the person with whom they are communicating when the topic is discussed. The collectivists, in contrast, use indirect verbal communication (e.g., being evasive, starting to talk about something else).

Before proceeding, one final aspect of privacy that must be mentioned briefly is the issue of crowding. Crowding is different from density. Density of population involves the concentration of people within a certain geographical area (e.g., the number of people per square mile). It is a physical indicator with no psychological meaning. *Crowding,* in contrast, is a psychological phenomenon; it is the subjective feeling associated with too little space. Altman and Chemers (1980a) argue that "crowding occurs when a privacy regulation system malfunctions, such that more social contact occurs than was originally desired" (p. 374). They contend that perceived crowding leads to psychological stress. This stress, in turn, motivates us to try to return to the desired level of social interaction.

Temporality

Cultures develop temporal patterns of life that are part of the psychological environment. These patterns define when it is appropriate to do certain things (e.g., sleep, eat, arrive for meetings), as well as how many things it is appropriate to do at the same time. Hall (1959) distinguishes between monochronic and polychronic time patterns. *Monochronic time* involves compartmentalization; people compartmentalize their time and schedule one event at a time. *Polychronic time,* in contrast, does not involve compartmentalization; people tend to engage in several activities at the same time. People in monochronic time cultures tend to perceive time as a linear progression, marching from the past into the future. They tend to treat time as a tangible, discrete entity, which can be "saved," "borrowed," "divided," "lost," and even "killed." People in polychronic time cultures, in contrast, tend to treat time in a more holistic way and to place a primary value on the activities occurring in time rather than the clock time itself. Polychronic time cultures stress completion of transactions rather than adherence to schedules. In many polychronic time cultures, punctuality is not as sacred as it is in monochronic time cultures. If something important needs to be completed, members of polychronic time cultures sacrifice the next scheduled activity to complete the current activity more readily than members of monochronic time cultures. It is not uncommon in monochronic time cultures to see some of the most exciting activities being stopped abruptly simply because "time is up."

Hall (1959) equates the use of monochronic time with cultures characterized by low levels of involvement among people and the use of polychronic time with cultures characterized by high levels of involvement among people. Cultures like those of the United States and most of Europe, which are characterized by relatively low levels of involvement among people, tend to have compartmentalized time schedules. Cultures like those in Latin America and the Arab states, in contrast, which are characterized by high levels of involvement among people, tend to use polychronic time patterns in which several activities are scheduled for the same time.

African cultures generally are viewed as polychronic time systems that are not very clock-bound. Africans do have objective time systems, but they are based more on seasonal cycles, natural events, and biological rhythms and generally are very flexible (Harris & Moran, 1979). Because of this relative flexibility, Africans tend to consider people in a hurry with suspicion and distrust. Since trust is very important among them, they want to sit and talk—get to know the others—even in business transactions.

The Sioux Indians provide another example of a differing orientation toward time. Hall (1959) gives an account of a Sioux Indian school superintendent concerning the time behavior of his culture:

> During a long and fascinating account of the many problems which his tribe was having in adjusting to our way of life, he suddenly remarked: "What would you think of a people who had no word for time? My people have no word for 'late' or for 'waiting,' for that matter. They don't know what it is to wait or to be late." (p. 25)

These differences may be due to the language spoken. This issue is discussed in more detail in Chapter 8.

Interaction Potential of the Environment

The final aspect of the psychological environment to be discussed is the "interaction potential" of the environment. The *interaction potential* is the potential the environment provides for interacting with strangers. The type of contact individuals have the opportunity to have with members of other groups depends on the structural conditions of the environment (Jaspars & Warnaen, 1982). Kanter (1977), for example, argues that feeling "different" depends on the relative numbers of people present. To illustrate, Kanter contends that when there are "tokens," or only a few people who are not part of the majority group (i.e., strangers) in organizations, these people feel a lot of pressure to conform. Because of this pressure, strangers may try to become invisible.

Blau and Schwartz (1984) argue that group memberships provide structural constraints in the establishment of intergroup relationships. They contend that the size of ingroups influences the amount of contact people have with members of outgroups; as the size of ingroups increases, the likelihood of contact with members of outgroups decreases and the ingroup members become more likely to interact with members of their ingroups. Blau and Schwartz also contend that the more heterogeneous the environment (i.e., increases in the number of different groups represented in the environment), the more intergroup contact occurs.

Blau and Schwartz's (1984) theory suggests that the more strangers from the same group there are in an environment, the less likely it is the strangers will interact with members of the ingroup. This argument is supported by extensive research. Hoffman (1985), for example, reports that as the relative number of strangers increases in organizations (i.e., there are more strangers), the strangers' communication with members of their ingroups increases. Hallinan and Smith (1985) also observe that opportunities for contact influence the development of interracial friendships in children. Children from the numerical minority group develop more interracial friendships than children from the numerical majority.

Another way of understanding the influence of the cultural composition of the environment is to look at the institutional completeness of the community. Breton (1964), for example, argues that the degree to which immigrants are assimilated into local communities depends on the availability of ethnic institutions (e.g., churches, markets, publications) to meet their needs. In comparing immigrants from 30 different ethnic backgrounds in Montreal, Breton reports that the more complete the ethnic institutional support for the immigrants, the more likely they are to develop personal ties within their ethnic groups and not with majority members of the local community. Inglis and Gudykunst's (1982) study comparing Korean immigrants in Hartford, Connecticut (which has a low level of institutional completeness), with Koreans from Kim's (1978) study in Chicago (which has a relatively complete institutional system) supports Breton's conclusion.

The differences between the networks we form with members of our own cultures and the networks we form with members of other cultures also can influence the interaction potential of the environment. Yum (1988c) proposes a theory designed to explain the differences in individuals' intracultural and intercultural networks. Yum points out that "in network theory, the focus is on positions and social relationships" (p. 240). She begins with the assumption that there is more variance in behavior between cultures than within cultures. There are six theorems in Yum's theory.

Yum's (1988c) first theorem posits that intercultural networks tend to be radial (individuals are linked to others who are not linked to each other) and intracultural networks tend to be interlocking (individuals are linked to others who are linked to each other). Theorem 2 predicts that intracultural networks are more dense (i.e., the ratio of actual direct links to number of possible links) than intercultural networks.

Yum's (1988c) third theorem proposes that intracultural networks are more multiplex (multiple messages flow through linkages) than intercultural networks. Theorem 4 states that "intercultural network ties are more likely to be weak ties than strong ties" (p. 250). Strong ties involve frequent and close contact (e.g., friendships). Links between acquaintances and people with whom individuals have intermittent role relationships (e.g., hairdressers) tend to be weak ties.

Theorem 5 in Yum's (1988c) theory states that "the roles of liaison and bridges will be more prevalent and more important for network connectedness in intercultural networks than in intracultural networks" (p. 251). Liaisons are individuals who link cliques (i.e., a group of connected individuals) but are not members of any of the cliques. Bridges are individuals who link cliques and are members of one of the cliques. Both are "intermediaries" and can form indirect linkages between members of different groups.

Yum's (1988c) final theorem suggests that "transivity will play a much smaller role in creating intercultural networks than intracultural networks" (p. 252). Transivity occurs when "my friend's friends are my friends" (p. 252). Since intercultural networks tend to be uniplex and involve weak ties, they do not facilitate forming networks with friends of outgroup members in the network.

To summarize, in order to understand strangers' behavior we must take into consideration their relative numbers in the environment. The fewer strangers from a particular group there are in the environment, the more likely the strangers are to seek out contact with members of the ingroup. As the number of strangers from a particular group increases, there is a tendency for them to associate with other strangers from their group. One of the major reasons for this is that people tend to be attracted to people who are similar to themselves, assuming there are other people in the environment who are like them.

SUMMARY

The environment and our perceptions of the environment influence our communication with strangers, as well as our communication as strangers. The physical environment, including geography, climate, landscape, and architecture, influences our feelings, emotions, and attitudes, which in turn influence our communication behavior. In addition, certain aspects of the physical environment have a direct impact on the predictions we make about strangers' behavior and the way we interpret incoming stimuli. A U.S. American exchange student (a stranger) visiting a Colombian family in the living room of their home, for example, probably will predict that informal behavior is called for in that setting and will act accordingly. Such a prediction, however, will not be accurate since the living room in a Colombian home is set aside for formal behavior. In order to make accurate predictions and correctly interpret incoming stimuli, we must know how the person with whom we are communicating defines the setting in which our communication is taking place. This is necessary when we are communicating with strangers on our "home turf," as well as when we are strangers on others' "home turf."

Situations are an important aspect of the environment that influences our behavior. The physical setting provides important cues that we use in determining how we should communicate. Our purpose in the situation also plays a large role in determining how we communicate in a particular situation. The people who are present and our relationship with them tell us whether we should speak formally or use a standard dialect, what topics we should discuss, and so forth.

The norms and rules of our culture tell us the prescribed and proscribed methods for behaving in specific situations. Since norms and rules tend to vary systematically across cultures, our behavioral expectations tend to be violated with greater frequency when we communicate with strangers than when we communicate with people who are known. Knowing the norms and rules guiding strangers' behavior, as well as those guiding our own behavior, can help us communicate more effectively with strangers.

Our perceptions of the environment also have a direct influence on how we interpret incoming stimuli and make predictions about strangers' behavior. People in some cultures perceive physical barriers (e.g., closed doors, fences) as regulators of their privacy, and people in other cultures do not perceive physical barriers as a mechanism of privacy regulation. Rather, they perceive privacy as being regulated by psychological barriers (e.g., pretending others are not there). Misunderstandings can occur whenever people from one type of culture find themselves to be strangers in the other type of culture. As strangers, they will be unable to find the privacy they want or desire because people of the host culture do not recognize the same barriers. Similarly, the hosts, in all likelihood, will misinterpret the strangers' behavior.

STUDY QUESTIONS

1. How do geography and landscape influence the way we communicate?
2. How do architecture and landscape influence our communication?
3. Why do the cues provided by the locale in which we communicate make our interactions smoother than they would be if we did not have these cues?
4. How do bystanders influence the way we communicate?
5. How does cooperation differ across cultures?
6. How does stigmatization influence communication?
7. Why do moderate dissimilarities when people are generally similar facilitate effective communication?
8. How does our own status and the other person's status influence communication?
9. How are norms and rules similar and different?
10. How do the dimensions of norms and rules vary across cultures?
11. How do the justice norms vary across cultures?
12. How does the reciprocity norm vary across cultures?
13. Why is achieving privacy a dialectical process?
14. How does privacy differ across cultures?
15. How does the use of territory differ across cultures?
16. How do monochronic and polychronic uses of time differ?
17. What factors influence the interaction potential of the environment?

SUGGESTED READINGS

Altman, I. (1975). *The environment and social behavior.* Monterey, CA: Brooks/Cole.
Altman, I., & Chemers, M. (1980). *Culture and environment.* Monterey, CA: Brooks/Cole.
Argyle, M., Furnham, A., & Graham, J. (1981). *Social situations.* Cambridge, UK: Cambridge University Press.
Forgas, J. (Ed.). (1985). *Language and social situations.* New York: Springer-Verlag.
Hall, E. T. (1983). *The dance of life.* New York: Doubleday.

PART THREE

INTERPRETING AND TRANSMITTING MESSAGES

Culture affects our communication in various ways. It provides us with patterned ways of dealing with information in our environment. It influences what we perceive, how we interpret, and how we respond to messages both verbally and nonverbally. Culture shapes and colors our image of reality and conditions the way we think.

Our communication patterns are often subtle, elusive, and unconscious. It is difficult for even well-informed members of a culture to explain why, in their own culture, the custom is thus-and-so rather than so-and-thus. It would be hard, for example, for one to explain the "rule" governing the precise time in a relationship when the other person becomes a friend. It simply "feels right." Fortunately, members of the same culture share a great number of such taken-for-granted assumptions about interpersonal relationships and the corresponding "appropriate" behavior.

For strangers, however, many of the hidden assumptions and modes of behavior are not shared. As many people who visit a foreign country soon discover, communicating with the natives can often be a challenging and novel experience. In the following chapters we present material designed to help us better understand our message interpreting and transmitting when we communicate with strangers. In Chapter 7, we examine interpreting messages, the most fundamental process of receiving and processing information from the environment. Specifically, we discuss the perceptual process, how we make sense of strangers' behavior (e.g., attribution processes), how our cognitive styles influence our interpreting of strangers' messages, and how our patterns of thought influence our perceptions of strangers. In Chapter 8, we take up language and verbal behavior. The focus there is on the Sapir-Whorf hypothesis, elaborated and restricted codes, and the factors that influence our language choices when we communicate with strangers (i.e., language vitality, language attitudes, second language competence, communication accommodation, and code-switching). Finally, in Chapter 9, we consider the recognition and expression of emotions, differences between contact and noncontact cultures, and what happens when our nonverbal behavioral expectations are violated when we communicate with strangers.

7

INTERPRETING MESSAGES

*What has been thought of as mind is actually
internalized culture. The mind culture process
which has evolved over the past four or more million
years is primarily concerned with "organization" and,
furthermore, the organization of "information" as it
is channeled (and altered by the senses) to the brain.*

Edward T. Hall

The way we interpret strangers' messages affects the way we respond to them. Interpreting messages involves perceiving the cues strangers transmit and attributing meaning to those cues. The way we perceive the cues strangers transmit and attribute meaning to those cues is influenced by our social cognitive styles (e.g., the way we think about people) and our patterns of thought, logic, and reasoning. We can increase the accuracy of our perceptions and our attributions about strangers' behavior if we are mindful of our communication behavior.

Initially, we discuss how we perceive strangers' behavior. Then we look at how we make sense of strangers' behavior—the process of making attributions. Next, we look at the cognitive styles that influence how we receive and organize information from the environment (i.e., field-independence/field-dependence, category width, uncertainty orientation, and cognitive complexity). Following this, we explore cultural variations in patterns of thought. Finally, we examine cultural variability in the systems of logic and patterns of reasoning.

PERCEPTUAL PROCESSES

Perception involves our awareness of what is taking place in the environment. There are three critical aspects of perceptions that influence our communication with strangers. First, our perceptions are selective. That is, we do not perceive all the information available to us in the specific environments in which our communication takes place. Second, our perceptions involve categorizations. When we perceive strangers communicating on automatic pilot, we unconsciously put them in categories. Third, rigid categories inhibit effective communication. To the extent that our categories are rigid (as opposed to flexible), we are unable to see individual characteristics of the strangers with whom we are communicating, and our communication, therefore, will not be as effective as it could be.

Our Perceptions Are Selective

If we had to pay attention to all the stimuli in our environments, we would experience information overload. In the interest of not overloading ourselves with too much information, we limit our attention to those aspects of strangers or the situations that are essential to what we are doing (Bruner, 1958). We might, for example, perceive the color of strangers' skin but not notice its texture. Watts (1966) points out that

> to notice is to select, to regard some bits of perception, or some features of the world, as more noteworthy, more significant than others. To these, we attend, and the rest we ignore— for which reason . . . attention is at the same time ignore-ance (i.e., ignorance) despite the fact that it gives us a vividly clear picture of what we choose to notice. Physically, we see, hear, smell, taste, and touch innumerable features that we never notice. (p. 29)

Our perceptions of strangers, therefore, are highly selective.

Bateson (1979) argues that the process of selecting information from the environment and forming images takes place unconsciously. We do not consciously decide on the things to which we pay attention. We are conscious of our perceptions (what we see), but we need to keep in mind that what we see is manufactured in our brains. What we see does not really exist because "all experience is subjective" (Bateson, 1979, p. 31). Presuppositions and expectations influence the cues we select from the environment and what we see (expectations were discussed in Chapter 5).

Ittelson and Cantril (1954) contend that our perceptions are always a function of our interactions with specific strangers in specific situations. We react to strangers on the basis of the way we perceive them in the interactions, *not* as entities independent of our interactions with them. Each of our perceptions is unique; they all are based on our cultures, ethnicities, genders, background experiences, and needs. To the extent that our perceptions overlap with those of strangers, our uncertainty is reduced. Our perceptions overlap with strangers' perceptions to the extent that we share common experiences (e.g., cultures, ethnicities, past interactions). We mistakenly assume that our perceptions are "real" and external to ourselves.

We also mistakenly assume that we perceive and observe strangers in unbiased ways. This, however, is not the case. Our perceptions are highly selective and biased. Assuming that our perceptions are unbiased leads us to make inaccurate predictions about strangers' behavior. Our group memberships and social identities (e.g., our cultures, ethnic groups, genders, ages) are major sources of bias in our perceptions. To illustrate, we unconsciously activate our social identities when we interact with strangers. When we communicate on automatic pilot, we perceive strangers' behavior on the basis of the social identities we have activated. If we meet strangers from other ethnic groups, for example, our ethnic identities guide our behavior. We unconsciously expect strangers' behavior to be based on their social identities as well. This leads to our perceptions' being highly selective, and we may not notice behavior inconsistent with our stereotypes of the strangers' ethnic groups.

Our past experiences are another source of bias in our perceptions. If, for example, our mothers were quiet before they exploded and got angry, we may perceive that strangers are getting angry when they are quiet. Our previous experiences with strangers also can bias our perceptions of their current behavior. Our emotional states also bias our perceptions. Moods provide a lens through which we interpret our own and strangers' behavior. Other biases in perceptions are a function of the categorization process and our expectations.

Perceptions Involve Categorizations

When we select information from the environment, we need to organize it in some way by finding meaningful patterns. This is accomplished by putting things or people into categories. As indicated in Chapter 2, categorization is a fundamental aspect of thought. Categorization allows "us to structure and give coherence to our general knowledge about people and the social world, providing typical patterns of behavior and the range of likely variation between types of people and their characteristic actions and attributes" (Cantor, Mischel, & Schwartz, 1982, p. 34).

When we categorize something, we group objects (people or things) on the basis of aspects they have in common and ignore aspects they do not have in common. Our categorizations are based on only selected aspects of the things or people being categorized. In categorizing, we have to ignore some aspects in order to classify people or things. Once we have created the category, we assume that things or people within the category are similar and that things or people in different categories are different. To illustrate, strangers can be classified as members of our cultures or not members of our cultures, but when we do this, other important qualities of the strangers (their ethnicities are similar to ours, their occupations are similar to ours, etc.) are ignored. Once formed, however, the categories influence how we respond to strangers.

When we categorize things or people, we draw distinctions among them and create boundaries between categories. Zerubavel (1991) points out that "things assume a distinctive identity only through being differentiated from other things, and their meaning is always a function of the particular mental compartment in which we place them" (p. 3). Once the categories are formed, we tend to take them for granted and assume there are gaps between them. These gaps enhance our viewing categories as separate and distinct. DeBono (1991) contends that the process of drawing distinctions often leads to drawing distinctions between things that actually are quite similar. When we create categories, we run the risk of treating them as solid and permanent (deBono refers to this as using "rock logic"). It is important to keep in mind, however, that we created the categories in the first place and that the gaps between the categories are a function of the way we created the categories. To illustrate, if we use color of skin to create the categories African American and European American, we must keep in mind that not all African Americans are dark-skinned and not all European Americans are light-skinned. Also, we must keep in mind that there are people who fit both categories (e.g., children of African American and European American parents).

Rigid Categories Inhibit Accurate Perceptions

Creating gaps between the categories formed is a natural part of the perceptual process. What creates problems in communication is the rigidity with which the boundaries between categories are maintained. Zerubavel (1991) points out that

> the most distinctive characteristic of the rigid mind is its unyielding, obsessive commitment to the mutual exclusivity of mental entities. The foremost logical prerequisite of a rigid classification is that a mental item belong to no more than one category . . . the rigid mind cherishes sharp, clear-cut distinctions among mental entities. (p. 34)

People with rigid categories try to classify everything and everyone into a single category. When something or someone does not clearly fit one category, it threatens the cognitive structure of people with rigid category systems. Forcing things or people into mutually exclusive categories biases perceptions. People with rigid category systems experience anxiety or fear when confronted with something or someone that cannot be categorized (Zerubavel, 1991).

If we hold categories rigidly, we will not recognize individual variations within our categories or consider recategorizing strangers' on the basis of new information. This leads to inaccurate predictions of strangers' behavior. If our categories are rigid, we may categorize strangers as disabled, for example, and then see *all* disabled people as alike. All disabled people, however, are not alike. To communicate effectively with strangers who are disabled, we must be able to recognize how they are like other disabled people *and* how they are different from other disabled people.

We draw boundaries and categorize strangers to make sense of the world. We draw boundaries between ourselves and strangers, for example, so that we feel distinct. We not only have a need to be distinct, we also have a need to feel connected. If we draw rigid boundaries between ourselves and strangers, we fail to see how we are connected to strangers. When we base our communication with strangers on our social identities, for example, we fail to see the human identities we share with strangers and we may become morally exclusive. Balancing our needs for distinction (autonomy) and connection requires flexible categories. Zerubavel (1991) argues that "flexibility entails the ability to be both rigid and fuzzy. Flexible people notice structures yet feel comfortable destroying them from time to time" (p. 120). If our mental structures are flexible and elastic, we can "break away from the mental cages in which we so often lock ourselves" (p. 122; DeBono, 1991, refers to this as using "water logic"). Having flexible categories is necessary to be mindful and communicate effectively. If we know we have rigid categories, we can choose consciously to be more flexible when we are mindful of our communication.

When we are mindful, one thing we can do to overcome the biases in our perceptions is to look for exceptions. Weiner-Davis (1992) points out that once we recognize a single exception, it helps us stop our cognitive distortions due to either/or thinking. If we categorize strangers as not talkative or quiet, for example, we would try to think of times when they are talkative. When we recognize that there are times when strangers are talkative, we will not view them in exactly the same way. Changing our perceptions leads to more accurate perceptions of strangers.

Perceptions of Groups

In Chapter 1, we pointed out that we all have implicit theories of communication. We also have implicit theories of groups that influence our perceptions of ingroups and outgroups (Lickel, Hamilton, & Sherman, 2001). Lickel et al. report that we perceive four types of groups in our implicit theories: "intimacy groups (e.g., family, friends, romantic partners), task groups (e.g., a work team, a jury), social categories (e.g., women, Blacks), and loose associations (e.g., people who like classical music, people in line at a bank)" (p. 131). This group typology is used when we perceive social information. We tend to assume that each type of group has specific characteristics associated with it and that these characteristics are different from those associated with the other types of groups.

Lickel et al. (2001) point out that social categories "are perceived as having long duration and low permeability but [are] rated as very large in size and fairly low in group member interaction, common goals, common outcomes, importance, and group member similarity" (p. 131). The extent to which we perceive that group members interact, have common goals, and are similar influences the extent to which we perceive the group as a coherent unit. The extent to which we perceive groups as coherent units influences how we process information about group members and the judgments we make about group members.

Levy et al. (2001) argue that our implicit theories of groups differ in terms of whether they are "static" (we assume that individuals' behavior is fixed and unchangeable) or "dynamic" (we assume that individuals' behavior is malleable and changeable). If our implicit theories are static, we focus on strangers' traits and tend to assume that those traits lead strangers' behavior to be consistent across time and situations. If our implicit theories are dynamic, in contrast, we tend to assume strangers' behavior is *not* consistent across time and situations. To understand strangers' behavior using dynamic implicit theories, we have to understand the situational and psychological factors influencing strangers. These differences lead people who use static implicit theories to believe social stereotypes more than people who use dynamic implicit theories.

Levy et al. (2001) also point out that our implicit theories of groups influence our perceptions of group homogeneity and intergroup differences. They suggest, for example, that people who use static implicit theories view groups as being more similar and exaggerate differences between ingroups and outgroups more than people who use dynamic implicit theories. Because they focus on strangers' traits, people who use static implicit theories commit the ultimate attribution error (attribute outgroup members' negative behavior to their group memberships; see below) more than people who use dynamic implicit theories. Using static implicit theories, therefore, leads people to be more biased toward their ingroups and engage in more prejudiced behavior toward outgroups than people using dynamic implicit theories.

MAKING ATTRIBUTIONS

Jones and Nisbett (1972) argue that people engaging in behavior interpret their behavior differently than people observing it. They suggest that people usually attribute their own behavior to situational factors and that observers attribute the behavior to qualities of the people being observed. Nisbett et al. (1973) offer two explanations for these divergent perspectives. The first is simply a perceptual one. The attention of people engaging in behavior is focused on situational cues with which their behavior is coordinated. It, therefore, appears to people engaging in behavior that their behavior is a response to those situational cues. For observers, however, it is not the situational cues that are salient, but rather the behavior. Observers are more likely to perceive the cause of strangers' behavior to be a trait or quality inherent in the people exhibiting it. This view suggests that when we communicate with strangers, our retroactive explanations of their behavior are likely to focus on characteristics of the strangers (e.g., their cultural backgrounds or group memberships).

The second explanation suggested by Nisbett et al. (1973) for the differential bias of people engaging in behavior and observers stems from a difference in the nature and extent of the information possessed. In general, the people engaging in behavior know more about their own past behavior and present experiences than do observers. This difference in information may prevent people engaging in behavior from interpreting their behavior in terms of personal characteristics while allowing observers to make such an interpretation. To illustrate,

> if an actor [or actress] insults another person, an observer may be free to infer that the actor [or actress] did so because the actor [or actress] is hostile. The actor [or actress], however, may know that he [or she] rarely insults others and may believe that his [or her] insult was a response to the most recent in a series of provocations from the person he [or she] finally attacked. The difference in information available to the actor [or actress] and observer is, of course, reduced when the actor [or actress] and observer know one another well but is always present to a degree. (Nisbett et al., 1973, p. 155)

It is important, therefore, to keep in mind when we are trying to make sense of strangers' behavior that the information we have about them is incomplete.

When we communicate with strangers, there is an increased likelihood that we will attribute the cause of their behavior to particular characteristics, namely, their cultural backgrounds or group memberships. Stated differently, we are not likely to attribute the cause of strangers' behavior to their cultures if they come from the same culture we do, but since strangers often come from other cultures or ethnic groups, their origins or backgrounds are plausible explanations for their behavior.

We begin our discussion of making sense of strangers' behavior by looking at the individual attribution process. Following this, we look at the social nature of attributions and the attribution errors we make in communicating with strangers.

Individual Attributions

Heider (1958) believes that we act as naive or intuitive scientists when we are trying to make sense of the world. He suggests that we are motivated by practical concerns such as our need to simplify and comprehend our environment and to predict others' behavior. To meet these needs, we try to get beneath external appearances to isolate stable underlying processes which he calls dispositional properties. Heider contends that others' motives are the dispositions we use most frequently in giving meaning to our experiences with them (e.g., children perform well in school because they are motivated to study hard). He also points out that it is not our experiences per se but our interpretations of our experiences that constitute our reality.

Kelley (1967) argues that when we are observing strangers' behavior we attempt to make attributions about the effect of the environment on their behavior by ruling out other explanations for the behavior. We use a covariation principle to assess the degree to which strangers' behavior occurs in the presence and absence of the various causes. The analysis of covariation is based on several principles. The *principle of consistency* deals with the extent to which others' behavior occurs across time and location, given the same stimulus. In other words, do others interact the same way with us in different situations and on different days? The *distinctiveness principle* involves the extent to which different objects bring about the same behavior. Do others, for example, behave the same way toward us and toward our best friends? The *consensus principle* deals with the degree to which people other than the person involved engage in the same behavior. To illustrate, do Person A and Person B behave the same way toward us?

It may appear that the attributional process takes a long time. In actuality, we go through this analysis very quickly when we have complete information. Kelley's principles of covariation explain our attributions when we have complete information, but they may not describe our everyday interactions when we do not have complete information. Kelley (1972) argues that in the presence of incomplete data, we infer meaning by using implicit theories, or preconceptions, we have about how specific causes are associated with specific effects. Our causal schemata permit "economical and fast attributional analysis, by providing a framework within which bits and pieces of information can be fitted in order to draw reasonably good inferences" (p. 152).

Social Attributions

Heider's (1958) and Kelley's (1967) explanations of the individual attribution process do not take into account that we are members of social groups. It, therefore, is necessary to look at the influence of group memberships on attribution processes. When group memberships are taken into consideration, the processes are called social attributions. *Social attributions* are concerned with how members of one social group explain the behavior of their own members and members of other social groups.

Hewstone and Jaspars (1984) isolate three propositions regarding the social nature of attributions:

1. Attribution is social in origin (e.g., it may be created by, or strengthened through, social interaction, or it may be influenced by social information).
2. Attribution is social in its reference or object (e.g., an attribution may be demanded for the individual characterized as a member of a social group, rather than in purely individual terms; or for a social outcome, rather than any behavior as such).

3. Attribution is social in that it is common to the members of a society or group (e.g., the members of different groups may hold different attributions for the same event). (pp. 379–380, italics omitted)

Hewstone and Jaspars argue that we enhance our social identities when we make social attributions. They also point out that our social attributions usually are based on the social stereotypes we share with other members of our ingroups. Our social attributions, however, also can be based on ethnocentrism.

Most writing on individual and social attributions is based on the assumption that observers know what the behavior they are observing means. This assumption, however, is questionable when we communicate with strangers. Detweiler (1975) points out that

there are unique factors which may yield different attributions interculturally than intraculturally. First, it is important to recognize that attributions are based upon our knowledge of cultural expectations. Hence, it is hypothesized that whether or not the actor [or actress] is from one's own culture or a different culture should have a major impact on the inference process. Second, to the degree that this cultural difference is recognized by the observer, inferences will be limited. (pp. 593–594)

The models proposed by individual attribution theorists, therefore, need modification for intercultural encounters.

In examining the nature of intercultural attributions, Jaspers and Hewstone (1982) conclude:

1. Behavior of members of other groups perceived as out-of-role and unexpected from the perspective of one's own group is more likely to lead to person attribution.
2. Since social categorization in terms of cultural differences is probably very salient in such situations, the person attribution will be associated with the perceived differences in culture.
3. The same behavior which gives rise to person attribution cross-culturally may lead to a situational attribution within a particular group or culture because social categorization does not covary with the behavior, but is constant. (p. 139)

Making attributions about strangers' behavior, therefore, introduces additional ways that we can make inaccurate attributions.

Hewstone and Brown (1986) argue that when we perceive ourselves and strangers in individual terms (our personal identities generate our behavior) or see strangers as atypical members of their groups, we tend to make person-based attributions. Person-based attributions, in turn, lead us to look for personal similarities and differences between us and strangers. When we perceive ourselves and others as members of groups (our social identities generate our behavior), we tend to make category-based attributions. Category-based attributions lead us to look for differences between our ingroups and strangers' outgroups.

The nature of the attributions we make is important and can determine whether our relations with strangers will improve. When members of different groups are working together and fail on their task, members of the ingroup usually blame the outgroup for the failure. Attributions like this do not help improve intergroup relations and can, in fact, have a negative influence. If ingroup members are somehow prevented from blaming the outgroup for the failure, cooperation that results in failure does not result in increased bias toward the outgroup (Worchell & Norwell, 1980).

Errors in Attributions

The attributions we make about strangers' behavior are often inaccurate. Our errors in explaining strangers' behavior occur because there are several biases that affect our attributional processes. We tend to see our own behavior as normal and appropriate (*egocentric bias;* Kelley, 1967). Strangers' behavior that is different from ours, therefore, is not viewed as "normal" or "appropriate."

We have a tendency to overestimate the influence of personal characteristics and underestimate the influence of situational factors when we explain strangers' behavior (*fundamental attribution error;* Ross, 1977). We are most likely to make the fundamental attribution error when we are explaining strangers' behavior that we perceive to be negative. Often when strangers engage in behavior that we perceive to be positive, we explain their behavior as a function of the situation. We tend to think that strangers behave positively because they have to as a result of situational demands. Smith and Bond (1993) argue that the fundamental attribution error is limited to individualistic cultures because members of collectivistic cultures have a situational bias (see below).

When we make the fundamental attribution error, we infer that others' personalities (dispositions) predict their behavior. This is called the *correspondence bias* (Fiske & Taylor, 1984). Krull et al. (1999) report that both individualists and collectivists exhibit the correspondence bias when they use dispositions to explain others' behavior and assume others have a choice about how to behave. Individualists, however, show a greater correspondence bias than collectivists when situational constraints are important (Choi & Nisbett, 1998).

We tend to explain our positive behavior or successes by using our personal characteristics and our negative behavior or failures by using situational factors (*ego-protective bias;* Kelley, 1967). When we act in a positive fashion, we explain it by thinking that we are "good people," but when we do something negative, such as yelling at another person, we do not think we are "bad people." Rather, we think that it was necessary given the situation.

We have a tendency to stop looking for explanations for our own or strangers' behavior once we have found a relevant and reasonable explanation for the behavior (*premature closure;* Taylor & Fiske, 1978). When we communicate on automatic pilot, we do not think about a large number of alternative explanations for our own or strangers' behavior. Rather, we tend to stop searching for explanations when we have found a reasonable one.

We also have a tendency to overemphasize negative information about strangers' behavior (*principle of negativity;* Kanouse & Hanson, 1972). When we try to explain strangers' behavior when communicating on automatic pilot, we tend to focus on those aspects of their behavior we perceive to be negative. We, therefore, often interpret strangers' behavior as more negative than it actually is.

The Ultimate Attribution Error

Pettigrew (1979) proposes that the *ultimate attribution error* is "a systematic patterning of intergroup misattributions shaped in part by prejudice" (p. 464). He points out that our tendency to attribute behavior to dispositional or personal characteristics is enhanced when strangers are perceived to engage in negative behavior. When strangers engage in what is perceived to be positive behavior, in contrast, our tendency is to treat them as "exceptions to the rule," and we discount dispositional explanations for the behavior. We, therefore, attribute the behavior to situational factors.

When our expectations are confirmed by strangers' behavior, we rely on strangers' dispositions associated with our stereotypes of their groups and do not bother to consider other explanations for their behavior (Pyszczynski & Greenberg, 1981). When strangers do not confirm our expectations, we tend to attribute their behavior to external factors (Stephan & Rosenfield, 1982).

The ultimate attribution error is illustrated in a study of perceptions of "shoving" (Duncan, 1976). In this study, students viewed a videotape of one person (either an African American or a European American) shoving another person (either an African American or a European American). European American respondents attribute shoving to dispositional causes (e.g., their ethnicity) when the person doing the shoving is African American, but not when the person is European American. The European Americans also think a shove is more violent when it is administered by an African American than when it is administered by a European American.

With respect to the ultimate attribution error, Pettigrew (1978) concludes that

across-group perceptions are more likely than within-group perceptions to include the following:

1. For acts perceived as antisocial or undesirable, behavior will be attributed to personal, dispositional causes. Often these internal causes will be seen as innate characteristics, and role requirements will be overlooked. ("He shoved the white guy, because blacks are born violent like that.")
2. For acts perceived as prosocial or desirable, behavior will be attributed either: (a) to the situation—with role requirements receiving more attention ("Under the circumstances, what could the cheap Scot do, but pay the check?"); (b) to the motivational, as opposed to innate, dispositional qualities ("Jewish students make better grades, because they try so much harder"); or (c) to the exceptional, even exaggerated "special case" individual who is contrasted with his/her group—what Allport (1954) called "fence-mending" ("She is certainly bright and hardworking—not at all like other Chicanos"). (p. 39, italics omitted)

It is likely that we will make the ultimate attribution error when communicating with strangers on automatic pilot. To reduce the possibility of making this error when making attributions about strangers' behavior, we must be mindful of our interpretations of their behavior.

Cultural Variability in Attribution Processes

Ehrenhaus (1983) argues that the types of attributions people make in individualistic and collectivistic cultures differ. Members of collectivistic cultures are sensitive to situational features and explanations and tend to attribute others' behavior to the context, the situation, or other factors external to individuals. Members of individualistic cultures, in contrast, are sensitive to dispositional characteristics and tend to attribute others' behavior to characteristics internal to individuals (e.g., personalities).

Miller (1984) observes that people in India (collectivistic) make greater reference to contextual factors and less reference to dispositional factors than people in the United States (individualistic) when explaining others' behavior. Similar results emerge in research on attributions about reasons for promotions and demotions in organizations in India and the United States (Smith & Whitehead, 1984) and the use of self-serving biases in dealing with success and failure experiences in Japan and the United States (Kashima & Triandis, 1986). Cha and Nam (1985) also report that U.S. Americans are more likely to make internal attributions than Koreans, and Al-Zohrani and Kaplowitz (1993) note that Saudis make more external attributions for others' behavior than U.S. Americans.

Morris, Menon, and Ames (2001) argue that individualists and collectivists have different implicit theories of agency (i.e., "conceptions of kinds of actors [or actresses], notions of what kinds of entities act intentionally or autonomously," p. 169). Menon et al. (1999), for example, report that Singaporeans are less likely than U.S. Americans to perceive that individuals have autonomy. Ames and Fu (cited by Morris et al., 2001) note that U.S. Americans perceive a wider variety of individual acts to be intentional than the Chinese. Ames et al. (cited by Morris et al., 2001) observe that the Japanese attribute intentionality and obligations to organizations more than U.S. Americans. Collectivists, therefore, tend to view collectivities or groups as having agency more than individualists. Morris et al. contend that individualists' and collectivists' implicit theories of agency are domain-specific (they apply to social objects or mechanical objects).

Forgas and Bond (1985) report that Chinese in Hong Kong differentiate among episodes based on equal/unequal (power distance) and communal/individual (individualism) dimensions. Australians also use equal/unequal to differentiate among episodes, but interpretations placed on the dimension are different from those of the Chinese and consistent with the difference between the two cultures' scores on Hofstede's (1980) power distance dimension of cultural variability.

Misattributions in Communicating with Strangers

To illustrate the misattributions that can occur when we communicate with strangers, consider the following example presented by Triandis (1975, pp. 42–43). The example is drawn from the files of his colleague George Vassiliou, a Greek psychiatrist, and it involves a segment of interaction between a supervisor from the United States and a subordinate from Greece. In the segment, the supervisor wants the employee to participate in decisions (a norm in the United States), while the subordinate expects to be told what to do (a norm in Greece):

Behavior	Attribution
[U.S.] American: How long will it take you to finish this report?	[U.S.] American: I asked him to participate. Greek: His behavior makes no sense. He is the boss. Why doesn't he tell me?
Greek: I do not know. How long should it take?	[U.S.] American: He refuses to take responsibility. Greek: I asked him for an order.
[U.S.] American: You are in the best position to analyze time requirements.	[U.S.] American: I press him to take responsibility for his own actions. Greek: What nonsense! I better give him an answer.
Greek: 10 days.	[U.S.] American: He lacks the ability to estimate time; this estimate is totally inadequate.
[U.S.] American: Take 15. It is agreed you willdo it in 15 days?	[U.S.] American: I offer a contract. Greek: These are my orders. 15 days.

In fact the report needed 30 days of regular work. So the Greek worked day and night, but at the end of the 15th day, he still needed one more day's work.

[U.S.] American: Where is my report?	[U.S.] American: I am making sure he fulfills his contract. Greek: He is asking for the report.
Greek: It will be ready tomorrow.	(Both attribute that it is not ready.)
[U.S.] American: But we agreed that it would be ready today.	[U.S.] American: I must teach him to fulfill a contract. Greek: The stupid, incompetent boss! Not only did he give me wrong orders, but he does not appreciate that I did a 30-day job in 16 days.
The Greek hands in his resignation.	The [U.S.] American is surprised. Greek: I can't work for such a man.

Clearly, the attributions the Greek and the U.S. American make for each other's behavior are incorrect. This leads to misunderstandings.

Triandis (1975) points out that if U.S. Americans do not understand Greeks' distinction between ingroup and outgroup, they cannot understand their politeness behavior:

Some [U.S.] Americans find Greeks extremely rude. They come to this conclusion from observations of Greeks in public settings—subways, buses, streets. They fail to recognize that Greeks have two sets of social behaviors; one set is used with their ingroup, and another with their outgroup. In an ingroup, which a Greek defines as "family and friends and other people who are concerned with my welfare," Greeks are extremely polite. In outgroups they are rude. If the sample of behavior to which a foreigner has access is limited to outgroup social behavior, he [or she] will mistakenly assume that all Greek social behavior is rude. This will, of course, have consequences for his [or her] own social behavior. Once he [or she] assumes that the other person is rude, he [or she] is likely to behave in a rude way toward him [or her], which will elicit rude behavior, thus confirming his [or her] perceptions. (p. 67)

Not understanding the ingroup-outgroup distinction in Greece leads U.S. Americans to make mistattributions about Greeks' behavior.

Another example of how differences in individualism-collectivism can lead to misunderstanding involves how face is negotiated. Face involves our public self-images (Ting-Toomey, 1988; face is discussed in detail in Chapter 11). Face can be based on our need for inclusion or our need for autonomy. Further, we can have a concern for our own face or a concern for others' face. Problems in communication may occur when there is a difference in interpretation of the face-concern being used. In collectivistic cultures, the concern for face is predominately other-oriented. In individualistic cultures, the concern is self-oriented. Misunderstandings may occur when individualists fail to give face to collectivists when they interact.

The issue of giving face, especially to people with higher status, is important in collectivistic cultures. When people from individualistic cultures violate this expectation, it can have major consequences for their relationships. Brislin et al. (1986) present an example of this in the context of business negotiations between individuals in Japan and the United States:

> Phil Downing . . . was involved in the setting up of a branch of his company that was merging with an existing Japanese counterpart. He seemed to get along very well with the executive colleagues assigned to work with him, one of whom had recently been elected chairman of the board when his grandfather retired. Over several weeks' discussion, they had generally laid out some working policies and agreed on strategies that would bring new directions needed for development. Several days later . . . the young chairman's grandfather happened to drop in. He began to comment on how the company had been formed and had been built up by the traditional practices, talking about some of the policies the young executives had recently discarded. Phil expected the new chairman to explain some of the new innovative and developmental policies they had both agreed upon. However, the young man said nothing; instead, he just nodded and agreed with his grandfather. Phil was bewildered and frustrated . . . and he started to protest. The atmosphere in the room became immediately tense. . . . A week later the Japanese company withdrew from the negotiations. (pp. 155–156)

The young chairman of the Japanese company was giving his grandfather face by agreeing with him. This did not, however, negate any of the negotiations he had with Phil. Phil obviously did not understand this. By protesting and disagreeing with the grandfather, Phil not only failed to give face to the grandfather, he threatened the grandfather's face.

Face issues also can lead to misunderstanding in interethnic encounters in the United States. In the European American, middle-class subculture, for example, refusing to comply with a directive given by a superior is considered a face-threatening act. In the African American subculture, however, "stylin" includes refusing to comply as part of a verbal game. This can be a problem when European American teachers interact with black students and neither party understands the other's communication style:

> The [European American] teachers, not realizing the play argument was a salient speech event in the children's speech community, took literally the child's refusal to comply, often

> with disastrous results for the child's reputation. Such children can be seen as recalcitrant and possibly emotionally disturbed [by European American teachers]. (Erickson, 1981, pp. 6–7)

Not understanding the communication rules strangers use often leads to misattributions for their behavior.

As indicated in Chapter 3, Hall (1976) sees interpersonal bonds in individualistic cultures as fragile and notes that people in these cultures move away or withdraw with relative ease if relationships are not developing satisfactorily. The bonds between people in a collectivistic culture, in contrast, are strong, and thus there is a tendency to allow for considerable bending of individual interests for the sake of ingroup relationships.

Not understanding the role of context in individualistic and collectivistic cultures also can lead to inaccurate interpretations of strangers' behavior. One area where misunderstandings may occur in communication between members of individualistic and collectivistic cultures is in the directness of speech used. As indicated in Chapter 3, members of individualistic cultures tend to use a direct style of speech. Members of collectivistic cultures, in contrast, tend to use an indirect style of speech. The problems when people from individualistic and collectivistic cultures interact is illustrated in Tannen's (1979) study of Greek–U.S. American communication. Tannen (1979) notes that Greeks tend to employ an indirect style of speech and interpret others' behavior on the basis of the assumption that they are using the same style. U.S. Americans, in contrast, use a direct style of speech and assume others are using the same style. Tannen observes that when Greeks and U.S. Americans communicate, there often are misunderstandings due to these differences in style of speech. She goes on to point out that overcoming misunderstandings due to direct-indirect style differences is difficult because "in seeking to clarify, each speaker continues to use the very strategy which confused the other in the first place" (p. 5). To resolve the misunderstandings, obviously one of the people involved must recognize that the differences in styles are creating the problem, try to interpret the other person's messages accurately, and then shift her or his style of speech.

Tannen observes that when Greeks and U.S. Americans communicate, there often are misunderstandings due to differences in style of speech. Tannen (1975) reports a conversation between a husband (nonnative speaker [NNS] of English who learned indirect rules) and a wife (native speaker [NS] using direct communication styles) that illustrates these differences:

> *NS (wife):* Bob's having a party. Wanna go?
> *NNS (husband):* OK
> *NS:* (later) Are you sure you wanna go?
> *NNS:* OK, let's not go. I'm tired anyway.

In this conversation, the husband interpreted the wife's questions as an indirect indication that she did not want to go.

Misattributions also result from the way people in individualistic and collectivistic cultures try to reduce uncertainty, particularly in initial interactions with strangers. To illustrate, consider how uncertainty is reduced in the United States and in Japan. In the European American, middle-class subculture in the United States, people try to obtain information about others' attitudes, feelings, and beliefs to reduce uncertainty.

In Japan, in contrast, people must know others' status and background in order to reduce uncertainty and know which version of the language to use (there are different ways to speak to superiors, equals, and inferiors). This leads Japanese to introduce themselves by saying things like " 'I belong to Mitsubishi Bank.' and immediately asking . . . 'What is your job?' 'How old are you?' and 'What is the name of your company?' " (Loveday, 1982, pp. 4–5). These questions are designed to gather the information necessary for a Japanese to communicate with strangers. They are perceived, however, as "rude" and "nosey" by U.S. Americans.

COGNITIVE STYLES

Cognitive style refers to the ways in which we structure our beliefs and attitudes about the world and the way we respond to incoming messages (Miller & Steinberg, 1975). In this section, we focus on four cognitive styles which have a major influence on the way we perceive incoming messages from strangers and make attributions about strangers' behavior: field-independence/field-dependence, category width, uncertainty orientation, and cognitive complexity.

Field-Independence and Field-Dependence

Field-dependence and *field-independence* refer to how we rely on visual or other information in making judgments (Witkin et al., 1962). Jahoda (1980) describes the salient features of field-independent individuals:

> Field-independent people have a higher ability to extract a constituent part than field-dependent people who find it difficult to break up such an organized whole analytically. Similarly, in the intellectual sphere, relatively field-independent people display greater skill in solving the particular type of problem which requires isolating certain elements from their context and making use of it in a different context [than field-dependent people]. It was also originally suggested that field-dependent individuals were more sensitive to the prevailing social field and therefore more likely to respond to social cues or conform to social pressures [than field-independent people]. (p. 100)

There is a clear linkage between these characteristics of the field-dependent and field-independent cognitive styles and high-context and low-context communication patterns. The field-dependent cognitive style corresponds closely to the perceptual mode of the high-context communication style, while the field-independent cognitive style is related closely to the perceptual pattern of the low-context communication style.

There appear to be cultural variations in field-independence and field-dependence. Witkin and Berry (1975) conclude that the evidence

> suggests that a relatively field-dependent cognitive style, and other characteristics of limited differentiation, are likely to be prevalent in social settings characterized by insistence on adherence to authority both in society and in the family, by the use of strict or even harsh socialization practices to enforce this conformance, and by tight social organizations. In contrast, a relatively field-independent cognitive style and greater differentiation are likely to be prevalent in social settings that are more encouraging of autonomous functioning, which are more lenient in their childrearing practices, and which are loose in social organization. (p. 46)

This analysis suggests that field-dependence should predominate in high power distance cultures, and field-independence in low power distance cultures (Gudykunst & Ting-Toomey, 1988).

Category Width

Category width "refers to the range of instances included in a cognitive category" (Pettigrew, 1982, p. 200). To illustrate, is a pane of glass in the wall that is 1 inch wide and 12 feet high a window? A narrow categorizer probably would say no, but a wide categorizer probably would say yes. Wide categorizers have more latitude than narrow categorizers in what they include in categories.

Detweiler (1978) summarizes the differences in narrow and wide categorizing, pointing out that category width

> is a term used to describe the amount of discrepancy tolerable among category members—how similar do things have to be to be called by the same name? A narrow categorizer might put only highly similar things in the same category, whereas a broad [or wide] categorizer might put more discrepant things in the same category. (p. 263)

Pettigrew (1982) suggests that individual differences in category width are related to more general information-processing strategies people use. Wide categorizers, for example, tend to perform better than narrow categorizers on tasks that require holistic, integrated information processing. Narrow categorizers, in comparison, tend to perform better than wide categorizers on tasks that require detailed, analytic information processing.

There are several other differences between narrow and wide categorizers that are worth noting. Rokeach (1951), for example, observes that wide categorizers include concepts like Buddhism, capitalism, Christianity, democracy, Judaism, and socialism in the same category (e.g., beliefs or doctrines), but that narrow categorizers do not. Rokeach also reports that narrow categorizers are more ethnocentric than wide categorizers. Narrow categorizers "react more to change, seek less prior information, and are more confident of their performances" than wide categorizers (Pettigrew, 1982, p. 207).

Detweiler (1975) demonstrates that category width influences the attributions European Americans make about people who are culturally similar (another European American) or culturally dissimilar (a person from Haiti) who engage in either positive or negative behavior. He indicates that narrow categorizers

> assume that the effects of behavior of a person from another culture tell all about the person, even though he [or she] in fact knows nothing about the actor's [or actress'] cultural background. He [or she] seems to make strong judgments based on the positivity or negativity of the effects of the behavior as evaluated from his [or her] own cultural viewpoint. Contrarily, when making attributions to a person who is culturally similar, the narrow [categorizer] seems to view the similarity as overshadowing the behavior. Thus, positive effects are seen as intended, and negative effects are confidently seen as unintended. (p. 600)

These findings suggest that narrow categorizers may have trouble making accurate attributions about messages from both people who are culturally similar and people who are culturally dissimilar.

Wide categorizers have a very different orientation. When making attributions about a culturally dissimilar person, a wide categorizer

> seems to assume that he [or she] in fact doesn't know enough to make "usual" attributions. Thus, behaviors with negative effect result in less confident and generally more neutral attributions when judgments are made about a person from a different culture. Conversely, the culturally similar person who causes a negative outcome is rated relatively more negatively with greater confidence by the wide [categorizer], since the behavior from one's own cultural background is meaningful. (Detweiler, 1975, p. 600)

Wide categorizers, therefore, are more likely than narrow categorizers to search for appropriate interpretations of strangers' behavior.

Uncertainty Orientation

Another cognitive style that influences our perceptions of strangers and our decoding of their messages is our orientation toward uncertainty. Sorrentino and Short (1986) point out

> that there are many people who simply are not interested in finding out information about themselves or the world, who do not conduct causal searches, who could not care less about comparing themselves with others, and who "don't give a hoot" for resolving discrepancies or inconsistencies about the self. Indeed, such people (we call them certainty oriented) will go out of their way not to perform activities such as these (we call people who *do* go out of their way to do such things uncertainty oriented). (pp. 379–380)

These differences influence how we think about ourselves and how we try to make sense of strangers' behavior.

Uncertainty-oriented people integrate new and old ideas and change their belief systems accordingly (Sorrentino & Short, 1986). They evaluate ideas and thoughts on their own merits and do not necessarily compare them with others. Uncertainty-oriented people want to understand themselves and their environment. Certainty-oriented people, in contrast, like to hold on to traditional beliefs and have a tendency to reject ideas that are different. Certainty-oriented people maintain a sense of self by not examining themselves or their behavior.

Uncertainty-oriented people tend to recall positive and negative events that occur in their interactions with strangers in unbiased and accurate ways. Certainty-oriented people, in contrast, tend to distort their recall of things that happened in ways that are consistent with their stereotypes of strangers' groups (Huber & Sorrentino, 1996). Certainty-oriented people also "are more likely to think in terms of categories or stereotypes and see greater differentiation between categories" than uncertainty-oriented people (p. 607).

When we communicate on automatic pilot, we tend to be certainty-oriented or uncertainty-oriented. For those of us who tend to be certainty-oriented, it is important to keep in mind that we can choose to be more uncertainty-oriented when we are mindful of our communication.

Cognitive Complexity

The complexity of our cognitive systems also affects the way we perceive strangers and interpret their messages (Applegate & Sypher, 1983). We use constructs to differentiate strangers when we communicate (Kelly, 1955). *Constructs* are perceptual categories used to organize our thoughts. A panhandler, for example, might use the construct looks generous–does not look generous in deciding who to approach to ask for money. When communicating with strangers, we might use constructs such as similar-dissimilar, empathic–not empathic, extroverted-introverted, honest-dishonest, trustworthy–not trustworthy, and so forth, in trying to understand their behavior. Cognitively complex people use more constructs to understand strangers than cognitively simple people.

It is not just the complexity of our cognitive system, however, that is important to how we communicate. The quality of the constructs we use in understanding strangers also is important (Clark & Delia, 1977). Determining quality is based on the relevance of the constructs to the situation in which we use them. If, for example, we are trying to improve the effectiveness of our communication with strangers, assessing whether they are generous–not generous will not be very useful, and, therefore, the quality of our contrasts will be low. Assessing the degree to which strangers are trustworthy–not trustworthy, in contrast, will be useful in improving the quality of our communication because this construct is directly related to communication.

Werner (1957) argues that "whenever development occurs it proceeds from a state of relative globality and lack of differentiation to a state of increasing differentiation, artic-ulation, and hierarchic integration" (p. 126). The more differentiations we make in an area, the more complex our cognitive systems. If we make a large number of differentia-tions, we are said to be cognitively complex; if we make only a few, cognitively simple.

Cognitively complex people form impressions of strangers that are more extensive and differentiated, and better represent the behavioral variability of strangers than cogni-tively simple people (O'Keefe & Sypher, 1981). Honess (1976) also points out that cognitively complex people seek out unique features of their environments more than cognitively simple people. Cognitively simple people tend to seek information that is con-sistent with their prior beliefs. Given these differences, it is argued that the more complex our cognitive systems, the more effective our communication (Wiseman & Abe, 1986).

In applying the concept of cognitive complexity to intercultural interactions, David-son (1975) argues that

> the relation between complexity and cross-cultural effectiveness is assumed to exist because a cognitively simple person has a single framework within which to evaluate the observed behavior of others in the target culture. Thus, when a behavior which he [or she] does not understand takes place, he [or she] is likely to evaluate it ethnocentrically. A complex per-son, on the other hand, has several frameworks for the perception of the same behavior. He [or she] might, for example, suspend judgment and obtain more information before evaluat-ing the behavior. (p. 80)

Detweiler's (1980) research supports this speculation.

Gudykunst (1995) argues that cognitive complexity is related directly to the man-agement of uncertainty and anxiety when communicating with strangers. He argues that the more complex our cognitions are, the greater our ability to manage our uncertainty and anxiety. It is important to keep in mind that if we tend to be cognitively simple when communicating on automatic pilot, we can choose to process information in a complex fashion when we are mindful of our communication.

PATTERNS OF THOUGHT

The way people in a culture think influences the way they interpret strangers' messages. In this section, we examine three aspects of our patterns of thought: world views, systems of logic, and systems of reasoning. These three aspects of patterns of thought are interrelated highly and are separated here only to organize our discussion.

World View

Kraft (1978) argues that "every social group has a world view—a set of more or less systematized beliefs and values in terms of which the group evaluates and attaches meaning to the reality that surrounds it" (p. 407). Kraft points out that the existence of a world view (*Weltanschauung* in the original German) is observed in every known group, but members of different groups vary in the degree to which they can articulate their world views. People have a difficult time articulating their world views mainly because they are learned as part of the socialization process and tend to be unconscious. World views are accepted without questioning as "the way things are."

Kraft (1978) argues that a world view serves five important functions for the people of a culture. First, a world view performs an explanatory function for the members of a culture; it provides "explanations of how and why things got to be as they are and why they continue that way" (p. 408). Second, a world view performs an evaluational and validating function; that is, it provides the criteria for evaluating and validating the ends and means of the group. The third function a world view performs is psychological reinforcement. A world view provides ways for people to gain reinforcement for their beliefs in times of anxiety and crisis. This reinforcement may take the form of rituals in which the people participate or of individual activities which reinforce basic beliefs. Fourth, a world view performs an integrating function. "It systematizes and orders for them their perceptions of reality into an overall design" (p. 410). Finally, a world view provides an adaptational function for members of a culture. In times of social change a world view gives people the means to adapt to the change that is taking place.

One way to illustrate differences in world views is to compare collectivistic and individualistic world views. Wei (1980) compares world views by looking at two specific dimensions: (1) cosmic patterns or ways of perceiving the world (Kraft's integrating function) and (2) philosophy of history (Kraft's explanatory function).

In individualistic cultures, people see the cosmos as created and controlled by a divine power. Since the cosmos is controlled by a supernatural power, there are laws of nature that must be followed. The view in collectivistic cultures, in contrast, is one of a "harmoniously functioning organism consisting of an orderly hierarchy of interrelated parts and forces which, though unequal in their status, are equally essential for the total process" (Wei, 1980, p. 4). The collectivistic view sees the cosmos as a self-operating system not controlled by an external source. Stemming from these general views of the cosmos are two epistemological questions: (1) What are the nature and source of knowledge? and (2) How do we come to know? In individualistic cultures "the fundamental question is how I can transcend myself to reach the other, either the external inanimated world or people surrounding me? In this question there is a basic dichotomy between the knower and things to be known" (Wei, 1980, p. 5). An example of the collectivistic view is seen in the Chinese orientation: "The Chinese distinguish two kinds of knowledge. The first is to investigate things, to know about the second is to know the illustrious way of the universe—the tao. The first kind of knowledge is one way of achieving the second, which is the true knowledge" (Wei, 1980, p. 8).

There also are differences between individualistic and collectivistic cultures with respect to the second aspect of world view: philosophy of history. The issue here is the meaning of history and the influence of specific events on history as a whole. In individualistic cultures, history is seen mainly as a "linear historical pattern toward progress" (Wei, 1980, p. 12). There are two different views: a sacred view stemming from the Judeo-Christian tradition and a secular view stemming from the philosophy of progress originating with Voltaire. In collectivistic cultures, in contrast, people see history as cyclical in nature. The themes of destruction and renovation, for example, are common throughout Buddhist and Hindu writings.

Systems of Logic

Observers of individualistic cultures characterize their predominant mode of thinking as logical, analytic, action mode, and linear. Their most characteristic form is known as scientific induction, which emphasizes concentrated attention on the "raw materials" provided by the senses and the application of rational principles to those raw materials to bring them into a more or less orderly and self-consistent whole. Gulick (1962) describes individualistic thinking as "the effort to make a coherent and verifiable 'world construct,' and to impose man's [or woman's] will on nature and society" (p. 127). Such mental characteristics of individualists have given great impetus to the development of natural science and technology.

An associated characteristic of individualistic cultures, particularly that of the United States, is the tendency to see the world in terms of dichotomies (Stewart, 1972). This characteristic is illustrated by the individualistic tendency to think in terms of good-evil, right-wrong, true-false, and beautiful-ugly. Stewart describes this tendency to polarize as "simplifying the view of the world, predisposing to action and providing individuals with a typical method of evaluating and judging by means of a comparison" (p. 29).

While sharing a great deal of commonality with thinking in individualistic cultures in general, thinking by the people in the United States is distinguishable from that of Europeans by its heavier emphasis on empirical facts, induction, and operationalism. Stewart (1972) comments:

> For [U.S.] Americans, the world is composed of facts—not ideas. Their process of thinking is generally inductive, beginning with facts and then proceeding to ideas. But the movement

from the concrete to the more abstract is seldom a complete success, for [U.S.] Americans have a recurrent need to reaffirm their theories and . . . their ideas require validation by application and by becoming institutionalized. (pp. 22–23)

The operational style of thinking tends to produce a stress on consequences and to result in a disregard for the empirical world as such. What is important is the ability of individuals to affect the empirical world. Such operationally oriented thinking in the United States has led to the prevailing cultural values of pragmatism and functionalism.

Europeans are characterized as attaching primacy to ideas and theories. Their deductive and abstract style of thinking gives priority to the conceptual world. Although the empirical world is not necessarily ignored, it often is treated with a symbolic and demonstrational attitude. Deductive thinkers are likely to have much more confidence in their ideas and theories, and so it suffices for them to show one or two connections between their concepts and the empirical world. They do not feel compelled to amass facts and statistics, as is the way in the United States, and they tend to generalize from one concept to another concept, or to facts, by means of logic. Europeans have faith and trust in the powers of thought, and people in the United States place significance on their methods of empirical observation and measurement (Stewart, 1972). Although the cultures of the United States and Western Europe are in some respects dissimilar, they share certain basic characteristics of field-independent, individualistic cultures. Even though the relative significance placed on empirical observation and verification and on the deductive and the inductive processes of deriving knowledge differs between the two cultural groups, both emphasize a fundamental cognitive pattern that is "logical", "categorical", "linear", and "analytic".

Compared with those of individualistic cultures, the thinking patterns used in collectivistic cultures are characterized as "relational," "integrative," "holistic," and "intuitive." Asians, for example, have a central mode of thinking that is not concerned as much with logic and analysis as it is with intuitive "knowing" and meditative introspection and contemplation. Asians tend to emphasize the unity between the subjective and the objective realms of the inner and the outer conditions and thus engage less in analyzing a topic divisively by breaking it down into smaller units as U.S. Americans often do. What seems to be of central importance in Asian thinking is a certain repose of the personality in which it "feels" it is "grasping" the inner significance of the object of contemplation. The direct sense of rapport with the outer object— whether a person, idea, or thing—is the primary end result of Asian thinking (Gulick, 1962, p. 127).

The intuitive thinking of collectivists tends to deemphasize the power of analysis, classification, precision, and abstraction, and the result is perhaps not as effective in attaining accurate "facts" about the object. Intuitive thinking, in contrast, allows holistic and intimate identification with all the contextual cues in a communication transaction, thus making the perceptual patterns of collectivists highly contextual. The intuitive style of thinking provides a powerful cognitive mechanism for developing a harmonious rapport with the other person and the environment. This mechanism enables collectivists to be sensitive to the most subtle undercurrents of emotion and mood in a particular communication event and interpersonal relationship without having to engage in a deliberate attempt to analyze the situation logically.

Okabe (1983) illustrates the differences between collectivistic and individualistic logic by comparing Japan and the United States:

[U.S.] American logic and rhetoric value "step-by-step," "chain-like" organization, as frequently observed in the "problem-solution" pattern or in the "cause-to-effect" or "effect-to-cause" pattern of organization. . . . By contrast, Japanese logic and rhetoric emphasize the importance of a "dotted," "point-like" method of structuring a discourse. No sense of rigidity . . . is required in the Japanese-speaking society, where there is instead a sense of leisurely throwing a ball back and forth and carefully observing each other's response. (pp. 29–30)

He goes on to point out that U.S. Americans rely on facts, figures, and quotations to support their arguments, while Japanese use more subjective and ambiguous forms of support.

Heimann (1964) compares logic in the United States and India. She argues that these differences are illustrated by comparing two Greek and Sanskrit terms:

the Greek term *heteros* means literally "the other." As such it gains with Aristotle the meaning of "the worse," "the lesser." Western logic clings to the established order and is reluctant to accept the vague otherness. The Sanskrit equivalent is *para*. It, too, means the "other" but as such the "higher and better." It is here where the fundamental difference between western and Indian logic and its ethical implications lies. The thing in hand, while being clearly observable and distinct, is of definite value for the Westerner. The "other" for him [or her] is thus something disquietingly vague, while the "other" is of positive value for the Indian because of its very vagueness. (p. 149)

These observations are consistent with the differences in low- and high-context communication discussed in Chapter 3.

Ornstein (1972) suggests a possible physiological explanation for the observed perceptual and cognitive variations across cultures. He believes the two cerebral hemispheres of the human brain process different kinds of information and that the operating characteristics of the two differ. The left hemisphere is involved predominantly with analytic, logical thinking, speech, and mathematical functions. Its mode of operation is primarily linear; it seems to process information sequentially. The right hemisphere is more holistic, direct, and relational in its mode of operation. It is responsible for orientation in space, intuition, and imagination and is able to integrate information in a nonlinear, diffused fashion. In normal people, of course, the two hemispheres operate interdependently, integrating both sides of the brain. The differential emphasis in the specialized hemispheric functions, however, appears to correspond very closely to the variations in the patterns of information processing in collectivistic and individualistic cultures.

The cultural variations in thinking isolated here do not mean individualists think using only logic and reason and collectivists think using only intuition. The differences discussed involve the *relative* emphasis that members of different cultures place on particular methods of thinking rather than absolute differences in kind. While collectivists do think and reason as well as use their intuitive mode of seeing things without logical analysis, the significance of knowledge through intuition is accepted and valued more extensively in collectivistic cultures than in individualistic cultures. Similarly, individualistic thinking involves intuitive processes, but individualists tend to deemphasize the importance of such awareness through intuition and to value instead the outcome of logical, analytic thinking processes.

Patterns of Reasoning

Glenn (1981) isolates two dimensions that can be used to describe patterns of reasoning across cultures: abstractive-associative and universalism-particularism. When knowledge is acquired through direct experience with the environment, it is associative. When thought is codified into precise meanings, abstraction takes place. Associative patterns are diffuse, indefinite, and rigid, while abstract patterns tend to be articulated, definite, and flexible. Glenn points out that

> associative reasoning is marked by "arbitrary" ties between informational units. Abstractive reasoning is marked by (1) the definition of information that is relevant to a given situation, and (2) the definition of the relationship between informational units. . . . The primary process for the acquisition of knowledge appears to be associative. Abstraction appears as the primary process of the organization of knowledge. (p. 57)

The use of associative thought does not readily allow new or novel information to be integrated. Triandis (1984) argues that associative patterns of information processing depend on oral, face-to-face communication and that those who depend on these patterns find it difficult to follow written instructions (which require abstraction).

Associative and abstract thought exist in all cultures, but one tends to predominate. An emphasis on associative thought is related to determining identity from ascription, and an emphasis on abstraction is related to deriving identity from achievement because achievement requires the use of abstraction (Gudykunst & Ting-Toomey, 1988).

Universalism involves seeing the world through conceptualizations that are reflected in definitions of words. Universalistic processing does not take into consideration experiences that make individuals different; it is abstract. Particularization, in contrast, recognizes specifics; it tends to be associative (Glenn, 1981). Particularistic information processing starts with specific observations and extracts generalizations, while universalistic processing begins with broad categories and determines how observations fit the categories. These tendencies correspond to inductive and deductive processes, respectively. Triandis (1984) points out that particularistic thought tends to be probabilistic and universalistic thought tends to be absolutistic. It appears that universalistic patterns of thought dominate in cultures high in uncertainty avoidance, while particularistic patterns of thought dominate in cultures low in uncertainty avoidance (Gudykunst & Ting-Toomey, 1988).

SUMMARY

In this chapter, we examined some of the factors that influence our interpretation of messages when we communicate with strangers. Perception involves our awareness of what is taking place in the environment. There are three critical aspects of perceptions that influence our communication with strangers. First, our perceptions are a function of the specific people and the specific environment in which our communication takes place. Second, our perceptions involve categorization. When we perceive people and objects while communicating on automatic pilot, we unconsciously put them in categories. Third, rigid categories inhibit effective communication. To the extent that our categories are rigid, we are unable to see individual characteristics of the people with whom we are communicating and our communication, therefore, will not be as effective as it could be.

The attributions we make about strangers' behavior are social in nature. When we communicate with strangers, we tend to overemphasize the importance of group memberships in explaining their behavior.

The way we interpret incoming messages from strangers is, in part, a function of our cognitive styles. The degree to which we are field-dependent or field-independent, the degree to which we are wide or narrow categorizers, the degree to which we are certainty- or uncertainty-oriented, and the degree to which we are cognitively simple or complex all influence the way we decode messages from strangers.

The way we interpret messages from strangers also is affected by the predominate patterns of thought in our culture. Whether we use chain-like or dot-like logic influences the way we draw inferences about the meaning of strangers' behavior.

STUDY QUESTIONS

1. Why are our perceptions biased?
2. What is the role of categorization in the perception process?
3. How do rigid categories inhibit effective communication?
4. How are individual and social attributions different?
5. What are the major errors that occur when we try to make sense of strangers' behavior?
6. What is the ultimate attribution error?
7. How do attributions differ in individualistic and collectivistic cultures?
8. How do differences in individualism and collectivism lead to misattributions?
9. How does category width influence our communication with strangers?
10. Why are cognitively complex people more effective than cognitively simple people?
11. How does uncertainty orientation influence our communication with strangers?
12. How are systems of logic different in individualistic and collectivistic cultures?
13. How does our pattern of reasoning influence our communication with strangers?

SUGGESTED READING

Bruner, J. (1986). *Actual minds, possible worlds.* Cambridge, MA: Harvard University Press.
DeBono, E. (1991). *I am right you are wrong: From rock logic to water logic.* New York: Viking.
Glenn, E. (1981). *Man and mankind.* Norwood, NJ: Ablex.
Kearney, M. (1984). *World view.* Novato, CA: Chandler & Sharp.
Zerubavel, E. (1991). *The fine line: Making distinctions in everyday life.* New York: Free Press.

8

VERBAL MESSAGES

Those who know do not talk.
Those who talk do not know.

Lao Tsu

Every culture has a language with which people are able to communicate with one another. The specific languages we speak are learned in our cultures and reflect our cultures. Over time, changes in our languages change our cultures and changes in our cultures lead to changes in our languages. We learn our languages as we are socialized into our cultures. The particular languages we learn exert powerful influences on how we interpret messages and our interactions with others. By specifying or highlighting what in the environment is relevant or irrelevant, the languages we speak influence the nature of our experiences.

Language and culture are so intertwined that Agar (1994) suggests that we use the term "languaculture" rather than treat language and culture separately (see Pinkey, 1994, for an alternative perspective). In this chapter, however, we separate the two and look at the role of language in our communication with strangers. We begin by looking at the nature of language. Next, we examine the factors that influence cross-cultural variations in language usage. Following this, we look at cultural variations in verbal messages (e.g., direct versus indirect messages, elaborated versus understated messages). We conclude by discussing our use of language when we communicate with strangers. In that section, we discuss dialects, ethnolinguistic vitality, code-switching, second language competence, and communication accommodation.

THE NATURE OF LANGUAGE

All human languages contain elements that are universal and elements that are unique. Languages are all rule-governed. There are *phonological rules* that tell us how the sounds of our languages are combined to form words. *Grammatical rules* tell us how to order words (e.g., nouns, objects, verbs) to form sentences. *Semantic rules* tell us the relationship between words and the things to which they refer. *Pragmatic rules* tell us how to interpret the meaning of utterances. The rules of languages are a function of the speech communities using the languages. *Speech communities* are groups of people who use similar rules to guide how they use language and interpret others' use of language (Hymes, 1974).

Within speech communities, there are *speech situations,* occasions when we speak to each other (Hymes, 1974). Different speech situations (e.g., parties, classes, job interviews) are characterized by different types of speech. Speech situations are composed of *speech events,* activities which have rules governing the use of our speech (e.g., getting-to-know-you conversations, formal speeches). The same speech event can take place in different speech situations (e.g., getting-to-know-you conversations take place at parties, at sporting events, in offices). Speech events are composed of speech acts. *Speech acts* involve uttering identifiable words that are perceived as coherent to members of our speech communities.

The languages spoken in speech communities serve at least three functions. First, the *informative* function of language is to provide others with information or knowledge. Second, the *expressive* function of language is to tell others our attitudes, feelings, and emotions. Third, the *directive* function of language is used to direct others (e.g., causing or preventing some action).

There are several characteristics of language important to understanding its role in communication (Hockett, 1958). First, the elements of languages can be combined in new meaningful utterances *(productivity).* Second, languages exhibit *discreteness* because we are able to perceive different sounds as discrete from one another. Third, languages are *self reflexive,* or can be used to refer to themselves. Fourth, languages can be used to refer to things that are not present *(displacement).* Fifth, languages are *arbitrary.* Words are symbols, and, therefore, there is not a direct connection between the words and the things they represent (see the discussion of symbols and meanings in Chapter 1).

CULTURAL VARIATIONS IN LANGUAGE USAGE

When we communicate with strangers from other linguistic or cultural groups, the degree of shared meaning is likely to be small, particularly when the differences between our two languages are large. English speakers, for example, have fewer commonalities with Chinese speakers than with German speakers. The similarity of our languages influences the degree to which we perceive the world in similar ways. One reason for this is that our languages influence the way we think. This is the basis for the Sapir-Whorf hypothesis.

The Sapir-Whorf Hypothesis

Drawing on the work of Sapir (1925), Whorf (1956) theorizes that languages are not merely instruments for expressing ideas; rather, they are shapers of ideas (see Gumperz & Levinson, 1996, for discussions of linguistic relativity). Whorf argues that languages play prominent roles in molding the perceptual world of the people who use them. He argues that

> we dissect nature along lines laid down by our native languages. The categories and types that we isolate from the world of phenomena we do not find there. On the contrary, the world is presented in a kaleidoscopic flux of impressions which has to be organized by our minds and this means largely by the linguistic systems in our mind. (Whorf, 1952, p. 5)

This view of the relationship between language and culture is commonly known as the Sapir-Whorf hypothesis.

Whorf (1956) concentrates on the structural differences between the Hopi language and European languages. In his analysis of plurality, for example, Whorf notes that English uses plural forms for both cyclic nouns (nouns that refer to days, years, or other units of time) and aggregate nouns (nouns that have a physical referent, such as apples). The Hopi, in contrast, do not use cyclic nouns in the same way they use aggregate nouns. In the Hopi language, cycles do not have plurals; they have duration. Thus the Hopi equivalent for the English "he stayed ten days" is "he stayed until the eleventh day." Further, the Hopi language does not possess tenses, which in most European languages place time in a sequence of distinct units of past, present, and future. English speakers express events happening in the present in one of two constructions, for example, "she runs" or "he is running." Hopi speakers can select from a much wider variety of present tenses, which depend on their knowledge or lack of knowledge concerning the validity of the statements being made; for instance, "I know that he [or she] is running at this very moment," "I know that he [or she] is running at this moment even though I cannot see him [or her]," "I am told that he [or she] is running," and so on (Farb, 1979, p. 445).

Another illustration of the role of language in the way people think about the world is how bilinguals answer questions asked in Japanese and English differently. Ervin-Tripp (1964), for example, reports responses to the same questions on different days in Japanese and English to Japanese women who are bilingual. One woman's responses are as follows:

1. WHEN MY WISHES CONFLICT WITH MY FAMILY . . .
   (Japanese) it is a time of great unhappiness.
   (English) I do what I want.
2. I WILL PROBABLY BECOME . . .
   (Japanese) a housewife.
   (English) a teacher.
3. REAL FRIENDS SHOULD . . .
   (Japanese) help each other.
   (English) be very frank. (p. 96)

These responses clearly indicate that different approaches to the world emerge when Japanese bilinguals think in Japanese and English. It should be noted, however, that Japanese world views do not disappear when Japanese speak in English. Beebe and Takahashi (1989), for example, argue that many Japanese perform face-threatening acts (e.g., threats to individuals' projected images; see Chapter 11) in a Japanese fashion in English.

The Sapir-Whorf hypothesis is accepted enthusiastically by some scholars and attacked by others. The weakness of the hypothesis lies in the impossibility of generalizing about entire cultures and then attributing those generalizations to the languages spoken in them. Farb (1979), for example, argues that the absence of clocks, calendars, and written histories suggests that Hopis have a different view of time than European language speakers, but such an observation is not the same as proving that these cultural differences are caused by the differences between the Hopi language and European languages.

Whorf (1956) does not attempt to draw inferences about the thought world of a people from the simple fact of the presence or absence of specific grammatical categories in a given language. Sapir and Whorf view the cultural significance of linguistic forms on a more submerged level than the overt one of definite cultural patterns. The concepts of time and matter for the Hopi "do not depend so much upon any one system (e.g., tense or nouns) within the grammar as upon the ways of analyzing and reporting experiences which have become fixed in the language as integrated 'fashions of speaking' and which cut across the typical grammatical classifications" (p. 44). Thus the true value of the Sapir-Whorf hypothesis is not in providing a definitive and deterministic relationship between specific linguistic categories and the thought patterns of the people in a cultural system but in articulating the alliance of language, mind, and the culture of the speech community. Clearly, the languages we speak influence, but do not determine, the way we look at the world. Few students of language doubt this interpretation of the hypothesis.

Restricted and Elaborated Codes

Bernstein (1966) provides a theoretical perspective that helps us understand the speech patterns (or verbal behaviors) of individuals in different groups. Bernstein hypothesizes that our speech patterns are necessarily conditioned by our social context. The social context is not only the specific interpersonal relational context in which a dyadic speech interaction occurs but also the broader social structure, such as society and the cultural environment. Bernstein argues that speech emerges in one of two types of codes: restricted and elaborated.

Restricted codes involve message transmission through verbal (word transmission) and nonverbal (intonation, facial features, gestures) channels. Restricted codes rely heavily on the hidden, implicit cues of the social context (such as interpersonal relationships, the physical and psychological environments, and other contextual cues). Bernstein (1966) explains that

> speech is played out against a backdrop of assumptions common to the speakers, against a set of closely shared interests and identifications, against a system of shared expectations; in short, it presupposes a local cultural identity which reduces the need for the speakers to elaborate their intent verbally and to make it explicit. (pp. 433–434)

Restricted codes resemble jargon or "shorthand" speech in which speakers are almost telegraphic. When we are with a close friend, for example, we often find ourselves making only a brief reference to something, yet we are reminded by such a reference of a wealth of experiences or concepts. The question "Kim, how was it?" can be responded to spontaneously by Kim without her having to ask what was meant by "it." An outsider would have difficulty understanding the question because of the lack of shared experiences. Jargon used by a given group also represents a type of restricted code. Code words used by doctors, engineers, prisoners, or street gangs or between family members and close friends are highly implicit in meaning and are known primarily to the members of such groups.

Speakers using elaborated codes employ verbal amplification to communicate, placing relatively little reliance on nonverbal and other contextual cues. New information emerges primarily through nonverbal channels with restricted codes, and the verbal channel is the dominant source of information with elaborated codes. Bernstein (1966) further explains elaborated codes by contrasting them to restricted codes:

> Speakers using a restricted code are dependent upon these shared assumptions. The mutually held range of identifications defines the area of common intent and also the range of the code. The dependency underpinning the social relation generating an elaborated code is not of this order. With an elaborated code the listener is dependent upon the verbal elaboration of meaning. (p. 437)

Context, therefore, is not critical in understanding elaborate codes.

Hall's (1976) high- and low-context messages, discussed in Chapter 3, are based on Bernstein's conceptualization of restricted and elaborated codes. As mentioned earlier, implicit messages (contextual cues) are emphasized in high-context messages and explicit verbal messages are of central importance in low-context messages. The heavy reliance of users of restricted codes on nonverbal and other contextual cues describes the common communication patterns used in collectivistic cultures; the primary reliance on elaborated, explicit verbal messages describes the predominant communication patterns used in individualistic cultures.

Hall (1976) characterizes the written Chinese language as a restricted or high-context language. To be literate in Chinese, one must understand the implicit meaning and significance of the characters and Chinese history. One also must know the spoken pronunciation system, in which there are four tones and a change of tone means a change of meaning. Understanding a restricted, high-context linguistic system such as Chinese requires not only a functional knowledge of the culture and history but also a sensitivity to the specific social context in which a particular communication transaction occurs.

Many Asian languages, such as Chinese, Japanese, and Korean, are sensitive to the social status of listeners. These languages implicitly or explicitly indicate others' social positions relative to speakers. This usually is done by using "honorific" prefixes or suffixes, by using certain words having respectful or derogatory implications, or by using particular verb endings. Certain nouns, pronouns, and verbs can be used only when speaking to or of a superior; a second group of words having the same basic meanings can be used only when speaking to or of an equal; a third group can be used only when speaking to or of an inferior. This verbal pattern reflecting a sensitivity to hierarchical context is absent from most contemporary European languages, with the exception of the formal and informal forms of *you,* such as *du* (casual) and *sie* (formal) in German and *tu* (casual) and *usted* (formal) in Spanish.

CULTURAL VARIATIONS IN VERBAL MESSAGES

In this section, we examine cultural variability in verbal messages. We begin by looking at cultural attitudes toward verbal messages. Next, we discuss the use of direct and indirect messages. Following this, we examine elaborated versus understated messages.

This is followed by a presentation of conversational constraints theory and the research supporting it. We conclude this section by looking at cultural differences in turn taking, topic management, and persuasive messages.

Cultural Attitudes toward Verbal Messages

Since all cultures have a system of language, the importance of verbal messages in interpersonal communication appears to be universally acknowledged. Cultures differ, however, in the importance placed on words and talk. The long tradition of the study of rhetoric in the United States and Europe demonstrates the importance given to verbal messages. This rhetorical tradition reflects the cultural pattern of logical, rational, and analytic thinking. In the United States, speech is considered to be an object of inquiry, more or less independent of its communicative context. Speakers and listeners are viewed as separate entities who are in a relationship defined primarily through the verbal messages. A primary function of speech in this tradition is for speakers to express their ideas and thoughts as clearly, logically, and persuasively as possible so that they can be fully recognized for their individuality in influencing others.

The systematic study of speech has not been developed as fully into a distinct academic discipline in collectivistic cultures as it has in individualistic cultures. The Asian attitude toward speech and rhetoric, for example, is characteristically a holistic one—the words are only part of, and are inseparable from, the total communication context, which includes the personal characters of the parties involved and the nature of the interpersonal relationships between them. This does not mean words are considered less important in Asian cultures than they are in the United States. Rather, verbal messages are considered an important and integral part of the total communication process in Asian cultures, inseparably interconnected with such concepts as ethics, psychology, politics, and social relations. In this holistic approach to speech and communication, verbal messages primarily serve the function of enhancing social integration and harmony rather than promoting speakers' individuality or self-motivated purposes. Dialogue aimed at social harmony, rather than at the well-being of specific speakers, naturally tends to lack arguments and persuasive fervor. Oliver (1971) observes that "perhaps most basic of all is the cardinal devotion of the Asian mind to the related concepts of unity and harmony" (p. 10).

Rather than encouraging the expression of individuality through the articulation of words, the tradition of collectivistic cultures stresses the value of strict adherence to culturally defined social expectations and rules. The primary emphasis is not placed on the technique of constructing and delivering verbal messages for maximum persuasiveness but on conformity to the already established social relationships defined by the positions of the communicators in the society. In such a rhetorical context, individuals are expected to possess moral and intellectual integrity and sensitivity to subtle and implicit contextual cues surrounding the total communication process. Without the contextual base, the speakers' verbal articulation and delivery are perceived as less meaningful, if not superficial or even deceitful.

A related attitude in collectivistic cultures is a strong recognition or acceptance of the limitations and biases inherent in the language used to express ideas, thoughts, and feelings. Unlike the case in the United States and other individualistic cultures, the orientation of collectivistic cultures can be characterized as bordering on a "mistrust" of words. Words are considered useful tools of human expression only to the extent that the users recognize their limitations and biases. In Buddhism, for example, language is considered deceptive and misleading with regard to the matter of understanding the truth. Similarly, Confucianism cautions that individuals should not speak carelessly and speech should be guided by the time and place. Even today, these religious teachings are deeply rooted in the minds of Asians. Commenting on Japanese communication patterns, Yoshikawa (1978) observes that

> what is often verbally expressed and what is actually intended are two different things. What is verbally expressed is probably important enough to maintain friendship, and it is generally called "Tatame" which means simply "in principle," but what is not verbalized counts most "Honne" which means "true mind." Although it is not expressed verbally, you are supposed to know it by "kan" [which means] "intuition." (p. 228)

When the true mind is not expressed, words cannot be trusted.

One area of research associated with cultural attitudes toward verbal communication is communication apprehension (i.e., fear or anxiety associated with verbally communicating). Members of Asian cultures tend to be higher in communication apprehension than U.S. Americans (Klopf, 1984; Kim et al., 2001). Kim et al. also report that emphasizing independent self construals is associated negatively with communication apprehension. Cultural differences in communication apprehension have to be interpreted with care. High levels of communication apprehension are problematic in individualistic cultures like the United States that emphasize verbal communication. Communication apprehension, however, is not necessarily problematic in Asian cultures. Elliot et al. (1982), for example, report that Koreans are more attracted to individuals who do not engage in a lot of verbal activity than to those who engage in a lot of verbal activity. Japanese have similar tendencies; they value *enryo* (being constrained or reserved).

Direct and Indirect Forms of Verbal Behavior

Attitudes toward verbal communication are related to the relative importance of context in the culture (Hall, 1976). The cautious attitude toward words in collectivistic cultures, for example, is manifested in moderate or suppressed expression of negative and confrontational verbal messages whenever possible. In general, members of collectivistic cultures tend to be concerned more with the overall emotional quality of interactions than with the meaning of particular words or sentences. Courtesy often takes precedence over truthfulness, and this is consistent with the cultural emphasis on maintaining social harmony as the primary function of speech. This leads members of collectivistic cultures to give an agreeable and pleasant answer to questions when literal, factual answers might be unpleasant or embarrassing (Hall & Whyte, 1979).

In certain high-context Asian languages (such as Chinese, Japanese, and Korean), the language structures themselves promote ambiguity. Kawashima and Kawashima (1998), for example, examine the use of pronouns in 39 languages. They report that cultures in which speakers can drop pronouns (e.g., pronouns indicating the subject of sentences) are more collectivistic than cultures in which speakers cannot drop pronouns. Dropping pronouns when speaking promotes ambiguity. In the Japanese language, verbs come at the end of sentences, and, therefore, listeners are not able to understand what is being said until the whole sentence has been uttered. In addition, Morsbach (1976) argues that their language allows the Japanese to talk for hours without clearly expressing their opinions to others. Even in ordinary conversation, Japanese may say *hai* ("yes") without necessarily implying agreement. Frequently, *hai* is intended by speakers, and is expected by listeners, to mean "I understand what you are saying," not agreement.

Okabe (1983) illustrates cultural differences in direct and indirect forms of communication by comparing the United States and Japan:

> Reflecting the cultural value of precision, [U.S.] Americans' tendency to use explicit words is most noteworthy in their communicative style. They prefer to employ such categorical words as "absolutely," "certainty," and "positively." . . . The English syntax dictates that the absolute "I" be placed at the beginning of the sentence in most cases, and that the subject-predicate relation be constructed in an ordinary sentence. . . . By contrast, the cultural assumptions of interdependence and harmony require that Japanese speakers limit themselves to implicit and even ambiguous use of words. In order to avoid leaving an assertive impression, they like to depend more frequently on qualifiers such as "maybe," "perhaps," "probably," and "somewhat." Since Japanese syntax does not require the use of a subject in a sentence, the qualifier-predicate is the predominant form of sentence construction. (p. 36)

The tendency among Asians to use subdued and ambiguous verbal expressions is not limited to communication situations in which one would express disagreement, embarrassment, doubt, or anger. Even when Asians are expressing strong personal affection, a style of hesitancy and indirectness commonly is preferred. Asians can even be suspicious of the genuineness of direct verbal expressions of love and respect. Excessive verbal praise or compliments sometimes are received with feelings of embarrassment.

Mizutani (1981) uses the example of a "higher-up" coming into a room that is cold and noticing that the window is open to illustrate how indirectness allows members of a Japanese group to maintain harmony. The higher-up might say something like " '*Samui-ja nai-ka, sono mado-o shimete-kure*' (Aren't you cold? Please close the window)" (p. 31), but this language does not take into consideration the human relations among the group. The higher-up can avoid giving a direct order by saying something like "*samui-nee*" (It's cold in here) and hope that one of the people in the room understands the unspoken meaning and responds with " '*A, soo-ka, mado-ga akete-atta*' (Oh that's right. The window's open)" (p. 31). Mizutani argues that not all Japanese would respond indirectly in this situation but that the majority of Japanese probably would unless there was a special relationship between themselves and the people in the room that would allow them to be direct.

Sometimes what appears to be ambiguous to outsiders is not ambiguous to insiders. Japanese, for example, often appears ambiguous to nonnative speakers because the meaning of Japanese sentences must be determined within the situational context in which the sentences are uttered (or written). Mizutani (1981) provides several examples. If guests enter a room (e.g., an office), the host might offer them a seat by just saying *doozo* ("please"). Clearly implied to another Japanese would be "have a seat."

If the guests do not recognize that the word please comes in a particular situational context, they will be confused. To further illustrate this tendency consider two people who are out drinking and there is only beer on the table. If one person says to the other, " *'Nomimasen-ka'* (Won't you have [some]?)" (p. 48), it would be understood that the referent is beer. If the person said "*'Biiru-o nomimasen-ka'* (Won't you have some beer?)" (p. 48), the other person would understand that other drinks are available but the person making the offer has selected beer.

Language use in Puerto Rico (a collectivistic culture) has many commonalities with language use in Asian cultures. Morris (1981) makes five generalizations about the use of discourse in Puerto Rico:

1. In Puerto Rican society, one's place and one's sense of oneself depends on an even, disciplined, and unthreatening style of behavior. . . .
2. In language one must take great care not to put oneself or others at risk, and one must reduce the risk of confrontation to the lowest degree possible. This implies a systematic blurring of meaning—that is, imprecision and indirectness. . . .
3. This implies a constant problem of interpretation, testing, probing, second-guessing, and investigation, but conducted indirectly. . . .
4. The personal value of the individual—and so the validity of his [or her] words—will be determined by what he [or she] actually *does,* not what he [or she] says. . . .
5. Information does not come in discrete "bits," but as complex indicators of fluid human relationships, the "bits" being inextricable from the constant, implicit negotiation of meaning. (pp. 135–136)

As with other forms of indirect communication, what is not said may be as important as what is said in Puerto Rico.

In comparison with Asian and Puerto Rican forms of verbal expression, U.S. Americans are more direct, explicit, and exact. Good and competent communicators are expected to say what they mean and mean what they say. If U.S. Americans discover that someone spoke dubiously or evasively with respect to important matters, they are inclined to regard the person as unreliable, if not dishonest. Most of the European individualistic cultures, such as the French, the German, and the English, show a similar cultural tradition. These cultures give a high degree of social approval to individuals whose verbal behaviors in expressing ideas and feelings are precise, explicit, straightforward, and direct.

Katriel (1986) argues that members of the Israeli Sabra culture use direct *dugri* speech ("straight talk") as a conscious form of communication. In Hebrew, *dugri* speech "involves a conscious suspension of face-concerns so as to allow the free expression of the speaker's thoughts, opinions, or preferences that might pose a threat to the addressee" (p. 11). *Dugri* speech implies a concern for sincerity in that it involves being true to oneself. Arabic speakers also use *dugri* speech. For Arabs, *dugri* speech is contrasted to *musayra*, which predominates in typical Arabic communication. *Musayra* "reflects a concern for harmonious social relations and for the social regulation of interpersonal conduct" (p. 111).

Holtgraves (1997) isolates two dimensions of indirectness in conversations. The first dimension is that "people can differ in terms of the extent to which they look for, and find, indirect meanings in the remarks of others" (p. 626). We all look for indirect meanings in what others say, and so this dimension deals with the degree to which we look for indirect messages. The second dimension "refers to a person's tendency to speak indirectly (i.e., convey nonliteral meanings) or directly" (p. 626). This dimension includes both the frequency and the amount of indirectness we use when we speak. The two dimensions are associated moderately. That is, those of us who speak indirectly tend to look for indirect messages in others' speech, and vice versa. Holtgraves reports that Koreans score higher on both dimensions than U.S. Americans. He argues that using indirect speech may be related to minimizing face-threats (face is discussed in detail in Chapter 11). Hara and Kim (2001) observe that emphasizing interdependent self construals is associated positively with both dimensions of conversational indirectness and emphasizing independent self construals is associated negatively with the tendency to speak indirectly.

Hall (1976) suggests that most of the time listeners can figure out what speakers mean when they are being indirect by using their knowledge of the context and the cultural system. Lim and Choi (1996) contend that this is not always the case in Korea. They point out that "Koreans who decide not to express their meanings explicitly do not want the other to figure out their meanings, or do not necessarily assume that the other will be able to figure out their intentions" (p. 131). Lim and Choi note that Koreans use *noon-chi* to figure out what others mean when others speak indirectly. Koreans "have to go through the *noon-chi* operation, which makes use of all kinds of world knowledge, the knowledge of the other, the knowledge of the context, the history of their interactions, and verbal and nonverbal messages" (p. 131). *Noon-chi,* therefore, is an element of Korean communication competence.

Cultural differences in the importance placed on context also influence the attention individuals pay to social roles when they use language. Okabe (1983), for example, points out that English is a person-oriented language and Japanese is a status-oriented language. When context is not emphasized (e.g., as in English), messages must be adapted to the specific person with whom we are communicating. When context is important (e.g., as in Japanese), messages must take the context into consideration. Status is a large part of the context in high power distance cultures. Albert's (1972) study of language use in Burundi (a collectivistic culture) illustrates the importance of roles. She observes that

> distinctions are made according to the social roles of those present: the degree of formality, publicity or privacy, and the objectives of the speech situation. Together, social role and situational prescriptions determine the order of precedence of speakers, relevant conventions of politeness, appropriate formulas and styles of speech, including extralinguistic signs, and topics of discussion. (p. 86)

In Burundi, language reflects the hierarchical social order that exists in the culture.

Direct and indirect forms of communication also are related to the use of a third-party person in social intercourse. Stewart (1972) cites an example in Thai culture where business between two people may be conducted indirectly by means of an emissary instead of directly by a face-to-face confrontation of the individuals involved. This indirectness extends to other aspects of social interaction, even those that strangers may consider rather personal, intimate, and sensitive, such as choosing a mate or attempting to resolve conflicts between spouses. The use of an intermediary allows both sides to accommodate one another or to withdraw without losing face. Stewart (1972) illustrates one implication of these different orientations (Asian indirectness and U.S. American preference for direct confrontation) in discussing the use of interpreters. He points out that U.S Americans see the interpreter "as a window pane that transmits the message from one language to the other; but in cultures where a third-person role is customary, the interpreter's role may become a much more active one, to the consternation of the [U.S.] American who is likely to interpret it as inefficiency or perhaps disloyalty" (p. 53).

Elaborate versus Understated Interaction Style

The elaborated versus understated dimension focuses on the degree to which talk is used (Gudykunst & Ting-Toomey, 1988). An *elaborated style* refers to the use of expressive language in everyday conversation. Expressive language can involve the use of exaggeration or animation. An *understated style,* in contrast, involves extensive use of silence, pauses, and understatements in conversation. The French, Arabs, Latin Americans, and Africans tend to use an exaggerated interaction style, while the Chinese, Japanese, Koreans, and Thai tend to use an understated interaction style. Individualists in the United States tend to fall somewhere in the middle of the continuum. To understand this dimension with respect to the communication style used by individualists in the United States, we need to make two types of comparisons: comparing the elaborate style with that used by individualists in the United States and comparing the understated style with that used by individualists in the United States.

As indicated earlier, the elaborate style can be based on either exaggeration or animation. Arabic verbal communication is an example of the exaggerated style:

> An Arab feels compelled to overassert in almost all types of communication because others expect him [or her] to. If an Arab says exactly what he [or she] means without the expected assertion, other Arabs may still think that he [or she] means the opposite. For example, a simple "No" by a guest to the host's request to eat more or drink more will not suffice. To convey the meaning that he is actually full, the guest must keep repeating "No" several times, coupling it with an oath such as "By God" or "I swear to God." . . . an Arab often fails to realize that others, particularly foreigners, may mean exactly what they say even though their language is simple. (Almaney & Alwan, 1982, p. 84)

The Arab proclivity to use verbal exaggerations probably is responsible for more diplomatic misunderstandings between the United States and Arab countries than any other single factor (Cohen, 1987).

The French also use an elaborate style in conversations with people close to them. The French style, however, is expressive in terms of animation, not exaggeration. For the French, a conversation must be "engaged, sustained, fueled, and revived if it is 'dragging.' Once we [the French] permit a conversation to begin, we owe it to ourselves to keep it from dying, to care for it, to guide it, to nourish it, and to watch over its development as if it were a living creature" (Carroll, 1988, p. 24). French conversations are like a spider's web: "we can see the exchanging words as playing the role of the spider, generating the threads which bind the participants. The ideal French conversation would resemble a perfect spider's web: delicate, fragile, elegant, brilliant, of harmonious proportions, a work of art" (Carroll, 1988, p. 25). This animated interaction style, however, is reserved for close relationships and is used in informal situations. In "serious conversations," long, uninterrupted responses and attentive listening are used.

There also are ethnic differences within the United States in the use of animated interactional styles. There are, for example, differences between European American and African American verbal interaction styles (Kochman, 1990). African Americans' verbal interaction style tends to be emotionally animated and expressive, and European Americans' verbal interaction style tends to be restrained and subdued. These style differences often lead to misunderstandings in intergroup encounters. Interethnic miscommunication arises when African Americans perceive European Americans as verbally detached and distant, and conversely, European Americans interpret the verbal style and tone of African Americans as emotionally threatening and intimidating. Even routine conversations can escalate to conflict because of the basic stylistic conversational differences when people communicate on automatic pilot. Recognizing and dealing with differences in verbal styles requires mindfulness.

The understated style involves the use of understatements, pauses, and silences in conversations (Gudykunst & Ting-Toomey, 1988). More generally, this style involves *not* emphasizing talk in interactions. European Americans see talk as more important and enjoyable than native-born Chinese or Chinese Americans (Wiemann, Chen, & Giles, 1986). European Americans are more likely than the other two groups to initiate conversations with others and to engage in conversations when opportunities present themselves. Chinese Americans are more likely to engage in these activities than native-born Chinese. European Americans also see talk as a means of social control, and native-born Chinese see silence as a control strategy. The differences in beliefs about talk between Chinese and European Americans are due to individualism-collectivism:

> Individualists have a choice among many groups . . . to which they do belong, and usually belong to these groups because they volunteer. Collectivists . . . are born into a few groups and are more or less stuck with them. So, the collectivists do not have to go out of their way and exert themselves to be accepted, while individualists have to work hard to be accepted. Hence, the individualists often speak more, try to control the situation verbally, and do not value silence. (Triandis quoted in Giles et al., 1992, p. 11)

This should not be taken to suggest that collectivists do not engage in small talk or gossip, because they do. Collectivists, however, do not see talk as being as important as individualists do in developing relationships with others. They also engage in a lot of talk with members of their ingroups.

Cultures that do not value talk tend to value silence. Silence tends to be valued more in collectivistic cultures than in individualistic cultures. Lebra (1987), for example, isolates four meanings of silence in Japan: truthfulness, social discretion, embarrassment, and defiance. Japanese view truth as occurring only inside the person. Activities regarding the outer self do not involve individuals' true feelings and, therefore, frequently involve distortion, deception, or "moral falsity." People who speak a little are trusted more than people who speak a great deal. In Japan, truthfulness emerges from silences, not words. Silence also allows Japanese to be socially discreet and "to gain social acceptance or to avoid social penalty" (Lebra, 1987, p. 347). At times, talking may be dangerous and require that Japanese tell the truth. In these instances, silence allows Japanese to avoid social disapproval. Silence also saves Japanese from embarrassment. Verbally expressing emotions to each other, for example, may cause a traditional married couple in Japan to become embarrassed. Japanese also may indicate disagreement or anger with someone else by being silent.

Hasegawa and Gudykunst (1998) report that Japanese have more negative attitudes toward silence when communicating with strangers than when communicating with close friends. The relationship, however, does not influence U.S. Americans' attitudes toward silence. Japanese also have more negative attitudes toward silence when communicating with strangers than U.S. Americans, but there are no cultural differences in attitudes toward silence when communicating with close friends. Hasegawa and Gudykunst also observe that U.S. Americans use silence more strategically (to accomplish goals) than Japanese. Members of both cultures use silence more strategically with strangers than with close friends.

Silence is valued by some groups within the United States. Asian Americans who hold collectivistic values, for example, value silence in conversations. Silence also is valued by many Native American tribes. To illustrate, Apache Indians see silence as appropriate in contexts where social relations between individuals are unpredictable and involve high levels of uncertainty. They also prefer silence over talk in situations where role expectations are unclear (Basso, 1970).

Stylistic differences with respect to succinctness and silence can create problems in interethnic communication. Native Americans in Canada and Alaska, for example, prefer more silence in conversations than European Americans (Scollon & Wong-Scollon, 1990). For the Native Americans, conversations are seen as threatening because other people may try to change them. Conversations, therefore, are avoided unless everyone's opinions are known in advance. European Americans, in contrast, "feel that the main way to get to know the point of view of people is through conversation with them" (Scollon & Wong-Scollon, 1990, p. 263). The conversational paradox in this case also lies in the fact that one of the primary functions of talk is to bridge relational distance for European Americans. European Americans tend to reserve silence for intimate relationships. For Native Americans, silence is used to protect the sense of vulnerable self from strangers, and talk is used when the relationship becomes more intimate.

Conversational Constraints

Conversations are goal-directed and require coordination between communicators in conversational constraint theory (CCT; Kim, 1995). We pursue a variety of goals in our interactions with others (e.g., gaining compliance, seeking information, altering relationships). In the pursuit of these goals, our messages are constrained by either personal or cultural factors. Conversational constraints influence the manner in which we construct messages and our conversational styles (Kim, 1993).

Kim (1993) isolates two conversational constraints: social-relational and task-oriented. *Social-relational constraints* emphasize speakers' concern for others that focuses on avoiding hurting hearers' feelings and minimizing impositions on hearers. *Task-oriented constraints* emphasize concerns for clarity (the degree to which the intentions of messages are communicated explicitly) (Kim, 1995).

Kim (1993) explains cross-cultural differences in the selection of communicative strategies. There are six propositions in her theory. Kim (1993) posits that collectivism influences the importance members of cultures place on relational concerns in conversations. The emphasis on relational concerns centers on face. Members of collectivistic cultures view face-supporting behavior (e.g., avoiding hurting the hearers' feelings, minimizing impositions, and avoiding negative evaluations by hearers) as more important than members of individualistic cultures when pursuing goals (proposition [P]1). Members of collectivistic cultures have higher thresholds for face support and select strategies that maximize face support more than members of individualistic cultures (P2, P3). Members of individualistic cultures, in contrast, view clarity as more important than members of collectivistic cultures when pursuing goals (P4). Members of individualistic cultures have higher thresholds and maximize concern for clarity more than members of collectivistic cultures (P5, P6).

At the individual level, Kim (1995) uses self construals to explain variability in conversational constraints. There are 11 propositions in this theory. Individuals who emphasize interdependent self construals have the desire to avoid the loss of face and be accepted by ingroup members. Individuals who emphasize independent self construals tend to be pointed, direct, clear, unambiguous, and concise in their choice of verbal tactics.

Kim (1995) argues that individuals who activate interdependent self construals view not hurting hearers' feelings and minimizing impositions on hearers in the pursuit of their goals as more important than individuals who activate independent self construals (P1, P2). Individuals who activate independent self construals view clarity as more important in pursuing goals than individuals who activate interdependent self construals (P3). Individuals who activate both self construals are concerned with both relational and clarity constraints (P4). Individuals who do not activate either self construal do not view either clarity or relational constraints as important (P5).

In addition to self construals, Kim (1995) uses the need for approval, the need for dominance, and gender roles to explain conversational constraints. The more individuals need approval, the more important they view being concerned with hearers' feelings and minimizing impositions on hearers (P6, P7). The more individuals need to be dominant, the more importance they place on clarity (P8). The more masculine individuals' psychological sex-roles, the more importance they place on clarity (P9). The more feminine individuals' psychological sex roles, the more importance they place on not hurting hearers' feelings and not imposing on hearers (P10, P11).

M. S. Kim (1994) reports that members of collectivistic cultures are concerned more with avoiding hurting others and imposing on them than are members of individualistic cultures. Members of individualistic cultures are more concerned with clarity in conversations (M. S. Kim, 1994) and view clarity as necessary for effective communication (Kim & Wilson, 1994) more than members of collectivistic cultures. Kim and Wilson (1994) note that members of individualistic cultures perceive direct requests as the most effective strategy for accomplishing their goals, while members of collective cultures perceive direct requests as the least effective. Kim, Sharkey, and Singelis (1994) observe that emphasizing interdependent self construals is associated with concern for others' feelings and that using independent self construals is associated with a concern for clarity in conversations. Kim et al. (1996) report that independent self construals are correlated with concerns for clarity and effectiveness and interdependent self construals are correlated with concern for hearers' feelings and concern for minimizing impositions on hearers.

Topic Management and Turn Taking in Conversations

In our conversations with others, we have to coordinate our turn taking, "that is, who speaks when and for how long. . . . Coordination is accomplished by a system that allows or obligates certain parties to talk at certain times" (Clark, 1985, p. 181). Turns must be managed sequentially in conversations on a moment-by-moment basis (Sacks, Schegloff, & Jefferson, 1974). There are several properties of conversations that are important in understanding turn taking (Sacks et al., 1974). Generally, one person talks at a time, and when one speaker is finished, another talks. While two (or more) people speaking at the same time is common in conversations, the overlaps do not last long. Generally, there is no gap, or only a small gap, between when one person finishes speaking and when another person begins (at least in English). The order and length of turns in conversations are not fixed. The relative distributions of turns in conversations also are not fixed.

Conversations are mutually constructed by the participants. The person speaking and the people listening have equal responsibilities for managing who talks when and what is discussed. Our conversations are "constructed on an utterance-by-utterance basis, with each subsequent utterance to some extent dependent on preceding ones for its sensibility and appropriateness" (Wiemann, 1985, p. 93). Scollon and Wong-Scollon (1994), however, argue that the basic structure of conversations in the East and the West are different:

> Asian conversations show a pattern . . . beginning with incidental topics and minor points. The main topic is introduced somewhat later. . . . It is quite customary after the introduction of the main topic for this to be followed by a final period of "small talk." . . . The western pattern, by contrast, begins with an early introduction of the initiator's main point. This is followed by a line of supportive developments or just small talk, but there is often a conclusion with a reiteration of the main or concluding point. (p. 135)

The sensibility and appropriateness of conversations, therefore, appear to differ in Asia and the United States.

We define our relationships with others by the way we communicate with them. How we hold conversations with others lays the foundation for our future relationships with them. If we want to develop relationships with others, we want to "get off on the right foot." This is accomplished, at least in part, by how we negotiate turn taking in our initial conversations. The way we take turns in conversations influences how cooperation will develop in relationships, and it also has implications for how control will be managed in relationships. By making choices about when to change speakers, we define who is in control of our conversations and relationships at that time (Wiemann, 1985). In dealing with turn taking in conversations, we often deal with control issues in relationships before we are consciously aware of them.

The ways we take turns and manage topics in conversations differ across cultures. Individualism-collectivism influences topic management and turn distribution in conversations. Japanese (collectivists), for example, "take short turns, distribute their turns relatively evenly, and continue to distribute their turns evenly regardless of who initiates a topic" (Yamada, 1990, p. 291). U.S. Americans (individualists), in contrast, "take long monologic turns, distribute their turns unevenly, and the participant who initiates a topic characteristically takes the highest proportion of turns in that topic" (p. 291). Collectivists organize topics interdependently, and individualists organize topics independently.

The way we manage conversations also is affected by individualism-collectivism. Collectivists use verbal and nonverbal complementary expressions and repetition to support others when they speak and maintain negotiations. Individualists, in contrast, use few synchronizing behaviors and repetition. Individualists tend to use feedback devices (e.g., questions, comments) to indicate they are attentive, and collectivists tend to use back channeling (i.e., brief utterances which make conversation flow smoothly) to accomplish this purpose. To illustrate, when U.S. American "speakers orient attention, they focus on the specific topical content. Japanese speakers only value the emphatic interactional behavior and tend to consider the message exchange secondary" (Hayashi, 1990, p. 188).

Collectivists send back channel signals to the people with whom they are communicating more than individualists (e.g., White, 1989). Back channel signals are the verbalizations we use to tell others that we are listening. To the extent that people are competent in using the back channeling techniques of members of other cultures when speaking their languages, effective communication is facilitated (LoCastro, 1987).

One area where problems occur when non-Japanese are speaking Japanese is in the use of *aizuchi*. *Aizuchi* is used frequently in Japanese conversations as a way for the listener to let the speaker know that he or she is listening. When the nonnative speaker is not aware of the rules for using *aizuchi,* it can create problems. Mizutani (1981, pp. 83–84) provides the following example to illustrate this point:

Japanese: Moshi moshi. (Hello.)
Foreigner: Moshi moshi. (Hello.)
Japanese: Ee, kochira, anoo, Yamamoto-desu-ga. (Uuh, this is err, Yamamoto.)
Foreigner: . . . .
Japanese: Moshi moshi. (Are you there?)
Foreigner: Moshi moshi. (Hello.)
Japanese: Kochira, Yamamoto-desu-ga. Johnsonsan-wa . . . (This is Yamamoto. Is Mr./Ms. Johnson . . .)
Foreigner: . . . .
Japanese: Moshi moshi. (Are you there?)

The caller identified himself or herself in the third line and expected that the listener would provide *aizuchi* to indicate that he or she was paying attention. When no *aizuchi* was provided, the caller assumed that the listener was not following the conversation. The caller, therefore, used *moshi moshi* to determine if the listener was still there. This pattern is repeated later in the conversation when no *aizuchi* is provided. When non-Japanese are able to use *aizuchi,* it decreases misunderstandings.

Some of the individualistic and collectivistic differences in conversational management also appear in ethnic conversations in the United States. Feldstein, Hennessy, and Bond (1981), for example, report that Chinese Canadians use longer periods of silence than Canadian English speakers, regardless of whether they are speaking Chinese or English. Chinese Canadians also use shorter periods of vocalization than English speakers, and their periods of vocalization are shorter when they speak English than when they speak Chinese.

Welkowitz, Bond, and Feldstein (1984) observe that Japanese American children take shorter turns than European American children in same-ethnicity dyads. They also note that Japanese American boys take fewer speaking turns of longer duration and use longer pauses than Japanese American girls. The results are inconsistent with traditional Japanese American sex roles. Welkowitz et al. suggest that Japanese American sex roles may not emerge by age eight (the age of the children studied). European American girls use fewer turns but take longer turns and have longer pauses than Japanese American girls in same-ethnicity dyads. Japanese American girls speak less with Japanese American boys and European American boys than with Japanese American girls. Welkowitz et al. argue that these differences may be due to Japanese American girls being more "feminine" than European American girls.

Persuasive Strategies

One important aspect of verbal communication that needs to be addressed before we look at language use in communicating with strangers is how the verbal strategies people use to persuade others vary across cultures. In the previous chapter, we examined patterns of thought. These patterns of thought can be linked to the strategies people use to persuade others. Universalism and abstraction (Glenn, 1981), for example, lead to an axiomatic-deductive style of persuasion (i.e., begin with generalities and proceed to specifics or start from fundamental principles and then discuss their implications). Particularism and associative thought, in contrast, are related to a factual-inductive style of persuasion (i.e., begin with relevant facts and draw conclusions from them). Both of these styles involve an affective neutrality orientation (Parsons, 1951) toward persuasion. An affective orientation toward persuasion is related to the affective-intuitive style of persuasion (i.e., using affective or emotional messages to persuade).

Members of collectivistic cultures take the context into consideration and select strategies that are appropriate to the context. Members of individualistic cultures, in contrast, focus on the person they are trying to persuade and use strategies that may be perceived as socially inappropriate (Gudykunst & Ting-Toomey, 1988).

Hirokawa and Miyahara (1986) examine the strategies managers in corporations in the United States and Japan use to persuade their subordinates. The first situation involves how the manager tries to persuade consistently tardy employees to change their behavior. Japanese managers indicate that they appeal to the employees' "duty" (e.g., "It is your duty as a responsible employee of this company to begin work on time"). U.S. American managers prefer to "threaten" the employees (e.g., "If you don't start reporting to work on time, I will have no choice but to dock your pay") or to give an "ultimatum" (e.g., "If you can't come to work on time, go find yourself another job").

The second situation in Hirokawa and Miyahara's (1986) study involves how the managers persuade employees to give their ideas and suggestions to managers. Japanese managers tend to prefer to use "altruistic" strategies (e.g., "For the sake of the company, please share your ideas and suggestions with us") or appeal to "duty" (e.g., "Remember that it is your duty as a good company employee to suggest how we can improve the overall performance of the company"). U.S. American managers prefer to make "direct requests" (e.g., "I want you to feel free to come to me with any ideas you have for improving the company"), to make "promises" (e.g., "Don't hesitate to offer ideas and suggestions because we always reward good suggestions"), or to "ingratiate" themselves with the employees (e.g., "You are one of our best people and I really value your judgment, so please feel free to come to me with ideas you have").

Shatzer et al. (1988) also compare compliance gaining in Japan and the United States (in a nonbusiness setting). They report that Japanese use explanation, positive esteem (e.g., people will think better of those who comply), moral appeal (e.g., people who do not comply are immoral), and negative altercasting (e.g., only people who are bad will not comply) more than U.S. Americans. U.S. Americans, in contrast, use positive self-feeling (e.g., people will feel better about themselves if they comply), allurement, bargaining, and direct request strategies more than Japanese. The items used in this study have an individualistic bias, but the results are generally compatible with what we would expect given the cultural differences in individualism-collectivism.

Burgoon et al. (1982) report that in comparison to European Americans, Asian Americans prefer to use the strategies of "promise" (e.g., "If you comply, I will reward you"), "positive expertise" (e.g., "If you comply, you will be rewarded by the nature of things"), "pregiving" (e.g., rewarding the person before a request), "liking" (e.g., person is friendly to get the other in a good frame of mind), "positive altercasting" (e.g., "A person with 'good' qualities would comply"), "negative altercasting" (e.g., "Only a person with 'bad' qualities would not comply"), "positive self-feeling" (e.g., "You will feel better about yourself if you comply"), and "positive self-esteem" (e.g., "People you value will think better of you if you comply"). All these strategies tend to involve high degrees of social acceptability.

Miller, Reynolds, and Cambra (1982) report that European Americans use aversive strategies more than Chinese Americans and Japanese Americans. European Americans also use threats, negative expertise, and negative self-feelings more than Japanese Americans. Japanese Americans use altruism less than Chinese Americans. They also note that respondents use a wider variety of strategies with members of other ethnic groups than with members of their own ethnic groups. Fong and Philipsen (2001) contend that Chinese Americans prioritize "indirect communication designed to influence the heart or will of another through face-saving strategies in order to maintain harmony. It reveals a cultural way to manifest caring for another strategically" (pp. 80–81).

Miller, Reynolds, and Cambra (1987) argue that the intensity of the language used influences the persuasive process. They report that ethnicity and gender combine to influence individuals' language intensity. Specifically, Chinese American men and Japanese American men use more intense language than Chinese American women and Japanese American women. There is, however, no difference in language intensity between European American men and women. The results of the study are consistent with the relative roles of men and women in the three ethnic groups.

Cialdini et al. (1999) look at two social influence principles (commitment/consistency and social proof) in individualistic and collectivistic cultures. The *commitment/consistency principle* suggests that we comply with others' request when we have engaged in the behavior in the past. We, therefore, comply to be consistent with our past behavior. The *social proof principle* suggests that we decide whether to comply with others' requests by looking at how people similar to us have responded. Cialdini et al. argue that the commitment/consistency principle is especially strong in individualistic cultures and the social proof principle is especially strong in collectivistic cultures. They report that both principles are used across cultures, and the data support their argument.

Cross-cultural research on advertising supports the argument made here. Han and Shavitt (1994), for example, report that magazine advertisements in the United States emphasize appeals to benefiting individuals, personal success, and independence more than Korean advertisements. Korean advertisements, in contrast, emphasize ingroup benefits, harmony, and family integrity more than advertisements in the United States. They also note that advertisements aimed at individual benefits are more persuasive than advertisements aimed at ingroup benefits in the United States, and the reverse is true in Korea.

Kim and Markus (1999) examine magazine advertisements in the United States and Asia. They find that ads in the United States show people rebelling against social institutions more than ads in Asia. Ads in Asia, in contrast, show people following expectations to be in harmony with ingroup members more than ads in the United States.

LANGUAGE USAGE IN COMMUNICATING WITH STRANGERS

Cross-cultural variations in languages and verbal communication styles influence how people from different cultures communicate. There also are language variations within cultures that influence the way people communicate. Each of us, for example, speaks a dialect. Chaika (1982) defines a *dialect* as "all the differences between varieties of a language, those in pronunciation, word usage, and syntax" (p. 132). Sometimes the difference between language and dialect is not clear-cut. Chaika (1982) points out that

> political boundaries, in themselves, often determine whether two speech varieties will be considered different languages or not. For instance, some varieties of Swedish and Norwegian are mutually comprehensible, but they are considered different languages because they are separated by national borders. Conversely, the so-called dialects of Chinese are as different as French from Italian, but being spoken in one country they are not considered different languages. (p. 133)

Chaika (1982) argues that how we speak is tied very closely to how we define ourselves. She points out that in highly mobile cultures like the United States, "speech is likely to be the most reliable determiner of social class or ethnic group" (p. 139). She goes on to say that this is critically important to people in the "middle class" who want to appear to be educated.

There are several aspects of language and dialect usage that are important in understanding our communication with strangers. Our attitudes toward other languages and dialects influence how we respond to others, whether we learn other languages, when we use other languages or dialects, and whether we accommodate to people with whom we are communicating. We begin our discussion of language in our communication with strangers by looking at the vitality of languages and linguistic groups.

Ethnolinguistic Vitality

Giles, Bourhis and Taylor (1977) argue that the degree to which group members will act as a group when interacting with members of outgroups is influenced by the group's *ethnolinguistic vitality,* the range and importance of the functions served by ethnic language usage. They isolate three factors that contribute to a group's vitality: the group's social status, the demographic characteristics of the group, and the institutional support for the group's language or dialect. The *social status* variables include those which exert an influence on the prestige of a language group, such as the economic, social, and language status of that particular social group. Giles et al. contend that the higher a group's social status, the greater its vitality. The *demographic* variables are those related to the size of the group and its distribution within specific areas and a country as a whole. Group size includes the group's absolute numbers, birth rate, mixed marriages, immigration, and emigration, while distribution refers to the concentration as well as proportion of the group compared to an outgroup. As would be expected, the larger the group, the greater its vitality (Giles et al., 1977). *Institutional support* refers to the representation of the language use in institutions such as churches, businesses, and government agencies. The greater the institutional support for a language group, the greater its validity (Giles et al., 1977).

Giles et al. (1977) isolate two types of group vitality: subjective and objective. Subjective group vitality is a group's societal position as perceived by its members, and objective group vitality is associated with the group's relative position based on the available "objective" data. They propose that the more vitality an ethnolinguistic group has, the more likely it is the group will survive as a distinctive linguistic group in multilingual settings. Conversely, an ethnolinguistic group that has little or no group vitality eventually will cease to exist as a distinctive group.

A number of researchers have compared different ethnic groups' perceptions of ethnolinguistic vitality within cultures. Giles, Rosenthal and Young's (1985) study of ethnolinguistic vitality perceptions of Greek and Anglo Australians, for example, reveals that the two groups agree that Anglos' vitality is higher on certain status and institutional support items but disagree about each other's socio-structural positions. Bourhis and Sachdev's (1984) research indicates that there is a relationship between perceived vitality and language, attitudes (discussed below). Young, Giles, and Pierson's (1986) research suggests that proficiency in the ingroup and outgroup languages also influences perceived vitality.

Gao, Schmidt, and Gudykunst (1994) report that ethnic identity has a significant influence on perceived group vitality; individuals who strongly identify with their ethnic groups perceive that their groups have higher vitality than do those who do not identify strongly with their groups. This pattern is compatible with social identity theory (e.g., Tajfel, 1978) and recent studies of the effect of social identity on language attitudes (e.g., Hogg, Joyce, & Abrams, 1984).

If members of groups perceive that their languages have high vitality, that strengthens their ethnic identities (Giles & Johnson, 1987). Because of its influence on strengthening identities, perceiving language vitality also decreases uncertainty and anxiety. Perceived vitality of languages also affects attitudes toward specific languages or dialects, whether individuals in "minority" groups are motivated to learn the language of the dominant group, and the language or dialect people choose to use when they communicate. We discuss language attitudes first.

Language Attitudes

The language or dialect we speak influences how others judge us and whether they are willing to help us. A study by Gaertner and Bickman (1971) illustrates the influence of dialect on whether others will help us. African American and European American callers made phone calls from a phone booth, pretending to have gotten a wrong number using the last of their change. After discovering they had a wrong number, the callers asked the person on the other end to help them by calling the correct number. The results indicate that African Americans who received phone calls were equally likely to help a European American or an African American caller. European Americans, in contrast, helped European Americans more frequently than they helped African Americans. Given that the only information the people receiving the call had about those making the call was their dialects, the results demonstrate that dialect influences the degree to which others will help.

Generally, speakers using a standard dialect are rated high on "competence," "intelligence," "industriousness," and "confidence," as well as other traits associated with competence and status. Speakers using nonstandard dialects, in contrast, are rated lower than standard speakers on these factors, even by speakers of nonstandard dialects (see Bradac, 1990, for a review). Speakers using nonstandard dialects are rated higher than speakers using the standard dialect on factors associated with ingroup solidarity (e.g., friendliness, likability). Other research suggests that standard dialect speakers are rated as qualified for high-status jobs and nonstandard dialect speakers are qualified only for low-status jobs (e.g., Kalin & Rayko, 1980).

Our social class influences our language attitudes. Chaika (1982) points out that speaking "properly"

> is a matter of great concern to the educated middle class, which above all wishes to be identified as educated. Its members' being recognized as those to be listened to hinges strongly on language. When people say they want to know the right way to speak, they do not mean the right way to communicate their ideas but, rather the right way to announce that those ideas are to be respected, to be listened to. (p. 239)

We, therefore, cannot understand others' language usage unless we take their social class into consideration.

Ryan, Giles, and Sebastian (1982) suggest that language attitudes can be characterized in terms of two interrelated dimensions: standardization and vitality. Ryan, Hewstone, and Giles (1984) summarize these dimensions as follows:

> Standardization is the more static dimension, referring to the extent to which norms for correct usage . . . have been codified, adopted, and promoted for a particular variety. This might be accomplished through the compilation of dictionaries and grammars while the acceptance of a variety may be advanced by elites and government. . . . Vitality is the more dynamic dimension, reflecting the range and importance of functions served by language varieties . . . and the social pressures toward shift in language use. (pp. 143–144)

Changes in languages attitudes are due mostly to changes in perceived vitality (changes in standardization also occur with changes in vitality). As people perceive the vitality of languages or dialects increasing, their use is viewed more positively.

Edwards (1985) draws several conclusions regarding the research on language attitudes. He points out that

> all language varieties can reflect [social] identity. There is a regularity in research findings here: non-standard forms attract high ratings in terms of group solidarity, while standard ones are seen to reflect higher competence. Thus, even dialects lacking in social prestige retain a claim upon their speakers. In this sense, a bidialectal person is like one for whom bilingualism is a stable quantity—identity can be carried in an original variety while another is added for instrumental reasons. . . . Dialectical adjustment according to the perceived demands of context reflects a motivation for success *and* original marker retention. (p. 167)

Our language attitudes clearly influence how we respond to strangers when they are not speaking the standard dialect.

Cargile and Bradac (2001) argue that our evaluations of strangers' language use involves more than just our attitudes toward their languages. They point out that our evaluations of speakers are based on our linguistic preferences, our expectations for speakers (e.g., based on our stereotypes), our goals in the interaction, the amount of attention we pay to speakers, and the depth with which we process what we hear.

Language attitudes are important in and of themselves. They also are important because they influence our desire to learn other languages.

Second Language Competence

There are numerous explanations of second language learning (see Gardner, 1985, for reviews of major theories), but only the intergroup model takes into consideration the intergroup factors relevant to second language learning. We, therefore, focus on that model here.

Giles and Byrne (1982) argue that second language learning cannot be explained unless the relations between the groups are taken into consideration. Garrett, Giles, and Coupland (1989) isolate five factors that contribute to members of a "minority" group learning the language of the "dominant" group.

The first factor in Garrett et al.'s (1989) model involves how the minority language is viewed. If members of ethnic groups identify weakly with their groups or do not view their languages as important parts of their identities, they are likely to try to learn the dominant language. If members of minority groups view their languages as an important part of their identities, they will try to learn the dominant language to the extent that it does not threaten their identities or they have other ways to preserve their ethnic identities.

Second, if members of ethnic groups perceive few alternatives to their "subordinate" status and view the chance of it changing as small, they will try to learn the dominant language. They also will try to learn the dominant language if they perceive cognitive alternatives to their status and realize that these alternatives can be met by learning the dominant language.

Third, members of minority groups will try to learn the dominant language to the extent that they perceive the boundaries between their groups and the dominant group to be soft and open. Stated differently, if they believe that learning the dominant language will help them be accepted in the dominant group, they will try to learn the language.

Fourth, members of minority groups will try to learn the dominant language to the extent that they derive satisfactory social identities from other group memberships. That is, if they are members of other social categories (e.g., occupations) that provide them with satisfactory identities.

Finally, if members of minority groups perceive the vitality of their groups to be low, they will attempt to learn the dominant group's language. They also will try to learn the dominant language if they believe learning it will contribute to the vitality of their ingroups.

In addition to these five intergroup factors, Garrett et al. (1989) isolate three sociolinguistic factors that contribute to second language learning. First, the more similar the dominant language and the minority language, the more likely members of minorities are to learn the dominant language. Second, there must be exposure to the dominant language for it to be learned (e.g., members of the minority groups must have contact with speakers of the dominant language). Third, there must be use of the dominant language for it to be learned (e.g., members of minority groups need to have the opportunity to use the dominant language in a variety of contexts).

Garrett et al.'s (1989) research generally supports the model they propose. Other support for the intergroup model is provided by Giles and Johnson (1987), Hall and Gudykunst (1986), and Kelley et al. (1993).

The theory outlined here is not limited to members of minority groups learning the dominant language; it applies equally to people from one culture learning the language of another culture. Once the dominant or second language is learned, there is the remaining issue of what effects its use has on the communication that takes place. If we are competent in strangers' languages, it reduces our uncertainty and anxiety when we communicate with them (Gudykunst, 1995). Linguistic competence also influences our ability to accommodate our communication and code-switch when we communicate with strangers. We discuss these issues in the next two sections.

Communication Accommodation

In attempting to provide a systematic explanation for the persistence of linguistic diversity, Tajfel (1974, 1978) suggests that when members of one ethnic group interact with strangers from another ethnic group, they compare themselves on a number of value dimensions with the strangers. He claims these intergroup social comparisons lead group members to search for characteristics of their own groups that will enable them to differentiate themselves favorably from the outgroups (as discussed in Chapter 4). Such positive ingroup distinctiveness not only allows individuals personal satisfaction in their own group memberships but also affords them positive social identities.

Communication accommodation theory (CAT) originated in Giles' (1973) work on accent mobility. Giles (1973) describes the tendency to accentuate (i.e., emphasize) linguistic differences as *speech divergence.* Some individuals in interaction with others shift their speech in their desire for their listeners' social approval. One tactic, consciously or unconsciously conceived, is for speakers to modify their speech in the direction of the listeners' speech patterns, a process Giles terms *speech convergence.*

Giles et al. (1977) suggest that when members of subordinate groups accept their inferior status, they attempt to converge into the dominant group socially and psychologically by means of speech convergence. If, in contrast, they consider their inferior status to be illegitimate and the intergroup situation to be unstable, they seek "psychological distinctiveness" by redefining their group attributes in a socially and psychologically more favorable direction. They also might do this linguistically and hence, in interaction with members of the outgroup, accentuate their own ingroup characteristics by means of speech divergence, using their own dialect, accent, jargon, or other form of speech variation.

CAT began as speech accommodation theory (SAT; e.g., Giles & Smith, 1979). SAT proposed that speakers use linguistic strategies to gain approval or to show distinctiveness in their interactions with others. The main strategies communicators use are speech convergence and divergence. These are "linguistic moves" to decrease or increase communicative distances, respectively. There is a tendency for members of ingroups to react favorably to outgroup members who linguistically converge toward them (Giles & Smith, 1979; see Jones et al., 1994, for evidence). This, however, is not always the case. Giles and Byrne (1982) point out that as outgroup members begin to learn the ingroup's speech style, ingroup members may diverge in some way to maintain linguistic distinctiveness. Reaction to outgroup members' speech convergence depends on the intent ingroup members attribute to the outgroup members (Simard, Taylor, & Giles, 1976). If outgroup members' intent is perceived to be positive, speech convergence is interpreted positively.

Genesse and Bourhis (1982) observe that ingroup members' evaluation of outgroup members' language usage in conversations is based on situational norms in the initial stages of conversations and on interpersonal accommodation later in the conversation. Bourhis (1985) claims that following situational norms is the strategy used most frequently in early stages of hostile intergroup encounters. In later stages of conversations, however, individuals adopt strategies based on their goals, their desire to assert their group identities, and their affective response to the other person.

Giles, Mulac, Bradac, and Johnson (1987) expanded speech accommodation theory in terms of the range of phenomena covered and relabeled it communication accommodation theory. They argue that communication convergence is a function of speakers' desire for (1) social approval, (2) high communication efficiency, (3) shared self-presentation or group presentation, and (4) an appropriate identity definition. For communication convergence to occur, there also needs to be a match between speakers' views of recipients' speech style and the actual style used, and the specific speech style used is appropriate for both speakers and recipients. Divergence, in contrast, is a function of speakers' desires (1) for a "contrastive" self-image, (2) to dissociate from recipients, (3) to change recipients' speech behavior, and (4) to define encounters in intergroup terms. Divergence also occurs when recipients use a speech style that deviates from a norm that is valued and consistent with the speakers' expectations regarding the recipients' performances. If strangers accommodate to our communication style and we perceive their intent to be positive, it will reduce our uncertainty and anxiety in communicating with them.

Coupland, Coupland, Giles, and Henwood (1988) adapted communication accommodation theory to intergenerational communication and incorporated additional modifications to the theory (e.g., conceptualizing speaker strategies as based on an "addressee focus" and incorporating addressees' attributions about speakers' behavior). Gallois, Franklyn-Stokes, Giles, and Coupland (1988) adapted Coupland et al.'s (1988) model to intercultural communication. This modification integrated predictions from ethnolinguistic identity theory (ELIT; e.g., Giles & Johnson, 1987) and emphasized the influence of situations on intercultural communication.

Gallois, Giles, Jones, Cargile, and Ota (1995) updated the 1988 version of the theory, incorporating research that had been conducted and cross-cultural variability in accommodative processes. This version of the theory contains 17 propositions, with several of the propositions subdivided into two based on the processes that are occurring (e.g., when interlocutors are evaluated positively or negatively). It is impossible to summarize all the propositions here. We, therefore, outline the theory (Gallois et al., 1995) and present representative propositions.

Communication accommodation theory begins with the "sociohistorical context" of the interaction. This includes the relations between the groups having contact and the social norms regarding contact (intercultural contact is one type of intergroup contact). This component also includes cultural variability. Gallois et al. (1995) argue that our cultural backgrounds affect how we respond to strangers' linguistic convergence. They suggest that

> individualists may react to convergence from outgroup interlocutors in a relatively positive manner, and converge toward the outgroup speaker reciprocally. With oftentimes softer group boundaries [than collectivists], their thresholds for allowing linguistic penetration by outgroup members may be lower [than collectivists' thresholds]. Conversely, people from collectivistic cultures, who perceive harder boundaries [than individualists], may react to attempts at communication convergence more negatively, and may diverge from them more if they perceive the convergence as overstepping a valued cultural or national boundary [than individualists]. (p. 131)

Members of collectivistic cultures, therefore, are more likely to diverge from outgroup members than members of individualistic cultures.

The second component of communication accommodation theory is the communicators' "accommodative orientation," or their tendencies to perceive encounters with outgroup members in interpersonal terms, intergroup terms, or a combination of the two. There are three aspects to accommodative orientations: (1) "intrapersonal factors" (e.g., social identities, personal identities), (2) "intergroup factors" (e.g., factors that reflect communicators' orientations to outgroups, such as perceived ingroup vitality), and (3) "initial orientations" (e.g., perceived potential for conflict, long-term accommodative motivation toward outgroups).

The perceived relations between groups influence communicators' tendencies to perceive encounters as interpersonal or intergroup. Similarly, members of dominant groups who have insecure social identities and perceive threats from outgroups tend to perceive convergence by members of subordinate groups negatively. Also, individuals who are dependent on their groups and feel solidarity with them tend to see encounters in intergroup terms and tend to emphasize linguistic markers of their groups.

The third component in communication accommodation theory is the "immediate situation." There are five aspects to the immediate situation: (1) "sociopsychological states" (e.g., communicators' interpersonal or intergroup orientation in the situation), (2) "goals and addressee focus" (e.g., motivations in the encounter, conversational needs, relational needs), (3) "sociolinguistic strategies" (e.g., approximation, discourse management), (4) "behavior and tactics" (e.g., language, accent, topic), and (5) "labeling and attributions." Convergence and divergence are viewed as approximation strategies in this version of the theory. The five aspects of the immediate situation are interrelated. To illustrate, Gallois et al. (1995) contend that "when intergroup concerns are salient, speakers are likely to attempt to attune (or counterattune) to their interlocutors through approximation, interpretability, discourse management, and interpersonal control strategies using group-marked behavior and behavior relevant to group differences and intergroup role relations" (p. 145).

The final component of communication accommodation theory is "evaluation and future intentions." The propositions here focus on communicators' perceptions of their interlocutors' behavior in the interaction. Convergent behavior that is perceived to be based on "benevolent intent," for example, tends to be evaluated positively. When interlocutors who are perceived to be typical group members are evaluated positively, individuals are motivated to communicate with the interlocutors and other members of their groups in the future.

Code-Switching

The code (i.e., language or dialect) people use is, in part, a function of the vitality of the languages or dialects of the speakers involved and the desire of the communicators to accommodate to the people with whom they are communicating. There are also "normative" factors that contribute to code choice. Studies of immigrants in the United States who speak English as a second language, for example, suggest that English is used in public formal settings and their native languages are used in informal, nonpublic settings (e.g., Ryan & Cananza, 1977). This conclusion is supported by research in other countries (e.g., Philippines, Sechrest, Flores, & Arellano, 1986; Israel, Herman, 1961) as well. Similarly, the topic of conversation affects the code used. People who speak more than one language tend to use their native languages when discussing stressful or exciting topics (e.g., Brook, 1973).

In addition to the topic of conversation and the setting, people may switch languages to show warmth and group identification (Gumperz & Hernandez-Chavez,

1972). Recall Rodriquez's explanation of the effect of speaking in Spanish on his feelings of being bonded to his family presented in the ethnic identity section of Chapter 4. Similarly, immigrants tend to use the first language when discussing life in the native country (e.g., Ervin-Tripp, 1968). Using the first language to discuss life in the native country reinforces cultural heritage and fills a need to "identify with compatriots" (Chaika, 1982, p. 239).

Chaika (1982) points out that people sometimes switch codes for emphasis or to see if a stranger belongs to the ingroup. She argues that

> the switch from one language to another, in itself, has meaning. No matter what else a switch means, it reinforces bonds between speakers. Such switching can obviously only occur between those who speak the same language. It may be done in the presence of nonspeakers as a way of excluding them, just as jargon may. (p. 238)

The language or dialect people select, therefore, reinforces their social identities.

Zentella (1985) isolates several aspects of how code-switching functions among Puerto Ricans in East Harlem. First, some Puerto Ricans use code-switching to hide fluency or memory problems in the second language, but this accounts for only about 10 percent of Puerto Ricans' code-switching. Second, code-switching is used to mark switching from informal situations (using native language) to formal situations (using English) or the reverse. Third, code-switching is used to exert control, especially between parents and children. Fourth, code-switching is used to align speakers with others in specific situations (e.g., "I'm now positioning my identity as Hispanic"). Johnson (2000) also points out that code-switching "functions to announce specific identities, create certain meanings, and facilitate particular interpersonal role relationships" (p. 184).

Scotton (1983) argues that individuals choose the code in which they speak in order to negotiate relationships with others. She believes that the choice is based on a *negotiation principle* which directs a person to "choose the form of your conversational contribution [i.e., the code] such that it symbolizes the set of rights and obligations which you wish to be in force between speaker and addressee for the current exchange" (p. 116). In any situation, one code is unmarked (i.e., considered to be the standard code in that situation) and other codes are considered marked to some degree. Which codes are considered marked or unmarked depends on the speakers and the situation. To illustrate, an upper-level management person in Nairobi speaking in an office transaction would choose English as the unmarked choice (Scotton, 1990). A lower-level employee, in contrast, would choose Swahili as an unmarked code.

Scotton (1990) contends that "making the unmarked choice in a conventionalized exchange is a negotiation of normative and predicted behavior" (p. 92). In conventionalized exchanges, the unmarked choice usually is relatively clear. Upper-level management employees in Nairobi, for example, would choose to speak in English to other upper-level employees if they want to negotiate predictable behavior. Employees, however, can choose to use an unmarked code in conventionalized exchanges. When this occurs, they are trying to negotiate outcomes different from the expected one. This strategy is used to change the social distance between people. To illustrate, lower-level employees in Nairobi choosing to speak to upper-level employees in English instead of Swahili might be attempting to decrease the social distance between themselves and the upper-level employees.

Switching from an unmarked choice in a conventionalized exchange involves trying to negotiate new rights and obligations in the situation. "Marked switches are always disruptive, because they are disputing the status quo" (Scotton, 1990, p. 98). They can have positive or negative consequences, depending on whether they increase or decrease the social distance between the participants. Scotton (1983) isolates two maxims which guide these changes. The *deference* maxim says to "show deference in your code choice to those from whom you desire something, especially to negotiate face-threatening acts" (Scotton, 1990, p. 98). The *virtuosity* maxim involves making a linguistic choice based on the linguistic ability of the speaker or person being addressed.

In nonconventionalized exchanges, the unmarked code is not necessarily clear (Scotton, 1990). In these situations, speakers propose an unmarked code, and if listeners accept this choice (i.e., respond in this code), they accept the rights and obligations that go with speaking in this code. If listeners choose another code, they are trying to negotiate a different identity with the speakers.

The degree to which different codes are mixed depends on how multilingual the society is. In the United States, European Americans do not engage in extensive code-switching. In other societies that are multilingual, there is extensive code-switching. Where there is extensive code-switching, code-switching tends to be motivated by maximizing the positive benefits of the code being used and minimizing the negative aspects of code usage. Southworth (1980), for example, points out that in southern India

> in many situations it is not only possible, but socially necessary, to use more than one language in the course of an interaction. Thus, rules of formality may indicate English, whereas ethnic solidarity demands Tamil or Malayalam. In other cases, informality (in a domestic context, for example) may require Tamil or Malayalam, but individuals of different ethnic backgrounds may require some speakers to add a certain proportion of another language to the mix. (p. 140)

Obviously, the degree to which code switches are made depends on the linguistic abilities of the people involved.

Code-switching is linked to ethnic identity in organizations. Banks (1987), for example, argues that the boundary (the line separating) between marked (use of ethnic dialect) and unmarked ("standard" dialect) ethnic discourse is soft and permeable, while the boundary between low- and high-power positions in the organization is relatively hard and not easily permeable. Banks draws four conclusions regarding ethnic discourse in organizations. First, members of minority groups must cross the soft boundary from ethnically marked to unmarked discourse before crossing the boundary from low- to high-power positions. Second, crossing the boundary from ethnically marked to unmarked discourse is a function of the individuals' strategies to maximize rewards, as well as the norms for discourse in the organization. Third, there is an implicit promise from the organization he studied that if members of minority groups cross the boundary from ethnically marked to unmarked discourse, they will have the opportunity to cross the boundary from low- to high-power position. Finally, individuals who cross the boundary from ethnically marked to unmarked discourse "subtract from" their ethnic identities (i.e., using unmarked discourse takes away from the strength of their ethnic identities).

San Antonio (1987) contends that language-in-use also is a marker of social identities in a United States company in Japan. In the company she observed, the official policy is that only English is to be spoken. While this is the official policy of the company, the actual English ability of the Japanese employees ranges from no ability to speak English to almost native proficiency. San Antonio suggests that the use of English by Japanese employees is a way the employees take on the identity of being a Japanese with whom the U.S. Americans can work. U.S. American managers interpret the use of English and following U.S. American communication rules (e.g., use of first names, joking) positively and not using English negatively. The Japanese who are fluent in English in this company "protect" employees who do not speak English by speaking up in meetings and answering U.S. Americans' questions. Speaking English, therefore, "adds" to their chosen identity in this situation.

Language and Power

Language and power are intertwined highly. Power, as we use it, means the ability of one person to influence another. Reid and Ng (1999) isolate ways in which power and language are related: "language *reflects* power," "language *creates* power," "language *depoliticizes* power," and "language *routinizes* power."

Language Reflects Power   Reid and Ng (1999) point out that "the prestige of a language rises or falls with the power of its users . . . a speaker's power or powerlessness is reflected in the content or style of language and the style of language reflects upon group membership" (p. 121). Powerless speech generally is described as involving being hesitant, using tag questions (e.g., "that was nice, *wasn't it?*"), and using hedges (e.g., "maybe"). When these characteristics are not present, it is powerful speech. Female speech often is equated with powerless speech, but Reid and Ng contend that people tend to view low-status speakers as using powerless speech.

Reid and Ng (1999) argue that the idea that language reflects power suggests that power is static, that it is embedded in language. They believe that power is dynamic and that "language, far from being a simple refection of power, underpins the creation of power, its maintenance, and change" (p. 123).

Language Creates Power   Reid and Ng (1999) contend that the "linguistic and paralinguistic processes that underlie the ability to gain conversational turns are acts of power" because they allow people to "control the context and direction of conversation" (p. 124). The more turns we take in conversations, the more power we are perceived to have (at least in individualistic cultures like the United States).

Reid and Ng (1999) argue that our ability to use conversational turns and be perceived as influential depends on what we say in specific contexts. They go on to point out that "to the extent that utterance content serves to confirm for speakers their respective social identities, as defined within the social context, they are granted speaking rights, and hence place themselves in a position to become influential" (p. 126). Reid and Ng believe that the reason what we say (the content of our utterances) needs to be consistent with our social identities in the context of being given speaking turns is that this confirms others' stereotypes of our groups. This suggests that low-status group members may need to use stereotypical linguistic forms (e.g., women using powerless language) to be given speaking turns, but, at the same time, in doing this they are reinforcing group stereotypes.

Language Depoliticizes Power Reid and Ng (1999) point out that "attempts at gaining influence and power are often covered up and/or justified through social categorizations, or stereotypes. This aspect of power is particularly insidious, because concealing acts of power enables the powerful to maintain control" (p. 121). This allows the powerful to depoliticize power because it is "hidden" in their language.

Reid and Ng (1999) suggest that "by invoking social categorizations or stereotypes within language, a speaker may place self and the ingroup in a position to be influential" (p. 128). One issue here is that categories are not fixed and are "constructed, represented, and misrepresented within language" (p. 129). People in power, therefore, often use language to construct categories where strangers (outgroup members) are viewed as "outsiders." This marginalizes low-power groups.

Language Routinizes Power Social dominance of one group tends to be "accompanied by linguistic dominance, in which the more dominant party imposes its own language . . . as the standard language to use" (Reid & Ng, 1999, pp. 121–122). The use of masculine pronouns as generic pronouns in English, for example, routinizes the power of men over women. Reid and Ng point out that "by obscuring the female category, a sexist language actively suppresses the ability of women to mobilize as a group and strive for social change" (p. 133).

If power differences are not stable, linguistic changes can lead to changes in the power structure. Ng and Bradac (1993) argue that "factors that increase the tendency for subordinate groups to contrast their language with that of the dominant group, to focus on language with high consciousness, or in other words, to view language as an opaque (not a transparent) phenomenon will work against linguistic routinization" (p. 188). To illustrate, if all U.S. Americans mindfully stopped using masculine generic pronouns (e.g., using plurals, he/she, her or him) and other forms of nonsexist language (e.g., use police officer instead of policeman; chairperson not chairman), linguistic routinization regarding sexist language would cease. Over time this would, in turn, influence sex role stereotypes and the power women have.

Miscommunication in Intercultural Discourse

Miscommunication implies that things have gone wrong in the interaction between two people. While miscommunication can occur when any two people communicate, it is likely when native speakers (NSs) of one language communicate with nonnative speakers (NNSs) of their language (e.g., when NSs of English communicate with NNSs whose native language is not English). Gass and Varonis (1991) divide problems of communication in NS-NNS interaction into two categories: nonengagement and miscommunication.

Gass and Varonis (1991) isolate two types of *nonengagement:* noncommunication and communication breakoff. *Noncommunication* occurs when a NS or NNS avoids communicating with the other person. This could involve going out of the way to avoid interacting with the other person or consciously choosing to speak to other members of the ingroup. One reason noncommunication might occur is that NSs perceive that the energy necessary to communicate with NNSs is greater than what they will gain from the interaction. *Communication breakoffs* occur when NSs or NNSs end a conversation that is taking place. The main reason this usually occurs is that the people breaking off the conversation perceive that continuing the conversation is not in their best interest.

Gass and Varonis (1991) also isolate two types of *miscommunication:* misunderstanding and incomplete understanding. *Misunderstanding* is a "simple disparity between the speaker's and hearer's semantic analysis of a given utterance" (Milroy, 1984, p. 15). When misunderstandings occur, the participants do not recognize that there is a problem. *Incomplete understanding,* in contrast, occurs when "one or more participants perceive that something has gone wrong" (Milroy, 1984, p. 15). When incomplete understanding occurs, at least one of the participants clearly recognizes that there is a problem.

When misunderstandings occur, neither participant recognizes that a problem occurs during the interaction. After the interaction is over, however, one or both of the participants might recognize that there was a problem. The person who recognizes the problem can choose to ignore the problem, or try to figure out what the problem was (for one method to do this, see the discussion of description, interpretation, and evaluation in Chapter 10). Once participants figure out what the problem was, they can choose to ignore the problem or to correct it. The decision that participants make probably depends on the nature of the relationship between the people with whom they are communicating and the importance of the conversation. To illustrate, if the relationship between the two people is not close, the participants may choose to ignore problems. If the relationship is close, in contrast, the participants may choose to correct problems. Similarly, the participants may choose to ignore problems in conversations they do not think are important and to correct problems in conversations they think are important.

When incomplete understandings occur, at least one of the participants recognizes that there is a problem during the conversation. This is more likely to occur when participants are mindful of their communication than when they communicate on automatic pilot. Participants who recognize problems can choose to ignore problems or to try to correct them. The factors that influence this choice probably are similar to those that influence the choices regarding miscommunication after the interaction. If a decision to correct problems is made, they must negotiate to correct the incomplete understanding. After attempting to negotiate the incomplete understanding, participants need to decide whether they have corrected problems. If they have not corrected problems, they must decide whether to try again or ignore problems.

When NNSs have low levels of competence in NSs' languages, both parties tend to assume that problems in communication will occur. When NNSs have high levels of competence, in contrast, there is an increased tendency for them not to recognize problems. Since the participants "assume they understand each other, they are less likely to question interpretations" of each other's messages (Gumperz & Tannen, 1979, p. 315).

Varonis and Gass (1985) argue that this is the most "dangerous" type of situation because participants are confident in their interpretations of others' messages but their interpretations actually are inaccurate.

Gass and Varonis (1984) argue that familiarity is one of the major factors that influence NSs' ability to comprehend NNSs. The more familiar NS are with the topic of the conversation, the easier it is for them to comprehend NNSs' speech. Familiarity with the NNSs' speech and accent also facilitates comprehension. To illustrate, the more familiar English speakers are with Japanese speaking English and their accents, the more easily they can comprehend specific Japanese speaking English. Finally, familiarity with specific NNSs facilitates NSs' comprehension of their speech.

Misunderstandings and incomplete understanding can emerge from pragmatic errors. As indicated earlier, pragmatic rules tell us how to interpret the meaning of utterances. Riley (1989) argues that *pragmatic errors* are "the result of an interactant imposing the social rules of his [or her] communicative behavior in a situation where the social rules of another culture would be more appropriate" (p. 234). He isolates four types of pragmatic errors we make in intercultural interactions: pragmalinguistic, sociopragmatic, inchoactive, and nonlinguistic (the first two originally were isolated by Thomas, 1983).

Pragmalinguistic errors are language-specific errors that involve the pragmatic force of an utterance having different meanings in two languages or that occur when speech strategies are transferred inappropriately from one language to another (Thomas, 1983). English speakers who speak aggressively when speaking in Japanese, for example, are making pragmalinguistic errors because Japanese speakers humble themselves. French hotel receptionists who hand back a passport to a foreign visitor saying "please" also are making these errors (e.g., translating what would be said in French into English).

Sociopragmatic errors "stem from cross-culturally different perceptions of what constitutes appropriate linguistic behavior" (Thomas, 1983, p. 99). These errors are a function of *not* perceiving the situation or categorizing the other people involved in accordance with the cultural norms they are using. To illustrate, if professors from Japan are visiting professors in the United States and immediately after introductions ask, "How old are you?" the Japanese professors are making a sociopragmatic error because they are using Japanese cultural communication rules (categorizing "American" professors on the basis of age) when they should be using "American" rules.

Inchoactive errors are a function of "a failure to appreciate the 'true' value of discourse" (Riley, 19889, p. 237). This type of error is a function of the cultural value placed on talk and silence discussed earlier in this chapter. Scollon and Scollon (1981), for example, argue that problems of communication between European Americans and Athbaskan Indians are due to different orientations toward talk and silence. European Americans "talk to strangers to get to know them," and Athbaskan Indians "get to know someone one in order to be able to speak." If we do not understand the values people place on talk and silence, we inevitably will make errors in interpreting their speech.

Nonlinguistic errors are errors that occur because of misinterpretations of the nonverbal cues strangers use (Riley, 1989). Riley argues that there are situations where responses to behaviors may require a verbal response and situations where no verbal response is required, but a nonverbal response is required. Nonverbal messages are discussed in the next chapter.

Riley (1989) argues that there are many strategies that can be used to correct pragmatic errors when they occur. Correcting errors, however, requires some awareness that errors have occurred. He isolates seven strategies for correcting pragmatic errors: (1) evasion (including message abandonment and change of focus); (2) paraphrase (including approximation, circumlocution, description, and word coinage); (3) transfer (including literal translation and language switch); (4) appeals (for assistance, clarification, or feedback); (5) nonverbal (gesture, drawing, writing); (6) checks (giving further information, examples); and (7) simplification (of grammar or vocabulary). Any of these strategies can be used to correct pragmatic errors and negotiate meanings when we communicate with strangers.

Language Usage and Uncertainty Reduction

The language strangers use influences how we reduce uncertainty. Berger and Bradac (1982) suggest four alternative models with respect to the relationship between language and uncertainty reduction:

Model 1 specifies that we use others' language to develop hypotheses about their group affiliations. On the basis of these hypotheses, judgments of similarity are made. The greater the similarity we perceive, the more our uncertainty is reduced.

Model 2 specifies that we use others' languages to make a judgment of their psychological traits. We then use these psychological traits to judge how similar others are to us. The more similarity we perceive, the more our uncertainty is reduced.

Model 3 combines Models 1 and 2. It posits that we use language to make a judgment of others' group memberships. Based on others' group memberships, we make assumptions about their psychological traits. Based on the traits, we make assumptions about how similar they are to us.

Model 4 suggests that we make judgments of similarity directly from the language others use.

These four models are valid in different situations (Berger & Bradac, 1982).

Gudykunst and Ting-Toomey (1990) suggest that the validity of the models varies depending on the interpersonal and intergroup characteristics of the interaction. When intergroup factors are very important and interpersonal factors are not very important, we tend to use language to make judgments of group affiliations which lead to judgments of similarity (Model 1). When intergroup factors are very important and interpersonal factors also are very important, a judgement of group membership is used to make judgments of psychological traits, which form the basis for judgments of similarity (Model 3). When intergroup factors are not very important and interpersonal factors are very important, language leads directly to judgments of psychological traits, which lead to judgments of similarity (Model 2). Finally, when neither interpersonal nor intergroup factors are very important, language usage leads directly to judgments of similarity (Model 4).

SUMMARY

In this chapter, we considered some of the cultural, sociological, and psychological dimensions of language and verbal behavior. The theoretical perspective provided by Sapir and Whorf warns us not to consider language to be merely a medium through which we express our thoughts and feelings. Language is much more than that. As we acquire language, we acquire culture, which, in turn, conditions our perception, thinking, and behavior.

Following Bernstein's conceptualization of language and social context, various languages can be placed on a continuum of restricted and elaborated codes. This continuum of linguistic variations closely coincides with Hall's continuum of high-context to low-context communication messages. While restricted codes are a predominant mode of linguistic and verbal behavior in collectivistic cultures, elaborated codes are relied on heavily for thinking processes and social interaction in individualistic cultures.

In addition, we noted how language ties us emotionally to the speech community to which we belong. Through group identification with our language, we develop both a sense of identification with our own speech community and a feeling of distinctiveness from other speech communities. Foreign diplomats visiting the United States (strangers) may choose to speak at a press conference in their own languages rather than in English. This deliberate choice of speech mode commonly is respected as a symbolic assertion of the national sovereignty represented by the diplomat. The heart-warming speech given by Pope John Paul II while visiting the United States, in contrast, constituted a friendly and respectful gesture to the public in that he addressed his audience in English.

When strangers move from one culture to another for an extended period of time, the first and foremost task is to acquire the host language. The acquisition of the host language is necessary not only to communicate and meet daily challenges but also to become acculturated into the new ways of living and begin to develop new group identities. Lambert (1963) states that "an individual successfully acquiring a second language gradually adopts various aspects of behavior which characterize members of another linguistic-cultural group" (p. 114).

Understanding cultural and subcultural variations in the social meaning of verbal behavior as outlined in this chapter is a crucial step toward gaining a greater understanding of ourselves and the strangers we meet. On the basis of such understanding, we may try to develop empathy and patience for strangers whose primary language and modes of verbal behavior are different from our own, thereby decreasing our anxiety and increasing our ability to understand and predict their behavior.

STUDY QUESTIONS

1. What is the Sapir-Whorf hypothesis?
2. How are restricted and elaborate code similar to low- and high-context messages?
3. Why is there little rhetorical tradition in Asian cultures?
4. How do direct and indirect styles of communication differ? Which styles predominate in individualistic and collectivistic cultures?

5. How do elaborate and understated styles of communication differ?
6. What does the way we take turns in conversations tell us about our relationships with others?
7. How do turn taking and topic management differ in individualistic and collectivistic cultures?
8. How does ethnolinguistic vitality influence the way members of different groups communicate with each other?
9. How are standard and nonstandard dialects evaluated?
10. What factors contribute to members of a minority group learning the majority group's language?
11. What factors contribute to our converging toward or diverging from others in conversations?
12. When do people who speak English as a second language tend to speak English, and when do they tend to speak their native languages?
13. What are the differences between misunderstanding and incomplete understanding?

SUGGESTED READINGS

Agar, M. (1994). *Language shock: Understanding the culture of conversation.* New York: Morrow.

Coupland, N., Giles, H., & Wiemann, J. (Eds.). (1991). *"Miscommunication" and problematic talk.* Thousand Oaks, CA: Sage.

Edwards, J. (1985). *Language, society, and identity.* Oxford, UK: Blackwell.

Fitch, K. L. (1998). *Speaking relationally: Culture, communication, and interpersonal connection.* New York: Guilford.

Giles, H., & Coupland, N. (1991). *Language: Contexts and consequences.* Pacific Grove, CA: Brooks/Cole.

Gumperz, J., & Levinson, S. (Eds.). (1996). *Rethinking linguistic relativity.* Cambridge, UK: Cambridge University Press.

Johnson, F. L. (2000). *Speaking culturally: Language diversity in the United States.* Thousand Oaks, CA: Sage.

Spencer-Oatey, H. (Ed.). (2000). *Culturally speaking: Managing rapport through talk across cultures.* London: Continuum.

9

NONVERBAL MESSAGES

How stupid [are they] who would
patch the hatred in [their] eyes
with the smile of [their] lips.

Kahlil Gibran

Just as our verbal behaviors are influenced by our cultures, our nonverbal behaviors reflect the cultural patterns we acquire throughout the socialization process. The way in which we move about in space when communicating with strangers is based primarily on our physical and emotional responses to environmental stimuli. Our verbal behaviors are mostly explicit and are processed cognitively, but our nonverbal behaviors are spontaneous, ambiguous, and often beyond our conscious awareness and control. When we communicate with strangers, our understanding of the interactions is limited by the strangers' unfamiliar nonverbal behaviors. From greetings to expressions of feelings, we may find ourselves feeling uncomfortable because of strangers' nonverbal behavior. Since our perceptions of nonverbal behaviors are rarely conscious, we may not know exactly why we are feeling uncomfortable.

Hall (1966) refers to the largely unconscious phenomenon of nonverbal communication as the "hidden dimension" of culture. It is considered hidden because, unlike verbal messages, nonverbal messages are embedded in the contextual field of communication. In addition to the situational and relational cues present in our interactions, nonverbal messages provide us with important contextual cues. Together with verbal and other contextual cues, nonverbal messages help us interpret the meaning of our communication with strangers.

Our purpose in this chapter is to examine cultural variability in nonverbal behaviors and how nonverbal behaviors influence our communication with strangers. We begin, however, with a brief overview of nonverbal communication.

THE NATURE OF NONVERBAL COMMUNICATION

Language and nonverbal cues are similar in some ways and different in others. First, nonverbal cues are discrete, as language is; nonverbal cues can be separated from one another. Second, some nonverbal cues are created on the basis of agreement among the members of a group using them and, therefore, are arbitrary, as symbols are. To illustrate, "the finger" is an obscene gesture in the United States, but other cultures use different gestures to mean the same thing as the finger. Other nonverbal cues are not arbitrary. A smile, for example, is recognized around the world to represent happiness (this is not to say that smiles cannot be used in other circumstances as well). Third, language involves displacement (i.e., the ability to use language to refer to things that are not present), but nonverbal cues do not. Nonverbal cues are limited to referring to things that are present. Finally, language and nonverbal cues differ in terms of their relative weight in determining meaning. In general, "adults place more reliance on nonverbal cues than verbal ones in determining meaning" (Burgoon, Buller, & Woodall, 1989, p. 155). This is especially true when the verbal and nonverbal messages are inconsistent.

Nonverbal cues serve several functions in interaction (Ekman & Friesen, 1969). First, nonverbal cues may *repeat* verbal messages. Second, nonverbal cues may *contradict* verbal cues. In English, if people tell us they love us in a flat tone of voice, we are likely to interpret the tone of voice as contradicting the verbal message. Third, nonverbal cues can *substitute* for the verbal messages. Fourth, nonverbal cues may *complement* verbal messages. Fifth, nonverbal cues can accent parts of verbal messages and regulate the flow of conversations.

There are various types of nonverbal behavior that we use when we communicate with strangers. First, our *physical appearance* provides nonverbal cues that others use to make judgments about us. Second, the way we use space (called *proxemics*) helps us regulate intimacy and control our sensory exposure to strangers. Third, the way we move our bodies (called *kinesic behavior*) gives strangers information about us. Fourth, the way we use our voices (called *paralanguage*) tells strangers how we define the relationships between ourselves and them. Fifth, the degree to which we *touch* strangers and the degree to which we allow strangers to touch us provide cues to how we see our relationships.

Often nonverbal behaviors are discussed as either universal or culture-bound. It, however, is not that simple. LaFrance and Mayo (1978) point out that there are at least three layers of nonverbal behavior:

> The innermost core represents nonverbal behaviors considered to be universal and innate; facial expressions of some emotional states belong to this core. Next come the nonverbal behaviors that show both uniformity and diversity; members of all cultures display affect, express intimacy, and deal with status but the particular signs of so doing are variable. Finally, there are culture-bound nonverbal behaviors which manifest great dissimilarity across cultures—language-related acts such as emblems [nonverbal cues with a direct verbal translation; e.g., "V" for victory], illustrators [nonverbal cues which directly accompany speech; e.g., cues which illustrate what is being said, such as nodding the head to accompany verbal agreement in the United States], and regulators [cues which regulate the back-and-forth flow of speaking and listening; e.g., looking at the speaker when listening and looking away when talking in European American culture] show diversity most clearly. (p. 73)

Nonverbal behaviors, therefore, vary from universality to dissimilarity across cultures.

CROSS-CULTURAL VARIABILITY IN NONVERBAL MESSAGES

In this section, we examine cultural variability in nonverbal messages. We begin by looking at the recognition and expression of emotions. Next, we examine how the desire for contact influences cultural differences in nonverbal behaviors. Following this, we discuss the process of interpersonal synchronization.

Emotion Expression and Recognition

People everywhere experience feelings such as happiness, sadness, and anger and exhibit a great deal of similarity in their expressions of these human emotions. Darwin (1872) observed certain similarities in the expressive behavior of humans with different cultural backgrounds and interpreted them as being due to characteristics inborn in all humans. Darwin contends that emotional facial expressions are inherited because they were biologically adaptive in earlier times. The main purpose of emotional expression today is to signal internal emotional states to others. Biologists, biologically oriented anthropologists, and psychologists repeatedly emphasize the innate similarities in human expressive behavior.

The innate view of emotional expression has been challenged repeatedly. La Barre (1947), for example, suggests that emotional expression is culturally based. Similarly, Birdwhistell (1963) argues that no expressive movement has a universal meaning and that all movements are a product of culture and are not biologically inherited or inborn.

Ekman (1972) integrates these two views on human emotional expression into a neuro-cultural theory of facial expressions of emotion. Ekman agrees that facial expressions of emotion are inherited. He also believes that cultural constraints play a very important role in shaping how emotions are expressed. Ekman suggests that cultural *display rules* that are learned within our cultures tell us when to express emotions and when not to express them. Cultural display rules lead us to intensify, deintensify, neutralize, or mask our facial displays to comply with the normative demands of specific situations in our cultures (see Bond, 1993, for cultural display rules in Chinese culture). There also are cultural *decoding rules* which tell us how to interpret others' emotions when they are displayed. Matsumoto and Kudoh (1993), for example, argue that U.S. Americans associate more positive characteristics with people who smile than the Japanese do.

Universals in Emotion Recognition   There has been extensive research on the universal aspects of emotion recognition. Izard (1968, summarized in Izard, 1980), for example, had individuals classify photographs of facial expressions into one of eight categories (interest-excitement, enjoyment-joy, surprise-startle, distress-anguish, disgust-contempt, anger-rage, shame-humiliation, and fear-terror) of emotions. His research reveals that there is high agreement on the category of emotion represented in the photographs in the United States, Germany, Sweden, France, Switzerland, Greece, and Japan. Data from Ekman and Friesen's (1971) study in Brazil, Chile, and Argentina yield similar results for six of the eight emotions (interest-excitement and shame-humiliation were omitted).

Ekman et al.'s (1987) study supports the argument that there are universal facial expressions of emotions. Research in 10 cultures (Estonia, Germany, Greece, Hong Kong, Italy, Japan, Scotland, Sumatra, Turkey, and the United States) indicates that agreement is not limited to conditions in which observers are limited to seeing one emotion for each facial expression. In this study there was agreement on which emotion was strongest and which was second strongest. Ekman et al. also observe agreement on the relative strength of the emotions expressed (see Matsumoto et al., 2001, for a list of the studies conducted).

Matsumoto, Wallbott, and Scherer (1989) summarize many of the findings that have emerged from the cross-cultural study of emotions. They contend that there is universality in the recognition of six emotions in facial expressions: anger, disgust, fear, happiness, sadness, and surprise. In addition to these six, they believe that recognition of contempt also probably is universal. Scherer and Wallbott (1994) argue that research in 37 cultures supports the universality of the expression of these seven emotions. Haidt and Keltner (1999) suggest there also may be universal recognition of embarrassment. Matsumoto et al. (1989) point out that people across cultures not only recognize the primary facial expressions but also recognize the secondary emotion being expressed. In addition to recognizing the emotion being expressed, people appear to agree on the relative intensity of the emotion being expressed.

In addition to recognition of facial expression of emotions, it appears that there is agreement on the recognition of vocal emotional expressions. Beier and Zautra (1972), for example, note that non-English-speaking Japanese and Polish students are as accurate at decoding vocal emotional expressions in English as students in the United States. A study by Bezooijen, Otto, and Heenan (1983) indicates that Dutch, Taiwanese, and Japanese adults are able to identify Dutch vocal expressions of emotion. Scherer, Banse, and Wallbott (2001) examine the vocal expression of anger, fear, joy, and sadness in nine countries. They report that there are "similar inference rules from vocal expression across cultures" (p. 76). Scherer et al. note that accuracy in inferring emotions from vocal cues decreases as a function of language dissimilarity.

Matsumoto et al. (1989) also isolate universal aspects of emotional experiences. There appears, for example, to be consistency in antecedents for some emotions. To illustrate, the birth of new family members elicits joy and strangers, novel situations, and risky situations tend to elicit fear. Further, anger and disgust appear to occur most frequently and fear least frequently across cultures. Situations leading to sadness appear to be experienced most intensely, and situations eliciting shame and guilt are experienced least intensely. Mesquita, Frijda, and Scherer (1997) conclude "that a large number of event types bear emotional meaning to many or most human beings, regardless of their cultural origin . . . there is a high degree of commonality in human emotional sensitivities" (p. 270).

Before discussing cultural differences in emotions, it is necessary to point out two caveats regarding accuracy in the recognition of emotions. Rosenthall and his associates' (1979) study indicates that the accuracy of interpreting role-plays of emotions varies but that respondents in all cultures are more accurate than would be expected by chance. The differences in accuracy that emerge appear to be a function of cultural similarity. The most accurate interpretations are made by respondents from cultures similar to the United States (e.g., Australia), where the role-plays were constructed, and the least accurate interpretations were from respondents in cultures very different from the United States (e.g., New Guinea). Ducci et al.'s (1983) study of the recognition of western emotions in Ethiopia suggests that familiarity with western culture is related to accuracy of recognizing western emotions.

To summarize, after reviewing research on the recognition and expression of emotions, Izard (1980) concludes that

> robust cross-cultural data . . . lend strong support to Darwin's thesis that the expressions of the emotions are innate and universal. Some studies suggest that universality is limited to

certain primary or fundamental emotions. However, even some blends (expressions representing components of two or more fundamental emotions) are correctly identified across certain cultures, though blends do not yield as high agreement as unitary expressions when naive judges are used. Although the expressions and inner experiences that characterize the fundamental emotions are innate and universal, there are numerous cultural differences in attitudes toward emotions and their expression. (p. 216)

Understanding the expression of emotions, therefore, requires that we also examine how culture influences the display rules used.

Cultural Differences in the Expression of Emotions   Matsumoto et al. (1989) isolate several differences in the expression of emotions. Rather than discussing differences between specific cultures, we focus here on systematic variations in emotions across cultures. There is some evidence that cultural differences in the expression of emotions, for example, may be related to the dimensions of cultural variability discussed in Chapter 3.

Gudykunst and Ting-Toomey (1988) note that attitudes toward some emotions are consistent with Hofstede's (1980) dimensions of cultural variability. To illustrate, they observe that people in masculine cultures tend to experience distress more than people in feminine cultures. They argue that since masculine cultures emphasize achievement and excelling, people in those cultures experience distress if they do not achieve or excel. Feminine cultures, in contrast, emphasize service and not trying to do better than others. Failure to accomplish those goals should not lead to distress.

Gudykunst and Ting-Toomey (1988) point out that people in high uncertainty avoidance cultures experience less joy from relationships than people in low uncertainty avoidance cultures. This finding is reasonable given that relationships are guided by strict rules in high uncertainty avoidance cultures and that the rules are relatively flexible in low uncertainty avoidance cultures.

Gudykunst and Ting-Toomey (1988) report that nonvocal (e.g., reactions that include the use of the body) and verbal reactions to emotions are associated with individualism. People in individualistic cultures display more nonvocal and vocal reactions to emotions than people in collectivistic cultures. This finding is consistent with the descriptions of individualistic and collectivistic cultures presented in Chapter 3.

Matsumoto (1989) extends Gudykunst and Ting-Toomey's research. He examines the perception of emotions in 15 cultures. Matsumoto concludes that

cultures high in power distance and low in individualism stress hierarchy and group cohesion ("collectivity"), while individuality is minimized. In these cultures, the communication of negative emotions threatens group solidarity and interpersonal social structure. On the other hand, cultures low in power distance and high in individualism may sanction the communication of these emotions more, as they relate to individual freedom to express and perceive negative emotions. As such, they do not threaten social structures and groups to the same extent found in high power distance, low individualism cultures. (p. 101)

Understanding cultural differences in emotion expression requires using at least two dimensions of cultural variability.

Matsumoto (1991) theoretically links individualism-collectivism and power distance to the expression of emotions. He argues that since subjugating individuals' goals to group goals is more important in collectivistic cultures than in individualistic cultures, members of collectivistic cultures will emphasize emotional displays that facilitate group cooperation, harmony, and cohesion more than members of individualistic cultures. He also points out that "members of individualistic cultures display a wider variety of emotional behaviors than members of collectivistic cultures. Collective cultures are not as tolerant of wide ranges of individual variations, and thus frown upon such variation" (p. 132).

The specific emotions displayed depend on the context and target of the emotion. Matsumoto (1991), for example, provides examples regarding expressing negative emotions when with a member of the ingroup in collectivistic cultures. In a public context it would be inappropriate to display the emotion because it would reflect negatively on the ingroup. In addition, if the emotion is a reaction to an ingroup member and is experienced in private with the ingroup member, it would be inappropriate to express the emotion because it would disturb the harmony of the group. If the emotion is a reaction to an outgroup member, however, it would be acceptable to express it because this would foster cohesion in the ingroup.

Matsumoto (1991) goes on to argue that people in individualistic cultures are more likely to express positive and not express negative emotions with members of the outgroup than are members of collectivistic cultures. We disagree with his argument. Members of collective cultures avoid establishing intimacy with members of outgroups and, therefore, would not display positive emotions in their presence. Virtually all analyses of individualism-collectivism suggest that members of collective cultures avoid negative behaviors with the ingroup or people of higher status but not with the outgroup. Friesen's (1972) study illustrates how negative emotions are avoided with members of the ingroup. He notes that students in Japan (collectivistic) and the United States (individualistic) experienced similar affect when viewing a stressful film alone. When viewing the film with a member of the ingroup, however, the students in the United States displayed more negative affect than the students from Japan.

Triandis et al. (1988) provide an explanation for the display of negative affect toward members of outgroups in collectivistic cultures. They point out that in collectivistic cultures a "do whatever you can get away with" orientation applies toward members of outgroups. Members of outgroups in collectivistic cultures often are treated as nonpersons (e.g., Nakane, 1974). Cole (1990) reports that members of collectivistic cultures are more dominating with members of outgroups when trying to resolve conflict than are members of individualistic cultures. Given this line of reasoning, we believe that members of collectivistic cultures are more likely to express negative emotions with members of outgroups in conflict situations than are members of individualistic cultures.

Matsumoto (1991) also links power distance to the expression of emotions. He argues that people in high power distance cultures will display emotions that preserve status differences, while people in low power distance cultures will display emotions that minimize status differences. To illustrate, people in high power distance cultures would express positive emotions to people higher in status and negative emotions to people lower in status. Matsumoto illustrates this by comparing Japan and the United States. He suggests that

> status differs among retail clerks, department managers, store managers, and regional directors in the retail business. Japanese department managers would not hesitate to display negative

emotions to their retail clerks (lower status). The retail clerks, meanwhile, would not dare display negative emotions back to the department manager. The combination of rules clearly differentiates status differences between the department manager and the clerks. [U.S.] American department managers, however, would be more likely to treat their clerks as equals, minimizing status differences by displaying less negative emotions and more positive emotions to reduce friction. (p. 133)

These speculations, however, must be considered tentative because there is little difference between Japan and the United States in terms of power distance (Hofstede, 1980).

The line of theorizing and research outlined in this section is in its infancy. The findings to date, however, suggest that individualism-collectivism and power distance provide coherent theoretical explanations for some of the similarities and differences in the display of emotions across cultures.

Before proceeding, an alternative explanation for cultural differences in the display of emotions needs to be presented. It is possible that individualism-collectivism and power distance do not directly influence the display of emotions but instead influence the way people perceive situations in which they experience emotions. The perceptions of the situation, in turn, influence the display of emotions. There is preliminary evidence from research in the United States and India to support this explanation. Roseman et al. (1995) report that the members of the two cultures respond with similar emotions when they perceive the situation the same way but that their perceptions of situations often differ. More research, however, is needed to test this explanation.

To summarize, there are many aspects of the perception and expression of emotions that appear to be universal. Even though this is true, our cultures shape our emotional lives. Mesquita et al. (1997) point out that

it should be acknowledged simultaneously that certain socially and individually important emotional response types are universal or near-universal, and that the experience, phenomenology, and social role of these response types may be different in essential regards. Even where universal patterns of appraisal and response exist, these universal cores may be submerged in the culturally determined contexts of experience, meaning, and social interaction. (p. 288)

Our emotional lives, therefore, are both similar to and different from those of members of other cultures.

Contact

In the preceding section, we used dimensions of cultural variability (e.g., individualism-collectivism) to explain similarities and differences in the display of emotions. One way to organize some of the research on nonverbal behavior is to use Hall's (1966) work on contact and noncontact cultures. Hall (1966) argues that people regulate intimacy by controlling sensory exposure through the use of interpersonal distance and space. He argues that cultures can be differentiated in terms of the degree of contact preferred by their members. Cultures in which the people tend to stand close and touch a lot are referred to as high-contact cultures, while cultures in which people stand apart and tend not to touch are referred to as low-contact cultures.

Andersen et al. (2001) suggest that Hall's (1966) distinction between contact and noncontact cultures is related to Mehrabian's (1971) immediacy dimension of meaning. *Immediacy* is the evaluative dimension of meaning, and it involves judgments of close-far, positive-negative, and good-bad that are used to indicate psychological closeness to others. Mehrabian contends that people approach persons and things high in immediacy and avoid persons or things low in immediacy. Immediacy behaviors reflect sensory stimulation, indicate attentiveness, and communicate liking (Mehrabian, 1971). The behaviors associated with immediacy are "(a) close conversational distance, (b) direct body and facial orientation, (c) forward lean, (d) increased and direct gaze, (e) positive reinforcers such as smiling, head nods, and pleasant facial expressions, (f) postural openness, (g) frequent gesturing, and (h) touch" (Burgoon et al., 1989, p. 315). In combination these behaviors suggest immediacy. Taken individually, however, they may indicate only the intensity of interaction. To illustrate, when we are angry with other people, we may engage in the same amount of eye contact as we do when we are attracted to them. When we are attracted to someone, we also will lean forward and have a pleasant look on our faces.

The immediacy nonverbal behaviors are highly interrelated. Increases in one of the behaviors may be associated with decreases in another in order to keep the message balanced (Burgoon et al., 1989). To illustrate, if we move closer to someone, we may decrease our eye contact to maintain the same degree of psychological closeness to the other person. When the various immediacy behaviors are combined, the psychological closeness is increased. It is important to recognize that the immediacy behaviors described here apply in the United States, especially in the European American subculture. Immediacy behaviors differ across cultures and across ethnic groups in the United States.

When Hall's (1966) and Mehrabian's (1971) schemes are combined, we can talk about cultures varying along a continuum from high contact to low contact. People in high-contact cultures evaluate "close" as positive and good and evaluate "far" as negative and bad. People in low-contact cultures evaluate "close" as negative and bad and "far" as positive and good. This conceptualization of the importance of contact helps us organize a lot of the past research on nonverbal behavior.

Territorality   Altman and Chemers (1980a) see *territorial behavior* as involving the "control or ownership of a place or object on a temporary or permanent basis" (p. 121). The place or object may be large or small, and it may be the possession of either a group or a person. Territorial behavior serves several functions, including providing status and identity for the people who own or control the territory. Altman and Chemers divide the types of territory we use into three categories: primary, secondary, and public.

Primary territories are controlled or owned by individuals or groups and are central to the lives of the people. Examples of primary territory include homes, offices, farms, and community property. Strangers must be invited into primary territories. Uninvited intrusions into primary territory leads to defensive behavior. Altman and Chemers (1980a) argue that the "inability to control a primary territory successfully may be a serious affront to the psychological well-being of a person or group" (p. 130).

Secondary territories are not as psychologically central to people. These territories may include places like the neighborhood street or bar, social clubs, and other places where there is a combination of public and private usage of the territory. Altman and Chemers (1980a) point out that secondary territories involve the potential for misunderstandings. Since they involve both public and private usage, strangers may not realize that there is a private aspect to secondary territories.

Public territories are available for people who have permission to use them on a temporary basis. Public territories include, but are not limited to, forms of public transportation (e.g., trains, planes, taxis), parks, tables in restaurants, beaches, and so forth. Public territories are not as central to people's lives as primary and secondary territories. Altman and Chemers (1980a) point out that in many "parts of the world certain groups within cultures are denied access to public facilities on the basis of their ethnicity, nationality, religion, or social class" (p. 135).

It is important to keep in mind that the way people mark their primary, secondary, and public territories varies across cultures. There also is variability across cultures in how the different forms of territories contribute to individuals' definitions of themselves. Native Americans in the northwestern part of North America, for example, use totem poles to mark their territories and reflect their clans and lineages—their social identities. Offices in the United States usually are decorated with photos, mementos, and so forth, to reflect the occupants' personal identities.

In addition to the use of territory in general, people vary in the way they use physical space—how they perceive, organize, and behave in their spatial environment. Hall (1966) suggests, for example, that human proxemic behavior can be classified into three general categories:

1. The *fixed feature,* such as spatial behavior in relation to an immovable and unchangeable environmental structure (e.g., organization of a town, architecture of a building)
2. The *semifixed feature,* which is conditioned by an environmental structure that is not permanently fixed (e.g., seating arrangement, furniture arrangement)
3. The *dynamic feature,* which is codetermined by an individual's movement in space and by the movements of others with whom the person interacts

These three categories, of course, are not mutually exclusive but are interrelated in any actual spatial behavior. To illustrate, the way two college roommates live in a dormitory is influenced by the space as structured by their room and the building, as well as by the physical conditions of the university campus and the town in which the campus is located.

Of particular interest here are the dynamic aspects of interpersonal space. The dynamic interpersonal space is controlled, in part, by the nature of the relationship between communicators. In general, the more intimate relationships are, the more people permit each other to come close. Ashcraft and Scheflen (1976) observe that "in the early stages of courtship, distance may be an issue of negotiation. But as courtship escalates, whatever the earlier distancing arrangements, the space between partners is reduced drastically. It disappears altogether in the physical union of copulation" (p. 7). It appears that the closer the distance between people, the closer their relationships are across cultures. The distance people expect to have between themselves and others in particular relationships (e.g., friendships), however, varies across cultures.

Hall (1966) proposes four spatial zones used in social relations in the United States:

1. *Intimate distance* (0–1.5 feet) usually is maintained only between intimates or close associates, and not often in public. At this distance, a rich array of cues can be exchanged, including heat, smell, fine visual details, and touch.
2. *Personal distance* (1.5–4 feet) is a transitional distance where rich communication possibilities still exist.
3. *Social distance* (4–12 feet) is the distance of business and general public contact. Office desks, furniture arrangements in public settings, and chair locations in homes generally put people somewhere in this zone. One can still receive a fair number of communication cues, but they are not fine-grained.
4. *Public distance* (12–25 feet) usually is reserved for formal occasions, public speakers, or high-status figures. At this distance, only gross cues are available, and such cues as smell, heat, and fine visual and vocal details are lost.

These spatial zones, however, are not the same in all cultures.

Sussman and Rosenfeld's (1982) study of how interpersonal distance is used by Japanese (low contact), U.S. Americans (moderate contact), and Venezuelans (high contact) indicates that when they speak their native languages, Japanese sit the farthest apart, Venezuelans sit the closest, and the U.S. Americans are in the middle. They also note that when speaking English, the Japanese and Venezuelans use interpersonal distances approximating that used by the U.S. Americans. Other research supports the conclusion from Sussman and Rosenfeld's study. Engebretson and Fullmer (1970), for example, observe that Japanese use greater interpersonal distances than Japanese Americans and European Americans in Hawaii. Watson and Graves' (1966) research suggests that Arabs prefer a closer sitting distance than U.S. Americans. Little (1968) notes that members of Mediterranean cultures (e.g., Greece, southern Italy; high contact) prefer closer interpersonal distances than Northern Europeans (moderate contact). Northern Europeans tend to use similar interactional distances similar to those of U.S. Americans (Sommer, 1968).

How people in different cultures react to violations of their personal space appears to be related to individualism-collectivism. Gudykunst and Ting-Toomey (1988), for example, suggest that "members of individualistic cultures tend to take an active, aggressive stance when their space is violated, while members of collectivistic cultures tend to assume a passive, withdrawal stance when their personal space is violated" (p. 125).

Sensory Involvement In general, people in high-contact cultures prefer greater sensory involvement with the person with whom they are communicating than people in low-contact cultures. Sussman and Rosenfeld (1982) conclude that sensory involvement is "high among South Americans, Southern and Eastern Europeans, and Arabs, and low among Asians, Northern Europeans, and U.S. Americans" (p. 66).

Almaney and Alwan (1982) compare the use of sensory information in Arab cultures (high contact) with that in other cultures. They contend that

to the Arab, to be able to smell a friend is reassuring. Smelling is a way of being involved with another, and to deny a friend his [or her] breath would be to act ashamed. In some rural Middle Eastern areas, when Arab intermediaries call to inspect a prospective bride for a relative, they sometimes ask to smell her. Their purpose is not to make sure she is freshly scrubbed; apparently what they look for is any lingering odor of anger or discontent. The Burmese [high contact] show their affection during greeting by pressing mouths and noses upon the cheek and inhaling the breath strongly. The Samoans [high contact] show affection by juxtaposing noses and smelling heartily. In contrast, [U.S.] Americans [moderate contact] seem to maintain their distance and suppress their sense of smell. (p. 17)

Differences in the use of smell can create misunderstandings when people from different cultures communicate. Hall (1983) points out that when Arabs interact with U.S. Americans, they often feel sensory deprivation and become alienated because of the lack of close social contact. U.S. Americans, in contrast, are anxious because of too much social contact.

Touch also is an aspect of sensory involvement. People in Latin American and Middle Eastern cultures engage in much more tactile behaviors than U.S. Americans and Northern Europeans (e.g., Engebretson & Fullmer, 1970; Shuter, 1976; Watson, 1970). People in Asian cultures, in contrast, tend to engage in less touching behavior than U.S. Americans and North Europeans (Barnlund, 1975; Sechrest, 1969). Watson (1970) argues that Far Eastern cultures are low touch, North American cultures are moderate touch, and Mediterranean cultures are high touch. To illustrate, Cohen (1987) compares Arab and U.S. American nonverbal behavior:

The Arab need for personal contact with his [or her] interlocutor is associated with an outlook that defines relationships in affective and familiar terms, not instrumental terms. . . . The [U.S.] Americans' distaste for tactile intimacy with strangers is clearly linked with the cultural primacy of personal autonomy and "privacy." Close contact with someone who is literally not one's intimate constitutes an invasion of one's living space. When Arab representatives meet, whether as friends or rivals, they do so as brothers. They embrace, hold hands, acquire a strong physical sense of the other's presence. Anything else leaves them "cold," uncomfortable and unable to relate to the issue at hand. (p. 41)

Arabs, therefore, emphasize close contact and touching in their nonverbal behavior.

In general, there is more touching behavior in high-contact cultures than in low-contact cultures. Other dimensions of cultural variability, however, influence the type of touching that occurs. Masculinity, for example, should affect the amount of touching that occurs between males and females. It would be expected that people in highly masculine cultures would avoid opposite-sex touching more than people in low masculine (feminine) cultures. Existing research appears to support this speculation. To illustrate, Jones and Remland's (1982) research indicates that people in the Far Eastern cultures (low contact, high masculinity) avoid touching members of the opposite sex the most, and that members of the Mediterranean cultures (high contact, moderate masculinity) avoid opposite-sex touching less than people in the Far Eastern cultures but more than people in the United States (moderate contact, low masculinity).

Smell and touch are not the only senses that differ across cultures. There also are differences in eye contact. The differences have to do with the extent to which people in engage in eye contact and when they engage in eye contact. Members of low-contact cultures (e.g., Asian cultures) tend to avoid eye contact when speaking and listening. Members of moderate-contact cultures (e.g., Australia, Northern Europe, United States), in contrast, engage in more eye contact than members of low-contact cultures (e.g., Hall, 1966; Noesjirwan, 1978). Members of high-contact cultures (e.g., Mediterranean cultures) engage in more eye contact than members of moderate-contact cultures (e.g., Watson & Graves, 1966).

People in individualistic cultures tend to learn to engage in eye contact when listening to others more than when speaking. The listeners' eye contact is interpreted as an indication that they are listening to the speaker. Members of other cultures (e.g., African cultures) learn to avoid eye contact when listening to others, especially when the person speaking is of higher status than the person listening (Byers & Byers, 1972). This pattern carries over to African Americans in the United States; that is, African Americans tend to look down (rather than engage in eye contact) to show respect when interacting with someone of higher status. European Americans often interpret this lack of eye contact as indicating that African Americans are inattentive or uninterested or that they are lying (European Americans learn to look people in the eye to indicate they are telling the truth). European Americans' eye contact behavior may be interpreted as aggressive by African Americans.

There is one final aspect of sensory involvement: how people use their voices. Members of high-contact cultures tend to speak loudly (Hall, 1959; Watson & Graves, 1966). In Arab cultures, for example, loudness is viewed as indicating strength and sincerity, while softness is viewed as reflecting deviousness and weakness. Members of moderate-contact cultures tend to speak more softly than members of high-contact cultures, and members of low-contact cultures tend to speak the softest.

Interpersonal Synchronization

Once people begin to interact, they unconsciously move together in synchrony (in whole or in part), and failing to do so is disruptive to others around them. Nonverbal cues are critical to providing rhythm to our interactions with others. Without rhythm in our interactions, we could not synchronize our behavior with others. *Interpersonal synchronization* refers to convergent rhythmic movements between two people on both the verbal and the nonverbal levels (Hall, 1983). Every facet of human behavior is involved in this rhythmic process. When synchronization occurs, our behavior is rhythmic and we are locked together in a dance that functions almost totally outside of awareness. A sense of synchronization in our interactions with others plays "a crucial role in our ability to talk to each other, to work with each other, and to fall and stay in love" (Douglis, 1987, p. 37).

Interpersonal synchrony or convergence is achieved when the nonverbal behavior between two individuals is unique to the dyad (two people), flexible, smooth, and spontaneous (Knapp, 1983). Interpersonal misalignment, or divergence, occurs when the nonverbal behavior between two individuals is stylized, rigid, awkward, and hesitant (Knapp, 1983). Interpersonal synchrony is related to liking, rapport, and attention, while interpersonal misalignment is related to disliking, and indifference.

Interpersonal synchronization is most evident when we watch two lovers talk:

> Without realizing it, after awhile they actually begin to mirror each other's movements. She, facing him, leans on her right elbow as he leans on his left. They shift postures at the same time. They reach for their wine glasses, raise them and drink simultaneously, an unthinking toast to their closeness.

> Rhythms may even betray love at first sight to a careful observer before the lovers themselves realize what is happening. Over the course of an evening, a newly acquainted but smitten couple will begin to synchronize first head and arm movements. Then more body parts will join the mating dance, until the two are dancing as one. (Douglis, 1987, p. 42)

Observing that other people's behavior is synchronized is a good predictor of their mutual involvement (Douglis, 1987).

It is important to recognize that the rhythms we expect in our interactions are learned in our cultures, our ethnic groups, and the regions of the country in which we live. Many problems that occur when people from different groups communicate can be traced to different rhythms of interaction. Nonnative speakers of English, for example, may stress the wrong words in a sentence or fail to stress words when they should. This misalignment in the vocal nonverbal behavior throws off the rhythm of a conversation. People from other cultures also might expect to stand at a distance closer than we expect. When they stand close, we move back without thinking about it. Again, these differences make coordinating behavior difficult.

Hall (1983) concludes that "1) conversational distances were maintained with incredible accuracy (to tolerances as small as a fraction of an inch); 2) the process was rhythmic; and 3) human beings were locked together in a dance which functioned almost totally out of awareness" (p. 141). Hall points out that people who use high-context communication are more conscious of their rhythmic movements than are people who use low-context communication. Gudykunst and Ting-Toomey (1988) argue that members of individualistic cultures stress verbal synchronization when they communicate, while members of collectivistic cultures emphasize nonverbal synchronization when they communicate.

Interpersonal syncing is a basis for an *action chain,* or a "sequence of events in which usually two or more individuals participate" (Hall, 1976, p. 41). Every action has a beginning, a climax, and an end and comprises a number of intermediate states. If any of the basic acts are left out or are too greatly distorted, the action must be started all over again. An action chain resembles a dance that is used as a means of reaching a common goal. Greeting, parting, engaging in serious discussion, becoming engaged, and buying something in a store are all examples of action chains of varying complexity.

Hall (1983) contends that the degree to which one is committed to complete an action chain varies across cultures. People in collectivistic cultures tend to be highly committed to completing action chains because of the high degree of involvement between people, the highly interrelated and cohesive nature of interpersonal relationships, and the overall sensitivity to nonverbal and other contextual cues in their cultures. The strong adherence to interpersonal syncing and the completion of action chains by people in collectivistic cultures result in great caution and often reluctance to begin something, particularly in situations or relationships that are not well known. European Americans and other people in individualistic cultures ordinarily do not feel bound to complete action chains regardless of the circumstances. Relatively speaking, many European Americans break action chains readily if they do not like the way things are going or if something or someone better comes along.

NONVERBAL CUES IN COMMUNICATING WITH STRANGERS

In the preceding sections, we focused on cross-cultural variability in nonverbal behaviors. In this section, we look at the influence of nonverbal behaviors when we communicate with strangers. When we communicate with strangers, they frequently use nonverbal behaviors that are different from ours. This often leads to misunderstandings. Burgoon et al. (1989), for example, point out that the use of different nonverbal behaviors by political leaders can lead to geopolitical embarrassment:

> A prime example is when then vice president Richard Nixon undertook a goodwill tour to Latin America. Photographers at his first airport stop flashed pictures of Nixon holding up both hands in the "A-OK" gesture. Unfortunately, that gesture in many Latin American countries means "screw you." . . . Nearly 15 years later, when Soviet premier Leonid Brezhnev visited the United States to meet with President Nixon, he exited his plane with his hands clenched over his head. This Russian emblem signifies gracious receipt of a tribute, and Brezhnev was acknowledging the welcoming ceremony he was receiving. But this emblem was inappropriate in the host culture, because in North America this emblem denotes superiority and victory. (pp. 27, 189)

Mistakes like these can easily create misunderstandings.

It is not only political leaders who use inappropriate nonverbal behaviors when interacting with members of other cultures. There is an unlimited number of examples of members of one culture or subculture causing miscommunication by using inappropriate nonverbal cues with strangers. In most cases, however, the people are unaware that their nonverbal behavior is inappropriate because nonverbal behavior takes place at low levels of awareness.

Gumperz (1982) illustrates the problems being discussed here with a case study of Indian and Pakistani women working in England:

> In a staff cafeteria at a major British airport, newly hired Indian and Pakistani women were perceived as surly and uncooperative by their supervisor as well as the cargo handlers whom they served. Observation revealed that while relatively few words were exchanged, the intonation and manner in which those words were pronounced were interpreted negatively. For example, when a cargo handler who had chosen meat was asked whether he wanted gravy, a British assistant would say "Gravy" using rising intonation. The Indian assistants, on the other hand, would say the word using falling intonation: "Gravy." (p. 173)

The Indian assistants did not recognize a difference between the way they pronounced the word "gravy" and the way the British assistants pronounced it. The supervisor, however, recognized the difference and pointed out that saying the word with a falling intonation would be interpreted as "This is gravy," which would be obvious and, therefore, would be interpreted as "rude."

Even though nonverbal behavior tends to be unconscious, members of one culture or subculture can learn to use nonverbal behavior appropriate in other cultures or subcultures. People from one culture or subculture who use nonverbal behavior that is appropriate when interacting with members of another culture or subculture are evaluated more positively than people who do not adjust their nonverbal behavior (Collett, 1971; Garrett, Baxter, & Rozelle, 1981).

While we can learn the nonverbal behavior used in other cultures or subcultures, we generally do not adapt our nonverbal behavior when communicating with strangers on automatic pilot. If strangers use their own nonverbal behavior and we use ours, we inevitably will violate each others' expectations regarding appropriate nonverbal behavior. To understand how this influences our uncertainty and anxiety, we look at Burgoon's (1992) nonverbal expectancy violations theory. We present her theory and examine its cross-cultural validity, and then we apply it to our communication with strangers.

Nonverbal Expectancy Violations Theory

Burgoon and her colleagues (e.g., Burgoon, 1992; Burgoon & Hale, 1988) have been developing a theory of nonverbal expectancy violations (see Burgoon, 1995, for evidence and cross-cultural examples). The theory is based on five assumptions and contains five propositions. Before we present the assumptions and propositions, it is important to recognize that Burgoon does *not* argue that the process she is explaining occurs at high levels of awareness. Stated differently, we are not necessarily mindful of our interpretations and evaluations of the violations of our nonverbal expectations. Given this caveat, we will summarize the theory and discuss the potential for cultural variability regarding the assumptions and propositions.

The first assumption is that "humans have competing approach and avoidance needs" (Burgoon, 1992, p. 56). Burgoon suggests that this assumption should be valid across cultures. This assumption is consistent with our discussion of privacy in Chapter 6 (and our discussion of approach-avoidance tendencies in Chapter 10). While the basic premise should hold across cultures, it is important to keep in mind that there will be cultural variations in how people in different cultures approach or avoid others. As indicated in Chapter 6, people in individualistic cultures will tend to use physical objects to avoid interaction and people in collectivistic cultures will use psychological mechanisms to control their privacy.

The second assumption is that "communicators evaluate the reward potential of others" (Burgoon, 1992, p. 57). This assumption is consistent with the perspective we outlined in Chapters 1 and 2. This assumption should hold true across cultures, but there will be variations in the criteria used to define what rewards are. In individualistic cultures, the criteria for evaluating rewards will be based on individual needs. In collectivistic cultures, the focus will be on rewards for the group.

Burgoon's (1992) third assumption is that "communicators develop expectations about the nonverbal behaviors of others" (p. 57). There is no reason to question the validity of this assumption across cultures. It is, however, necessary to recognize that the specific expectations which are developed do vary across cultures. Burgoon points out that members of cultures that value physical contact will expect to have contact during greetings while members of cultures that do not value contact will expect that contact will be minimized during greetings.

The fourth assumption is that "nonverbal behaviors have associated evaluations ranging from extremely positive to extremely negative" (Burgoon, 1992, p. 58). Like the earlier assumptions, this assumption should be universal. Burgoon suggests that the evaluations may be instinctive (e.g., feeling fear when threatened), culturally learned, or unique to the individual. She goes on to point out that there is little firm evidence for how nonverbal behaviors are evaluated (e.g., judgments of good/bad) differently across cultures. While there is little research in this area, it is clear that there are cultural variations in how specific nonverbal behaviors are evaluated. Recall, for example, the relationship between contact and immediacy discussed earlier in this chapter. People in high-contact cultures value "close" and evaluative it positively and, at the same time, evaluate "far" negatively.

The final assumption is that "nonverbal behaviors have socially recognized meaning" (Burgoon, 1992, p. 59). There is no reason to question the validity of this assumption across cultures. Burgoon suggests that, in comparison to individualistic cultures, there may be "greater room for multiplicity of meaning and ambiguity in collectivist cultures" (p. 5). While this is probably true, the context provides for relatively agreed upon meanings for ambiguous messages in collectivistic cultures.

Five propositions are derived from the assumptions outlined. The first proposition in nonverbal expectancy violation theory is that "expectancy violations are arousing and distracting, diverting attention to communicator and/or relationship characteristics and behaviors" (Burgoon, 1992, p. 60). Burgoon argues that communicators' characteristics (e.g., group memberships) and the implicit meaning of the nonverbal behavior are more important when our expectations are violated than when they are not. Recall, however, that we may not be highly aware that we have become aroused and that our attention has shifted. The process suggested in the proposition should be valid across cultures, but cross-cultural differences in the specific content are to be expected. Burgoon, for example, points out that nonverbal communication is important in determining meaning in collectivistic cultures. To illustrate, Doi (1973) claims that "for Japanese verbal communication is something that accompanies nonverbal communication and not the other way around" (p. 181). The violation of nonverbal expectations, therefore, should take on greater significance in collectivistic cultures than in individualistic cultures.

Burgoon's (1992) second proposition is that "communicator reward valence [moderates] the interpretation of ambiguous or multi-meaning nonverbal behaviors" (p. 61). Reward valence refers to whether the rewards or costs associated with the people with whom we are communicating are greater. If the rewards are greater, there is a positive valence; if the costs are greater, there is a negative valence. Burgoon differentiates between nonverbal behaviors that have relatively agreed upon social meanings within a culture (e.g., averting the gaze; note that this example is agreed upon only within selected subcultures in the United States) and those that are open to multiple interpretations within a culture (e.g., personal space). When communicators who can provide rewards violate our expectations regarding nonverbal behaviors that are open to multiple meanings, their violations will be interpreted positively, as opposed to the negative interpretations that would occur with violations committed by people who cannot provide rewards.

The third proposition is that "communicator reward valence [moderates] the evaluation of nonverbal behavior" (Burgoon, 1992, p. 61). Burgoon points out that nonverbal behaviors that have relatively common meanings may be valued differently. The way they are evaluated, however, is influenced by whether the violator can provide rewards.

Burgoon argues that the cognitive processes of evaluation should be used by people in all cultures but that content of the evaluations of specific nonverbal behaviors will vary across cultures (e.g., the different evaluations of "close" and "far" in high- and low-contact cultures).

The fourth proposition in Burgoon's (1992) expectation violation theory is stated as follows:

> The ultimate evaluation of a violation is a function of the magnitude and direction of the discrepancy between the evaluation of the expected behavior and the evaluation of the actual behavior such that (a) enacted behaviors that are more positively valenced than expected behaviors produce positive violations and (b) enacted behaviors that are more negatively valenced than expected behaviors produce negative violations. (p. 62)

This proposition suggests that we compare the nonverbal behavior that individuals use with our expectations. If actual nonverbal behaviors are viewed more positively than expected behaviors, this leads to positive violations. When actual behaviors are viewed more negatively than expected behaviors, negative violations occur.

The final proposition in Burgoon's (1992) theory is that "positive violations produce favorable communication outcomes, while negative violations produce negative consequences" (p. 63). Burgoon argues that positive violations of expectations can lead to increases in "credibility, attraction, persuasion, and comprehension" (p. 7).

To summarize, the assumptions and propositions in Burgoon's (1992) theory appear to be valid across cultures. At the same time, however, there are cultural variations regarding the expectations, interpretations, and evaluations of specific nonverbal behaviors. The distance individuals expect others to stand from them when they are talking, for example, varies between contact and noncontact cultures. People in contact cultures expect others to stand only inches away, and people in noncontact cultures expect others to stand at least an arm's length away. Since we are not highly aware that the expectancy violation processes outlined in the assumption and propositions are occurring, cultural differences in expectations, interpretations, and evaluations create misunderstandings when people from different cultures communicate. In the next section, we focus on what happens when our expectations regarding nonverbal behavior are violated when we communicate with strangers.

Nonverbal Violations in Communicating with Strangers

Nonverbal expectancy violations theory has clear implications for our communication with strangers. We tend to avoid strangers more than we tend to avoid people who are familiar (Assumption 1) because of the uncertainty and anxiety present when we communicate with strangers (we discuss approach-avoidance in detail in Chapter 10). One of the factors that affect our approach-avoidance behavior with strangers, for example, is the cultural/ethnic differences in the ways people indicate that they do not want to be approached. We may be sending signals indicating that we do not want to be approached, but strangers do not recognize these signals.

Unless we are attracted to people who are dissimilar to us for some reason, strangers generally have lower reward value than people who are familiar (Assumption 2). The costs of interacting with strangers generally are viewed as greater than any rewards associated with interacting with them (Knapp, cited in Crockett & Friedman, 1980). This reinforces our desire to avoid strangers rather than seek out interaction with them.

Our expectations for appropriate nonverbal behavior also may be different from those of strangers (Assumption 3). We *may* recognize when strangers violate our expectations, but they probably will not realize that they have violated our expectations unless we tell them. Similarly, strangers *may* recognize when we violate their expectations, but we will not unless we receive some indication from them. It is important to recognize that we will not always recognize consciously that our expectations have been violated. If the violation is not a major one, we probably will interpret the strangers' behavior negatively without consciously thinking about it and may not realize consciously that our expectations were violated. When this occurs, misunderstandings are likely.

We tend to recognize major violations of our expectations consciously. When we consciously recognize these violations, we try to figure them out. If we are mindful of our communication, the possibility of effective communication is increased. This suggests that major violations of our nonverbal expectations may not be as problematic as minor violations of our nonverbal expectations when we communicate with strangers.

There is cultural variability in how explicit expectations are. Since rules are less explicit in individualistic cultures than in collectivistic cultures (as indicated in Chapter 3), strangers from collectivistic cultures may have trouble figuring out what the expectations are in individualistic cultures. Further, strangers from collectivistic cultures will emphasize the context more than is appropriate when interpreting the behavior of people in individualistic cultures.

Burgoon (1992) argues that we are aroused and we attune to the characteristics of the person with whom we are communicating when our expectations are violated (Proposition 1). This suggests that our uncertainty and anxiety increase when our expectations are violated. We may not, however, be consciously aware that this is happening. As indicated in Chapter 2, high uncertainty and anxiety (particularly if they are above our maximum thresholds) lead to ineffective communication. Attuning to the characteristics of the person with whom we are communicating also leads to problems when we communicate with strangers. The most prominent characteristic on which we focus is the strangers' group memberships (e.g., their cultures or ethnicities). Focusing on strangers' group memberships, in turn, increases the likelihood that we will commit the ultimate attribution error (see Chapter 7).

Strangers' reward valences influence how we interpret their violations of our expectations. Since strangers generally have negative reward valences, we tend to interpret their violations of our nonverbal expectations negatively. To illustrate, consider the case of someone from the United States (a moderate-contact culture) communicating with a stranger from a high-contact culture. The stranger from the high-contact culture probably will stand closer than the person from the United States expects. Since strangers have negative reward valence, this will be interpreted negatively, and the stranger will be viewed as "pushy." If the person from the United States was interacting with a superior, the reaction would be different. The superior would have positive reward valence, and standing closer than expected probably would be interpreted as the superior showing liking for the subordinate.

If the nonverbal behavior in which others engage is more positively valenced than the expected behavior, a positive violation of expectations occurs; if the nonverbal behavior in which others engage is more negatively valenced than the expected behavior, a negative violation occurs (Proposition 4). Our expectations regarding strangers' nonverbal behavior are influenced by our stereotypes. If we view the strangers' groups as "pushy," for example, and the strangers with whom we interact engage in behavior we interpret as polite, we will see this as a positive violation of our expectations. Positive violations like this, however, usually lead us to see particular strangers with whom we are interacting as "an exception to the rule" rather than changing our stereotype of the strangers' groups. If our stereotypes of strangers' groups are that they are "polite" and strangers are "pushy," in contrast, a negative violation of our expectation occurs. Negative violations like this increase the chance that we will make the ultimate attribution error (they are all like that).

Positive violations of our expectations lead to positive communication outcomes, and negative violations lead to negative outcomes (Proposition 5). We believe that negative violations of expectations tend to occur more than positive violations when we communicate with strangers. This suggests that our communication with strangers is likely to have more negative communication outcomes than our communication with people who are familiar. The consequences of negative evaluations include, but are not limited to, an inability to synchronize our behavior with that of strangers and ineffective communication.

As suggested in the section on the recognition of emotions, the similarity of strangers' cultures and ours, as well as the familiarity we have with their cultures and the familiarity they have with ours, may moderate the negative outcomes. The more similar our cultures and the more familiar we are with each other's cultures, the greater the chance is that we will be able to interpret each other's nonverbal cues accurately.

As indicated earlier, we are less aware of our nonverbal behavior than we are of our verbal behavior. We rarely stop and think about what happens when our nonverbal behavior expectations are violated. Rather, we interpret the violation from our own frames of reference. To increase the likelihood of positive outcomes (e.g., effective communication), we must become mindful of our communication. In other words, we must stop and think about what the strangers' behavior that violated our expectation means to strangers (e.g., we need to reduce our explanatory uncertainty). We cannot do this if we are highly anxious, however. When we become mindful, we must manage our emotional reactions to the behavior (e.g., our anxiety) cognitively. Cognitively managing our emotional reactions and understanding what the behavior means to strangers are necessary for effective communication to occur. We discuss effective communication in more detail in Chapter 10.

SUMMARY

The recognition of at least six primary emotions (anger, disgust, fear, happiness, sadness, and surprise) in facial expressions appears to be universal. Recognition of contempt and embarrassment also may be universal. In addition to agreement on the emotions expressed, there is agreement on the relative intensity of the emotions across cultures. There also are, however, cross-cultural differences in the display rules guiding the expression of emotions. Recent work suggests that individualism-collectivism and power distance can be used to explain many of these differences.

In addition to the display of emotions, cultures differ in the emphasis they place on the need for contact among members. High-contact cultures emphasize close interpersonal distances, extensive touching behavior, and sensory involvement of communicators. Low-contact cultures, in contrast, emphasize far interpersonal distances, avoidance of touching others, and little sensory involvement between communicators.

One of the major functions that nonverbal behaviors perform is the synchronization of communication. Since people learn different nonverbal behaviors across cultures, it often is difficult for us to synchronize our behavior when we communicate with strangers. Lack of synchronization disrupts communication.

When strangers violate our nonverbal expectations, we tend to interpret those violations negatively. These negative interpretations decrease the effectiveness of our communication with strangers. To communicate effectively with strangers, we must learn to interpret their nonverbal behavior and their violations of our expectations accurately. This requires that we manage our anxiety mindfully and try to reduce our explanatory uncertainty regarding strangers' behavior.

STUDY QUESTIONS

1. What are the similarities and differences between language and nonverbal cues?
2. What are the functions of nonverbal cues?
3. Why are some aspects of the expression and recognition of emotions universal and some not?
4. What are the differences between contact and noncontact cultures?
5. What is the role of immediacy in our relationships with others?
6. How does the use of interpersonal distance differ across cultures?
7. How does the use of touch differ across cultures?
8. How does the use of territory differ across cultures?
9. How does the use of sensory involvement differ across cultures?
10. How does the use of interpersonal synchronization differ across cultures?
11. How do nonverbal expectancy violations affect our communication with strangers?

SUGGESTED READINGS

Hall, E. T. (1959). *The silent language.* New York: Doubleday.

Hall, E. T. (1966). The *hidden dimension.* New York: Doubleday.

Matsumoto, S. (1996). *Unmasking Japan: Myths and realities about the emotions of the Japanese.* Stanford, CA: Sanford University Press.

Morris, D. (1994). *Body talk: The meaning of human gesture.* New York: Crown.

Scherer, K., Wallbott, H., & Summerfield, A. (Eds.). (1986). *Experiencing emotion: A cross-cultural study.* Cambridge, UK: Cambridge University Press.

PART FOUR

INTERACTION WITH STRANGERS

In the first three parts, we examined the major influences on our communication with strangers and the ways in which communication patterns vary across cultures. In Part Two, we pointed out that our predictions and interpretations of strangers' behavior and the anxiety we experience are influenced by our cultures, by our group memberships, and our social identities (the sociocultural influences). Further, our anxiety, predictions, and interpretations are influenced by stereotypes and the intergroup attitudes we hold (the psychocultural influences), as well as by the environments in which we are communicating. In Part Three, we examined interpreting messages—both verbal messages and nonverbal messages.

The focus of Part Four is selected aspects of our interactions with strangers. In the chapters in this part, we address a series of important questions. To illustrate, what factors influence our effectiveness in communicating with strangers? How do we manage conflict with strangers successfully? What happens when we come into contact with strangers? What factors contribute to the development of our interpersonal relationships with strangers? How do strangers who find themselves in new and unfamiliar cultural environments cope with and adapt to the many uncertainties of their new lives? What are some of the changes occurring in strangers as a consequence of their adaptive experiences in a new environment? How can we become more "intercultural" as a result of our communication with strangers? How can we develop community with strangers?

In Chapter 10, we focus on factors that contribute to communicating effectively with strangers. Once we understand what is necessary to be effective, we have the basis for managing conflict and negotiating face with strangers successfully, the focus of Chapter 11. The first two chapters provide the foundation for developing interpersonal relationships with strangers (Chapter 12). In Chapter 13, we examine how strangers adapt to new cultural environments. Adapting to new cultural environments leads to personal changes and provides the foundation for becoming intercultural, the focus of Chapter 14. We conclude by examining how we can build community with strangers in Chapter 15.

10

COMMUNICATING
EFFECTIVELY
WITH STRANGERS

To be surprised, to wonder, is to begin to understand.

Jose Ortega Y Gasset

Our desire to communicate with strangers and the nature of our relationships with them depend on the degree to which we can communicate effectively with them. We cannot manage conflict with strangers or develop relationships with them if we do not communicate relatively effectively. We, therefore, begin our discussion of our interactions with strangers by looking at effective communication.

Our purpose in this chapter is to elaborate on our view of communicating with strangers by examining the factors that contribute to communication effectiveness. We divide our discussion of effectiveness into three sections. In the first section, we define what we mean by effective communication and differentiate it from competence and being perceived as competent communicators. Next, we provide an overview of ways in which communication effectiveness and intercultural competence have been studied. We present our view of the factors that contribute to being perceived as competent communicators in the third section.

DEFINING COMMUNICATION EFFECTIVENESS AND COMPETENCE

In the movie *Cool Hand Luke,* Paul Newman plays Luke, a man put in prison for destroying parking meters. While in prison, Luke constantly gets into trouble with the prison staff. At one point when Luke has not done something that the warden told him to do, the warden says to Luke, "What we have here is a failure to communicate." On the surface, the warden's statement makes sense. It is, however, incomplete. The warden and Luke communicated, but they did not communicate effectively.

Communication Effectiveness

To say that we communicated does not imply an outcome. Communication is a process involving the exchange of messages and the creation of meaning. No two people ever attach the same meaning to messages. Whether communication is effective depends on the degree to which the participants attach similar meanings to the messages exchanged. Stated differently, *effective communication* involves minimizing misunderstandings. Fisher (1978) argues that "to say that meaning in communication is never totally the same for all communicators is not to say that communication is impossible or even difficult—only that it is imperfect" (p. 257).

When we communicate, we attach meaning to (or interpret) messages we transmit to strangers. We also attach meaning to (or interpret) messages we receive from strangers. We are not always aware of this process, but we do it nevertheless. To say that two people communicated effectively requires that the two attach relatively similar meanings to the messages sent and received (they interpret the messages similarly). Powers and Lowrey (1984) refer to this as *basic communication fidelity,* "the degree of congruence between the cognitions [or thoughts] of two or more individuals following a communication event" (p. 58). Similarly, Triandis (1977) argues that effectiveness involves making isomorphic attributions (isomorphic implies being similar; attributions involve assigning a quality or characteristic to something).

Ineffective communication can occur for a variety of reasons when we communicate with strangers. We may not transmit our messages in ways that can be understood by strangers, strangers may misinterpret what we say, or both can occur simultaneously. The problems that occur may be due to pronunciation, grammar, familiarity with the topic being discussed, familiarity with strangers, familiarity with strangers' native languages, fluency in the other person's language, and/or social factors (Gass & Varonis, 1984). If we are familiar with and/or fluent in strangers' languages, for example, we usually can understand them better when they speak our languages than we can if we know nothing about their languages.

Generally, the greater our cultural and linguistic knowledge of strangers' cultures and groups, and the more our beliefs overlap with those of the strangers with whom we communicate, the less the likelihood is that there will be misunderstandings. Lack of linguistic and cultural knowledge contributes to misunderstandings because we "listen to speech, form a hypothesis about what routine is being enacted, and then rely on social background knowledge and co-occurrence expectations to evaluate what is intended and [the] attitudes [that] are [being] conveyed" (Gumperz, 1982, p. 171).

When we communicate on automatic pilot, we interpret incoming messages on the basis of the symbolic systems we learned as children. A large part of this system is shared with other members of our cultures, our ethnic groups, our religions, and our families, to name only a few of our group memberships. A part of our symbolic systems, however, is unique and is based on our specific life experiences. No two people share the same symbolic system. Much of our habitual or scripted behavior involves superficial interactions with other members of our cultures or ethnic groups in which we rely mainly on cultural or sociocultural data. The meanings we attach to specific messages and the meanings others attach to those messages are relatively similar. This is due, in part, to the fact that the scripts we enact provide us with shared interpretations of our behavior. While there are differences in our meanings, the differences are not large enough to make our communication ineffective. Under these conditions, we do not need to think consciously about our communication to be relatively effective.

In addition to following scripts, the categories in which we place strangers can be a source of our going on automatic pilot. As indicated in Chapter 4, we categorize strangers into groupings that make sense to us. These categories often are based on physical (e.g., gender, race, ethnicity) or cultural (e.g., cultural or ethnic background) characteristics, but as Trungpa (1973) indicates, we also can categorize others in terms of their attitudes or approaches to life:

> We adopt sets of categories which serve as ways of managing phenomena. The most fully developed products of this tendency are ideologies, the systems of ideas that rationalize, justify, and sanctify our lives. Nationalism, communism, existentialism, Christianity, Buddhism—all provide us with identities, rules of action, and interpretations of how and why things happen as they do. (Trungpa, 1973, p. 6)

Using only *broad* categories to predict and interpret strangers' behavior inevitably leads to ineffective communication.

The categories in which we place strangers affect our interpretations. Once we place strangers in categories, our stereotypes of people in those categories influence the predictions we make and how we interpret strangers' behavior. Basing our predictions on broad categories usually leads to mindless behavior. That is, we rely on our expectations based on categories to guide our behavior and interpretations and are not conscious of our communication behavior. Categorical information is useful in making predictions, but strangers can be placed into many different categories. To communicate effectively, we have to understand which identity is guiding strangers' communication.

When we are communicating with strangers and basing our interpretations on our symbolic systems, ineffective communication often occurs. Consider a European American teacher interacting with African American students raised in the lower-class subculture in the United States. The teacher asks the students a question. In answering the question, the students do not look the teacher in the eyes. The teacher, in all likelihood, would interpret the students' behavior as disrespectful and/or assume that the students are hiding something. Establishing eye contact is expected in the mainstream, middle-class subculture in the United States when European Americans are telling the truth and being respectful. The students' intention, in contrast, may have been to show respect to the teacher given that children in the lower-class African American subculture in the United States are taught not to make eye contact with people they respect. Situations like this lead to misunderstanding and ineffective communication.

To summarize, effective communication involves minimizing misunderstandings. To be effective in communicating with strangers we must be mindful. Communicating effectively and appropriately is an important aspect of being perceived as a competent communicator. We can, however, communicate effectively and not be perceived as competent communicators.

Perceived Competence

There are at least two views of the nature of competence. One view suggests that competence is "within" communicators, and the second suggests that competence is "between" communicators. Kim (1991) takes the first position. She argues that intercultural communication competence

> should be located *within* a person as his or her overall *capacity* or *capability* to facilitate the communication process between people from differing cultural backgrounds and to contribute to successful interaction outcomes. Here [intercultural communication competence] is

considered a necessary, but not sufficient, condition for achieving success in intercultural encounters—just as a highly competent driver may not always be able to prevent accidents due to factors external to the driver (such as hazardous road conditions or serious mistakes made by other incompetent drivers). (p. 263)

In this view, competence is internal to the person.

The second view of competence assumes that judgments of competence emerge from the interactions in which we engage. Gudykunst (1991), for example, points out that communicators' views of their communication competence may not be the same as those of the strangers with whom they are communicating. You, for example, might see yourself as a very competent communicator, but when you interact, your partner may perceive you as not being very competent. An outside observer might have still a different perception of your competence. Understanding communication competence, therefore, minimally requires that we take into consideration our own and strangers' perspectives.

If we can have different views of our competence than the strangers with whom we are communicating, then competence is an impression we have of ourselves and strangers. Stated differently, "competence is not something intrinsic to a person's nature or behavior" (Spitzberg & Cupach, 1984, p. 115). There are several implications of this view of competence:

> First, competence does not actually reside in the performance; it is an *evaluation* of the performance by someone. . . . Second, the fact that *someone* is making the evaluation means that it is subject to error, bias, and judgment inferences; different judges using the same criteria may evaluate the performance differently. Third, since the evaluation always must be made with reference to some set of implicit or explicit *criteria,* the evaluation cannot be understood or validated without knowledge of the criteria being employed; thus, the same performance may be judged to be competent by one standard and incompetent by another. (Mc Fall, 1982, pp. 13–14)

This view of competence clearly suggests that the specific skills we have do not ensure that we will be perceived as competent in any particular interaction. Our skills, however, do increase the likelihood that we are able to adapt our behavior so that strangers see us as competent (Wiemann & Bradac, 1989).

Even if people from different cultures use the same criteria (e.g., appropriateness) to judge individuals' competence, they still may evaluate the same performance differently. Consider a Japanese asking "How old are you?" during an initial interaction with a U.S. American. Another Japanese observing this interaction probably would evaluate the Japanese speaker's question as appropriate. The U.S. American who is asked the question, in contrast, is likely to see the question as inappropriate.

The standards used to judge competence also vary across cultures. Carroll (1988), for example, argues that the French value animated conversations that are fast-moving and have frequent interruptions. Often, the speakers ask questions and do not wait for answers. U.S. Americans, however, prefer fuller answers to questions, fewer interruptions, and more continuity in the conversation than the French. The French may interpret U.S. Americans' readiness to discuss serious topics in social gatherings as inappropriate (and incompetent) because serious conversations occur in contexts other than social situations and require a strong commitment between individuals. U.S. Americans may view the French style of frequent interruptions and short answers to their questions as inappropriate and, therefore, incompetent.

To further illustrate differences in perceived competence, consider the role of assertiveness in Japan and in the United States (Singhal & Nagao, 1993). People who are perceived as assertive are viewed as competent communicators in the United States, and people who are reticent are not perceived to be highly competent. In Japan, in contrast, people who are reticent are perceived as more competent than people who are assertive. Japanese, therefore, may perceive U.S. American assertiveness as incompetent, and U.S. Americans may perceive Japanese reticence as incompetent.

The competence-as-impressions view of competence suggests that the specific skills we have do not ensure that we are perceived as competent in any particular interaction. Our skills, however, do increase the likelihood that we are able to adapt our behavior so that others see us as competent (Wiemann & Bradac, 1989).

As you can see from the preceding overview of the two positions on the nature of competence, we (the two authors) disagree. Both of us agree, however, that individuals possess motivation, knowledge, and skills which can contribute to the effectiveness of their communication. We both also agree that individuals make judgments of each other's competence. For the purposes of this chapter, we, therefore, focus on effective communication and *perceived competence*.

APPROACHES TO THE STUDY OF EFFECTIVE COMMUNICATION

There have been several attempts to specify the characteristics of the people who can communicate effectively with strangers (i.e., competence is in the person). Gardner (1962), for example, characterizes people who are effective in communicating with strangers as "universal communicators." He describes these people as possessing five characteristics: "(1) an unusual degree of integration or stability, (2) a central organization of the extrovert type, (3) a value system which includes the 'value of all men [and women],' (4) socialized on the basis of cultural universals, and (5) a marked telepathic or intuition sensitivity" (p. 248). Similarly, Kleinjans (1972) takes the position that effective communicators (1) see people first and representatives of cultures second, (2) know people are basically good, (3) know the value of other cultures as well as that of their own, (4) have control over their visceral reactions, (5) speak with hopefulness and candor, and (6) have inner security and are able to feel comfortable being different from other people. Both Gardner and Kleinjans, therefore, characterize competence in communicating with strangers in terms of individual traits within communicators.

Ruben (1976) suggests that several behavioral dimensions are important to communication competence in intercultural interactions: (1) Display of respect involves the ability to show positive regard and express respect for another person, (2) interaction posture is the "ability to respond to others in a descriptive, nonevaluating, and nonjudgmental way" (p. 340), and (3) interaction management "is displayed through taking turns in discussion and initiating and terminating interaction based on a reasonably accurate assessment of the needs and desires of others" (p. 341). Ruben and Kealey (1979) report that successful adaptation to other cultures can be predicted by individuals' empathy, respect, ability to perform role behaviors, non-judgmentalness, openness, tolerance for ambiguity, and interaction management.

Hawes and Kealey's (1981) research suggests there is a difference between adaptation and effectiveness. People can adapt to other cultures and not be effective. They argue that effectiveness is a function of professional expertise, adaptation, and intercultural interaction (i.e., interest in and capacity for interacting with host nationals).

Gudykunst, Wiseman, and Hammer (1977) argue that people who are effective in communicating with strangers do not use the perspective of their own cultures when interpreting the behavior of strangers. Rather, effective communicators use a "third-culture perspective," which acts as a psychological link between their cultural perspectives and strangers' cultural perspectives. Gudykunst et al. argue that people who use a third-culture perspective

> can be characterized as follows: (1) they are open-minded toward new ideas and experiences, (2) they are empathic toward people from other cultures, (3) they accurately perceive differences and similarities between the host culture and their own, (4) they tend to describe behavior they don't understand rather than evaluating unfamiliar behavior as bad, nonsensical, or meaningless, (5) they are relatively astute noncritical observers of their own behavior and that of others, (6) they are better able to establish meaningful relationships with people from the host culture, and (7) they are less ethnocentric (i.e., they try first to understand and then evaluate the behavior of host nationals based upon the standards of the culture they are living in). (p. 424)

Gudykunst et al. recognize that people are not always able to use a third-culture perspective when they communicate. Their view suggests that individuals' knowledge and skills contribute to effective communication but does not suggest that such knowledge and skills constitute competence.

Hammer, Gudykunst, and Wiseman (1978) isolate three behavioral dimensions associated with perceived effectiveness: (1) "the ability to deal with psychological stress," (2) "the ability to effectively communicate," and (3) "the ability to establish meaningful interpersonal relationships." The dimension of being able to deal with psychological stress includes the ability to deal with frustration, stress, anxiety, pressures to conform, social alienation, financial difficulties, and interpersonal conflict. The dimension of being able to communicate effectively includes the ability to enter into meaningful dialogue with strangers, to initiate interaction with strangers, to deal with communication misunderstandings, and to deal with different communication styles. The ability to establish meaningful interpersonal relationships includes the ability to develop satisfying interpersonal relationships with strangers, to maintain satisfying relationships with strangers, to understand strangers' feelings, to work effectively with strangers, and to deal with different social customs. Hammer et al. suggest that having these skills contributes to effective communication. They do not contend that these skills define competence.

Partial cross-cultural support for Hammer et al.'s (1978) findings comes from Abe and Wiseman's (1983) replication of their study with Japanese tourists in the United States. Abe and Wiseman's research reveals five dimensions to effectiveness, with all five dimensions being related closely to the three dimensions displayed in the earlier study. The differences that exist in the findings can be explained easily by the length of the individuals' experiences in another culture (the original study examined long-term visitors, while Abe and Wiseman studied tourists). Hammer's (1987) research confirms the three-dimensional explanation. The dimensions are similar across cultures, but the specific behaviors will differ. To illustrate, the ways people establish relationships across cultures clearly are different (see Chapter 12).

Kealey (1990) proposes a model to explain understanding when we are in other cultures. He contends that our individual skills, desire for contact with members of the host culture, altruistic motives, and positive expectations influence our interactions. The extent to which we are satisfied with our interactions and minimize our stress, in turn, influences our understanding of host nationals.

Individual traits alone can be used as a good predictor of communication effectiveness only if they yield consistent behavior across situations and throughout our lives. This, however, does not appear to be the case. Rather, individual traits often do not lead to consistent behavior across situations or throughout our lives (Mischel, 1973). Explanations of effectiveness, therefore, cannot rely solely on individual traits; they must include other factors, such as the interaction that takes place between the people.

Prior research on effective communication with strangers and/or intercultural competence has not been organized in a systematic way. Given our focus on managing uncertainty and anxiety when communicating with strangers, we focus on factors that are related directly to these processes. To isolate these factors, it is necessary to look at the components that contribute to being perceived as competent communicators.

COMPONENTS OF PERCEIVED COMPETENCE

Spitzberg and Cupach (1984) isolate three components of perceived competence: motivation, knowledge, and skills. *Motivation* refers to our desire to communicate appropriately and effectively with others. Of particular importance to the present analysis is our motivation to communicate with strangers. *Knowledge* refers to our awareness or understanding of what needs to be done in order to communicate appropriately and effectively. *Skills* are our abilities to engage in the behaviors necessary to communicate appropriately and effectively.

We may be highly motivated and lack the knowledge and/or skills necessary to communicate appropriately and effectively. We also may be motivated and have the necessary knowledge but not the skills. If we are motivated and have the knowledge and skills, this does not ensure that we will communicate appropriately or effectively. There are several factors that may intervene to affect our behavior. We may, for example, have a strong emotional reaction to something that happens. Our emotional reaction, in turn, may cause us to "act out" a script we learned earlier in life that is dysfunctional in the situation in which we find ourselves. To illustrate, consider European Americans who are served snake in another culture. They are likely to have strong negative reactions to eating this meat. If they are unable to control their emotional reactions cognitively (i.e., mindfully), there is little chance that they will behave in ways that are perceived as competent by people in the other culture.

The strangers with whom we are communicating also may be a factor in our ability to be perceived as competent. If strangers communicate with us in a way that suggests we are not competent, in all likelihood we will act in an incompetent fashion. It is also possible that we may act appropriately and effectively without actually having the knowledge necessary to engage in the behaviors by imitating strangers' behavior. This can work in communicating with strangers when we do not have sufficient knowledge of strangers' groups, but it is not the best strategy. Wiemann and Kelly (1981) point out that "knowledge without skill is socially useless, and skill cannot be obtained without the cognitive ability to diagnose situational demands and constraints" (p. 290).

Our motivation, knowledge, and skills interact with outcomes of our interactions with strangers to yield perceptions of competence. We have mentioned two outcomes—appropriateness and effectiveness—already. Other potential outcomes include, but are not limited to, interpersonal attraction, trust, satisfaction with our communication, the development of interpersonal relationships (e.g., intimacy), managing conflict, adapting to other cultures, and building community. The remainder of this chapter is devoted to the three components of competence.

Motivation

J. H. Turner (1988) suggests that certain basic needs motivate us to interact with others. *Needs* are "fundamental states of being in humans which, if unsatisfied, generate feelings of deprivation" (p. 23). The needs that serve as motivating factors are (1) our need for a sense of security as human beings, (2) our need for a sense of predictability (e.g., I trust you will behave as I think you will), (3) our need for a sense of group inclusion, (4) our need to avoid diffuse anxiety, (5) our need for a sense of a common shared world, (6) our need for symbolic/material gratification, and (7) our need to sustain our self-conceptions. We vary in the degree to which we are conscious of our various needs. We are the least conscious of the first three, moderately conscious of the fourth, and the most conscious of the last three.

Each of our needs, separately and in combination, influences how we want to present ourselves to strangers, the intentions we form, and the habits or scripts we follow. The needs also can influence each other. Anxiety, for example, can result from not meeting our needs for group inclusion, predictability, security, and/or sustaining our self-concepts. J. H. Turner argues that our overall level of motivational energy is a function of our levels of anxiety produced by these four needs. Three of these needs are critical in our communication with strangers and warrant further discussion.

Need for Predictability   One of the major reasons we often are not motivated to communicate with strangers is that we do not see their behavior as predictable. J. H. Turner (1988) contends that we "need to 'trust' others in the sense that, for the purposes of a given interaction, others are 'reliable' and their responses 'predictable' " (p. 56). When strangers' behavior is predictable, we feel that there is a rhythm to our interactions with them. When strangers' behavior is not predictable, there is no rhythm to our interaction and we experience diffuse anxiety.

If we do not feel a part of interaction taking place (e.g., our need for inclusion is not met), we will have a difficult time seeing strangers' behavior as predictable. One reason we may not feel part of the interaction is that we have learned different communication rules than strangers and we often follow our own rules even when communicating in strangers' languages. If Japanese follow their cultural norms regarding silence in conversations when speaking English, for example, U.S. Americans will feel that the rhythm of the conversation is off and will not feel part of the conversation taking place.

If we do not recognize that predictability will be lower when we are getting to know strangers compared with members of our own groups, the low level of predictability will lead to low motivation to communicate with strangers. One way we can deal with this problem is to be mindful when we communicate with strangers. When we are mindful, we need to remind ourselves that the lack of predictability may not be due to the strangers; rather, there may be group differences influencing our communication. After recognizing this, we can try to gather information that will help us understand what is happening and, therefore, increase the predictability of strangers' behavior. In addition, we should recognize that "from a mindful perspective . . . uncertainty [lack of predictability] creates the freedom to discover meaning. If there are meaningful choices, there is uncertainty" (Langer, 1997, p. 130).

Need to Avoid Diffuse Anxiety   J. H. Turner (1988) views *diffuse anxiety* as a "generalized or unspecified sense of disequilibrium" (lack of balance) (p. 61). Anxiety stems from feeling uneasy, tense, worried, or apprehensive about what might happen. It is an emotional (affective) response to situations based on a fear of negative consequences (Stephan & Stephan, 1985). Turner argues that feelings of diffuse anxiety stem from deprivations in meeting our needs for security, predictability, group inclusion, and self-confirmation. He contends that if we have not met our needs for security, predictability, and group inclusion, the focus of our behavior is on trying to deal with the diffuse anxiety associated with not meeting these needs. Because we are not highly aware of our needs for security, predictability, and group inclusion, however, we have a hard time pinpointing the source of the anxiety. The net result is that "considerable interpersonal energy can be devoted to meeting these needs as they grope around for a solution to their often vague feelings of discomfort" (p. 63).

Anxiety is an important motivating factor in intergroup encounters. If our anxiety is too high, we avoid communicating with strangers as a way to deal with our anxiety. If our anxiety is too low, there is not enough adrenaline flowing through our systems to motivate us to communicate. To be motivated to communicate with strangers, we have to manage our anxiety if it is too high or if it is too low. This requires that we be mindful. When we are mindful, there are several things we can do to manage our anxiety. We discuss these techniques in the section on the ability to manage anxiety later in this chapter.

Need to Sustain Our Self-Conceptions   Another consequence of high anxiety is that our need to sustain our self-conceptions becomes important (J. H. Turner, 1988). Sustaining our self-conceptions is much more difficult, however, when we communicate with strangers than when we communicate with members of our own groups. Schlenker (1986) explains that our self-conceptions are made up of the various identities we have and our theories of ourselves:

> Identity, like any theory, is both a *structure,* containing the organized contents of experience, and an active *process* that guides and regulates one's thoughts, feelings, and actions. . . . It influences how information is perceived, processed, and recalled . . . it acts as a script to guide behavior . . . and it contains the standards against which one's behavior can be compared and evaluated. (p. 24)

Our self-conceptions, therefore, influence how we communicate with strangers and the choices (conscious and unconscious) we make when we form relationships.

J. H. Turner (1988) contends that we try to maintain our self-conceptions, even going to the point of using defense mechanisms (e.g., denial) to maintain our views of ourselves. Our need for self-concept support directly influences our communication. Cushman, Valentinsen, and Dietrich (1982), for example, suggest that we are attracted to strangers who support our self-concepts. Perceiving that strangers support our self-concepts is necessary if we are going to form or maintain relationships with them.

One of the problems in intergroup encounters is that one or both of the communicators perceive that others do not support their self-concepts. If we are communicating on automatic pilot, we are likely to respond negatively in this situation. When we are mindful of our communication, however, we can recognize that strangers might emphasize different aspects of their self-concepts than we do. Individualists, for example, stress their personal identities, and collectivists emphasize their social identities. Failure to support each other's self-concepts, therefore, may be due not to lack of concern but to a failure to understand group differences in what each considers to be important aspects of the self. To illustrate, Japanese are likely to ask questions about U.S. Americans' social identities when U.S. Americans expect questions about their personal identities. If U.S. Americans perceive this as lack of self-concept support, they will not be motivated to interact with Japanese. If U.S. Americans are mindful of their communication, however, they can recognize that this is just a cultural difference. This interpretation should not have a negative effect on U.S. Americans' motivation to communicate with Japanese.

Approach-Avoidance Tendencies   Most us spend the vast majority of our time interacting with people who are relatively similar to us. Our actual contact with people who are different is limited; it is a novel form of interaction (Rose, 1981). If our attempts to communicate with strangers are not successful and we cannot get out of the situations in which we find ourselves easily, our unconscious need for group inclusion becomes unsatisfied. This leads to anxiety about ourselves and our standing in a group context (J. H. Turner, 1988). One way we deal with this anxiety is to retreat into known territory and limit our interactions to people who are similar to us. At the same time, most of us want to see ourselves as nonprejudiced and caring people. We may, therefore, want to interact with strangers to sustain our self-concepts. Holding both attitudes at the same time is not unusual. The combination of our need to avoid diffuse anxiety and our need to sustain our self-conceptions often leads us to an approach-avoidance orientation toward intergroup encounters.

Knowledge

The knowledge component of communication competence refers to our awareness of what we need to do to communicate in an appropriate and effective way. This includes a specific awareness of the skills discussed in the next section and how they can be used when communicating with strangers. When communicating with strangers, we also need to have knowledge about strangers' groups. We begin this section by looking at how we can gather information about strangers and their groups so that we can interpret their messages accurately. While our focus is on gathering information about strangers, the processes outlined apply equally to gathering information about people who are similar.

Knowledge of How to Gather Information   Marris (1996) points out that "because uncertainty so often arises from not knowing enough to predict what will happen, searching for more information or deeper understandings is one of the most powerful ways to contain it" (p. 10). Berger (1979) isolates three general types of strategies we can use to gather information about others and manage our uncertainty about them and the way they will interact with us: passive, active, and interactive strategies. To illustrate this process, assume that we want to find out about Yuko, a Japanese to whom we have just been introduced. We are using an intercultural example, but the strategies discussed can be used to gather information about anyone.

When we use *passive strategies,* we take the role of "unobtrusive observers" (i.e., we do not intervene in the situation we are observing; Berger, 1979). Obviously, the type of situation in which we observe Yuko influences the amount of information we gain about her. If we observe Yuko in a situation where she does not have to interact with others, we will not gain much information about her. Situations in which she is interacting with several people at once, in contrast, allow us to make comparisons of how Yuko interacts with the different people.

If we know any of the people with whom Yuko is interacting, we can compare how Yuko interacts with the people we know and how she might interact with us. It also should be noted that if other Japanese are present in the situation, we can compare Yuko's behavior with theirs to try to determine how she is similar to and different from other Japanese.

There is one other aspect of the situations that will influence the amount of information we obtain about Yuko's behavior. If situations are formal, her behavior is likely to be a function of the role she is filling in the situations and we will not learn much about Yuko as an individual. Informal situations where behavior is not guided by roles or social protocol, in contrast, will provide useful information about Yuko's behavior.

The preceding examples all involve our taking the role of an observer. The *active strategies* for managing uncertainty require us to do something to acquire information about Yuko without actually interacting with her (Berger, 1979). One thing we could do to get information about Yuko is to ask questions of someone who knows her. When we ask others about someone, we need to keep in mind that the information we receive may not be accurate. The other person may intentionally give us wrong information or may not know Yuko well.

We also can gather information about other groups by asking people who have had contact with those groups or gathering information from the library. In this example, we could gather information on Japan by questioning someone we know who has lived in Japan, reading a book on Japanese culture, or completing a Japanese cultural assimilator (i.e., a programmed learning course that teaches readers about the Japanese culture). This would give us information about Yuko's cultural background and allow us to make cultural-level predictions about her behavior. Again, we need to keep in mind that our informant may or may not have good information about Japan and that Yuko may not be a typical Japanese.

This raises the issue of how we can select good informants to learn about other groups. People who have a lot of informal social contact with members of the other group, for example, are better informants than people who have little informal contact or even a lot of contact in formal settings. We also would do well to select informants who have been successful in their interactions with members of other groups. To illustrate, if there are two members of our group who have frequent contact with the group in which we are interested, we would select the one who appears to be most successful in interacting with members of the other group (based on our observations of their interactions or their reports of their interactions).

When we use active strategies to gather information, we do not actually interact with the people about whom we are trying to gather information. The *interactive strategies* of verbal interrogation (question asking) and self-disclosure, in contrast, are used when we interact with strangers (Berger, 1979).

One obvious way we can gather information about strangers is to use *interrogation,* that is, ask them questions (Berger, 1979). When we are interacting with someone from our own group, there are limitations to this strategy that have to be kept in mind. First, we can ask only so many questions. We may not be sure what the exact number is, but we always know when we have asked too many. Second, our questions must be appropriate to the nature of the interaction we are having and the relationship we have with the stranger.

When we are communicating with strangers, the same limitations are present, and there are others. The number and type of questions that strangers consider acceptable may not be the same as what we consider acceptable (recall the example of the questions the Japanese asked in the previous chapter). Strangers also may not be able to answer our questions, especially if our questions deal with why they behave the way they do (the ultimate answer to why questions is "because!" or "that is the way we do it here"). When we are interacting with strangers, there is also the added problem of our not wanting to appear stupid or be rude. We, therefore, often avoid asking strangers questions.

If we can overcome our fear of looking stupid, asking questions is an excellent way to gather information about strangers. Generally speaking, strangers will probably respond in a positive way as long as they perceive that our intent is to learn about them personally or their group and *not* to judge them. This requires mindfulness. Langer (1997) asks, "How can we know if we do not ask? Why should we ask if we are certain we know? All answers come out of the questions. If we pay attention to our questions, we increase the power of mindful learning" (p. 139).

The other way we can gather information about strangers when interacting with them is through *self-disclosure*—telling strangers unknown information about ourselves (Berger, 1979). Self-disclosure works as an information-gathering strategy because of the reciprocity norm. Essentially, the reciprocity norm states that if we do something for you, you will reciprocate and do something for us. The reciprocity norm appears to be a cultural universal; it exists in all cultures.

In conversations between people who are not close (e.g., people we meet for the first time, acquaintances), we tend to reciprocate and tell each other the same information about ourselves that others tell us. If we disclose our opinions on a topic when communicating with strangers, they probably will disclose their opinions on the same topic. There will, however, be some differences when we communicate with strangers and when we communicate with people from our own group. The topics that are appropriate to be discussed, for example, vary from culture to culture and ethnic group to ethnic group. If we self-disclose on a topic with strangers and they do not reciprocate, there is a good chance we have found an inappropriate topic of conversation in strangers' groups. Since the timing and pacing of self-disclosure vary across cultures and ethnic groups, it is also possible that our timing is off or we have tried to self-disclose at an inappropriate pace.

Knowledge of Group Differences   Many people assume that to communicate effectively with members of other groups, we should focus only on similarities. This, however, is not the case. If strangers strongly identify with their groups, they will feel that their self-concepts are not being confirmed if we focus only on similarities. This is true whether strangers come from different cultures, ethnic groups, disability groups, age groups, or social classes. To communicate effectively, we must understand real differences between our groups and strangers' groups. We often are aware of differences based on our ethnocentrism, prejudice, sexism, ageism, and stereotypes. These differences, however, may not be real (e.g., our stereotypes may not be accurate, or strangers may be atypical members of their groups).

Recognizing differences often facilitates effective communication. Coleman and DePaulo (1991), for example, point out that

> there is evidence to suggest that [nondisabled] people would rather work and socialize with disabled people who acknowledge their disability than with those who do not acknowledge it. . . . Although acknowledgement of the disability on the part of the disabled person does not always lead to acceptance . . . it does reduce uncertainty and tension and enhances the attractiveness of the disabled person. Interactions proceed less problematically when a disabled person "appropriately" self-discloses about the disability. (p. 82)

A similar argument can be made for other group differences.

To communicate effectively, we need to be aware of the actual differences that exist between our groups and strangers' groups and between ourselves and individual strangers. One way we can isolate these actual differences is to learn all we can about strangers' groups (e.g., become an expert on other cultures or ethnic groups). This approach, however, is not practical. How can we be experts on all the groups of which the strangers with whom we have contact are members? Obviously, we cannot.

When we are communicating with strangers from other cultures, we can use the dimensions of cultural variability discussed in Chapter 3 to develop a preliminary understanding of the real differences between our cultures and other cultures. To illustrate, Gudykunst and Nishida (1994) isolate several cultural differences that would help U.S. Americans better understand Japanese communication:

1. Recognizing that Japan is a collectivistic culture where people conceptualize themselves as interdependent with one another. This leads to an emphasis on *wa* [harmony] in the in-group, as well as an emphasis on *enryo* [reticence] and *amae* [dependence] in interactions with others. The importance of *wa* also leads to drawing a distinction between *tatemae* [what is stated in public] and *honne* [what is truly believed].

2. High-context messages are used more frequently in Japan than low-context messages. This leads to an emphasis on indirect forms of communication, as opposed to an emphasis on direct forms of communication in the United States. *Sasshi* [the ability to guess] is necessary to understand indirect messages.
3. Japan is a high uncertainty avoidance culture. This leads to an emphasis on rituals and the specification of relatively clear rules in most communication situations. People who deviate from the rules are viewed as dangerous and, therefore, are avoided whenever possible.
4. Japan is a high power distance culture. This leads to an emphasis on status (e.g., position, age) in communication. Power distance also leads to an emphasis on *on* and *giri* [obligations] in relationships between individuals in Japan.
5. Japan is a highly masculine culture. This leads to an emphasis on communicating with members of the same-sex, and separation of the sexes in many social situations. (p. 112)

These five conclusions are not all-inclusive, but they summarize the way the major dimensions of cultural variability influence Japanese communication.

Broad generalizations like those isolated here can help us understand the differences between ourselves and strangers from other cultures if the strangers are relatively typical members of their cultures. To communicate effectively with specific strangers, however, we must understand how they view their cultures. We also must go a step further and try to understand the personal differences between us.

Knowledge of Personal Similarities While understanding differences is important, we also have to understand similarities if we are going to communicate effectively with strangers. Understanding similarities at the group level is important, but finding similarities at the individual level is critical if we want to develop relationships with strangers (this issue is discussed in more detail in Chapter 12). Isolating similarities requires that we be mindful of our communication.

One way we can be mindful is by creating new categories (Langer, 1989). One way to create new categories is to develop subcategories of broad categories (e.g., separating Chicanos and Chicanas from Mexican Americans in our stereotype of people from Mexico). The smaller our categories, the more effectively we can communicate with strangers in the categories. We create new categories when we consciously search for similarities we share with strangers rather than focusing only on differences. Do strangers, for example, have children who go to the same school as ours? Do strangers belong to the same social clubs we do? Do strangers experience similar frustrations in their professional and personal lives as we do? Do strangers have similar worries about their families? The first two questions search for shared group memberships, and the second two focus on shared values, attitudes, or beliefs.

Bellah, Madsen, Sullivan, Swidler, and Tipton (1985) point out that we need to seek out commonalities because "with a more explicit understanding of what we have in common and the goals we seek to attain together, the differences between us that remain would be less threatening" (p. 287). Finding commonalities requires that we be mindful of our prejudices. Brodie (1989) contends that "racism and sexism and homophobia and religious and cultural intolerance . . . are all ways of denying that other people are the same kind as ourselves" (p. 16).

The position that Bellah et al. (1985) advocate vis-à-vis cultural and/or ethnic differences is consistent with Langer's (1989) contention that

> because most of us grow up and spend our time with people like ourselves, we tend to assume uniformities and commonalities. When confronted with someone who is clearly different in one specific way, we drop that assumption and look for differences. . . . The mindful curiosity generated by an encounter with someone who is different, which can lead to exaggerated perceptions of strangeness, can also bring us closer to that person if channeled differently. (p. 156)

Langer suggests that once individuals satisfy their curiosity about differences, understanding can occur. She, therefore, argues that what is needed is a way to make mindful curiosity about differences not taboo. One way that each of us can contribute to the acceptance of mindful curiosity is by accepting strangers' questions about us and our groups as "requests for information" until we are certain there is another motivation.

Knowledge of Alternative Interpretations Effective communication requires that we minimize misunderstandings or maximize the similarity in the ways messages are interpreted. To accomplish this, we must recognize that there are many ways that messages can be interpreted, and often these interpretations involve evaluations of strangers' behavior. (Note: Awareness of alternative perspectives is one component of being mindful, a skill discussed in the next section.)

The problem of misinterpreting strangers' behavior is compounded when we communicate with strangers because we tend to interpret strangers' behavior on the basis of our own frames of reference. Lakoff (1990) illustrates the problems that emerge when we interpret strangers' behavior on the basis of our frames of reference:

> We see all behavior from our internal perspective: what would that mean if I did it? And, of course, if I, as a member of my own group, did what that person did in the presence of other members of my group, it would be strange or bad. . . . We don't usually extrapolate, we don't say, "Yes, but in *his* [or her] frame of reference, what would it mean? We assume the possibility of direct transfer of meaning, that a gesture or act in Culture A can be understood in the same way by members of Culture B. Often this is true: there are universals of behavior, but often that is a dangerous assumption; and by cavalierly ignoring the need for translation, we are making misunderstanding inevitable. (pp. 165–166)

It is important to keep in mind that we tend to make the assumption of direct transfer of meaning when we communicate on automatic pilot. Understanding strangers' perspectives requires that we be mindful of our communication.

When we communicate on automatic pilot, we interpret strangers' behavior by using our perspectives. Recognizing strangers' perspectives requires understanding the differences among the three cognitive processes involved in our perception of strangers' behavior: description, interpretation, and evaluation. To communicate effectively, it is necessary to distinguish among these three processes. By *description* we mean an actual report of what we have observed with the minimum of distortion and without attributing social significance to the behavior. Description includes what we see and hear and is accomplished by counting and/or recording observations.

In order to clarify these processes, consider the following example:

Description
Kim stood six inches away from me when we talked.

This statement is descriptive in nature. It does not attribute social significance to Kim's behavior; it merely tells what the observer saw. If we attributed social significance to this statement or made an inference about what we saw, we would be engaged in *interpretation.* In other words, interpretation is what we think about what we see and hear. The important thing to keep in mind is that multiple interpretations can be made for any particular description of behavior. Returning to our example, we have the following:

Description
Kim stood six inches away from me when we talked.
Interpretations
Kim is aggressive.
Kim violated my personal space.
Kim likes me.

Each of these interpretations can have several different evaluations. *Evaluations* are positive or negative judgments concerning the social significance we attribute to behavior; whether we like it or not. To illustrate this, we can use the first interpretation given above:

Interpretation
Kim is aggressive.
Evaluations
I like that; Kim stands up for herself or himself.
I don't like that; Kim should not violate my rights by standing so close.

Of course, several other evaluations could be made, but these two are sufficient to illustrate potential differences in evaluations that can be made regarding any one interpretation.

If we are unable to distinguish among these three cognitive processes, it is likely that we will skip the descriptive process and jump immediately to either interpretation or evaluation when confronted with different patterns of behavior. This leads to misattributions of meaning and, therefore, to ineffective communication. Being able to distinguish among the three processes, in contrast, increases the likelihood that we are able to see alternative interpretations, thereby increasing our ability to communicate effectively. Differentiating among the three processes also increases the likelihood of our making more accurate predictions of strangers' behavior. If we are able to describe strangers' behavior, we can make more accurate predictions because we are able to see alternative interpretations of behavior patterns.

If we do not separate descriptive and interpretive processes, misunderstandings are inevitable. When we communicate on automatic pilot, we usually interpret strangers' behavior without describing it. Our interpretations are based on our cultural, ethnic, and social class upbringing. Our interpretations of strangers' behavior, however, may be very different from what they intended by the behavior. When we think there might have been a misunderstanding, we need to stop and describe the behavior in question. Once we have described the behavior, we need to look for alternative interpretations. After we have thought of some alternative interpretations, we can ask strangers which interpretation is correct. If we cannot ask strangers, we can make an educated guess as to what they meant on the basis of our knowledge of them or the groups of which they are members. Separating descriptions and interpretations, as we are suggesting here, requires that we be mindful.

Skills

The skills necessary to communicate effectively and appropriately with strangers are those that are directly related to managing our uncertainty and anxiety. Managing our anxiety requires at least three skills: ability to be mindful, ability to tolerate ambiguity, and ability to manage anxiety. Managing uncertainty minimally requires four skills: ability to be mindful, ability to empathize, ability to adapt our behavior, and ability to make accurate predictions and explanations of strangers' behavior (the first two skills, however, are necessary to develop the third). Since the ability to be mindful is common to managing both anxiety and uncertainty, we begin with it.

Ability to Be Mindful   By now it should be clear that we believe becoming mindful is an important aspect of communicating effectively with strangers. We must be cognitively aware of our communication if we are to overcome our tendencies to interpret strangers' behavior on the basis of our own frames of reference. At the outset, it is important to recognize that we are seldom highly mindful of our communication. Even when we communicate with people close to us, we are not mindful of the process. Csikszentmihalyi (1990) contends that

> there are few things as enjoyable as freely sharing one's most secret feelings and thoughts with another person. Even though this sounds commonplace, it in fact requires concentrated attention [mindfulness], openness, and sensitivity. In practice, the degree of investment of psychic energy in a friendship is unfortunately rare. (p. 188)

He goes on to argue that we must control our own lives if we want to improve our relationships with others. Such control requires that we be mindful.

As indicated in Chapter 2, Langer (1989) isolates three qualities of *mindfulness:* "(1) creation of new categories; (2) openness to new information; and (3) awareness of more than one perspective" (p. 62). (Note: Since knowledge of alternative perspectives was discussed in the preceding section, only the first two components are discussed here.)

Langer (1989) points out that "categorizing is a fundamental and natural human activity. It is the way we come to know the world. Any attempt to eliminate bias by attempting to eliminate the perception of differences is doomed to failure" (p. 154). She argues that what we need to do is learn to make more, not fewer, distinctions. To illustrate, Langer uses an example of people who are in the category "cripple." If we see all people in this category as the same, we start treating the category in which we place strangers as their identities. If we draw additional distinctions within this category (i.e., create new categories), in contrast, it stops us from treating strangers as a category. If we see strangers with a "lame leg," we do not necessarily treat them as "cripples."

We can become open to new information by modifying our expectations. If, for example, we have an inflexible negative stereotype of strangers' groups, we can either modify the content of the stereotype or hold it more flexibly. Harvey, Hunt, and Schroder (1961) argue that people differ in the degree to which they are willing to modify the stereotypes they hold, or in other words, the degree of "openness-closedness" of their stereotypes. In applying this concept to interactions across national boundaries, Scott (1965) argues that

> an image is "closed" to the extent that the person regards the attributes included in it as completely defining the object. . . . The more "open" the image, the more is the person willing to entertain the possibility that essential features of the object have not yet been recognized by him [or her], and that these additional attributes would reveal new similarities and differences in relation to other objects. (p. 81)

Holding closed stereotypes is linked directly to inaccurate interpretations and predictions of strangers' behavior. Holding open stereotypes, in contrast, increases the likelihood of making accurate interpretations and predictions of strangers' behavior. More specifically, if our stereotypes are open, we will be open to perceiving behavior not associated with the stereotype, thereby making it possible for us to interpret and predict strangers' behavior more accurately. We also need to recognize consciously that our stereotype may be inaccurate and does not apply to *all,* or even most, members of the other groups (see Burgoon, Berger, & Waldron, 2000, for a discussion of mindfulness and reducing stereotyping).

Sometimes when we communicate with strangers, we are mindful of our communication. Our focus, however, is usually on the outcome ("Will I make a fool of myself?") rather than the process of communication. As you will recall, however, focusing on the outcome does not facilitate effective communication. For effective communication to occur, we must focus on the process. Langer (1989) argues that

> an outcome orientation in social situations can induce mindlessness. If we think we know how to handle a situation, we don't feel a need to pay attention. If we respond to the situation as very familiar (as a result, for example, of overlearning), we notice only minimal cues necessary to carry out the proper scenarios. If, on the other hand, the situation is strange, we might be so preoccupied with the thought of failure ("what if I make a fool of myself?") that we miss nuances of our own and others' behavior. In this sense, we are mindless with respect to the immediate situation, although we may be thinking quite actively about outcome related issues. (p. 34)

Langer believes that focusing on the process (e.g., how we do something) forces us to be mindful of our behavior and pay attention to the situations in which we find ourselves. It is only when we are mindful of the process of our communication that we can determine how our interpretations of messages differ from strangers' interpretations of those messages.

We often are mindful of our behavior when we communicate with strangers because they may act in a deviant or unexpected fashion or we do not have a script to guide our communication with them. The "problem" is that we usually are mindful of the outcome, not the process. Since we tend to interpret strangers' behavior on the basis of our own frames of reference, to communicate effectively with strangers we need to become mindful of our process of communication, even when we are engaging in habitual behavior. We are not suggesting that we try to be mindful at all times. This would be impossible. Rather, we are suggesting that when there is a high potential for misunderstanding, we need to be mindful and consciously aware of the process of communication that is taking place.

Effective communication with strangers requires that we develop mindful ways of learning about our communication with strangers. Langer (1997) argues that

> the concept of mindfulness revolves around certain psychological states that are really different versions of the same thing: (1) openness to novelty; (2) alertness to distinctions; (3) sensitivity to different contexts; (4) implicit, if not explicit, awareness of multiple perspectives; and (5) orientation in the present. Each leads to the others and back to its self. Learning a subject or skill with an openness to novelty and actively noticing differences, contexts, and perspectives—sideways learning—makes us receptive to changes in an ongoing situation. In such a state of mind, basic skills and information guide our behavior in the present, rather than run like a computer program. (p. 23)

Engaging in these behaviors will lead us to focus on the process of communication rather than getting hung up on the possible outcomes of the interaction.

Langer (1997) points out that we do not want to be overly vigilant when we are mindful. If we become overly vigilant (concentrate with all our will), we lock strangers in our attention but our attention tends to be static and we become fatigued. If we engage in "soft vigilance," in contrast, we are open to novelty in our interactions with strangers and take in new information. When we see novelty in our interactions with strangers, our interactions are enjoyable. Our enjoyment, in turn, leads us to pay attention to our interactions.

When we become mindful, there are several things we can do to improve our communication effectiveness. We can, for example, negotiate meanings with strangers. *Negotiating meanings* involves seeking clarification of meanings in the middle of a conversation when we realize a misunderstanding has occurred (Varonis & Gass, 1985). Attempts to negotiate meanings usually are initiated by the person whose native language is being spoken. Another technique we can use is repairs. *Repairs* involve asking strangers to repeat what was said when we do not understand (Gass & Varonis, 1985). Repair sequences usually are initiated by people speaking in their second languages.

Negotiating meaning and repairs are forms of metacommunication—communicating about our communication. Another aspect of metacommunication that is relevant when we are mindful of our communication is feedback. When we are mindful, we can give the strangers with whom we are communicating feedback about how we are interpreting their messages and request feedback about how they are interpreting our messages. Closely related is the issue of effective listening. When we communicate on automatic pilot, we do not listen effectively. To listen effectively, we must be mindful of our communication and focus on understanding strangers' perspectives.

Being mindful is the single most important skill in communicating effectively with strangers. When we are mindful, we make conscious choices about what we need to do in specific situations in order to communicate effectively. Mindless behavior, no matter how well motivated or skillful, cannot substitute for mindful behavior. We always will be more effective when we are mindful than when we are on automatic pilot (i.e., mindless) (Langer, 1997).

Ability to Tolerate Ambiguity *Tolerance for ambiguity* implies the ability to deal successfully with situations even when a lot of information needed to interact effectively is unknown (see Furnham & Ribchester, 1995, for a review). Budner (1962) argues that *lack* of tolerance for ambiguity involves perceiving ambiguous situations as threatening and undesirable. Our tolerance for ambiguity affects the type of information we gather about strangers. If we have a low tolerance for ambiguity, we tend to base our judgments of strangers on first impressions, which are formed prematurely before all information is available (Smock, 1955). We also seek out information that supports our beliefs when we have a low tolerance for ambiguity (McPherson, 1983). If we have a high tolerance for ambiguity, in contrast, we tend to seek objective information about the situation and the strangers in it. Further, we tend to be open to new information about ourselves and strangers if we have a high tolerance for ambiguity (Pilisuk, 1963).

The greater our tolerance for ambiguity, the more comfortable we feel in situations where we do not have all the information we would like. Ruben and Kealey (1979) point out that

> the ability to react to new and ambiguous situations with minimal discomfort has long been thought to be an important asset when adjusting to a new culture. . . . Excessive discomfort resulting from being placed in a new or different environment—or from finding the familiar environment altered in some critical ways—can lead to confusion, frustration and interpersonal hostility. Some people seem better able to adapt well in new environments and adjust quickly to the demands of the changing milieu. (p. 19)

Ruben and Kealey's research indicates that the greater our tolerance for ambiguity, the more effective we are in completing task assignments in other cultures.

Our tolerance for ambiguity affects the type of information we try to find out about strangers. People with a low tolerance for ambiguity try to gather information that supports their own beliefs. People with a high tolerance for ambiguity, in contrast, seek objective information from strangers (McPherson, 1983). Objective information is necessary to understand strangers and predict their behavior accurately.

Ability to Manage Anxiety As indicated earlier, the amount of anxiety we experience when we communicate with strangers influences our motivation to communicate with them. If our anxiety is above our maximum thresholds or below our minimum thresholds, we will not be able to communicate effectively. If our anxiety is too high, we will be preoccupied with managing it to communicate effectively. If our anxiety is too low, we will not have enough adrenaline flowing to want to communicate with strangers.

Kennerley (1990) isolates two general issues in managing anxiety: (1) controlling bodily symptoms and (2) controlling worrying thoughts or cognitive distortions. There are several physical symptoms associated with anxiety. When we are highly anxious, we may experience respiratory problems (difficulty in breathing), palpitations of the heart, dry mouth, muscular tension, or a tension headache.

To manage our anxiety, Prather (1986) suggests the most important thing we can do is break away from the situation in which we feel anxious. This might mean excusing ourselves to leave the room or mentally withdrawing for a short period of time. Once we have withdrawn, we need to calm ourselves and remember that our anxiety is not going to harm us. We can allow our anxious feelings to pass and then return to the situation.

If our anxiety does not dissipate quickly, we need to do something that will restore our calm. We can use various techniques to control the physical symptoms associated with our anxiety. These include, but are not limited to, yoga, hypnotism, meditation, and progressive muscular relaxation (relaxing the various muscle groups in our bodies in a systematic fashion). Respiratory control also can be used to manage the physical symptoms of anxiety. One way to practice controlled breathing is to sit up straight and concentrate on your breathing. Mindfully draw in a long breath and focus on your inhaling. Then let out the breath, focusing on your exhaling.

We can control our worrying thoughts by overcoming our cognitive distortions. When we interpret our own and others' behavior, our perceptions often are distorted because of the ways we think about our feelings and behavior. Burns (1989) isolates 10 forms of cognitive distortions that influence the ways we interpret behavior: (1) all-or-nothing thinking, (2) making overgeneralizations, (3) using mental filters, (4) discounting the positive and focusing only on the negative, (5) jumping to conclusions, (6) using magnification, or making problems bigger than they are, (7) using emotional reasoning, (8) using "should" statements (e.g., I should be a better person), (9) labeling, and (10) blaming ourselves or others. To overcome our worrying thoughts, we need to be mindful of our communication. When we are mindful, we need to replace the worrying thoughts with a rational response. Unless we stop distorting our thought processes, we will *not* be able to manage our anxiety consistently over long periods of time.

Ability to Empathize   The one skill that consistently emerges in discussions of effective communication with strangers is empathy. Bell (1987) argues that *empathy* is multifaceted, involving cognitive (thinking), affective (feeling), and communication components:

> Cognitively, the empathic person takes the perspective of another person, and in so doing strives to see the world from the other's point of view. Affectively, the empathic person experiences the emotions of another; he or she *feels* the other's experiences. Communicatively, the empathic individual signals understanding and concern through verbal and nonverbal cues. (p. 204)

The cognitive, affective, and communication components are highly interrelated, and all must be present for others to perceive that we are being empathic.

Empathy involves (1) carefully listening to strangers, (2) understanding strangers' feelings, (3) being interested in what strangers say, (4) being sensitive to strangers' needs, and (5) understanding strangers' points of view (Hwang, Chase, & Kelley, 1980). These indicators of empathy include verbal components, but we tend to rely on nonverbal behavior more than verbal behavior when we interpret others' behavior as empathic (Bell, 1987).

When we are *empathic,* we imagine how strangers are feeling. Sympathy often is confused with empathy. When we are *sympathetic,* we imagine how we would feel in strangers' situations. Bennett (1979) argues that the "Golden Rule"—"Do unto others as you would have them do unto you"—many people are taught as children involves a sympathetic response to others, not an empathic response. He proposes that we follow the "Platinum Rule"—"Do unto others as they would have you do unto them"—which involves an empathic response. This is a reasonable approach as long as what others want done unto them does not violate our basic moral principles or universally accepted principles of human rights.

Stephan and Finlay (1999) point out that "empathy leads to prosocial behavior" (p. 732) (e.g., helping strangers, inhibiting aggression). Cognitive empathy with strangers may reduce perceptions of dissimilarities and feeling threatened by strangers, which, in turn, leads to reductions in prejudice. Emotional empathy with strangers may "arouse feelings of injustice," and this "counteracts prejudice" (p. 735). Stephan and Finlay, however, argue that empathizing with strangers without respecting them can be problematic (e.g., it can lead to condescension).

Ability to Adapt Our Behavior   To gather information about and adapt our behavior to strangers, we must be flexible in our behavior. We must be able to select strategies that are appropriate to gather the information we need about strangers in order to communicate effectively with them. This requires that we have different behavioral options for gathering information open to us.

We also must be able to adapt and accommodate our behavior to people from other groups if we are going to be successful in our interactions with them. Langer (1997) points out that "when we are mindful, we are implicitly aware that in any particular situation there is no absolute optimum standard for action. From a mindful perspective, one's response to a particular situation is not an attempt to make the best choice from among available options but to create options" (p. 114, italics omitted).

Duran (1983) argues that *communication adaptability* involves "1) The requirement of both cognitive (ability to perceive) and behavioral (ability to adapt) skills; 2) Adaptation not only of behaviors but also interaction goals; 3) The ability to adapt to the requirements posed by different communication contexts; and 4) The assumption that perceptions of communicative competence reside in the dyad" (p. 320).

Triandis, Brislin, and Hui (1988) provide suggestions for how individualists and collectivists might want to consider adapting their behavior and ways of thinking when communicating with each other. *For individualists to communicate effectively with collectivists,* Triandis and his associates suggest that individualists (1) recognize that collectivists pay attention to group memberships and use group memberships to predict collectivists' behavior; (2) recognize that when collectivists' group memberships change, their behavior changes; (3) recognize that collectivists are comfortable in vertical, unequal relationships; (4) recognize that collectivists see competition as threatening; (5) recognize that collectivists emphasize harmony and cooperation in the ingroup; (6) recognize that collectivists emphasize face (public self-image) and help them preserve face in interactions; (7) recognize that collectivists do not separate criticism from the person being criticized and avoid confrontation whenever possible; (8) cultivate long-term relationships; (9) be more formal than usual in initial interactions; and (10) follow collectivists' guide in disclosing personal information.

For collectivists to interact effectively with individualists, Triandis, Brislin, and Hui (1988) suggest that collectivists (1) recognize that individualists behavior cannot be predicted accurately from group memberships; (2) recognize that individualists will be proud of their accomplishments and say negative things about others; (3) recognize that individualists are emotionally detached from their ingroups; (4) recognize that individualists prefer horizontal, equal relationships; (5) recognize that individualists do not see competition as threatening; (6) recognize that individualists are not persuaded by arguments emphasizing harmony and cooperation; (7) recognize that individualists do not form long-term relationships and that initial friendliness does not indicate an intimate relationship; (8) recognize that individualists maintain relationships when they receive more rewards than costs; (9) recognize that individualists do not respect others on the basis of position, age, or sex as much as collectivists; and (10) recognize that outgroups are not viewed as highly different from the ingroup. Suggestions also could be based on the other dimensions of cultural variability presented in Chapter 3.

Often the adaptations we make when interacting with strangers do not improve the effectiveness of our communication (see, for example, the discussion of communicative distance in Chapter 5). Kraut and Higgins (1984) argue that the "adjustments majority speakers make when speaking to minority members often give the impression that the speaker is patronizing and distant and, in turn, affect the recipients' behavior and conversational style" (p. 114). If strangers perceive we are patronizing, they will become defensive, and communication cannot be effective when one of the individuals is defensive. To be more effective we must adapt our messages to the specific strangers with whom we are communicating. Strangers understand our messages better when they are constructed for them than when we do not adapt our messages.

One important aspect of adapting our behavior is the ability to speak another language (or at least use phrases in another language). If we always expect strangers to speak our languages, we cannot be effective in communicating with them. Boyer (1990) points out that we "should become familiar with other languages and cultures so that [we] will be better able to live, with confidence, in an increasingly interdependent world" (p. B4).

Triandis (1983) points out that the importance of speaking another language depends, at least in part, on where we are:

> In some cultures foreigners are expected to know the local language. A Frenchman [or woman] who arrives in the United States without knowing a word of English, or an American who visits France with only a bit of French, is bound to find the locals rather unsympathetic. For example, I have found a discrepancy between my friends' and my own experience in Paris. Their accounts stress discourtesy of the French, while I have found the French to be quite courteous. I suspect the difference is that I speak better French than the majority of visitors and am therefore treated more courteously. In contrast, in other cultures the visitor is not expected to know the local language. In Greece, for example, one is not expected to know the language although a few words of Greek create delight, and increase by order of magnitude (a factor of ten) the normal hospitable tendencies of that population. (p. 84)

Some attempt at using local languages is necessary to indicate interest in the people and/or culture. It is important to keep in mind, however, that members of other cultures may prefer to speak our languages. To illustrate, Ross and Shortreed (1990) report that Japanese who speak English do not view responding in Japanese to non-Japanese-speaking Japanese, even those relatively fluent, to be empathic or efficient.

The need to adapt our behavior is not limited to speaking another language. If European Americans are communicating with strangers from another culture who want to stand closer than the European Americans want them to stand (e.g., strangers from

Latin or Arab cultures), the European Americans have two options if they are mindful of their communication. First, the European Americans can choose to try to use their own interpersonal distances (e.g., strangers should stand at least at arm's length). If strangers keep trying to use their distances, however, they will dance the European Americans around the room (e.g., the strangers move forward, the European Americans move back; to compensate and be at a distance that is comfortable for them, the strangers move closer). If the European Americans are not mindful of their communication, this is what is likely to occur. Alternatively, the European Americans can choose to use a different pattern of behavior. They can decide to stand closer to strangers than they would if they were communicating with someone from their own culture. This option, in all likelihood, will lead to effective communication. When people are following different norms, at least one of the parties has to adapt for effective communication to occur.

You may be asking yourself, Why do I have to adapt? Why don't strangers adapt, especially if they are foreigners in the United States? The strangers could adapt, and strangers from other cultures visiting or living in the United States usually do to some extent. As members of the human community, nevertheless, we have to make choices about whether to adapt and when to adapt to others. We believe that if we know what can be done to improve the chances for effective communication, have the skills to do what needs to be done, and choose not to adapt our communication, we have to take responsibility for the misunderstandings that occur as a result. There are obviously situations where this principle may not hold. If the behavior required, for example, goes against our moral standards or violates another's human rights, some other option must be found.

Ability to Make Accurate Predictions and Explanations   The final skill is the ability to make accurate predictions and explanations of strangers' behavior. If we can empathize, have the ability to adapt our communication, and are mindful, we can gather the information necessary to manage our uncertainty. Managing uncertainty requires that we be able to describe strangers' behavior, select accurate interpretations of their messages, predict their behavior accurately, and be able to explain their behavior accurately.

Karniol (1990) points out that we assume that strangers' thoughts, feelings, and behavior are rule-governed. If we do not make such an assumption, we could not ever predict strangers' thoughts, feelings, or behavior. The problem with the accuracy of our predictions is that we know only a limited number of rules that we can use to understand strangers' thoughts, feelings, and behavior. Since we may not know the rules that strangers are using, we assume that they are the same as ours when we are on automatic pilot. To understand the rules that strangers are using to guide their thoughts, feelings, and behavior, we must be mindful. When we are mindful, we need to be empathic and use active listening in order to try to understand strangers' rules. Once we understand the rules strangers are using, we can make accurate predictions and explanations of their behavior.

When we are on automatic pilot, our predictions of and explanations for strangers' behavior are based on our stereotypes, attitudes, and previous experiences with the individuals involved. We may be highly confident of our predictions and explanations when we are on automatic pilot, but our predictions and explanations may *not* be accurate. If our predictions are based only on our stereotypes of strangers' groups, for example, our predictions will not be accurate if our stereotypes are inaccurate or strangers are not typical members of their groups. Accurate predictions or explanations of strangers' behavior require that we use cultural, social, and personal information.

To make accurate predictions and explanations, we must be able to gather accurate information about strangers. When our anxiety is too high, we are not able to gather accurate information about strangers (Wilder & Shapiro, 1989). If our anxiety is too low, we also will have problems gathering accurate information about strangers. To gather accurate information, we must mindfully manage our anxiety so that it is below our maximum thresholds and above our minimum thresholds. The accuracy of our predictions and explanations for strangers' behavior also are dependent upon our knowledge of group differences, our knowledge of similarities, and our knowledge of alternative interpretations. Our accuracy also is affected by our expectations. If we expect the interactions to be negative, for example, our anxiety will be high, probably above our maximum thresholds, and we will not be able to make accurate predictions or explanations. We also are better able to make accurate predictions and explanations if our needs (see the motivation section in this chapter) have been met.

Another factor that influences the accuracy of our predictions and explanations is our view of our ingroups and outgroups. We tend to view our ingroups as being more differentiated than outgroups. The more familiar we are with outgroups, however, the greater our perceived differentiation of the outgroups (Linville et al., 1989). The more variability we perceive in outgroups, the less our tendency to treat all members in a similar negative fashion (Johnston & Hewstone, 1991). The variability we perceive in outgroups provides information about the strangers with whom we are communicating and, therefore, increases the accuracy of our predictions.

Our perceptions of strangers' intentions toward us also affect the accuracy of our predictions and explanations of their behavior. We tend to be more accurate, for example, in perceiving strangers' intentions when they are negative than when they are positive. Bodenhauser, Gaelick, and Wyer (1987) argue that "intentions to convey hostility are perceived more accurately than intentions to convey positive feelings" (p. 159). Our accuracy in interpreting strangers' intentions also is lower if we have been dissatisfied with our previous interactions with them than if we have been satisfied with our previous interactions.

SUMMARY

Effective communication involves minimizing misunderstandings. To be an effective communicator requires that we be motivated and have the appropriate knowledge and skills. We must be motivated to approach strangers and communicate effectively. Our motivation is a function of meeting our needs for predictability, avoiding anxiety, and sustaining our self-concepts. If we are not able to meet these needs, we will not be motivated to communicate with strangers.

To communicate effectively also requires that we have certain knowledge. We must know how to gather appropriate information about strangers, have knowledge of group differences and personal similarities, and know how strangers are interpreting messages. If we know how to gather information, we can gain the other types of knowledge from our interactions with strangers.

There are several skills that are particularly important in managing our uncertainty and anxiety. To manage our anxiety, we must be able to be mindful, be able to tolerate ambiguity, and be able to manage our anxiety. To manage our uncertainty, we must be able to empathize, be able to adapt our behavior, and be able to make accurate predictions and explanations of strangers' behavior.

STUDY QUESTIONS

1. How do we know where we have communicated effectively?
2. Why is competence based on our impressions of ourselves and others?
3. What are the components of perceived competence? Why are all three necessary to communicate effectively?
4. How do meeting our needs for predictability, avoiding anxiety, and sustaining our self-conceptions influence our motivation to communicate with strangers?
5. How does our knowledge of how to gather information influence our communication with strangers?
6. How does our knowledge of group differences influence our communication with strangers?
7. How does our knowledge of personal similarities influence our communication with strangers?
8. How does our knowledge of alternative interpretations influence our communication with strangers?
9. How does our ability to be mindful influence our communication with strangers?
10. How does our ability to tolerate ambiguity influence our communication with strangers?
11. How does our ability to manage our anxiety influence our communication with strangers?
12. How does our ability to empathize (not sympathize) influence our communication with strangers?
13. How does our ability to adapt our behavior influence our communication with strangers?

SUGGESTED READINGS

Langer, E. (1989). *Mindfulness*. Reading, MA: Addison-Wesley.

Langer, E. (1997). *The power of mindful learning*. Reading, MA: Addison-Wesley.

Spitzberg, B., & Cupach, W. (1984). *Interpersonal communication competence*. Beverly Hills, CA: Sage.

Wiseman, R., & Koester, J. (Eds.). (1993). *Intercultural communication competence*. Thousand Oaks, CA: Sage.

11

MANAGING CONFLICT
AND NEGOTIATING FACE

*As long as groups are in conflict, the casting
of blame by either side will lead to a vicious
circle of mutual recriminations.*

Musafer Sherif

Elie Wiesel, a recipient of the Nobel Peace Prize, believes that hate directed toward members of different cultures and ethnic groups is the major source of conflict between members of different groups in today's world. Conflict is occurring between people of different groups everywhere we look. To illustrate, nationality conflicts are taking place in the former Soviet Union (e.g., between the Azerbaijanis and the Armenians); ethnic conflict is occurring among the Serbians, Croatians, and Muslims in the former Yugoslavia; conflict between neo-Nazis and immigrants in Germany is leading to violence; conflict between Protestants and Catholics in Northern Ireland is still taking place; and conflict between Palestinians and Jews in Israel has not stopped, to name only a few of the intergroup conflicts occurring in the world today.

In the United States, there also is racial harassment on university campuses and in society at large, hate crimes are being committed against members of different groups (e.g., members of different ethnic groups, homosexuals), and there is conflict between pro-choice and right-to-life groups at abortion clinics. The animosity among the various groups is aggravated by the hate programs appearing on public-access cable television in the United States (e.g., *Race and Reason;* see Zoglin, 1993).

The specific causes of the conflicts occurring throughout the world differ depending on the situation, but all the incidents have one thing in common: polarized communication. *Polarized communication* occurs when the communicators have "the inability to believe or seriously consider one's view as wrong and the other's opinion as truth. Communication within [the] human community becomes typified by the rhetoric of 'we' are right and 'they' are misguided or wrong" (Arnett, 1986, pp. 15–16). Polarized communication, therefore, exists when groups or individuals look out for their own interests and have little or no concern for others' interests. Tannen (1993) believes that

> the devastating group hatreds that result in so much suffering in our own country and around the world are related in origin to the small intolerances in our everyday conversations—our readiness to attribute good intentions to ourselves and bad intentions to others; to believe there is one right way and ours is it; and to extrapolate from frustration with an individual in order to generalize to a group. (p. B5)

We express these small intolerances in our everyday conversations without being highly aware of doing so.

The small intolerances in our everyday communication with strangers often lead to conflict. In this chapter, we examine factors related to managing conflict and negotiating face (e.g., individuals' public images) with strangers. Face is included here because conflict threatens participants' faces. We begin by looking at the nature of conflict. Next, we look at cultural and ethnic differences in conflict. Following this, we discuss face and facework across cultures. We then summarize face-negotiation theory as an explanation for cultural differences in conflict and face. We conclude by looking at intergroup conflict.

THE NATURE OF CONFLICT

Conflict "exists whenever incompatible activities occur" (Deutsch, 1973, p. 10). When one person's actions are incompatible with another person's activities, those actions obstruct or interfere with one or both people's attempts to accomplish their goals. This involves a wide range of situations. Conflicts can range from minor disagreements, such as differences of opinion with individuals with whom we have ongoing relationships, to wars. Understanding the nature of conflict and how our cultures and ethnicities influence our approaches to conflict is critical to developing and maintaining relationships with strangers.

Conflict is inevitable in any ongoing relationship; it is going to happen whether we want it to or not. Roloff (1987) isolates several sources of conflict. First, conflicts occur when people misinterpret each other's behavior. Misinterpreting spouses' intent, for example, is one of the major causes of discontent in marriages (Gottman et al., 1976). Second, conflict can arise from perceptions of incompatibility, such as perceiving that personalities or group characteristics are not compatible. Third, conflict arises when people disagree on the causes of their own or other people's behavior. As indicated in Chapter 7, we tend to explain our own positive behavior on the basis of our personal characteristics and tend to attribute strangers' positive behavior to situational demands. We tend to attribute our own negative behavior to situational demands, and we tend to explain strangers' negative behavior by using their group memberships.

When conflicts occur, neither of the parties, one of the parties, or both parties may recognize that a conflict exists. If neither of the parties recognizes that conflicts exist, conflicts may not create problems for the relationships. If only one of the parties recognizes that conflicts exist, they can create problems for the relationships, depending on the conflicts and how the people handle them. To illustrate, if the person who recognizes the conflict decides that the issue is not important, that person can ignore the problem and it will not create problems in the relationship. If, however, the person thinks the conflict is important and ignores it, in all likelihood it will create problems in the relationship. If it does not come out in any other way, it will come out in how the person reacts to the person with whom there is a conflict.

Communication is the medium through which conflict is created and managed. The way we communicate with strangers often creates conflict. The way we communicate with strangers reflects whether we are having conflicts with them. Conflict in relationships can be overt and out in the open (manifest conflict) or can be out of sight (latent conflict). When conflict is out of sight, it is easy to avoid addressing it. In fact, avoidance is probably the most widely used strategy for dealing with conflict. It has been estimated that college students avoid 50 percent of their conflicts with others (Sillars et al., 1982). One reason we avoid conflict is that many of us view conflict negatively. Conflict itself, however, is not positive or negative. How we manage the conflicts we have, in contrast, can have positive or negative consequences for our relationships with strangers.

Our conflicts with strangers often seem to get out of control without our realizing it. Donohue (1993) isolates four aspects of conflict development that contribute to this result. First, once conflicts start, they tend to perpetuate themselves, especially if there are already problems between the people involved. Conflict breeds conflict unless it is managed successfully. Second, conflicts always take place within contexts, but we often are not aware of how the contexts contribute to our conflicts with strangers. To manage conflicts, we have to understand the contexts in which they occur. Third, our conflicts always have implications for our relationships with strangers. When the conflicts are over, our relationships change in some way, but we often do not recognize that it is how we manage conflicts that is critical to how they will affect our relationships. Fourth, conflicts get out of control because we do not recognize that manifest conflict actually serves many positive functions in our lives. If two people have conflicts with a common enemy, for example, it brings them closer together. Our conflicts with strangers also help define our roles and help us understand our feelings about strangers.

CULTURAL AND ETHNIC DIFFERENCES IN MANAGING CONFLICT

Our cultures influence the ways we think about conflicts and our preferences for managing them. We begin this section by looking at the assumptions members of different cultures make about the nature of conflict. Next, we look at the ways members of different cultures manage conflict. We conclude this section by looking at ethnic differences in managing conflict.

Assumptions about Conflict

The major reasons conflicts occur differ across cultures. Olsen (1978) argues that conflicts arise from either instrumental or expressive sources. *Expressive conflicts* arise from a desire to release tension, usually generated from hostile feelings. *Instrumental conflicts,* in contrast, stem from a difference in goals or practices. Ting-Toomey (1985) believes members of individualistic cultures "are more likely to perceive conflict as instrumental rather than expressive in nature" and that members of collectivistic cultures "are more likely to perceive conflict as expressive rather than instrumental in nature" (p. 78).

Members of individualistic cultures often separate the issues on which they have conflicts from the people with whom they have conflicts. Members of collectivistic cultures, in contrast, generally do not make this distinction. To illustrate, Nishiyama

(1971) points out that Japanese managers take criticism and objections to ideas they express as personal attacks. U.S. American managers, in contrast, do not take criticism of their ideas as personal attacks unless they are highly defensive.

The conditions under which conflicts occur differ across cultures. Ting-Toomey (1985) argues that in individualistic cultures conflicts are likely to occur when individuals' expectations for appropriate behavior are violated. Conflicts in collectivistic cultures, in contrast, are likely to occur when a group's normative expectations for behavior are violated. The reason for this difference lies in the role of context in providing information in the two types of cultures. Context plays a crucial role in providing meaning to communication messages in collectivistic cultures, but context plays a less crucial role because more information is provided in the message in individualistic cultures. The more important the context is, the more often violations of collective normative expectations lead to conflict. The less important the context is, the more often violations of individuals' expectations lead to conflict.

The attitudes of the participants toward dealing with conflicts vary across cultures. Ting-Toomey (1985) takes the position that members of individualistic cultures are "likely to possess a confrontational, direct attitude toward conflicts" and that members of collectivistic cultures are "likely to possess a non-confrontational, indirect attitude toward conflicts" (p. 9). A direct approach to conflict in individualistic cultures probably stems from the "doing" orientation and the use of linear logic. Members of collectivistic cultures have a strong desire for ingroup harmony and tend to use indirect forms of communication to maintain harmony and, therefore, tend to prefer nonconfrontational approaches to conflict.

Ting-Toomey (1994a) argues that the self construals which guide individuals in managing conflicts differ across cultures. Members of individualistic cultures tend to deal with conflict on the basis of independent self construals, and members of collectivistic cultures tend to deal with conflict on the basis of interdependent self construals. Members of individualistic cultures think only of themselves and the specific person with whom they have a conflict when their behavior is guided by their independent self construals. Members of collectivistic cultures, in contrast, think about themselves and the members of their ingroups when their behavior is guided by their interdependent self construals. Members of collectivistic cultures cannot separate themselves from the ingroups of which they are members when their behavior is guided by their interdependent self construals.

Ting-Toomey (1994a) believes that members of individualistic cultures take a short-term view of managing conflicts while members of collectivistic cultures take a long-term view of managing conflicts. Members of individualistic cultures are concerned with the immediate conflict situations. Once conflicts are managed, they can move on to other issues in their relationships with those with whom they have conflicts. Members of collectivistic cultures, in contrast, focus on long-term relationships with others. The immediate conflict is important, but the critical issue for collectivists is whether they can depend on others over the long term.

Ting-Toomey (1994a) also contends that members of collectivistic cultures prefer to use mediators to manage conflicts more than members of individualistic cultures. The use of mediators allows conflicts to be managed without direct confrontation. If confrontation can be avoided, harmony in the relationship can be maintained. Members of individualistic cultures do use mediators to manage conflicts. When individualists use mediators, they prefer formal mediators (e.g., lawyers) more than members of collectivistic cultures. Members of collectivistic cultures, in contrast, prefer informal mediators more than members of individualistic cultures.

Kozan and Ergin's (1998) research supports the assumption that collectivists prefer to use mediators. They report that collectivists (i.e., Turks) prefer to manage conflicts through intermediaries more than individualists (i.e., U.S. Americans) and individualists prefer to address conflict directly more than collectivists. Similarly, Bond et al.'s (1985) study reveals that the Chinese would advise an executive to meet with an insulter and the target of the insult separately so that conflict between the two could be avoided. U.S. Americans, in contrast, would advise an executive to have a joint meeting so that the problem between the insulter and the target of the insult could be resolved face-to-face. Leung (1987; Leung & Lind, 1986) also reports that Chinese prefer bargaining and mediation more than U.S. Americans and that U.S. Americans prefer adjudicatory procedures more than Chinese.

Oetzel (1998c) reports that European Americans initiate more conflicts than Japanese in small group discussions. Smith et al. (1998) contend that individualists rely on their own experiences and training in handling disagreements more than collectivists and that collectivists rely on formal rules and procedures more than individualists in handling disagreements. Gabrielidis et al. (1997) point out that collectivists (i.e., Mexicans) emphasize others' outcomes more than individualists (i.e., U.S. Americans). Collectivists also have a greater desire to maintain self-other bonds and are concerned with others' evaluations of them more than individualists. Pearson and Stephan (1998) observe that Brazilians also emphasize others' outcomes more than U.S. Americans.

Conflict Styles

Conflict styles refer to our typical modes of managing conflicts in different situations (Ting-Toomey, 1988). Glenn, Witmeyer, and Stevenson (1977) outline three persuasive styles used to manage conflicts: factual-inductive, axiomatic-deductive, and affective-intuitive. The *factual-inductive* method begins with the important facts and inductively moves toward a conclusion. This is the predominant style used in the United States. The *axiomatic-deductive* style begins with general principles and deduces the implications for specific situations, and the *affective-intuitive* style is based on the use of emotional or affective messages. These two styles predominate in the Soviet Union. Ting-Toomey (1985) argues that members of individualistic cultures are likely to use both the factual-inductive and axiomatic-deductive styles in managing conflicts. She believes that members of collectivistic cultures, in contrast, are "likely to use affective-intuitive styles in conflict" (p. 82).

Ting-Toomey (1988) predicts cultural differences in conflict on the basis of Rahim's (1983) five styles of conflict. Rahim's styles are based on the degree of concern for self and concern for others inherent in the way individuals try to manage conflict. An *integrating* style of managing conflict involves a high concern for self and a high concern for others. When we use this style, we try to find solutions that are acceptable to both parties. A *compromising* style involves a moderate concern for self and a moderate concern for others. When we use this style, we try to find an agreement that is acceptable to ourselves and others, but the agreement may not be either party's first choice. Both integrating and compromising styles reflect a solution orientation to conflict (Putnam & Wilson, 1982). A *dominating* style reflects a high concern for self and a low concern for others. When we use this style, we try to control or dominate the conflict situation. An *obliging* style involves a low concern for self and a high concern for others. When we use this style, we give in to what others want in conflict situations. Finally, an *avoiding* style involves a low concern for self and a low concern for others. When we use this style, we avoid the conflict topic or situation. (Note: Ting-Toomey and Kurogi [1998] point out that viewing avoiding as involving low concern for self and others is based on an individualistic bias. In collectivistic cultures, avoiding conflict might represent high concern for self and others.) Obliging and avoiding styles of conflict involve nonconfrontation of conflict (Putnam & Wilson, 1982).

Ting-Toomey (1988) argues that members of individualistic cultures prefer direct styles of dealing with conflict, such as integrating and compromising. Members of collectivistic cultures, in contrast, prefer indirect styles of dealing with conflict that allow all parties to preserve face (see below). They tend to use obliging and avoiding styles of conflict resolution or avoid conflicts altogether. These predictions are consistent with Barnlund's (1975) description of conflict strategies in Japan and the United States. He concludes that people in the United States

> prefer to defend themselves actively, employing or developing the rationale for positions they have taken. When pushed they may resort to still more aggressive forms that utilize humor, sarcasm, or denunciation. Among Japanese, the reactions are more varied, but defenses tend to be more passive, permit withdrawal, and allow greater concealment. (p. 423)

Ting-Toomey, Trubisky, and Nishida's (1989) study of conflict in Japan and in the United States supports Ting-Toomey's (1988) predictions and Barnlund's descriptions of conflict.

Obuchi, Fukushima, and Tedeshi (1999) report that individualists (i.e., U.S. Americans) are concerned with justice when managing conflicts more than collectivists (i.e., Japanese) and that collectivists are concerned with their relationships with others more than individualists. Obuchi et al. also note that individualists prefer assertive styles for dealing with conflicts more than collectivists and that collectivists prefer avoiding conflict more than individualists. These results are compatible with Ting-Toomey's argument. There also are differences across collectivistic cultures. Miyahara et al. (1998), for example, point out that Koreans are more collectivistic with respect to managing conflicts than Japanese. This is consistent with Hofstede's scores for these two cultures (i.e., Korea is more collectivistic than Japan).

Research in several other cultures is consistent with Ting-Toomey's (1988) predictions. Chiu and Kosinski (1994), for example, report that Chinese are less direct and less confrontational than U.S. Americans. Similarly, Knutson, Hwang, and Jeng (2000) note that Taiwanese use indirect, nonconfrontational styles more than U.S. Americans and that U.S. Americans use direct solution-oriented styles more than Taiwanese. Leung et al. (1990, 1992) observe that Canadians and Dutch (both individualistic cultures) prefer negotiation and compliance less and accusing more than Spanish and Japanese (both collectivistic cultures). Elsayed-Ekhouly and Buda (1996) find that Arabs use the avoiding style more than U.S. Americans and that U.S. Americans use the dominating and obliging styles more than Arabs. Similar differences emerge when people in the United States and Mexico are compared. Specifically, Mexicans tend to avoid or deny that conflict exists, and people in the United States tend to use direct strategies to deal with it (e.g., McGinn, Harburg, & Ginsburg, 1973).

Not all research is consistent with Ting-Toomey's (1988) predictions. Trubisky, Ting-Toomey, and Lin's (1991) study, for example, suggests that Taiwanese use obliging and avoiding styles more than U.S. Americans but that Taiwanese also use integrating and compromising styles more than U.S. Americans. Ting-Toomey et al.'s (1991) study also provides some inconsistent findings. Gire and Carment (1993) report that Canadians (individualists) prefer negotiation more than Nigerians (collectivists) while Nigerians prefer threats more than Canadians. One explanation for the inconsistent findings in these studies is that some of the members of the collectivistic cultures might have used independent self construals when dealing with conflicts and some of the members of individualistic cultures might have used interdependent self construals when dealing with conflicts. This explanation is supported by Gire and Carment's research. The Canadians in their study were more collectivistic toward friends (e.g., were more allocentric; see Chapter 3) than the Nigerians, and the conflict studied involved roommates.

Individual-level factors that mediate the influence of cultural individualism-collectivism appear to be related to the selection of conflict styles. Leung (1987), for example, observes that the more allocentric individuals are, the more they view mediation and bargaining as effective ways to reduce animosity. Oetzel (1998a, 1998c) reports that groups composed of members who emphasize independent self construals use competitive conflict tactics more and cooperative tactics less than groups composed of members who emphasize interdependent self construals. Oetzel (2001) notes that emphasizing interdependent self construals is associated positively with cooperative group interaction. Oetzel (1998b) observes that self construals are better predictors of conflict styles than ethnicity. He also reports that emphasizing independent self construals is associated with the use of dominating conflict styles and that emphasizing interdependent self construals is associated with the use of avoiding, obliging, and compromising conflict styles.

A second explanation for the inconsistent findings on conflict styles across cultures is that people across cultures may want to avoid conflict. Studies of college students in the United States, for example, indicate that students avoid over 50 percent of the conflicts they have with others (Sillars et al., 1982). Similarly, Leung (1987) notes that Chinese and U.S. Americans want to reduce animosity between themselves and the people with whom they have conflicts. Chinese, however, see bargaining and mediation as more viable ways to reduce animosity than U.S. Americans. Gire and Carment (1993) report similar tendencies to want to avoid conflict when comparing Nigerians and Canadians.

A third explanation for the inconsistent findings on conflict styles predicted on the basis of individualism-collectivism is that other dimensions of cultural variability are involved. Leung et al. (1990), for example, argue that members of feminine cultures prefer harmony-enhancing procedures for managing conflict more than members of masculine cultures. Members of masculine cultures, in contrast, prefer confrontation procedures such as threats more than members of feminine cultures. The rationale for this argument is that interpersonal cooperation and a friendly atmosphere are valued in feminine cultures, while achievement and challenging others are valued in masculine cultures.

Smith, Dugan, Peterson, and Leung (1998) also link power distance to conflict management. They report that individuals rely on subordinates and coworkers in handling disagreements in low power distance cultures more than in high power distance cultures. Bond et al. (1985) also argue that the level of power distance in a culture mediates how collectivists respond to someone who insults members of the ingroup. They note that Chinese are less critical than U.S. Americans of people insulting ingroup members when they have higher status than the ingroup member compared to when their status is lower than the ingroup members' status. Bond et al. also observe that U.S. Americans make less of a distinction as a function of an insulter's status or group membership than Chinese.

Kozan (1989) reports that Turkish managers (high power distance) tend to use power tactics such as forcing when they have conflicts with subordinates more than when they have conflicts with superiors. This difference does not occur in the United States (relatively low power distance). Tse et al. (1994) also note that subordinates in high power distance cultures may rely on their superiors to resolve conflicts. Ury, Brett, and Goldberg (1988) point out that superiors in high power distance cultures may use the status imbalance between themselves and their subordinates to push particular solutions to conflicts, possibly because it is the quickest way to manage them.

The research discussed so far has not taken into consideration whether conflict is with member of ingroups or members of outgroups. Leung (1988) reports that Chinese are less likely to pursue a conflict with an ingroup member and more likely to pursue a conflict with an outgroup member than U.S. Americans. Similarly, Pearson and Stephan (1998) point out that Brazilians are more likely to avoid conflicts with ingroup members than with outgroup members and that U.S. Americans treat ingroups and outgroups the same. Singhal and Nagao (1993) observe that Japanese are more assertive with ingroup members than with outgroup members and that there is no difference between ingroup and outgroup assertiveness in the United States. Han and Park (1995) report that collectivistic Koreans draw a greater distinction between ingroups and outgroups when managing conflicts than individualistic Koreans.

Espinoza and Garza (1985) report that collectivists are more comptitive with outgroup members than individualists. Similarly, Cole (1990) notes that European American students in the United States tend to use integrating and obliging styles more with members of ingroups than with members of outgroups. He also observes that Japanese students studying in the United States tend to use an obliging style more with members of ingroups than with members of outgroups and tend to use a dominating style more with members of outgroups than with members of ingroups.

The differences in how collectivists deal with ingroup and outgroup conflicts may be related to different concerns in the two situations. Leung (1997) argues that there are two different concerns regarding managing conflict in collectivistic cultures: animosity reduction and disintegration avoidance. He suggests that when conflicts are relatively intense (which usually happens with outgroup members), collectivists are concerned with animosity reduction. When conflicts exist with ingroup members or members of outgroups with whom collectivists have ongoing relationships, collectivists are concerned with disintegration avoidance because they want to maintain the relationships. Leung predicts that when collectivists are concerned with animosity reduction, they use problem-solving and compromising conflict strategies. When collectivists are concerned with disintegration avoidance, in contrast, they use avoiding and yielding conflict strategies. Previous research on conflict across cultures, however, has not examined these issues.

Before concluding this section, it is important to make an additional point. Given our discussion so far, some readers may have the impression that conflicts do not occur in collectivistic cultures. This is simply not the case. We only have to look at television dramas from collectivistic cultures to know that conflicts exist in those cultures. Maynard (1997), for example, illustrates the nature of conflict in Japan:

> Everyday conflicts are mostly among *uchi* members [insiders, or close ingroup members]. Blatant and blunt confrontations often occur among close friends, where the *amae* [psychological and emotional dependence] relationship is well established. Here the raw emotions and hard feelings that may result from confrontations and conflict are usually assured of being mended. The *amae* relationship is expected to survive day-to-day emotional skirmishes among its members.
>
> Conflict between people who do not share the *amae* relationship, however, can be potentially harmful, even destructive. Strongly voiced disagreements with people to whom one is expected to show deference are considered especially damaging. (p. 156)

Maynard points out that "*amae* can be seen as that part of the social contract that allows emotions to be freely expressed with approval" (p. 35). *Amae* occurs only in close ingroup relationships in Japan. There are similar relationships in most, if not all, collectivistic cultures in which conflict can be expressed.

To summarize, it appears that there are relatively consistent patterns with respect to preferences for conflict styles based on cultural individualism-collectivism and power distance. To date, these patterns have not been linked to cultural norms and rules in the cultures that have been studied. Further, there must be some freedom of choice in the use of conflict styles across cultures because individual-level factors that mediate the influence of cultural individualism-collectivism (e.g., self construals) are related to preferences for conflict styles.

Business Negotiations

In the last 20 years there has been extensive research on business negotiations (see Cai & Drake, 1998, for a review) that is related to conflict management. Graham (1985), for example, reports that Brazilians make more extreme initial offers, say "no" more, interrupt others more, and use silence less than Japanese or U.S. American negotiators. Graham et al. (1988) note that using problem-solving tactics is related to the negotiating partners' satisfaction in Korean and U.S. American negotiations and that Japanese, Korean, and U.S. American negotiators reciprocate the use of problem-solving tactics.

Adler, Graham, and Gehrke (1987) report that Mexican negotiators' partners are more satisfied than Anglo Canadians' and Franco Canadians' partners. Franco Canadians perceive themselves to be more cooperative than Anglo Canadian and Mexican negotiators. Adler, Brahm, and Graham (1992) observe that U.S. American negotiators ask fewer questions, interrupt less, and say "no" more than Chinese negotiators.

Cai, Wilson, and Drake (2000) contend that the negotiators' position (i.e., buyer or seller) influences negotiations. Neale, Huber, and Northcraft (1987), for example, report that U.S. American buyers gain more profits than U.S. American sellers. Graham and colleagues find similar results but note that the differences between buyers and sellers are more pronounced in collectivistic cultures than in individualistic cultures, for example, in comparisons between U.S. Americans and Japanese (Graham, 1983), Koreans (Graham et al., 1988), and Mexicans (Graham et al., 1987). Cai et al. suggest that these differences may be due to buyers having more power than sellers and that collectivism encourages integrative bargaining. Wilson, Cai, and Drake (1995) observe that collectivism is associated positively with negotiators' profit in 21 studies and that when partners are high in collectivism, joint profits are highest. Cai, Wilson, and Drake (1996) report that buyers in high-collectivism dyads use fewer distributive tactics than buyers in low-collectivism dyads (there is no effect for sellers).

Adler and Graham (1989) argue that there are different negotiation processes in intracultural and intercultural contexts. Brett and Okumura (1998), for example, report lower joint outcomes in intercultural negotiations than in intracultural negotiations. Cai et al. (2000) note that sellers' collectivism in intercultural negotiations facilitates joint profits (but not buyers' collectivism). They conclude that "seller collectivism leads to (a) the seller asking [for] more information, which is positively associated with higher joint profits, (b) the seller using fewer distributive tactics, which is negatively associated with joint profits, and (c) the seller giving less directional information, which is negatively associated with higher joint profits" (p. 609).

Ethnic Differences in Conflict Management

There also are differences in conflict styles across ethnic groups in the United States. African Americans, for example, prefer a controlling conflict resolution style more than European Americans, and European Americans prefer a solution-oriented style more than African Americans (Ting-Toomey, 1986a). Kagan et al. (1982) report that Mexican Americans prefer passive or avoidance styles for dealing with conflict. Cox, Lobel, and McLeod (1991) note that members of collectivistic ethnic groups (e.g., Asian Americans, African Americans, Latino[a] Americans) make more cooperative choices than European Americans.

The styles that members of ethnic groups in the United States use to manage conflict is influenced by the strength of their ethnic identities and the strength of their cultural identities (Ting-Toomey et al., 2000). Ting-Toomey et al., for example, report that individuals who have strong cultural identities use integrating and compromising conflict styles more than individuals who have weak cultural identities. Individuals with strong ethnic identities, however, also use integrating styles more than individuals with weak ethnic identities. The results for cultural and ethnic identities also vary by ethnic group.

To illustrate, Asian Americans with weak ethnic identities and strong cultural identities use a compromising style more than Asian Americans with strong ethnic identities and weak cultural identities. Asian Americans who strongly identify with their ethnic groups and weakly identify with their culture use an avoidance strategy more than Asian Americans who strongly identify with their culture and ethnic groups.

Kim and Kitani (1998) report that European Americans use the dominating conflict style more in romantic relationships than Asian Americans. Asian Americans, in contrast, use integrating, avoiding, obliging, and compromising styles in romantic relationships more than European Americans. They also note that emphasizing independent self construals is related to using the dominating style and emphasizing interdependent self construals is related to using the integrating, obliging, avoiding, and compromising styles.

Kochman (1981) describes differences in how European Americans and African Americans argue that influence how they manage conflicts. Where European Americans "use the relatively detached and unemotional *discussion* mode to engage an issue, [African Americans] use the more emotionally intense and involving mode of *argument*. Where [European Americans] tend to *underestimate* their exceptional talents and abilities, [African Americans] tend to *boast* about theirs" (Kochman, 1981, p. 106). African Americans favor forceful outputs such as high volume, and European Americans prefer subdued outputs. African Americans interpret European Americans' subdued responses as lifeless, and European Americans interpret African Americans' responses as being in bad taste (Kochman, 1981).

There are several other areas where European Americans' and African American's styles of communication may differ when they communicate with each other, particularly in a conflict situation. One area of importance for dealing with conflict is how members of the two groups view their responsibilities to the other people's sensibilities and feelings. Differences in reactions to an assignment in an interpersonal communication class where students were told to confront each other and comment on their perceptions of the other person's style of communication illustrate the two approaches (Kochman, 1981). The students' responses to the assignment divided basically along ethnic lines:

> Twelve of the fourteen [European American] students argued for the right of students *not* to hear what others might want to say about them—thus giving priority to the protection of individual sensibilities, those of others as well as their own, even if this might result in forfeiting their own chance to say what they felt. . . . The eight [African American] students and the remaining two [European American] students, on the other hand, argued for the rights of those students to express what they had to say about others even if the protection of all individual sensibilities would be forfeited in the process. On this last point, one [African American] woman said: "I don't know about others, but if someone has something to say to me, I want to hear it." (Kochman, 1981, pp. 122–123)

Withdrawing the protection of sensibilities is seen as insensitive or cruel by European Americans, while African Americans interpret European Americans' failure to say what they think as lack of concern for African Americans' real selves.

One of the major implications of these differences is what happens when African Americans and European Americans are involved in an interethnic conflict situation.

African Americans have a tendency to express themselves more forcefully than European Americans. The tendency "to receive and manipulate the forceful assertions of others gives them greater leverage in interracial encounters" (Kochman, 1981, p. 126). When African Americans offend European Americans' social sensibilities, European Americans demand an apology. African Americans see this demand as weak and inappropriate. Part of the difference is in who is considered responsible when people are upset. When European Americans are upset, they tend to see the cause as the other person. African Americans, in contrast, see themselves as responsible for their feelings. African Americans "will commonly say to those who have become angry, '*Others* did not make you angry'; rather, 'You *let yourself* become angry' " (Kochman, 1981, p. 127).

To summarize, there appear to be relatively clear patterns regarding preferred conflict styles across ethnic groups in the United States. Specifically, preferred styles across ethnic groups are related to the individualistic or collectivistic cultural heritage of the ethnic groups. The preferred styles, however, probably are not used by all members of ethnic groups. We would expect, for example, that individuals who strongly identify with their ethnic groups will use the preferred styles of their cultural heritages. Individuals who weakly identify with their ethnic groups may not follow these patterns.

FACE AND FACEWORK

The concept of face originated in China, but it has been used extensively by social scientists in the United States. Ho (1976) defines face in China as

> the respectability and/or deference which a person can claim for himself [or herself] from others, by virtue of the relative position he [or she] occupies in his [or her] social network and the degree to which he [or she] is judged to have functioned adequately in that position and acceptably in his [or her] general conduct. (p. 883)

Ho points out that face is not an "individual thing." Face has to be considered in relation to the people in individuals' social networks. Face does not emerge when a person is independent of others; rather, it emerges when a person is interdependent with others.

Ho's (1976) conceptualization of face is based in the Chinese culture. Goffman (1955) adapted the concept for use in the United States. He defines face as "the positive social value a person effectively claims for himself [or herself] . . . Face is an image of self delineated in terms of approved social attributes" (p. 213). Goffman argues that face can be lost, saved, and/or given. Goffman draws a distinction between self-face (e.g., our own face) and other-face (e.g., the face of people with whom we interact). He suggests that we defend our self-face and protect other(s)-face during interactions and that face emerges in the flow of events in our interactions with others.

Brown and Levinson (1978) link face to politeness. They view face as individuals' public self-images. Brown and Levinson argue that three situational factors influence our politeness: social distance, relative power, and how much of an imposition is being made on others. They suggest that high social distance, high differences in power, and/or high levels of imposition (e.g., making a big request of others) can be perceived as serious face-threats and require polite behavior.

Cultural Differences in Face Concern

Ting-Toomey (1988) views face as the projected image of one's self in a relational situation. In addition to distinguishing between self-face and other-face, Ting-Toomey argues that there also is "mutual-face." She contends that members of individualistic cultures emphasize self-face maintenance more than members of collectivistic cultures. Members of collectivistic cultures, in comparison, emphasize mutual-face and other-face maintenance more than members of individualistic cultures.

Morisaki and Gudykunst (1994) argue that face in individualistic and collectivistic cultures is not this simple. They point out that Goffman (1955) and Brown and Levinson (1978) treat face as if it is a trait of individuals, but Chinese writers on face (e.g., Ho, 1976; Hu, 1944) define face as an interdependent phenomenon. Morisaki and Gudykunst go on to argue that face is based on the independent self construal in individualistic cultures and is based on the interdependent self construal in collectivistic cultures. To illustrate, if a student fails in school (does not pass to the next grade) in individualistic cultures, the student loses face but the family does not lose face. In collectivistic cultures, in contrast, the whole family loses face if a student fails.

Face in Asian Cultures   Face is particularly important in Asian cultures. Engaging in appropriate behavior, for example, is important in China. If Chinese behavior is perceived as inappropriate by others, others will make negative remarks about the people engaging in the inappropriate behavior and those people will lose face (Gao, 1996). "Face need," therefore, is a major factor that regulates behavior in China. Face need also influences self-disclosure in China. To illustrate, Chinese will not expose family disgraces to outsiders because this would lead to loss of face for their families. This suggests that face in China is not an individual concern but rather a concern for the ingroup.

Hu (1944) draws a distinction between two types of face in China: *lien* and *mien-tzu*. *Lien* "refers to the confidence of society in the moral character of ego" (p. 61). *Mien-tzu* refers to the social reputation which is "achieved through getting on in life, through success and ostentation" (p. 45). Loss of *lien* puts individuals outside the boundary of what society considers "decent human beings." Loss of *mien-tzu* involves a loss of confidence in individuals' character. Hu points out, though, that it is not just individuals who lose *mien-tzu;* members of individuals' ingroups do as well. Gao and Ting-Toomey (1998) point out that *lien* has a moral dimension and is internalized, while *mien-tzu* involves individuals' social images and is extenalized. Morizsaki and Gudykunst (1994) contend that Japanese have two uses of face as well: *mentsu* and *taimen*. *Mentsu* is similar to the Chinese notion of *mien-tzu,* and *taimen* is similar to Goffman's (1955) use of the term *face* (the appearance we present to others).

Gao and Ting-Toomey (1998) illustrate how face is reflected in Chinese conversations:

A: Are you going to see that show on Saturday?
B: I'm afraid not. Because I was invited to a piano recital.
A: I thought you didn't like that kind of music.
B: It's true, but I feel I need to show up to give my friend [face]. (p. 56)

In this case, one person's actions (i.e., attending the recital) reflect on another's face (i.e., the person giving the recital). Gao and Ting-Toomey point out that Chinese employ face (*mien-tzu*) to make requests and gain others' compliance (e.g., Please give me face and help my friend).

Bond and Lee's (1981) research supports the ingroup basis of face in China. Chinese students in Hong Kong are empathetic to fellow students (members of an ingroup) who do not perform well on mock presentations, and the students actively try to help the presenters save face. Bond and Lee also report that Chinese whose ingroups are insulted engage in greater rebuttal and retaliation than Chinese who are personally insulted.

There is a distinction between personal and positional face in Korea (Lim & Choi, 1996). Personal face is similar to face in the United States (e.g., it is negotiated in interactions). Positional face, however, is different. Positional face is attached to the positions Koreans fill in the social system (e.g., professor, physician), and Koreans filling those positions are expected to behave in certain ways across situations. The amount of positional face is a function of how high the social position is in the social system. The amount of face attached to a position is static. Individual professors, for example, cannot increase their positional face. All they can do is maintain or fail to maintain their positional face. They maintain their positional face if they behave in ways that meet the social expectations of professors in Korea (e.g., conducting their lives in a way professors are expected to act). They lose their positional face if they behave in ways that are inappropriate for professors.

The preceding describes the types of face that exist in Asian cultures. Lebra (1976) provides specific descriptions of how Japanese maintain face. She isolates two general ways of maintaining face: "defensive" and "displaying." Lebra points out that Japanese can defend their face by avoiding behavior that may cause them shame. She isolates nine strategies that Japanese can use to defend their face:

1. *Mediated communication.* This strategy involves asking another person to negotiate with the target person (the person with whom one is negotiating) so that no direct face-to-face contact has to take place (e.g., using a mediator).
2. *Refracted communication.* This strategy involves talking to a third person in the presence of the target person. In doing this, it is expected that the target person will understand the real intentions. Lebra suggests that this occurs when husbands and wives negotiate by talking to their children.
3. *Acting as a delegate.* This strategy involves meeting with the target person but pretending to be a delegate for someone else (e.g., an acquaintance of higher status). Again, the target person is expected to understand the true intentions.
4. *Anticipatory communication.* This strategy involves expecting the target person to anticipate what is wanted. Lebra points out that "the higher one's status, the more others strive to anticipate his [or her] wants" (p. 123). Empathy facilitates this strategy.
5. *Self-communication.* This strategy involves "avoiding the risk of face-to-face exposure" (p. 123). Here Japanese write their thoughts on paper (e.g., in a diary) as though they were not meant to be read by others but with the expectation that others may read them.
6. *Correspondence.* This strategy involves an exchange of letters. Lebra contends that letters make the communication indirect and spare the writers the embarrassment of face-to-face contact.

7. *Understatement.* This strategy involves using the implicit qualities of the Japanese language (e.g., omitting the subject). In doing this, Japanese can avoid verbal commitments and retract what is said easily if the target person disagrees.

8. *Unobtrusive behavior.* The more obtrusive Japanese people's behavior, the greater the possibility they can lose face. Lebra points out that "humility, besides being a virtue, is a social weapon to defend one's own or another's face" (p. 125).

9. *Ritualism.* Lebra contends that "face is most vulnerable in unpredictable situations" (p. 125). Ritualistic behavior maximizes predictability because social norms and rules are being followed. Ritualized behavior minimizes the possibility of inappropriate behavior.

All these strategies are ways in which Japanese can defend or protect face in interactions with other Japanese.

As indicated earlier, Lebra (1976) isolates three ways that Japanese can display face, or promote themselves:

1. *Conspicuous generosity.* Lebra argues that "generosity in rendering help, gift-giving, or entertaining guests is considered by most Japanese a necessary measure to maintain or upgrade one's face" (pp. 126–127).

2. *Self-praise.* This strategy involves Japanese praising themselves to others (e.g., boasting).

3. *Arrogance.* Lebra argues that this strategy involves Japanese promoting their dignity by demoting others' dignity.

Lebra contends that conspicuous generosity is the only socially acceptable strategy for displaying face in Japan. Self-praise violates the expectation that Japanese will demonstrate humility and modesty in their interactions with others. Arrogant Japanese are described as *ibaru* ("overbearing") and can elicit retaliation by people who lose face.

Research on Face across Cultures   The way individuals manage their face varies across cultures. Cocroft and Ting-Toomey (1994), for example, report that U.S. Americans use antisocial, self-presentation, and self-attribution face-maintenance strategies more than Japanese and that Japanese use indirect face-maintenance strategies more than U.S. Americans. Cupach and Imahori (1993b) note that U.S. Americans are more likely than Japanese to use humor and aggression to manage social predicaments where face is lost and that Japanese are more likely than U.S. Americans to apologize. Imahori and Cupach (1994) observe that U.S. Americans use humor as a way to maintain face in embarrassing situations more than Japanese. Japanese, in contrast, use remediation (the correction of behavior) as a way to manage face more than U.S. Americans.

Holtgraves and Yang (1992) report that Koreans are influenced by others' power and the relational distance between themselves and others more than U.S. Americans in determining when to be polite. U.S. Americans, therefore, may assume a closer distance than Koreans when they interact and use less politeness behavior than Koreans expect. Koreans may interpret the lack of politeness as a claim to power in the relationship.

Ting-Toomey et al. (1991) report that Chinese, Koreans, and Taiwanese have more other-face concern than U.S. Americans and Japanese. U.S. Americans, Chinese, Japanese, and Taiwanese have more self-face concern than Koreans. These findings do not exactly fit expectations, perhaps because the respondents in Japan were highly individualistic and/or the measures used in the study did not assess collectivistic aspects of face fully.

Oetzel et al. (2000) report that Chinese have higher other-face concerns than members of the other three cultures and that Japanese have higher other-face concerns than Germans. They also note that Japanese have lower self-face concerns than members of the other three cultures. Further, Oetzel et al. observe that self construals are better predictors of face concerns than cultural individualism-collectivism. Emphasizing independent self construals is associated positively with self-face concern, and emphasizing interdependent self construals is associated positively with other-face and mutual-face concerns.

Oetzel, Ting-Toomey, and Chew (1999) examine face concerns during a conflict with parents and siblings in Germany, Japan, Mexico, and the United States. They note that Japanese have lower self-face concerns than members of the other three cultures. They also report that self construals are better predictors of face-concern than cultural individualism-collectivism. The patterns are the same as in Oetzel et al.'s (2000) study.

In addition to face-concerns, a few studies also have looked at facework tactics used in managing conflicts. Facework tactics are the strategies used to threaten or support others' face and protect self-face when conflicts are managed. Oetzel et al. (1999), for example, report that Germans and U.S. Americans do not avoid conflict and use direct, confrontational facework tactics (e.g., problem solving). Japanese and Mexicans, in contrast, prefer to avoid conflicts and use tactics that indicate to others that the conflict does not exist. These findings are consistent with cultural individualism-collectivism. Oetzel et al. also observe that emphasizing interdependent self construals is associated positively with using problem-solving, respect, apologizing, and third-party help facework tactics and is associated negatively with using aggressive facework tactics. They conclude that self construals are better predictors of facework tactics than cultural individualism-collectivism.

Oetzel et al. (2000) report that Chinese tend to use avoiding, obliging, and aggression facework tactics; Germans use direct and confrontational facework tactics; Japanese use facework tactics that allow them to avoid direct confrontation; and U.S. Americans use respect and expression of feelings facework tactics. Emphasizing independent self construals is associated with defending and remaining calm facework tactics. Emphasizing interdependent self construals is associated with problem-solving, respect, apologizing, pretending, private discussion, and giving in facework tactics. Oetzel et al. find that self construals are better predictors of facework tactics than cultural individualism-collectivism.

Oetzel et al. (in press) link face-concerns and facework tactics. Across cultures (Japan and the United States), self-face concerns are associated with aggressive and defensive facework tactics; other-face concerns are associated with giving in, avoiding, pretending, and third-party facework tactics; and mutual-face concerns are associated with problem-solving, private discussion, apologizing, and compromising facework tactics.

Apologies Apologies are one of the major strategies individuals use to save face. Barnlund and Yoshioka (1990) report that both Japanese and U.S. Americans use direct forms of apology. Japanese, however, use a wider variety of apologizing strategies than U.S. Americans and Japanese adapt their strategies on the basis of others' status more than U.S. Americans. The most preferred Japanese strategy for apologizing is offering to do something for the offended person. U.S. Americans, in contrast, prefer to explain their actions when they apologize. Barnlund and Yoshioka also note that apologies restored relations between people to the way they were before the incident requiring the apology in Japan.

Sugimoto (1997) observes that Japanese use more elaborate apology strategies than U.S. Americans. U.S. Americans and Japanese both give accounts to explain the transgression requiring the apology, but their accounts are different. U.S. Americans emphasize that they had no control over the situation or that the offense occurred because they were forgetful. Japanese, in contrast, emphasize that the offense occurred because of uncontrollable forces or that they did not intend to "wrong" the victim. Japanese also use statements of remorse, requests for forgiveness, reparation, compensation, and promise not to repeat the actions more than U.S. Americans.

Ethnic Differences in Face-Concerns

There have not been a lot of studies examining ethnic differences in face-concerns. There are, however, a few we can summarize. Tata (2000), for example, reports that Mexican Americans emphasize other-face concerns less than European Americans when communicating with subordinates. When communicating with superiors, in contrast, Mexican Americans emphasize other-face concerns more than European Americans. These results appear to be due to power distance.

Yeh and Huang (1996) argue that Asian Americans have high face-concerns. They suggest that "face includes the positive image, interpretations, or social attributes that one claims for oneself or perceives others to have accorded one. If one does not fulfill expectations of the self, then one loses face" (p. 651). Shon and Ja (1982) point out that Asian Americans with high face-concerns are likely to try to conform to interpersonal expectations that others have for them. When Asian Americans have high face-concerns, they tend to use shame to control their own and others' behavior. Kwan and Sodowsky (1997) contend that fear of loss of face is related to ethnic identities for Chinese immigrants; the stronger their ethnic identities, the greater their face-concerns.

When individuals lose face, they feel shame or guilt (Morisaki & Gudykunst, 1994). Liem (1997) argues that "guilt accompanies moral transgressions, acts that violate ethical standards" (p. 369). Shame, in contrast, "is provoked by exposure of the self to an audience, real or symbolic, in whose eyes the actor [or actress] experiences his or her total being as profoundly flawed" (p. 369). Liem contends that guilt for European Americans emerges when they do something they know is wrong and no one knows about it. European Americans experience shame as being "embarrassed" or feeling "ashamed." Shame for European Americans emerges when something they do wrong becomes public. European Americans' shame is not shared with others; it is based on the independent self construal. Liem (1997) claims that guilt for Asian Americans emerges from moral transgressions in hierarchical relationships. Asian Americans experience guilt when they feel they have not done their duty. Shame for Asian Americans emerges when the wrongdoing becomes public. Shame for Asian Americans is shared by ingroup members; it is based on the interdependent self construal.

Closely related to shame is embarrassment. Embarrassment involves threats to individuals' public images (their face). Singelis and Sharkey (1995) examine susceptibility to embarrassment among Asian Americans and European Americans. They report that emphasizing interdependent self construals is associated positively and emphasizing independent self construals is associated negatively with susceptibility to embarrassment across ethnic groups. When self construals are held constant, European Americans perceive that they are less susceptible to embarrassment than Chinese Americans, Filipino Americans, Japanese Americans, and Korean Americans (there is no difference across Asian American ethnic groups). Singels and Sharkey contend that self construals are better predictors of susceptibility to embarrassment than ethnicity.

Scollon and Scollon (1981) observe that European Americans are less polite than Athabaskan Indians when members of the two groups interact. European Americans' politeness behavior is guided by how close they think they are to the other person. They often use less politeness than Athabaskan Indians expect. The Athabaskan Indians interpret the lack of politeness as being due to the European Americans thinking they are culturally superior.

FACE-NEGOTIATION THEORY

Originally a theory focusing on cultural differences in conflict (Ting-Toomey, 1985), face-negotiation theory (FNT) has been expanded to integrate cultural-level dimensions and individual-level attributes to explain face-concerns, conflict styles, and facework behaviors (e.g., Ting-Toomey, 1988; Ting-Toomey & Kurogi, 1998; also see Ting-Toomey & Oetzel, 2001a, 2001b). It provides an explanatory framework for the material we have discussed so far in this chapter.

Ting-Toomey (1988) argues that conflict is a face-negotiation process because individuals engaged in conflict have their situated identities or "faces" threatened or questioned. Face is "a claimed sense of favorable social self-worth that a person wants others to have of her or him" (Ting-Toomey & Kurogi, 1998, p. 187). Although only mentioned briefly in the 1988 version of the theory, the concept of face is an integral part of the most recent version of the theory (Ting-Toomey & Kurogi, 1998).

Face-negotiation theory (Ting-Toomey & Kurogi, 1998) includes 32 propositions (20 propositions are based on dimensions of cultural variability, and 12 are based on individual-level mediators of cultural variability). Ting-Toomey and Kurogi (1998) argue that members of collectivistic cultures use other-oriented face-saving strategies and use other-face enhancement strategies more than members of individualistic cultures. Conversely, members of individualistic cultures use more self-oriented face-saving strategies and use self-face approval-seeking strategies more than members of collectivistic cultures.

Members of low power distance cultures defend and assert their personal rights more than members of high power distance cultures (Ting-Toomey & Kurogi, 1998). Members of high power distance cultures, in contrast, perform their ascribed duties responsibly more than members of low power distance cultures. Members of low power distance cultures tend to minimize the respect-deference distance (e.g., treat others as equals) more than members of high power distance cultures. Members of high power distance cultures are concerned with vertical facework interactions (e.g., they maximize the respect-deference distance via formal interaction) more than members of low power distance cultures.

Ting-Toomey and Kurogi (1998) contend that members of collectivistic cultures use relational, process-oriented conflict strategies (e.g., yielding, smoothing) more than members of individualistic cultures. Members of individualistic cultures, in contrast, tend to use substantive, outcome-oriented conflict strategies (e.g., solution orientation) more than members of collectivistic cultures. High-status members of high power distance cultures tend to use verbally indirect facework strategies (e.g., indirect questioning and relational pressuring) more than low-status members of high power distance cultures. High-status members of low power distance cultures tend to use verbally direct strategies (e.g., criticism, reprimands) more than high-status members of low power distance cultures.

Ting-Toomey and Kurogi (1998) also link individual-level mediators of the dimensions of cultural variability to face behaviors and conflict styles. Emphasizing self-face leads to using dominating/competing conflict styles and substantive conflict resolution modes. Emphasizing other-face leads to using avoiding/obliging conflict styles and relational conflict resolution modes.

Ting-Toomey and Kurogi (1998) argue that individuals who emphasize the independent self construal and not the interdependent self construal tend to use dominating/competing conflict styles and substantive conflict resolution modes. Individuals who emphasize the interdependent self construal and not the independent self construal tend to use avoiding/obliging conflict styles and relational conflict resolution modes. Individuals who are high on both self construals use substantive and relational conflict resolution modes, and individuals who are low on both self construals tend not to use specific styles.

INTERGROUP CONFLICT

Intergroup conflict is occurring at high rates throughout the world today (see Boucher, Landis, & Clark, 1987; Horowitz, 1985; for discussions of some of these specific conflicts). Understanding why intergroup conflicts occur is necessary if we are to be able to manage them successfully. To begin, we look at the characteristics of intergroup conflict.

Characteristics of Intergroup Conflict

Intergroup conflict is similar to interpersonal conflict in some ways, but there are important differences. Condor and Brown (1988) point out that

> intergroup conflict is, by definition, a collective phenomenon. . . . The psychological factors associated with intergroup hostility are best sought in *collective* social cognition and motivation. It is an important task . . . to examine the relationship between individual drives and cognition and those associated with the groups to which they belong. (p. 19)

Condor and Brown, therefore, argue that intergroup conflict takes place between different *groups* and that interpersonal conflict takes place between *individuals*. (Note: Cross-cultural differences in conflict discussed earlier are mainly interpersonal conflicts.) Some forms of conflict combine interpersonal and intergroup qualities, for example, conflicts between individuals who are members of different groups.

Landis and Boucher (1987) outline several characteristics of interethnic conflict that appear to apply to other forms of intergroup conflict as well. First, intergroup conflict involves perceived (not necessarily real) group differences which lead to the activation of social identities and stereotypes. Second, intergroup conflicts often involve claims to a given territory. Third, intergroup conflicts tend to be based on group differences in power and resources. Fourth, intergroup conflicts may involve disagreements over language usage or language policies. Fifth, intergroup conflicts are exacerbated by group differences in endorsement of the process preferred for resolving conflicts (e.g., members of one culture may prefer to resolve conflicts through a third party, while members of another culture do not use third parties and prefer direct confrontation). Sixth, intergroup conflicts often are exacerbated by religious differences. Conflicts are intensified, for example, when religious differences are compounded with other group differences (e.g., in Sri Lanka the Tamil-Sinhalese conflict is intensified because Tamils are Hindu and Sinhalese are Buddhist).

Lilli and Rehm (1988) point out that social categorization leads individuals to make evaluative judgments about members of ingroups and outgroups. When conflict occurs, social categorizations are particularly important, and this heightens the ingroup bias. Social categorizations lead to emphasizing social identities over personal identities. When social identities are enhanced by intergroup comparisons, the devaluation of the outgroup can lead to conflicts. The persistence of "being negatively categorized (labeled) may cause conflicts" (p. 35). Social categorizations also lead to deindividuation. Deindividuation can initiate conflicts or escalate conflicts that already exist. Social categorization also influences the way information about outgroups is processed; it is simplified (e.g., outgroups are seen as homogeneous, and only stereotypical information about outgroups is obtained). Simplified information processing can lead to arguments which maintain and justify conflicts.

We divide the remainder of the chapter into two sections. In the first section, we examine explanations for group-level conflicts (e.g., between Protestants and Catholics in Northern Ireland and between Israelis and Palestinians). In the second section, we look at conflict between individuals who are members of different groups.

Group-Level Conflicts

Group-level conflict is different from individual-level conflict in that group-level conflict occurs between groups. The relations between the groups in society at large influence any conflict between individual members of the groups. We begin with realistic conflict theory.

Realistic Conflict Theory   Realistic conflict theory (RCT; Sherif, 1966; Sherif et al., 1961) is concerned with how conflict arises between groups, the processes involved in the conflicts that arise, and the various ways those conflicts can be resolved.

The emphasis in RCT is on conflict between groups with equal power. RCT is based on three assumptions about human behavior: (1) Groups try to maximize their own rewards, (2) conflict arises from incompatible interests, and (3) the social psychological aspects of intergroup behavior are determined by the compatibility of group interests.

Sherif (1966) contends that intergroup behavior occurs "whenever individuals belonging to one group interact, collectively or individually, with another group or its members *in terms of their group identification*" (p. 12). Intergroup behavior, therefore, can occur when individual members from different groups interact. The way individual members interact is affected by the functional relations between the groups. In RCT, it is the perception of competition between groups that leads to hostility and conflict. There may not be any actual competition between the groups.

Sherif (1966) argues that "the bounds for the attitudes of members of different groups towards one another are set by the functional relations between the groups" (p. 63). Competition for scarce resources leads to bias against outgroups (e.g., prejudice, negative stereotypes). The resources over which groups compete vary from concrete resources such as territory to abstract resources such as status. Competition does not arise between groups when goals are complementary (e.g., each group can reach its goal without help from the other group). When ingroups and outgroups compete over scarce resources, being close to outgroups and contact with outgroups increase hostility toward outgroups. Also, the more ingroup members perceive threats from outgroup members and have conflicts with outgroup members, the more hostility ingroup members demonstrate toward outgroup members. RCT suggests that intergroup cooperation emerges when the members of the groups work on superordinate goals. When goals are superordinate, groups can achieve mutually desired goals only when they work together.

The Instrumental Model of Group Conflict   Esses, Jackson, and Armstrong (1998) build on RCT to develop the instrumental model of group conflict. They state that the instrumental model "suggests that the combination of resource stress and the salience of a potentially competitive outgroup leads to perceived group competition for resources. In turn, this perceived competition leads to attempts to remove the source of competition, using a variety of strategies" (p. 702). Resource stress refers to the perception that access to resources in society is limited to certain groups. The resources include things like money, jobs, and power.

Eses et al. (1998) isolate several factors that determine the extent to which individuals perceive resource stress: (1) perceptions of scare resources, (2) unequal distribution of resources in society leading low-status groups to perceive that their access to resources is limited, and (3) "the *desire* for an unequal distribution of resources among groups" (p. 702). Resource stress leads to competition for resources among groups; "outgroups that are salient and distinct from one's own group are . . . likely to stand out as potential competitors" (p. 704). Esses et al. argue that when there is resource stress and salient/distinct outgroups, there will be group competition. The group competition is based on zero-sum beliefs (if one group gains, the other loses) that are accompanied by anxiety and fear.

Esses et al. (1998) view the model as "an instrumental model of group conflict because [they] propose that attitudes and behaviors toward the competitor outgroup reflect attempts to remove the source of the competition" (p. 704). They argue that groups use three strategies to accomplish this. First, members of the ingroup try to decrease the outgroup competitiveness (e.g., by convincing people that the outgroup is worthless, practicing discrimination toward the outgroup). This leads ingroup members to feel less competitive with outgroups. Second, ingroup members may increase their own group's competitiveness (e.g., improving ingroup members' skills). Third, ingroup members may decrease an outgroup's competitiveness by increasing the distance between ingroups and outgroups (e.g., denying immigration to members of outgroups).

Esses et al. (1998) report data on attitudes toward immigrants that support the instrumental model of group conflict. They conclude that "media coverage of immigration" can influence the strength of the negative attitudes toward immigrants. Esses et al. contend that having negative attitudes toward immigrants is a form of prejudice; "in particular, when the scarcity of resources is publicized [e.g., poor economic conditions, high unemployment] and, ironically, when immigrants are described as faring well, these effects are likely to be exacerbated" (p. 719).

The Common Ingroup Identity Model Sherif's (1966) realistic conflict theory suggests that when members of different groups work on superordinate goals, conflict can be minimized. The common ingroup identity model (e.g., Dovidio, Maruyama, & Alexander, 1998; Gaertner & Dovidio, 2000) suggests an alternate approach. This model "proposes that influencing the ways in which group members conceive of group boundaries can reduce intergroup bias and conflict, but through recategorization rather than decategorization. Recategorization involves using an alternate, superordinate social category to think about both the ingroup and the outgroup" (Dovidio et al., pp. 838–839).

Dovidio et al. (1998) point out that group members do not have to give up their group identities to share common ingroup identities with members of outgroups; they can have dual identities. Sharing common ingroup identities has positive effects on intergroup relations. Dovidio et al. (1997), for example, report that perceiving a common group identity leads to positive attitudes toward outgroup members, as well as self-disclosure to outgroup members and being helpful to outgroup members. Dovidio et al. (1998) point out that "because self-disclosure and helping typically produce reciprocal responses from others, these behaviors may have longer term, reverberating effects for resolving conflicts between groups" (p. 840).

Attributional Bases of Intergroup Conflict Hewstone (1988) argues that group members' attributions can lead to intergroup conflict. He suggests that "vicarious personalism sets the scene for sustained intergroup conflict" (p. 63). *Vicarious personalism* is defined as "one group's perception that the other group's actions are aimed specifically at them" (p. 49). Vicarious personalism leads ingroup members to have a hostile view of the outgroup and negative expectations for outgroup members' behavior. When outgroup members' behavior confirms ingroup members' negative expectations, ingroup members attribute outgroup members' behavior to stable internal causes (e.g., their group memberships), and this maintains the conflict. Alternatively, ingroup members' negative expectations for outgroup members' behavior can lead ingroup members to modify their behavior, which, in turn, affects outgroup members' behavior. This can lead to a self-fulfilling prophecy (i.e., outgroup members confirm ingroup members' expectations). When this occurs, ingroup members attribute outgroup members' behavior to stable internal causes, and this leads to continued conflict.

Hewstone (1988) suggests that outgroup members' behavior also may disconfirm ingroup members' expectations. One way ingroup members can explain outgroup members' unexpected behavior is to attribute it to external factors (e.g., the situation). This maintains the conflict because ingroup members have no reason to expect outgroup members' behavior to change unless the external factors change. Alternatively, ingroup members may attribute outgroup members' unexpected behavior to internal factors. If outgroup members are perceived as atypical group members, ingroup members tend to see them as special cases, and their behavior has little influence on changing the conflict situation. If ingroup members perceive the outgroup members as typical group members, in contrast, there is a possibility that ingroup members' perceptions of unexpected behavior will change their attitudes toward the outgroup and provide the potential for managing the conflict (e.g., ingroup members develop more positive attitudes toward the outgroup, which improves relations between the groups).

Models of Intergroup Conflict Management   Cross and Rosenthal (1999) isolate three models used in intergroup conflict management: distributive bargaining, integrative bargaining, and interactive problem solving. We present the three models separately, but in practice they often are used in combination.

Cross and Rosenthal (1999) point out that the distributive bargaining model originated in labor negotiations. *Distributive bargaining* "is a competitive, position-based, agreement-oriented approach to dealing with conflicts that are perceived as 'win/lose' or zero sum disputes" (p. 564). In this model, the negotiators are "adversaries" who make concessions to reach an agreement. Each negotiator is trying to maximize individual gain; if one party gains, the other loses.

Integrative bargaining also originated in labor negotiations. *Integrative bargaining* "is a cooperative, interest-based, agreement-oriented approach to dealing with conflicts that are intended to be viewed as 'win/win' or mutual gain disputes" (Cross & Rosenthal, 1999, p. 565). This model involves joint problem solving. Using this model involves "searching for mutually profitable alternatives." Negotiators take on the role of partners who are searching for a "fair" agreement. "This approach encourages the generation of, and commitment to, workable, equitable, and durable solutions" (p. 565). Cross and Rosenthal contend that this is the most widely used model for managing intergroup conflicts.

Interactive problem solving is a form of informal mediation that has been applied to a wide variety of international conflicts (e.g., Northern Ireland). *Interactive problem solving* is a "nongovernmental third-party approach [that] emphasizes analytical dialogue, joint problem solving, and transformation of the conflict relationship" (Cross & Rosenthal, 1999, p. 565). The third party helps the disputing parties analyze their motivations, needs, and fears related to their identities guiding the conflict. This process helps the disputing parties engage in analysis and problem solving before engaging in binding negotiations. Interactive problem solving is "devoted to improving the process of communication, increasing perspective taking and understanding, and enabling the parties to reframe their substantive goals and priorities, and ultimately, to engage in more creative problem solving" (p. 566).

Cross and Rosenthal (1999) compare the three models with respect to the Israeli-Palestinian dispute about Jerusalem. They report that the Arab and Israeli participants using the interactive problem-solving model are less pessimistic about the possible outcome of the dispute over Jerusalem and have the most positive attitude change toward members of the other group than the participants using the two other models. They conclude, however, that serious intergroup conflicts may require the use of all three models. When the three models are used, negotiators might start with the interactive problem-solving model to help participants analyze their motivations and needs and then use integrative bargaining to find mutually acceptable alternatives. Unresolved issues may need to be dealt with using distributive bargaining.

Herbert Kelman (1999) has been conducting problem-solving workshops between Israelis and Palestinians for the last 30 years to help establish peace in the Middle East. His workshops involve a combination of the three models outlined here. There is evidence that the problem-solving workshops are reasonably successful at the individual level (see Kelman, 1999, for studies describing and testing the effects of the workshops). The current workshops focus on identity negotiation, using an approach similar to the common ingroup identity model (e.g., Gaertner & Dovidio, 2000) discussed earlier (but Kelman does not make the linkage to the common ingroup identity model).

Contact and Conflict

Intergroup contact often is promoted as a way to manage intergroup conflicts. The contact hypothesis suggests that when intergroup contact takes place under favorable conditions (e.g., equal status, intimate contact, rewarding contact; see Stephan, 1987, and Chapter 5 for a summary), contact leads to a decrease in prejudice and discrimination. Tzeng and Jackson's (1994) research further indicates that interethnic contact under favorable conditions reduces intergroup hostilities across ethnic groups in the United States.

Related research on norm violations and intergroup hostility (DeRidder & Tripathi, 1992) also suggests that perceptions that ingroup norms have been violated lead members of ingroups to make negative attributions about outgroups. The negative attributions that ingroup members make lead outgroup members to make negative inferences about ingroup members. Norm violations, therefore, can lead to cycles of escalating conflict. Escalations are most likely when individuals strongly identify with their ingroups, when negative intergroup attitudes exist, when one group has feelings of relative deprivation, and when the group violating the norms has power over the group whose norms are violated.

Harmonious interpersonal contact can take place between members of different groups even when there is a history of intergroup conflict (e.g., Trew's, 1986, study in Ireland; Taylor, Dube, & Bellerose's, 1986, work in Quebec). This does not always occur, however, as Foster and Finchilescu's (1986) research in South Africa indicates.

Pettigrew (1986) points out that "the use of intergroup contact as a means of alleviating conflict is largely dependent on the social structure that patterns relations between the groups" (p. 191).

To explain cross-cultural variability in this process, it is necessary to isolate the dimensions of cultural variability that apply to structural relations. Structural tightness is "the degree of hierarchical structure among sociocultural elements in a society" (Witkin & Berry, 1975, p. 11). Boldt and Roberts (1979) argue that role relatedness (the degree to which roles are interrelated) defines a culture as loose or tight. Gudykunst (1988a) contends that Ireland and Canada have a high degree of role relatedness with respect to the roles members of different groups fill, while South Africa did not have a high degree of role relatedness between blacks and whites when Foster and Finchilescu's (1986) research was conducted. He suggests that contact has a greater influence on reducing intergroup conflict in tight cultures than in loose cultures.

Individual-Level Conflict

The preceding discussion focused on conflict at the group level. In this section, we focus on conflict between individuals who are members of different groups. This form of conflict is similar to interpersonal conflict, but it differs in that individuals' group memberships do not have a major influence on interpersonal conflicts. Cox (1993) suggests that individual-level interethnic conflicts can be analyzed by using group-level perspectives. The reason for this is that when the conflicts occur, ethnic identities are activated, and the conflicts that occur may reflect group-level processes occurring in society.

The Relational Model of Conflict   Tyler and Lind (1992) argue that we approach conflict differently depending upon whether the person with whom we have a conflict is a member of our ingroup or an outgroup. They contend that we are concerned about our relationships with members of groups with which we identify. How others in those groups treat us provides information about where we "stand in the group." Tyler and Lind believe that we pay close attention to make sure that our interactions with ingroup members are free of discrimination, that other ingroup members can be trusted to treat us benevolently, and that there are indications that we are respected members of our ingroups. These three issues all involve "relational concerns." We are especially concerned with how "authority" figures in our ingroups treat us. If the authority figures treat us well, our self-esteem is enhanced.

Tyler et al. (1998) contend that we attend to relational concerns when we interact with ingroup members more than when we interact with outgroup members. With respect to conflicts, "the relational prediction is that people will be more concerned with relational aspects of disputing when they share some salient social category with the other person (or people) and/or the authority involved in the dispute" (p. 138).

Ohbuchi, Chiba, and Fukushima's (1996) multiple goals theory makes similar predictions. They contend that there are three goals in conflict situations: (1) resource goals which involve outcomes, (2) relational goals which involve maintaining the relationship, and (3) identity goals which involve issues of face or self-esteem (which are related to issues of politeness). Identity goals correspond to relational concerns in Tyler et al.'s (1998) relational model. Ohbuchi et al. suggest that protecting face and maintaining relationships motivate us when we have relationships with the people with whom we have conflicts (e.g., ingroup members) and not when we do not have relationships with them (e.g., outgroup members).

Tyler et al. (1998) test these predictions in intercultural and interethnic disputes. They report that both studies support the predictions, namely, that relational concerns are more important in disputes with ingroup members than in disputes with outgroup members.

Issues in Intercultural Conflict   There has been extensive research on cross-cultural differences in conflict management but very little research on intercultural or interethnic conflict. The lack of research on intercultural and interethnic conflict is surprising given the extensive writing on workplace diversity in the United States (Leung & Chan, 1999).

Bochner and Hesketh (1994) examine how cultural power distance influences communication with superiors in multinational organizations in Australia. They report that employees from high power distance cultures (e.g., Hong Kong, the Philippines) are not as open with their supervisors as are employees from low power distance cultures (e.g., Finland, England). Employees from high power distance cultures do not question their superiors' decisions and are more cautious about discussing problems with supervisors from other cultures than are employees from low power distance cultures. These communication patterns should be manifested in intercultural conflicts as well.

Weldon et al. (1996; cited by Leung & Chan, 1999) report that employees use different strategies in intra- and intercultural conflicts in U.S.–China joint ventures. The Chinese indicate they use indirect strategies such as raising the issue in a meeting or informing the boss when they have conflicts with U.S. Americans. U.S. Americans, in contrast, indicate that they interact directly with the Chinese with whom they have conflicts. The Chinese managers also report that they use direct, vindictive strategies that tend to intensify the conflict. The U.S. Americans also say they are concerned about maintaining the relationships with the Chinese with whom they have conflicts. The Chinese response can be explained by recognizing that the U.S. Americans are members of outgroups. As you may recall, collectivists may respond competitively to outgroup members.

Leung and Chan (1999) isolate three dimensions that influence intercultural conflict management: motivational, cognitive, and normative. One major motivational factor they isolate is intercultural anxiety. As you will recall from Chapter 2, high anxiety (e.g., above our maximum thresholds) leads us to want to avoid interacting with members of other groups (Stephan & Stephan, 1985). High anxiety also leads to simple information processing and relying on stereotypes. Both hinder effective problem solving with members of other cultures or ethnic groups. As indicated in Chapter 10, we can manage our anxiety when it is above our maximum thresholds.

The second motivational factor Leung and Chan (1999) isolate is instrumental concerns. Tyler, Boeckmann, Smith, and Huo (1997) argue that when members of groups (cultures) see others as members of outgroups, instrumental concerns become important (e.g., they become concerned with the outcomes of their interactions). Leung and Chan suggest that if members of groups try to maximize their outcomes in intercultural conflicts, it will make it difficult to manage intercultural conflicts.

The second domain that Leung and Chan (1999) isolate is cognitive. They argue there are cognitive biases that hinder intercultural conflict management that are not present in interpersonal conflicts. First, Leung and Chan contend there is an "ethnocentric fairness bias." Individuals have a tendency to perceive ingroup members' actions as "fairer" than outgroup members' behavior. Second, cultural differences in attributions may cause members of different cultures to perceive the cause of conflicts differently. Third, "misattributions based on negative stereotypes may divert attention from the real causes of the conflict and thus recreate unnecessary animosity among members of different cultural groups" (p. 182).

The third domain that may cause problems in intercultural conflicts is the normative domain. Leung and Chan (1999) argue that members of different cultures may have different desirable outcomes: U.S. American "negotiators often regard the outcome of a negotiation as very important, whereas many cultural groups, including Chinese, Malaysians, and Japanese, regard establishing a cordial relationship between the negotiators as very important" (p. 182). They also contend that members of different cultures use different norms to allocate resources. The equity norm, for example, is used by individualists with ingroups and outgroups and the equality norm is used by collectivists, especially with ingroup members. These differences make it difficult to arrive at decisions on how to allocate resources that are considered fair by members of different cultures.

Intercultural Conflicts between Collectivists and Individualists   Ting-Toomey (1994b) argues that individualists and collectivists can adapt their behavior to increase their effectiveness when they have intercultural conflicts. Individualists can make several adaptations that will increase the likelihood of success in managing conflicts with collectivists. First, individualists need to remember that collectivists tend to use interdependent self construals to guide their behavior. Their actions reflect on their ingroups, and they have to take their ingroups into consideration in managing conflicts. Second, individualists should try to deal with conflicts when they are small rather than allow them to become large issues and recognize that collectivists may want to use a third party to mediate a conflict. Third, individualists need to help collectivists maintain face (public image) during the conflict. This means not humiliating or embarrassing collectivists, especially in public. Fourth, individualists need to pay attention to collectivists' nonverbal behavior and implicit messages. Collectivists tend not to express their opinions directly. Fifth, individualists need to listen when collectivists talk and try to figure out their implicit meanings. Sixth, individualists need to use indirect messages more than they typically do. This means using qualifier words such as "maybe" and "possibly," being more tentative, and avoiding bluntly saying no. Seventh, individualists need to let go of conflict if collectivists do not recognize that the conflict exists or do not want to deal with it (recall that avoiding is the preferred collectivist strategy).

Collectivists also need to make adaptations when dealing with individualists (Ting-Toomey, 1994b). First, collectivists need to recognize that individualists often separate the conflict from the people with whom they are having the conflict. Second, collectivists need to focus on the substantive issues involved in the conflict. Third, collectivists need to use an assertive, rather than nonassertive, style when dealing with conflicts. Fourth, collectivists need to be more direct than they usually are. This involves using "I messages" and directly stating their opinions and feelings more than they usually do. Fifth, collectivists need to provide verbal feedback to individualists and focus on the verbal aspects of communication more than they typically do. Sixth, collectivists need to recognize that individualists do not value silence in conversations. Seventh, collectivists need to try to manage conflicts when they arise rather than avoiding them.

If one or both of the parties in intercultural conflicts between individualists and collectivists do not adapt their behavior, there is no chance the conflicts can be managed successfully. The people who usually are expected to adapt the most are the strangers (i.e., the people not in their home cultures), but both parties must adapt to some degree for conflicts to be managed successfully.

SUMMARY

Conflicts often arise from the small intolerances expressed in our everyday communication. It is inevitable in any ongoing relationship. Our conflicts with strangers often get out of hand before we realize it. One reason for this is that there are cultural and ethnic differences in how conflict is viewed and managed.

Members of individualistic cultures tend to separate conflict issues from the people with whom they have conflicts; members of collectivistic cultures tend not to make this distinction. Conflict tends to arise when personal expectations are violated in individualistic cultures and when normative expectations are violated in collectivistic cultures. Members of individualistic cultures tend to approach conflict directly, and members of collectivistic cultures tend to approach conflict indirectly or avoid it. Members of individualistic cultures tend to take a short-term view of conflict, and members of collectivistic cultures tend to take a long-term view.

Members of individualistic cultures emphasize self-face, and members of collectivistic cultures emphasize other-face and mutual-face. Face in individualistic cultures is based on the independent self construal, and face in collectivistic cultures is based on the interdependent self construal. Self construals appear to be better predictors of face concerns than cultural individualism-collectivism. Face-negotiation theory appears to provide a plausible explanation for cultural differences in conflict management and face-negotiation.

Intergroup conflict is different from interpersonal conflict. Intergroup conflicts involve perceived group differences, claims to territory, and disagreements over languages and may be exacerbated by religious differences. We focus on relational concerns when managing conflicts with ingroup members. Managing intergroup conflicts is facilitated when members of different groups work on superordinate goals or have a common ingroup identity.

STUDY QUESTIONS

1. Why is conflict inevitable in our ongoing relationships with strangers?
2. How do people from individualistic cultures deal with conflict differently than people from collectivistic cultures?
3. How are individualistic and collectivistic face concerns different?
4. How does face-negotiation theory explain cultural differences in conflict management and face-negotiation?
5. How are interpersonal and intergroup conflicts different?
6. How does working on superordinate goals influence the management of intergroup conflicts?
7. Why do we not focus on relational concerns in conflicts with outgroup members?
8. How does having a common ingroup identity influence managing intergroup conflict?
9. How can individualists and collectivists adapt their behavior to manage conflicts with each other?

SUGGESTED READINGS

Boucher, J., Landis, D., & Clark, K. (Eds.). (1987). *Ethnic conflict.* Newbury Park, CA: Sage.

Deutsch, M. (1973). *The resolution of conflict.* New Haven, CT: Yale University Press.

Hewstone, M., & Brown, R. (Eds.). (1986). *Contact and conflict in intergroup encounters.* Oxford, UK: Blackwell.

Hocker, J. L., & Wilmot, W. W. (1991). *Interpersonal conflict* (3rd ed.). Dubuque, IA: Wm. C. Brown.

Kochman, T. (1981). *Black and white: Styles in conflict.* Chicago: University of Chicago Press.

Strobe, W., Kruglanski, A., Bar-Tal, D., & Hewstone, M. (Eds.). (1988). *The social psychology of intergroup conflict.* New York: Springer-Verlag.

Ting-Toomey, S. (Ed.). (1994). *The challenge of facework.* Albany: State University of New York Press.

Ting-Toomey, S., & Oetzel, J. (2001). *Managing intercultural conflicts effectively.* Thousand Oaks, CA: Sage.

12

DEVELOPING RELATIONSHIPS WITH STRANGERS

Under cherry trees
there are
no strangers

Issa

Interpersonal relationships are sources of social contact and intimacy, two important elements of human survival in any culture. We form many different types of relationships with others. We develop some relationships we call acquaintances and some we call friendships. Friendships, however, should not be confused with friendly relations. Kurth (1970) points out that friendly relations are an outgrowth of role relationships and may be a prelude to friendship and that friendships are intimate relationships involving two people as individuals. Friendships, therefore, are more intimate than friendly relations.

Friendly relations involve a present orientation and a focus on the encounter that is taking place (Kurth, 1970). In friendships, participants engage in interactions regarding the past and future, as well as the present. The two types of relations also differ with respect to the normative specifications guiding them. There are cultural norms and rules specifying what constitutes friendly relations, but "the development of friendship is based upon private negotiations and is not imposed through cultural values or norms" (Bell, 1981, p. 10). Suttles (1970) takes a similar position; he claims friendships are the least culturally programmed relationships we form. We do not mean to suggest that culture plays no role in the development of friendships; rather, culture plays a much less important role in friendships than it does in friendly relations.

Wright (1978) argues that friendships are entered into voluntarily and that friends informally agree to get together often in the absence of external constraints or pressures. Friendships also involve a focus on the person; friends react to each other as whole persons, not just as members of social groups. The argument we make in this chapter is that our group memberships, including our cultures, influence the early stages of our relationships with strangers more than the later stages. If we form close friendships with strangers, they are similar to our close friendships with people from our own groups.

We begin by looking at dimensions of relationships that appear to be universal (i.e., consistent across cultures). Next, we examine cross-cultural variability in communication in interpersonal and romantic relationships. Following this, we discuss the development of interpersonal relationships with strangers. We conclude this chapter by discussing romantic relationships with strangers.

UNIVERSAL ASPECTS OF RELATIONSHIPS

Triandis (1977) isolates four dimensions of social relations that appear to be universal. The first dimension is association-dissociation. *Associative behaviors* include being helpful, supportive, or cooperative, and *dissociative behaviors* involve fighting or avoiding others. The second universal dimension is superordination-subordination. *Superordinate behaviors* include criticizing or giving orders, and *subordinate behaviors* involve asking for help, agreeing, or obeying. The third dimension is intimacy-formality. *Intimate behaviors* include self-disclosure, expressing emotions, or touching, and *formal behaviors* involve sending written invitations to others and similar activities. The final dimension of universal social behavior is overt-covert. *Overt behaviors* are visible to others, and *covert behaviors* are not visible to others.

These four aspects of behavior are universal, but the degree to which they are manifested varies across cultures. Triandis (1984) argues that the association-dissociation dimension is related to Kluckhohn and Strodtbeck's (1961) human nature value orientation. Associative behaviors predominate in cultures where people assume that human nature is inherently good, and disassociative behaviors predominate in cultures where people assume that human nature is inherently evil.

The superordination-subordination dimension is related to Hofstede's (1980) power distance dimension of cultural variability. Triandis (1984) argues that being superordinate and being subordinate are viewed as natural and a function of the characteristics of the people in high power distance cultures. Superordinate and subordinate behaviors are not viewed as natural in low power distance cultures. In low power distance cultures, being superordinate or subordinate is viewed as a function of the roles people play, not as characteristics with which they are born.

Intimacy-formality can be related to the general issue of contact. Triandis (1984) argues that in contact cultures "people touch a lot, they stand much closer to each other, they orient their bodies so they face each other, they look each other in the eye, and they employ greater amplitudes of emotional expression" (p. 324). Noncontact cultures involve the opposite pattern: little touching, standing far apart, little eye contact, and low levels of emotional expression. People in contact cultures tend to express their emotions openly, and members of noncontact cultures tend to suppress them.

Triandis (1984) suggests that the overt-covert dimension varies as a function of loose-tight cultural variations. As indicated in Chapter 3, Boldt (1978) defines structural tightness in terms of role diversity (the number of roles and role relationships) and role relatedness (the nature of the bonds among the roles). The more roles there are and the more tightly they are bonded together, the more structurally tight the social structure is. Triandis contends that there is greater overt behavior in loose cultures than in tight cultures and greater covert behavior in tight cultures than in loose cultures. Triandis, however, points out that cultures may be loose with regard to some behaviors and tight with regard to others.

Adamopoulos and Bontempo (1986) focus on the universality of three dimensions of interpersonal relations by using literary material from different historical periods. They note that affiliation and dominance appear to be universal, without much change over the last 3,000 years. Intimacy, in contrast, also appears universal, but the behaviors that are considered intimate have changed over the years.

Foa and Foa (1974) take a different approach to isolating universal dimensions of behavior. They argue that the resources individuals exchange during interaction can be classified into six groups arranged in a circle: love (12 o'clock, using the face of a clock to represent the circle), services (2 o'clock), goods (4 o'clock), money (6 o'clock), information (8 o'clock), and status (10 o'clock). These resources vary along two dimensions: (1) *particularism*—the importance of the individual's (receiver or giver) identity in the exchange (runs vertically up and down the face of the clock, with least particularism at 6 o'clock and most at 12 o'clock) and (2) *concreteness*—the degree to which the resource has face value versus symbolic value (runs horizontally across clock's face, with least concreteness at 9 o'clock and most at 3 o'clock).

The closer the resources in Foa and Foa's (1974) framework are to each other, the more similar they are perceived to be and the greater the satisfaction that emerges when resources are exchanged. Foa and Foa's research indicates that the resource structure is applicable across cultures.

Fiske (1991) isolates four elementary forms of human relations that exist in all cultures: communal sharing, equality matching, authority ranking, and market pricing. *Communal sharing* is "a relationship of equivalence in which people are merged (for the purpose at hand) so that the boundaries of individual selves are indistinct" (p. 13). *Equality matching* is an equal relationship between people who are distinct from each other and are peers. *Authority ranking* is an asymmetrical relationship between two people who are not equals. *Market pricing* is a relationship mediated by the values of some "market system." The market system, for example, might be based on people's actions, services, or products. Fiske argues that these four models provide the basic "grammars" for social relationships and give order to the way individuals think about their social interactions. Fiske's (1993) research supports this claim. The four elementary forms of social behavior are the basis for all other types of relationships and are universal across cultures.

Fiske (1991) argues that all forms of behavior can be used in any situation in any culture. Members of cultures, however, learn preferences for particular forms of behavior in particular situations. Triandis (1994) contends that people in collectivistic cultures learn to use communal sharing and authority ranking more than equality matching and market pricing. Members of individualistic cultures, in contrast, learn to use equality matching and market pricing more than the other two. Authority ranking also can be seen as a function of power distance (Triandis, 1994). Smith and Bond (1993) argue that market pricing is related to Hofstede's (1980) masculine orientation and equality matching is related to a feminine orientation.

CROSS-CULTURAL VARIATIONS IN INTERPERSONAL AND ROMANTIC RELATIONSHIPS

There are dimensions of social relations that appear to be universal, but there also are many differences in interpersonal relations across cultures. Our focus here is on cultural differences in how we categorize others, differences in the intimacy of interpersonal relationships, self-disclosure and social penetration, anxiety/uncertainty management, and communication in romantic relationships.

Categories of Interpersonal Relationships

The way people categorize types of interpersonal relationships varies across cultures. The type of behavior expected of people in the same category (e.g., acquaintance) also may vary across cultures. Wish, Deutsch, and Kaplan (1976) suggest that people tend to use four dimensions to distinguish among different types of relationships in the United States: (1) cooperative-friendly to competitive-hostile, (2) equal to unequal, (3) intense to superficial, and (4) socioemotional-informal to task-oriented-formal. Of primary concern here is the intense-to-superficial dimension. Another way of looking at this dimension is to think of it as addressing the issue of the degree of intimacy present in a relationship.

In contrast to the categorization of interpersonal relationships in the United States, Nakane (1974) contends that Japanese distinguish among three different categories of people: "(1) those people within one's own group; (2) those whose background is fairly well known, and (3) those who are unknown, the strangers" (p. 124). As one would expect, the style of communication in the first group (the ingroup), which includes not only family members but also coworkers, is generally informal; however, "as a personal relationship becomes more distant, the style becomes more formal, employing more honorific expressions" (p. 125). Nakane (1974) argues that communication with people within one's own group is generally very effective (i.e., there is little "miscommunication"). This is at least partly due to the stability of people's reference groups in Japan, where individuals may live in the same place and work for the same company all their lives. Since individuals spend the majority of their lives within the same ingroups, they are concerned with how others react.

With people in the second group (people whose background is known), communication is more formal than it is with people in the ingroup and "more universal forms of Japanese etiquette" are used (Nakane, 1974, p. 127). This category includes an indefinite number of people who are not actually known personally, for example, people who went to the same university or grew up in the same rural town. Even though the people may not be known, their backgrounds are. Nakane (who taught at the University of Tokyo at the time) cites an example that illustrates communicating with a person in this group. In the example she tells of visiting another university (one she had not been to before) to give a lecture. When she arrives, she is met by an unknown professor who greets her by saying, "You must be Professor Nakane. I am also from Tokyo. Please do come into my office." She immediately recognizes that the professor is telling her he went to Tokyo University. Because they share this group membership, the professor moves from being a stranger to being a person whose background is known. Because the professor's background was known, Nakane could make reliable predictions about his behavior.

The third category of people in Japan—strangers—are totally unknown. Japanese "do not feel the necessity of applying any particular code of etiquette" to strangers, and "Japanese rarely greet or smile at a stranger, even if they share the same table in a crowded restaurant" (Nakane, 1974, p. 128). Contact with strangers is avoided because there is no way to predict how they will behave. Strangers are, to a certain extent, nonpersons. When in a train crowded with strangers, for example, Japanese act as though the other people are not there. If they bump into strangers, there is no reason to say "excuse me," because strangers are nonpersons.

The interpersonal behavior patterns discussed here are due, at least in part, to the role of context in Japanese communication. Because of the contexting process, people in collectivistic cultures such as Japan draw greater distinctions between insiders and outsiders than people in individualistic cultures such as the United States. Hall (1976) points out that people in collectivistic cultures expect the person to whom they are talking to know what is on their minds. People in collectivistic cultures will talk indirectly about what is on their minds, giving the other person all the necessary information except the crucial piece. Figuring out the final piece and putting it all together are the responsibility of the other person. Obviously, only insiders can perform these expected functions effectively. Strangers invariably find themselves frustrated in a situation like this.

Intimacy of Interpersonal Relationships

Gudykunst and Nishida (1986b) compare the intimacy ratings of interpersonal relationships in the United States with those in Japan on a scale of 1 to 9 (1 = intimate, 9 = nonintimate). To illustrate the differences, consider the following findings:

	United States	Japan
Interpersonal Relationships		
Stranger	8.35	7.99
Acquaintance	6.79	4.95
Friend	3.67	3.42
Best friend	2.51	1.73
Boy/girlfriend	1.70	3.32
Lover	1.25	2.81
Ingroup Relationships		
Coworker	5.76	5.27
Colleague	5.33	4.76
Classmate	5.72	3.84

These findings illustrate several of the differences that can be expected based on the dimensions of cultural variability discussed in Chapter 3. In collectivistic cultures, for example, ingroup membership is valued highly and there is a greater difference between communication with members of ingroups and communication with members of outgroups than there is in individualistic cultures. It will be noted that, as expected, the Japanese perceive the three ingroup relationships listed as more intimate than the respondents in the United States.

Differences due to masculinity-femininity can also be illustrated here. The Japanese rate the two opposite-sex interpersonal relationships (boy/girlfriend and lover) as less intimate than people in the United States. This would be expected, since Japan is a highly masculine culture and the United States tends to be a feminine culture. In masculine cultures there is relatively little informal communication in opposite-sex relationships, and these relationships, therefore, are not considered highly intimate because of the sex role rigidity that exists in masculine cultures.

Differences in the intimacy ratings of interpersonal relationships are reflected in the communication that occurs in these relationships. Gudykunst and Nishida (1986b), for example, note that there are greater differences in Japan than in the United States between ingroups and outgroups in the degree to which they talk about personal things, are able to coordinate their communication, and experience difficulties when communicating. This finding is supported by extensive research (e.g., Gudykunst et al., 1992; Gudykunst, Schmidt & Nishida, 1989; Gudykunst, Yoon, & Nishida, 1987). Consistent with the masculinity-femininity findings, Gudykunst and Nishida (1986b) observe greater differences between communication in same-sex and opposite-sex relationships in Japan than in the United States.

Before proceeding, there is one additional point that needs to be made about Gudykunst and Nishida's (1986b) data. If you look at the scores for the first four interpersonal relationships within each culture, you will note that the same pattern exists in Japan and the United States: Stranger relationships are seen as the least intimate, acquaintance relationships are next, followed by friend and then by best friend relationships. There is consistency in the ratings of the relative intimacy of the four relationships. There is not a consistent pattern, however, when the two romantic relationships are included. People in the United States tend to view boy/girlfriend and lover relationships as more intimate than close friendships, and Japanese tend to view close friendships as more intimate than romantic relationships. These findings are consistent with Gudykunst and Nishida's (1993) research, which indicates that U.S. Americans tend to select romantic relationships as their closest relationships and Japanese tend to select friendships as their closest relationships. These differences are consistent with cultural differences in masculinity-femininity.

Patterns of intimacy ratings of interpersonal relationships are reflected in the communication that occurs in the relationships. Gudykunst and Nishida (1986b), for example, observe the most personalization and synchronization and the least difficulty in best friend relationships in Japan and the United States. These relationships are followed (in descending order) by friendships, acquaintances, and stranger relationships.

Anxiety/Uncertainty Management

Anxiety/uncertainty management (AUM) theory (e.g., Gudykunst, 1995) suggests that effective interpersonal and intergroup communication is a function of the how individuals manage the anxiety and uncertainty they experience when communicating with others. *Uncertainty* involves individuals' ability to predict and/or explain others' feelings, attitudes, and behavior (Berger & Calabrese, 1975). Managing uncertainty is a cognitive process. Berger and Calabrese (1975) argue that "when strangers meet, their primary concern is one of uncertainty reduction or increasing predictability about the behavior of both themselves and others in the interaction" (p. 100). The reduction of uncertainty leads to changes in the nature of the communication that takes place; for example, it brings about increases in the amount of communication and increases in the amount of interpersonal attraction. It also can be argued that if the amount of uncertainty present in initial interactions is not reduced, further communication between the people, in all likelihood, will not take place.

Anxiety is the affective equivalent of uncertainty. It stems from feeling uneasy, tense, worried, or apprehensive about what might happen and is based on a fear of potential negative consequences (Stephan & Stephan, 1985). To date there is little research on cross-cultural differences in anxiety in interpersonal relationships. It can be argued, however, that members of high uncertainty avoidance cultures experience higher anxiety in communicating with strangers than members of low uncertainty avoidance cultures (Gudykunst, 1995). Since there are few cross-cultural studies of anxiety, our focus in this section is on cultural and ethnic differences in uncertainty. We begin by looking at cultural differences.

Cultural Differences in Uncertainty   The extent to which uncertainty is valued varies across cultures. Basso (1979), for example, points out that Western Apaches do not find uncertainty distressing. Keenan (1976) suggests that men in a Malagasy community generate messages to create uncertainty and value ambiguity in interactions. Lim and Choi (1986) also claim that Koreans sometimes create ambiguous messages to others cannot "figure out their meanings" (p. 131). Morris (1981) argues that Puerto Rico is "a society of continuities where things are kept open, where things are not so clearly defined as to exclude other interpretations" (p. 119). In Puerto Rico, leaving interpretations open is viewed as a sign of respect. Cultural differences in the extent to which uncertainty is valued should be a function of Hofstede's (1980) uncertainty avoidance dimension of cultural variability. Uncertainty should be acepted or valued in low uncertainty avoidance cultures more than in high uncertainty avoidance cultures.

Gudykunst (1983c) suggests that the typical pattern of initial interactions in the individualistic culture of the United States may not be generalizable to collectivistic cultures. Members of collectivistic cultures do try to reduce uncertainty in initial interactions, but the nature of the information they seek appears to be different from the information sought when two people meet for the first time in the United States. Since much of the information necessary for communication in collectivistic cultures resides in the context or is internalized in the individual (as opposed to being mostly in the message in individualistic cultures), members of collectivistic cultures are more cautious concerning what they talk about with strangers than are members of individualistic cultures.

Gudykunst's (1983c) research further indicates that members of collectivistic cultures have a greater tendency to make assumptions about strangers on the basis of cultural background than members of individualistic cultures. This finding is consistent with Hall's (1976) argument that members of collectivistic cultures are more aware of culture's screening process and, therefore, make greater distinctions between insiders and outsiders than members of individualistic cultures. Gudykunst's research also suggests that people from collectivistic cultures ask more questions about others' backgrounds and engage in less nonverbal activity than members of individualistic cultures. These findings are consistent with Nakane's (1974) argument that it is the background information that allows members of collectivistic cultures to determine whether a person is indeed unknown.

The ways individuals gather information to reduce uncertainty differ in individualistic and collectivistic cultures. Members of individualistic cultures seek out person-based information to reduce uncertainty about strangers (Gudykunst & Nishida, 1986a). The *person-based* information used to reduce uncertainty involves knowing others' attitudes, beliefs, feelings, values, and past behaviors. Members of collectivistic cultures seek out group-based information to reduce uncertainty (Gudykunst & Nishida, 1986a). The *group-based* information used to reduce uncertainty involves knowing others' age, status, and group memberships. The focus on person-based information leads members of individualistic cultures to search for personal similarities when communicating with outgroup members more than members of collectivistic cultures (Gudykunst, 1995). The focus on group-based information, in contrast, leads members of collectivistic cultures to search for group similarities when communicating with outgroup members more than members of individualistic cultures.

Gelfand et al. (2000) examine the utility of individuating information (e.g., person-based) and relational information (e.g., group-based) in making social predictions in the United States and China. U.S. Americans find that individuating information such as beliefs and accomplishments is more useful than relational information such as group memberships and social status in "predicting how others will behave and their degree of trustworthiness" (p. 509). The Chinese, in contrast, find relational information more useful than individuating information.

There also are differences in how members of individualistic and collectivistic cultures explain others' behavior. Members of collectivistic cultures emphasize the importance of context in explaining others' behavior more than members of individualistic cultures (e.g., Kashima, Siegel, Tanaka, & Kashima, 1992). The emphasis on context in collectivistic cultures affects other aspects of communication as well. To illustrate, adapting and accommodating to the context in which they are communicating are important parts of the high-context communication patterns used in collectivistic cultures (Hall, 1976). Norenzayan, Choi, and Nisbett (2002) point out that members of collectivistic cultures use situation-based information to make social inferences more than members of individualistic cultures when situational information is salient (also see Choi et al., 1999, for a discussion of cultural differences in causal attributions).

There also are predictable differences in how uncertainty is managed in ingroup and outgroup relationships in individualistic and collectivistic cultures. Gudykunst and Nishida (1986a), for example, report that Japanese students have more attributional confidence (the inverse of uncertainty) regarding classmates (members of an ingroup in Japan) than students in the United States, while the reverse pattern exists for strangers (potential members of an outgroup in Japan). Gudykunst, Nishida, and Schmidt (1989) note differences in uncertainty reduction processes between ingroup and outgroup relationships in Japan, but not in the United States. Gudykunst, Gao, Nishida, Bond, Leung, Wang, and Barraclough's (1992) study of uncertainty reduction processes in ingroup and outgroup relationships in Australia, Japan, Hong Kong, and the United States supports the earlier findings. Group membership (ingroup versus outgroup) influences uncertainty reduction in Japan and Hong Kong, but not in the United States and Australia. To illustrate, uncertainty is lower for communication with members of ingroups than for communication with members of outgroups in Japan and Hong Kong, but there is no difference in Australia and the United States.

There also are cultural differences in the factors that are related to reducing uncertainty. Gudykunst and Nishida (1986b), for example, report that frequency of communication predicts uncertainty reduction in individualistic cultures, but not in collectivistic cultures. Sanders, Wiseman, and Matz (1991) note that self-disclosure does not predict uncertainty reduction in collectivistic cultures but does in individualistic cultures. These findings are compatible with the differences between individualistic and collectivistic cultures discussed in Chapter 3.

Ethnic Differences in Uncertainty   Gudykunst and Hammer (1987) report that there are no differences in the amount of uncertainty European Americans and African Americans experience when communicating with members of their own ethnic group they do not know. There are, however, differences in what influences uncertainty reduction. Asking questions leads to uncertainty reduction for European Americans, but not for African Americans. Reducing uncertainty leads to attraction toward the other person for European Americans, but not for African Americans.

Sanders and Wiseman (1991) report ethnic differences in predicting uncertainty reduction. Their research suggests that the amount of information others disclose predicts uncertainty reduction across ethnic groups. Positive nonverbal expressiveness predicts uncertainty reduction for European Americans, Latino(a) Americans, and Asian Americans, but not African Americans. Self-disclosure predicts uncertainty reduction for European Americans and Latino Americans, but not the other two groups. Finally, asking questions of the other person reduces uncertainty for European Americans, but not the other three groups. The finding for question asking is consistent with Gudykunst and Hammer's (1987) research and Gudykunst, Sodetani, and Sonoda's (1987) research, which suggest that the relationship between interrogation and uncertainty reduction may be limited to European Americans.

Cultural Differences in Perceptions of Effective Communication   What is perceived as effective communication differs in individualistic and collectivistic cultures. Tominaga, Gudykunst, and Ota (2002) report that U.S. Americans perceive effective communication to involve (from most to least frequent): (1) understanding, (2) compatibility between communicators, (3) positive dispositions, (4) a lot of communication, (5) positive outcomes, (6) positive nonverbal communication, and (7) adapting messages to others. Japanese, in contrast, perceive effective communication to involve (from most to least frequent): (1) compatibility between communicators, (2) appropriate behavior, (3) good relations between communicators, (4) positive outcomes, (5) a lot of communication, (6) positive dispositions, (7) understanding, (8) positive nonverbal communications, and (9) clear messages.

Clearly there are similarities and differences in what U.S. Americans and Japanese perceive as effective communication. Tominaga et al.'s (2002) study suggests that the largest group of U.S. Americans associate effective communication with cognitive understanding. Only a small percentage of the Japanese, in contrast, view effective communication as involving understanding (the focus was on understanding others' feelings). Japanese tend to associate compatibility, appropriate behavior, and good relations with effective communication. These factors all have an emotional component. It, therefore, appears that U.S. Americans emphasize cognitive understanding and Japanese emphasize good emotional relations between communicators.

Self-Disclosure and Social Penetration

Self-disclosure involves individuals telling information about themselves to others that the other people do not know (Altman & Taylor, 1973). Closely related to self-disclosure is Altman and Taylor's notion of social penetration. They argue that as relationships become more intimate, there is an increase in social penetration; that is, as relationships become more intimate, participants engage in self-disclosure on a greater variety of topics and with more depth. In this section, we examine cultural and ethnic differences in self-disclosure and social penetration. We begin with cultural differences.

Cultural Differences Generally, self-disclosure is associated with direct communication styles that predominate in individualistic cultures rather than with the indirect communication styles that predominate in collectivistic cultures (Gudykunst & Ting-Toomey, 1988). Intuitively, it appears that individualists would engage in more self-disclosure than collectivists. Barnlund's (1975) research in Japan and the United States supports this contention. Barnlund begins with the assumption that the Japanese prefer an interpersonal style in which little information about the self is made accessible to others in everyday interactions (e.g., the public self is relatively small), while the majority of information one knows about oneself is kept private (e.g., the private self is relatively large). Barnlund hypothesizes, in contrast, that the preferred interpersonal style in the United States is one in which large portions of information about the self are made available to others (e.g., the public self is relatively large), while little of such information is kept to oneself (e.g., the private self is relatively small).

Barnlund (1975) compares six topics of self-disclosure (interests/tastes, work/studies, opinions on public issues, financial matters, personality, and physical condition) and six targets of self-disclosure (same-sex friend, opposite-sex friend, mother, father, stranger, and untrusted acquaintance) among college students from Japan and the United States. This research suggests there are similarities between the two groups of students in terms of what they consider appropriate topics for self-disclosure. Specifically, tastes and opinions are seen as being most appropriate by both groups, while physical attributes and personality traits are least preferred. Further, the hierarchy of preferences is the same in the United States and Japan: same-sex friend, opposite-sex friend, mother, father, stranger, and untrusted acquaintance. Barnlund, however, finds that the level of self-disclosure is higher for college students from the United States than it is for college students from Japan. This pattern is consistent across all six topics of conversation and all six target persons. Barnlund concludes that "interpersonal distance, as estimated by self-disclosure, was substantially greater among Japanese than Americans" (p. 79).

Consistent with Barnlund, Ting-Toomey's (1991) research in France, Japan, and the United States, as well as Chen's (1995) research in China and the United States, indicates that individualists self-disclose more than collectivists. Wheeler, Reis, and Bond (1989), however, report that Chinese in Hong Kong engage in more self-disclosure in everyday communication than U.S. Americans. On the surface, this finding appears inconsistent with the claim that self-disclosure is associated with direct communication, but this is not necessarily the case. Wheeler et al. point out that most of the Chinese respondents' contacts are with members of their ingroups and that communication in ingroups in collectivistic cultures tends to be intimate (e.g., involves high levels of self-disclosure). Most of the U.S. American respondents' contacts, in contrast, are with superficial acquaintances, where high levels of self-disclosure are not expected.

Gudykunst, Gao, Schmidt, et al. (1992) observe more self-disclosure with ingroup members than with outgroup members in two Chinese samples, both high in collectivism. There is, however, no difference in ingroup and outgroup self-disclosure in the Australian and United States samples, both high in individualism. The Japanese data, in contrast, do not fit the expected pattern. Wheeler et al. (1989) argue that this reversal of expectation may be due to other dimensions of self-disclosure mediating the process of self-disclosure. To illustrate, the expected findings might not be observed in collectivistic cultures, like Japan, that are high in masculinity and/or uncertainty avoidance (discussed later in this chapter). Alternatively, Wheeler et al. point out that the findings for Japan may be due to the homogeneity of the Japanese culture. Barnlund (1975) contends that "the greater the cultural homogeneity, the greater the meaning conveyed in a single word, the more that can be implied rather than stated" (p. 162). This implies that explicit self-disclosure is not needed to convey intimate information.

Gudykunst and Nishida's (1986b) data on social penetration are consistent with Triandis' (1988) description of the focus on ingroup relationships in collectivistic cultures. Japanese report greater differences in personalization (e.g., knowing personal information), synchronization (e.g., coordination), and difficulty of communication between ingroup (classmate) and outgroup (stranger) relationships than U.S. Americans. Gudykunst, Yoon, and Nishida (1987) also examine the influence of individualism on social penetration in ingroup and outgroup relationships in Japan, Korea, and the United States. They note that the greater the degree of collectivism present in a culture, the greater the differences between ingroup (i.e., classmate) and outgroup (i.e., stranger) communication in terms of amount of personalization (e.g., intimacy of communication) and synchronization (e.g., coordination of communication) and difficulty in communication.

Ethnic Differences   European Americans tend to disclose at higher rates than African Americans (Diamond & Hellcamp, 1969; Jourard, 1958; Littlefield, 1974; Wolken, Moriwaki, & Williams, 1973). Additionally, Littlefield (1974) finds that African Americans tend to self-disclose at a higher rate than Mexican Americans. These differences, however, may be attributable to social class rather than to racial factors, an interpretation suggested by Jaffee and Polanski's (1962) finding that no significant differences exist between lower-class African Americans and lower-class European Americans.

Gudykunst and Hammer (1987) report that European Americans engage in more self-disclosure with people they do not know than African Americans when social class is controlled for statistically. By the time close friendships are formed, however, the pattern reverses. Gudykunst (1986) observes that African Americans self-disclose more with friends than European Americans. Hammer and Gudykunst (1987) also note that African Americans engage in more overall social penetration with their best friends than European Americans. These findings are consistent with Hecht and

Ribeau's (1984) research on communication satisfaction. They argue that "[African Americans] seem to require deeper, more intimate topical involvement than [European American] respondents. This intimacy must be seen as intrinsic to the relationship, therapeutic, and involving trust" (p. 147).

Communication in Romantic Relationships

Dion and Dion (1988, 1996) suggest that individualism-collectivism is the major dimension of cultural variability that influences similarities and differences in romantic relationships across cultures. They point out that in individualistic cultures like the United States the idea of being dependent on someone else either is viewed negatively or receives a neutral response. This, however, is not the case in collectivistic cultures. Doi (1973), for example, relates the Japanese concept of *amae* to love. *Amae* refers to the tendency to depend on another person and/or presume upon that person's benevolence. Doi claims that "*amae,* generally speaking, is an inseparable concomitant of love" (p. 118). Hsu (1981) makes a similar observation about love in Chinese culture.

Dion and Dion (1988) isolate several problems that arise in individualistic cultures regarding love relationships:

> First, one can "lose" one's self and the feeling of personal autonomy in a love relationship, feeling used and exploited as a result. Second, satisfying the autonomous needs of two "separate" individuals in a love relationship obviously becomes a balancing act. Third, the spirit of [U.S.] American individualism makes it difficult for either partner in a relationship to justify sacrificing or giving to the other more than one is receiving. Finally, and inevitably, [U.S.] Americans confront a fundamental conflict trying to reconcile personal freedom and individuality, on the one hand, with obligations and role requirements of marital partner and parent, on the other. (p. 286)

These problems would not necessarily arise in collectivistic cultures, where dependence on the spouse is valued.

Dion and Dion (1993) suggest that romantic love is less likely to be considered an important reason for marriage in collectivistic cultures than it is in individualistic cultures. In individualistic cultures, romantic love is considered the main reason for marriage. In collectivistic cultures, however, having a family tends to be the main reason for marriage. If having a family is the most important consideration, the acceptability of the potential mate to the family is critical. This explains the emphasis on arranged marriages in collectivistic cultures. (Note: There is a tendency in many collectivistic cultures for young people to want to marry on the basis of love.) Dion and Dion also contend that psychological intimacy is more important to marital satisfaction in individualistic cultures than in collectivistic cultures.

Dion and Dion's research (cited in Dion & Dion, 1993) suggests that the greater our psychological individualism, the less positive our attitudes toward marriage. Dion and Dion's research (1991) indicates that the greater our self-contained individualism (e.g., a tendency to dislike any form of dependency and to want total control over our lives), the less love, care, need, trust, and physical attraction we experience with partners in romantic relationships.

Dion, Pak, and Dion (1990) suggest that individualism-collectivism influences the stereotyping of members of the opposite sex on the basis of physical attractiveness. They contend that collectivism leads individuals to stereotype members of the opposite sex on group-related attributes (e.g., the other person's position in a social network and family memberships) rather than on individual attributes such as physical attractiveness.

Wheeler and Kim (1997) report that U.S. Americans perceive attractive targets to be higher in "potency" (e.g., strong, assertive, dominant) than Koreans. Koreans, in contrast, perceive attractive targets to be higher in "integrity" and "concern for others" than U.S. Americans. They conclude that the physical attractiveness stereotype applies in Korea but that the content of Koreans' stereotypes is different than U.S. Americans' stereotypes. Sheffer, Crepoz, and Sun (2000) note that Taiwanese use physical attractiveness as a basis for making inferences about personalities more than U.S. Americans. These researchers did not assess the respondents' individualistic and collectivistic tendencies. It is possible, therefore, that the respondents in the Asian cultures have individualistic tendencies (an issue that Shaffer et al. raise in discussing their results).

Sprecher et al. (1994) report that U.S. Americans emphasize romantic, passionate love and love based on friendship more than Japanese and Russians. U.S. Americans and Russians score higher on romantic beliefs than Japanese. Further, U.S. Americans rate physical appearance, similarity, family and friend approval, personality, affection, and mystery as more important than Russians and Japanese. With the exception of friend and family approval, these findings support Dion and Dion's (1993) speculations.

Gao (2001) notes that individualism-collectivism influences love and intimacy in romantic relationships. Specifically, partners in romantic relationships in the United States report more passion than partners in romantic relationships in China. Partners in romantic relationships in China, in contrast, report more intellectual intimacy than partners in U.S. American relationships.

Gao and Gudykunst (1995) observe greater high-context attributional confidence (i.e., reducing uncertainty indirectly) in Chinese romantic relationships than in European American romantic relationships. They also note that perceived attitude similarity is higher among European Americans than among Chinese. Finally, they observe that others socially react to European American romantic partners as a couple more than they do to Chinese romantic partners.

In addition to the research cited here, there is research on the use of power strategies (i.e., ways of persuading others to do something) in romantic relationships that is consistent with individualism-collectivism. Belk et al. (1988) suggest that individuals in the United States use direct power strategies such as persistence, persuasion, and telling more than Mexicans. Mexicans, in contrast, use bilateral-indirect strategies more than people in the United States. Belk et al. also report that Mexican men use more indirect-unilateral power strategies than men in the United States. This last difference may be a function of masculinity-femininity.

Most of the research to date supports Dion and Dion's (1988, 1991, 1993) speculations regarding differences in love in individualistic and collectivistic cultures (see Levine et al., 1995, for an 11-culture study; Neto et al., 2000, for an 8-culture study). There is one study that does not support their speculations. Doherty et al.'s (1994) research indicates that individual-level individualism is correlated negatively with passionate love among members of different ethnic groups in Hawaii.

THE DEVELOPMENT OF INTERPERSONAL RELATIONSHIPS WITH STRANGERS

Most of our close interpersonal relationships are with people who are relatively similar to us. We tend to develop close relationships with members of our own cultures and members of our ethnic groups (Pogrebin, 1987). Safilios-Rothchild (1982) also points out that "there is considerable evidence that very often people do not want to enter unpredictable, and therefore, stressful interactions with visibly disabled people, and they avoid doing so by extending only 'fictional acceptance' which does not go beyond a polite, inhibited, and overcontrolled interaction" (p. 44). Fussell (1983) claims that class differences similarly hinder members of different social classes from developing close relationships. Tamir (1984) argues that age segregation in society "has hampered the opportunity for young and old to come to know one another. Hence, when they do come into contact, well-worn and often detrimental stereotypes may persist, and participants must make an active effort to dispel these preconceptions for a healthy dialogue to take place" (p. 39).

One reason why we do not have close relationships with strangers is that we do not have a lot of contact with them. Another reason is that our initial interactions and superficial contacts with strangers often result in ineffective communication. Since our communication with strangers is not as effective and satisfying as we would like, we do not *try* to develop intimate relationships with strangers. If we understand the process of relationship development, however, we can make an informed conscious decision as to whether we want to have intimate relationships with strangers. In making such a decision, it is important to keep in mind that the more we know about strangers, the more accurately we can predict their behavior (Honeycutt, Knapp, & Powers, 1983).

In examining how communication influences the development of interpersonal relationships with strangers, we must keep in mind that there are both similarities and differences in communication across cultures. In this section, we examine how our expectations influence the relationships we form, how we reduce uncertainty and anxiety in communicating with strangers, and the role of self-disclosure and similarity in relationship development. We conclude by presenting a summary of the relationship development process. To begin, we look at how our expectations influence our interactions with strangers.

Expectations

Since proximity is one of the major factors involved in interpersonal attraction (Bersheid & Walster, 1969), strangers may be attracted to us simply because we are nearer to them than members of their own groups. In interacting with us, strangers may expect that they have nothing to lose; "the costs of pursuing a dissimilar relation are negligible relative to the rewards [for strangers]" (Knapp, cited in Crockett & Friedman, 1980, p. 91). We may, however, expect that we have something to lose when interacting with strangers since the rewards may be negligible and the costs high. Specifically, we may expect that if we interact with strangers, we may be looked down on by members of our ingroups. Regardless of any actual or potential sanctions, however, some of us expect positive interactions with strangers.

Hoyle, Pinkley, and Insko (1989) report that people expect interpersonal encounters (i.e., interactions with ingroup members) to be more agreeable and less abrasive than intergroup encounters. These expectations generalize to Japan (Gudykunst, Nishida, Morisaki, & Ogawa, 1999) and Greece (Broome, 1990). In Greece, for example, ingroup members are expected to be cooperative, polite, reliable, and warm, while outgroup members are expected to be competitive, deceitful, hostile, and untrustworthy. Gudykunst and Shapiro (1996), however, report that expectations become more positive as relationships with strangers become more intimate. Hubbert et al. (1999) also observe that expectations become more positive over time in intergroup encounters.

Our expectations for interactions with strangers can create self-fulfilling prophecies. Negative expectations can lead us to want to avoid interacting with strangers or to keep our interactions as short as possible. Positive expectations, in contrast, can lead us to look for positive aspects of our interactions with strangers. If we find positive aspects of the interaction, we want to interact more. Whether we want to continue our interaction also depends on our ability to manage our anxiety and uncertainty.

Uncertainty and Anxiety Management

Once a decision is made to interact with strangers, our major concern during the initial stages of interaction is the management of uncertainty and anxiety. Managing uncertainty is necessary if we are to arrive at a basis for predicting strangers' responses to our communication behavior and interpret strangers' behavior accurately. Managing anxiety is necessary to decrease our tendency to avoid interacting with strangers and to motivate us to want to communicate.

Uncertainty   There are differences in uncertainty reduction processes when we communicate with strangers as opposed to when we communicate with people who are familiar. Initial interactions with people who are familiar are different from initial interactions with strangers. Gudykunst (1983a) reports that students in the United States tend to make more assumptions about others on the basis of cultural background in initial interactions with strangers than they do in initial interactions with people who are familiar. This result is to be expected, since the major difference between the two forms of interaction is the communicators' cultural backgrounds. Gudykunst also notes that students in the United States prefer to do more of the talking in initial encounters with people who are familiar and prefer to ask more questions in initial encounters with strangers.

Lee and Boster (1991) report that people in the United States perceive strangers from other cultures as less attractive than people from their own culture and have less confidence in predicting the behavior of strangers in initial interactions than in predicting the behavior of people who are familiar. Lee and Boster also note that individuals ask for more intimate information from partners who are familiar than from strangers.

Gudykunst and Shapiro (1996) observe that there is greater uncertainty in intergroup encounters (interethnic and intercultural) than in intragroup encounters. They also observe that uncertainty is associated negatively with positive expectations, communication satisfaction, and quality of communication. Uncertainty is associated positively with the degree to which social identities are activated in the interaction and with the amount of anxiety experienced. Hubbert, Gudykunst, and Guerrero (1999) note that uncertainty decreases over time in intergroup encounters. Gudykunst, Nishida, and Chua (1986) report that uncertainty decreases as the intimacy of intercultural relationships increases. Similarly, Gudykunst (1985c) notes that there is less uncertainty in intercultural friendships than in intercultural acquaintance relationships.

Our social identities influence the reduction of uncertainty when we communicate with strangers (Gudykunst & Hammer, 1988b; Gudykunst, Sodetani, & Sonoda, 1987). Gudykunst and Hammer, for example, report that the more positive individuals' relevant social identities (e.g., ethnic identities when interacting with someone from a different ethnic group), the more they are able to reduce uncertainty when communicating with strangers. This finding, however, holds only when strangers are seen as typical members of their groups and when group differences are recognized. If strangers are viewed as atypical members of their groups and/or group differences are not recognized, personal identities, not social identities, influence the interaction.

Anxiety   Actual or anticipated interaction with members of other ethnic groups can lead to anxiety. Stephan and Stephan (1985) argue that individuals fear four types of negative consequences: negative psychological consequences (e.g., frustration), negative behavioral consequences (e.g., exploitation), negative evaluations by members of outgroups (e.g., negative stereotyping), and negative evaluations by members of their ingroups (e.g., disapproval).

Stephan and Stephan (1985, 1989, 1992) contend that the amount of anxiety we experience when interacting with strangers is, in part, a function of our intergroup attitudes. The greater our prejudice and ethnocentrism, for example, the greater our anxiety about interacting with strangers. Contact with strangers, however, leads to decreases in anxiety (Islam & Hewstone, 1993; Stephan & Stephan, 1992).

Gudykunst and Shapiro (1996) note that greater anxiety is experienced in intergroup encounters (interethnic and intercultural) than in intragroup encounters. They report that anxiety is associated negatively with positive expectations, communication satisfaction, and quality of communication. Anxiety is associated positively with the degree to which social identities are activated in the interaction and the amount of uncertainty experienced. Hubbert et al. (1999) report that anxiety decreases over time in intergroup encounters with strangers as a function of the communication that takes place when there are not hostile relations between the groups.

As indicated earlier, we experience more anxiety in our initial interactions with members of other groups than with members of our own groups. Managing anxiety is associated closely with developing trust. *Trust* is "confidence that one will find what is desired from another, rather than what is feared" (Deutsch, 1973, p. 149). When we trust others, we expect positive outcomes from our interactions with them; when we have anxiety about interacting with others we fear negative outcomes from our interactions with them. When we first meet someone, "trust is often little more than a naive expression of hope" (Holmes & Rempel, 1989, p. 192). For us to have hope about the relationship, our anxiety must be below our maximum thresholds. For relationships to become close,

> most people need to act *as if* a sense of [trust] were justified, and set their doubts aside. To do so requires a "leap of faith" in the face of evidence that can never be conclusive. Thus

trust becomes . . . an emotionally charged sense of closure. It permits an illusion of control . . . where one can plan ahead without anxiety. (Holmes & Rempel, 1989, p. 204)

Without some minimal degree of trust, relationships cannot become close.

Effective Communication   Gudykunst (1995) argues that the effectiveness of communication with strangers is a function of our ability to manage our anxiety and uncertainty. Hubbert et al.'s (1999) research indicates that perceived effectiveness of communication is affected by the amount of uncertainty and anxiety present in the interaction. The less the uncertainty and anxiety, the greater the perceived quality and effectiveness of communication. This pattern holds across time and holds for both European Americans and non-European Americans. Unreported data from Hubbert et al.'s study also indicate that the perceived effectiveness of communication the first time individuals communicate influences the amount of anxiety and uncertainty they experience the second time they communicate.

Gudykunst and Shapiro (1996) report that perceived effectiveness of communication is greater in intercultural friendships than in intercultural acquaintance relationships. Gudykunst and Nishida (2001) also observe that anxiety and uncertainty are associated negatively with perceived effectiveness of communication in ingroup and outgroup relationships in Japan and the United States.

Quality of communication refers to the extent to which our communication is relaxed, is smooth, involves understanding, and involves minimal communication breakdown (Duck et al., 1991). Gudykunst and Shapiro (1996) report that perceptions of the quality of communication are higher in intragroup relationships than in intergroup relationships. Hubbert et al. (1999) observe that perceived quality of communication increases as anxiety and uncertainty decrease and that quality of communication increases over time as a function of the interaction. Gudykunst and Shapiro also note that perceived quality increases as intergroup relationships become more intimate.

Li (1999a) compares how information is communicated in intracultural and intercultural interactions. The results indicate that individuals communicate more information in intracultural encounters than in intercultural encounters. Li (1999b) reports that the more individuals engage in "grounding" activities, the more effectively speakers communicate with listeners in both intracultural and intercultural encounters. Grounding activities refer to updating "common understanding of what is exchanged in the ongoing conversation" (p. 196).

Language and Cultural Knowledge

If strangers approach us and do not speak our language, it will be almost impossible to reduce uncertainty about their behavior, and this will inhibit the development of any possible relationship between us (Kertamus, Gudykunst, & Nishida, 1991; Gudykunst, Gao, Sudweeks, Ting-Toomey, & Nishida, 1991; Sudweeks, Gudykunst, Ting-Toomey, & Nishida, 1990). In Gudykunst et al.'s (1991) study, U.S. Americans' acceptance of Japanese partners' inability to speak English well and/or the U.S. American's offers to help the Japanese partners in improving their English is one of the major factors in allowing relationships to move past the acquaintance stage.

The development of personal relationships with strangers requires more than knowledge of linguistic codes. Knowledge of culturally appropriate rules for conducting the process of acquaintance formation also is necessary. Strangers, in all likelihood, have learned different rules for the process of acquaintance formation than we have. Lack of knowledge of strangers' cultures inhibits the development of interpersonal relationships. Miller and Sunnafrank (1982), for example, argue that "knowledge about another person's culture—its language, dominant values, beliefs, and prevailing ideology—often permits predictions of the person's probable response to certain messages. . . . Upon first encountering . . . [people from another culture], cultural information provides the only grounds for communicative predictions" (pp. 226–227).

Similarity

The ease with which initial interactions take place depends, at least in part, on the degree of similarity (including cultural, racial, sexual, and attitudinal similarity) between the two participants. It is not the actual similarity between participants that is important, but the degree of *perceived similarity,* the degree to which people think they are similar to others. As would be expected, the degree of perceived similarity is higher in intragroup relationships than in intergroup relationships (Gudykunst, 1986; Gudykunst et al., 1987).

Rokeach (1960) argues that the primary factor in the social distance between two people is the degree of similarity perceived. Similarly, Byrne (1971) views attraction as a function of the proportion of similar opinions two people hold. Brewer (1968) reports that similarity of beliefs accounts for social distance among members of East African tribes. Byrne et al. (1971) note that although culture influences the level of attraction, similarity also has a significant influence on attraction to strangers. More generally, perceived similarity is associated with intergroup interactions (e.g., Osbech et al., 1997). Tan and Singh's (1995) study suggests that the similarity-attraction hypothesis generalizes to collectivistic cultures. Kim's (1991) research indicates that perceived attitude similarity is a stronger predictor of attraction to strangers than even perceived competence in the ingroup language.

Knapp points out that dissimilarity "is enjoyable when the interaction is brief, when the differences are few and on peripheral beliefs, and when the chance of rejection is small, that is, when the costs of pursuing dissimilar relations are negligible relative to the rewards" (cited in Crockett & Friedman, 1980, p. 91). Knapp (1978) also suggests several qualifications that must be made with respect to the general principle of similarity and attraction:

> In the early stages of a relationship, similarity may be based upon a wide range of background factors and relatively superficial opinions and interests. As the relationship intensifies, certain topics, beliefs, and values may emerge as the most critical areas of similarity; those areas must be similar if the relationship is to continue. . . . Other qualifications include those people who are attracted to others dissimilar from themselves . . . there are instances in which we seek out people who are known to be different. (pp. 102–103)

In Knapp's view, then, dissimilarities may not hinder our initial interactions with strangers.

Rogers and Bhowmik (1971) argue that "in a free choice situation, when a source can interact with any one of a number of different receivers, there is a strong tendency for him [or her] to select a receiver who is like himself [or herself]" (p. 528). They go on to suggest that communication between people who are similar is generally more effective than communication between dissimilar people. Although this finding is accepted widely, moderate dissimilarities between communicators who are generally similar leads to the most effective communication (Simons, Berkowitz, & Moyer, 1970).

Simard's (1981) study of French/English intraethnic and interethnic initial interactions in Canada indicates that

> when focusing on a potential friend from the other group [French and English respondents] perceive it as more difficult to know how to initiate a conversation, to know what to talk about during interaction, to be interested in the other person, and to guess in which language they should talk, than when they considered a person from their own group. (p. 183)

Further, Simard's research suggests that both groups (Anglophones and Francophones in Canada) find attitude and language similarity more important than occupational and social class similarity in the development of interethnic acquaintances. The results of her research "may imply that the dissimilarity in terms of ethnic affiliation may have been compensated for by increased similarity along a number of other dimensions or that so much dissimilarity was expected that after the actual encounters the overall similarity surprised the [respondents]" (p. 187).

Sunnafrank and Miller (1981) report that "individuals paired with an attitudinally similar partner were more attracted to the partner than individuals paired with an attitudinally dissimilar partner, but only when they had not engaged in initial interaction" (p. 22). We are attracted to dissimilar strangers if we have a chance to interact with them, but we are not attracted to them if interaction does not take place. Hubbert et al.'s (1999) research supports this argument. They report that perceived similarity increases over time as a function of the communication that takes place.

We filter potential relational partners on the extent to which we perceive that they are similar to us (Duck, 1977). In the initial stages of getting to know others, we probably focus on general attitudes and opinions that we hold. If we perceive that our attitudes are similar to those of others, we will be attracted to them because the similarity in attitudes validates our view of the world (Byrne, 1971). As we get to know others, we search for similarities in central aspects of our world views (e.g., our core values).

Probably one of the most important similarities we search for in potential relational partners is similarity in our orientations toward interpersonal interactions (Sunnafrank, 1991). If we perceive similarities in our orientations toward communication, we are likely to form close relationships with others. Burleson, Samter, and Lucchetti's (1992) research suggests that close friends have similar orientations toward five specific communication activities: conflict management, ways to comfort each other, ways to persuade each other, ways to support each other's self-concepts, and ways to tell stories and jokes. Lee and Gudykunst (2001) report that perceived similarity in communication styles, perceived self-concept support, lack of uncertainty, strength of ethnic identities, and positive intergroup expectations predict interethnic attraction.

To summarize, cultural dissimilarity may complicate initial interactions, but it clearly does not preclude the development of more intimate relationships. Following Rokeach, Smith, and Evans (1960), it appears reasonable to argue that cultural and ethnic similarity is not a necessary prerequisite for friendship formation. In the absence of cultural similarity, however, similarity in other areas (e.g., attitudes, interests, communication styles) is necessary for relationships to develop. The degree of similarity between communicators plays another important role in initial interactions in that it influences the reduction of uncertainty (Berger & Calabrese, 1975) and the reduction of anxiety present when we communicate with strangers (Stephan & Stephan, 1985)

It appears reasonable to argue that our initial interactions with strangers will move toward the development of more intimate relationships if we perceive some minimum level of similarity between ourselves and the strangers and are able to reduce some of the uncertainty present in our initial interactions. If we do not perceive sufficient similarity, the relationship probably will take a trajectory leading to a relationship that does not change in the level of intimacy over time; for example, we may remain acquaintances for the entire length of time we know each other.

Self-Disclosure and Social Penetration

One of the major factors which contribute to the development of personal relationships with strangers is self-disclosure. One type of interaction where self-disclosure is an important issue occurs when nondisabled and disabled people communicate. Thompson (1982), for example, argues that nondisabled people react more positively to disabled people who self-disclose than to those who do not self-disclose, especially when the self-disclosure is about the disability. Thompson and Seibold (1978), however, point out that self-disclosure does not necessarily reduce tension, although it does increase the nondisabled people's acceptance of disabled people.

Braithwaite (1991) contends that disabled people tend to disclose about their disabilities in response to nondisabled people's questions about their disabilities if they perceive that the disclosure is appropriate to the relationship and the context in which they are communicating. Disabled people, however, prefer to have nondisabled people get to know them as individuals before answering questions about their disabilities. To accomplish this, disabled people may try to direct the conversation and suggest topics for conversation other than their disabilities. If disabled people perceive that a nondisabled person with whom they are communicating is experiencing great discomfort, they may choose to disclose about their disabilities to make the other person more comfortable (Braithwaite, 1991).

The age of the communicators also affects self-disclosure. Dickson-Markman (1986), for example, believes that older people tend to disclose more than younger people, especially with respect to negative feelings. Self-disclosure in intergenerational encounters does not necessarily follow the same patterns that it follows in encounters between members of the same generation (Giles et al., 1992). When older people interact with younger people, they tend to self-disclose more than the younger people, especially about painful information such as accidents, deaths in the family, and medical problems. When older people self-disclose to younger people they do not know, the younger people do not necessarily reciprocate self-disclosures at the same rate they do when communicating with other younger people. When young people self-disclose, in contrast, older people tend to reciprocate.

Gudykunst and Nishida (1984) report that there is a greater intention to disclose information in initial intercultural encounters than in initial intracultural encounters. This pattern, however, does not hold when self-disclosure in intracultural and intercultural acquaintances and friendships is compared. Gudykunst (1985c), for example, observes no difference between the amount of self-disclosure in intercultural and intracultural acquaintances and/or friendships. There is, nevertheless, more self-disclosure in both intracultural and intercultural friendships than in intracultural or intercultural acquaintances. Gudykunst's (1985b) research also reveals moderate to high associations between social penetration in close friendships with culturally similar partners and social penetration in close friendships with culturally dissimilar partners.

The research summarized here can be explained by using Altman and Taylor's (1973) conceptualization of the social penetration process. Communication in close friendships is characterized by freewheeling and loose exchange and "facile switching from one mode of communication to another" (p. 139). Altman and Taylor also point out that in close friendships "the dyad has moved to the point where interaction is relatively free in both peripheral and in more central areas of the personality. Cultural stereotypy is broken down in these more intimate areas and there is a willingness to move freely in and out of such exchanges" (pp. 139–140). If cultural stereotypy is indeed broken down, the culture from which strangers come should not be a major factor influencing the interaction. Close relationships between culturally similar communicators, therefore, should not be expected to differ dramatically from those between culturally dissimilar communicators.

Another explanation for the research on self-disclosure comes from Miller and Steinberg's (1975) developmental theory of interpersonal communication. Specifically, it can be inferred that when communicators making predictions move from the cultural and sociocultural levels of data to the use of psychocultural data, the culture from which people come is not a major variable affecting the predictions made about their communication behavior. Given this, it would be expected that when predictions are made mainly on the basis of psychocultural data (e.g., in close friendships), the degree of social penetration should not necessarily differ in culturally similar and dissimilar relationships. The differences that do exist in close friendships are best attributed to the specific characteristics of the dyad and the people involved, not to their cultural background.

Gudykunst, Nishida, and Chua's (1986) study of social penetration processes in intercultural dyads supports the argument made here. It reveals that as intercultural relationships become more intimate (i.e., move from acquaintances to friends to close friends), social penetration increases. Social penetration in intercultural relationships influences the degree of communication satisfaction individuals have when they communicate with strangers.

Interaction Involvement

Chen (1995) examines interaction involvement in initial intracultural and intercultural interactions. She reports that communicators in initial intercultural encounters are less perceptive (e.g., understanding meanings others attribute to messages) and less responsive (e.g., knowing what to say and when to say it) than communicators in initial intracultural encounters. Communicators use alignment talk (e.g., telling partners how to interpret messages) more in intercultural encounters than in intracultural encounters (Chen, 1997). Alignment talk is used to increase clarity and understanding. Chen points out that we tend to take clarity and understanding for granted in intracultural encounters.

Chen and Cegala (1994) report that U.S. Americans discuss explicit and accessible topics and engage in information exchange more in intercultural interactions than in intracultural interactions. They also note that topic sharing is associated positively with interaction involvement and the perception of intercultural accommodation (e.g., that others adjust to us). Chen and Cegala suggest that perceived accommodation and interaction involvement in initial interactions may be factors that lead communicators to have future interactions.

Communication Satisfaction

Whether we are able to manage our uncertainty and anxiety, find similarities, and engage in social penetration influences whether participants are satisfied with their communication. Satisfaction is an affective (i.e., emotional) reaction to communication that meets or fails to meet our expectations (Hecht, 1978). The way strangers respond to us influences our satisfaction in communicating with them. Hodges and Byrne (1972), for example, point out that responses to strangers are most positive when they express attitudes in open-minded rather than dogmatic (closed-minded) terms. Broome (1981) argues that "responses to differences stated in an open manner will be less defensive than responses stated in a non-open manner" (p. 231).

Hecht and Ribeau and their associates study satisfaction with interethnic conversations in the United States. Hecht, Ribeau, and Alberts (1989), for example, isolate factors that contribute to African Americans' satisfaction with their conversations with European Americans. To be satisfied, African Americans need to feel that they are respected, confirmed, and accepted by the European Americans with whom they communicate. Satisfying conversations with European Americans also include emotional expression and the European Americans being authentic (i.e., European Americans in satisfying conversations are perceived as genuine, and European Americans in dissatisfying conversations are perceived as evasive). African Americans also perceive that there is understanding (i.e., shared meanings) and goal attainment in satisfying conversations. They perceive negative stereotyping and feel powerless (e.g., manipulated or controlled) in dissatisfying conversations.

Hecht, Ribeau, and Sedano (1990) report a similar study with Latino(a) Americans. Similar to African Americans, Latino(a) Americans see acceptance as an important aspect of satisfying conversations. Satisfying conversations with European Americans also include the expression of feelings and behaving rationally. The presence of self-expression and relational solidarity also contribute to satisfaction in conversations. Negative stereotyping and failure to discover a shared world view (i.e., absence of perceived similarities) emerge as important factors in dissatisfying conversations.

Gudykunst, Nishida, and Chua's (1986, 1987) research indicates that the more communication in intercultural relationships is personalized and synchronized and the less difficulty people experience in communicating with strangers, the more satisfied they are with the communication in their relationships. It also suggests that the more partners self-disclose to each other, the more they are attracted to each other, the more similarities they perceive, and the more they reduce uncertainty about each other, the more satisfied they are. Finally, the more competent the partners judge each other's communication to be, the more satisfied they are.

Gudykunst and Shapiro (1996) report that satisfaction is higher in intragroup encounters than in intergroup encounters. They also note that satisfaction increases as relationships become more intimate. Hubbert et al. (1999) also observe that satisfaction increases over time in intergroup encounters for non-European-Americans but remains relatively constant for European Americans.

Patterns of Relationship Development

What is it about our initial interactions and our communication with acquaintances who are from other groups that allows the relationship to develop into a friendship? Research suggests that we must communicate in a way that signals we accept strangers, we must express our feelings, and we must avoid negative stereotyping. All of these factors combined suggest that our communication with strangers helps them have positive personal and social identities. Stated differently, we support their self-concepts.

As pointed out earlier, there must be linguistic competence, there has to be some degree of cultural knowledge, and we must perceive some degree of similarity between ourselves and strangers if intimate relationships are to develop (Kertamus et al., 1991; Gudykunst et al., 1991; Sudweeks et al., 1990). The display of empathy and mutual accommodation regarding differences in communication styles (i.e., adapting each other's style to the other person) also appear to be critical.

Other factors that appear to be important are similar to those in developing relationships with people from our own groups. We must, for example, make time available to interact with strangers (Kertamus et al., 1991; Gudykunst et al., 1991; Sudweeks et al., 1990). In addition to making time to interact, consciously or unconsciously attempting to increase the intimacy of our communication (i.e., talking about things that are important to us) is necessary if we are going to develop interpersonal relationships with strangers.

The stages relationships go through provide additional insight into the development of interpersonal relationships with strangers. Altman and Taylor (1973), for example, propose a four-stage model of interpersonal relationship development: (1) orientation, (2) exploratory affective exchange, (3) full affective exchange, and (4) stable exchange. The orientation stage is characterized by responses that often are stereotypical and reflect superficial aspects of the personalities of the actors involved. The content of the interaction at this stage is limited to the "outer public areas" of the individuals' personalities. The second stage, exploratory affective exchange, is typified by those relationships labeled casual acquaintances and nonintimate friends. Relationships at this stage are generally friendly and relaxed, but commitments are only temporary. The third stage, full affective exchange, is characteristic of close friendships and courtship relationships. These relationships involve loose and freewheeling verbal interaction and an increase in self-disclosure concerning the central areas of the individuals' personalities. As was pointed out previously, this is the stage in which cultural stereotypy is broken down. The final stage, stable exchange, is achieved in very few relationships. If it is achieved, however, Altman and Taylor argue that there are very few instances of miscommunication between the partners because they have described themselves fully to each other.

Given Altman and Taylor's (1973) model, it can be argued that the initial stages of our relationships (i.e., the first two stages) with strangers are different from those of our relationships with people who are familiar. This arises because the early stages are dominated by cultural stereotypes, and, therefore, when we communicate with strangers, differences are bound to emerge. This is not to say that our relationships with strangers do not go through these stages, because they do. Rather, the argument is that they may go through them in different ways.

If cultural stereotypy is indeed broken down in the stage of full affective exchange, it can be argued that the culture from which strangers come will not be a major factor influencing our relationships. Once relationships reach the stage of friendship, the majority of interaction has a personalistic focus, a focus on strangers as unique communicators (Wright, 1978). To put this in slightly different terms, the communicators in a friendship have moved from using mainly cultural and sociocultural levels of data for making predictions to using mainly psychocultural data (Miller & Steinberg, 1975). When the data used in making predictions are mainly psychocultural, the culture from which strangers come is not a major factor influencing our predictions.

This is not to say that our relationships with strangers and those with people who are familiar are the same. No two friendships are exactly the same; friendships are based on private negotiations, follow idiosyncratic rules, and are all slightly different. The argument put forth is that since friendship is a relationship in which cultural stereotypy is broken down and there is a personalistic focus, the differences in our behavior in the two types of friendships can be attributed to personal characteristics of the person with whom we are interacting or to other factors, not to the person's cultural background.

Before concluding, it should be noted that relationships do not always develop along a smooth course from superficial to intimate. Altman, Vinsel, and Brown (1981) point out that "although people may exhibit relatively stable openness (or closedness) for a time, it is likely that openness eventually gives way to closedness and that closedness is eventually followed by openness. Such cyclical variations in accessibility of people to one another are affected by factors internal and external to an individual" (p. 139). They go on to argue that different patterns of openness-closedness may be adaptive over the life span of a relationship. Lerner (1979) also makes the point that relationships go through cycles with respect to other dimensions, including affection, trust, and sharing. How a particular relationship ultimately develops, therefore, is influenced by the degree to which the people involved have synchrony in timing and content with respect to the openness-closedness in their interaction (Altman, Vinsel, & Brown, 1981), as well as by whether there is synchrony with respect to their display of affection and trust (Lerner, 1979). Following Hall (1983), we believe that establishing synchrony is easier with people who are familiar than it is with strangers. It can be established with strangers, however.

When we communicate on automatic pilot, we often filter out members of other groups as potential friends simply because they are different and our communication with them is not as effective as our communication with people from our own groups. Whether we want to act differently depends on our motivation. Pogrebin (1985) points out that pluralistic friendships celebrate

> *genuine* differences arising out of life experiences and culture but reject *socially constructed* differences resulting from stereotypes or discrimination. . . .
>
> Ethnicity is friendship-enhancing when it does not make another group into an "Other" group.
>
> Ethnicity is friendship-enhancing when we make it an "and" not a "but." The difference is palpable: "She's my friend *and* she's Jewish" allows me the pride of difference that a "but" would destroy.
>
> Group pride spawns both pride *and* prejudice. What makes a group special also makes it different. For some people, "different" must mean "better" or it is experienced as "worse." But people who do not need ethnic supremacy to feel ethnic pride find comfort and attitudinal regeneration among their "own kind" and also are able to make friends across racial and ethnic boundaries. (pp. 187–188)

Pogrebin's comments on ethnicity apply to other group differences (e.g., disability, age, social class) that affect relationship development as well.

Do we want to approach people who are different or continue to avoid them? We believe that relationships with strangers provide a chance for us to grow as individuals (see Chapter 14). The choice about developing these relationships, however, is an individual one. We encourage you to make a conscious choice about whether you want to communicate effectively and develop relationships with strangers rather than relying on your unconscious, mindless decisions. If you choose to approach strangers and are mindful of your communication, you will recognize real differences and eventually discover similarities between yourselves and the strangers with whom you communicate. The similarities you discover will provide the foundation for developing intimate relationships.

ROMANTIC RELATIONSHIPS WITH STRANGERS

Much of the material discussed in the preceding section on the development of interpersonal relationships also applies to the development of romantic relationships with strangers. In this section we, therefore, focus on selected aspects of communication with strangers that are unique to romantic relationships. We begin by examining dating relationships with strangers. We conclude with an examination of intercultural marriages.

Intergroup Dating Relationships

Lampe's (1982) research on interethnic dating (European American/African American, European American/Latino(a) American, African American/Latino(a) American) in the United States indicates that the major motivation for interethnic dating is the same as that for intraethnic dating, namely, personal liking for the other person. In fact, no other reason for interethnic dating comes close to personal liking in terms of the percentage of respondents giving it (personal liking is reported by 60 percent of the respondents; no other reason is given by more than 16 percent of the respondents). Lampe's study, in contrast, reveals no consistent reason against interethnic dating; "the most commonly cited reason given by both males and females was a lack of desire" (p. 118). This response was given by less than 35 percent of the respondents. The most common reasons against interethnic dating given by European Americans study are "no desire," "don't know any well enough," and "no chance." The most common reasons given by African Americans are "no desire," "hadn't thought of it," and "no chance." Mexican Americans give "don't know any well enough," "no desire," and "no chance" as the most common reasons against interethnic dating.

Recent research supports Lampe's (1982) findings (e.g., Guring & Duong, 1999; Shibozaki & Bremman, 1998). These studies suggest that partners in interethnic dating relationships enter the relationships for the same reason partners enter intraethnic dating relationships (e.g., personal liking, common interests) and report similar levels of intimacy and satisfaction in their relationships.

Spickard (1989) suggests that generation in the United States is one of the major factors that influence Asian Americans' interethnic dating. He claims that Asian Americans' interethnic dating with European Americans is prevalent among third-generation Asian Americans who do not live in ethnic enclaves and those who live outside the western part of the United States (e.g., away from large groups of Asian Americans). Nagata (1993) observes that California *Sansei* (third-generation Japanese Americans) are more likely to have dated another Japanese American than *Sansei* living in other parts of the country. She suggests this is because of the higher concentration of Japanese Americans in California than in other parts of the country. Johnson and Ogasawara (1984) also point out that Asian Americans from higher socioeconomic groups are more likely to date out of their ethnic groups than those from lower socioeconomic groups.

Fujino (1997) also notes that Asian American women who date European Americans come from families that have lived in the United States longer than the families of those who do not date European Americans. Only 41 percent of the first-generation Asian American women had "significant" dating relationships with European Americans, 65 percent of the second-generation Asian American women had "significant" dating relationships with European Americans, and 77 percent of the third-generation Asian American women had "significant" dating relationships with European Americans.

Liu, Campbell, and Condie (1995) contend that Asian Americans prefer to date European Americans over members of other ethnic groups (e.g., of those not from their own group). Similarly, Revilla (1989) reports that only 31 percent of Filipino Americans prefer to date/marry members of their own group, and a vast majority of those who prefer non-Filipino Americans prefer European Americans. One reason for preferring European Americans may be that Asian Americans perceive them to be attractive. Fujino (1992), for example, reports that both European Americans and Asian Americans rate European Americans as more attractive than Asian Americans.

Kitano, Young, Chai, and Hatanaka (1984) point out that Asian American women date outside their ethnic groups more than Asian American men. This finding is supported by extensive research (e.g., Kitano & Chai, 1982; Lee & Yamamaka, 1990). Two studies (Shinagawa & Pang, 1996; Tuan, 1998) suggest that the rate is leveling off for young Asian Americans. There are a couple of possible explanations for women dating outside their ethnic groups more than men.

One reason Asian American women may date out of their ethnic groups more than Asian American men has to do with gender stereotypes. Weiss (1970), for example, claims that European American men have positive stereotypes of Chinese American women (e.g., "sexy," "quiet," "subservient"). Chinese American women in turn have negative stereotypes of Chinese American men (e.g., "weak," "traditional," "old-fashioned") and positive stereotypes of European American men (e.g., "suave," "cool," "sophisticated," "sexy"). When asked why they date Chinese American men, Chinese American women say things like "parental coercion," "respect for tradition," and "race consciousness." When asked about dating European American men, Chinese American women say things like they are "more fun on dates" and "more considerate" than Chinese American men and have "easygoing personalities." The combination of stereotypes and preconceptions facilitates Chinese American women dating European American men.

The influence of stereotyping on interethnic dating also may involve Asian American women not fitting Asian American men's stereotypes. One Japanese American woman who is married to a European American says:

> [European Americans] were the only guys I was attracted to, felt more comfortable with. I always would feel that Japanese guys [pause] I just wasn't what they were looking for, and they weren't what I was looking for either because I didn't fit into that conforming mold. I never kept up with all the things that were important to Japanese girls so I don't think I was desirable to them [Japanese guys], that I was ever on the list. And all the guys liked the same girls. There'd really be like a list of who was not desirable. I'm too outspoken and too intimidating. (Tuan, 1998, p. 121)

This woman's preference may be a function of both her stereotypes of Japanese American men and Japanese American men's stereotypes of Japanese American women.

Another potential explanation for Asian American women engaging in interethnic dating more than Asian American men involves issues of racism. Fujino (1992) suggests that Asian American men are expected to initiate dates. Since they are expected to initiate dates, Asian American men who perceive that they are subject to racism may not tend to initiate dates with European American women. Asian American women, in contrast, can determine whether European American men who approach them are highly racist and choose not to date those who are. Fujino argues that Asian American women's dating patterns, therefore, are not as influenced by racism as Asian American men's dating patterns.

Fujino (1997) examines interethnic dating among Chinese Americans, European Americans, and Japanese Americans at the University of California, Los Angeles. Overall, she finds that Japanese Americans date out of their ethnic group more than Chinese Americans, who date out of their group more than European Americans. A large percentage of all three groups, however, had at least one interethnic date: Japanese American men (86.5 percent), Japanese American women (85.7 percent), Chinese American men (75.3 percent), Chinese American women (69.2 percent), European

American men (62.5 pecent), and European American women (52.6 percent). The pattern is a little different when the overall percentage of dates *not* from their own ethnic groups is examined: Japanese Americans (64 percent), Chinese Americans (54 percent), European Americans (22 percent).

Fujino (1997) reports that Asian American women prefer to date and marry members of their own ethnic groups, followed by European Americans and then by other Asian Americans. Asian American men also prefer to date and marry members of their own groups, followed by other Asian Americans and then by European Americans. Fujino also observes that Asian Americans who date European Americans had more European Americans in their high schools and neighborhoods than those who do not date European Americans. Asian American women who date European Americans have more liberal attitudes toward women's roles and place higher value on dating partners' attractiveness than those who do not date European Americans.

Tucker and Mitchell-Kernan (1995) report that over half the African Americans, Latino/Latina Americans, and European Americans in their survey conducted in southern California date members of other ethnic groups. Their survey indicates that interethnic dating is associated with being a young male who is highly educated and perceiving the possibility of marrying members of other ethnic groups. Their data also suggest that African Americans and Latino/Latina Americans are more likely to engage in interethnic dating than European Americans.

Alba (1976) argues that the strength of individuals' ethnic identities is related to their outgroup dating and marriage. Specifically, he contends that those with weaker identities have a greater tendency to date/marry out of their group than those with strong identities. Parsonson's (1987) research supports this contention but also suggests that there may be ethnic differences. Her data suggest that this relationship may not hold for non-Anglos in Canada.

Chung and Ting-Toomey (1999) report that "ethnic exclusivity" (the opposite of cultural identity) interacts with the ethnicity of the dating partner to influence relational expectations. Their data suggest that Asian Americans who are strong in ethnic exclusivity have negative expectations for interethnic dates with European Americans (expect European American dates to be dominant, distant, low in intimacy, low in trust) but that they do not have negative expectations for intraethnic dates.

Another factor that influences the decision to date strangers is the degree to which they are perceived to be typical members of their culture. Gudykunst et al. (1991) report that individuals in intercultural romantic relationships see their partners as atypical of their cultures. The Japanese respondents, for example, view their U.S. American partners as different from other U.S. Americans and as possessing some Japanese characteristics.

Garcia and Rivera (1999) examine racially similar and dissimilar couples among African Americans and Latino(a) Americans. They report that perceptions of same-race couples are more positive than perceptions of different-race couples. Different-race couples are perceived as "significantly more likely to dissolve, less compatible, less attractive, and less likely to receive approval" than same-race couples (p. 81). Garcia and Rivera also note that different-race friendships are perceived more positively than different-race engagements.

Intergroup Marriages

Interracial marriages have always been legal in some states, but 38 states had antimiscegenation laws at one time. California, for example, passed a law prohibiting marriages between people of European decent and "Negroes," "Mulattos," "Indians," "Mongolians," and people of "mixed blood" in 1880. The law was amended in 1934 to include "Malays." The California law was found unconstitutional in 1948. Like California, 21 other state laws were overturned or repealed, but it was not until 1967 that the last 16 state laws were declared unconstitutional (U.S. Supreme Court, Loving v. Virginia). Between 1960 and 1997, the percentage of all marriages that were interethnic marriages increased almost sixfold (1960 = 0.49 percent; 1997 = 2.3 percent; U.S. Census Bureau, 1997).

Even though interethnic marriage is legal, there is still opposition to it in the United States. Fang, Sidanus, and Pratto (1998), for example, report that European Americans score 2.97 (5 = very much opposed) regarding interethnic marriages with Asian Americans, 2.80 with respect to Latino(a) Americans, and 3.17 with respect to African Americans. Asian Americans score 2.69 with respect to interethnic marriages with European Americans, 2.91 with respect to Latino(a) Americans, and 3.19 with respect to African Americans. Latino(a) Americans score 2.44 with respect to interethnic marriages with European Americans, 2.79 with respect to Asian Americans, and 2.95 with respect to African Americans. African Americans score 2.26 with respect to European Americans, 2.48 with respect to Asian Americans, and 2.48 with respect to Latino(a) Americans.

The decision to date or become friends with strangers is not the same as the decision to marry strangers. A marriage with strangers requires a lifelong commitment to live with someone who is culturally or ethnically different. Any marriage calls for adjustments, but marriages to strangers generally demand more adjustments on the part of both partners than do marriages to members of ingroups. One of the adjustments necessary is adjusting to the ingroup's reaction to intergroup couples. European Americans in the United States, however, are becoming more tolerant of interethnic marriages (National Opinion Research Center, 1991). In 1970, European American disapproval of laws prohibiting interethnic marriages was only 48 percent. In 1990, 77 percent of European Americans disapproved of such laws. Even though there is more disapproval of these laws, many people still consider interethnic relationships taboo (Johnson & Warren, 1994).

Kitano et al. (1998) isolate the best predictors of Asian Americans' interethnic marriages by using data from Los Angeles. They report that generation is the best predictor of interethnic marriage across Asian American ethnic groups. The later the generation in the United States, the greater the interethnic marriage rate. Second-generation Asian Americans are three times more likely to marry outside their ethnic groups than first-generation Asian Americans. Third-generation Asian Americans are five times more likely to marry outside their ethnic groups than first-generation Asian Americans.

Kitano et al. (1998) also observe that ethnicity influences interethnic marriage. Korean Americans are less likely to marry outside their group than Japanese Americans. Among women, Chinese Americans and Filipino Americans are more likely to marry outside their groups than Japanese Americans. Younger Asian American men are more likely to marry outside their ethnic groups than older Asian American men.

People get married for a wide variety of reasons. When one chooses to marry a stranger, it is often, like the decision to date, based on the same reasons for which one would choose to marry a person who is familiar (e.g., for love or upward mobility). People in interracial marriages, for example, report being attracted to their partners because they hold similar values and have similar interests (Kouri & Lasswell, 1993) or get along well (Rosenblatt et al., 1995). There are, however, other motivations that come into play in marriages to strangers that may not be factors in marriages to people who are familiar (Char, 1977). To illustrate, while chance and availability play a major role in any marriage, these reasons often take on increased importance in marriages to strangers. When strangers are living in or visiting another culture, they are in close proximity to potential marriage partners from the host culture and far away from any from their home culture (Char, 1977). Often marriages to strangers take place simply because people from another culture are the only available partners; for example, United States military personnel living overseas may marry host-country nationals because they are the only available candidates.

Related to chance and availability are practical reasons for marrying strangers. Char (1977) cites the following as an example of a practical reason: "A poor . . . German girl may consent to marry [an African American] soldier stationed in post-war Germany for the material benefits he can give her, and the opportunity to escape from her unhappy home and come to America" (p. 35). In citing this example, Char does not imply this is the only reason a white German woman might marry an African American serviceman from the United States, only that it is one possible reason.

Another reason for marrying strangers is the beliefs we hold about their culture. These beliefs, of course, may be based on actual characteristics of the strangers' cultures or may not be grounded in reality. To illustrate, a European American "male might marry a Japanese woman because he feels a Japanese female can better satisfy his desire to have a wife who is willing to wait on him" (Char, 1977, p. 37). Such a belief may be based on messages be received from his parents or the mass media. Parents, for example, may consciously or unconsciously suggest that members of another culture are desirable or undesirable marriage partners.

No matter what the motivation for entering into a marriage, once married, the partners must learn to adjust to living with each other. Disapproval by family, friends, and members of the community is not a problem unique to intercultural marriages, but the resulting rejection and discrimination are (Stuart & Abt, 1973). Fontaine and Dorch's (1980) research reveals that interethnic marriages have more severe problems than intraethnic marriages. Similarly, Markoff (1977) observes that partners in intercultural marriages have difficulty in communication and coping with external disapproval. Graham, Moeai, and Shizuru (1985) also report that there are more external problems in intercultural marriages than in intracultural marriages even though both groups are equally satisfied with their marriages.

In addition to adjusting to external demands, the success of a marriage depends on the ability of each party to adjust to living with the other person. In interracial marriages the problem of racism cannot be ignored. Partners' racist beliefs may come out accidentally when they are angry. Rosenblatt et al. (1995) point out that overcoming racism, even in interracial marriages, is a lifelong project.

Another problem in marriages between strangers is that very often the individuals are not prepared to recognize cultural differences (Tseng, 1977). When confronted with a particular situation, both partners react on the basis of their cultural backgrounds, neither recognizing that the other is reacting from a different set of cultural standards. Tseng argues that

> any problems or differences which may exist within an intercultural marriage will not be solved easily just because cognitively the persons are aware of the reason for the differences and strategically there is a prescribed solution for it. Culture is something which is learned through experiences in early life. An individual has developed strong emotional attachments to his [or her] culture—associated with his [or her] belief system, values, and habits—his [or her] style of life. In the process of intercultural marriage adjustment, he [or she] has to learn how to overcome, correct, and adjust his [or her] emotional reaction to the necessary change and expansion of his [or her] cultural behavior. (pp. 96–97)

What Tseng says about marriage between culturally dissimilar partners also can be applied to the development of friendships between strangers.

Tseng (1977) describes five general patterns of adjustment in marriages between culturally dissimilar partners: (1) one-way adjustment, (2) alternative adjustment, (3) mid-point compromise, (4) mixing, and (5) creative adjustment. The *one-way adjustment* pattern takes place when one spouse totally adopts the cultural patterns of the other. Such an adjustment may be with regard to one particular aspect of a culture (e.g., religion, food, or language) or to the whole constellation of cultural behaviors. This pattern of adjustment is common when one culture is extremely dominant; also, it often is selected because of the practicality of everyday life.

Alternative adjustment occurs when both spouses insist that their cultural patterns be followed and when it is impossible for either to mix or give up cultural behavior (Tseng, 1977). Again, this pattern may involve only one aspect of a culture or both cultures as a whole. Tseng cites an example of a couple (one Catholic, one Buddhist) who decide to have two wedding ceremonies to meet the requirements of both of their cultures.

Mid-point compromise occurs when the partners compromise or meet in the middle. Tseng (1977) cites a couple in which the husband is from China and the wife is from the United States. The husband feels an obligation to send his family in China $100 a month, but the wife objects because she thinks they cannot spare the money (the nuclear family is most important). In order to address both of their needs, they settle on a mid-point compromise—the husband sends his family $50 a month rather than $100 as he originally planned.

Couples also can *mix* the two cultures in their marriage. This mixing might be random and awkward or balanced and harmonious. While such a mixing is most obvious in concrete matters (e.g., home furnishings, eating patterns, religious behavior), it also may involve concepts and ideas (Tseng, 1977). That is, the partners may develop their own values, norms, and rules of behavior, which are a mix of their original cultures.

Creative adjustment takes place when a couple give up both of the original cultures and decide to "invent" new behaviors for their marriage (Tseng, 1977). This pattern of adjustment may be necessary because of conflict between the couple's cultures (e.g., traditional dinner eating patterns in the United States and in some eastern cultures are not highly compatible), or it may come about because neither partner is satisfied with his or her own culture.

Marriages between culturally dissimilar partners do have unique problems of adjustment, but they should not be viewed simply as problematic. There is also a positive side to such marriages. They can be a source of personal growth for the partners, as well as a source of social change for the cultures in which they take place.

SUMMARY

In this chapter we examined selected aspects of the interpersonal relationships we develop with strangers. Cultural similarity is not a requirement for the development of an interpersonal relationship. In the absence of cultural similarity, linguistic similarity and similarity along other dimensions (e.g., occupation, attitudes) may be necessary. If sufficient similarity is perceived during initial interactions, culturally dissimilar communicators may meet again, thereby making possible the development of a more intimate relationship.

The initial stages of our relationships with strangers may be different from those of our relationships with people who are familiar. Depending on the culture from which strangers come, for example, they may reduce uncertainty differently than we do. Strangers from collectivistic cultures will seek demographic information, and those from individualistic cultures will seek information regarding attitudes and values.

If our relationships with strangers reach the stage of friendship, the culture from which the strangers come becomes less important. Stated differently, since friendships have a personalistic focus in which cultural stereotypes are broken down, the culture from which the stranger comes is not a major factor in predicting behavior in a close relationship. Friendships with strangers and those with people who are familiar, therefore, exhibit more similarities than differences. The differences that do exist are best attributed to the idiosyncratic rules and structure of particular relationships.

There are similarities and differences in romantic relationships across cultures. It appears that openness, involvement, shared nonverbal meanings, and relational assessment are themes in romantic relationships across cultures. At least some of the differences which exist are related to individualism-collectivism. Physical attractiveness of the partner, for example, is more important in individualistic cultures than in collectivistic cultures.

People in the United States appear to be more tolerant of intercultural marriages than they were in the past. Intercultural couples, however, still face discrimination. If intercultural marriages are to succeed, the partners must learn to accommodate to each other's cultural patterns of behavior.

STUDY QUESTIONS

1. How are friendships different from friendly relations?
2. What are the elementary forms of social relationships that exist across cultures?
3. How do the categories of relationships used in the United States and Japan differ?
4. How do the intimacy ratings of relationships differ in Japan and the United States?
5. How is uncertainty reduced in individualistic and collectivistic cultures?
6. How does self-disclosure differ in individualistic and collectivistic cultures?
7. How is effective communication different in individualistic and collectivistic cultures?
8. How do romantic relationships differ in individualistic and collectivistic cultures?
9. How do our expectations influence our interactions with strangers?
10. How does uncertainty reduction differ when we communicate with strangers and when we communicate with people who are familiar?
11. What factors influence our anxiety when we communicate with strangers?
12. How do linguistic and cultural knowledge contribute to developing relationships with strangers?
13. What factors contribute to African Americans' and Latino(a) Americans' satisfaction when communicating with European Americans?
14. How does perceived similarity contribute to developing relationships with strangers?
15. What are the major patterns of adjustment couples use when the spouses come from different cultures?

SUGGESTED READINGS

Gudykunst, W. B., & Ting-Toomey, S., with Chua, E. (1988). *Culture and interpersonal communication.* Beverly Hills, CA: Sage.

Gudykunst, W. B., Ting-Toomey, S., & Nishida, T. (Eds.). (1996). *Communication in personal relationships across cultures.* Thousand Oaks, CA: Sage.

Hatfield, E., & Rapson, R. (1995). *Love and sex: A cross-cultural perspective.* Boston: Allyn & Bacon.

Pogrebin, L. (1987). *Among friends.* New York: McGraw-Hill.

Rosenblatt, P., Karis, T., & Powell, R. (1995). *Multiracial couples.* Thousand Oaks, CA: Sage.

Ting-Toomey, S., & Korzenny, F. (Eds.). (1991). *Cross-cultural interpersonal communication.* Newbury Park, CA: Sage.

13

ADAPTING TO NEW CULTURES

Be bent, and you will remain straight.
Be vacant, and you will remain full.
Be worn, and you will remain new.

Lao Tsu

In the preceding chapter, we discussed various aspects of developing interpersonal relationships with strangers. We now focus our attention on strangers and examine how they adapt to a new and unfamiliar cultural environment and how their communication activities influence their adaptation. Conversely, we become strangers ourselves and must undergo the same adaptation process when we move to an unfamiliar culture. Usually this adaptation is associated with major cultural gaps that occur as a result of strangers' relocation from one society or subsection of a society to another, as well as with changes in their social environments.

Examples of situations that involve cross-cultural adaptation include temporary sojourning, long-term settling, subcultural mobility, and cultural change in society. While the first two involve geographical mobility, the other two do not. Examples of *in situ* changes requiring adaptation include such situations as starting at a university, making the transition from school to work, changing profession, marrying, divorcing, retiring, and aging. Also included are the processes of accepting major social and technological innovations such as the rapidly changing ethnic compositions of urban centers and the ubiquitous presence of the Internet and other computerized information-processing systems relaying many of the traditional ways of carrying out everyday life activities, from finding social support by "chatting" with others on topics of common interest to carrying out commercial transactions such as banking and purchasing goods. There are also situations in which strangers are incorporated into a new social system, including the military services, religious orders, residential universities, mental hospitals, rehabilitation centers, prisons, and concentration camps.

Situations that result from moving to new locations include those of international students, Peace Corps volunteers, foreign business personnel, missionaries, military personnel stationed in foreign countries, diplomats, and technical advisors or administrators, as well as the increasing number of individuals who seek employment or retire overseas for prolonged periods of time. There are also immigrants and refugees who have voluntarily or involuntarily moved to another country intending to start a new life on a more or less permanent basis. Also, individuals moving from a small, ethnically homogeneous rural town to a large metropolitan area with various ethnic communities, or vice versa, are in a situation that requires a degree of cross-cultural adaptation. International migration, whether for a long or a short term, represents a classic situation where the newly arrived strangers are required to face substantial challenges of uncertainty. Because of the relatively greater severity of cultural change, the experiences of immigrants, refugees, and sojourners provide us with comprehensive insights into the process of cross-cultural adaptation that can be extended to understanding other, less drastic adaptation situations.

The following examination, therefore, focuses on the adaptation process that takes place in the context of international migration and is based primarily on Y. Kim's theory that describes and explains the cross-cultural adaptation process from an interdisciplinary communication perspective (Y. Kim, 1988, 1995a, 1995b, 2001).

CROSS-CULTURAL ADAPTATION

Situations involving international migration and the motives for such migration vary widely (Berry, 1990; Berry & Sam, 1997; Furnham, 1988; Volkan, 1993). An abrupt and involuntary cultural transition, for instance, is experienced by refugees around the world who have left their homelands involuntarily due to war or natural disasters. Owing to the sudden nature of their departure, most refugees have little chance to prepare themselves for life in the host country. At least during the initial resettlement phase, many suffer from a deep psychological dislocation and sense of loss.

Even when the transition is made voluntarily, international migrants differ in their motivations to relocate and to make the host societies their "second homes." The motivation to adapt depends largely on the degree of permanence of the new residence. In the case of immigrants, they must reestablish their life conditions and attain permanent membership in the host society. They need to be concerned with their relationship to the new environment in the same way the members of the native population are. A peripheral contact with the new culture, in contrast, is typical of the situation of many sojourners. The reasons for a sojourn are often specifically to pursue a vocation, to obtain a degree, or merely to enhance one's prestige in the eyes of the folks back home. Such reasons may require less motivation to adapt to the host cultural system. International students, for example, can reduce their adaptation to the bare minimum as they pursue a degree by confining their social contact to fellow students from the home country. Similarly, many military personnel and their families in foreign countries may perceive less of a need to adapt to the host culture since their stay is only temporary and their contacts are confined largely to the military base.

Regardless of the circumstantial and motivational variations, every stranger in a new environment must respond to the challenges of finding ways to function in that environment. Every stranger must undergo a process of adaptation that makes such functioning possible.

The Process of Adaptation

Throughout the socialization process, we learn and acquire "all the factors and processes which make one human being fit to live in the company of others" (Kelvin, 1970, p. 270). Socialization involves conditioning and programming in the basic processes of communication, including decoding (perceptual and cognitive) patterns and encoding (verbal and nonverbal) training. The form of this training depends on the particular culture and is embedded in the process of *enculturation,* in which the forms for expressing and comprehending basic social behavior are internalized from the teachings of early "significant others," with a strong emotional overtone and identification. The process of socialization provides children with an understanding of their world and the culturally patterned modes of responding to it. The familiar culture, then, is the "home world," which is associated closely with the family or significant others. An unfamiliar culture, in contrast, is one that is out of harmony with one's basic understanding of self and reality.

When strangers who are socialized in this manner move into a new and unfamiliar culture and interact with it, the process of resocialization, or *acculturation,* occurs. Gradually, strangers begin to detect similarities and differences within the new surroundings. They become acquainted with and adopt some of the norms and values of salient reference groups in the host society. As acculturation takes place, however, some unlearning of old cultural patterns occurs as well, at least in the sense that new responses are adopted in situations that previously would have evoked different ones. This unlearning of the original cultural habits is called *deculturation.* As the dynamic interplay of acculturation and deculturation continues, newcomers undergo a cross-cultural adaptation process. Of course, a change in their basic values is extremely difficult, slow, and rare. As Brim (in Brim & Wheeler, 1966) suggests, more common adaptive changes in strangers take place in more superficial areas, such as the overt role behaviors expected or required at workplaces. Yet a person cannot be forced to accept and appreciate the values underlying such role behaviors. Goffman (1961) also doubts whether true resocialization occurs in practice even in a "total institution" such as a prison.

Even with the limit in acculturative changes, however, a new culture does have a substantial impact on the psychological and social behaviors of strangers. Through group support, institutional legitimization of the new identity, and the presence of new significant others to replace those of childhood, strangers may adopt the cultural patterns of the host society to a significant degree. Even then, the acculturative change is accomplished only slowly and in stages. It normally brings conflict, a struggle between the desire to retain old customs and keep the original cultural identity on the one hand and the desire to adopt new ways to seek harmony with the changed milieu on the other hand (Boekestijn, 1988). This conflict is, in essence, between the need for acculturation and the resistance to deculturation, the push of the new culture and the pull of the old, and the existing conditions inside the strangers and the demands of the external environment. It is, then, a conflict that is not unlike the experiences of members of the older generations who often find themselves in the situation of "involuntary immigrants from the past to the present" (Mead, 1963).

Adaptation and Change

The core of cross-cultural adaptation, therefore, is change. Unlike the native-born members of the host society, who often attempt to change and succeed in changing portions of the environment to better suit their needs, strangers are almost exclusive bearers of the burden of making adjustments themselves. The power of individual strangers to change the host environment is minuscule, at least in the short run, compared to the pervasive influence of the host culture on them. Clearly, a reason for the essentially one-sided change is the diffference between the size of the population sharing a given stranger's original culture and that of the population sharing the host culture. To the extent that the dominant power of the host culture controls the daily survival and functioning of strangers, it presents a coercive pressure on them to adapt.

The direction of acculturative change in strangers is toward *assimilation,* that is, a state of a high degree of acculturation into the host milieu and a high degree of deculturation of the original culture. It is a state that reflects a maximum convergence of strangers' internal conditions with those of the natives and a minimum maintenance of the original cultural habits. Studies of historical change in immigrant communities have demonstrated the long-term assimilative trend of the cross-cultural adaptation process, particularly across generations (e.g., Y. Kim, 1980, 1990; McGuire & McDermott, 1988; Subervi-Velez, 1986; Szalay & Inn, 1988; Ward, Kennedy, & Kojima, 1998). A study by the American Jewish Committee, for example, shows a significant increase in the members' merging into non-Jewish organizations and a substantial decrease in their Jewish identification (Zweigenhaft, 1979–1980). Masuda (1970) demonstrates that ethnic identification among Japanese Americans in the United States shows a gradual decrease from the first generation to the third.

As summarized in Figure 13.1, then, the cross-cultural adaptation process involves a continuous interplay of deculturation and acculturation that brings about change in strangers in the direction of assimilation, the highest degree of adaptation theoreticially conceivable. It is that process by which strangers are resocialized into a new culture so as to attain an increasing compatibility and functional fitness. For most people, even for natives, complete adaptation is a lifetime goal, and individuals vary in the degree of adaptation achieved. The adaptation of strangers, therefore, properly should be thought of as falling at some point on a continuum ranging from minimally adapted to maximally adapted.

FIGURE 13.1
Key terms associated with cross-cultural adaptation
(*Source:* Y. Kim, 2001, p. 53).

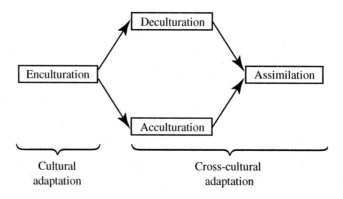

THE CENTRALITY OF COMMUNICATION

Underlying the adaptation process described above is the communication process: Adaptation occurs in and through communication. Just as natives have acquired their cultural patterns through interaction with others, strangers over time acquire the new cultural patterns by participating in the host communication activities. Conversely, strangers' communication patterns reveal their adaptation. Through prolonged and varied experiences in communication, strangers gradually learn and internalize the symbols and practices of the host communication system. The acquired communicative capabilities, in turn, serve as a set of adaptive tools that help strangers satisfy their personal and social needs. Through effective communication, strangers are able to increase control over their own behavior and over the host environment.

Because communication, by definition, involves interaction of the person and the environment, we can examine the role of strangers' communication in the adaptation process in terms of two interrelated processes: personal (or intrapersonal) communication and social communication.

Personal Communication

Personal (or intrapersonal) communication refers to the three interrelated psychological processes—cognitive, affective, and operational—by which we organize ourselves in a sociocultural milieu. Through personal communication, we develop ways of understanding and responding to our environment. As Ruben (1975) notes, "Personal communication is thought of as sensing, making sense, or acting toward the objects and people in one's milieu. It is the process by which the individual informationally fits himself [or herself] into (adapts and adapts to) his [or her] environment" (pp. 168–169).

In the context of cross-cultural adaptation, personal communication can be viewed as the process of organizing adaptive experiences into identifiable cognitive, affective, and operational patterns that are consistent or compatible with the cultural patterns of the host environment. Individual strangers' personal communication patterns, thus, can be conceived in terms of their *host communication competence,* that is, the ability to communicate in ways that are consistent with the communication codes, rules, and practices operating in the host culture. As strangers develop their host communication competence, they increasingly are empowered to participate in the host cultural processes with fidelity and effectiveness. The level of strangers' host communication competence at a given time, in turn, should reflect their overall adaptation level, while the lack of such competence manifests itself in various forms of "miscommunication" on the part of strangers (Banks, Gao, & Baker, 1991; Gass & Varonis, 1991).

The Cognitive Process   One of the most fundamental adaptive changes in personal communication (or host communication competence) occurs in the cognitive structure through which strangers process information from the environment. Communication between strangers and hosts is successful to the extent that the strangers are able to comprehend the categorizing system of the hosts and match their own cognitive activities to those of the hosts.

Because of their unfamiliarity with the cognitive process of the host culture, strangers frequently find the mindset of the natives difficult to understand. Their difficulty stems from the fact that, particularly during the initial phases of adaptation, their perceptions of the host environment are simplistic. Gross stereotypes are salient in strangers' perception of the host cultural patterns. The "thinking-as-usual," as we may call it, often becomes unworkable in dealing with the host environment since strangers do not share the common underlying assumptions of the native population. The uncertainty and the accompanying anxiety are two of the most basic challenges that confront strangers. In Schuetz's (1944) words,

> the cultural pattern of the approached group is to the stranger not a shelter but a field of adventure, not a matter of course but a questionable topic of investigation, not an instrument for disentangling problematic situations but a problematic situation itself and one hard to master. (p. 108)

Gudykunst and associates (Gao & Gudykunst, 1990; Gudykunst, 1988, 1995; Gudykunst & Hammer, 1988b; Gudykunst & Sudweeks, 1992) have identified these two factors as central to explaining intercultural communication effectiveness in general and cross-cultural adaptation in particular.

To the extent that culture is a learned phenomenon, however, strangers can increase their understanding of the host cognitive system. Cultural learning enables them to recognize their cognitive structures as distinct from those of the host culture and increase their ability in "perspective taking" (Fogel, 1979) and to develop a mental "coorientation relation" with members of the host society (H. S. Kim, 1986; Pearce & Stamm, 1973). Empirical data from Y. Kim's study (1977a) of Korean immigrants suggest that as the strangers' cultural knowledge becomes increasingly extensive, accurate, and refined, their cognitive structure in perceiving the host culture also becomes more discriminating and integrative. The increased cognitive complexity, in turn, has been found to lead to a greater capacity to understand the host culture and seek information from appropriate sources (Yum, 1982).

The Affective Process   Over time, strangers learn to acquire not only cognitive complexity but also the affective patterns of the host culture. The affective cultural patterns are embodied in the common emotional orientations, aesthetic sensibilities, motivational drives, attitudes, and values held by the native members of the host society. Taft (1977) identifies this affective process as the "dynamic" aspect of culture:

> There are certain universal human needs and modes of functioning that must be satisfied in all cultures. In broad terms, these needs refer to the maintenance of life processes, the need to maintain a structural society to enhance as well as regulate social relationships, and to provide for the self-expressive needs of individuals. While these needs are universal, each culture prescribes different models for satisfying them. (p. 134)

Because all personal and social activities in the host society involve some measure of affective experiences, strangers must understand and participate in these activities not only intellectually but also affectively. Mansell (1981) stresses this point by focusing on the fulfillment of aesthetic needs in an alien culture:

> The concept of aesthetic awareness is linked with ineffable, intuitive feelings of appreciation and celebration. This form of awareness creates a consciousness which transforms individuals' perceptions of the world and imparts a sense of unity between self and surrounding. . . . It is in this transformative mode of experiencing that many people create access to the momentary peaks of fulfillment which make life meaningful. (p. 99)

Needs of this sort are often difficult to gratify within an unfamiliar culture. Many newly arrived strangers experience a decline in emotional well-being as they find themselves unable to engage fully in the new aesthetic milieu (Ying & Liese, 1991). One way strangers compensate for this psychological difficulty is by withdrawing from the host nationals and affiliating with other conationals or by communicating with their families and friends back home. In fact, ethnic communities commonly serve as a refuge for emotionally and aesthetically needy immigrants by offering a range of familiar cultural elements—from food, language, music, and entertainment to activities of socializing through churches and social clubs. Yet only when the affective process is integrated successfully with the cognitive process do strangers achieve an adequate psychological and social orientation that enables them to appreciate and participate in the natives' experiences of joy, hope, and excitement, as well as their anger, pain, and disappointment.

The Operational Process   What is ultimately required of strangers in the host society is the operational (or behavioral) ability that enables them to display behaviors that are in accordance with the host cultural norms (Ruben, 1976; Ruben & Kealey, 1979). Doing so requires a capacity to act and react appropriately in various social situations in addition to the relevant cognitive and affective abilities. Taft (1977) describes such behavioral capacity in terms of two types of "skills": technical and social. *Technical skills* include basic practical skills such as language skills, job skills, academic skills, and others that are essential to performing one's particular social role. A study of Japanese sojourners in the United States (Diggs & Murphy, 1991), for example, shows that the inability to drive a car is one of the significant factors that correlated with the subjects' level of satisfaction. *Social skills* are more general and are crucial to all social interactions in that they encompass a wide range of capabilities, from initiating a simple conversation and adjusting to the behavioral patterns of different interaction parterns to developing and solidifying a relationship and managing conflicts.

Strangers who are competent in technical skills may, nonetheless, be deficient in social skills. Even the natives of a culture who perform various social roles naturally often are unable to explain the specific patterns involved in certain situations. Strangers, therefore, need to formulate "action plans" before dealing with the situations they face. American businesspeople visiting a Japanese company, for example, must rely on their own understanding of the way Japanese business is conducted and figure out how to behave in performing the role of a business negotiator.

Through trial and error, and through cumulative acquisition of the cognitive and affective orientations of the host culture, strangers can and do increase their social skills over time to enact appropriate and effective behaviors. Their action plans gradually become refined and integrated into sequences that can be used in a relatively automatic form. Well-adapted strangers can perform the required social roles in accordance with the host cultural norms without having to formulate a mental plan of action. As they internalize many of the culturally patterned behaviors, they are able to achieve harmonious interpersonal synchronization in their interactions with the natives (Y. Kim, 1992, 1993). Insofar as these automatic actions are executed successfully, strangers experience satisfaction and success in carrying out their daily activities.

The operational skills, together with the the cognitive and affective orientations, constitute the overall host communication competence. As previously noted, this competence is the very capacity of a stranger to cope with various challenges of the new life, to achieve a cohesive functional relationship with the host society, and to enjoy participating in the emotional/aesthetic experiences of host nationals. Mastery of host communication competence, then, is key to achieving full membership in the host communication processes.

Social Communication

Personal communication, or host communication competence, is linked to social communication in a reciprocal relationship. Strangers interacting with local people have opportunities to learn about the host communication system and assess their own cognitive, affective, and behavioral patterns. Their improved communication competence, in turn, increases the likelihood of success in subsequent encounters. Participation in the host social communication processes can take many forms—from simple observations of people on the street or reading about people and events in newspapers and magazines to engaging actively in face-to-face encounters. Broadly, we will examine the various forms of social communication in two categories: *interpersonal communication* and *mass communication*. Interpersonal communication occurs through direct face-to-face contact or via various forms of communication channels, such as telephone calls, letters, e-mails, and faxes. Mass communication, in contrast, is a more generalized form of social communication by which people interact with their environment without direct involvement with any particular person. Individuals participate in mass communication processes through various media, such as radio, television, newspapers, magazines, movies, theaters, museums, and lectures, as well as the Internet and audiotapes and videotapes, among others.

Interpersonal Communication Communication in interpersonal contact situations is central to life. As Fogel (1993) argues, individuals develop and mature psychologically and socially through their relationships with others. Communication in this context is particularly vital to the cultivation of cognitive, affective, and operational capabilities. Through formal and informal contacts and relationships, strangers also can find social support in attempting to handle difficulties and opportunities for finding additional contacts (Adelman, 1988; Jou & Fukada, 1995; McPherson & Popielarz, 1991; Pescosolido, 1992; Wellman, 1992). At the same time, interpersonal networks exert social control by controlling the language strangers must use and conveying implicit or explicit messages of social approval and disapproval (Heckathorn, 1990; Ho & Sung, 1990; Milroy, 1980).

One can infer strangers' level of adaptation from their interpersonal communication activities involved in the relationships they have at a given time. An immigrant with a mainly ethnic relational network, for example, tends to be less adapted and probably less competent in the host communication system than someone whose associates are primarily members of the host society. Also, the degree of intimacy in the relationships developed with members of the host society is an important indicator of strangers' host communication competence.

Considerable research evidence exists to link strangers' adaptation levels and their interpersonal relationship patterns. Studies of international students and visitors indicate a positive association between the number of natives in strangers' relational networks and strangers' positive feelings toward the host society at large. Also, the degree of interpersonal involvement with host nationals has been found to be an important indicator of sojourners' cognitive learning. Selltiz and her associates (1963), for example, report that international students in the United States who associate extensively with and form close friendships with host nationals score higher on measures of adjustment than do those who have less association with host nationals or do not have host friends. In Morris' (1960) study, students who are high on measures of social relations with host nationals score high on an index of satisfaction with various aspects of their experience in the host country (see also Coelho, 1958; Pool, 1965).

A similar linkage between interpersonal communication and elements of host communication competence is observed in studies of long-term settlers in the United States and elsewhere (e.g., Y. Kim, 1976, 1977a, 1979a, 1980, 1989, 1990; Leslie, 1992; Oehlkers, 1991; Searle & Ward, 1990; Shah, 1991; Ward, Okura, Kennedy, & Kojima, 1998). A consistent conclusion from these studies is a positive relationship of participation in host interpersonal communication activities to other aspects of adaptation, such as variables of host communication competence and psychological health. Wen (1976), in a study of Chinese immigrants, observes that the degree of mental illness tends to vary with the degree of social isolation from the host culture. Yum's (1982) study of Korean immigrants in Hawaii suggests that the immigrants' ability to acquire information necessary for their functioning in the United States is influenced positively by their "communication diversity," or the level of integration of Hawaiians in the immigrants' information sources. In addition, a study of Native Americans in Oklahoma (Y. Kim, Lujan, & Dixon, 1998) indicates that the subjects' psychological adaptation in the predominantly European American environment is closely linked to the level of inclusion of non-Native American acquaintances and friends.

With respect to *intraethnic communication* activities, researchers generally agree that extensive and prolonged ethnic involvements impede the adaptation process in the long run. This observation is made despite the fact that the ethnic community often plays a vital role in assisting in the initial stages of adaptation of newly arrived strangers. In many ethnic communities in the United States, new arrivals often find necessary emotional and social support and information from their family members, relatives, and other compatriots (Mortland & Ledgerwood, 1988). Y. Kim's studies of Korean immigrants (1977a, 1977b, 1978a) and Indochinese refugees (1979a, 1980,

1990) have shown the subjects' heavy reliance on ethnic ties during the first several years in the United States, even though the numbers of both ethnic and host acquaintances tend to increase simultaneously during this period. Further supporting the adaptation-retarding long-term effect of extensive involvement in ethnic communication activities are the findings from Bates's (1994) study of Asian immigrants; Leslie's (1992) study of Central American immigrants; Hsu, Grant, and Huang's (1993) study of foreign students; Shah's (1991) study of Asian Indians; and Okazaki-Luff's study (1991) of Japanese sojourners. This insulating effect has been found to be even stronger when the strangers' ethnic ties consist primarily of coethnics who are themselves poorly adapted (Hsu, Grant, & Huang, 1993).

On the basis of these and related research findings, Y. Kim (1988, 1995a, 2001) postulates that strangers' interpersonal networks change over time from a primarily intraethnic composition to an increasing integration of ties with host nationals. In this regard, the role of involvement with persons from the same culture is considered to promote ethnicity and, in the long run, slow adaptation in the host society. This conclusion concurs with the observation of Shibutani and Kwan (1965) that "to the extent that . . . a minority group participated in different sets of communication channels, they develop different perspectives and have difficulty in understanding each other" (p. 582). Broom and Kitsuse (1955) similarly argue that "a large part of the acculturation experience of the members of an ethnic group may be circumscribed by the ethnic community" (p. 45).

Mass Communication   Many studies of immigrants in the United States have shown that, along with the development of nonethnic interpersonal ties, the use of the mass media of the host society increases over time and that such increased media use facilitates the adaptation process (e.g., Hong, 1980; Kapoor & Williams, 1979; J. Kim, 1980; J. Kim, Lee, & Jeong, 1982; Y. Kim, 1977a, 1977b, 1978a, 1980, 1990; Pedone, 1980; Subervi-Velez, 1986; Walker, 1993; Yang, 1988). Participation in the host mass communication processes enables strangers to learn about a broader spectrum of the elements of the host culture not easily discernible from the immediate environment. In transmitting messages that reflect aspirations, historical forces, myths, work and play, and specific issues and events, the mass media explicitly and implicitly convey societal values, norms, and traditional perspectives for interpreting the larger environment.

Exposure to information-oriented media messages such as news items, analyses of social issues, and documentaries is particularly facilitative of stgrangers' adaptation, compared with exposure to primarily entertainment-oriented messages (J. Kim, 1982; Y. Kim, 1976, 1979a). The overall adaptation function of mass communication is relatively more limited than that of interpersonal channels (Y. Kim, 1976, 1979a). This limitation is due to the often stereotypical, undifferentiated images of the host culture that the mass media depict (G. Miller, 1988). In addition, interpersonal communication activities (particularly those that take place in direct face-to-face encounters) provide strangers with unsolicited feedback messages that subtly, yet powerfully, let the strangers recognize inadequacies in their behaviors.

The intensity inherent in many face-to-face communication situations may be too stressful to strangers poorly equipped in host communication competence. They may shy away from participating in direct encounters with the natives. Accordingly, mass media provide alternative, less stressful channels of communication through which strangers with inadequate communication competence can absorb some elements of the host culture.

Along with the mass media of the host society, *ethnic media* are available to most strangers, including newspapers, magazines, audiotapes, and videotaped television programs and movies imported from the home country. Some of them may be available on the Internet. Many large ethnic communities in the United States also offer locally produced newspapers, radio programs, and television programs (S. Miller, 1987; Suverbi-Velez, 1986). Research has shown consistently that in direct contrast to the increasing use of the host mass media over time, the level of interest in and the perceived utility of ethnic media decrease as strangers become familiar with the host language and culture.

The processes of personal and social communication discussed above are summarized in Figure 13.2. Communication processes are essential and central to the cross-cultural adaptation process. Just as native-born persons undergo the enculturation process through communication, strangers undergo the deculturation-acculturation interplay. In this process, strangers acquire and internalize some of the cognitive, affective, and behavioral

FIGURE 13.2
Interrelated processes of personal and social communication
(*Source:* Y. Kim, 2001, p. 143).

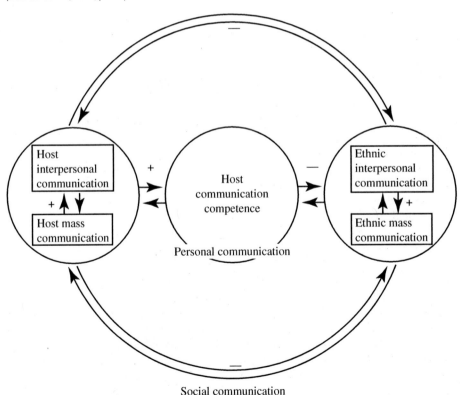

communication patterns operating in the host society. The acquired host communication competence, in turn, facilitates their participation in the host social communication processes, both interpersonally and via the mass media. Strangers may benefit from the interpersonal and mass communication activities within their ethnic communities; prolonged and excessive ethnic communication activities are likely to hinder their long-term success in adapting to the host society at large.

THE ROLE OF PREDISPOSITION AND ENVIRONMENT

Strangers respond differently to a new cultural environment in terms of their prior experiences, accepting what promises to be rewarding and rejecting what seems to be unworkable or disadvantageous. At the same time, strangers' experiences are conditioned further by the host environment. The nature of the dynamic interaction between personal factors and environmental factors shapes the patterns of subsequent adaptive changes in strangers.

Predisposition

One of the predispositional factors that need to be considered in understanding strangers' adaptation is the degree of *ethnic proximity* (or distance), that is, the overall similarity (or difference) and compatibility (or incompatibility) between their ethnicity and the dominant ethnicity in the host society. To the extent that the original ethnic characteristics coincide with those of the host nationals, fewer potential barriers are expected. The larger the disparity between the two, the more difficulty strangers are likely to face. Differences in physical appearance, language, verbal and nonverbal behaviors, rules and norms of social engagement, and economic and political ideology, as well as religious beliefs, ceremonies, and rituals, are some of the major ethnicity gaps to be overcome in the adaptation process. Of particular importance is the degree of *salience* of noticeable "ethnic markers," including distinct speech patterns and physical characteristics (e.g., skin color, facial features, and physique). Such markers often add to the overall "foreignness" of strangers, playing a favorable or unfavorable role in the strangers' subsequent communication with host nationals. An Irish immigrant in the United States, for example, is likely to present less psychological distance to native-born North Americans than someone from India. Accordingly, Lysgaard (1955) and Sewell and Davidsen (1961) describe Scandinavian students as having little difficulty in adapting to life in the United States, while Lambert and Bressler (1956) and Bennett, Passin, and McKnight (1958) report considerable difficulty on the part of students from India and Japan, respectively. Similar results are reported by Furnham and Bochner (1982) for international students in England.

Along with ethnicity, the *personality* of individual strangers plays an important role in their adaptation. Everyone possesses a set of certain basic personality dispositions that are enduring but also adaptive. Personality patterns make all individuals unique, and such uniquenesses reveal themselves dramatically when a person is struggling to adapt to a new environment. When strong prejudice or actual enmity exists in the host society toward a particular ethnic group, some members of that group are able to win a position of respect and goodwill while others respond with hostility and withdrawal.

Various personality attributes have been observed in research to be associated with adaptation. Among such attributes are tolerance for ambiguity and risk taking (Fiske & Maddi, 1961), gregariousness (Bradburn, 1969), an internal locus of control (Johnson & Sarason, 1978; Yum, 1988), and a hardy or resilient personality (Quisumbing, 1982). Yum (1988), for example, reports a finding that immigrants' internal locus of control (the tendency to place the responsibility for events within themselves) is associated positively with the extent to which they develop host national acquaintances. In addition, characteristics that reflect extroversion, a positive orientation, respect for people in general, and self-control have been identified as contributing to effective adaptation in the new culture.

These and related personal attributes share considerable semantic redundancy and are consolidated by Y. Kim (1988, 1995a, 2001) into three higher-level constructs: openness, strength, and positivity. *Openness* as a personality construct serves as the inclusive generic baseline for specific attributes such as flexibility, open-mindedness, tolerance for ambiguity, gregariousness, optimism, and extroversion. *Strength* represents concepts of narrower meanings, such as an internal locus of control, tolerance for ambiguity, persistence, hardiness, resourcefulness, and self-confidence. Both openness and strength of personality are closely associated with the third adaptive personality characteristic, positivity—an affirmative and optimistic outlook, or the internal capacity to defy negative predictions (Dean & Popp, 1990). Strangers with a positive personality can better endure many stressful encounters with a belief that things will turn out as they should. It is a kind of idealism—a belief in possibilities and a faith in the goodness of life and people in general—as opposed to being overcome by unwarranted defeatist cynicism. Positivity thus encourages acceptance of others despite differences and is expressed in the form of self-esteem, self-trust, or "general self-efficacy" (Harrison, Chadwick, & Scales, 1996).

Together, openness, strength, and positivity present a psychological profile of individuals who possess inner resources with which to facilitate the adaptation process. Strangers who are open, strong, and positive are less likely to give up easily and more likely to take risks willingly under challenging situations in the host environment. They are better equipped to work toward developing host communication competence as they continually seek new ways to handle their life activities. In doing so, they are better able to make necessary adjustments in themselves. A serious lack of these personality attributes, in contrast, would handicap their adaptive capacity by serving as a self-imposed barrier against adaptation.

In addition to the factors of personality and ethnicity, the adaptive potential of strangers is also a matter of *preparedness* for change prior to entering the new environment (Y. Kim, 1976, 1977a, 1988, 1995a, 2001). Strangers move to a new environment with differing levels of realism in their expectations and knowledge about it (Brabant, Palmer, & Gramling, 1990). Many cross-cultural training and orientation programs, thus, emphasize familiarizing trainees with the host culture (Brislin & Yoshida, 1994; Landis & Brislin, 1983). Peace Corps volunteers are among the best prepared for cross-cultural adaptation in that they go through an intensive screening process and extensive language and cultural training before being given an overseas assignment. Sewell and Davidsen (1961) have found that the guidance international students receive prior to coming to the United States positively influences their academic adjustment and satisfaction with the sojourn.

Certain demographic characteristics also tend to increase strangers' adaptive potential. In studies of immigrants, *age* is considered an element that influences subsequent adaptation. The older strangers are, the greater the difficulty they experience in adapting to a new culture and the slower they are in acquiring new cultural patterns (Kim, 1976, 1977a; Rogler et al., 1980; Szapocznik & Kurtines, 1980; Szapocznik, Kurtines, & Fernandez, 1980; Searle & Ward, 1990). This inverse relationship between age and adaptation can be attributed to the greater rigidity (or lesser openness) of the personality structure that tends to grow as we get older.

Another important demographic factor is the *educational level* of strangers prior to migration. Education, regardless of its cultural context, appears to expand our mental capacity for new learning and for the challenges of life in general. In many cases, strangers' education in the home country includes training in the language of the host country, which provides added leverage for building communication competencies after moving into the new system (Y. Kim, 1976, 1977a, 1980; Yum, 1982).

Environment

The adaptation process is influenced not only by strangers' adaptive predisposition but also by the conditions existing or developing in the host society (Y. Kim, 1979c, 1988, 1995a, 1995b, 2001). The adaptation process involves an interactive "push and pull" between the strangers and the environment. The adaptation experiences of two very similar persons may differ in two different environments.

The environment influences strangers' adaptation by defining the "interaction potential," that is, the degree of opportunity provided to strangers by the immediate physical and social environment (Y. Kim, 1976, 1977a; Y. Kim, Lujan, & Dixon, 1998). Ordinarily, if a situation is to have any interaction potential at all, it must provide for physical proximity. Beyond this basic requirement, social contexts differ greatly in interaction potential. People in the United States, for example, usually do not engage in extensive conversation with strangers sitting next to them in the subway or on a bus. In contrast, strangers who attend local church services or are assigned to work with colleagues on a collaborative task soon cease to be unknown. Such organized social contexts are high in interaction potential, almost demanding communication of some sort and making it easy to go beyond superficial exchanges if strangers wish to do so.

Strangers whose living arrangements offer little interaction potential are likely to have relatively fewer interactions with host nationals. Ting-Toomey (1981), in her study of Chinese American college students, reports that the students' friendship formation is influenced significantly by the availability of European Americans within the school environment. Similarly, U.S. military personnel who live in a predominantly military town have limited access to local people in their daily activities. Peace Corps volunteers, in contrast, whose primary responsibility is to help local residents improve their health practices, have a greater interaction potential and develop more meaningful interpersonal relationships with the host nationals.

The interaction potential for strangers depends on the *receptivity* of the host society toward them (Y. Kim, 1988, 1995a, 1995b, 2001). Receptivity refers to the attitude present in the host environment that shows openness toward and acceptance of strangers. Strong hostility against a group minimizes the receptivity of the host society toward individual members of that group, making communication more difficult for them. The attitudes of the native population toward a specific group may be due to long-standing historical animosity. New developments in international relationships may change a traditionally held attitude between groups abruptly, as has been the case in the increased openness among Americans toward Russians.

Sometimes the attitude or sentiment of the host society toward an outside group may be influenced by its own domestic economic or political situation, such as a high unemployment rate or surging nationalistic sentiment. Mass media play a particularly important role in shaping the emotional mood of the host society toward other cultural groups. Media news coverage of various international and domestic events tends to influence public opinion concerning certain groups. Once a societal climate is developed, some unusual situations may arise in the host society regarding specific groups of strangers, such as segregation in housing, discrimination in employment, and isolation by exclusion from intimate and sympathetic social contacts. These and other discriminatory practices in the host environment can make the already difficult adaptation of strangers even more trying.

The adaptation process of strangers is influenced further by the degree of *conformity pressure* the host society exerts on strangers (Y. Kim, 1988, 1995a, 2001). The extent to which the host society expects strangers to conform to its existing cultural norms and values varies from society to society. Strangers entering a totalitarian society or one that follows extreme ideological orthodoxy may be forced to conform rapidly to assigned roles that cover many aspects of their daily activities. Relatively freer and more pluralistic societies such as the United States, in contrast, allow a greater latitude or tolerance for cultural differences.

A similar observation can be made about the differences in the cultural rigidity of the small rural town and the openness of the large metropolitan cultural milieu toward diverse lifestyles. The heterogeneous and cosmopolitan cultural milieu of the metropolitan area exhibits greater freedom for new and different elements. One cannot point to this or that particular type of relationship and behavior as forming the basis of the social and cultural system of a city since many types contribute to this end, no one of which may be excluded. In contrast, the presence of cultural strangers can be a matter of keen interest in villages, and the strangers may be subjected to close scrutiny. If strangers are to be accepted by the villagers, they are likely to find it hard not to learn and conform to the accepted norms and practices of the local people.

The degree to which a given host environment extends receptivity to and exerts conformity pressure on a stranger is influenced strongly by *the strength of the stranger's ethnic group* relative to the host environment at large (Y. Kim, 1995a, 2001). An insight into ethnic group strength has been provided by a number of investigators, such as the sociologists Clarke and Obler (1976), who describe ethnic communities developing from the stages of initial economic adjustment and community building to the subsequent stage of aggressive self-assertion and promotion of identity. An additional insight has been offered in theories of "institutional completeness" (Breton, 1964, 1991; Goldenberg & Haines, 1992) and of ethnolinguistic vitality and intergroup behavior (Giles & Johnson, 1987). These theories point to the ecological conditions of a strong ethnic group and its influence on the psychology and communication behavior of its individual members.

The strength of an ethnic group tends to discourage strangers' development of host communication competence and participation in host social communication processes. Inglis and Gudykunst (1982) have examined the interpersonal communication patterns of Korean immigrants in the Hartford, Connecticut, area and compared them with the findings from Y. Kim's (1976, 1977a, 1977b) studies of the same group in the Chicago area. The comparison shows a significant difference between the two groups' interactions with other Koreans. Members of the smaller and less organized Hartford-area Korean community are found to have far fewer Korean acquaintances than do those in the more established Chicago-area Korean community, where there is an extensive system of ethnic organizations and communication activities. A study of Korean communities in southern California (Shim, 1994) has reported a similar ethnicity-reinforcing function of the immigrants' usage of Korean newspapers.

ADAPTATION AND PSYCHOLOGICAL HEALTH

A healthy psychological state involves a dynamic fitting of parts of the internal system and external realities, that is, an attainment of internal harmony and a meaningful relationship to the outside world. The psychological health of strangers is associated directly with their ability to communicate and their functional fitness in the new environment. Thayer (1968) explains that

> successful communication with self and others implies correction by others as well as self-correction. In such a continuous process, up-to-date information about the self, the world, and the relationship of the self to the world leads to the acquisition of appropriate techniques, and eventually increases the individual's chances of mastery of life. Successful communication therefore becomes synonymous with adaptation and life. (p. 18)

The internal and external congruence is difficult for strangers to achieve initially. Newly arrived strangers experience a substantial amount of communication breakdown in the host environment because they are poorly equipped with a cohesively developed system of host communication competence. One or more of the cognitive, affective, and operational elements of their host communication competence may be lacking, while others may be strong. Some strangers may be quite knowledgeable about the host culture but may find it almost impossible to understand and share many of the aesthetic sensibilities. Others may be adequately skilled in performing social roles but may find some of the operant values in their role performances disagreeable. Yet others may be sufficiently capable of participating in the emotional and aesthetic experiences of the natives but may be unable to express such experiences adequately through verbal and nonverbal performances.

The lack of host communication competence accounts for many of the psychological problems associated with strangers' maladaptation, including a negative self-image, low self-esteem, low morale, social isolation, dissatisfaction with the life in the host society, and the frustration of being a helpless "victim" of circumstances (Hedge, 1998) and related distresses such as depression (Berry, 1990; Dyal & Dyal, 1981; Furnham & Bochner, 1986; Hurh & K. Kim, 1990; Searle & Ward, 1990). Strangers' psychological distress can be manifested further in the form of hostility and aggression toward the host environment. As suggested in the "frustration-aggression hypothesis"

(Zajonc, 1952), strangers who face a need to conform and feel blocked by the host society may respond to such pressure by aggressively devaluating the host society.

In contrast, achievement of psychological health is reflected in strangers' smooth and effective dealings with the host environment. As Erikson (1969) notes, a "healthy personality" requires the ability "to perceive the world and himself [or herself] correctly" (p. 31). For strangers to be psychologically healthy, they must concentrate on improving their host communication competence and participate in local interpersonal and mass communication processes.

Studies of immigrants and sojourners have documented a close link between indicators of strangers' psychological health (such as satisfaction and happiness) and stress (such as alienation), their host communication competence, and their social communication activities, particularly those within interpersonal networks (e.g., Arevalo, 1987; Nishida, 1985; Searle & Ward, 1990; van Oudenhoven & Eisses, 1998; Ward et al., 1998). Indeed, most strangers are able to achieve, over time, a higher level of internal integration—a sense of inner cohesion and confidence (Church, 1982; Nishida, 1985). Even those who interact with the natives with the intention of confining themselves to only superficial relationships are likely to see their experience of the host environment improve at least minimally "in spite of themselves" (p. 150).

SUMMARY

The process of adapting to a new and unfamiliar culture is essentially a journey of personal change in which strangers who are socialized in one culture (enculturation) cultivate an inroad into another culture. Once strangers enter the new environment, the adaptation process is set in motion and will continue as long as they stay in direct contact with that environment. Gradually and imperceptibly, strangers acquire and internalize new learning (acculturation) as well as suspend and unlearn some of the old practices (deculturation) to move in the direction of increased functional fitness and ultimately a state of assimilation in the host society in the case of long-term resettlers such as immigrants. At the heart of the adaptation process lies the communication activities linking newcomers to the new environment. In turn, strangers' cognitive, affective, and operational capacity to communicate (host communication competence) enables them to partake in various social communication processes (interpersonal and mass communication) of the host society.

Given the centrality of personal and social communication processes in cross-cultural adaptation, strangers must recognize that each person's adaptation experiences are unique to some extent. The quantity and the quality of individual strangers' communicative relationships with the host environment are influenced by the interplay of factors attributable to both the strangers and the conditions of the environment. We can predict that those strangers who possess an ethnic (physical, linguistic, and cultural) background similar to the mainstream ethnicity of the host society, who are familiar with the host language and culture prior to moving, and whose personalities are characteristically open, strong, and positive are more likely to be successful in the adaptation process. Also, those who are better educated and younger find it easier to adapt to a new environment. If all other factors are equal, the strangers are likely to be better adapted in an environment that provides greater receptivity toward them but, at the same time, exerts a greater conformity pressure on them. Strangers, however, are less likely to feel the conformity pressure from the host environment when their own ethnic communities have a strong presence in the host society with a highly organized ethnic communication system and exert their own conformity pressure on their members.

The cross-cultural adaptation process is seldom a smooth and easy process. Yet it is a process that strangers must undertake if they are to carry on their life activities in sync with the forces of the host milieu and attain a state of mind that is healthy and at ease.

STUDY QUESTIONS

1. Describe the various cross-cultural situations that require at least some level of cross-cultural adaptation.
2. Compare the situations identified above in terms of the relative degrees of strangers' adaptation that generally are expected to take place.
3. Define and compare the meanings of these key terms: *acculturation, adaptation, enculturation, deculturation,* and *assimilation.* How are these terms interrelated?
4. What role does personal communication, or host communication competence, play in the cross-cultural adaptation process? Explain the three processes of personal communication: cognitive, affective, and operational.
5. What role do the two social communication processes—interpersonal communication and mass communication—play in cross-cultural adaptation? What deliberate efforts can strangers make in each area to facilitate their cross-cultural adaptation?
6. How do strangers' active and prolonged communication activities within their ethnic communities affect their adaptation to the larger society?
7. What factors in individual strangers' predispositions facilitate or retard their communication and adaptation in the host society? How do these factors affect their communication behavior?
8. What are the factors in the host environment that facilitate or retard strangers' communication and adaptation? How do these environmental factors affect their communication behavior?
9. How is strangers' increased adaptation to the host environment related to their psychological health? Why?

SUGGESTED READINGS

Kim, Y. Y. (2001). *Becoming intercultural: An integrative theory of communication and cross-cultural adaptation.* Thousand Oaks, CA: Sage.

Liu, Z. (1984). *Two years in the melting pot.* San Francisco: China Books.

Miller, M. (1988). *Reflections on reentry after teaching in China* (Occasional Papers in Intercultural Learning No. 14). New York: AFS Center for the Study of Intercultural Learning.

Minatoya, L. (1992). *Talking to high monks in the snow: An Asian American odyssey.* New York: HarperCollins.

Torbiorn, I. (1982). *Living abroad.* New York: Wiley.

14

BECOMING
INTERCULTURAL

There is a tide in the affairs of men [or women]
which, taken at the flood, leads on to fortune. . . .
On such a sea we are now afloat,
and we must take the current when it serves,
or lose our ventures.

      Julius Caesar, William Shakespeare

We live in a "world of simultaneous events and overall awareness" (McLuhan, 1962, p. 40). Through remarkable advancements in communications technology, we constantly are exposed to international affairs. What happens in a small nation anywhere in the world can be, directly and indirectly, a significant factor in the political and economic reality of many nations around the world. Diplomats and international business personnel work closely with strangers from other cultures and need to be aware of the changing conditions of the world. In urban centers, many of us find ourselves working side by side with strangers from various national, racial, ethnic, and religious backgrounds.

In addition to adjusting to the technological connectedness of our international and domestic environments, each of us has to make changes in many aspects of our lives—in social structure, values, politics, and, most of all, human relations. Even in less technological societies, change has encroached on nearly every pattern of traditional values, the structure and functions of the family, and the relations between generations, genders, and other social groups. Every index suggests that the rate of change will continue to increase up to the as yet untested limits of human adaptability. Our relationship to our personal and collective past is increasingly becoming one of dislocation, of that peculiar mixture of freedom and loss that inevitably leads to massive change. The culture of our youth no longer can be depended on to produce reliable predictions about what other people are going to do next. Indeed, "modernity has made all of us immigrants in our own homes" (Pearce & Kang, 1988, p. 40).

When faced with new circumstances, however, most of us prefer to continue in our familiar cultural ways without a clear and objective vision and without a readiness to embrace the different and the unfamiliar. Each of us acquires a personality and a culture in childhood, long before we are capable of comprehending either of them (Barnlund, 1991). Efforts to cope with the changes and complexities of the contemporary world often lack an understanding of its fundamental dynamics and direction for change. Even though the problems we face demand a new orientation and new ways of dealing with one another, we often try to force our own cultural ways on others. Such is the case with many international and domestic clashes of divergent cultural forces as well as our attempts to resolve them.

To be more effective in this changing world, we need to make a conscious decision concerning our basic views of ourselves and our relationships to others and to the world at large. Accepting this challenge means we need to search for a new definition of ourselves that will help us develop specific strategies for daily activities and problems. Reorienting ourselves is, of course, a serious challenge. Most of us who have been enculturated into one culture during our formative years find it extremely difficult to change the inertia of our habits even if we are willing to do so. Yet it is crucial that we do our utmost in reassessing our customary, ethnocentric ways and reformulating our habitual practices if we are to increase our functional fitness and psychological health in this changing world. To be profitable business managers in a multinational company, for example, we cannot insist on our own ways of doing business. To be effective teachers in a multiethnic urban school, we must be able to deal with children and parents whose cultural attributes are different from ours. To be successful ambassadors overseas, we must be effective communicators with a great deal of cultural sensitivity and understanding and with the necessary social skills of the local culture.

In this chapter, we extend our discussion from Chapter 13 on cross-cultural adaptation and examine how it is possible for individuals to undergo a fundamental psychic transformation through prolonged intercultural communication and adaptation experiences. Information and insights we gain from the experiences of immigrants and sojourners will serve as a main source of our understanding of the psychodynamics of change. We also will examine the concept of "intercultural personhood" (Y. Kim, 1988, 1995a, 1995b, 2001; Y. Kim & Ruben, 1988) as a model of human development in this increasingly interconnected world.

ENCOUNTERING DIFFERENT CULTURES

All of us came into this world knowing literally nothing of what we need to know to function acceptably in human society. Through the process of enculturation, cultural patterns are etched into our nervous systems and become part of our personalities and behavior. This internalized learning enables us to interact easily with other members of our culture who have a similar image of reality. That is, the culture of our youth provides a common pattern for our cognitive, affective, and behavioral structure and processes, so that persons belonging to the same culture tend to have a similar understanding of and similar responses to reality. It is culture that programs us to define what is real, what is true, what is right, what is beautiful, and what is good.

Cultural Unconscious

We remain largely unconscious of the cultural imprinting that governs our personalities and behavior. Our cultural unconscious can be understood only through detailed analysis. We automatically treat what is most characteristically our own as though it were innate. We are programmed to think, feel, and behave as though anyone whose behavior is not predictable or is peculiar in any way is strange, improper, irresponsible, or inferior. In this sense, all of us have a natural tendency to be ethnocentric as a result of our profound and inseparable relationship to our culture.

We become aware of our hidden control system when things do not follow the hidden program. Boulding (1956) argues that the human nervous system is structured in such a way that the patterns that govern behavior and perception come into consciousness only when there is a deviation from the familiar. To be functional and mature in a given culture, we must experience a multitude of challenges, and the full impact of the process is not experienced until we have "cut the apron strings" and established ourselves as separate from our parents (Hall, 1976, p. 225). Similarly, the only time we become fully aware of the hidden control system of our own culture is when we distance ourselves mentally or physically from our culture and face experiences that challenge our taken-for-granted images and assumptions.

Encounters with strangers bring surprises (uncertainty) and stresses (anxiety). Some of the surprises may shake our self-concepts and cultural identities and bring the anxiety of temporary rootlessness. Likewise, when we are strangers in other cultures, we are confronted with situations in which our mental and behavioral habits are called into question. Such situations produce a conflict in which we are forced to suspend temporarily or abandon our identification with the cultural patterns that have symbolized who are and what we are. Ill equipped to deal with such inconsistencies, most of us are, temporarily at least, in a state of mental and physical disturbance. The many examples of confusion experienced by international students, Peace Corps volunteers, and international business personnel suggest a wide spectrum of responses and reactions to new cultural surroundings. Similarly, a woman who returns to work after many years of being out of the work force may experience some of these transitional problems.

Culture Shock

Reactions to such situations have been called culture shock. Fictional as well as first-person accounts have been written depicting the bewildering experiences of being foreign in foreign lands (e.g., Dublin, 1993; Lewis & Jungman, 1986). It is Oberg (1960), however, who first coined the term *culture shock,* in connection with the experience of anthropologists who must learn to manage the violation of their social reality implicit in alien social norms, values, and mores. This violation represents a challenge to their primary socialization. As Lundstedt (1963) describes it, culture shock is "a form of personality maladjustment, a reaction to a temporary unsuccessful attempt to adjust to new surroundings and people" (p. 8). Many other writers, notably Furnham and Bochner (1986), have investigated a wide range of psychological, social, and physical reactions associated with culture shock.

In an overview of various studies of culture shock, Taft (1977) has identified a number of common reactions, including (1) "cultural fatigue," manifested by irritability, insomnia, and other psychosomatic disorders; (2) a sense of loss arising from being uprooted from one's familiar surroundings; (3) rejection by the individual of members of the new environment; and (4) a feeling of impotence from being unable to deal competently with the environmental unfamiliarity. Others describe the reactions of people to stressful situations under more severe conditions, such as those of concentration camp inmates, hostages captured by political terrorists, and returned prisoners of war. In each case, the features associated with the change are the "shock" effects involving heightened emotions and intense suffering.

Bennett (1977) expanded the meaning of culture shock and regarded it as part of the general *transition shock,* a natural consequence of the state of a person's inability to interact with the new and changed environment in an effective manner. According to Bennett, transition shock occurs in various situations, such as divorce, relocation, the death of a loved one, and a change of values associated with rapid social innovation, as well as the loss of a familiar frame of reference in intercultural encounters. Further, the concepts culture shock and transition shock have been extended to include *reentry shock,* or the emotional and physiological difficulties an individual may experience on returning home from overseas. Gullahorn and Gullahorn (1963) suggest that reentry difficulties are likely to be more severe a short time after returning than immediately on returning to the home culture.

At the heart of these "shock" phenomena is the lack of fitness between strangers' subjective experiences and the commonly accepted modes of experience in the unfamiliar surroundings. Everyone requires the ongoing validation of his or her experiences, and being unable to meet this basic human need can lead to symptoms of mental, emotional, and physical disturbance (Berger & Kellner, 1970; Williams & Westermeyer, 1986). The shifting of the self-world relationship brings about heightened levels of inner conflict through an increased awareness of the split between internal, subjective experiences and external, objective circumstances. In this sense, our experiences of culture shock and related phenomena are basically a form of "self-shock" (Zaharna, 1989), a form of existential dilemma in response to the painful discrepancy between what is and what should be.

THE PROCESS OF INTERCULTURAL TRANSFORMATION

Many investigators of sojourner adaptation have attempted to understand the short-term adaptive changes that follow the initial shock phase. Oberg (1960), for example, has identified four stages: (1) a "honeymoon" stage characterized by fascination, elation, and optimism; (2) a stage of hostility and emotionally stereotyped attitudes toward the host society and increased association with fellow sojourners; (3) a recovery stage characterized by increased language knowledge and ability to get around in the new cultural environment; and (4) a final stage in which adjustment is about as complete as possible, anxiety is largely gone, and new customs are accepted and enjoyed.

These and other similar characterizations of adaptation stages also have been described in "curves" that indicate the patterns of adaptive change over time. Researchers have measured adaptive change mainly in terms of the level of satisfaction or positive attitudes toward the host environment, and their findings generally support a "U-curve" hypothesis to predict the psychological change in sojourners. The U-curve depicts the initial optimism and elation in the host culture, the subsequent dip in the level of adaptation, and the following gradual recovery (Deutsch & Won, 1963; Lysgaard, 1995). As shown in Figure 14.1, this popularized U-curve pattern of adaptive change in the new environment has been extended to the "W-curve" (Gullahorn & Gullahorn, 1963; Trifonovitch, 1977) with the addition of a reentry (or return-home) phase of the sojourn experience.

FIGURE 14.1
The U-curve and W-curve adaptive change of sojourners.

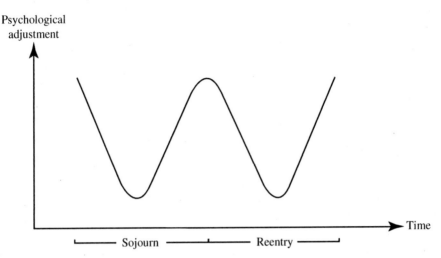

The U-curve and W-curve patterns of adaptive change, however, may not be applicable to all strangers' personal experiences. Church (1982) notes that support for the U-curve hypothesis is somewhat inconclusive and overgeneralized. Not all studies, for instance, report that sojourners begin their intercultural experiences with a period of elation and optimism (Klineberg & Hull, 1979; Ward, Okura, Kennedy, & Kojima, 1998). Even those studies supporting the hypothesis show marked differences in the time parameters of the curve, making the U-curve description less than precise in its ability to predict specific incidents of cross-cultural sojourn.

The Stress-Adaptation-Growth Dynamic

Despite the difficulty in identifying the adaptive process with precision, the process is one of the most profound and even painful life experiences. Adler (1987) argues that culture shock is not necessarily a "disease for which adaptation is the cure, but is at the very heart of the cross-cultural learning experience, self-understanding, and change" (p. 29). Intercultural learning and growth are, in this view, the core or essence of the sojourn experience. Strangers are capable not only of adapting to new cultures but also, and more important, of undertaking modifications within themselves. Through culture shock experiences, individuals confront the physiological, psychological, social, and philosophical discrepancies between their own internalized dispositions and those of the host culture. The sojourn experience, accordingly, is an experience of personal transformation, or a psychological "movement from a state of low self- and cultural awareness to a state of high self- and cultural awareness" (Adler, 1987, p. 15).

How can a person brought up to be a certain type of cultural being through the primary enculturation process ever overcome the existing barriers in order to cope with an unfamiliar culture? An answer lies in the profound plasticity and adaptability of the human organism. From the moment of birth, we are active agents in our own development, constructing the very reality in which we live. As we change, there is a progression of stages, where each stage in the developmental sequence is a necessary result of the preceding stage and integrates previous behaviors, concepts, and actions into a present condition. We simultaneously go through qualitative changes and maintain integrity throughout the life span, although it is still not clearly understood how such qualitative changes occur between stages.

In this framework of human development, successive levels and forms of equilibrium are conceived as levels of adaptation, with change being caused by a mismatch or discrepancy between our internal worlds and the external reality (Fogel, 1979; Ford & Lerner, 1992). This adaptive principle governing the human organism is evidenced most dramatically in individuals who have gone through such extreme life circumstances as prisons and death camps. Many inmates manage to cope in such settings with resilience. Numerous immigrants, refugees, and missionaries also demonstrate that they gradually learn to create for themselves appropriate situations and relationships.

Because cross-cultural adaptation necessitates both acculturation (learning) and deculturation (unlearning), the psychological movement of strangers often produces forms of *stress*. Stress, after all, is a natural human response whenever one has to let go of familiar and routine habits and whenever one's internal capabilities are challenged by the demands of the environment (Y. Kim, 1988, 2001). Because strangers' cultural identities and habits are placed against the systematic forces of the host culture, the strangers are at least temporarily in an unsettling state of "disequilibrium" manifested in many emotional "lows" of uncertainty and confusion. Indeed, the challenges of handling daily activities are most severe during the initial phases, as has been shown in studies of culture shock.

In the state of stress, a so-called defense mechanism is activated in strangers to hold the internal structure in balance. They try to avoid or minimize the anticipated or actual "pain" of disequilibrium through some kind of psychological maneuvering, such as selective attention, self-deception, denial, avoidance, and withdrawal as well as hostility, cynicism, and compulsive altruism (Lazarus, 1966; Lazarus, Averill, & Opton, 1974; Lazarus et al., 1980). Yet defensive stress reactions such as these are generally temporary; if they are prolonged, they become counterproductive to the strangers' functioning in the host environment. Such reactions must, and generally do, accompany adaptive responses as well.

Temporary psychic disintegration is identified by Y. Kim (1988, 1995a, 1995b, 2001) as the very basis for subsequent *adaptation*. She argues that experiences of stress prompt adaptation because when the environment continues to threaten internal conditions, individuals by necessity strive to meet the challenge by adding to the existing system of ideas and reconfigurating it into a new set of coping abilities. With the reflexive and self-reflexive capacity of the human mind that reviews, anticipates, generalizes, analyzes, and plans, we are capable of transforming our internal conditions creatively. What follows such adaptive responses is a subtle internal *growth*, according to Y. Kim. The periods of stress will pass in time as the strangers work out new ways of handling problems. A crisis, once managed, presents strangers with an opportunity to strengthen their internal capacity.

The interdependence of stress, adaptation, and subsequent internal transformation is referred to by Y. Kim as the *stress-adaptation-growth dynamic*. As depicted in Figure 14.2, this psychological dynamic is one that is fueled by a continual and cyclic tension between stress and adaptation, resulting in a form of psychic growth. It is a process of "draw-back-to-leap," similar to the movement of a wheel. Each stressful experience is responded to with a "draw back," which then activates the adaptive energy to help reorganize oneself and "leap forward." The process presents a continual resolution of the dialectical relationship between push and pull, or engagement and disengagement, in which the "opposite" psychological forces bring about a qualitative transformation—a greater personality integration and maturity (Heath, 1977; Kao, 1975; Wrightsman, 1994).

The process, if successful, enables the individual to grow into a new kind of person at a higher level of integration. Even extreme mental illness can be viewed as a process of a potentially positive disintegration that will be reintegrated with new material at a higher level (Dabrowski, 1968). Jourard (1974) refers to this phenomenon as the "integration-disintetgration-reintegration" process:

> Growth is the disintegration of one way of experiencing the world, followed by a reorganization of this experience, a reorganization that includes the new disclosure of the world. The

FIGURE 14.2
The stress-adaptation-growth dynamic.
(*Source:* Y. Kim, 2001, p. 59)

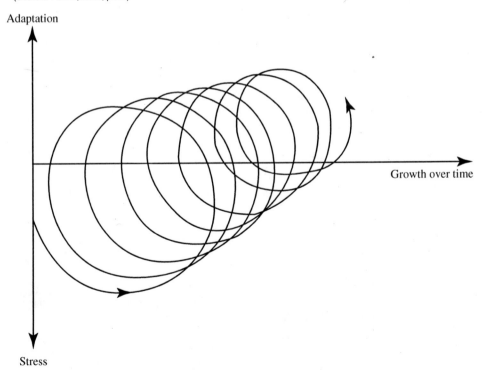

Adaptation

Growth over time

Stress

disorganization, or even shattering, of one way to experience the world, is brought on by new disclosures from the changing being of the world, disclosures that were always being transmitted, but were usually ignored. (p. 456)

The stress-adaptation-growth dynamic that is central to Y. Kim's theory of intercultural transformation echoes Mezirow's (1984, 1991) idea of "transformation learning" of adults. Mezirow emphasizes the capacity of adults to develop a higher level of self-understanding through reflection and in so doing "emancipate" themselves from the constraints of various limited, conventional perspectives. Kim's theory further converges with what Hall (1976) calls the "identity-separation-growth dynamics" and what Phinney (1993) refers to as the "differentiation-conflict-integration" process.

Research Evidence

Few systematic studies have directly examined the phenomenon of the process of intercultural identity development described above. Yet some scientific evidence is available that offers indirect support for the phenomenon of the process of intercultural transformation. Among such studies is the report by Eaton and Lasry (1978) that the stress level of more upwardly mobile immigrants tends to be greater than that of immigrants who are less upwardly mobile. Similarly, among Japanese Americans (Marmot & Syme, 1976) and Mexican American women (Miranda & Castro, 1977), the better-adapted immigrants initially experience a somewhat greater frequency of stress-related symptoms (such as anxiety and the need for psychotherapy) than the less adapted group. Findings from the study of Ruben and Kealey (1979) further suggest that even in the case of temporary sojourners (Canadian technical advisors in Nigeria), those who are ultimately the most effective in the new environment tend to be those who have undergone the most intense culture shock during the transition period.

These and other similar research findings lack the important detail concerning the subtle and intricate psychological dynamic of stress, adaptation, and growth and the gradual and often unquantifiable identity transformation depicted in Figure 14.2. Yet they do offer valuable "snapshots" of the evolutionary process, particularly when we examine them in the context of the many studies (some of which have been discussed in this chapter and in the preceding chapter) that consistently point to the upward-forward progression accompanying an increased level of functional fitness (greater adaptation) and psychological health (less adaptive stress). As noted earlier, these studies point to the fact that once the initial phase has been managed successfully, strangers almost always develop increasingly refined and positive views of their relationships to the host society. They also have been found to develop, over time, more behavioral capacities to manage themselves and function effectively in the host environment and to experience fewer feelings of alienation and hostility vis-à-vis the environment.

An additional source of validation of the stress-adaptation-growth dynamic is provided by the extensive body of research studies that have investigated the phenomenon of personal constructs and cognitive complexity originally theorized by Kelly (1955). Kelly argues that personal constructs are the conceptual tools we use in understanding and differentiating among similar or adjacent objects in the psychological environment. The cognitive schemes we employ define our intentions and imply alternative lines of action in a given situation. The greater the number of constructs present in our cognitive system is, the more discriminating and mindful we are in experiencing each communicative reality accurately and fully. Bieri (1955) applies the term *cognitive complexity* to describe this psychological construct. Cognitive complexity, according to Bieri, is the "degree of differentiation of the construct system" (p. 263). From subsequent research, three structural features of the complexity-simplicity continuum have been identified: (1) differentiation of the number of dimensions in one's personal constructs, (2) the relative articulation (or abstraction) of dimensions or the number of categories in a behavioral dimension that a person can discriminate (Rigney, Bieri, & Tripodi, 1964), and (3) integration of various dimensions of cognition into a meaningful whole, which is called "integrative complexity" (Schroder, Driver, & Streufert, 1967).

An important aspect of human cognition relevant to the present discussion is the intrinsically social and developmental nature of its structure. Schroder and his associates (1967) explain that the level of cognitive complexity in a given area is not necessarily static over time but develops further with new learning experiences. In other words, our cognitive structure is developed through various social experiences, creating a relatively differentiated, articulated (or abstracted), and integrated schematic structure. This developmental principle has been demonstrated in the research on immigrant adaptation. Just as comparative analyses of children, adolescents, and adults reveal increasing cognitive complexity, research indicates that in general, immigrants' perceptions of the new culture become more complex and refined in time with increased interactions with the host environment. Through the cumulative experiences of adaptation, strangers gradually attain a significant degree of cognitive capacity to differentiate between the original culture and the host culture along increasingly more dimensions and categories and to synthesize the cultures and their dimensions into an integrated whole.

What is significant about successfully adjusted immigrants and sojourners is that, as strangers separate themselves mentally and physically from their original cultures, they become less like strangers and more like insiders in the new culture. They simultaneously go through a process of transforming their original cultural identities and becoming intercultural. This transformation brings about a reorganization of their psychic patterns on a higher level of cognitive complexity, allowing for a greater capacity to overcome cultural parochialism. Empirical validation of this development has been offered in Y. Kim's (1976, 1977a) study of Korean immigrants. When asked to compare the meaning of "friendship" among Koreans with that among Americans, the subjects who were relatively new to the United States were able to offer fewer and more stereotypical comments, focusing only on the differences between the two cultures. In comparison, the subjects who had lived in the United States longer addressed both the similarities and the differences in a more elaborate, differentiated, and accurate manner. This research finding suggests a pattern of perceptual development in strangers over time toward greater clarity, depth, scope, balance, and integration (see also Grotevant, 1993).

INTERCULTURAL PERSONHOOD

Emerging from the process of intercultural transformation is the image of *intercultural personhood,* a special kind of personal orientation that promises greater fitness in our increasingly intercultural world (Y. Kim, 1988, 1995b, 2001; Y. Kim & Ruben, 1988). The "intercultural person" projects the fundamental outlook of a person who has achieved a high level of identity transformation through a prolonged process of stress, adaptation, and growth experiences through intercultural encounters.

A Psychological Profile

The intercultural person possesses internal attributes that are not defined rigidly by any single culture. Instead, he or she is someone who has internalized different cultural elements and is open to further intercultural growth. The term *intercultural person* is employed here as a generic term that embraces other similar concepts, such as "international" person (Lutzker, 1960), "universal" person (Walsh, 1973), "multicultural" person (Adler, 1987), and "species identity" (Boulding, 1990), as well as "meta-identity" and "transcultural identity." Walsh's (1973) concept of the "universal" person, for instance, emphasizes three aspects of a "cosmopolitan" viewpoint: (1) respect for all cultures, (2) understanding of what individuals in other cultures think, feel, and believe, and (3) appreciation for differences among cultures. Adler (1987) explains the unique characteristics of the multicultural person:

> The identity of [the] multicultural [person] is based, not on "belongingness" which implies either owning or being owned by culture, but on a style of self-consciousness that is capable of negotiating ever new formations of reality. In this sense [the] multicultural [person] is a radical departure from the kinds of identities found in both traditional and mass societies. He [or she] is neither totally a part of nor totally apart from his [or her] culture; he [or she] lives, instead, on the boundary. (p. 391)

These terms indicate a *nondualistic, noncategorical, and metacontextual definition of self and others* rather than rigid boundedness within any particular category. As such, the intercultural person manifests a mindset that is less stereotypical, less ethnocentric, and more individualized. Having experienced the dilemma between identity maintenance and adaptive change, these people possess a mental outlook that exhibits greater cognitive differentiation (Amerikaner, 1978; Boekestijn, 1988; Y. Kim, 1988, 1995a, 1995b, 2001). Such an outlook allows the openness that embraces different cultural and other group-based characteristics without being dictated to by them. The intercultural person can thus step into and "imaginatively participate in the other's world view" (Bennett, 1977, p. 49).

As we become increasingly intercultural in our internal systems, we gain new perspectives and outlooks that reflect *an integrative and creative "third-culture" perspective* (Gudykunst, Wiseman, & Hammer, 1977; Casmir, 1999). In this realm of psychic growth, differences and distinctions between human groups are taken less as polarities and opposites without relationships. The intercultural person is better able to seek and find a creative way to reconcile seemingly contradictory elements of peoples and cultures and transform them into complementary parts of an integrated whole. The nature of this psychic evolution presents a potential for achieving what Harris (1979, 1980) defines as "optimal communication competence." As one achieves a significant level of interculturalness, one may be better able to make deliberate choices of actions in specific situations rather than simply being bound by the culturally normative courses of behavior. Harris argues that an optimally competent communicator has a sophisticated metasystem for critiquing his or her own managing system and interpersonal system. The very existence of the metasystem makes the difference between the optimal level and the other two levels of competence a qualitative one (p. 31).

The achievement of an increasingly *inclusive and transcendental perception and awareness* is seen as one of the highest aims of humans in the spiritual traditions of the eastern cultures. Suzuki (1968) writes:

> The fundamental idea of Buddhism is to pass beyond the world of opposites, a world built up by intellectual distinctions and emotional defilements, and to realize the spiritual world of non-distinction, which involves achieving an absolute point of view. (p. 18)

As such, a virtuous person in the eastern philosophical tradition is not one who undertakes the impossible task of striving for the good and eliminating the bad, but rather one who is able to maintain a dynamic balance between good and bad. This notion of dynamic balance is emphasized extensively by the Chinese sages in their symbolism of the archetypal poles of yin and yang. They call the unity lying beyond yin and yang the tao and see it as a process that brings about the interplay of the two poles (Yoshikawa, 1988).

In becoming intercultural, we rise above the hidden forces of culture and discover that there are many ways to be "good," "true," and "beautiful." In this developmental process, we acquire a greater capacity to overcome cultural parochialism and develop *a wider circle of identification,* approaching the limits of many cultures and ultimately of humanity itself. The process of becoming intercultural, then, is like climbing a high mountain. As we reach the mountaintop, we see that all the paths below ultimately lead to the same summit and that each path presents unique scenery. Becoming intercultural is a gradual process of liberating ourselves from our limited and exclusive interests and viewpoints and striving to attain a perspective in which we see ourselves as a part of a larger, more inclusive whole.

The present psychologicial profile of intercultural persons is captured by Muneo Yoshikawa's (1978) observation of his own intercultural transformation. Yoshikawa was born in Japan and has been teaching at a university in the United States for many years. As Yoshikawa explains:

> I am now able to look at both cultures with objectivity as well as subjectivity; I am able to move in both cultures, back and forth without any apparent conflict. . . . I think that something beyond the sum of each [cultural] identification took place, and that it became something akin to the concept of "synergy"—when one adds 1 and 1, one gets three, or a little more. This something extra is not culture-specific but something unique of its own, probably the emergence of a new attribute or a new self-awareness, born out of an awareness of the relative nature of values and of the universal aspect of human nature. . . . I really am not concerned whether others take me as a Japanese or an [North] American; I can accept myself as I am. I feel I am much freer than ever before, not only in the cognitive domain (perception, thoughts, etc.), but also in the affective (feeling, attitudes, etc.) and behavioral domains. (p. 220)

Case Illustrations

Bearing concrete witness to the concept of the intercultural person are the many individuals' experiences of crossing cultures that have been told in case studies, memoirs, biographical stories, and essays of self-reflection and self-analysis (e.g., Ainslie, 1994; Copelman, 1993; Keene, 1994; Miller, 1988; O'Halloran, 1994; Schwimmer & Warren, 1993). Such accounts often present vivid testimonials and special insights into the emotional ebb and flow and the progressive and eventual realization of intercultural transformation.

One story of intercultural transformation is told by a former Peace Corps volunteer, Vicki Holmsten, and was published in the *Chicago Tribune* (May 27, 1978). The following excerpts from the diary illustrate the author's gradual transformation, from her initial culture shock experiences to an outlook that has grown beyond her original cultural identity.

December 12, 1975

I am visiting the town that I have been assigned to—it's in the bush! A small town called Foequellie, it's about 27 miles and an hour of dirt roads out of Gbarnga, the Bong County capital. Here I am to spend the next two years. To be honest, I have a bad case of culture shock. Not much English spoken in town—the language is Kpelle, the people here mostly of the tribe of the same name. No electricity. Kerosene lamps and battery-run radios seem to be modern touches. The running water is provided by the houseboy who brings the buckets from the well.

January 5, 1976

Why am I doing this? Why, why, why? We stayed in Monrovia long enough to shop for household necessities, then the members of our group took off for various parts of the country. . . . I move into a house in Foequellie and wait for school to begin.

May 11, 1976

What is it all for? I don't know. One of my students is dying. Life and death, the essence here. It's getting enough food to keep going and watching people die because there's no way to prevent it. I'm hurting very badly. Am I doing the right thing by being here? I know I'm not doing my best. I'm not even sure what that is anymore.

October 17, 1976

I think I am only now coming to terms with Africa. It is a very alive place. Life-giving and deadly at the same time. Life and death all out in the open, nothing muted or subtle. I am excited to be a part of it. I will never be African, but I am a part of it because I am investing myself in the future of the continent. One small part of Africa is mine. I am in one small part African.

January 16, 1977

Eleven months to go, I'm sure now that I can do it. Positive feelings about being here. Good ideas about what to do in my teaching, the ability and self-confidence to implement them that are gradually coming with experience.

March 25, 1977

Today I ate roasted termites. Not bad.

September 10, 1977

I'm enjoying life here now. I finally belong, I'm accepted. I am at last Vicki Holmsten to the people of Foequellie, not the "Peace Corps volunteer." It's almost time for me to leave. I'm not sure I really want to.

December 6, 1977

I'm sad to be going home but nevertheless feel that the time is ripe. The school had a going away party for me Saturday night. It was absurdly perfect. People all over the house, palm wine, tear-jerking farewell speeches, appropriate exits and entrances at calculated moments. I was presented with a beautiful African country cloth robe—it is probably the most precious thing I will ever own. It's over now, time to pack up and go.

Another story of intercultural transformation is told by a Cambodian refugee and described in Gail Sheehy's book *The Spirit of Survival* (1987). At the age of 12, Mohm was one of the first Cambodian refugees to be settled in New York City, arriving in September 1982. Having lived through the genocidal regime of Pol Pot, during which her entire family, with the possible exception of a brother, was wiped out, Mohm became the author's adopted daughter. Mohm's diary during the first two years in the United States is interspersed with the author's own reflections, and tells a compelling story about Mohm's stress, adaptation, and growth experiences. Her inner conflict continues throughout the period, although in an increasingly hopeful and confident tone.

After one month:

I don't like to live here, all Americans, all big apartments, no children, and I can't speak. Everything I know seems so far away, cannot ever get it back. My family is gone, part of me is torn away. I'm already broken. But I healed some of that wound, brought some of those parts back together and made the beginning of a new life. . . . (p. 214)

After three months:

My mind is still in my little world, of the [refugee] camp, where you could walk to everything. Anything you need, you could just call out for it and people will hear you and you can hear them. When I walk down the street in New York, there's another street like it and another and another as far as I look—it's endless. But I'm beginning to know which direction is right and wrong. I want to find my way. (p. 234)

After six months:

Things begin to fall into place little by little. And I'm not scared anymore of doing things, that I'll make a bad mistake. Even I'm able to communicate with people, a little bit. It isn't going to be as bad as I think. I have the feeling if I want to be myself badly enough, I can be someday—but not soon. Life is not as ugly as I think. It could be as beautiful as I want, if I make it. (p. 243)

Clearly, over time, Mohm was able to affirm herself and her new world as she began to reinvent herself. Toward the end of her first two years in the United States, an intercultural identity begins to emerge in Mohm. The author reflects:

Mohm did not emerge as a little cutout of an American teenager, made to order to fit some empty place in a middle-aged woman's life, with a miserable Cambodian child inside screaming to get out. She was, and is today, able to embrace her brand new American-ness while retaining her essential Cambodian-ness, knowing that is what makes her special. (p. xvii)

PROMOTING INTERCULTURAL GROWTH

The process of intercultural development exemplified in these personal stories can be credited in large part to each individual. The power and responsibility for their transformation ultimately rest within themselves, as each one is the captain of his or her own intercultural journey. Their stories clearly demonstrate that becoming intercultural is not a mere theoretical possibility or a romantic ideal but a concrete reality— one that all of us can attain if we are prepared to undergo the stressful challenges inherent in the process.

Intercultural persons have a special place in our increasingly pluralistic world as the "cross-links" (Molina, 1978), "mediating persons" (Bochner, 1981), and sustaining core of agents of positive social change (Lum, 1982). They provide the hub and glue of the moral infrastructure that is necessary to hold together divergent groups, to facilitate individual freedom, to discourage excessive claims for social categories, and to help build communities where individuals with disparate identities are given their respective places without losing sight of common aspirations. They possess the creative mindset that can reconcile and unite cultural differences and integrate the roles required by each cultural context. Such a mindset embodies the requisite attributes of an effective facilitator and catalyst. Even short-term sojourners such as exchange students who have returned home from abroad have been observed to have developed the capacity to serve as mediating persons (Wilson, 1985).

Just as democracy is an ideal state of government, the intercultural person is an ideal toward which we can strive. The process of psychic growth from monocultural to intercultural is a process of change in which we continually integrate new elements of life. The process necessitates openness to the dynamics of change and possession of attitudes that welcome new cultural learning with a commitment to the "uncommitted potentiality for change" (Bateson, 1972, p. 497) and the ability to doubt our own culturally colored perceptions by suspending our own value priorities.

Each of us is different, of course, in the degree to which our perceptions and interests are flexible. Some react with curiosity and delight to unpredictable events. Others are disturbed or uncomfortable in the presence of confusing and complex information. Some show strong resilience and tolerance for ambiguity, while others become extremely insecure. A crucial factor influencing the rigidity or flexibility of our psyche is age. As discussed in Chapter 13, age at the time of sojourn or immigration significantly affects the subsequent adaptation in the host society. A study of children of Hispanic cultural background (Seelye & Wasilewski, 1981) suggests that well-adjusted immigrant children already manifest a type of character structure on which a different but integrated intercultural personality can be built. Some of the children in the study demonstrate a noticeable amount of "situational flexibility" and a wide enough behavioral repertoire to negotiate differences of opinion in the multitude of cultural contexts of their daily activities, including the home, school, and street environments.

Efforts to promote intercultural development can be directed most effectively to our younger generations. The educational system has a monumental task of projecting and cultivating a new direction for human character formation. If sucessful, the educational system can help members of future generations embrace the intercultural world and its diversity and give up outdated national, racial, ethnic, and territorial perspectives. The educational system of the United States has begun to respond to this challenge by emphasizing the international/intercultural dimension throughout the curricula and by developing special programs such as foreign language programs, bilingual-bicultural education programs, ethnic studies, area studies, and studies of world regions and cultures. Many of these programs, although useful for enlarging appreciation of diverse cultures and societies, are not aimed directly at cultivating fundamental character formation and a clear direction for change. Lum (1982) inquires with regard to the bilingual-bicultural programs of the United States:

> Will they produce students who live in, between, and beyond cultures? That is, will they produce people who will make our pluralistic society and world survive? What will these pupils look like? How will we know we have produced children with non-separatist outlooks? (p. 384)

If intercultural personhood is deemed a valid educational goal, and we believe that it is, an extensive search for ways to articulate and implement intercultural human development must be undertaken. The propagation of the goal must go beyond the educational process directly to the political processes and the mass media. Media, in particular, can play a pivotal role in the spread of interculturalness as a human social value and thus produce a gradual change in the mindset of the general public. Y. Kim and Ruben (1988) state that

> there is a special privilege to think, feel, and behave beyond the parameters of any single culture. This accomplishment . . . has an intrinsic merit in dealing with our increasingly complex intercultural world. In this frame of mind, the tension, stress, and effort necessarily present in overcoming intercultural difficulties can be more willingly accepted and endured. (p. 318)

SUMMARY

In this chapter we have examined the process of the development of intercultural personhood through the experience of intercultural communication. In this process, we witness the human spirit at work, at once struggling and being triumphant as individuals undergo the dynamic interplay of stress, adaptation, and growth. Intercultural personhood presents a model of human development toward less cultural rigidity and more openness, less ethnocentrism and more understanding of the fundamental oneness of all human beings. We argue that this kind of fundamental personal change is necessary for us to be functional in our increasingly intercultural world, that is, to be better able to accept and appreciate cultural variations, to resolve and integrate conflicting views from the basis of a perspective broader than any one particular cultural perspective.

Reaching this goal would take a lifetime commitment, and visible short-term results may be limited. Yet numerous immigrants and sojourners around the world already have accomplished the long and difficult journey of becoming intercultural, leaving us with little doubt that being an intercultural person is a viable goal toward which all of us may strive. Through the personal testimonials presented in this chapter and those of many others with similar transformative experiences, we learn about the reality of the continual juxtapositions of stress and adaptation. Despite the often unsettling nature of the transformation process, we see in their experiences the triumphant human spirit that embraces new elements of life. While the process of becoming inter-cultural is largely the work of each individual, it needs to be promoted as an important public value that can be propagated through the educational and mass communciation institutions of each society.

STUDY QUESTIONS

1. Explain how the changing circumstances of today's world necessitate a new self-definition and a new orientation toward others.
2. What are the various symptoms of culture shock?
3. What are the general stages that strangers tend to undergo in the face of culture shock? How have they been characterized graphically in the research literature?
4. Describe Y. Kim's theory of intercultural transformation. How do intercultural experiences facilitate the growth process?
5. What kinds of research evidence are available concerning Kim's theory?
6. Identify at least one prominent person whom you consider highly intercultural. What characteristics of this person qualify him or her as an intercultural person?
7. How can intercultural persons benefit the community on local, national, and international levels?
8. How can people in leadership positions promote intercultural personhood as a public value? How can ordinary citizens in a democratic society participate in this effort?

SUGGESTED READINGS

Bochner, S. (Ed.). (1981). *The mediating person.* Cambridge, MA: Schenkman.

Csikszentmihalyi, M. (1993). *The evolving self: A psychology for the third millennium.* New York: HarperCollins.

Furnham, A., & Bochner, S. (1986). *Culture shock: Psychological reactions to unfamiliar environments.* London: Methuen.

Keene, D. (1994). *On familiar terms: A journey across cultures.* New York: Kodansha International.

Kim, Y. Y. (2001). *Becoming intercultural: An integrative theory of communication and cross-cultural adaptation.* Thousand Oaks, CA: Sage.

Seelye, H., & Wasilewski, J. (1996). *Between cultures: Developing self-identity in a world of diversity.* Lincolnwood, IL: NTC Business Books.

15

BUILDING COMMUNITY

In and through community lies the salvation of the world.

M. Scott Peck

Conflict between people of different ethnic and cultural groups is occurring throughout the world today. While the specific causes of intergroup conflict differ depending on the situation, all incidents share one thing in common; they involve polarized communication. Polarized communication occurs when we are not willing to question our assumption that we are right and strangers are wrong (Arnett, 1986). Polarized communication, therefore, exists when groups or individuals look out for their own interests and have little concern for strangers' interests. Lack of concern for strangers' interests leads to moral exclusion.

Lack of concern for strangers and moral exclusion are a function, at least in part, of the spiritual deprivation (i.e., the feeling of emptiness associated with separation from our fellow humans) that the late Mother Teresa saw as the major problem facing the world today (Jampolsky, 1989). Many people tend to think that our connections to our fellow humans have decreased because of cultural and ethnic diversity. These people think that cultural and ethnic diversity inevitably lead to polarized communication and hinder the development of community. This, however, is not the case. Diversity is necessary not only for community to exist but for community to develop.

The term *community* is derived from the Latin *communitas,* which has two related but distinct interpretations: (1) the quality of "common interest and hence the quality of fellowship" and (2) "a body of people having in common an external bond" (Rosenthal, 1984, p. 219). Yankelovich (1984) argues that community evokes the "feeling that 'Here is where I belong, these are my people, I care for them, they care for me, I am part of them' . . . its absence is experienced as an achy loss, a void . . . feelings of isolation, falseness, instability, and impoverishment of spirit" (p. 227). Selznick (1992) argues that "communities provide settings within which people grow and flourish and within which subgroups are nourished and protected" (p. 360). Wuthnow (1991), however, points out that even though people in the United States talk a lot about community, they live their lives in ways that say individual freedom is more important to them than community.

Our purpose in this chapter is to examine community building among culturally and ethnically diverse groups of people. First, we introduce Martin Buber's suggestions for developing community. Second, we review characteristics of community. Third, we look at issues of community and public life and civic engagement. Fourth, we discuss ethical issues in developing community with strangers. We conclude by presenting a set of principles for community building with strangers.

WALKING A NARROW RIDGE

Buber (1958, 1965) sees community as a choice around a common center, the voluntary coming together of people in a relationship that involves a concern for the self, a concern for others (including strangers), and a concern for the community. He believes that community must begin in small groups and that it cannot be forced on organizations or nations. At the same time, Buber contends that some form of community is necessary to make life worth living.

Buber (1965) claims that a community is *not* a group of like-minded people; rather, it is a group of individuals with complementary natures who have differing minds. Extending Buber's analysis, Friedman (1983) draws a distinction between a community of otherness and a community of affinity. A *community of affinity* is a group of like-minded people who have come together for security. Friedman argues that they feel safe because they use a similar language and the same slogans but that they do not have close relations with one another. A *community of otherness,* in contrast, begins from the assumption that each member has a different point of view that contributes to the community. Members are not alike, but they share common concerns.

Buber sees openness, *not* intimacy, as one of the keys to developing community: "A real community need not consist of people who are perpetually together; but it must consist of people who, precisely because they are comrades, have mutual access to one another and are ready for one another" (quoted by Friedman, 1986, p. xiii). The importance of openness becomes clear when we look at the distinctions Buber draws among three forms of conversations: monologues, technical dialogues, and dialogues.

Monologues are self-centered conversations in which strangers are treated as objects. Buber (1965) says that monologues are conversations "characterized by the need neither to communicate something, not to learn something, not to influence someone, not to come into connection with someone, but solely by the desire to have one's own self-reliance confirmed" (p. 20). When we engage in monologues, we do not see strangers as unique human beings and do not take their needs into consideration. If we are thinking of what we are going to say when strangers are talking, we are engaged in monologues.

Technical dialogues are information-centered conversations. In technical dialogues, our goal is to exchange information with strangers, not establish contact with them. Buber (1965) sees these types as a function of "modern existence." Monologues and technical dialogues are necessary and appropriate at times, but problems emerge when they are used too frequently (e.g., there is a lack of connection between the participants), and community, therefore, cannot develop.

For community to develop, dialogues are necessary (Buber, 1958). *Dialogues* involve communication between individuals. The goal of dialogues is not to change strangers but to understand them. Buber (1965) contends that in dialogue "each of the participants really has in mind the other or others in their present or particular being and turns to them with the intention of establishing a living mutual relationship between himself [or herself] and them" (p. 19). In dialogues, there is a search for mutuality. The focus is on what is happening between the two people. In dialogues, each participants' feelings of control and ownership are minimized; each participant confirms the other, even when conflict occurs. Buber argues that it is the mutual confirmation that occurs in dialogues that allows us to feel human.

When we communicate on automatic pilot, most of our conversations are monologues or technical dialogues. Engaging in these types of conversations exclusively does not allow us to make contact with strangers (or members of our own ingroups). For most of us, engaging in dialogue requires that we be mindful of our communication. When we are mindful, we need to focus on the process of communication, not worry about the outcomes. If we focus on what is happening between ourselves and strangers and do not think about our goals, we can engage in dialogue with strangers.

Developing community requires engaging in dialogue with strangers, and it also requires a commitment to values higher than our own (Arnett, 1986). Tinder (1980) suggests that the values of civility and of tolerance of plurality and diversity are necessary for community. When we hold these values, we accept that our own needs are not always met (Arnett, 1986).

The key to building community in Buber's (1965) view is for individuals to walk a narrow ridge. The concept of the *narrow ridge* involves taking both our own and strangers' viewpoints into consideration in our dealings with strangers. Arnett (1986) uses the metaphor of tightrope walkers to illustrate the narrow ridge concept. If tightrope walkers lean too much in one direction, they will begin to lose their balance. To regain their balance, tightrope walkers must compensate by leaning in the other direction. The same is true of walking the narrow ridge in our dealings with strangers. If we give our own opinions too much weight in conversations, we must compensate by giving strangers' opinions equal weight if we are going to walk a narrow ridge.

In walking the narrow ridge, we must try to understand strangers' points of view. Buber (1965) does *not* advocate that we take nonjudgmental or relativistic attitudes toward strangers. Rather, he argues that we openly listen to strangers, but if we are not persuaded by their arguments, we should maintain our original position; if we are persuaded, we should modify our opinions. There is a subtle difference between listening openly and not changing our minds and being close-minded. The difference depends on our intentions. If our intentions are to consider strangers' opinions seriously, we are walking the narrow ridge; if our intentions are not to consider strangers' opinions, we are close-minded. It is our dual concern for self and strangers in walking the narrow ridge that stops polarized communication and allows community to develop (Arnett, 1986).

Buber (1965) argues that we should avoid accepting strangers' opinions just for the sake of peace. Rather, he suggests that we should accept strangers' opinions or compromise if that is the way to the best solution. Our commitment must be to principles, not false peace. Buber, however, does not suggest that we accept everything strangers say unquestioningly. Suspicion sometimes is warranted, but problems occur when suspicion becomes a norm of communication. When suspicion is always present, existential mistrust exists.

Bellah et al. (1991) argue that trust cannot be taken for granted. They point out that "if we are dominated by mistrust we cannot attend or interpret adequately, we cannot act accountably, and we will rupture, not strengthen, the solidarity of the community or communities we live in" (p. 284). Bellah et al. go on to suggest that "since we only attend to those we trust, we cannot interpret accurately, we cannot be accountable to, we cannot grow in solidarity with those we have put outside of our circle of trust" (p. 284).

One factor that contributes to mistrust in individualistic cultures like the United States that value direct communication is looking for hidden meanings. Suspicion and looking for hidden meanings are only two of the factors that lead to mistrust. No matter how mistrust emerges, it always polarizes communication. Understanding strangers requires "a willing suspension of disbelief" (Trilling, 1968, p. 106).

CHARACTERISTICS OF COMMUNITY

Peck (1987) takes a slightly different approach to community than Buber (1965), but the two approaches are compatible. Peck sees community as critical to peace and intergroup harmony:

> In and through community lies the salvation of the world. Nothing is more important. Yet it is virtually impossible to describe community meaningfully to someone who has never experienced it—and most of us have never had an experience of true community. The problem is analogous to an attempt to describe the taste of artichokes to someone who has never eaten one. (p. 17)

Peck restricts the use of the term *community* to "a group of individuals who have learned how to communicate honestly with each other, whose relationships go deeper than their masks of composure, and who have developed some significant commitment to 'rejoice together, mourn together' and to 'delight in each other, make others' conditions our own' " (p. 59). Peck isolates several characteristics of true communities.

1. *Inclusivity.* Consistent with Buber's (1965) argument that communities are not made up of the like-minded, Peck (1987) contends that different types of people, ideas, and emotions must be present in a community. Exclusivity is the enemy of a community. When individuals are excluded, cliques are formed, and cliques are defensive bastions against community.

2. *Commitment.* Peck (1987) argues that commitment involves "a willingness to coexist together and hang in there when the going gets rough" (p. 62). It is commitment to the community that allows the differences among the members of the community to be absorbed.

3. *Consensus.* Communities seek agreement among all the members (Peck, 1987). Developing a consensus requires that differences be confronted and discussed. A consensus cannot emerge if differences are ignored or if conflict is suppressed. In a community, differences are transcended, *not* obliterated or demolished. Peck suggests that "perhaps the most necessary key to transcendence is the appreciation of differences. In community, instead of being ignored, denied, hidden, or changed, human differences are celebrated as gifts" (p. 62).

4. *Contemplation.* Members of a community examine it. Peck (1987) argues that "the essential goal of contemplation is increased awareness of the world outside oneself, the world inside oneself, and the relationship between the two" (p. 66). The need for contemplation is consistent with Socrates' claim that "the life which is unexamined is not worth living." Nozick (1989) believes that this position is unnecessarily harsh, but he agrees that it is necessary to examine *our* lives, if we are to live our own lives, not someone else's.

5. *Safe place.* Peck (1987) argues that once communities are developed, members perceive them as "safe places." Peck contends that it is rare for any of us to feel completely safe; we spend most of our lives feeling only partly safe. Members of communities feel like they are accepted and can speak from their hearts because they feel safe. Feeling safe allows them be vulnerable.

6. *Vulnerability.* As indicated earlier, for community to develop, members must drop their masks of composure. Peck (1987) contends that the development of community requires that we expose our inner selves to strangers and that we be affected by strangers when they expose their inner selves to us.

7. *Graceful fighting.* A community cannot exist without conflict. The management of the conflict which occurs, however, must be based on a real desire to listen and understand each other's opinions, not to being right. Peck (1987) makes the point that people tend to believe the fantasy that "If we can resolve our conflicts, then someday we will be able to live together in a community" (p. 72). He suggests, however, that this fantasy has the relationship between conflict and community backward. The goal should be: "If we can live together in community, then someday we shall be able to resolve our conflicts" (p. 72).

Peck (1987) contends that community can occur by accident but that it also can occur by design. He sees the process through which a group becomes a community as one that can be taught and learned. Peck isolates four stages in the development of community: pseudocommunity, chaos, emptiness, and community. In *pseudocommunity,* members of the group are pleasant to each other and avoid conflict. What emerges is not true community but pseudocommunity because conflict is avoided. The focus of the second stage, *chaos,* involves misguided attempts to help others or convert them to our way of thinking. In this stage, individual differences are out in the open and there is a perceived vacuum in leadership.

Peck (1987) specifies two ways out of the chaos stage. One way is through organization (e.g., assigning a leader). While organization will help a group out of chaos, it does not lead to community. Community emerges from "emptiness." By *emptiness,* Peck is referring to "the need to empty [ourselves] of barriers to [effective] communication" (p. 95). Barriers to effective communication include expectations, preconceptions, prejudices, ideology, theology, the need to convert, and the need to control. When the individuals in the group overcome the barriers to effective communication, community can emerge.

The barriers to effective communication that Peck (1987) isolates are consistent with those discussed by many other authors. Prather (1986), for example, makes the point that all expectations are judgments and that for people to unite, they must let go of their expectations. We agree with Prather's sentiment, but we also think it is important to recognize that we probably cannot let go of all of our expectations, prejudices, and so forth, especially when we communicate on automatic pilot. Being aware of our expectations and prejudices and how they influence the way we communicate, however, is necessary for effective communication and community building. For most of us, this requires that we are mindful.

COMMUNITY AND PUBLIC LIFE

Bellah, Madsen, Sullivan, Swidler, and Tipton (1985) argue that without community, "there may be very little future to think about at all" (p. 286). They see a community as an inclusive group of people who share their public and private lives or, more specifically, as "a group of people who are socially interdependent, who participate together in discussion and decision-making and who share certain practices that both define the community and nurture it" (p. 333). A genuine community (e.g., a marriage, a university, a whole society) is defined by its practices.

Practices refer to "shared activities that are not undertaken as a means to an end but are ethically good in themselves" (Bellah et al., 1985, p. 335). This definition is similar to Aristotle's use of the term *praxis*. Bellah et al. argue that genuine practices virtually always involve commitment because they involve activities that are ethically good.

Consistent with Buber (1965) and Peck (1987), Bellah and his associates (1985) view communities as consisting of different types of people, even though we have a tendency to want to be with people who are similar to us. They point out that "the [U.S.] American search for spontaneous community with the like-minded is made urgent for fear that there may be no way at all to relate to those who are different. . . . the public realm still survives, even though with difficulty, as an enduring association of the different" (p. 251). At times, the associations in the public realm may approach community. Bellah and his associates cite the civil rights movement and the response to Martin Luther King, Jr., as an example:

> The powerful response King elicited, transcending simple utilitarian calculations, came from the reawakened recognition by many [U.S.] Americans that their own sense of self was rooted in companionship with others who, though not necessarily like themselves, nevertheless shared with them a common history and whose appeals to justice and solidarity made powerful claims on their loyalty. (p. 252)

Developing community, therefore, requires that we value justice and loyalty and recognize the commonalities we share.

Selznick (1992) argues that there are two sources of moral integration which serve as the foundation for community: civility and piety. *Civility* involves being "guided by the distinctive virtues of public life. These include, especially, moderation in pursuit of one's own interests, and concern for the common good. More particularly, civility signals the community's commitment to dialogue as the preferred means of social decision" (p. 391). Selznick contends that civility "presumes diversity, autonomy, and potential conflict" and that "norms of civility are predicated on a regard for the integrity and independence of individuals and groups" (p. 391). Peck (1993) argues that civility emerges out of being conscious of our behavior (i.e., mindful) and is based on ethical behavior toward strangers. *Piety* involves a "reflection of the need for coherence and attachment. The distinctive virtues of piety are humility and loyalty" (Selznick, 1992, p. 387). Dewey (1934) views piety as respect for human interdependence.

Bellah et al. (1985) believe that commitment to public life and community will not emerge unless large numbers of individuals go through personal transformations (e.g., are willing to change). These transformations must be not only be transformations of consciousness but also transformations of actions.

One of the transformations of actions necessary for the development of community is giving of ourselves to others. Mahatma Gandhi states that "consciously or unconsciously, every one of us does render some service or other. If we cultivate the habit of doing this service deliberately, our desire for service will steadily grow stronger, and will make not only for our own happiness, but for that of the world at large" (quoted by Lynberg, 1989, p. 19). Lynberg points out that

> the importance of giving, the path to a greater sense of success and fulfillment, is also a central lesson of the world's great religions. "They who give have all things," says a Hindu proverb, "they who withhold have nothing." In the Buddhist scriptures it is written, "The man [or woman] of wisdom who did good, the man [or woman] of morals who gave gifts, in this world and the next one too, they will advance to happiness." In the Koran, Mohammed conveys that "a man's [or woman's] true wealth is the good he [or she] does in this world." In the Torah, it is said that the Lord gives to every man [or woman] according to his [or her] ways, according to the fruit of his [or her] doings." And in Christianity we learn that "it is more blessed to give than to receive" and that "he [or she] who is greatest among you shall be your servant." (p. 18)

Lynberg concludes that it is not possible to live a "great life" without serving others.

Wuthnow (1991) points out that serving others is not inconsistent with individualism. He reports that both people who value "being able to do what you want" and people who do not hold this value in the United States say that "helping people in need" is important. Wuthnow argues that individualism "embodies inner strength, a strong and clear sense of personal identity. It is this self-confidence that allows one to give. . . . It is, therefore, possible to live in community without giving up one's individuality" (p. 114).

Individuals must give of their own accord, but the support of a community engaging in the same behavior makes it easier. Bellah et al. point out that "individuals need the nurture of groups that carry a moral tradition reinforcing their own aspirations" (p. 286). They also contend that we need to develop a conception of the common good because "with a more explicit understanding of what we have in common and the goals we seek to attain together, the differences between us that remain would be less threatening" (p. 287). Finding commonalities requires that we be mindful of our prejudices. Brodie (1989) contends that "racism and sexism and homophobia and religious and cultural intolerance . . . are all ways of denying that other people are the same kind as ourselves" (p. 16).

The position that Bellah and his associates advocate vis-à-vis cultural and/or ethnic differences is consistent with Langer's (1989) contention that

> because most of us grow up and spend our time with people like ourselves, we tend to assume uniformities and commonalities. When confronted with someone who is clearly different in one specific way, we drop that assumption and look for differences. . . . The mindful curiosity generated by an encounter with someone who is different, which can lead to exaggerated perceptions of strangeness, can also bring us closer to that person if channeled differently. (p. 156)

Langer's research suggests that once individuals satisfy their curiosity about differences, understanding can occur. Harman (1987) points out that "with modernity has

come the need on behalf of the modern stranger to recognize community with potential others and negotiate membership on the basis of minimal indicators of commonality" (p. 127).

CIVIC ENGAGEMENT

Putnam (2000) argues that individuals in the United States today feel disconnected
from others. To understand why this is happening, he analyzes civic engagement (e.g.,
involvement in community organizations) over the last several decades. Putnam contends that there have been ups and downs in civic engagement in the United States
over its history, especially in the last 100 years:

> For the first two-thirds of the twentieth century a powerful tide bore [U.S.] Americans into
> ever deeper engagement in the life of their communities, but a few decades ago—silently,
> without warning—that tide reversed and we were overtaken by a treacherous rip current.
> Without at first noticing, we have been pulled apart from one another and from our commu-
> nities over the last third of the century. (p. 27)

These changes affect all aspects of society in the United States (e.g., how well schools
work, democracy in the country, the health and happiness of people living in the
United States).

Putnam (2000) summarizes the results of several surveys regarding civic engagement. He reports that three-quarters of the U.S. work force viewed "the breakdown of
community" and "selfishness" as "serious" or "very serious" problems in 1992. Several surveys conducted in 1999 reveal that two-thirds of U.S. Americans say that
"civic life has weakened in recent years" and that there is more emphasis on the individual than on the community. Further, "more than 80 percent said that there should
be more emphasis on community, even if that put more demands on individuals"
(p. 25).

The concept of social capital is central to Putnam's (2000) analysis. *Social capital*
"refers to connections among individuals—social networks and the norm of reciprocity and trustworthiness that arise from them" (p. 19). There are both public and private
components of social capital. The connections we form with others benefit each of us
individually (e.g., help us find jobs, provide social support; the private good). The
connections we form with others also provide benefits to society (e.g., if neighbors are
connected to each other, they watch each other's houses, and this leads to decreases in
the crime rate in the neighborhood; the public good). Putnam contends that the "touch-
stone" of social capital "is the principle of generalized reciprocity—I'll do this for you
now, without expecting anything immediately in return and perhaps without even
knowing you, confident that down the road you or someone else will return the favor"
(p. 134). Generalized reciprocity leads to trustworthiness among members of society
and provides benefits to individuals.

Putnam (2000) analyzes trends in civic engagement and social capital in terms of
political participation, civic participation (e.g., Rotary Club, environmental associations, Boy Scouts, Girl Scouts), religious participation, connections in the workplace,

informal social connections, volunteering, philanthropy, small groups, social movements, and the internet. His analysis reveals that U.S. Americans' civic engagement and connections with others generally declined in the last third of the twentieth century. There was, in contrast, a tendency for an increase in mass membership organizations (e.g., American Association of Retired Persons, National Wildlife Foundation) where there are no "local" chapters where individuals meet face-to-face in recent years. Putnam points out that "active participation in face-to-face organizations has plummeted" (p. 163); the rates of participation have been cut in half in a few decades. Similar trends emerge for most of the other areas examined. There are, however, exceptions (i.e., volunteering, small groups, social movements, the internet). The decrease in civic engagement has led to a decrease in social capital (e.g., connections among individuals) and generalized reciprocity in the society.

One area where there has not been a decline in civic engagement is volunteering (Putnam, 2000). The increase in volunteering, however, is centered in the generation who are the parents of the "baby boomers" (e.g., the parents of the generation born immediately after World War II). Also, the types of activities for which people volunteer have changed. Individual-oriented volunteering (e.g., "reading to shut-ins") has decreased less fast than collective-oriented volunteering (e.g., refurbishing community gardens). U.S. Americans are engaging in individual activities more than in activities where they have to work with others.

Three other areas are counter to the trend of a decrease in civic engagement: participation in small groups, growth in social movements, and use of the internet (Putnam, 2000). Participation in selected types of small groups has increased in recent years (e.g., self-help, support groups). Self-help groups based on "12-step" programs (e.g., Alcoholics Anonymous, Gamblers Anonymous) and support groups (e.g., support groups for people with specific diseases, commercial support groups like Jenny Craig) have increased in recent years. Putnam points out that "self-help groups certainly provide emotional support and interpersonal ties that are invaluable to participants" (p. 150), and "in some respects support groups substitute for other intimate ties that have been weakened in our fragmented society, serving people who are disconnected from more conventional social networks" (p. 151). He claims that divorced and single people participate in support groups at rates two to four times those of married people. Putnam suggests that self-help and support groups involve the use of social capital as a way to address "previously neglected problems."

Putnam (2000) argues that self-help and support groups are different from other forms of civic engagement. Participation in these groups is not associated with participation in other forms of civic engagement. Wuthnow (1994) points out that small groups "are more fluid and more concerned with the emotional states of the individual" (p. 3) than other forms of civic engagement (also see Wuthnow, 1998). He also claims that small groups may only provide a place for individuals to focus on themselves "in the presence of others." Putnam, however, contends that social movements are related closely to social capital. Individuals who organize social movements must rely on social networks. He suggests that "social movements also *create* social capital, by fostering new identities and extending social networks" (p. 153).

The internet is the final exception to the general trend of a decline in civic engagement. Putnam (2000) points out that "the internet is a powerful tool for the transmission of information among physically distant people," but he questions whether it "fosters social capital and genuine community" (p. 172). Putnam claims that virtual communities are more egalitarian than face-to-face communities. Virtual communities are heterogeneous with respect to social factors such as ethnicity, gender, and age, but they are homogeneous with respect to "interests and values." For the internet to contribute to the development of true community, electronic contact needs to reinforce face-to-face contact.

Putnam (2000) tries to isolate the reasons for the changes in civic engagement in the United States in the last third of the twentieth century. He finds four general causes. First, pressures regarding changes in work (e.g., people needing more money, working more and having less leisure time), especially two-career families, contributed to the changes in civic engagement. Second, suburbanization and individuals having to commute to work have decreased the time available for civic engagement. Third, electronic entertainment, especially television, has decreased the time people spend in civic engagement. Fourth, there has been a generational change. The baby boomers' parents are involved more in civic engagement than their children (the baby boomers) or their grandchildren. Putnam concedes that he cannot prove these are the causes of the changes in civic engagement, but they are his "best guesses."

Putnam (2000) provides several suggestions to increase civic engagement, social capital, generalized reciprocity, and community in the United States. First, he suggests that we develop programs that will increase the civic engagement of U.S. Americans over what it is today. One way to do this is through community service programs in schools. Putnam points out that volunteering in our youth is one of the best ways to establish lifelong volunteering patterns. Second, he suggests that workplaces become more "family-friendly and community-oriented" than they are today. This will allow workers to help "replenish our stocks of social capital both within and outside the workplace" (p. 406, italics omitted). Third, U.S. Americans need to become more involved with their neighbors than they are today and develop spaces in public areas that encourage "casual socializing." Fourth, U.S. Americans need to become more involved in spiritual communities and be more tolerant of other spiritual communities than they are today. Fifth, U.S. Americans need to "spend less leisure time sitting passively alone in front of glowing screens and more time in active connection with fellow citizens" than they do today (p. 410, italics omitted). Putnam also suggests that new forms of electronic entertainment that foster community be developed. Sixth, U.S. Americans need to engage in more cultural activities (e.g., artistic activities such as community theater) than they do today. Seventh, U.S. Americans need to be more involved in public life than they are today (e.g., serving on community committees, attending public meetings).

Each of these activities will increase civic engagement and social capital in the country. Increasing social capital will increase generalized reciprocity and trustworthiness among members of the society. These changes will, in turn, improve intergroup relations in the country and facilitate community building.

ETHICAL ISSUES IN BUILDING COMMUNITY WITH STRANGERS

The practices in which we engage are critical to the development of community. One area where there may be a conflict in practices when we communicate with strangers is ethical behavior. Barnlund (1980) suggests that

> the moral issues that attend intercultural encounters are not simply more complicated, they are of an entirely new dimension. Despite the pervasiveness of cross-cultural contact, these complications remain overlooked and unexplored in any systematic way. The ethical vacuum that confronts us reflects not merely a failure of specialists within this evolving field, nor the negligence of outside agencies to give support to such ethical study, but is due in large part to difficulties that are inherent in the cross-cultural context. (pp. 9–10)

He goes on to argue that there is not a metaethic which can be used by people from different cultures when ethical dilemmas arise.

Since ethical principles tend to be culture-specific, Barnlund (1980) suggests that when we communicate with strangers, we tend to approach ethical questions in one of two ways: (1) We make ethical judgments using our own cultural standards, or (2) we use the frames of reference of the strangers' culture. Both of these methods are unsatisfactory because

> either fosters a truncated morality that is incomplete and ethnocentric, for it subordinates the ethical premises of one culture or the other. And it thereby fails to fully illuminate or to fairly adjudicate conflicts in which people of different moral orientations must accommodate their differences and create ways of collaborating on common tasks. (p. 10)

Barnlund contends that what is needed is a metaethic, one prescribing standards applicable to both cultures.

One reason Barnlund (1980) argues that ethical judgments cannot be made regarding people in one culture by people in another culture is that he has extended the descriptive theory of cultural relativity to the domain of ethics. The theory of cultural relativism asserts that the behavior of people in different cultures can be understood only in the context of those cultures (Barnsley, 1972; see Chapters 1 and 5). Stated differently, if we want to understand the behavior of people in other cultures, we have to do it from their frames of reference (i.e., we have to avoid being ethnocentric). Many of the early writers discussing cultural relativism, however, incorporated the idea of tolerance of different practices in their discussions of cultural relativism. Herskovits (1950), for example, maintains that cultural relativism "is a philosophy which, in recognizing the values set up by every society to guide its own life, lays stress on the dignity in every body of custom, and on the need for tolerance of conventions though they may differ from one's own" (p. 76).

Renteln (1988) points out that incorporating tolerance in the theory of cultural relativity was due to the time in which the idea of cultural relativity was developed. She points out that "cultural relativism was introduced in part to combat . . . racist, Eurocentric notions of progress" (p. 37), for example, viewing people from "less developed" cultures as "savages" or "primitive." Barnsley (1972) points out, however, that it is necessary to draw a distinction between the evaluative and descriptive aspects of ethical relativity:

> Descriptive relativism . . . merely asserts the factual diversity of customs, of moral beliefs and practices. . . . The thesis itself, however, is purely a factual one. It may be termed, therefore, cultural relativism. . . . Ethical relativism proper, on the other hand, is an evaluative thesis, affirming that the value of actions and the validity of moral judgments are dependent upon their sociocultural context. The two theses are logically distinct, though not unrelated. (pp. 326–327)

In other words, Barnsley takes the position that saying ethics develop out of culture and vary across cultures (cultural relativism) is different from saying that valid moral judgments can be made only within a particular cultural context (ethical relativism).

Berger argues that cultural relativity "does not, of course, free the individual from finding his [or her] own way morally. That would be another instance of 'bad faith,' with the objective fact of relativity being taken as an alibi for the subjective necessity of finding those single decisive points at which one engages one's whole being" (cited by Barnsley, 1972, p. 355). Like Berger, Renteln (1988) contends that cultural relativism

> does not force its adherents to foreswear moral criticism. Relativists, like everyone else, are ethnocentric . . . and remain true to their own convictions. There is no reason why the relativist should be paralyzed [from making moral judgments]. . . . But the relativist will acknowledge that the criticism is based on his [or her] own ethnocentric standards and realizes also that the condemnation may be a form of cultural imperialism. Under extreme circumstances, meaning that an action in another culture violates one of the relativist's most deeply held beliefs, the relativist may decide that criticism and even intervention are lesser evils than either ethnocentrism or cultural imperialism. (pp. 63–64)

Even if we accept cultural diversity, in other words, we still must make ethical judgments in our interactions with strangers.

There is not a metaethic upon which there is agreement to guide our moral judgments, but there are cultural universals that can be used to guide our behavior when we communicate with strangers. Bidney (1968), for example, suggests that there may be universals regarding prohibitions against activities such as treason, murder, rape, and incest because "in all cultures the perpetuation of society takes precedence over the life of the individual" (p. 545). Selznick (1992) argues that a long list of moral universals can be constructed. Such a list would include "the ideal of preserving human life; looking to the well-being of close relatives; prohibiting murder and theft; valuing affection and companionship; reciprocity in helping and being helped; and hospitality" (p. 96). Selznick goes on to point out that "there can be no effective social life without widespread commitment to responsible conduct, which requires virtues of truthfulness, courage, fidelity, and respect" (p. 101). There is general agreement on these values across cultures, but the ways that values are practiced may differ.

In discussing the moral constraints necessary for peace, Bok (1989) suggests additional areas where there may be cultural universals in ethical behavior:

> Of the four, two are the widely acknowledged curbs on violence and deceit. . . . To cement agreement about how and to whom those curbs apply, and to keep them from being ignored or violated at will, a third constraint—on breaches of valid promises, contracts, laws, and treaties—is needed.

Whether expressed in religious or secular form, these three values are shared by every civilization, past and present. Any community, no matter how small or disorganized, no matter how hostile toward outsiders, no matter how cramped its perception of what constitutes, say, torture, has to impose at least *some* internal curbs on violence, deceit, and betrayal in order to survive. But because persons acting clandestinely easily bypass or ignore these constraints, a fourth is necessary on excessive secrecy. (pp. 81–82)

The constraint on violence is obvious. For peace to exist, however, we also must not lie to each other or break our promises. Lying or breaking our promises can destroy peace because it makes us untrustworthy. We also must not be overly secretive. If there are too many secrets, others can be violent, lie, or break promises and we will not know about it. The practice of Bok's moral constraints in a group provides an environment in which peace and community can be nurtured (for extended discussions of the importance of nonviolence, see Gandhi, 1948; King, 1958).

Etzioni (2001) takes a different position with respect to making ethical judgments across cultures. The ideas of "moral voice" and "moral dialogues" are central to his position. Etzioni argues that "the *moral voice* is a peculiar form of motivation that encourages people to adhere to values to which they already subscribe" (p. 240). He contends that when we are tempted to ignore values we hold, we hear our moral voices. Hearing our moral voices does not mean we always listen to them, but our moral voices can influence our behavior. Etzioni also argues that "*moral dialogues* occur when a group of people engage in a process of sorting the values that guide their lives" (p. 240). Shared world views of what is "good" evolve from moral dialogues. Etzioni contends that "moral dialogues are not merely a matter of reasonable people coming to terms, but of people of divergent convictions finding a common normative ground" (p. 241).

Etzioni (2001) points out that moral dialogues generally take place within nations but that they can occur across national boundaries as well. He argues that moral voices that reflect the views of people in a culture can be expressed to members of other cultures. Etzioni claims that "rather than muting the cross-cultural moral voice, as the [ethical] relativists do, all societies should respect the right of others to lay moral claims on them just as they are entitled to do to others" (p. 242). When members of different cultures use their moral voices and engage in moral dialogues, there is a possibility of a "global moral base" being negotiated. Etzioni points out, however, that using moral voices across cultures does not "legitimize berating" people in other cultures. He concludes that "the moral voice is most compelling when it is firm but not screeching, judging but not judgmental, critical but not self-righteous" (p. 244).

PRINCIPLES OF COMMUNITY BUILDING

To review, a community consists of diverse individuals who are honest and open with each other, trust each other, engage in ethical behavior, and are committed to living together. Members of a community are civil to each other, they value diversity, and at the same time, they search for the commonalities humans share. Community makes life worth living, and the existence of community makes peace and intergroup harmony possible. Community occurs in groups, but individuals must take the responsibility for building community in their marriages, workplaces, schools, cities, and nations, as well as the world. Finally, members of a community behave ethically.

Assumptions

To conclude the chapter and the book, we synthesize the information presented into a set of principles for community building (this section is based on Gudykunst, 1994). The principles presented are based on several assumptions.

Assumption 1   Community is necessary to make life worth living and increase the potential for peace in the world. Peace is not possible without community. As the Peck (1987) quote at the beginning of the chapter suggests, community building may be the "salvation of the world."

The more we develop communities in our lives, the greater the potential for peace. Staub (1989) points out that "our experience of connection and community shape who we are, how we experience other people, and how we bear the stresses of both ordinary and extraordinary events" (p. 269). When we have community in our lives, we treat people who are not members of our communities better than when we do not have community in our lives.

Assumption 2   Developing community is the responsibility of individuals. Each of us must take the responsibility for building community in our own lives. Most of us, however, do not try to build community in our lives. The major reason for this is that we engage in our interactions with strangers mainly on automatic pilot, or if we are mindful, we are mindful of the outcome, not the process of communication. Given the individualistic emphasis in the United States, we focus on ourselves as individuals when we are on automatic pilot. Building community requires conscious effort. We must invest consciously in building social capital with strangers (e.g., forming connections with strangers; Putnam, 2000).

Staub (1989) argues that "people who fully develop and harmoniously integrate their capabilities, values, and goals will be connected to others. The full evolution of the self . . . requires relationships and the development of deep connections and community—as well as the capacity for separateness" (p. 269). Kegley (1997) points out that "individuals without community are without substance, while communities without individuals are blind" (p. 37).

Assumption 3   Cultural diversity and ethnic diversity (and all other forms of diversity as well) are necessary resources for building community. When we interact on automatic pilot, we assume that cultural diversity and ethnic diversity (and other types of diversity) inhibit the development of community. This, however, is not the case. Variety and diversity are the basis of excellence (Gould, 1996).

Lippmann (1937) argues that we need to work toward developing communities that respect and encourage diversity. A true community cannot exist without diversity. Gardner (1991), however, points out that "to prevent the wholeness from smothering diversity, there must be a philosophy of pluralism, an open climate for dissent, and an opportunity for subcommunities to retain their identity and share in setting of larger goals" (p. 11).

Assumption 4   Communities can be any size (e.g., a marriage, social organization, university, town, country, or even the world). We often mistakenly assume that community exists only in large groups. The feeling of community, however, can exist in any relationship we have.

We must start building community in the smaller groups of which we are members (e.g., families) and work toward developing community in the larger groups (e.g., universities, societies). If we cannot build community in the small groups of which we are members, we cannot build it in the larger groups.

Assumption 5   We are what we think. Jampolsky (1989), among others, points out that "everything in life depends on the thoughts we choose to hold in our minds and our willingness to change our belief systems" (p. 31). Similarly, Buddha said that "our life is shaped by our minds; we become what we think" in *The Dhammapada.*

The way we think about strangers influences how we interact with them. If we have negative expectations for our interactions with strangers, the outcomes of our interactions with strangers probably will be negative. If we have positive expectations for our interactions with strangers, in contrast, positive outcomes are probable. Building community is one positive outcome.

Assumption 6   Community cannot exist without conflict. Hampshire (1989) argues that we should expect "ineliminable and acceptable conflicts, and . . . rationally controlled hostilities, as the normal condition" (p. 189). We need to be able to manage and reconcile the conflicts that occur, especially the conflicts that emerge from the diversity of our community (Lippmann, 1937).

Peck (1987) points out that "if we can live together in community, then someday we shall be able to resolve our conflicts" (p. 72). To develop community, therefore, we must engage in "graceful fighting"; we must try to persuade each other but not coerce each other.

Assumption 7   Fisher and Brown (1988) suggest that one person can change a relationship and, by extension, start the development of community in a relationship. If people in relationships change their behavior toward strangers, strangers eventually will change the way they interact. We can, therefore, change our relationships with strangers and develop community with them by changing our behavior toward them.

Rather than waiting for strangers to take the first step, we can take the first step and try to develop community with them. If we follow the principles suggested below in our relationships with strangers, there is a good possibility we can develop community in our relationships with strangers.

Principles

Given the seven assumptions and the material summarized throughout the book, we present seven community-building principles. The principles are not presented in any order of priority; all are necessary for community to develop.

Principle 1: Be Committed   We must be committed to the principle of building community in our lives, as well as to the strangers with whom we are trying to develop a community (Peck, 1987). Commitment to strangers is a prerequisite for community to exist. Being committed to strangers presupposes that we have connections with strangers. If we are committed, we will not abandon our relationships when there are problems. If we are not committed, strangers will sense this and it will affect the quality of our relationships with them. Without commitment, there cannot be trust.

We also need to be committed to dialogue as a way of solving problems (Selznick, 1992). Without commitment to forming relationships with strangers and to dialogue, we cannot manage our conflicts with them constructively. It is the commitment present in a community that allows the differences inherent in its diversity to be absorbed (Peck, 1987). We need to be committed to the our collective (social) identities associated with our communities and to a participatory mode of politics within the community (Taylor, 1991). The community identities need to be common ingroup identities for all members and incorporate lower-level identities. We must be committed to cooperating with strangers on our shared goals. We also need to be committed to principles, not being right (Buber, 1958).

Principle 2: Be Mindful   We must pay attention to what we do and say and how we interpret strangers' behavior. Bellah et al. (1991) point out that "when we are giving our full attention to something, when we are really attending, we are calling on all of our resources of intelligence, feeling, and moral sensitivity. . . . We are not thinking about ourselves, because we are completely absorbed in what we are doing" (p. 254). They go on to point out that "attention implies an openness to experience, a willingness to widen the lens of apperception" (p. 256). Bellah and his colleagues believe that a "good society is one in which attention takes precedence over distraction" (p. 273).

When we communicate on automatic pilot, we interpret strangers' behavior by using our own frames of reference and evaluating them rather than trying to understand them. This makes it impossible to develop community. When we are mindful, we need to focus on the process of our communication with strangers, not the outcomes (Langer, 1989). Our emphasis should be on adapting our messages so that strangers can understand us and interpreting strangers' messages by using their frames of reference.

Principle 3: Be Unconditionally Accepting   For community to develop, we must accept strangers as they are and not try to change or control them (Fisher & Brown, 1988). If we try to change strangers, they will become defensive and building community will not be possible. If we accept strangers, they will sense this. Feeling accepted will allow strangers to be open with us and be concerned with our welfare.

We must accept strangers' diversity and not judge them only on the basis of their group memberships. We need to recognize and support the personal and social identities strangers claim for themselves. If we do not support strangers' self-concepts, we cannot develop satisfying relationships with them. We need to minimize our expectations, prejudices, suspicion, and mistrust (Peck, 1987). Bellah et al. (1991) point out that trusting others is necessary for community to develop. This can be accomplished only when we are mindful.

Principle 4: Be Concerned for Both Ourselves and Others Communities are inclusive; they are *not* groups of like-minded people. We must develop connections with strangers and be concerned about their welfare. If we think we are better than strangers and try to exclude them from our lives, we are being morally exclusive. If we are morally exclusive, we accept physically or psychologically harming strangers as acceptable behavior. We must walk a narrow ridge in our interactions with strangers whenever practical (Buber, 1958). This means that we avoid polarizing communication with strangers (Arnett, 1986), actively listen to strangers when they speak, and engage in dialogue whenever possible (Buber, 1958, 1965).

Our survival depends on the survival of the communities of which we are members (Loewry, 1993). Being authentic (e.g., self-fulfilled, empowered) and identifying with strangers and our communities are *not* incompatible (Taylor, 1991). We must consult strangers on issues that affect them and be open to their ideas (Fisher & Brown, 1988). We must take strangers into consideration when there is a conflict and fight gracefully (Peck, 1987). We also need to be contemplative in examining our own behavior and that of the communities of which we are members (Peck, 1987).

Principle 5: Be Understanding We need to strive to understand strangers as completely as possible. Martin Luther King, Jr. (1963) argues that "shallow understanding from people of good will is more frustrating than absolute misunderstanding from people of ill will" (p. 88). To be understanding, we must determine how strangers' interpretations of events and/or behaviors are different from and similar to our own.

We also must recognize how culture, ethnicity, and other forms of diversity affect the way we think and behave. We must understand real differences between our groups and strangers' groups, not base our interpretations of differences on our stereotypes and prejudices. Building community requires "the appreciation of differences. In community, instead of being ignored, denied, hidden, or changed, human differences are celebrated as gifts" (Peck, 1987, p. 62). We also need to search for commonalities on which community can be built (Bellah et al., 1985). In our communication, we must balance emotion, anxiety, and fear with reason (Fisher & Brown, 1988).

Principle 6: Be Ethical We must engage in behavior that is not a means to an end but behavior which is morally right in and of itself (Bellah et al., 1985). We have to be reliable in what we say and do (Fisher & Brown, 1988). We must recognize that being moral takes precedence over all other concerns (Pritchard, 191). Behaving morally means we must protect our own and strangers' dignity and remember that strangers' sense of dignity may be different from ours.

We must be morally inclusive (Optow, 1990), not be evil (Staub, 1989), and engage in service to others (Lynberg, 1989). Staub (1989) points out that "starting with common everyday acts and moving on to acts requiring greater sacrifice . . . can lead to genuine concern and a feeling of responsibility for people" (p. 276). This is not to say that we should not make moral judgments. We cannot avoid making ethical judgments, but we need to understand strangers' behavior by using their frames of reference before we make judgments. A community is based on its moral principles (Etzioni, 1993).

Principle 7: Be Peaceful Bok (1989) contends that for peace to exist, we must *not* be violent, be deceitful, breach valid promises, or be secretive (Bok, 1989). Even if others engage in these behaviors toward us, we are not justified in engaging in these behaviors toward them (Fisher & Brown, 1988). Socrates points out that retaliation is never justified (Vlastos, 1991).

We must strive for internal peace (Prather, 1986) and peace in our relations with strangers. Hanh (1991) suggests that by "practicing mindfulness in each moment of our daily lives, we can cultivate our own peace. With clarity, determination, and patience . . . we can sustain a life of action and be real instruments of peace" (p. 99). If we are peaceful, everyone with whom we come into contact will benefit from our peace.

Conclusion

These seven principles are ideals toward which we can strive. The more we are able to put them into practice individually, the greater the chance for community and peace in the world. We must not, however, punish ourselves when we fail to achieve these ideals. Achieving these ideals is a lifetime's work and requires extensive practice.

If we are to tolerate strangers, we must begin by accepting our own mistakes. Prather (1986) points out that when we find that we are not engaging in behaviors we want to practice (e.g., building community), we must forgive ourselves and start anew at practicing those behaviors. For most of us, this will occur numerous times a day initially. The behaviors suggested in these ideals are different from those we have learned from birth. To engage in these behaviors consistently, we must unlearn many of our normal behaviors (e.g., behaviors that occur at low levels of awareness such as reacting defensively and looking out only for ourselves). The critical thing is *not* the outcome but the process. If we behave in a way consistent with these ideals (the process), community (the desirable outcome) will occur.

SUMMARY

Polarized communication predominates in the world today. There is a lack of concern for others present in the world today which often leads to strangers' being morally excluded. Communities, however, are inclusive, and cultural diversity and ethnic diversity are resources for building community. The development of community requires that we walk a narrow ridge when communicating with others. To develop community in our lives, we must be committed, mindful, unconditionally accepting, concerned for both ourselves and others, understanding, ethical, and peaceful.

To conclude, we have tried to present material that we think will help you understand your communication with strangers. Understanding is a necessary prerequisite for effective communication. If we do not understand how strangers are different from and similar to ourselves, we cannot communicate effectively with them. To understand strangers (and people who are familiar), we must be able to manage the anxiety we experience when we communicate with them. Understanding strangers (and people who are familiar), therefore, requires that we are mindful of our communication.

We generally are not mindful when we communicate with strangers or people who are familiar. When we are mindful when communicating with strangers, we tend to focus on the outcome. When we are mindful of the process, however, we can manage our anxiety cognitively and figure out how our interpretations of messages differ from those of strangers with whom we are communicating. Deciding whether we want to make the effort is up to each of us. We can continue our normal patterns of communication— communicating on automatic pilot and interpreting strangers' messages by using our frames of reference. Making this choice ensures that a large proportion of our communication with strangers will be ineffective. If we choose to try to understand strangers, the likelihood of our communication with strangers being effective increases. Understanding strangers does not mean that we have to accept behavior we find objectionable. Rather, we need to understand what the behavior means to strangers before we judge them and realize that our judgments may be ethnocentric.

Attempting to understand strangers increases the chance that we will be able to build community in our lives and foster peace on the planet. While these are idealistic goals, they are achievable if each of us does his or her part. Let us begin!

STUDY QUESTIONS

1. Why are communities *not* composed of people who are like-minded?
2. What are the differences among monologues, technical dialogues, and dialogues? Which contributes to building community? Why?
3. What is involved in walking a narrow ridge?
4. What are the characteristics of community?
5. What is the role of civility in building community?
6. Why are individualism and community not inconsistent?
7. Why are diversity and commonality important in developing community?
8. Why is ethical relativity not necessary for building community?
9. What are potential cultural universal ethical principles?
10. Why is conflict a necessary part of building community?
11. What are the principles of building community?

SUGGESTED READINGS

Arnett, R. (1986). *Communication and community.* Carbondale: Southern Illinois University Press.

Bellah, R., Madsen, R., Sullivan, W., Swidler, A., & Tipton, S. (1985). *Habits of the heart.* Berkeley: University of California Press.

Bellah, R., Madsen, R., Sullivan, W., Swidler, A., & Tipton, S. (1991). *The good society.* New York: Knopf.

Etzioni, A. (1993). *The spirit of community.* New York: Crown.

Etzioni, A. (2001). *The monochrome society.* New York: Simon & Schuster.

Peck, M. S. (1987). *The different drum: Community making and peace.* New York: Simon & Schuster.

Putnam, R. (2000). *Bowling alone: The collapse and revival of American community.* New York: Simon & Schuster.

Selznick, P (1992). *The moral commonwealth.* Berkeley: University of California Press.

Staub, E. (1989). *The roots of evil.* New York: Cambridge University Press.

Taylor, C. (1992). *The ethics of authenticity.* Cambridge, MA: Harvard University Press.

Wuthnow, R. (1998). *Loose connections: Joining together in America's fragmented communities.* Cambridge, MA: Harvard University Press.

REFERENCES

Abe, H., & Wiseman, R. (1983). Cross-cultural confirmation of the dimensions of intercultural effectiveness. *International Journal of Intercultural Relations, 7,* 53–68.

Abelson, R. (1976). Script processing in attitude formation and decision making. In J. Carroll & J. Payne (Eds.), *Cognition and social behavior.* Hillsdale, NJ: Erlbaum.

Aberson, C., Healy, M., & Romero, V. (2000). Ingroup bias and self-esteem. *Personality and Social Psychology Review, 4,* 157–173.

Abrahams, R. (1976). *Talking black.* Rowley, MA: Newbury House.

Adamopoulos, J., & Bontempo, R. (1986). Diachronic universals in interpersonal structures. *Journal of Cross-Cultural Psychology, 17,* 169–189.

Adelman, M. B. (1988). Cross-cultural adjustment. *International Journal of Intercultural Relations, 12,* 183–204.

Adelman, M. B., & Lustig, W. (1981). Intercultural communication problems as perceived by Saudi Arabian and American managers. *International Journal of Intercultural Relations, 5,* 365–381.

Adler, N., Brahm, R., & Graham, J. (1992). Strategy implementation. *Strategic Management Journal, 13,* 449–466.

Adler, N., & Graham, J. (1989). Cross-cultural interaction. *Journal of International Business Studies, 20,* 515–537.

Adler, N., Graham, J., & Gehrke, T. (1987). Business negotiations in Canada, Mexico, and the United States. *Journal of Business Research, 15,* 411–429.

Adler, P. S. (1975). The transitional experience: An alternative view of culture shock. *Journal of Humanistic Psychology, 15,* 13–23.

Adler, P. S. (1987/1982). Beyond cultural identity: Reflections on cultural and multicultural man. In L. Samovar & R. Porter (Eds.), *Intercultural communication: A reader* (4th ed.). Belmont, CA: Wadsworth.

Ady, J. (1995). Toward a differential demand model of sojourner adjustment. In R. Wiseman (Ed.), *Intercultural communication theory.* Thousand Oaks, CA: Sage.

Agar, M. (1994). *Language shock.* New York: Morrow.

Ainslie, R. (1994). Notes on the psychodynamics of acculturation. *Mind & Human Interaction, 5*(2), 6–67.

Aitken, T. (1973). *The multinational man: The role of the manager abroad.* New York: Wiley.

Akimoto, S., & Sanbonmatsu, D. (1999). Differences in self-effacing behaviors between European and Japanese Americans. *Journal of Cross-Cultural Psychology, 30,* 159–177.

Alba, R. (1976). Social assimilation among American Catholic national origin groups. *American Sociological Review, 41,* 1030–1046.

Alba, R. (1990). *Ethnic identity.* New Haven: Yale University Press.

Albert, E. (1972). Culture patterning in Burundi. In J. Gumperz & D. Hymes (Eds.), *Directions in sociolinguistics.* New York: Holt, Rinehart, and Winston.

Alberty, R., & Emmons, M. (1990). *Your perfect right* (6th ed.). San Louis Obispo, CA: Impact.

Allen, B. P. (1976). Race and physical attractiveness as criteria for white subjects' dating choices. *Social Behavior and Personality, 4,* 289–296.

Allen, I. (1983). *The language of ethnic conflict.* New York: Columbia University Press.

Allen, I. (1990). *Unkind words.* New York: Bergin and Garvey.

Allport, G. W. (1954). *The nature of prejudice.* New York: Macmillan.

Almaney, A., & Alwan, A. (1982). *Communicating with the Arabs.* Prospect Heights, IL: Waveland.

Altman, I. (1975). *The environment and social behavior.* Monterey, CA: Brooks/Cole.

Altman, I. (1977). Privacy regulation. *Journal of Social Issues, 33,* 66–84.

Altman, I., & Chemers, M. (1980a). *Culture and environment.* Monterey, CA: Brooks/Cole.

Altman, I., & Chemers, M. (1980b). Cultural aspects of environment-behavior relationships. In H. Triandis & R. Brislin (Eds.), *Handbook of cross-cultural psychology* (Vol. 5). Boston: Allyn and Bacon.

Altman, I., & Gauvain, M. (1981). A cross-cultural dialectical analysis of homes. In L. Luben, A. Patterson, & N. Newcombe (Eds.), *Spatial representation and behavior across the life span.* New York: Academic Press.

Altman, I., & Taylor, D. (1973). *Social penetration.* New York: Holt, Rinehart, and Winston.

Altman, I., Vinsel, A., & Brown, B. (1981). Dialectical conceptions in social psychology: An application to social penetration and privacy regulation. In L. Berkowitz (Ed.), *Advances in experimental social psychology* (Vol. 14). New York: Academic Press.

Altouchi, J., & Altouchi, L. (1995). Polyfaceted psychological acculturation in Cook Islanders. *Journal of Cross-Cultural Psychology, 26,* 426–440.

Al-Zahrani, S., & Kaplowitz, S. (1993). Attributional bias in individualistic and collectivistic cultures. *Social Psychology Quarterly, 56,* 223–233.

Amerikaner, M. (1978). *Personality integration and the theory of open systems.* Ph.D. dissertation, University of Florida.

Andersen, P., Hecht, M., Hoobler, G., & Smallwood, M. (2001). Nonverbal communication across cultures. In W. B. Gudykunst & B. Mody (Eds.), *Handbook of international and intercultural communication* (2nd ed.). Thousand Oaks, CA: Sage.

Andersen, P, Lustig, M., & Andersen, J. (1990). Changes in latitude, changes in attitude. *Communication Quarterly, 38,* 291–311.

Applegate, J., & Sypher, H. (1983). The constructivist approach. In W. Gudykunst (Ed.), *Intercultural communication theory.* Beverly Hills, CA: Sage.

Ardener, S. (1975). *Perceiving women.* London: Malaby.

Argyle, M. (1982). Intercultural communication. In S. Bochner (Ed.), *Cultures in contact.* Elmsford, NY: Pergamon.

Argyle, M. (1991). *Cooperation.* London: Routledge.

Argyle, M., Furnham, A., & Graham, J. (1981). *Social situations.* Cambridge: Cambridge University Press.

Argyle, M., & Henderson, M. (1984). The rules of relationships. In S. Duck & D. Perlman (Eds.), *Understanding personal relationships.* Beverly Hills, CA: Sage.

Argyle, M., Henderson, M., Bond, M., Iizuka, Y., & Contarelo, A. (1986). Cross-cultural variations in relationship rules. *International Journal of Psychology, 21,* 287–315.

Arnett, R. (1986). *Communication and community.* Carbondale: Southern Illinois University Press.

Arnoff, C. (1974). Old age in prime time. *Journal of Communication, 24,* 86–87.

Aronson, E. (1972). *The social animal.* San Francisco: W. H. Freeman.

Asch, S. (1956). Studies of independence and conformity. *Psychological Monographs, 70*(9) (whole no. 416).

Ashcraft, N., & Scheflen, E. (1976). *People space: The making and breaking of human boundaries.* Garden City, NY: Anchor Press.

Atkenson, P. (1970). Building communication in intercultural marriage. *Psychiatry, 33,* 396–408.

Atwater, E. (1983). *Psychology and adjustment.* Englewood Cliffs, NJ: Prentice-Hall.

Austin, C. (1983). *Cross-cultural reentry: An annotated bibliography.* Abilene, TX: Abilene Christian University.

Baddassare, M., & Feller, S. (1975). Cultural variation in personal space. *Ethos, 3,* 481–503.

Baker, J., & Gudykunst, W. (1990). *Privacy regulation in Japan and the United States.* Paper presented at the International Communication Association convention.

Baker, N. (2001). Of samurai an sisterhood. *Tricycle, X*(3), 58–63.

Ball-Rokeach, S. (1973). From pervasive ambiguity to definition of the situation. *Sociometry, 36,* 378–389.

Ball-Rokeach, S., Rokeach, M., & Grube, J. (1984). *The great American values test.* New York: Free Press.

Banks, S. (1987). Achieving "unmarkedness" in organizational discourse. *Journal of Language and Social Psychology, 6,* 171–190.

Banks, S., Gao, G., & Baker, J. (1991). Intercultural encounters and miscommunication. In N. Coupland, H. Giles, & J. Wiemann (Eds.), *"Miscommunication" and problematic talk.* Thousand Oaks, CA: Sage.

Barbato, C., & Feezel, J. (1987). The language of aging in different age-groups. *Gerontological Society of America, 27,* 527–531.

Barnes, J. (1954). Class and communities in a Norwegian island parish. *Human Relations, 7,* 39–58.

Barnett, G., & Kincaid, D. L. (1983). A mathematical theory of cultural convergence. In W. Gudykunst (Ed.), *Intercultural communication theory.* Beverly Hills, CA: Sage.

Barnlund, D. (1962). Toward a meaning-centered philosophy of communication. *Journal of Communication, 2,* 197–211.

Barnlund, D. (1968). *Interpersonal communication.* Boston: Houghton Mifflin.

Barnlund, D. (1975). *Public and private self in Japan and the United States.* Tokyo: Simul Press.

Barnlund, D. (1980). The cross-cultural arena: An ethical void. In N. Asuncion-Lande (Ed.), *Ethical perspectives and critical issues in intercultural communication.* Falls Church, VA: Speech Communication Association.

Barnlund, D. (1991). Communication in a global village. In L. Samovar & R. Porter (Eds.), *Intercultural communication: A reader* (6th ed.). Belmont, CA: Wadsworth.

Barnlund, D., & Yoshioka, M. (1990). Apologies: Japanese and American styles. *International Journal of Intercultural Relations, 14,* 193–206.

Barnsley, J. (1972). *The social reality of ethics.* London: Routledge and Kegan Paul.

Barringer, F. (1993, May 16). Pride in a soundless world. *New York Times,* pp. 1, 14.

Bar-Tal, D., (1997). Formation and change of ethnic and national stereotypes. *International Journal of Intercultural Relations, 21,* 491–524.

Barth, F. (1969). *Ethnic groups and boundaries.* London: Allen and Unwin.

Basso, K. (1970). To give up on words. *Southern Journal of Anthropology, 26,* 213–230.

Bates, T. (1994). Social resources generated by group support networks may not be beneficial to Asian immigrant-owned small businesses. *Social Forces, 72,* 671–689.

Bateson, G. (1972). *Steps to an ecology of mind.* New York: Ballantine Books.

Bateson, G. (1978). The pattern which connects. *Co-Evolution Quarterly, 18,* 4–15.

Bateson, G. (1979). *Mind and nature.* New York: Dutton.

Bavelas, J., Black, A., Chovil, N., & Mullett, J. (1990). *Equivocal Communication.* Newbury Park, CA: Sage.

Beardsley, R. K. (1965). Cultural anthropology. In J. Hall & R. Beardsley (Eds.), *Twelve doors to Japan.* New York: McGraw-Hill.

Beck, A (1976). *Cognitive therapy and the emotional disorders.* New York: International Universities Press.

Beck, A. (1988). *Love is never enough.* New York: Harper and Row.

Beebe, L., & Takahashi, T. (1989). Sociolinguistic variations in face threatening acts. In M. Eisenstein (Ed.), *The dynamic interlanguage.* New York: Plenum.

Beier, E., & Zautra, A. (1972). Identification of vocal communication of emotion across cultures. *Journal of Consulting and Clinical Psychology, 34,* 166.

Belk, S., Snell, W., Garcia-Falconi, R., Hargrove, L., & Holzman, W. (1988). Power strategies use in the intimate relationships of women and men from Mexico and the United States. *Personality and Social Psychology Bulletin, 14,* 439–447.

Bell, R. (1981). *Worlds of friendship.* Beverly Hills, CA: Sage.

Bell, R. (1987). Social involvement. In J. McCrosky & J. Daly (Eds.), *Personality and interpersonal communication.* Beverly Hills, CA: Sage.

Bellah, R., Madsen, R., Sullivan, W., Swidler, A., & Tipton, S. (1985). *Habits of the heart.* Berkeley: University of California Press.

Bellah, R., Madsen, R., Sullivan, W., Swidler, A., & Tipton, S. (1991). *The good society.* New York: Knopf.

Bem, S. (1970). Case study of nonconscious ideology. In D. Bem (Ed.), *Beliefs, attitudes, and human affairs.* Belmont, CA: Brooks/Cole.

Bem, S. (1974). The measurement of psychological androgyny. *Journal of Consulting and Clinical Psychology, 42,* 155–162.

Bem, S. (1993). *The lens of gender.* New Haven, CT: Yale University Press.

Benedict, R. (1934). *Patterns of culture.* Boston: Houghton Mifflin.

Benedict, R. (1946). *The chrysanthemum and the sword.* Boston: Houghton Mifflin.

Bennett, J. (1977). Transition shock. In N. Jain (Ed.), *International and intercultural communication annual* (Vol. IV). Falls Church, VA: Speech Communication Association.

Bennett, J., Passin, J., & McKnight, R. (1958). *In search of identity: Japanese overseas scholars in the United States.* Minneapolis: University of Minnesota Press.

Bennett, M. (1979). Overcoming the golden rule: Sympathy and empathy. In D. Nimmo (Ed.), *Communication yearbook 3.* New Brunswick, NJ: Transaction.

Benson, P., & Vincent, S. (1980). Development and validation of the sexist attitude toward women scale. *Psychology of Women Quarterly, 5,* 276–291.

Berger, C. (1979). Beyond initial interaction. In H. Giles & R. St. Clair (Eds.), *Language and social psychology.* Oxford, England: Blackwell.

Berger, C., & Bradac, J. (1982). *Language and social knowledge.* London: Edward Arnold.

Berger, C., & Calabrese, R. (1975). Some explorations in initial interaction and beyond. *Human Communication Research, 1,* 99–112.

Berger, C., & Douglas, W. (1982). Thought and talk: "Excuse me, but have I been talking to myself?" In F. Dance (Ed.), *Human communication theory.* New York: Harper and Row.

Berger, C., Gardner, R., Parks, M., Schulman, L., & Miller, G. (1976). Interpersonal epistemology and interpersonal communication. In G. Miller (Ed.), *Explorations in interpersonal communication.* Beverly Hills, CA: Sage.

Berger, P., & Kellner, H. (1970). Marriage and construction of reality. In H. Dreitzel (Ed.), *Recent sociology, no. 2: Patterns of communication behavior*. New York: Macmillan.

Berger, P., & Luckman, T. (1967). *The social construction of reality*. New York: Doubleday.

Berger, J., Wagner, D., & Zelditch, M. (1985). Introduction: Expectation states theory. In J. Berger & M. Zelditch (Eds.), *Status, rewards, and influence*. San Francisco: Josey-Bass.

Berlin, B., & Kay, P. (1969). *Basic color terms: Their universality and evolution*. Berkeley: University of California Press.

Berlo, D. K. (1960). *The process of communication*. New York: Holt, Rinehart, and Winston.

Berlyne, D. (1980). Psychological aesthetics. In H. Triandis & W. Lambert (Eds.), *Handbook of cross-cultural psychology* (Vol. 3). Boston: Allyn and Bacon.

Bernstein, B. (1966). Elaborated and restricted codes. In A. Smith (Ed.), *Communication and culture*. New York: Holt, Rinehart, and Winston.

Bernstein, B. (1971). *Class, codes and control*. Boston: Routledge and Kegan Paul.

Berreman, G. (1972). Race, caste and other invidious distinctions in social stratification. *Race, 13,* 385–414.

Berry, D., Pennebaker, J., Mueller, J., & Hiller, W. (1997). Linguistic bases of social perception. *Personality and Social Psychology Bulletin, 23,* 526–537.

Berry, J. (1980). Acculturation as varieties of adaptation. In A. Padilla (Ed.), *Acculturation: Theory, models and some new findings*. Boulder, CO: Westview Press.

Berry, J. (1990). Psychology of acculturation. In R. Brislin (Ed.), *Applied cross-cultural psychology*. Newbury Park, CA: Sage.

Berry, J., & Kim, U. (1987). Acculturation and mental health. In P. Dasen, J. Berry, & N. Sartorious (Eds.), *Health and cross-cultural psychology*. Thousand Oaks, CA: Sage.

Berry, J., Kim, U., & Boski, P. (1988). Psychological acculturation of immigrants. In Y. Kim & W. Gudykunst (Eds.), *Cross-cultural adaptation*. Newbury Park, CA: Sage.

Berry, J., & Sam, D. (1997). Acculturation and adaptation. In J. Berry, M. Segall, & C. Kagitcibisi (Eds.), *Handbook of cross-cultural psychology* (2nd ed., Vol. 3). Boston: Allyn and Bacon.

Berscheid, E. (1985). Interpersonal attraction. In G. Lindzey & E. Aronson (Eds.), *Handbook of social psychology* (3rd ed., Vol. 2). New York: Random House.

Berscheid, E., Granziano, W., Monson, T., & Dermer, M. (1976). Outcome dependency. *Journal of Personality and Social Psychology, 34,* 978–989.

Berscheid, E., & Walster, E. (1969). *Interpersonal attraction*. Reading, MA: Addison-Wesley.

Best, D., & Williams, J. (1984). A cross-cultural examination of self and ideal self descriptions in Canada, England, and the United States. In R. Diaz-Guerrero (Ed.), *Cross-cultural and national studies in social psychology*. New York: Elsevier.

Best, D., & Williams, J. (1997). Sex, gender, and culture. In J. Berry, M. Segall, & C. Kagitcibisi (Eds.), *Handbook of cross-cultural psychology* (2nd ed., Vol. 3). Boston: Allyn & Bacon.

Bezooijen, R., Otto, S., & Heenan, T. (1983). Recognition of vocal expressions of emotions. *Journal of Cross-Cultural Psychology, 14,* 387–406.

Bidney, D. (1968). Cultural relativism. In D. Sills (Ed.), *International encyclopedia of the social sciences* (Vol. 3). New York: Free Press.

Bieri, J. (1955). Cognitive complexity-simplicity and predictive behavior. *Journal of Abnormal and Social Psychology, 51,* 263–268.

Billig, M. (1987). *Arguing and thinking*. Cambridge, England: Cambridge University Press.

Billig, M. (1995). *Banal nationalism*. London: Sage.

Billig, M., Condor, S., Edwards, D., Gane, M., Middleton, D., & Radley, A. (1988). *Ideological dilemmas*. Newbury Park, CA: Sage.

Birdwhistell, R. (1963). The kinesis level in the investigation of the emotions. In P. H. Knapp (Ed.), *Expressions of the emotions in man*. New York: International University Press.

Birdwhistell, R. (1970). *Kinesics in context*. Philadelphia: University of Pennsylvania Press.

Birenbaum, A., & Sagarin, E. (1976). *Norms and human behavior*. New York: Praeger.

Biswas, A. (1984). *Climate and development*. Dublin: Tycoly.

Blanchard, F., Lilly, T., & Vaughn, L. (1991). Reducing the expression of racial prejudice. *Psychological Science, 2,* 101–105.

Blau, P., & Schwartz, B. (1984). *Cross-cutting social circles*. New York: Academic Press.

Boas, F. (1911). Introduction. In *Handbook of American Indian languages* (Vol. 40). Washington, DC: Smithsonian Institute.

Bochner, S. (Ed.). (1981). *The mediating person*. Cambridge, MA: Schenkman.

Bochner, S. (1994). Cross-cultural differences in self-concept. *Journal of Cross-Cultural Psychology, 25,* 273–283.

Bochner, S., & Hesketh, B. (1994). Power distance, individualism/ collectivism, and job related attitudes in a culturally diverse work group. *Journal of Cross-Cultural Psychology, 25,* 233–257.

Bodenhausen, G., Gaelick, L., & Wyer, R. (1987). Affective and cognitive factors in intragroup and intergroup communication. In C. Hendrick (Ed.), *Group processes and intergroup relations*. Newbury Park, CA: Sage.

Bodenhausen, G., & Macrae, C. (1996). The self-regulation of intergroup perceptions. In C. Macrae, C. Stagnor, & M. Hewstone (Eds.), *Stereotypes and stereotyping*. New York: Guilford.

Boekestijn, C. (1988). Intercultural migration and the development of personal identity. *International Journal of Intercultural Relations, 12*(2), 83–105.

Bogardus, E. (1959). *Social distance.* Yellow Springs, OH: Antioch Press.

Bok, S. (1989). *A strategy for peace.* New York: Pantheon.

Boldt, E. (1978). Structural tightness and cross-cultural research. *Journal of Cross-Cultural Psychology, 9,* 151–165.

Boldt, E., & Roberts, L. (1979). Structural tightness and social conformity. *Journal of Cross-Cultural Psychology, 10,* 221–230.

Bolton, R. (1979). *People skills.* New York: Simon & Schuster.

Bond, M. (1988). Finding universal dimensions of individual variations in multinational studies of values. *Journal of Personality and Social Psychology, 55,* 1009–1015.

Bond, M. (1993). Emotions and their experience in Chinese culture. *Journal of Nonverbal Behavior, 17,* 245–262.

Bond, M., & Cheung, T. (1983). College students' spontaneous self-concept. *Journal of Cross-Cultural Psychology, 14,* 153–171.

Bond, M., & Lee, P. (1981). Face-saving in Chinese culture. In A. King & R. Lee (Eds.), *Social life and development in Hong Kong.* Hong Kong: Chinese University Press.

Bond, M., & Venus, C. (1991). Resistance to group or personal insults in an ingroup and outgroup context. *International Journal of Psychology, 26,* 83–94.

Bond, M., Wan, K., Leung, K., & Giacalone, R. (1985). How are the responses to verbal insults related to cultural collectivism? *Journal of Cross-Cultural Psychology, 16,* 111–127.

Bond, R., & Smith, P. (1996). Culture and conformity. *Psychological Bulletin, 119,* 111–137.

Bosmajian, H. (1974). *The language of oppression.* Washington, DC: Public Affairs Press.

Bostain, J. (1973). *"How to read a foreigner."* Videotaped presentation. Intercultural Relations Course, Naval Amphibious School, Coronado, CA.

Boucher, J., Landis, D., & Clark, K. (Eds.). (1987). *Ethnic conflict.* Newbury Park, CA: Sage.

Boulding, E. (1990). *Building a global civic culture.* Syracuse: Syracuse University Press.

Boulding, K. (1956). *The image.* Ann Arbor: University of Michigan Press.

Bourhis, R. (1985). The sequential nature of language choices in cross-cultural communication. In R. Street & J. Cappella (Eds.), *Sequence and pattern in communicative behavior.* London: Edward Arnold.

Bourhis, R., Giles, H., Leyens, J., & Tajfel, H. (1979). Psycholinguistic distinctiveness. In H. Giles & R. St. Clair (Eds.), *Language and social psychology.* Oxford: Blackwell.

Bourhis, R., Giles, H., & Rosenthal, D. (1981). Notes on the construction of a "subjective vitality questionnaire" for ethnolinguistic groups. *Journal of Multilingual and Multicultural Development, 2,* 145–155.

Bourhis, R., & Sachdev, I. (1984). Vitality perceptions and language attitudes. *Journal of Language and Social Psychology, 3,* 97–126.

Boyer, E. (1990, June 20). Letter to the editor. *Chronicle of Higher Education,* p. B4.

Brabant, S., Palmer, C., & Grambling, R. (1990). Returning home. *International Journal of Intercultural Relations, 14,* 387–404.

Bradac, J. (1990). Language attitudes and impression formation. In H. Giles & P. Robinson (Eds.), *Handbook of language and social psychology.* London; Wiley.

Bradburn, N. (1969). *The structure of psychological well-being.* Chicago: Aldine.

Braithwaite, D. (1991). "Just how much did that wheelchair cost?" *Western Journal of Speech Communication, 55,* 254–274.

Braithwaite, D., & Thompson, T. (Eds.). (2000). *Handbook of communication and people with disabilities.* Mahwah, NJ: Erlbaum.

Bram, J. (1955). *Language and society.* Garden City, NY: Doubleday.

Branham, R. (1980). Ineffability, creativity and communication competence. *Communication Quarterly, 3,* 11–21.

Branscombe, N., & Wann, D. (1994). Collective self-esteem consequences of outgroup derogation when a values social identity is on trial. *European Journal of Social Psychology, 24,* 641–657.

Brein, M., & David, K. (1971). Intercultural communication and the adjustment of the sojourner. *Psychological Bulletin, 76,* 215–230.

Breton, R. (1964). Institutional completeness of ethnic communities and the personal relations of immigrants. *American Journal of Sociology, 40,* 193–205.

Breton, R. (1991). *The governance of ethnic communities.* Westport, CT: Greenwood.

Brett, J., & Okumura, T. (1998). Inter- and intracultural negotiations. *Academy of Management Journal, 41,* 495–510.

Brewer, M. (1968). Determinants of social distance among East African tribal groups. *Journal of Personality and Social Psychology, 10,* 279–289.

Brewer, M. (1979). Ingroup bias in the minimal intergroup situation. *Psychological Bulletin, 86,* 307–324.

Brewer, M. (1991). The social self. *Personality and Social Psychology Bulletin, 17,* 475–482.

Brewer, M. (1999). The psychology of prejudice. *Journal of Social Issues, 55*(3), 429–444.

Brewer, M., & Brown, R. (1998). Intergroup relations. In D. Gilbert, S. Fiske, & G. Lindsey (Eds.), *Handbook of social psychology* (4th ed., Vol. 2). New York: McGraw-Hill.

Brewer, M., & Campbell, D. (1976). *Ethnocentrism and intergroup attitudes.* New York: Wiley.

Brewer, M., & Gaertner, S. (2001). Toward reduction of prejudice. In R. Brown & S. Gaertner (Eds.), *Intergroup processes.* Oxford, UK: Blackwell.

Brewer, M., & Miller, N. (1988). Contact and cooperation. In P. Katz & D. Taylor (Eds.), *Eliminating racism.* New York: Plenum.

Brewer, M., & Pickett, C. (1999). Distinctiveness motives as a source of the social self. In T. Tyler, R. Kramer, & O. John (Eds.), *The psychology of the social self.* Hillsdale, NJ: Erlbaum.

Brewer, M., & Roccas, S. (2001). Individual values, social identity, and optimal distinctiveness. In C. Sedikides & M. Brewer (Eds.), *Individual self, relational self, and collective self.* Philadelphia: Psychology Press.

Brim, O., & Wheeler, S. (1966). *Socialization through the life cycle.* New York: Wiley.

Brislin, R. (1979). Increasing the range of concepts in intercultural research: The example of prejudice. In W. Davey (Ed.), *Intercultural theory and practice.* Washington, DC: Society for Intercultural Education, Training and Research.

Brislin, R. (1981). *Cross-cultural encounters.* Elmsford, NY: Pergamon.

Brislin, R., Cushner, K., Cherrie, C., & Yong, M. (1986). *Intercultural interactions.* Beverly Hills, CA: Sage.

Brislin, R., & Yoshida, T. (1994). *Intercultural communication training.* Thousand Oaks, CA: Sage.

Brodie, H. (1989, September 9). No we're not taught to hate, but we can overcome the instinct to fear "the other." *Los Angeles Times,* Part II, p. 16.

Brook, G. (1973). *Varieties of English.* London: Macmillan.

Broom, L., & Kitsuse, J. (1955). The validation of acculturation. *American Anthropologist, 57,* 44–48.

Broome, B. (1981). Facilitating attitudes and messages characteristic in the expression of differences in intercultural encounters. *International Journal of Intercultural Relations, 5,* 215–238.

Broome, B. (1990). "Palevome": Foundations of struggle and conflict in Greek interpersonal communication. *Southern Journal of Communication, 55,* 260–275.

Brown, P., & Fraser, C. (1979). Speech as a marker of situation. In K. Scherer & H. Giles (Eds.), *Social markers in speech.* Cambridge, UK: Cambridge University Press.

Brown, P., & Levinson, S. (1978). Universals in language usage. In E. Goody (Ed.), *Questions and politeness.* Cambridge, UK: Cambridge University Press.

Brown, R. (1966). *Words and things.* Glencoe, IL: Free Press.

Bruner, J. (1957). On perceptual readiness. *Psychological Review, 64,* 123–152.

Bruner, J. (1958). Social psychology and perception. In E. Maccoby, T. Newcomb, & E. Hartley (Eds.), *Readings in social psychology* (3rd ed.). New York: Holt, Rinehart, and Winston.

Bruner, J., Goodnow, J., & Austin, G. (1956). *A study of thinking.* New York: Wiley.

Bruner, J., Oliver, R., & Greenfield, P. (1966). *Studies in cognitive growth.* New York: Wiley.

Bruner, J., & Perlmutter, H. (1957). Compatriot and foreigner. *Journal of Abnormal and Social Psychology, 55,* 253–260.

Buber, M. (1958). *I and thou.* New York: Scribner.

Buber, M. (1965). *Between man and man.* New York: Macmillian.

Budner, S. (1962). Intolerance of ambiguity as a personality variable. *Journal of Personality, 30,* 29–50.

Burk, J. (1976). The effects of ethnocentrism on intercultural communicators. In F. Casmir (Ed.), *International and intercultural communication annual* (Vol. III). Falls Church, VA: Speech Communication Association.

Burgoon, J. (1992). Comparatively speaking: Applying a comparative approach to nonverbal expectancy violations theory. In J. Blumler, J. McCleod, & K. Rosengren (Eds.), *Communication and culture across time and space.* Newbury Park, CA: Sage.

Burgoon, J. (1995). Cross-cultural and intercultural applications of expectancy violations theory. In R. Wiseman (Ed.), *Intercultural communication theory.* Thousand Oaks, CA: Sage.

Burgoon, J., Berger, C., & Waldron, V. (2000). Mindfulness and interpersonal communication. *Journal of Social Issues, 56*(1), 105–128.

Burgoon, J., Buller, D., & Woodall, W. (1989). *Nonverbal communication.* New York: Harper & Row.

Burgoon, J., & Hale, J. (1988). Nonverbal expectancy violations. *Communication Monographs, 55,* 58–79.

Burgoon, M., Dillard, J., Doran, N., & Miller, J. (1982). Cultural and situational influences on the process of persuasive strategy selection. *International Journal of Intercultural relations, 6,* 85–99.

Burleson, B., Samter, W., & Lucchetti, A. (1992). Similarity in communication values as predictors of friendship choices. *Southern Communication Journal, 57,* 260–276.

Burns, D. (1989). *The feeling good handbook.* New York: William Morrow.

Burridge, K. (1956). Friendship in Tangu. *Oceana,* 177–189.

Butler, R. (1969). Age-ism: Another form of bigotry. *Gerontologist, 9,* 243–246.

Byers, P., & Byers, H. (1972). Nonverbal communication and the education of children. In C. Cozden et al. (Eds.), *Functions of language in the classroom.* New York: Teachers College Press.

Byrne, D. (1971). *The attraction paradigm.* New York: Academic Press.

Byrne, D., Goumax, C., Griffitt, W., Lamberth, J., Murakawa, N., Prasad, M., Prasad, A., & Ramirez, M. (1971). The ubiquitous relationship: Attitude similarity and attraction. *Human Relations, 24,* 201–207.

Byrne, D., & Wong, T. (1962). Racial prejudice, interpersonal attraction and assumed dissimilarity of attitudes. *Journal of Abnormal and Social Psychology, 65,* 246–253.

Cai, D., & Drake, L. (1998). The business of business negotiations. In M. Roloff (Ed.), *Communication yearbook 21.* Thousand Oaks, Sage.

Cai, D., Wilson, S., & Drake, L. (1996). *Individualism/collectivism and joint gain.* Paper presented at the International Association for Conflict Management convention.

Cai, D., Wilson, S. & Drake, L. (2000). Culture in the context of intercultural negotiation. *Human Communication Research, 26,* 591–617.

Cameron, J., Alvarez, J., Ruble, D., & Fuligni, A. (2001). Children's lay theories about ingroups and outgroups. *Personality and Social Psychology Review, 5,* 118–128.

Campbell, D. T., & Levine, R. A. (1968). Ethnocentrism and intergroup relations. In R. Abelson, E. Aronson, W. McGuire, T. Newcomb, M. Rosenberg, & P. Tannenbaum (Eds.), *Theories of cognitive consistency: A sourcebook.* Chicago: Rand McNally.

Cantor, N., Mischel, W., & Schwartz, J. (1982). Social knowledge. In A. Isen & A. Hastorf (Eds.), *Cognitive social psychology.* New York: Elsevier.

Capozza, D., Voci, A., & Luciardello, D. (2000). Individualism, collectivism, and social identity theory. In D. Capozza & R. Brown (Eds.), *Social identity processes.* London: Sage.

Capra, F. (1975). *The tao of physics.* Boulder, CO: Shambhala.

Carbaugh, D. (1993). Competence as cultural pragmatics. In R. Wiseman & J. Koester (Eds.), *Intercultural communication competence.* Thousand Oaks, CA: Sage.

Cargile, A., & Bradac, J. (2001). Attitudes toward language. In W. B. Gudykunst (Ed.), *Communication yearbook 25.* Mahwah, NJ: Erlbaum.

Carroll, R. (1988). *Cultural misunderstandings.* Chicago: University of Chicago Press.

Casmir, F. (1999). Foundations for the study of intercultural communication based on a third-culture building model. *International Journal of Intercultural Relations, 23,* 91–116.

Catton, W. R. (1961). The functions and dysfunctions of ethnocentrism. *Social Problems, 8,* 201–211.

Cegala, D., & Waldron, V. (1992). Study of the relationship between communicative performance and conversational participants' thoughts. *Communication Studies, 43,* 105–123.

Cha, J., & Nam, K. (1985). A test of Kelly's cube theory of attribution. *Korean Social Science Journal, 12,* 151–180.

Chaika, E. (1982). *Language: The social mirror.* Rowley, MA: Newbury House.

Chan, K., & Lam, L. (1987). Psychological problems of Chinese Vietnamese refugees resettling in Quebec. In K. Chan & D. Indra (Eds.), *Uprooting, loss, and adaptation.* Ottawa: Canadian Public Health Association.

Char, W. (1977). Motivations for intercultural marriages. In W. Tseng, J. McDermott, & T. Maretzki (Eds.), *Adjustment in intercultural marriage.* Honolulu: University of Hawaii Press.

Chatman, J., & Barsade, S. (1995). Personality, organizational culture, and cooperation. *Administrative Science Quarterly, 40,* 423–443.

Chen, G. (1995). Differences in self-disclosure patterns among Americans versus Chinese. *Journal of Cross-Cultural Psychology, 26,* 84–91.

Chen, L. (1995). Interaction involvement and patterns of topical talk. *International Journal of Intercultural Relations, 19,* 463–482.

Chen, L. (1996). Cognitive complexity, situational influences, and topic selection in intracultural and intercultural dyadic interactions. *Communication Reports, 9,* 1–12.

Chen, L. (1997). Verbal adaptive strategies in U.S. American dyadic interactions with U.S. Americans or East-Asian partners. *Communication Monographs, 64,* 302–323.

Chen, L., & Cegala, D. (1994). Topic management, shared knowledge, and accommodation. *Research in Language and Social Interaction, 27,* 389–417.

Cheng, A. (1974). Clashes in courtship across cultures. *East-West Center Magazine,* Summer, 11–12.

Chin, J. (1983). Diagnostic considerations in working with Asian Americans. *American Journal of Orthopsychiatry, 53,* 100–109.

Chinese Culture Connection. (1987). Chinese values and the search for culture-free dimensions of culture. *Journal of Cross-Cultural Psychology, 18,* 143–164.

Chiu, R., & Kosinski, F. (1994). Is Chinese conflict-handling behavior influenced by Chinese values? *Social Behavior and Personality, 22,* 81–90.

Choi, I., & Nisbett, R. (1998). Situational salience and cultural differences in the correspondence bias and actor-observer bias. *Personality and Social Psychology Bulletin, 24,* 949–960.

Choi, I., & Nisbett, R., & Norenzayan, A. (1991). Casual attributions across cultures. *Psychological Bulletin, 125,* 47–63.

Choi, S. C., & Choi, S. H. (1990). *Che-myon: Korean's social face.* Unpublished paper, Chung-Ang University, Seoul, South Korea.

Chung, L., & Ting-Toomey, S. (1999). Ethnic identity and relational expectations among Asian Americans. *Communication Research Reports, 16,* 157–166.

Church, A. (1982). Sojourner adjustment. *Psychological Bulletin, 91,* 540–572.

Cialdini, R., Wosinska, W., Barret, D., Butner, J., & Gornik-Durose, M. (1999). Compliance with a request in two cultures. *Personality and Social Psychology Bulletin, 25,* 1242–1253.

Cissna, K., & Sieburg, E. (1981). Patterns of interactional confirmation and disconfirmation. In C. Wilder-Mott & J. Weakland (Eds.), *Rigor and imagination.* New York: Praeger.

Clark, H. (1985). Language use and language users. In G. Lindzey & E. Aronson (Eds.), *Handbook of social psychology* (3rd ed., Vol. II). New York: Random House.

Clark, H., & Marshall, C. (1981). Definite reference and mutual knowledge. In A. Joshi, B. Webber, & I. Sag (Eds.), *Elements of discourse understanding.* New York: Cambridge University Press.

Clark, R., & Delia, J. (1977). Cognitive complexity, social perspective-taking and functional persuasive skills in second-to-ninth grade children. *Human Communication Research, 3,* 128–134.

Clarke, S., & Obler, J. (1976). Ethnic conflict, community building, and the emergence of ethnic political traditions in the United States. In S. Clarke & J. Obler (Eds.), *Urban ethnic conflict.* Chapel Hill: University of North Carolina Press.

Clatterbuck, G. (1979). Attributional confidence and uncertainty in initial interactions. *Human Communication Research, 5,* 147–157.

Clement, R., Noels, K., & Karine, G. (1994). *Media influence in minority group acculturation.* Paper presented at the Fifth International Conference on Language and Social Psychology.

Cocroft, B., & Ting-Toomey, S. (1994). Facework in Japan and the United States. *International Journal of Intercultural Relations, 18,* 469–506.

Cody, M., & McLaughlin, M. (1985). The situation as a construct in interpersonal communication. In M. Knapp & G. Miller (Eds.), *Handbook of interpersonal communication.* Beverly Hills, CA: Sage.

Coelho, G. (1958). *Changing images of America.* Glencoe, IL: Free Press.

Cohen, E. (1972). Toward a sociology of international tourism. *Social Research, 39,* 164–182.

Cohen, R. (1987). Problems in intercultural communication in Egyptian-American diplomatic relations. *International Journal of Intercultural Relations, 11,* 29–47.

Cole, M. (1990). *Relational distances and personality influences on conflict communication styles.* Paper presented at the Speech Communication Association convention.

Coleman, L., & DePaulo, B. (1991). Uncovering the human spirit: Moving beyond disability and "missed" communication. In N. Coupland, H. Giles, & J. Wiemann (Eds.), *"Miscommunication" and problematic talk.* Newbury Park, CA: Sage.

Collett, P. (1971). On training Englishmen in the nonverbal behavior of Arabs. *International Journal of Psychology, 6,* 209–215.

Collier, M., Ribeau, S., & Hecht, M. (1986). Intracultural communication rules and outcomes within three domestic cultures. *International Journal of Intercultural Relations, 10,* 439–458.

Collier, M., & Thomas, M. (1988). Cultural identity. In Y. Kim & W. Gudykunst (Eds.), *Theories in intercultural communication.* Newbury Park, CA: Sage.

Condon, J., & Kurata, K. (1973). *In search of what's Japanese about Japan.* Tokyo: Shufunotomo.

Condon, J., & Yousef, F. (1975). *An introduction to intercultural communication.* Indianapolis, IN: Bobbs-Merrill.

Condor, S., & Brown, R. (1988). Psychological processes in intergroup conflict. In W. Strobe, A. Kruglanski, B. Bar-Tal, & M. Hewstone (Eds.), *The social psychology of intergroup conflict.* New York: Springer-Verlag.

Coon, H., & Kemmelmeir, M. (2001). Cultural orientations in the United States. *Journal of Cross-Cultural Psychology, 32,* 348–364.

Copelman, D. (1993). The immigrant experience. *Mind & Human Interaction, 4*(2), 76–82.

Coupland, J., Nussbaum, J., & Coupland, N. (1991). The reproduction of aging and ageism in intergenerational talk. In N. Coupland, H. Giles, & J. Wiemann (Eds.), *"Miscommunication" and problematic talk.* Newbury Park, CA: Sage.

Coupland, N. (1980). Style-shifting in a Cardiff work setting. *Language in Society, 9,* 1–12.

Coupland, N., Coupland, J., Giles, H., & Henwood, K. (1988). Accommodating the elderly. *Language in Society, 17,* 1–42.

Cousins, S. (1989). Culture and self perception in Japan and the United States. *Journal of Personality and Social Psychology, 56,* 124–131.

Covey, H. (1988). Historical terminology used to represent older people. *Gerontologist, 28,* 291–297.

Cowan, G., & Hodge, C. (1996). Judgments of hate speech. *Journal of Applied Social Psychology, 26,* 355–374.

Cox, T., Jr. (1993). *Cultural diversity in organizations.* San Francisco: Berret-Koehler.

Cox, T. H., Lobel, S., & McLeod, P. (1991). Effects of ethnic group cultural differences on cooperative and competitive behavior on a group task. *Academy of Management Journal, 34,* 827–847.

Crisp, R., Hewstone, M., & Rubin, M. (2001). Does multiple categorization reduce intergroup bias? *Personality and Social Psychology Bulletin, 27,* 76–89.

Crocker, J., & Luhtanen, R. (1990). Collective self-esteem and ingroup bias. *Journal of Personality and Social Psychology, 58,* 60–67.

Crocker, J., Major, B., & Steele, C. (1998). Social stigma. In D. Gilbert, S. Fiske, & G. Lindsey (Eds), *Handbook of social psychology* (4th ed., Vol. 2). New York: McGraw-Hill.

Crocker, J., Voekl, K., Testa, M., & Major, B. (1991). Social Stigma: The affective consequences of attributional ambiguity. *Journal of Personality and Social Psychology, 60,* 218–228.

Crockett, W., & Friedman, P. (1980). Theoretical explorations of the process of initial interactions. *Western Journal of Speech Communication, 44,* 86–92.

Crosby, F., Bromley, S., & Saxe, L. (1980). Recent unobtrusive studies of black and white discrimination and prejudice. *Psychological Bulletin, 87,* 546–563.

Cross, S., & Rosenthal, R. (1999). Three models of conflict resolution. *Journal of Social Issues, 55*(3), 561–580.

Cross, W. (1970). The Negro to black conversion experience. *Black World, 20,* 13–27.

Crowe, P. (1991). *Sociocultural units in progress.* Paper presented at the annual meeting of the International Society for the Comparative Study of Civilizations.

Csikszentmihalyi, M. (1990). *Flow: The psychology of optimal experiences.* New York: Harper & Row.

Cupach, W., & Imahori, T. (1993a). Identity management theory. In R. Wiseman & J. Koester (Eds.), *Intercultural communication competence.* Thousand Oaks, CA: Sage.

Cupach, W., & Imahori, T. (1993b). Managing social predicaments created by others. *Western Journal of Communication, 57,* 431–444.

Cushman, D., Valentinsen, B., & Dietrich, D. (1982). A rules theory of interpersonal relationships. In F. Dance (ed.), *Human communication theory.* New York: Harper and Row.

Cushman, D., & Whiting, G. (1972). An approach to communication theory: Toward a consensus on rules. *Journal of Communication, 22,* 217–233.

Dabrowski, K. (1968). *Theory of positive disintegration.* Audio recording. Big Sur Recordings No. 1120.

Dance, F. (1982). A speech theory of human communication. In F. Dance (Ed.), *Human communication theory.* New York: Harper & Row.

Dance, F., & Larson, C. (1972). *Speech communication.* New York: Holt, Rinehart, and Winston.

Darwin, C. (1872). *Journal of researches into natural history and geology of the countries visited during the voyage of H.M.S. "Beagle" round the world, under the command of Capt. Fitzroy, R.N.* London: Ward, Lock and Bowden.

Davidson, A. (1975). Cognitive differentiation and culture training. In R. Brislin, S. Bochner, W. Lonner (Eds.), *Cross-cultural perspectives on learning.* Beverly Hills, CA: Sage.

Davidson, A., & Thompson, E. (1980). Cross-cultural studies of attitudes and beliefs. In H. Triandis & R. Brislin (Eds.), *Handbook of cross-cultural psychology* (Vol. 5). Boston: Allyn and Bacon.

Davis, F. (1977). Deviance disavowal. In J. Stubbins (Ed.), *Social and psychological aspects of disability.* Baltimore: University Park Press.

Dean, O., & Popp, G. (1990). Intercultural communication effectiveness as perceived by American managers in Saudi Arabia and French managers in the U.S. *International Journal of Intercultural Relations, 14,* 405–424.

Deaux, K. (1991). Social identities. In R. Curtis (ed.), *The relational self.* New York: Guilford.

Deaux, K. (1993). Reconstructing social identity. *Personality and Social Psychology Bulletin, 19,* 4–12.

Deaux, K., & Ethier, K. [Dimensions of social identity]. Unpublished raw data reported in Deaux (1991).

Deaux, K., & Perkins, T. (2001). The kaleidoscopic self. In C. Sedikides & M. Brewer (Eds.), *Individual self, relational self, collective self.* Philadelphia: Psychology Press.

Deaux, K., Reid, A., Mizirahi, K., & Ethier, K. (1995). Parameters of social identity. *Journal of Personality and Social Psychology, 68,* 280–291.

DeBono, E. (1991). *I am right and you are wrong.* New York: Viking.

Deregowski, J. (1980). Perception. In H. Triandis & W. Lonner (Eds.), *Handbook of cross-cultural psychology* (Vol. 3). Boston: Allyn and Bacon.

DeRidder, R., & Tripath, R. (1992). *Rules to live by: Escalation and de-escalation of intergroup hostility.* Oxford, UK: Clarendon.

Derricotte, T. (1999, November 17). Racism: Invisible thoughts and trusted hearts. *Chronicle of Higher Education*, p. B11.

Detweiler, R. (1975). On inferring the intentions of a person from another culture. *Journal of Personality, 43*, 591–611.

Detweiler, R. (1978). Culture, category width and attributions. *Journal of Cross-Cultural Psychology, 9*, 259–284.

Detweiler, R. (1980). Intercultural interaction and the categorization process. *International Journal of Intercultural Relations, 4*, 275–293.

Deutsch, M. (1954). Field theory in social psychology. In G. Lindzey (Ed.), *Handbook of social psychology* (Vol. 1). Reading, MA: Addison-Wesley.

Deutsch, M. (1961). The interpretation of praise and criticism as a function of their social context. *Journal of Abnormal and Social Psychology, 62*, 391–400.

Deutsch, M. (1973). *The resolution of conflict*. New Haven, CT: Yale University Press.

Deutsch, S., & Won, G. (1963). Some factors in the adjustment of foreign nationals. *Journal of Social Issues, 19*(3), 115–122.

De Verthelyi, R. (1995). International students' spouses. *International Journal of Intercultural Relations, 19*, 387–411.

Devine, P. (1989). Stereotypes and prejudice. *Journal of Personality and Social Psychology, 56*, 5–18.

Devine, P., & Elliot, A. (1995). Are racial stereotypes really fading? *Personality and Social Psychology Bulletin, 21*, 1139–1150.

Devine, P., Evett, S., & Vasquez-Suson, K., (1996). Exploring the interpersonal dynamics of intergroup contact. In R. Sorrentino & E. Higgins (Eds.), *Handbook of motivation and cognition* (Vol. 3). New York: Guilford.

DeVos, G. (1975). Ethnic pluralism. In G. DeVos & L. Romanucci-Ross (Eds.), *Ethnic identity*. Palo Alto, CA: Mayfield.

DeVos, G. (1978). Selective permeability and reference group sanctioning. In J. Yinger & S. Cutler (Eds.), *Major social issues*. New York: Free Press.

Dewey, J. (1934). *A common faith*. New Haven, CT: Yale University Press.

Diamond, R., & Hellcamp, D. (1969). Race, sex, ordinal position of both and self-disclosure in high school students. *Psychological Report, 25*, 235–238.

Dickson-Markman, F. (1986). Self-disclosure with friends across the life cycle. *Journal of Social and Personal Relationships, 3*, 259–264.

Diggs, N., & Murphy, B. (1991). Japanese adjustment to American communities. *International Journal of Intercultural Relations, 15*, 103–116.

Dion, K. K., & Dion, K. L. (1991). Psychological individualism and romantic love. *Journal of Social Behavior and Personality, 6*, 17–33.

Dion, K. K., & Dion, K. L. (1993). Individualistic and collectivistic perspectives on gender and the cultural context of love and intimacy. *Journal of Social Issues, 49*(3), 53–69.

Dion, K. K., & Dion, K. L. (1996). Cultural perspectives on romantic love. *Personal Relationships, 3*, 5–17.

Dion, K. K., Pak, A., & Dion, K. L. (1990). Stereotyping and physical attractiveness. *Journal of Cross-Cultural Psychology, 21*, 378–398.

Dion, K. L. (1990). The joy of ethnicity. *International Society for the Study of Personal Relationships Bulletin, 7*(1), 3–7.

Dion, K. L., & Dion, K. K. (1988). Romantic love: Individual and cultural perspectives. In R. Sternberg & M. Barnes (Eds.), *The psychology of love*. New Haven: Yale University Press.

Doherty, K., Hatfield, E., Thompson, K., & Choo, P. (1994). Cultural and ethnic influences on love and attachment. *Personal Relationships, 1*, 391–398.

Doi, T. (1973). *The anatomy of dependence*. Tokyo: Kodansha.

Doi, T. (1976). The Japanese patterns of communication and the concept of amae. In L. Samovar & R. Porter (Eds.), *Intercultural communication: A reader* (2nd ed.). Belmont, CA: Wadsworth.

Doi, T. (1986). *The anatomy of the self*. Tokyo: Kodansha.

Donohue, W., with Kolt, R. (1993). *Managing interpersonal conflict*. Newbury Park, CA: Sage.

Doosje, B., Branscombe, N., Spears, R., & Manstead, A. (1998). Guilty by association. *Journal of Personality and Social Psychology, 75*, 872–886.

Dorfman, P., & Howell, J. (1988). Dimensions of national cultures and effective leadership patterns. In R. Farmer & E. McGown (Eds.), *Advances in international comparative management* (Vol. 3). Greenwich, CT: JAI Press.

Douglis, C. (1987, November). The beat goes on. *Psychology Today*, pp. 37–42.

Dovidio, J., & Gaertner, S. (1986). Prejudice, discrimination, and racism: Historical trends and contemporary approaches. In J. Dovidio & S. Gaertner (Eds.), *Prejudice, discrimination, and racism*. Orlando, FL: Academic Press.

Dovidio, J., Gaertner, S., Niemann, Y., & Snider, K. (2001). Racial, ethnic, and cultural differences in responding to distinctiveness and discrimination on campus. *Journal of Social Issues, 57*(1), 167–188.

Dovidio, J., Gaertner, S., Validzic, A., Matoka, A., Johnson, B., & Frazier, S. (1997). Extending the benefits of · recategorization. *Journal of Experimental Social Psychology, 33*, 401–420.

Dovidio, J., Maruyama, G., Alexander, M. (1998). A social psychology of national and international group relations. *Journal of Social Issues, 54*(4), 831–846.

Downs, J. (1971). *Cultures in crisis*. Chicago: Glencoe Press.

Downs, R., & Stea, D. (Eds.). (1973). *Image and environment.* Chicago: Aldine.

Downs, R., & Stea, D. (1977). *Maps in minds.* New York: Harper & Row.

Driberg, H. (1935). The "best friend" among the Dianja. *Man, 35,* 101–102.

Driver, E. (1973). Self-conceptions in India and the United States. *Sociological Quarterly, 14,* 576–588.

Dublin, T. (1993). *Immigrant voices.* Urbana: University of Illinois Press.

Dubos, R. (1981). *Celebrations of life.* New York: McGraw-Hill.

Ducci, L., Arcuri, L., W/Georgis, T., & Sineshaw, D. (1982). Emotion recognition in Ethiopia. *Journal of Cross-Cultural Psychology, 13,* 340–351.

Duck, S. (1977). *The study of acquaintance.* Farnborough, UK: Saxon House.

Duck, S., Rutt, D., Hurst, M., & Strejc, H. (1991). Some evident truths about conversations in everyday relationships. *Human Communication Research, 18,* 228–267.

Duncan, B. (1976). Differential social perception and attribution of intergroup violence. *Journal of Personality and Social Psychology, 34,* 590–598.

Duran, R. (1982). Communicative adaptability. *Communication Quarterly, 31,* 230–236.

Dyal, J., & Dyal, R. (1981). Acculturation, stress and coping. *International Journal of Intercultural Relations, 5,* 301–328.

Earley, P. (1997). *Face, harmony, and social structure.* New York: Oxford University Press.

Eaton, W., & Lasry, J. (1978). Mental health and occupational mobility in a group of immigrants. *Science and Medicine, 12,* 53–58.

Edgerton, R. (1985). *Rules, expectations, and social order.* Berkeley: University of California Press.

Edwards, J. (1985). *Language, society, and identity.* Oxford: Blackwell.

Efron, D. (1972/1941). *Gestures and environment.* New York: King's Crown Press.

Ehrenhaus, P. (1983). Culture and the attribution process. In W. Gudykunst (Ed.), *Intercultural communication theory.* Beverly Hills, CA: Sage.

Ehrlich, H. (1973). *The social psychology of prejudice.* New York: Wiley.

Eibl-Eibesfeldt, L. (1979). Similarities and differences between cultures in expressive movements. In S. Weitz (Ed.), *Nonverbal communication* (2nd ed.). New York: Oxford University Press.

Eisenberg, E. (1984). Ambiguity as a strategy in organizational communication. *Communication Monographs, 51,* 227–242.

Eisenstadt, E. (1954). *The absorption of immigrants.* London: Routledge and Kegan Paul.

Ekman, P. (1972). Universals and cultural differences in facial expressions of emotion. In J. Cole (Ed.), *Nebraska symposium on motivation* (Vol. 19). Lincoln: Nebraska University Press.

Ekman, P. (1978). Facial expressions. In A. Siegman & S. Feldstein (Eds.), *Nonverbal behavior and communication.* Hillsdale, NJ: Erlbaum.

Ekman, P., & Friesen, W. (1969). The repertoire of nonverbal behavior: Categories, origins, usage, and coding. *Semiotica, 1,* 49–98.

Ekman, P., & Friesen, W. (1971). Constants across cultures in the face and emotion. *Journal of Personality and Social Psychology, 17,* 124–129.

Ekman, P, Friesen, W., O'Sullivan, M., Chan, A., Diacoyanni-Tarlatzis, I., Heider, K., Krause, R., LeCompte, W., Pitcairn, T., Ricci-Bitti, P., Scherer, K., Tomita, M., & Tzavaras, A. (1987). Universals and cultural differences in the judgment of facial expressions of emotions. *Journal of Personality and Social Psychology, 53,* 712–717.

Ellingsworth, H. (1977). Conceptualizing intercultural communication. In B. Ruben (Ed.), *Communication yearbook 1.* New Brunswick, NJ: Transaction Books.

Elliot, S., Scott, M., Jensen, A., & McDonald, M. (1982). Perceptions of reticence. In M. Burgoon (Ed.), *Communication yearbook 5.* New Brunswick, NJ: Transaction Books.

Ellis, D. (1999). *Crafting society.* Mahwah., NJ: Erlbaum.

Ellis, J., & Wittenbaum, G. (2000). Relationship between self construal and verbal promotion. *Communication Research, 27,* 704–722.

Elsayed-Ekhouly, S., & Buda, R. (1996). Organizational conflict. *International Journal of Conflict Management, 7,* 71–81.

Embree, J. (1950). Thailand—A loosely structured social system. *American Anthropologist, 52,* 181–193.

Emerson, R. (1960). *From empire to nation.* Cambridge, MA: Harvard University Press.

Engebretson, D., & Fullmer, D. (1970). Cross-cultural differences in territoriality. *Journal of Cross-Cultural Psychology, 1,* 261–269.

Enloe, W., & Lewin, P. (1987). Issues of integration abroad and readjustment to Japan of Japanese returnees. *International Journal of Intercultural Relations, 11,* 223–248.

Epstein, S. (1984) Controversial issues in emotion theory. In P. Shaver (Ed.), *Review of personality and social psychology* (Vol. 5). Beverly Hills, CA: Sage.

Erickson, F. (1981). *Anecdote, rhapsody, and rhetoric.* Paper presented at the Georgetown University Roundtable on Linguistics.

Ervin-Tripp, S. (1964). Interaction of language, topic, and listener. *American Anthropologist, 66,* 86–102.

Ervin-Tripp, S. (1968). An analysis of the interaction of language, topic, and listener. In J. Fishman (Ed.), *Readings in the sociology of language*. The Hague: Mouton.

Espinoza, J., & Garza, R. (1985). Social group salience and interethnic cooperation. *Journal of Experimental Social Psychology, 21*, 697–715.

Espiritu, Y. (1992). *Asian American panethnicity*. Philadelphia: Temple University Press.

Esses, V., Jackson, L., & Armstrong, T. (1998). Intergroup competition and attitudes toward immigrants and immigration. *Journal of Social Issues, 54*(4), 699–724.

Ethier, K., & Deaux, K. (1994). Negotiating social identity when contexts change. *Journal of Personality and Social Psychology, 67*, 243–251.

Etzioni, A. (1993). *The spirit of community*. New York: Crown.

Etzioni, A. (2001). *The monochrome society*. Princeton, NJ: Princeton University Press.

Fang, C., Sidanius, J., & Pratto, F. (1998). Romance across the social status continuum. *Journal of Cross-Cultural Psychology, 29*, 290–305.

Farb, P. (1979). Man at the mercy of language. In D. Mortensen (Ed.), *Basic readings in communication theory* (2nd ed.). New York: Harper & Row.

Faulkender, P. (1985). Relationship between Bem sex-role inventory and attitudes of sexism. *Psychological Reports, 57*, 227–235.

Feather, N. (1990). Bridging the gap between values and action. In E. Higgins & R. Sorrentino (Eds.), *Handbook of motivation and cognition* (Vol. 2). New York: Guilford.

Feather, N. (1995). Values, valences, and choice. *Journal of Personality and Social Psychology, 68*, 1135–1151.

Feig, J., & Blair, J. (1975). *There is a difference*. Washington, DC: Meriden International House.

Feldman, R. (1968). Response to compatriot and foreigner who seek assistance. *Journal of Personality and Social Psychology, 10*, 202–214.

Feldstein, S., Hennessy, B., & Bond, R. (1981). *Conversational chronography and interpersonal perception in Chinese and English dyads*. Paper presented at the American Psychological association convention (cited by Welkowitz et al., 1984).

Fernandez, D., Carlson, D., Stepina, L., & Nicholson, J. (1997). Hofstede's country classification 25 years later. *Journal of Social Psychology, 137*(1), 43–54.

Fernandez-Collado, C., Rubin, R., & Hernandez-Sampieri, R. (1991). *A cross-cultural examination of interpersonal communication motives in Mexico and the United States*. Paper presented at the International Communication Association convention.

Festinger, L. (1957). *A theory of cognitive dissonance*. Evanston, IL: Row, Peterson.

Fisher, B. A. (1978). *Perspectives on human communication*. New York: Macmillan.

Fisher, R., & Brown, S. (1988). *Getting together*. New York: Houghton Mifflin.

Fiske, A. (1991). *Structures of social life*. New York: Free Press.

Fiske, A. (1993). Social errors in four cultures. *Journal of Cross-Cultural Psychology, 24*, 463–494.

Fiske, D., & Maddi, S. (Eds.). (1961). *Functions of varied experiences*. Homewood, IL: Dorsey.

Fiske, S., & Morling, B. (1996). Stereotyping as a function of personal control motives and capacity constraints. In R. Sorrentino & E. Higgins (Eds.), *Handbook of motivation and cognition* (Vol. 3). New York: Guilford.

Fiske, S., Morling, B., & Stevens, L. (1996). Controlling self and others. *Personality and Social Psychology Bulletin, 22*, 115–123.

Fiske, S., Xu, J., Cuddy, A., & Glick, P. (1999). (Dis)respecting versus (dis)liking. *Journal of Social Issues, 55*(3), 473–489.

Fitch, K., & Sanders, R. (1994). Culture, communication, and preferences for indirectness in expression of directives. *Communication Theory, 4*, 219–245.

Foa, U., & Foa, E. (1974). *Societal structures of the mind*. Springfield, IL: Charles Thomas.

Fogel, A. (1993). *Developing through relationships*. Chicago: University of Chicago Press.

Fogel, D. (1979). *Human development and communication competencies*. Paper presented at the Speech Communication Association convention.

Fong, M., & Philipsen, G. (2001). A Chinese American way of speaking. *Intercultural Communication Studies, X*(2), 65–84.

Fontaine, G., & Dorch, E. (1980). Problems and benefits of close interpersonal relationships. *International Journal of Intercultural Relations, 4*, 329–338.

Ford, D., & Lerner, R. (1992). *Developmental systems theory*. Newbury Park, CA: Sage.

Forgas, J., & Bond, M. (1985). Cultural influences on perceptions of interaction episodes. *Personality and Social Psychology Bulletin, 11*, 75–88.

Foster, D., & Finchilescu, G. (1986). Contact in a "noncontact" society. In M. Hewstone & R. Brown (Eds.), *Contact and conflict in intergroup encounters*. Oxford, UK: Blackwell.

Frable, D., Blackstone, T., & Sherbaum, C. (1990). Marginal and mindful. *Journal of Personality and Social Psychology, 59*, 140–149.

Frager, R. (1970). Conformity and anticonformity in Japan. *Journal of Personality and Social Psychology, 15,* 203–210.

Freeberg, A., & Stein, C. (1996). Felt obligation toward parents in Mexican-American and Anglo-American adults. *Journal of Social and Personal Relationships, 13,* 457–471.

French, J., & Raven, B. (1959). The basis of social power. In D. Cartwright (Ed.), *Studies in social power.* Ann Arbor, MI: Institute for Social Research.

Frey, D., & Gaertner, S. (1986). Helping and the avoidance of inappropriate interracial behavior. *Journal of Personality and Social Psychology, 50,* 1083–1090.

Friedman, M. (1974). *The hidden human image.* New York: Dell.

Friedman, M. (1983). *The confirmation of otherness.* New York Pilgrim Press.

Friedman, M. (1986). Foreword. In R. Arnett, *Communication and community.* Carbondale: Southern Illinois University Press.

Friesen, W. (1972). *Cultural differences in facial expression in a social situation.* Unpublished doctoral dissertation, University of California, San Francisco.

Frymier, A., Klopf, D., & Ishii, S. (1990). Japanese and Americans compared on the affect orientation construct. *Psychological Reports, 66,* 985–986.

Fuentes, C. (1992). *The buried mirror.* Boston: Houghton Mifflin.

Fujino, D. (1992). *Extending exchange theory: Effects of ethnicity and gender on Asian American heterosexual relationships.* Doctoral dissertation, University of California, Los Angeles.

Fujino, D. (1997). The rates, patterns and reasons for forming heterosexual interracial dating relationships among Asian Americans. *Journal of Social and Personal Relationships, 14,* 809–828.

Furnham, A. (1986). Situational determinants of intergroup communication. In W. Gudykunst (Ed.), *Intergroup communication.* London: Edward Arnold.

Furnham, A. (1988). The adjustment of sojourners. In Y. Kim & W. Gudykunst (Eds.), *Cross-cultural adaptation.* Newbury Park, CA: Sage.

Furnham, A., & Bochner, S. (1982). Social difficulty in a foreign culture. In S. Bochner (Ed.), *Cultures in contact.* Elmsford, NY: Pergamon.

Furnham, A., & Bochner, S. (1986). *Culture shock.* New York: Routledge.

Furnham, A., & Ribchester, T. (1995). Tolerance of ambiguity: A review of the concept, its measurement, and applications. *Current Psychology, 14*(3), 179–199.

Fussell, P. (1983). *Class.* New York: Summit Books.

Gabrenya, W., & Wang, Y. (1983). *Cultural differences in self schemata.* Paper presented at the Southeast Psychological Association convention.

Gabrielidis, C., Stephan, W., Ybarra, O., Pearson, V., & Villareal, L. (1997). Preferred styles of conflict resolution: Mexico and the United States. *Journal of Cross-Cultural Psychology, 28,* 661–677.

Gaertner, S., & Dovidio, J. (1986). The aversive form of racism. In J. Dovidio & S. Gaertner (Eds.), *Prejudice, discrimination, and racism.* Orlando, FL: Academic Press.

Gaertner, S., & Dovidio, J. (2000). *Reducing intergroup bias: The comon ingroup identity model.* Philadelphia: Psychology Press.

Gaetz, L., Klopf, D., & Ishii, S. (1990). *Predispositions toward verbal behavior of Japanese and Americans.* Paper presented at the Communication Association of Japan conference.

Gaines, S., Granrose, C., Rios, D., Garcia, B., Yoon, M., Farris, K., & Bledsoe, K. (1999). Patterns of attachment and responses to accommodative dilemmas among interethnic/interracial couples. *Journal of Social and Personal Relationships, 16,* 275–285.

Gaines, S., Marelich, W., Bledsoe, K., Steers, W., Henderson, M., Granrose, C., Barayos, L., Hicks, D., Lyde, M., Takahashi, Y., Yum, N., Rios, D., Garcia, B., Farris, K., & Page, K. (1997). Links between race/ethnicity and cultural values as mediated by race/ethnic identity and moderated by sender. *Journal of Personality and Social Psychology, 72,* 1460–1476.

Gallois, C. (1994). Group membership, social rules, and power. *Journal of Pragmatics, 22,* 301–324.

Gallois, C., Franklyn-Stokes, A., Giles, H., & Coupland, N. (1988). Communication accommodation theory and intercultural encounters. In Y. Kim & W. Gudykunst (Eds.), *Theories in intercultural communication.* Newbury Park, CA: Sage.

Gallois, C., Giles, H., Jones, F., Cargile, A., & Ota, H. (1995). Accommodating intercultural encounters. In R. Wiseman (Ed.), *Intercultural communication theory.* Thousand Oaks, CA: Sage.

Galston, M. (1991). Rights do not equal rightness. *Responsive Community, 1,* 78.

Gandhi, M. (1948). *Nonviolence in peace and war.* Ahmedabad, India: Garland.

Gao, G. (1990). *A dyadic analysis of romantic relationships in China and the United States.* Unpublished doctoral dissertation, Arizona State University.

Gao, G. (1991). Stability of romantic relationships in China and the United States. In S. Ting-Toomey & F. Korzenny (Eds.), *Cross-cultural interpersonal communication.* Newbury Park, CA: Sage.

Gao, G. (1996). Self and OTHER: A Chinese perspective. In W. Gudykunst, S. Ting-Toomey, & T. Nishida (Eds.), *Communication in personal relationships across cultures*. Thousand Oaks, CA: Sage.

Gao, G. (2001). Intimacy, passion, and commitment in Chinese and U.S. American relationships. *International Journal of Intercultural Relations, 25,* 329–342.

Gao, G., & Gudykunst, W. B. (1990). Uncertainty, anxiety, and adaptation. *International Journal of Intercultural Relations, 14,* 301–317.

Gao, G., & Gudykunst, W. B. (1995). Attributional confidence, perceived similarity, and network involvement in Chinese and European American romantic relationships. *Communication Quarterly, 43,* 431–445.

Gao, G., Schmidt, K., & Gudykunst, W. (1994). The influence of strength of ethnic identity on perceived ethnolinguistic vitality. *Hispanic Journal of Behavioral Sciences, 16,* 332–341.

Gao, G., & Ting-Toomey, S. (1998). *Communicating effectively with the Chinese*. Thousand Oaks, CA: Sage.

Gaertner, S. & Bickman, L. (1971). Effects of race on the elicitation of helping behavior. *Journal of Personality and Social Psychology, 20,* 218–222.

Gans, H. (1979). Symbolic ethnicity. *Ethnic and Racial Studies, 2,* 1–20.

Garcia, S., & Rivera, S. (1999). Perceptions of Hispanic and African American couples at the friendship or engagement stage of relationship. *Journal of Social and Personal Relationships, 16,* 65–86.

Gardner, G. (1962). Cross-cultural communication. *Journal of Social Psychology, 58,* 241–256.

Gardner, J. (1991). *Building community*. Washington, DC: Independent Sector.

Gardner, R. (1985). *Social psychology and second language learning*. London: Edward Arnold.

Gardner, W., Gabriel, S., & Lee, A. (1999). "I" value freedom but "we" value relationships. *Psychological Science, 10,* 321–326.

Garratt, G., Baxter, J., & Rozelle, R. (1981). Training university police in black-American nonverbal behavior. *Journal of Social Psychology, 113,* 217–229.

Garrett, P., Giles, H., & Coupland, N. (1989). The contexts of language learning. In S. Ting-Toomey & F. Korzenny (Eds.), *Language, communication, and culture*. Newbury Park, CA: Sage.

Garvin, B., & Kennedy, C. (1986). Confirmation and disconfirmation in nurse-physician communication. *Journal of Applied Communication Research, 14,* 1–19.

Gass, S., & Varonis, E. (1984). The effect of familiarity on the comprehensibility of nonnative speech. *Language Learning, 34,* 65–89.

Gass, S., & Varonis, E. (1985). Variations in native speaker speech modification on nonnative speakers. *Studies in Second Language Acquisition, 7,* 37–58.

Gass, S., & Varonis, E. (1991). Miscommunication in nonnative speaker discourse. In N. Coupland, H. Giles, & J. Wiemann (Eds.), *"Miscommunication" and problematic talk*. Thousand Oaks, CA: Sage.

Gaw, K. (2000). Reverse shock in students returning from overseas. *International Journal of Intercultural Relations, 24,* 83–104.

Gebart-Eaglemont, J. (1994). *Acculturation and stress in immigrants*. Paper presented at the Fifth International Conference on Language and Social Psychology.

Gerbner, G., Gross, L., Morgan, M., & Signorielli, N. (1980). The "mainstreaming" of America. *Journal of Communication, 30,* 10–29.

Geertz, C. (1966). *Person, time, and conduct in Bali*. New Haven, CT: Yale Southeast Asia Studies Program.

Geertz, C. (1973). *The interpretation of culture*. New York: Basic Books.

Geertz, C. (1975). On the nature of anthropological understanding. *American Scientist, 63,* 47–53.

Gelfand, M., Spurlock, D., Sniezel, J., & Shao, L. (2000). Culture and social prediction. *Journal of Cross-Cultural Psychology, 31,* 498–516.

Genesse, F., & Bourhis, R. (1982). The social psychological significance of code switching in cross-cultural communication. *Journal of Language and Social Psychology, 1,* 1–28.

Gerbner, G. (1978). The dynamics of cultural resistance. In G. Tuchman et al. (Eds.), *Health and home*. New York: Oxford University Press.

Geyer, R. (1980). *Alienation theories: A general systems approach*. New York: Pergamon.

Gibb, J. (1961). Defensive communication. *Journal of Communication, 11,* 141–148.

Gibbs, J. (1965). Norms: The problem of definition and classification. *American Journal of Sociology, 70,* 586–594.

Gil, A., Vega, W., & Dimas, J. (1994). Acculturative stress and person adjustment among Hispanic adolescent boys. *Journal of Community Psychology, 22,* 43–54.

Gilbert, G. (1951). Stereotype persistence and change among college students. *Journal of Abnormal and Social Psychology, 46,* 245–254.

Giles, H. (1973). Accent mobility. *Anthropological Linguistics, 15,* 87–105.

Giles, H., Bourhis, R., & Taylor, D. (1977). Toward a theory of language in ethnic group relations. In H. Giles (Ed.), *Language, ethnicity and intergroup relations*. London: Academic Press.

Giles, H., & Byrne, J. (1982). The intergroup theory of second language acquisition. *Journal of Multilingual and Multicultural Development, 3,* 17–40.

Giles, H., & Coupland, N. (1991). *Language: Contexts and consequences.* Pacific Grove, CA: Brooks/Cole.

Giles, H., Coupland, N., Coupland, J., Williams, A., & Nussbaum, J. (1992). Intergenerational talk and communication with older people. *International Journal of Aging and Human Development, 34,* 271–297.

Giles, H., Coupland, N., & Wiemann, J. (1992). "Talk is cheap . . ." but "my word is my bond." In R. Bolton & H. Kwok (Eds.), *Sociolinguistics today.* London: Routledge.

Giles, H., & Hewstone, M. (1982). Cognitive structures, speech, and social situations. *Language Sciences, 4,* 187–219.

Giles, H., & Johnson, P. (1981). The role of language in ethnic relations. In J. Turner & H. Giles (Eds.), *Intergroup behavior.* Chicago: University of Chicago Press.

Giles, H., & Johnson, P. (1987). Ethnolinguistic identity theory. *International Journal of the Sociology of Language, 68,* 69–90.

Giles, H., Mulac, A., Bradac, J., & Johnson, P. (1987). Speech accommodation theory. In M. McLaughlin (Ed.), *Communication yearbook 10.* Newbury Park, CA: Sage.

Giles, H., Rosenthall, D., & Young, L. (1985) Perceived ethnolinguistic vitality: The Anglo- and Greek-Australian setting. *Journal of Multilingual and Multicultural Development, 6,* 253–269.

Giles, H., & Smith, P. (1979). Accommodation theory. In H. Giles & R. St. Clair (Eds.), *Language and social psychology.* Oxford: Blackwell.

Gimenez, M., Lopez, F., & Munoz, C. (Eds.). (1992). The politics of ethnic construction. *Latin American Perspectives, 19*(4).

Gire, J., & Carment, D. (1993). Dealing with disputes. *Journal of Social Psychology, 133,* 81–95.

Glazer, N. (1993). Is assimilation dead? *Annals of the American Academy of Political and Social science, 530,* 122–136.

Glazer, N., & Moynihan, D. (1975). *Ethnicity.* Cambridge, MA: Harvard University Press.

Glenn, E. (1981). *Man and mankind.* Norwood, NJ: Ablex.

Glenn, E., Witmeyer, D., & Stevenson, K. (1977). Cultural styles and persuasion. *International Journal of Intercultural Relations, 1,* 52–66.

Glick, P., & Fiske, S. (1996). The ambivalent sexism inventory. *Journal of Personality and Social Psychology, 70,* 461–512.

Glidden, H. (1972). The Arab world. *American Journal of Psychiatry, 128,* 984–988.

Gmelch, G. (1997). Crossing cultures: Student travel and personal development. *International Journal of Intercultural Relations, 21,* 475–490.

Goffman, E. (1955). On face-work. *Psychiatry, 18,* 213–231.

Goffman, E. (1959). *The presentation of self in everyday life.* Hammondsworth, UK: Penguin.

Goffman, E. (1961). *Asylums.* New York: Doubleday.

Goffman, E. (1963). *Stigma.* Englewood Cliffs, NJ: Prentice Hall.

Goffman, E. (1967). *Interaction ritual.* Garden City, NY: Anchor.

Goldenberg, S., & Haines, V. (1992). Social networks and institutional completeness. *Canadian Journal of Sociology, 17,* 301–312.

Gonzalez, D. (1992, November 15). What's the problem with Hispanics? Just ask a Latino. *Los Angeles Times,* p. E6.

Goodwin, S., Operario, D., & Fiske, S. (1998). Situational power and interpersonal dominance facilitate bias and inequality. *Journal of Social Issues, 54*(4), 677–698.

Gorden, M. (1964). *Assimilation in American life.* Oxford: Oxford University Press.

Gorden, R. (1974). *Living in Latin America.* Skokie, IL: National Textbooks.

Gotanda, P. K. (1991). Interview with Philip Kan Gotanda. *Los Angeles Performing Arts, 25(1),* 10–11.

Gottman, J., Notarius, C., Markman, H., Bank, S., Yoppi, B., & Rubin, M. (1976). Behavioral exchange theory and marital decision making. *Journal of Personality and Social Psychology, 34,* 14–23.

Gould, S. (1996). *Full house: The spread of excellence from Plato to Darwin.* New York: Three Rivers Press.

Gouldner, A. (1960). The norm of reciprocity. *American Sociological Review, 25,* 161–179.

Graafsma, T., Bosma, H., Grotevant, H., & deLevita, D. (1994). Identity and development: An interdisciplinary view. In H. Bosma, T. Graafsma, & D. deLevita (Eds.), *Identity and development.* Thousand Oaks, CA: Sage.

Graham, J. (1983). Brazilians, Japanese, and American business negotiations. *Journal of International Business Studies, 14,* 47–61.

Graham, J. (1985). Cross-cultural marketing negotiations. *Marketing Science, 4,* 130–146.

Graham, J., Kim, D., Lim, C., & Robinson, M. (1988). Buyer-seller negotiations around the Pacific Rim. *Journal of Consumer Research, 15,* 48–54.

Graham, M., Moeai, J., & Shizuru, L. (1985). Intercultural marriages. *International Journal of Intercultural Relations, 9,* 427–434.

Grant, P., & Holmes, J. (1981). The integration of implicit theory schemes and stereotype images. *Social Psychology Quarterly, 44,* 107–115.

Greenland, K., & Brown, R. (1999). Categorization and intergroup anxiety in contact between British and Japanese nationals. *European Journal of Social Psychology, 29,* 503–521.

Greenland, K., & Brown, R. (2000), Categorization and intergroup anxiety in intergroup contact. In D. Capozza & R. Brown (Eds.), *Social identity processes.* London: Sage.

Grice, H. (1975). Logic and conversation. In P. Cole & J. Morgan (Eds.), *Syntax and semantics* (Vol. 3). New York: Academic Press.

Grieve, P., & Hogg, M. (1999). Subjective uncertainty and intergroup discrimination in the minimal group situation. *Personality and Social Psychology Bulletin, 25,* 926–940.

Grotevant, H. (1993). The integrative nature of identity. In J. Kroger (Ed.), *Discussions on ego identity.* Hillsdale, NJ: Erlbaum.

Grove, T., & Werkman, D. (1991). Communication with able-bodied and visually disabled strangers. *Human Communication Research, 17,* 507–534.

Gudykunst, W. B. (1983a). Similarities and differences in perceptions of initial intracultural and intercultural encounters. *Southern Speech Communication Journal, XLIX,* 49–65.

Gudykunst, W. B. (1983b). Toward a typology of stranger-host relationships. *International Journal of Intercultural Relations, 7,* 401–415.

Gudykunst, W. B. (1983c). Uncertainty reduction and predictability of behavior in low- and high-context cultures. *Communication Quarterly, 31,* 49–55.

Gudykunst, W. B. (1985a). A model of uncertainty reduction in intercultural encounters. *Journal of Language and Social Psychology, 4,* 79–98.

Gudykunst, W. B. (1985b). An exploratory comparison of close intracultural and intercultural friendships. *Communication Quarterly, 33,* 236–251.

Gudykunst, W. B. (1985c). The influence of cultural similarity, type of relationship, and self-monitoring on uncertainty reduction processes. *Communication Monographs, 52,* 203–217.

Gudykunst, W. B. (1986). Toward a theory of intergroup communication. In W. B. Gudykunst (Ed.), *Intergroup communication.* London: Edward Arnold.

Gudykunst, W. B. (1987). Cross-cultural comparisons. In C. R. Berger & S. Chaffee (Eds.), *Handbook of communication science.* Newbury Park, CA: Sage.

Gudykunst, W. B. (1988a). Intergroup communication across cultures. In M. Bond (Ed.), *The cross-cultural challenge to social psychology.* Beverly Hills, CA: Sage.

Gudykunst, W. B. (1988b). Uncertainty and anxiety. In Y. Y. Kim & W. B. Gudykunst (Eds.), *Theories in intercultural communication.* Newbury Park, CA: Sage.

Gudykunst, W. B. (1989). Culture and communication in interpersonal relationships. In J. Anderson (Ed.), *Communication yearbook 12.* Newbury Park, CA: Sage.

Gudykunst, W. B. (1991). *Bridging differences.* Newbury Park, CA: Sage.

Gudykunst, W. B. (1993). Toward a theory of interpersonal and intergroup communication. In R. Wiseman & J. Koester (Eds.), *Intercultural communication competence.* Thousand Oaks, CA: Sage.

Gudykunst, W. B. (1994). *Bridging differences* (2nd ed.). Thousand Oaks, CA: Sage.

Gudykunst, W. B. (1995). Anxiety/uncertainty management (AUM) theory. In R. Wiseman (Ed.), *Intercultural communication theory.* Thousand Oaks, CA: Sage.

Gudykunst, W. B. (1998). Applying anxiety/uncertainty management (AUM) theory to intercultural adjustment training. *International Journal of Intercultural Relations, 22,* 227–250.

Gudykunst, W. B. (2001). *Asian American ethnicity and communication.* Thousand Oaks, CA: Sage.

Gudykunst, W. B. (forthcoming). Anxiety/uncertainty management (AUM) theory: Making the mesh of the net finer. In W. B. Gudykunst (Ed.), *Theorizing about communication and culture.* Thousand Oaks, CA: Sage.

Gudykunst, W. B., Chua, E., & Gray, A. (1987). Cultural dissimilarities and uncertainty reduction processes. In M. McLaughlin (Ed.), *Communication yearbook 10.* Newbury Park, CA: Sage.

Gudykunst, W. B., Gao, G., & Franklyn-Stokes, A. (1996). Self-monitoring in China and England. In J. Pandy, D. Sinha, & D. Bhawuk (Eds.), *Asian contributions to cross-cultural psychology.* New Delhi: Sage.

Gudykunst, W. B., Gao, G., Nishida, T., Bond, M. H., Leung, K., Wang, G., & Barraclough, R. A. (1989). A cross-cultural study of self-monitoring. *Communication Research Reports, 6* (1), 7–12.

Gudykunst, W. B., Gao, G., Nishida, T., Nadamitsu, Y., & Sakai, J. (1992). Self-monitoring in Japan and the United States. In S. Iwaki, Y. Kashima, & K. Leung (Eds.), *Innovations in cross-cultural psychology.* The Hague: Swets and Zeitlinger.

Gudykunst, W. B., Gao, G., Schmidt, K. L., Nishida, T., Bond, M. H., Leung, K., Wang, G., & Barraclough, R. (1992). The influence of individualism-collectivism on communication in ingroup and outgroup relationships. *Journal of Cross-Cultural Psychology, 23,* 196–213.

Gudykunst, W. B., Gao, G., Sudweeks, S., & Ting-Toomey, S., & Nishida, T. (1991). Developmental themes in opposite-sex Japanese-North American relationships. In S. Ting-Toomey & F. Korzenny (Eds.), *Cross-cultural interpersonal communication.* Newbury Park, CA: Sage.

Gudykunst, W. B., & Hammer, M. (1987). The effect of ethnicity, gender, and dyadic composition on uncertainty reduction in initial interactions. *Journal of Black Studies, 18,* 191–214.

Gudykunst, W. B., & Hammer, M. (1988a). Strangers and hosts. In Y. Kim & W. Gudykunst (Eds.), *Cross-cultural adaptation*. Newbury Park, CA: Sage.

Gudykunst, W. B., & Hammer, M. (1988b). The influence of social identity and intimacy of interethnic relationships on uncertainty reduction processes. *Human Communication Research, 14,* 569–601.

Gudykunst, W. B., & Lim, T. S. (1985). Ethnicity, sex, and self-perceptions of communicator style. *Communication Research Reports, 2,* 68–75.

Gudykunst, W. B., & Lim, T. S. (1986). A perspective for the study of intergroup communication. In W. Gudykunst (Ed.), *Intergroup communication*. London: Edward Arnold.

Gudykunst, W. B., Matsumoto, Y., Ting-Toomey, S., Nishida, T., Kim, K., & Heyman, S. (1996). The influence of cultural individualism-collectivism, self construals, and individual values on communication styles across cultures. *Human Communication Research, 22,* 510–543.

Gudykunst, W., & Nishida, T. (1983). Social penetration in close friendships in Japan and the United States. In R. Bostrom (Ed.), *Communication yearbook 7*. Beverly Hills, CA: Sage.

Gudykunst, W. B., & Nishida, T. (1984). Individual and cultural influences on uncertainty reduction. *Communication Monographs, 51,* 23–36.

Gudykunst, W. B., & Nishida, T. (1986a). Attributional confidence in low- and high-context cultures. *Human Communication Research, 12,* 525–549.

Gudykunst, W. B., & Nishida, T. (1986b). The influence of cultural variability on perceptions of communication behavior associated with relationship terms. *Human Communication Research, 13,* 147–166.

Gudykunst, W. B., & Nishida, T. (1993). Closeness in interpersonal relationships in Japan and the United States. *Research in Social Psychology, 8*(2), 85–97.

Gudykunst, W. B., & Nishida, T. (1994). *Bridging Japanese/North American differences*. Thousand Oaks, CA: Sage.

Gudykunst, W. B., & Nishida, T. (1999). The influence of culture and strength of cultural identity on individual values in Japan and the United States. *Intercultural Communication Studies, IX*(1), 1–18.

Gudykunst, W. B., & Nishida, T. (2001). Anxiety, uncertainty and perceived effectiveness of communication across relationships and cultures. *International Journal of Intercultural Relations, 25,* 55–72.

Gudykunst, W. B., & Nishida, T. (2002). *The influence of general and family-specific self construals on family communication styles in Japan and the United States*. Paper presented at the International Communication Association convention.

Gudykunst, W. B., Nishida, T., & Chua, E. (1986). Uncertainty reduction in Japanese-North American dyads. *Communication Research Reports, 3,* 39–46.

Gudykunst, W. B., Nishida, T., & Chua, E. (1987). Perceptions of social penetration in Japanese-North American dyads. *International Journal of Intercultural Relations, 11,* 171–190.

Gudykunst, W. B., Nishida, T., Koike, H., & Shiino, N. (1986). The influence of language on uncertainty reduction: An exploratory study of Japanese- Japanese and Japanese-North American interactions. In M. McLaughlin (Ed.), *Communication yearbook 9*. Beverly Hills, CA: Sage.

Gudykunst, W. B., Nishida, T., Morisaki, S., & Ogawa, N. (1999). The influence of students' personal and social identities on their perceptions of interpersonal and intergroup encounters in Japan and the United States. *Japanese Journal of Social Psychology, 15,* 47–58.

Gudykunst, W. B., Nishida, T., & Schmidt, K. (1989). Cultural, relational, and personality influences on uncertainty reduction processes. *Western Journal of Speech Communication, 53,* 13–29.

Gudykunst, W. B., & Shapiro, R. (1996). Communication in everyday interpersonal and intergroup encounters. *International Journal of Intercultural Relations, 20,* 19–45.

Gudykunst, W. B., & Sodetani, L. L., & Sonoda, K. T. (1987). Uncertainty reduction in Japanese-American Caucasian relationships in Hawaii. *Western Journal of Speech Communication, 51,* 256–278.

Gudykunst, W. B., & Sudweeks, S. (1992). Applying a theory of intercultural adaptation. In W. Gudykunst & Y. Kim (Eds.), *Readings on communicating with strangers*. New York: McGraw-Hill.

Gudykunst, W. B., & Ting-Toomey, S., with Chua, E. (1988). *Culture and interpersonal communication*. Newbury Park, CA: Sage.

Gudykunst, W. B., & Ting-Toomey, S. (1990). Ethnicity, language, and communication breakdowns. In H. Giles & P. Robinson (Eds.), *Handbook of language and social psychology*. London: Wiley.

Gudykunst, W. B., Ting-Toomey, S., Hall, B. J., & Schmidt, K. L. (1989). Language and intergroup communication. In M. K. Asante & W. B. Gudykunst (Eds.), *Handbook of international and intercultural communication*. Newbury Park, CA: Sage.

Gudykunst, W. B., Ting-Toomey, S., Sudweeks, S., & Stewart, L. (1995). *Building bridges: Interpersonal skills for a changing world*. Boston: Houghton-Mifflin.

Gudykunst, W. B., Wiseman, R., & Hammer, M. (1977). Determinants of a sojourner's attitudinal satisfaction. In B. Ruben (Ed.), *Communication yearbook 1*. New Brunswick, NJ: Transaction.

Gudykunst, W. B., Yang, S. M., & Nishida, T. (1985). A cross-cultural test of uncertainty reduction theory. *Human Communication Research, 11,* 407–454.

Gudykunst, W. B., Yang, S. M., & Nishida, T. (1987). Cultural differences in self-consciousness and self-monitoring. *Communication Research, 14,* 7–36.

Gudykunst, W. B., Yoon, Y. C., & Nishida, T. (1987). The influence of individualism-collectivism on perceptions of communication in ingroup-outgroup relationships. *Communication Monographs, 54,* 295–306.

Gulick, S. (1962). *The East and the West: A study of their psychic and cultural characteristics.* Rutland, VT: Charles E. Tuttle.

Gullahorn, J. T., & Gullahorn, J. E. (1963). An extension of the U-curve hypothesis. *Journal of Social Issues, 19(3),* 33–47.

Gumperz, J. (1982). *Discourse strategies.* New York: Cambridge University Press.

Gumperz, J., & Hernandez-Chavez, E. (1972). Bilingualism, bidialectism and classroom interaction. In C. Cazden et al. (Eds.), *Functions of language in the classroom.* New York: Teacher's College Press.

Gumperz, G., & Hymes, D. (1972). *Directions in sociolinguistics.* New York: Holt, Rinehart, & Winston.

Gumperz, J., & Levinson, S. (Eds.). (1996). *Rethinking linguistic relativity.* Cambridge, UK: Cambridge University Press.

Gumperz, J., & Tannen, D. (1979). Individual and social differences in language use. In C. Fillmore, D. Kempler, & W. Wang (Eds.), *Individual differences in language ability and language behavior.* New York: Academic Press.

Gurin, P., Peng, T., Lopez, G., & Nagda, B. (1999). Context, identity, and intergroup relations. In D. Prentice & D. Miller (Eds.), *Cultural divides.* New York: Russell Sage Foundation.

Gurung, R., & Duong, T. (1999). Mixing and matching. *Journal of Social and Personal Relationships, 16,* 639–657.

Gutmann, A. (1992). Introduction. In A. Gutmann (Ed.), *Multiculturalism and the politics of recognition.* Princeton, NJ: Princeton University Press.

Haidt, J., & Keltner, D. (1999). Culture and facial expression. *Cognition and Emotion, 13,* 225–266.

Hale, C. L. (1980). Cognitive complexity-simplicity as a determinant of communication effectiveness. *Communication Monographs, 47,* 304–311.

Hall, B., & Gudykunst, W. B. (1986). The intergroup theory of second language ability. *Journal of Language and Social Psychology, 5,* 291–302.

Hall, E. T. (1959). *The silent language.* New York: Doubleday.

Hall, E. T. (1966). *The hidden dimension.* New York: Doubleday.

Hall, E. T. (1976). *Beyond culture.* New York: Doubleday.

Hall, E. T. (1983). *The dance of life.* New York: Doubleday.

Hall, E. T., & Whyte, W. F. (1979). Intercultural communication. In C. D. Mortenson (Ed.), *Basic readings in communication theory* (2nd ed.). New York: Harper & Row.

Hallinan, M., & Smith, S. (1985). The effects of classroom racial composition on students' interracial friendliness. *Social Psychology Quarterly, 48,* 3–16.

Hamilton, D., Sherman, S., & Ruvolo, C. (1992). Sterotyped based expectancies. In W. Gudykunst & Y. Kim (Eds.), *Readings on communicating with strangers.* New York: McGraw-Hill. (Originally published in *Journal of Social Issues, 46(2),* 35–60).

Hammer, M. (1987). Behavioral dimensions of intercultural effectiveness. *International Journal of Intercultural Relations, 11,* 65–88.

Hammer, M., & Gudykunst, W. (1987). The influence of ethnicity, sex, and dyadic composition on communication in friendships. *Journal of Black Studies, 17,* 418–437.

Hammer, M., Gudykunst, W., & Wiseman, R. (1978). Dimensions of intercultural effectiveness. *International Journal of Intercultural Relations, 2,* 382–393.

Hampshire, S. (1989). *Innocence and experience.* Cambridge: Harvard University Press.

Han, G., & Park, B. (1995). Children's choice in conflict. *Journal of Cross-Cultural Psychology, 26,* 298–313.

Han, S., & Shavitt, S. (1994). Persuasion and culture. *Journal of Experimental Social Psychology, 30,* 326–350.

Hanh, T. N. (1991). *Peace in every step.* New York: Bantam.

Hara, K., & Kim, M. S. (2001). *The effect of self construals on conversational indirectness.* Paper presented at the International Communication Association convention.

Harman, L. (1987). *The modern stranger.* New York: Mouton de Gruyter.

Harris, L. (1979). *Communication competence: An argument for a systematic view.* Paper presented at the International Communication Association convention.

Harris, L. (1980). *Communication competence: An empirical test of a systematic model.* Paper presented at the International Communication Association convention.

Harris, P., & Moran, R. (1979). *Managing cultural differences.* Houston, TX: Gulf.

Harrison, J., Chadwick, M., & Scales, M. (1996). The relationship between cross-cultural adjustment and the personality variables of self-efficacy and self-monitoring. *International Journal of Intercultural Relations, 20,* 167–188.

Harvey, O., Hunt, D., & Schroder, H. (1961). *Conceptual systems and personality organization.* New York: Wiley.

Hasegawa, T., & Gudykunst, W. B. (1998). Silence in Japan and the United States. *Journal of Cross-Cultural Psychology, 29,* 668–684.

Haselden, K. (1968). *Morality and the mass media.* Nashville, TN: Broadman Press.

Haslett, B. (1990). Social class, social status, and communicative behavior. In H. Giles & W. Robinson (Eds.), *Handbook of language and social psychology.* Chichester, UK: Wiley.

Hass, R., Katz, I., Rizzo, N., Bailey, J., & Moore, L. (1992). When racial ambivalence evokes negative affect. *Personality and Social Psychology Bulletin, 18,* 786–797.

Hawes, F., & Kealey, D. (1981). An empirical study of Canadian technical assistance. *International Journal of Intercultural Relations, 5,* 239–258.

Hayano, D. (1981). Ethnic identification and disidentification. *Ethnic Groups, 3,* 157–171.

Hayashi, R. (1990). Rhythmicity, sequence, and synchrony of English and Japanese face-to-face conversations. *Language Sciences, 12,* 155–195.

Hearn, L. (1956). *Japan: An attempt at interpretation.* Tokyo: Charles Tuttle.

Heath, D. (1977). *Maturity and competence.* New York: Gardner.

Hecht, M. (1978). The conceptualization and measurement of communication satisfaction. *Human Communication Research, 4,* 253–264.

Hecht, M., Andersen, P., & Ribeau, S. (1989). Cultural dimensions of nonverbal communication. In M. Asante & W. Gudykunst (Eds.), *Handbook of international and intercultural communication.* Newbury Park, CA: Sage.

Hecht, M., & Ribeau, S. (1994). Sociocultural roots of ethnic identity. *Journal of Black Studies, 12,* 501–513.

Hecht, M., Ribeau, S., & Alberts, J. (1989). An Afro-American perspective on interethnic communication. *Communication Monographs, 56,* 385–410.

Hecht, M., Ribeau, S., & Sedano, M. (1990). A Mexican-American perspective on interethnic communication. *International Journal of Intercultural Relations, 14,* 31–55.

Hedge, R. (1998). Swinging trapeze: The negotiation of identity among Asian Indian immigrant women in the United States. In D. Tanno & A. Gonzalez (Eds.), *Communication and identity across cultures.* Thousand Oaks, CA: Sage.

Heider, F. (1958). *The psychology of interpersonal relations.* New York: Wiley.

Heimann, B. (1964). *Facets of Indian thought.* New York: Schocken.

Heine, S., & Lehman, D. (1999). Culture, self-discrepancies and self-satisfaction. *Personality and Social Psychology Bulletin, 25,* 915–925.

Heine, S., Takata, T., & Lehman, D. (2000). Beyond self-presentation. *Personality and Social Psychology Bulletin, 26,* 71–78.

Heckathorn, D. (1990). Connective sanctions and compliance norms. *American Sociological Review, 55,* 366–384.

Henley, N., Hamilton, M., & Thorne, B. (1985). Womanspeak and manspeak. In A. Sargent (Ed.), *Beyond sex roles.* New York: West.

Henley, N., & Kramarae, C. (1991). Gender, power, and miscommunication. In N. Coupland, H. Giles, & J. Wiemann (Eds.), *"Miscommunication" and problematic talk.* Thousand Oaks, CA: Sage.

Henry, W. (1990, April 9). Beyond the melting pot. *Time,* pp. 28–31.

Herman, S. (1961). Explorations in the social psychology of language choice. *Human Relations, 4,* 149–164.

Herman, S., & Schield, E. (1960). The stranger group in a cross-cultural situation. *Sociometry, 24,* 165–176.

Herskovits, M. (1955). *Cultural anthropology.* New York: Knopf.

Herskovits, M. (1966). *Cultural dynamics.* New York: Knopf.

Herskovits, M. (1973). *Cultural relativism.* New York: Random House.

Hettema, P. (1979). *Personality and adaptation.* New York: North Holland.

Hetts, J., Sakuma, M., & Pelham, B. (1999). Two roads to positive regard. *Journal of Experimental Social Psychology, 35,* 512–559.

Hewstone, M. (1988). Attributional bases of intergroup conflict. In W. Strobe, A. Kruglanski, D. Bar-Tal, & M. Hewstone (Eds.), *The social psychology of intergroup conflict.* New York: Springer-Verlag.

Hewstone, M., & Brown, R. (1986). Contact is not enough. In M. Hewstone & R. Brown (Eds.), *Contact and conflict in intergroup encounters.* Oxford: Blackwell.

Hewstone, M., & Giles, H. (1986). Stereotypes and intergroup communication. In W. Gudykunst (Ed.), *Intergroup communication.* London: Edward Arnold.

Hewstone, M., & Jaspars, J. (1984). Social dimensions of attributions. In H. Tajfel (Ed.), *The social dimension* (Vol. 2). Cambridge, England: Cambridge University Press.

Hirokawa, R., & Miyahara, A. (1986). A comparison of influence strategies utilized by managers in American and Japanese organizations. *Communication Quarterly, 34,* 250–265.

Ho, D. (1976). On the concept of face. *American Journal of Sociology, 81,* 867–884.

Ho, T., & Sung, K. (1990). Role of infrastructure networks in supporting social values to sustain economic success in newly-industrialized nations. *International Journal of Psychology, 25,* 887–900.

Hocker, J., & Wilmot, W. (1991). *Interpersonal conflict* (3rd ed.). Dubuque, IA: Wm. C. Brown.

Hockett, C. (1958). *A course in modern linguistics.* New York: Macmillan.

Hockett, C. F. (1968). Chinese vs. English. In P. Gleeson & N. Wakefield (Eds.), *Language and culture.* Columbus, OH: Charles E. Merrill.

Hodges, H. H. (1964). *Social stratification.* Cambridge, England: Schenkman.

Hodges, L., & Byrne, D. (1972). Verbal dogmatism as a potentiator of intolerance. *Journal of Personality and Social Psychology, 21,* 312–317.

Hoebel, E. (1960). *The Cheyenne.* New York: Holt, Rinehart, and Winston.

Hoffman, E. (1985). The effect of race-relation composition on the frequency of organizational communication. *Social Psychology Quarterly, 48,* 17–26.

Hofman, T. (1985). Arabs and Jews, blacks and whites. *Journal of Multilingual and Multicultural Development, 6,* 217–237.

Hofstede, G. (1979). Value systems in forty countries. In L. Eckensberger, W. Lonner, & Y. Poortinga (Eds.), *Cross-cultural contributions to psychology.* Lisse, Netherlands: Swets & Zeitlinger.

Hofstede, G. (1980). *Culture's consequences.* Beverly Hills, CA: Sage.

Hofstede, G. (1983). Dimensions of national cultures in fifty countries and three regions. In J. Deregowski, S. Dzuirawiec, & R. Annis (Eds.), *Explications in cross-cultural psychology.* Lisse, Netherlands: Swets & Zeitlinger.

Hofstede, G. (1991). *Cultures and organizations.* London: McGraw-Hill.

Hofstede, G. (1998). *Masculinity and femininity.* Thousand Oaks, CA: Sage.

Hofstede, G. (2001). *Culture's consequences* (2nd ed.). Thousand Oaks, CA: Sage.

Hofstede, G., & Bond, M. (1984). Hofstede's culture dimensions. *Journal of Cross-Cultural Psychology, 15,* 417–433.

Hogg, M., Joyce, N., & Abrams, D. (1984). Diglossia in Switzerland. *Journal of Language and Social Psychology, 3,* 185–196.

Hoijer, H. (1954). *Language in culture.* Chicago: University of Chicago Press.

Hoijer, H. (1976). The Sapir-Whorf hypothesis. In L. Samovar & R. Porter (Eds.), *Intercultural communication: A reader* (2nd ed.). Belmont, CA: Wadsworth.

Holmes, J., & Rempel, J. (1989). Trust in close relationships. In C. Hendrick (Ed.), *Close relationships.* Newbury Park, CA: Sage.

Holmes, L. (1965). *Anthropology.* New York: Ronald Press.

Holtgraves, T. (1992). The linguistic realization of face management. *Social Psychology Quarterly, 55,* 141–159.

Holtgraves, T. (1997). Styles of language usage. *Journal of Personality and Social Psychology, 30,* 620–640.

Holtgraves, T., & Yang, J. (1992). The interpersonal underpinnings of request strategies. *Journal of Personality and Social Psychology, 62,* 246–256.

Honeycutt, J., Knapp, M., & Powers, W. (1983). On knowing others and predicting what they say. *Western Journal of Speech Communication, 47,* 157–174.

Hong, K. S. (1980). The interest level and exposure to informational contents of mass media. *Shin-Moon-Hak-Bo (Journal of Mass Communication),* 83–93 (in Korean).

Honess, T. (1976). Cognitive complexity and social prediction. *British Journal of Social and Clinical Psychology, 15,* 22–31.

Hornsey, M., & Hogg, M. (2000). Assimilation and diversity. *Personality and Social Psychology Review, 4,* 143–156.

Horowitz, D. (1985). *Ethnic groups in conflict.* Berkeley: University of California Press.

Howell, W. (1982). *The empathic communicator.* Belmont, CA: Wadsworth.

Hoyle, R., Pinkley, R., & Insko, C. (1989). Perceptions of social behavior. *Personality and Social Psychology Bulletin, 15,* 365–376.

Hraba, J., & Hoiberg, E. (1983). Origins of modern theories of ethnicity. *Sociological Quarterly, 24,* 381–391.

Hsu, F. (1971). *The challenge of the American dream: The Chinese in the United States.* Belmont, CA: Wadsworth.

Hsu, F. (1981/1953). *Americans and Chinese* (3rd ed.). Honolulu: University of Hawaii Press.

Hsu, T., Grant, A., Huang, W. (1993). The influence of social networks on the acculturation behavior of foreign students. *Connections, 16*(1–2), 23–30.

Hu, H. (1944). The Chinese concept of "face." *American Anthropologist, 46,* 45–64.

Hubbert, K., Gudykunst, W., & Guerrero, S. (1999). Intergroup communication over time. *International Journal of Intercultural Relations, 23,* 13–46.

Huber, G., & Sorrentino, R. (1996). Uncertainty in interpersonal and intergroup relations. In R. Sorrentino & E. Higgins (Eds.), *Handbook of motivation and cognition* (Vol. 3). New York: Guilford.

Hudson Institute (1987). *Workforce 2000.* Washington, DC: United States Department of Labor.

Hunter, J., & Bowman, C. (1996). *The state of disunion: 1996 survey of American political culture.* Ivy, VA: In Media Res Educational Foundation.

Huntington, E. (1945). *Mainsprings of civilizations.* New York: Wiley.

Hurh, W., & Kim, K. (1988). *Uprooting and adjustment.* Washington, DC: National Institute of Mental Health.

Huston, T. (1973). Ambiguity of acceptance, social desirability, and dating choice. *Journal of Experimental Social Psychology, 9,* 32–42.

Hwang, J., Chase, L., & Kelly, C. (1980). An intercultural examination of communication competence. *Communication, 9,* 70–79.

Hymes, D. (1971). Sociolinguistics and the ethnography of speaking. In E. Ardener (Ed.), *Social anthropology and language*. New York: Tavistock.

Hymes, D. (1974). Ways of speaking. In R. Bauman & J. Sherzer (Eds.), *Explorations in the ethnography of speaking*. Cambridge, UK: Cambridge University Press.

Hymes, D. (1979). On communication competence. In J. Pride & J. Holmes (Eds.), *Sociolinguistics*. New York: Penguin.

Ickes, W. (1984). Composition in black and white. *Journal of Personality and Social Psychology, 47,* 330–341.

Imahori, T., & Cupach, W. (1994). A cross-cultural comparison of the interpretation and management of face. *International Journal of Intercultural Relations, 18,* 193–220.

Inglis, M., & Gudykunst, W. (1982). Institutional completeness and communication acculturation. *International Journal of Intercultural Relations, 6,* 251–272.

Inkeles, A. (1974). *Becoming modern.* Cambridge, MA: Harvard University Press.

Islam, M., & Hewstone, M. (1993). Dimensions of contact as predictors of intergroup anxiety, perceived outgroup variability, and outgroup attitude. *Personality and Social Psychology Bulletin, 19,* 700–710.

Ittelson, W. (1973). Environment perception and contemporary perceptual theory. In W. Ittelson (Ed.), *Environment and cognition*. New York: Seminar Press.

Ittelson, W., & Cantril, H. (1954). *Perceptions, a tranactional approach.* Garden City, NY: Doubleday.

Ittelson, W., Prochansky, H., Rivlin, L., & Winkel, G. (1974). *Introduction to environmental psychology.* New York: Holt, Rinehart, & Winston.

Izard, C. (1968). *The emotions as a culture-common framework of motivational experiences and communicative cues.* Washington, DC: Office of Naval Research.

Izard, C. (1971). *The face of emotion.* New York: Apppleton-Century-Crofts.

Izard, C. (1980). Cross-cultural perspectives on emotion and emotion communication. In H. Triandis & W. Lonner (Eds.), *Handbook of cross-cultural psychology* (Vol. 3). Boston: Allyn and Bacon.

Jackman, M., & Jackman, R. (1983). *Class awareness in the United States.* Berkeley: University of California Press.

Jackson, J. (1964). The normative regulation of authoritative behavior. In W. Grove & J. Dyson (Eds.), *The making of decisions*. New York: Free Press.

Jackson, L., Esses, V., & Burris, C. (2001). Contemporary sexism and discrimination. *Personality and Social Psychology Bulletin, 27,* 48–61.

Jacobson, E., Kumata, H., & Gullahorn, J. (1960). Cross-cultural contributions to attitude research. *Public Opinion Quarterly, 24,* 205–233.

Jacobson, M. (1998). *Whiteness of a different color.* Cambridge, MA: Harvard University Press.

Jaffee, L., & Polanski, N. (1962). Verbal inaccessibility in young adolescents showing delinquent trends. *Journal of Health and Social Behavior, 3,* 105–111.

Jahoda, G. (1980). Theoretical and systematic approaches. In H. Triandis & W. Lambert (Eds.), *Handbook of cross-cultural psychology* (Vol. 1). Boston: Allyn and Bacon.

Jampolsky, G. (1989). *Out of darkness and into the light.* New York: Bantam.

Janis, I. (1971). *Stress and frustration.* New York: Harcourt, Brace, Jovanovich.

Janis, I., & Mann, L. (1977). *Decision making.* New York: Free Press.

Janis, I., & Smith, M. (1965). Effects of education and persuasion on national and international images. In H. Kelman (Ed.), *International behavior*. New York: Holt, Rinehart, and Winston.

Jantsch, E. (1980). *The self-organizing universe: Scientific and human implications of the emerging paradigm of evolution.* New York: Pergamon.

Jaspers, J., & Hewstone, M. (1982). Cross-cultural interaction, social attribution, and inter-group relations. In S. Bochner (Ed.), *Cultures in contact*. Elmsford, NY: Pergamon.

Jaspars, J., & Warnaen, S. (1982). Intergroup relations, social identity, and self-evaluation in India. In H. Tajfel (Ed.), *Social identity and intergroup relations*. Cambridge, England: Cambridge University Press.

Jeffries, L., & Hur, K. K. (1981). Communication channels within ethnic groups. *International Journal of Intercultural Relations, 5,* 115–132.

Jen, G. (1997, May 23). A person is more than the sum of her social facts. *Chronicle of Higher Education,* p. B11.

Johnson, C., & Johnson, F. (1975). Interaction rules and ethnicity. *Social Forces, 54,* 452–466.

Johnson, D. (1986). *Reaching out* (3rd ed.). Englewood Cliffs, NJ: Prentice-Hall.

Johnson, D., & Johnson, F. (1982). *Joining together* (2nd ed.). Englewood Cliffs, NJ: Prentice-Hall.

Johnson, F. (2000). *Speaking culturally: Language diversity in the United States.* Thousand Oaks, CA: Sage.

Johnson, H. G., Ekman, P., & Friesen, W. V. (1975). Communicative body movements: American emblems. *Semiotica, 15,* 335–353.

Johnson, J., & Sarason, I. (1978). Life stress, depression and anxiety. *Journal of Psychosomatic Research, 22,* 205–208.

Johnson, K. (1976). Black kinesics. In L. Samovar & R. Porter (Eds.), *Intercultural communication: A reader* (2nd ed.). Belmont, CA: Wadsworth.

Johnson, R., & Ogasawara, G. (1984). Group size and group income as influences on marriage patterns in Hawaii. *Social Biology, 31,* 101–107.

Johnson, W., & Warren, D. (1994). Introduction. In W. Johnson & D. Warren (Eds.), *Inside the mixed marriage.* Lanham, MD: University Press of America.

Johnston, L., & Coolen, P. (1995). A dual processing approach to stereotype change. *Personality and Social Psychology Bulletin, 21,* 660–673.

Johnston, L., & Hewstone, M. (1991). Intergroup contact. In D. Abrahms & M. Hogg (Eds.), *Social identity theory.* New York: Springer-Verlag.

Johnston, L., & Macrae, C. (1994). Changing social stereotypes. *European Journal of Social Psychology, 24,* 581–592.

Jones, E., & Davis, K. (1965). From acts to dispositions. *Personality and Social Psychology Bulletin, 4,* 200–206.

Jones, E., Gallois, C., Barker, M., & Callan, V. (1994). Evaluations of interactions between students and academic staff: Influence of communication accommodation, ethnic group, and status. *Journal of Language and Social Psychology, 13,* 158–191.

Jones, E., & Nisbett, R. (1972). *The actor and the observer.* Morristown, NJ: General Learning Press.

Jones, T., & Remland, M. (1982). *Cross-cultural differences in self-reported touch avoidance.* Paper presented at the Eastern Communication Association convention.

Jou, Y., & Fukada, H. (1995). Effects of social support on adjustment of Chinese students in Japan. *Journal of Social Psychology, 135,* 39–47.

Jourard, S. (1958). A study of self-disclosure. *Scientific American, 198,* 77–82.

Jourard, S. (1961). Self-disclosure patterns in British and American college females. *Journal of Social Psychology, 54,* 315–320.

Jourard, S. (1971). *Self-disclosure.* New York: Wiley.

Jourard, S. (1974). Growing awareness and the awareness of growth. In B. Patton & K. Giffin (Eds.), *Interpersonal communication.* New York: Harper & Row.

Kagan, S., Knight, G., & Martinez-Romero, S. (1982). Culture and the development of conflict negotiation style. *Journal of Cross-Cultural Psychology, 13,* 43–59.

Kalin, R., & Rayko, D. (1980). The social significance of speech in job interviews. In R. St. Clair & H. Giles (Eds.), *The social and psychological contexts of language.* Hillsdale, NJ: Erlbaum.

Kanagawa, C., Cross, S., & Markus, H. (2001). "Who am I?" The cultural psychology of the conceptual self. *Personality and Social Psychology Bulletin, 27,* 90–103.

Kanno, Y. (2000). *Kikokishijo* as bi-cultural. *International Journal of Intercultural Relations, 24,* 361–382.

Kanouse, D., & Hanson, L. (1972). Negativity in evaluations. In E. Jones, D. Kanouse, H. Kelley, R. Nisbett, S. Valins, & L. Petrullo (Eds.), *Attribution.* Morristown, NJ: General Learning Press.

Kanter, R. (1977). *Men and women of the corporation.* New York: Basic Books.

Kao, C. (1975). *Search for maturity.* Philadelphia: Westminister.

Kapoor, S., & Williams, W. (1979). *Acculturation of foreign students by television.* Paper presented at the International Communication Association convention.

Karbins, M., Coffman, T., & Walters, G. (1969). On the fading of social stereotypes. *Journal of Personality and Social Psychology, 13,* 1–16.

Karniol, R. (1990). Reading people's minds. In M. Zanna (Ed.), *Advances in experimental social psychology* (Vol. 23). New York: Academic Press.

Kashima, E., & Hardie, E. (2000). The development and validation of the relational, individual, and collective self-aspects (RIC) scale. *Asian Journal of Social Psychology, 3,* 19–47.

Kashima, E., & Kashima, Y. (1998). Culture and language. *Journal of Cross-Cultural Psychology, 29,* 461–486.

Kashima, Y. (1989). Conceptions of persons. In C. Kagitcibasi (Ed.), *Growth and progress in cross-cultural psychology.* The Hague: Zwets and Zeitlinger.

Kashima, Y., Siegel, M., Tanaka, K., & Kashima, E. (1992). Do people believe behaviors are consistent with attitudes? *British Journal of Social Psychology, 31,* 111–124.

Kashima, Y., & Triandis, H. C. (1986). The self-serving bias in attributions as a coping strategy. *Journal of Cross-Cultural Psychology, 17,* 83–97.

Kashima, Y., Yamaguchi, S., Kim, U., Choi, S.-C., Gelfand, M., & Yuki, M. (1995). Culture, gender, and the self. *Journal of Personality and Social Psychology, 69,* 925–937.

Katriel, T. (1986). *Talking straight.* New York: Cambridge University Press.

Katz, D. (1960). The functional approach to the study of attitudes. *Public Opinion Quarterly, 24,* 164–204.

Katz, D., & Braly, K. (1933). Racial stereotyping of 100 college students. *Journal of Abnormal and Social Psychology, 28,* 280–290.

Katz, I., Hass, R., & Wackenhut, J. (1986). Racial ambivalence, value duality, and behavior. In J. Dovidio & S. Gaertner (Eds.), *Prejudice, discrimination, and racism.* New York: Academic Press.

Kawakami, C., White, J., & Langer, E. (2000). Mindful and masculine. *Journal of Social Issues, 56*(1), 49–64.

Kealey, D. (1990). *Cross-cultural effectiveness.* Quebec: International Development Agency.

Keene, D. (1994). *On familiar terms.* Tokyo: Kodansha.

Keesing, R. (1974). Theories of culture. *Annual Review of Anthropology, 3,* 73–97.

Kegley, J. (1997). *Genuine individual and genuine communities.* Nashville, TN: Vanderbilt University Press.

Kellermann, K. (1993). Extrapolating beyond. In S. Deetz (Ed.), *Communication yearbook 16.* Newbury Park, CA: Sage.

Kelley, H. (1967). Attribution theory in social psychology. *Nebraska Symposium on Motivation, 15,* 192–238.

Kelley, H. (1972). Causal schemata and the attribution process. In E. Jones, D. Kanouse, H. Kelley, R. Nisbett, S. Valins, & L. Petrullo (Eds.), *Attribution.* Morristown, NJ: General Learning.

Kelly, C., Sachdev, I., Kottsieper, P., & Ingram, M. (1993). The role of social identity in second language proficiency and use. *Journal of Language and Social Psychology, 12,* 288–301.

Kelly, G. A. (1955). *The psychology of personal constructs.* New York: Norton.

Kelman, H. (1999). The interdependence of Israeli and Palestinian national identities. *Journal of Social Issues, 55*(3), 581–600.

Kelvin, P. (1970). *The bases of social power.* New York: Holt, Rinehart, and Winston.

Kennerley, H. (1990). *Managing anxiety.* New York: Oxford University Press.

Kertamus, L., Gudykunst, W., & Nishida, T. (1991). *Themes in male-male Japanese-North American relationships.* Paper presented at the Conference on Communication in Japan and the United States, California State University, Fullerton.

Kim, H., & Markus, H. (1999). Deviance or uniqueness, harmony or conformity? *Journal of Personality and Social Psychology, 77,* 785–800.

Kim, H. K. (1991). Influence of language and similarity on initial intercultural attraction. In S. Ting-Toomey & F. Korzenny (Eds.), *Cross-cultural interpersonal communication.* Newbury Park, CA: Sage.

Kim, H. S. (1986). Coorientation and communication. In B. Dervin & M. Voight (Eds.), *Progress in communication science* (Vol. VII). Norwood, NJ: Ablex.

Kim, J., Lee, B., & Jeong, W. (1982). *Uses of mass media in acculturation.* Paper presented at the Association for Education in Journalism convention, Athens, OH.

Kim, J. K. (1980). Explaining acculturation in a communication framework. *Communication Monographs, 47,* 155–179.

Kim, J. K., Lee, B. H., & Jeong, W. J. (1982). *Use of mass media in acculturation.* Paper presented at the Association for Education in Journalism conference.

Kim, M. S. (1993). Culture-based interactive constraints in explaining intercultural strategic competence. In R. Wiseman & J. Koester (Eds.), *Intercultural communication competence.* Thousand Oaks, CA: Sage.

Kim, M. S. (1994). Cross-cultural comparisons of the perceived importance of conversational constraints. *Human Communication Research, 21,* 128–151.

Kim, M. S. (1995). Toward a theory of conversational constraints. In R. Wiseman (Ed.), *Intercultural communication theory.* Thousand Oaks, CA: Sage.

Kim, M. S., Aune, K., Hunter, J., Kim, H.-J., & Kim, J.-S. (2001). The effects of culture and self construals on predispositions toward verbal communication. *Human Communication Research, 27,* 382–408.

Kim, M. S., Hunter, J., Miyahara, A., Horvath, A., Bresnahan, M., & Yoon, H. (1996). Individual vs. culture-level dimensions of individualism and collectivism: Effects on preferred conversational styles. *Communication Monographs, 63,* 29–49.

Kim, M. S., & Kitani, K. (1998). Conflict management styles of Asian- and Caucasian-Americans in romantic relationships in Hawaii. *Journal of Asian Pacific Communication, 8,* 51–68.

Kim, M. S., Sharkey, W., & Singelis, T. (1994). The relationship between individuals' self construals and perceived importance of interactive constraints. *International Journal of Intercultural Relations, 18,* 117–140.

Kim, M. S., & Wilson, S. (1994). A cross-cultural comparison of implicit theories of requesting. *Communication Monographs, 61,* 210–235.

Kim, U. (1994). Individualism and collectivism: Conceptual clarification and elaboration. In U. Kim, H. Triandis, C. Kagitcibisi, S. Choi, & G. Yoon (Eds.), *Individualism-collectivism.* Thousand Oaks, CA: Sage.

Kim, Y. Y. (1976). *Communication patterns of foreign immigrants in the process of acculturation.* Unpublished doctoral dissertation, Northwestern University.

Kim, Y. Y. (1977a). Communication patterns of foreign immigrants in the process of acculturation. *Human Communication Research, 4,* 66–77.

Kim, Y. Y. (1977b). Interethnic and intraethnic communication. In N. Jain (Ed.), *International and intercultural communication annual* (Vol. 4). Falls Church, VA: Speech Communication Association.

Kim, Y. Y. (1978a). *Acculturation and patterns of interpersonal communication relationships.* Paper presented at the Speech Communication Association convention.

Kim, Y. Y. (1978b). Toward a communication approach to the acculturation process. *International Journal of Intercultural Relations, 2,* 197–224.

Kim, Y. Y. (1979a). *Mass media and acculturation.* Paper presented at the Eastern Communication Association convention.

Kim, Y. Y. (1979b). Toward an interactive theory of communication-acculturation. In D. Nimmo (Ed.), *Communication yearbook 3.* New Brunswick, NJ: Transaction.

Kim, Y. Y. (1979c). *Dynamics of intrapersonal and interpersonal communication: A study of Indochinese refugees in the initial phase of acculturation.* Paper presented at the Speech Communication Association convention.

Kim, Y. Y. (1980). *Psychological, social, and cultural adjustment of Indochinese refugees.* Vol. IV of Indochinese refugees in the State of Illinois (5 vols.). Chicago: Travelers Aid Society of Metropolitan Chicago.

Kim, Y. Y. (1985). Communication, information, and adaptation. In B. Ruben (Ed.), *Information and behavior* (Vol. 1). New Brunswick, NJ: Transaction.

Kim, Y. Y. (Ed.). (1986a). *Interethnic communication.* Newbury Park, CA: Sage.

Kim, Y. Y. (1986b). Understanding the social context of intergroup communication: A personal network approach. In W. Gudykunst (Ed.), *Intergroup communication.* London: Edward Arnold.

Kim, Y. Y. (1987). Facilitating immigrant adaptation: The role of communication. In T. Albrecht & M. Adelman (Eds.), *Communicating social support.* Newbury Park, CA: Sage.

Kim, Y. Y. (1988). *Communication and cross-cultural adaptation: An integrative theory.* Clevedon, England: Multilingual Matters.

Kim, Y. Y. (1989). Communication and adaptation of Asian Pacific refugees in the United States. *Journal of Pacific Rim Communication, 1,* 191–207.

Kim, Y. Y. (1990). Psychological, social, and economic adaptation: The case of 1975–1979 arrivals in Illinois. In D. Haines (Ed.), *Refugees as immigrants: Survey research on Cambodians, Laotians, and Vietnamese in America.* Totowa, NJ: Rowman & Littlefield.

Kim, Y. Y. (1991). Intercultural communication competence. In S. Ting-Toomey & F. Korzenny (Eds.), *Cross-cultural interpersonal communication.* Newbury Park, CA: Sage.

Kim, Y. Y., (1992). Synchrony and intercultural communication. In D. Crookall & K. Arai (Eds.), *Global interdependence.* New York: Springer-Verlag.

Kim, Y. Y. (1993). *Synchrony and intercultural communication competence.* Paper presented at the International Communication Association convention.

Kim, Y. Y. (1994a). Interethnic communication. In S. Deetz (ed.), *Communication yearbook 17.* Thousand Oaks, CA: Sage.

Kim, Y. Y. (1994b). Intercultural personhood. In L. Samovar & R. Porter (Eds.), *Intercultural communication: A reader* (7th ed.). Belmont, CA: Wadsworth.

Kim, Y. Y. (1995a). Cross-cultural adaptation. In R. Wiseman (Ed.), *Intercultural communication theory.* Thousand Oaks, CA: Sage.

Kim, Y. Y. (1995b). Identity development. In H. Mokros (Ed.), *Information and behavior* (Vol. 5). New Brunswick, NJ: Transaction Books.

Kim, Y. Y. (2001). *Becoming intercultural: An integrative theory of communication and cross-cultural adaptation.* Thousand Oaks, CA: Sage.

Kim, Y. Y., & Gudykunst, W. B. (Eds.). (1988a). *Cross-cultural adaptation: Current approaches.* Newbury Park, CA: Sage.

Kim, Y. Y., & Gudykunst, W. B. (Eds.). (1988b). *Theories in intercultural communication.* Newbury Park, CA: Sage.

Kim, Y. Y., Lujan, P., & Dixon, L (1998). "I can walk both ways": Identity integration of American Indians in Oklahoma. *Human Communication Research, 25,* 252–274..

Kim, Y. Y., & Ruben, B. (1988). Intercultural transformation: A systems theory. In Y. Kim & W. Gudykunst (Eds.), *Theories in intercultural communication.* Newbury Park, CA: Sage.

King, M. L., Jr. (1958). *Stride toward freedom.* New York: Harper & Row.

King, M. L., Jr. (1963). Letter from Birmingham jail. In *Why we can't wait.* New York: Harper and Row.

Kirschner, G. (1994). Equilibrium process: Creativity and depression. *Mind and Human Interaction, 5,* 165–171.

Kitano, H., & Chai, L. (1982). Chinese interracial marriage. *Marriage and Family Review, 5,* 75–89.

Kitano, H., Fujino, D., & Sato, J. (1998). Interracial marriages. In L. Lee & N. Zane (Eds.), *Handbook of Asian American psychology.* Thousand Oaks, CA: Sage.

Kitano, H., Young, W., Chai, L., & Hatanaka, H. (1984). Asian American interracial marriage. *Journal of Marriage and the Family, 46,* 179–190.

Kitayama, S., & Burnstein, E. (1988). Automaticity in conversations. *Journal of Personality and Social Psychology, 54,* 219–224.

Kitayama, S., Markus, H., Matsumoto, H., & Norasakkunkit, V. (1997). Individual and collective processes in the construction of the self. *Journal of Personality and Social Psychology, 72,* 1245–1267.

Klass, M., & Hellman, H. (1971). *The kinds of mankind.* New York: Lippincott.

Kleg, M. (1993). *Hate, prejudice, and racism.* Albany: State University of New York Press.

Klineberg, O., & Hull, W. F. (1979). *At a foreign university.* New York: Praeger.

Kleinjans, E. (1972). Opening remarks at a conference on world communication held at the East-West Center, Honolulu, HI.

Klopf, D. (1984). Cross-cultural apprehension research. In J. Daly & J. McCroskey (Eds.), *Avoiding communication.* Beverly Hills, CA; Sage.

Kluckhohn, F., & Strodtbeck, F. (1960). *Variations in value orientations.* New York: Row, Peterson.

Knapp, M. (1973). Dyadic relationship development. In J. Wiemann & R. Harrison (Eds.), *Nonverbal interaction.* Beverly Hills, CA: Sage.

Knapp, M. (1978). *Social intercourse.* Boston: Allyn and Bacon.

Knapp, M. (1983). Dyadic relationship development. In J. Wiemann & R. Harrison (Eds.), *Nonverbal interaction*. Beverly Hills, CA: Sage.

Knapp, M., Ellis, D., & Williams, B. (1980). Perceptions of communication behavior associated with relationship terms. *Communication Monographs, 47,* 262–278.

Knapp, M., & Hall, J. (1992). *Nonverbal communication in human interaction* (3rd ed.). New York: Harcourt Brace.

Knutson, T., Hwang, J., & Deng, B. (2000). Perception and management of conflict. *Intercultural Communication Studies, IX*(2), 10–31.

Kochman, T. (1981). *Black and white: Styles in conflict*. Chicago: University of Chicago Press.

Kochman, T. (1990). Force fields in black and white communication. In D. Carbaugh (Ed.), *Cultural communication and intercultural contact*. Hillsdale, NJ: Erlbaum.

Kohn, M. (1969). *Class and conformity: A study in values*. Homewood, IL: Dorsey Press.

Korten, D. (1972). *Planned change in a traditional society*. New York: Praeger.

Korzybski, A. (1948). *Science and sanity* (3rd ed.). Lakeville, CT: International Non-Aristotelian Library.

Kosmitzki, C. (1996). The reaffirmation of cultural identity in cross-cultural encounters. *Personality and Social Psychology Bulletin, 22,* 238–248.

Kouri, K., & Lasswell, M. (1993). Black-white marriage. *Marriage and Family Review, 19,* 241–255.

Kozan, M. (1989). Cultural influences on styles of handling interpersonal conflict. *Human Relations, 42,* 787–799.

Kozan, M., & Ergin, C. (1998). Preference for third-party help in conflict management in the United States and Turkey. *Journal of Cross-Cultural Psychology, 29,* 525–539.

Kraft, C. (1978). Worldview in intercultural communication. In F. Casmir (Ed.), *International and intercultural communication*. Washington, DC, University Press of America.

Kramarae, C. (1981). *Women and men speaking*. Rowley, MA: Newbury House.

Krauss, R., & Fussell, S. (1991). Constructing shared communicative environments. In L. Resnick, J. Levine, & S. Brhrend (Eds.), *Perspectives on socially shared cognition*. Washington, DC: American Psychological Association.

Kraut, R., & Higgins, E. (1984). Communication and social cognition. In R. Wyer & T. Srull (Eds.), *Handbook of social cognition* (Vol. 3). Hillsdale, NJ: Erlbaum.

Kristeva, J. (1991). *Strangers to ourselves*. New York: Colombia University Press.

Krober, A., & Kluckhohn, C. (1952). *Culture: A critical review of the concept and its definition*. Cambridge, MA: Peabody Museum.

Kroger, J. (1993). On the nature of structural transition in the identity formation process. In J. Kroger (Ed.), *Discussions on ego identity*. Hillsdale, NJ: Erlbaum.

Kruglanski, A. (1989). *Lay epistemics and human knowledge*. New York: Plenum.

Krull, D., Loy, M., Lin, J., Wang, C., Chen, S., & Zhao, X. (1999). The fundamental fundamental attributional bias. *Personality and Social Psychology Bulletin, 25,* 1208–1219.

Kurth, S. (1970). Friendships and friendly relations. In G. McNall (Ed.), *Social relationships*. Chicago: Aldine.

Kwan, K., & Sodowsky, G. (1997). Internal and external ethnic identity and their correlates. *Journal of Multicultural Counseling and Development, 25*(1), 51–67.

LaBarre, W. (1947). The cultural basis of emotions and gestures. *Journal of Personality, 16,* 49–68.

LaBarre, W. (1976). Paralinguistics, kinesics, and cultural anthropology. In L. Samovar & R. Porter (Eds.), *Intercultural communication: A reader* (2nd ed.). Belmont, CA: Wadsworth.

Labrie, N., & Clement, R. (1986). Ethnolinguistic vitality, self-confidence, and second language proficiency. *Journal of Multilingual and Multicultural Development, 7,* 269–282.

Lackoff, R. (1975). *Language and woman's place*. New York: Harper & Row.

Lackoff, R. (1990). *Talking power*. New York: Basic Books.

LaFrance, M., & Mayo, C. (1978). Cultural aspects of nonverbal behavior. *International Journal of Intercultural Relations, 2,* 71–89.

Laing, D. (1961). *The self and others*. New York: Pantheon.

Lambert, R., & Bressler, M. (1956). *Indian students on an American campus*. Minneapolis: University of Minnesota Press.

Lambert, W. (1963). Psychological approaches to the study of language. *Modern Language Journal, 14,* 51–62.

Lambert, W. (1972). *Language, psychology, and culture*. Stanford, CA: Stanford University Press.

Lampe, P. (1982). Interethnic dating: Reasons for and against. *International Journal of Intercultural Relations, 6,* 115–126.

Landis, D., & Boucher, J. (1987). Themes and models of conflict. In J. Boucher, D. Landis, & K. Clark (Eds.), *Ethnic conflict*. Newbury Park, CA: Sage.

Landis, D., & Brislin, R. (Eds.). (1983). *Handbook of intercultural training* (Vol. I–III). New York: Pergamon.

Landry, R., & Bourhis, R. (1997). Linguistic landscale and ethnolinguistic vitality. *Journal of Language and Social Psychology, 16,* 23–49.

Lane, H. (1993). The medicalization of cultural deafness in historical perspective. In R. Fisher & H. Lane (Eds.), *Looking back*. Hamburg: Signum Press.

Langer, E. (1978). Rethinking the role of thought in social interaction. In J. Harvey, W. Ickes, & R. Kidd (Eds.). *New directions in attribution research* (Vol. 2). Hillsdale, NJ: Erlbaum.

Langer, E. (1989). *Mindfulness.* Reading, MA: Addison-Wesley.

Langer, E. (1997). *The power of mindful learning.* Reading, MA: Addison-Wesley.

Larkey, L., & Hecht, M. (1995). A comparative study of African American and European American ethnic identity. *International Journal of Intercultural Relations, 19,* 483–504.

Larkey, L., Hecht, M., & Martin, J. (1993). What's in a name? *Journal of Language and Social Psychology, 12,* 302–317.

Lazarsfeld, P., & Merton, R. (1954). Friendship as a social process. In M. Berger et al. (Eds.), *Freedom and control in modern society.* New York: Octagon Books.

Lazarus, R. (1966). *Psychological stress and the coping process.* New York: McGraw-Hill.

Lazarus, R. (1991). *Emotions and adaptation.* New York: Oxford University Press.

Lazarus, R., Averill, J., & Opton, E. (1974). The psychology of coping. In G. Coelho, D. Hamburg, & J. Adams (Eds.), *Coping and adaptation.* New York: Basic Books.

Lazarus, R., Cohen, R., Folkman, S., Kanner, A., & Schaefer, C. (1980). Psychological stress and adaptation. In H. Selye (Ed.), *Seyle's guide to stress research* (Vol. 1). New York: Van Nostrand Reinhold.

Leary, M., Kowalski, R., & Bergen, D. (1988). Interpersonal information acquisition and confidence in first encounters. *Personality and Social Psychology Bulletin, 14,* 68–77.

Lebra, T. (1976). *Japanese patterns of behavior.* Honolulu: University of Hawaii Press.

Lebra, T. (1987). The cultural significance of silence in Japanese communication. *Multilingua, 6,* 343–357.

Lee, C., & Gudykunst, W. B. (2001). Attraction in initial interethnic encounters. *International Journal of Intercultural Relations, 25,* 373–387.

Lee, D. (1950). Lineal and nonlineal codifications of reality. *Psychosomatic Medicine, 12,* 89–97.

Lee, D. (1959). *Freedom and culture.* Englewood Cliffs, NJ: Prentice-Hall.

Lee, H., & Boster, F. (1991). Social information for uncertainty reduction during initial interactions. In S. Ting-Toomey & F. Korzenny (Eds.), *Cross-cultural interpersonal communication.* Newbury Park, CA: Sage.

Lee, L., & Ward, C. (1998). Ethnicity, idiocentrism-allocentrism, and intergroup attitudes. *Journal of Applied Psychology, 28,* 109–123.

Lee, S., & Yamanaka, K. (1990). Patterns of Asian American intermarriage and marital assimilation. *Journal of Comparative Studies, 21,* 287–305.

Leets, L., & Giles, H. (1997). Words as weapons—when do they wound? *Human Communication Research, 24,* 260–301.

Leets, L., & Giles, H. (1999). Harmful speech in intergroup encounters. In M. Roloff (Ed.), *Communication yearbook 22.* Thousand Oaks, CA: Sage.

Leets, L., Giles, H., & Noels, K. (1999). Attributing harm to racist speech. *Journal of Multilingual and Multicultural Development, 20,* 209–215.

Lerner, R. (1979). A dynamic interactional concept of individual and social relationship development. In R. Burgess & T. Huston (Eds.), *Social exchange in developing relationships.* New York: Academic Press.

Leung, C., & Ward, C. (2000). Identity conflict in sojourners. *International Journal of Intercultural Relations, 24,* 763–776.

Leung, K. (1987). Some determinants of reaction to procedural models for conflict resolution. *Journal of Personality and Social Psychology, 53,* 898–908.

Leung, K. (1988). Some determinants of conflict avoidance. *Journal of Cross-Cultural Psychology, 19,* 125–136.

Leung, K. (1997). Negotiation and reward allocation across cultures. In P. Earley & M. Erez (Eds.), *New perspectives on international industrial/organizational psychology.* San Francisco: Jossey-Bass.

Leung, K., Au, Y., Fernandez-Dol, J., & Iwawaki, S. (1992). Preferences for methods of conflict processing in two collectivistic cultures. *International Journal of Psychology, 27,* 195–209.

Leung, K., & Bond, M. (1982). How Chinese and Americans reward task-related contributions. *Psychoogia, 25,* 32–39.

Leung, K., & Bond, M. (1984). The impact of cultural collectivism on reward allocation. *Journal of Personality and Social Psychology, 49,* 793–804.

Leung, K., Bond, M., Carment, D., Krishman, L., & Liebrand, W. (1990). Effects of cultural femininity on preference for methods of conflict processing. *Journal of Experimental Social Psychology, 26,* 373–388.

Leung, K., & Lind, E. (1986). Procedural justice and culture. *Journal of Personality and Social Psychology, 50,* 1134–1140.

Leung, K., & Chan, D. (1999). Conflict management across cultures. In J. Adamopoulos & Y. Kashima (Eds.), *Social psychology and cultural context.* Thousand Oaks, CA: Sage.

Levin, J., & Levin, W. (1980). *Ageism.* Belmont, CA: Wadsworth.

Levine, D. (1965). *Wax and gold.* Chicago: University of Chicago Press.

Levine, D. (1979). Simmel at a distance. In W. Shack & E. Skinner (Eds.), *Strangers in African societies.* Berkeley: University of California Press.

Levine, D. (1985). *The flight from ambiguity.* Chicago: University of Chicago Press.

Levine, R., & Campbell, D. (1972). *Ethnocentrism.* New York: Wiley.

Levine, R., Sato, S., Hashimoto, T., & Verma, J. (1995). Love and marriage in eleven cultures. *Journal of Cross-Cultural Psychology, 26,* 554–571.

Levy, S., Plaks, J., Chiu, C., & Dweck, C. (2001). Static versus dynamic theories and the perception of groups. *Personality and Social Psychology Review, 5,* 156–168.

Lewin, K. (1936). *Principles of topological psychology.* New York: McGraw-Hill.

Lewin, K. (1948). Some social-psychological differences between the United States and Germany. In G. Lewin (Ed.), *Resolving social conflicts.* New York: Harper.

Lewin, K. (1951). *Field theory in social science.* New York: Harper and Row.

Lewis, T., & Jungman, R. (Eds.). (1986). *On being foreign.* Yarmouth, ME: Intercultural Press.

Li, H. Z. (1999a). Communicating information in conversations. *International Journal of Intercultural Relations, 23,* 387–410.

Li, H. Z. (1999b). Grounding and information communication in intercultural and intracultural dyadic discourse. *Discourse Processes, 28*(3), 195–215,

Li, H. Z. (2001). *Gaze and mutual gaze in inter- and intra-cultural conversations.* Paper presented at the International Communication Association convention.

Lickel, B., Hamilton, D., & Sherman, S. (2001). Elements of a lay theory of groups. *Personality and Social Psychology Review, 5,* 129–140.

Lieberson, S. (1985). *Making it count.* Berkeley: University of California Press.

Liem, N. D. (1980). *Vietnamese-American intercultural communication.* Paper presented at the International Communication Association convention.

Liem, R. (1997). Shame and guilt among first- and second-generation Asian Americans and European Americans. *Journal of Cross-Cultural Psychology, 28,* 365–392.

Lilli, W., & Rehm, J. (1988). Judgmental processes as bases of intergroup conflict. In W. Strobe, A. Kruglanski, D. Bar-Tal, & M. Hewstone (Eds.), *The social psychology of intergroup conflict.* New York: Springer-Verlag.

Lim, T. S., & Choi, S. H. (1996). Interpersonal relationships in Korea. In W. Gudykunst, S. Ting-Toomey, & T. Nishida (Eds.), *Communication in personal relationships across cultures.* Thousand Oaks, CA: Sage.

Lindgren, H., & Marrash, J. (1970). A comparative study of intercultural insight and empathy. *Journal of Social Psychology, 80,* 135–141.

Linville, P., Fisher, G., & Salovey, P. (1989). Perceived distributions of the characteristics of in-group and out-group members. *Journal of Personality and Social Psychology, 57,* 165–188.

Lippman, W. (1922). *Public opinion.* New York: Macmillan.

Lippman, W. (1937). *The good society.* Boston: Little, Brown.

Lipset, S. (1963). The value patterns of democracy. *American Sociological Review, 28,* 515–531.

Little, K. (1968). Cultural variations in social schemata. *Journal of Personality and Social Psychology, 10,* 1–7.

Littlefield, R. (1974). Self-disclosure among Negro, white and Mexican-American adolescents. *Journal of Counseling Psychology, 21,* 133–136.

Liu, J., Campbell, S., & Condie, H. (1995). Ethnocentrism in dating preferences for an American sample. *European Journal of Social Psychology, 25,* 95–115.

LoCastro, V. (1987). *Aizuchi:* A Japanese conversational routine. In L. Smith (Ed.), *Discourse across cultures.* Englewood Cliffs, NJ: Prentice-Hall.

Loewy, E. (1993). *Freedom and community.* Albany: State University of New York Press.

Longmore, P. (1987). Screening stereotypes. In A. Gartner & T. Jol (Eds.), *Images of the disabled.* New York: Praeger.

Lonner, W. (1980). The search for psychological universals. In H. Triandis & W. Lambert (Eds.), *Handbook of cross-cultural psychology* (Vol. 1). Boston: Allyn and Bacon.

Loomis, C. (1938). Political and occupational cleavages in a Hanoverian village. *Sociometry, 1,* 375–419.

Loveday, L. (1982). Communicative interference. *International Review of Applied Linguistics in Language Teaching, 20,* 1–16.

Luhtanen, R., & Crocker, J. (1992). A collective self-esteem scale. *Personality and Social Psychology Bulletin, 18,* 302–318.

Lukens, J. (1978). Ethnocentric speech. *Ethnic Groups, 2,* 35–53.

Lum, J. (1982). Marginality and multiculturalism. In L. Samovar & R. Porter (Eds.), *Intercultural communication: A reader* (3rd ed.). Belmont, CA: Wadsworth.

Lundstedt, S. (1963). An introduction to some evolving problems in cross-cultural research. *Journal of Social Issues, 14,* 1–9.

Lutzker, D. (1960). Internationalism as a predictor of cooperative behavior. *Journal of Conflict Resolution, 4,* 426–430.

Lynberg, M. (1989). *The path with heart.* New York: Fawcett.

Lysgaard, S. (1955). Adjustment in a foreign society. *International Social Science Bulletin, 7,* 45–51.

Madon, S., Guyll, M., Aboufadel, K., Montiel, E., Smith, A., Palumbo, P., & Jussim, L. (2001). Ethnic and national stereotypes. *Personality and Social Psychology Bulletin, 27,* 996–1010.

Mahler, I., Greenberg, L., & Hayashi, H. (1981). A comparative study of rules of justice. *Psychologia, 24,* 1–8.

Maltz, D. & Borker, R. (1982). A cultural approach to male-female miscommunication. In J. Gumperz (Ed.), *Language and social identity.* Cambridge, UK: Cambridge University Press.

Mansell, M. (1981). Transcultural experience and expressive response. *Communication Education, 30,* 93–108.

Mare, L. (1990). *Ma* and Japan. *Southern Communication Journal, 55,* 319–328.

Markoff, R. (1977). Intercultural marriage. In W. Tseng, J. McDermott, & T. Martzki (Eds.), *Adjustment in intercultural marriages.* Honolulu: University of Hawaii Press.

Markus, H., & Kitayama, S. (1991). Culture and the self. *Psychological Review, 98,* 224–253.

Markus, H., & Kitayama, S. (1994a). The cultural construction of self and emotion. In S. Kitayama & H. Markus (Eds.), *Culture, self, and emotion.* Washington, DC: American Psychological Association.

Markus, H., & Kitayama, S. (1994b). A collective fear of the collective. *Personality and Social Psychology Bulletin 20,* 568–579.

Marmot, M., & Syme, S. (1976). Acculturation and coronary heart disease in Japanese-Americans. *American Journal of Epidemiology, 104,* 225–247.

Marris, P. (1996). *The politics of uncertainty.* London: Routledge.

Martin, J. (1984). The intercultural reentry. *International Journal of Intercultural Relations, 8,* 115–134.

Martin, J. (1986). Communication in the intercultural reentry. *International Journal of Intercultural Relations, 10,* 1–22.

Martin, J., Krizek, R., Nakayama, T., & Bradford, L. (1996). Exploring whiteness: A study of self labels for white Americans. *Communication Quarterly, 44,* 125–144.

Maruyama, M. (1998). *Cross-cultural adaptation and host environment: A study of international students in Japan.* Unpublished doctoral dissertation, University of Oklahoma.

Maslow, A. H. (1970/1954). *Motivation and personality* (2nd ed.). New York: Harper & Row.

Maslow, A. H. (1971). *The farther reaches of human nature.* New York: Viking.

Masterpasqua, F., & Perna, P. (1997). *The psychological meaning of chaos.* Washington, DC: American Psychological Association.

Masuda, M. (1970). Ethnic identity in three generations of Japanese Americans. *Journal of Social Psychology, 81,* 199–207.

Matsuda, M., Lawrence, C. Delgado, R., & Crenshaw, K. (1993). *Words that wound.* Boulder, CO: Westview.

Matsumoto, D. (1989). Cultural influences on the perception of emotion. *Journal of Cross-Cultural Psychology, 20,* 92–104.

Matsumoto, D. (1991). Cultural influences on the facial expression of emotions. *Southern Communication Journal, 56,* 128–137.

Matsumoto, D., Franklyn, B., Choi, J., Rogers, D., & Tatani, H. (2001). Cultural influences on the expression and perception of emotion. In W. Gudykunst & B. Mody (Eds.), *Handbook of international and intercultural communication* (2nd ed.). Thousand Oaks, CA: Sage.

Matsumoto, D., & Kudoh, T. (1993). American-Japanese cultural differences in attributions based on smiles. *Journal of Nonverbal Behavior, 17,* 231–243.

Matsumoto, D., Wallbott, H., & Scherer, K. (1989). Emotions in intercultural communication. In M. Asante & W. Gudykunst (Eds.), *Handbook of international and intercultural communication.* Newbury Park, CA: Sage.

May, R. (1977). *The meaning of anxiety.* New York: Washington Square Press.

Maynard, S. (1997). *Japanese communication.* Honolulu: University of Hawaii Press.

Mazur, A. (1977). Interpersonal spacing on public benches in contact vs. noncontact cultures. *Journal of Social Psychology, 101,* 53–58.

McArthur, L. (1982). Judging a book by its cover. In A. Hastorf & A. Isen (Eds.), *Cognitive social psychology.* New York: Elsevier.

McClelland, D. (1961). *The achieving society.* Princeton, NJ: Van Nostrand.

McConahay, J. (1986). Modern racism, ambivalence, and the modern racism scale. In J. Dovidio & S. Gaertner (Eds.), *Prejudice, discrimination, and racism.* New York: Academic Press.

McConnel-Ginet, S. (1978). Address forms in sexual politics. In D. Butturff & E. Epstein (Eds.), *Women's language and styles.* Akron, OH: L&S Books.

McFall, R. (1982). A review and reformulation of the concept of social skills. *Behavioral Assessment, 4,* 1–33.

McGill, M. (1986). *The McGill report on male intimacy.* New York: Harper & Row.

McGinn, N., Harburg, E., & Ginsburg, G. (1973). Responses to interpersonal conflict by middle class males in Guadalajara and Michigan. In F. Jandt (Ed.), *Conflict resolution through communication.* New York: Harper & Row.

McGuire, M., & McDermott, S. (1988). Communication in assimilation, deviance, and alienation states. In Y. Kim & W. Gudykunst (Eds.), *Cross-cultural adaptation.* Newbury Park, CA: Sage.

McGuire, W. (1969). The nature of attitudes and attitude change. In G. Lindzey & E. Aronson (Eds.), *Handbook of social psychology* (2nd ed., Vol. 3). Reading, MA: Addison-Wesley.

McLemore, S. (1970). Simmel's "stranger": A critique of the concept. *Pacific Sociological Review, 13,* 86–94.

McLuhan, M. (1962). *The Gutenberg galaxy*. New York: New American Library.

McNaughton, W. (1974). *The Confucian vision*. Ann Arbor: University of Michigan Press.

McPherson, J. (1991). *Opportunities for contact and network diversity*. Paper presented at the Sunbelt Social Network conference.

McPherson, K. (1983). Opinion-related information seeking. *Personality and Social Psychology Bulletin, 9,* 116–124.

Mead, M. (1963). Culture change and character structure. In M. Stein et al. (Eds.), *Identity and anxiety*. Glencoe, IL: Free Press.

Meggers, B. J. (1954). Environmental limitations on the development of culture. *American Anthropologist, 56,* 801–824.

Mehrabian, A. (1971). *Silent messages*. Belmont, CA: Wadsworth.

Melikan, L. (1962). Self-disclosure among university students in the Middle East. *Journal of Social Psychology, 57,* 257–263.

Menon, T., Morris, M., Chiu, C., & Hong, Y. (1999). Culture and the construal of agency. *Journal of Personality and Social Psychology 76,* 701–717.

Merrigan, G. (2000). Negotiating personal identities among people with and without disabilities. In D. Braithwaite & T. Thompson (Eds.), *Handbook of communication and people with disabilities*. Mahwah, NJ: Erlbaum.

Merritt, A. (2000). Culture in the cockpit: Do Hofstede's dimensions replicate? *Journal of Cross-Cultural Psychology, 31,* 283–301.

Merton, R. K. (1957). *Social theory and social structure*. New York: Free Press.

Mesquita, B., Frijda, N., & Scherer, K. (1997). Culture and emotion. In J. Berry, P. Dazen, & T. Saraswathi (Eds.), *Handbook of cross-cultural psychology* (2nd ed, Vol. 2). Boston: Allyn & Bacon.

Mezirow, J. (1984). A critical theory of adult learning and education. In S. Merriam (Ed.), *Selected writings on philosophy and adult education*. Malabar, FL: Robert E. Krieger.

Mezirow, J. (1991). *Transformative dimensions of adult learning*. San Francisco: Jossey-Bass.

Milgram, S. (1970). The experience of living in cities. *Science, 167,* 461–468.

Miller, G. (1988). Media messages and information processing in interpersonal communication. In B. Ruben (Ed.), *Information and behavior* (Vol. 2). New Brunswick, NJ: Transaction Books.

Miller, G., & Steinberg, M. (1975). *Between people*. Chicago: Science Research Associates.

Miller, G., & Sunnafrank, M. (1982). All is for one but one is not for all: A conceptual perspective of interpersonal communication. In F. Dance (Ed.), *Human communication theory*. New York: Harper & Row.

Miller, J. (1984). Culture and the development of everyday social explanations. *Journal of Personality and Social Psychology, 46,* 961–978.

Miller, M., Reynolds, R., & Cambra, R. (1982). *The selection of persuasive strategies in multicultural groups*. Paper presented at the Speech Communication Association convention.

Miller, M., Reynolds, R., & Cambra, R. (1987). The influence of gender and culture on language intensity. *Communication Monographs, 54,* 101–105.

Miller, S. (1987). *The ethnic press in the United States*. New York: Greenwood.

Milroy, L. (1980). *Language and social networks*. Baltimore: University Park Press.

Milroy, L. (1984). Comprehension and context. In P. Trudgill (Ed.), *Applied sociolinguistics*. London: Academic Press.

Mintz, N. (1956). Effects of aesthetic surroundings II. *Journal of Personality, 41,* 459–466.

Miranda, M., & Castro, F. (1977). Culture distance and success in psychotherapy with Spanish speaking clients. In J. Martinez (Ed.), *Chicano psychology*. New York: Academic Books.

Mischel, W. (1973). Toward a cognitive social learning reconceptualization of personality. *Psychological Review, 80,* 252–283.

Miyahara, A. (1995). Metatheoretical issues in conceptualization of Japanese communication competence. *Keio Communication Review, 17,* 63–82.

Miyahara, A., Kim, M. S., Shin, H., & Yoon, K. (1998). Conflict resolution styles among "collectivistic" cultures. *International Journal of Intercultural Relations, 22,* 505–525.

Miyamoto, Y., & Kuhlman, N. (2001). Ameliorating culture shock in Japanese expatriate children in the US. *International Journal of Intercultural Relations, 25,* 21–40.

Mizutani, O. (1981). *Japanese: The spoken language*. Tokyo: Japan Times.

Molina, J. (1978). Cultural barriers and interethnic communication in a multiethnic neighborhood. In E. Ross (Ed.), *Interethnic communication*. Athens: University of Georgia Press.

Montagu, A. (1952). *Man's most dangerous myth*. New York: Harper & Row.

Montagu, A. (1972). *Statement on race*. New York: Oxford University Press.

Monteith, M., Sherman, J., & Devine, P. (1998). Suppression as a stereotype control strategy. *Personality and Social Psychology Review, 2,* 63–82.

Moos, R. (1976). *Human adaptation*. Lexington, MA: Heath.

Morisaki, S., & Gudykunst, W. B. (1994). Face in Japan and the United States. In S. Ting-Toomey (Ed.), *The challenge of facework*. Albany: State University of New York Press.

Morris, M., Menon, T., & Ames, D. (2001). Culturally conferred conceptions of agency. *Personality and Social Psychology Review, 5,* 169–182.

Morris, M. L. (1981). *Saying and meaning in Puerto Rico.* Elmsford, NY: Pergamon.

Morris, R. T. (1960). *The two-way mirror.* Minneapolis: University of Minnesota Press.

Morrison, T. (1992). *Playing in the dark.* Cambridge, MA: Harvard Univerity Press.

Morsbach, H. (1976). Aspects of nonverbal communication in Japan. In L. Samovar & R. Porter (Eds.), *Intercultural communication: A reader* (2nd ed.). Belmont, CA: Wadsworth.

Mortland, C., & Ledgerwood, J. (1988). Refugee resource acquisition. In Y. Kim & W. Gudykunst (Eds.), *Cross-cultural adaptation.* Newbury Park, CA: Sage.

Mosel, J. (1973, May 17). *Status and role analysis.* Lecture to Japan and East Asia Area Studies Course, Foreign Service Institute, Washington, DC.

Mulac, A., Bradac, J., & Gibbons, P. (2001). Empirical support for the gender as culture hypothesis. *Human Communication Research, 27,* 121–152.

Mummendey, A., & Wenzel, M. (1999). Social discrimination and tolerance in intergroup relations. *Personality and Social Psychology Review, 3,* 158–174.

Myrdal, G. (1944). *An American dilemma* (2 vols.). New York: Harper & Row.

Nagata, D. (1993). *Legacy of silence.* New York: Plenum.

Nakane, C. (1970). *Japanese society.* Berkeley: University of California Press.

Nakane, C. (1974). The social system reflected in interpersonal communication. In J. Condon & M. Saito (Eds.), *Intercultural encounters with Japan.* Tokyo: Simul Press.

National Opinion Research Center (1991). Race relations responses to General Social Survey. Reported in *Los Angeles Times,* January 9, 1991, p. A 15.

Nayo, L. (1995, July 7). Making monsters of ordinary men. *Los Angeles Times,* p. B7.

Neale, M., Huber, V., & Northcraft, G. (1987). The framing of negotiations. *Organizational Behavior and Human Decision Processes, 39,* 228–241.

Neisser, U. (1976). *Cognition and reality.* San Francisco: W. H. Freeman.

Neto, F., Mullet, E., Deschamps, J., Barros, J., Benuvido, R., Camino, L., Falconi, A., Kagibanga, V., & Machado, M. (2000). Cross-cultural variations in attitudes toward love. *Journal of Cross-Cultural Psychology, 31,* 626–635.

Neuberg, S. (1989). The goal of forming accurate impressions. *Journal of Personality and Social Psychology, 56,* 374–386.

Ng, S., & Bradac, J. (1993). *Power in language.* Newbury Park, CA: Sage.

Nilsen, A. (1977). Sexism as shown through English vocabulary. In A. Nilsen, H. Bosmajian, H. Gershuny, & J. Stanley (Eds.), *Sexism and language.* Urbana, IL: National Council of Teachers of English.

Nilsen, A., Bosmajian, H., Gershuny, H., & Stanley, J. (Eds.). (1977). *Sexism and language.* Urbana, IL: National Council of Teachers of English.

Nisbett, R., Caputo, C., Legant, P., & Marecek, J. (1973). Behavior as seen by the actor and as seen by the observer. *Journal of Personality and Social Psychology, 27,* 154–165.

Nishida, H. (1985). Japanese intercultural communication competence and cross-cultural adjustment. *International Journal of Intercultural Relations, 9,* 247–270.

Nishiyama, K. (1971). Interpersonal persuasion in a vertical society. *Speech Monographs, 38,* 148–154.

Noesjirwan, J. (1978). A rule-based analysis of cultural differences in social behavior. *International Journal of Psychology, 13,* 305–316.

Noller, P. (1980). Misunderstanding in marital communication. *Journal of Personality and Social Psychology, 39,* 1135–1148.

Noller, P. (1993). Gender and emotional communication in marriage. *Journal of Language and Social Psychology, 12,* 132–152.

Norenzayan, A., Choi, I., & Nisbett, R. (2002). Cultural similarities and differences in social inference. *Personality and Social Psychology Bulletin, 28,* 109–120.

Norton, R. (1978). Foundations of a communicator style construct. *Human Communication Research, 4,* 99–112.

Nozick, R. (1989). *The examined life.* New York: Simon & Schuster.

Nuessel, F. (1984). Ageist language. *Maledicta, 8,* 17–28.

Oberg, K. (1958). *Culture shock and the problem of adjustment to new cultural environments.* Washington, DC: Department of State, Foreign Service Institute.

Oberg, K. (1960). Culture shock and the problems of adjustment to new cultural environments. *Practical Anthropology, 7,* 170–179.

Oehlkers, P. (1991). *Networks of social support and the adjustment of Japanese sojourners in the United States.* Paper presented at the Speech Communication Association convention.

Oetzel, J. (1998a). Culturally homogeneous and heterogeneous groups. *International Journal of Intercultural Relations, 22,* 135–161.

Oetzel, J. (1998b). The effects of self construals and ethnicity on self-reported conflict styles. *Communication Reports, 11,* 133–144.

Oetzel, J. (1998c). Explaining individual communication processes in homogeneous and heterogeneous groups through individualism-collectivism and self construals. *Human Communication Research, 25,* 202–224.

Oetzel, J. (2001). Self construals, communication processes, and group outcomes in homogeneous and heterogeneous groups. *Small Group Research, 32,* 19–54.

Oetzel, J., Ting-Toomey, S., & Chew, M. (1999). *Face and facework in conflicts with parents and siblings: A cross-cultural comparison of Germans, Japanese, Mexicans, and U.S. Americans.* Paper presented at the National Communication Association convention.

Oetzel, J., Ting-Toomey, S., Masumoto, T., Yokochi, Y., Pan, X., Takai, J., & Wilcox, R. (2000). *Face and facework in conflict: A cross-cultural comparison of China, Germany, Japan, and the United States.* Paper presented at the International Communication Association convention.

Oetzel, J., Ting-Toomey, S., Yokochi, Y., Masumoto, T., & Takai, J. (in press). A typology of facework behaviors in conflicts with best friends and relative strangers. *Communication Quarterly.*

Ogawa, N., & Gudykunst, W. B. (1999). Politeness rules in Japan and the United States. *Intercultural Communication Studies, IX*(1), 47–68.

O'Halloran, M. (1994). *Pure heart, enlightened mind.* Tokyo: Tuttle.

Ohbuchi, K., Chiba, S., & Fukushima, O. (1996). Mitigation of interpersonal conflicts. *Personality and Social Psychology Bulletin, 22,* 1035–1042.

Ohbuchi, K., Fukushima, O., & Tedeschi, J. (1999). Cultural values in conflict management. *Journal of Cross-Cultural Psychology, 30,* 51–71.

Ohbuchi, K., & Takahashi, Y. (1994). Cultural styles of conflict management in Japanese and Americans. *Journal of Applied Social Psychology, 24,* 1345–1366.

Okabe, K. (1987). Indirect speech acts of Japanese. In D. Kincaid (Ed.), *Communication theory from eastern and western perspectives.* New York: Academic Press.

Okabe, R. (1983). Cultural assumptions of East and West: Japan and the United States. In W. Gudykunst (Ed.), *Intercultural communication theory: Current perspectives.* Beverly Hills, CA: Sage.

Okazaki-Luff, M. (1994). On the adjustment of Japanese sojourners. *International Journal of Intercultural Relations, 15,* 85–102.

O'Keefe D., & Sypher H. (1981). Cognitive complexity measures and the relationship of cognitive complexity to communication. *Human Communication Research, 8,* 72–92.

Oliver, R. (1962). *Culture and communication.* Springfield, IL: Charles C Thomas.

Oliver, R. (1971). *Communication and culture in ancient India and China.* Syracuse, NY: Syracuse University Press.

Olsen, M. (1978). *The process of social organization* (2nd ed.). New York: Holt, Rinehart, and Winston.

Omi, M., & Winant, H. (1994). *Racial formation in the United States.* New York: Routledge.

Operario, D., & Fiske, S. (2001a). Ethnic identity moderates perceptions of prejudice. *Personality and Social Psychology Bulletin, 27,* 550–562.

Operario, D., & Fiske, S. (2001b). Stereotypes: Content, structures, processes and context. In R. Brown & S. Gaertner (Eds.), *Intergroup processes.* Oxford, UK: Blackwell.

Optow, S. (1990). Moral exclusion and injustice. *Journal of Social Issues, 46*(1), 1–20.

Orbe, M (1998a). *Constructing co-cultural theory.* Thousand Oaks, CA: Sage.

Orbe, M. (1998b). From the standpoint(s) of traditionally muted groups. *Communication Theory, 8,* 1–26.

Ornstein, R. (1972). *The psychology of consciousness.* New York: Pelican Books.

Ortega y Gasset, J. (1957). *Man and people* (W. Trask, trans.). New York: Norton.

Osbeck, L., Moghaddam, F., & Perreault, S. (1997). Similarity and attraction among majority and minority groups in a multicultural context. *International Journal of Intercultural Relations, 21,* 113–123.

Osgood, C., May, H., & Miron, S. (1972). *Cross-cultural universals of affective meaning.* Urbana: University of Illinois Press.

Oudenhoven, J. (2001). Do organizations reflect national cultures? *International Journal of Intercultural Relations, 25,* 89–107.

Oyserman, D., Gant, L., & Ager, J. (1995). A socially contextualized model of African American identity. *Journal of Personality and Social Psychology, 69,* 1216–1232.

Page, J. (1994, January–February). Japanese Brazilian style. *Americas,* 34–41.

Palisi, B. (1966). Ethnic patterns of friendship. *Phylon,* 217–225.

Palmore, E. (1962). Ethnophaulisms and ethnocentrism. *American Journal of Sociology, 67,* 442–445.

Palmore, E. (1982). Attitudes toward the aged. *Research on Aging, 4,* 333–348.

Pandy, J. (1990). The environment, culture, and behavior. In R. Brislin (Ed.), *Applied cross-cultural psychology.* Newbury Park, CA: Sage.

Park, R. (1930). Assimilation. *Encyclopedia of the Social Sciences, 2,* p. 282.

Park, R. (1939). Reflections on communication and culture. *American Journal of Sociology, 44,* 191–205.

Park, R. (1950). Our racial frontier in the Pacific. In R. Park (Ed.), *Race and culture.* New York: Free Press.

Parrillo, V. N. (1980). *Strangers to these shores.* Boston: Houghton Mifflin.

Parsons, T. (1951). *The social system.* Glencoe, IL: Free Press.

Parsons, T. (1953). Some comments on the state of the general theory of action. *American Sociological Review, 18,* 618–631.

Parsons, T., & Shils, E. (1951). *Toward a general theory of action.* Cambridge, MA: Harvard University Press.

Parsonson, K. (1987). Intermarriage. *Journal of Cross-Cultural Psychology, 18,* 363–371.

Pascale, R., & Athos, A. (1981). *The art of Japanese management.* New York: Simon & Schuster.

Patai, R. (1976). *The Arab mind.* New York: Scribner's.

Patterson, O. (1977). *Ethnic chauvinism.* New York: Stein and Day.

Pearce, W. B., & Kang, K. (1988). Conceptual migrations. In Y. Kim & W. Gudykunst (Eds.), *Cross-cultural adaptation.* Newbury Park, CA: Sage.

Pearce, W. B., & Stamm, K. (1973). Communication behavior and co-orientation relations. In P. Clark (Ed.), *New models for communication research.* Beverly Hills, CA: Sage.

Pearson, V., & Stephan, W. (1998). Preferences for styles of negotiation. *International Journal of Intercultural Relations, 22,* 67–83.

Peck, M. S. (1987). *The different drum: Community making and peace.* New York: Simon & Schuster.

Peck, M. S. (1993). *A world waiting to be born: Civility rediscovered.* New York: Bantam.

Pedone, R. (1980). *The retention of minority language in the United States.* Washington, DC: National Center for Educational Statistics.

Pelto, P. (1968, April). The difference between "tight" and "loose" societies. *Transaction,* pp. 37–40.

Peng, F. (1974). Communicative distance. *Language Sciences, 31,* 32–38.

Pescosolidio, B. (1992). Beyond rational choice. *American Journal of Sociology, 97,* 1096–1138.

Pettigrew, T. (1958). Personality and sociocultural factors in intergroup attitudes. *Journal of Conflict Resolution, 2,* 29–42.

Pettigrew, T. (1978). Three issues in ethnicity. In J. Yinger & S. Cutler (Eds.), *Major social issues.* New York: Free Press.

Pettigrew, T. (1979). The ultimate attribution error. *Personality and Social Psychology Bulletin, 5,* 461–476.

Pettigrew, T. (1982). Cognitive styles and social behavior. In L. Wheeler (Ed.), *Review of personality and social psychology* (Vol. 3). Beverly Hills, CA: Sage.

Pettigrew, T. (1986). The intergroup contact hypothesis reconsidered. In M. Hewstone & R. Brown (Eds.), *Contact and conflict in intergroup encounters.* Oxford, UK: Blackwell.

Philipsen, G. (1981). *The prospect for cultural communication.* Paper presented at the Seminar on Communication Theory from Eastern and Western Perspectives, East-West Center, Honolulu (a revised version was published in D. Kincaid [Ed.], *Communication theory from eastern and western perspectives.* New York: Academic Press, 1987).

Philipsen, G. (1989). Speech and the communal function in four cultures. In S. Ting-Toomey & F. Korzenny (Eds.), *Language, culture, and communication.* Newbury Park, CA: Sage.

Philipsen, G. (1992). *Speaking culturally.* Albany: State University of New York Press.

Philipsen, G. (2001). Cultural communication. In W. B. Gudykunst & B. Mody (Eds.), *Handbook of international and intercultural communication* (2nd ed.). Thousand Oaks, CA: Sage.

Phillips, H. (1965). *Thai peasant personality.* Berkeley: University of California Press.

Phinney, J. (1993). Multiple group identities. In J. Kroger (Ed.), *Discussions on ego identity.* Hillsdale, NJ: Erlbaum.

Pike, K. L. (1966). Etic and emic standpoints for the description of behavior. In A. Smith (Ed.), *Communication and culture.* New York: Holt, Rinehart, and Winston.

Piker, S. (1968). Friendship to the death in rural Thai society. *Human Organization,* 200–204.

Pilusuk, M. (1963). Anxiety, self acceptance, and open-mindedness. *Journal of Clinical Psychology, 19,* 386–391.

Pinker, S. (1994). *The language instinct.* New York: Harper.

Planalp, S., Rutherford, D., & Honeycutt, J. (1988). Events that increase uncertainty in relationships. *Human Communication Research, 14,* 516–547.

Pleck, J. (1977). The psychology of sex roles. *Journal of Communication, 26,* 193–200.

Plog, S. (1965). The disclosure of self in the United States and Germany. *Journal of Social Psychology, 65,* 193–203.

Pogrebin, L. (1985). *Among friends.* New York: McGraw-Hill.

Pool, I. de Sola (1965). Effects of cross-national contact on national and international images. In H. Kelman (Ed.), *International behavior.* New York: Holt, Rinehart, and Winston.

Powers, W., & Lowry, D. (1984). Basic communication fidelity. In R. Bostrom (Ed.), *Competence in communication.* Beverly Hills, CA: Sage.

Prather, H. (1986). *Notes on how to live in the world and still be happy.* New York: Doubleday.

Presidential Commission on Foreign Language and International Studies. (1979). *Strength through wisdom.* Washington, DC: U.S. Government Printing Office.

Pritchard, M. (1991). *On becoming responsible.* Lawrence: University of Kansas Press.

Putnam, L., & Wilson, C. (1982). Communication strategies in organizational conflicts. In M. Burgoon (Ed.), *Communication yearbook 6.* Beverly Hills, CA: Sage.

Putnam, R. (2000). *Bowling alone: The collapse and revival of American community.* New York: Simon & Schuster.

Pyszczynski, T., & Greenberg, J. (1981). Role of disconfirmed expectancies in the instigation of attributional processing. *Journal of Personality and Social Psychology, 40,* 31–38.

Quisumbing, M. (1982). *Life events, social support and personality: Their impact upon Filipino psychological adjustment.* Doctoral dissertation, University of Chicago.

Rahim, A. (1983). A measure of styles of handling interpersonal conflict. *Academy of Management Journal, 26,* 368–376.

Rahula, W. (1959). *What the Buddha taught.* New York: Grove Press.

Ralston, D. (1985). Employee ingratiation. *Academy of Management Review, 10,* 447–487.

Rapoport, A. (1969). *House form and culture.* Englewood Cliffs, NJ: Prentice-Hall.

Read, K. (1955). Morality and the concept of the person among the Gahuku-kama. *Oceana, 25,* 233–282.

Reagan, T. (1995). A sociocultural understanding of deafness. *International Journal of Intercultural Relations, 19,* 239–281.

Reece, D., & Palmgreen, P. (1996). *Coming to America: The influence of cultural variables on media use among Indian sojourners in the US.* Paper presented at the International Communication Association convention.

Redmond, M., & Bunyi, J. (1993). The relationship of intercultural communication competence with stress and the handling of stress as reported by international students. *International Journal of Intercultural Relations, 17,* 235–254.

Reid, S., & Ng, S. (1999). Language, power, and intergroup relations. *Journal of Social Issues, 55*(1), 119–140.

Reina, R. (1959). Two patterns of friendship in a Guatemalan community. *American Anthropologist, 44*–61.

Renteln, A. (1988). Relativism and the search for human rights. *American Anthropologist, 90,* 56–72.

Revilla, L. (1989). Dating and marriage preferences among Filipino Americans. *Journal of the Asian American Psychological Association, 13,* 72–79.

Rhee, E., Uleman, J., & Lee, H. (1996). Variations in collectivism and individualism by group and culture. *Journal of Personality and Social Psychology, 71,* 1037–1054.

Richards, Z., & Hewstone, M. (2001). Subtyping and subgrouping. *Personality and Social Psychology Review, 5,* 52–73.

Rigney, J., Bieri, J., & Tripodi, T. (1964). Social concept attainment and cognitive complexity. *Psychological Reports, 15,* 503–509.

Riley, P. (1989). Well don't blame me! On the interpretation of pragmatic errors. In W. Oleksy (Ed.), *Contrastive pragmatics.* Philadelphia: John Benjamins.

Rivera-Sinclair, E. (1997). Acculturation/biculturalism and its relationship to adjustment in Cuban-Americans. *International Journal of Intercultural Relations, 21,* 379–391.

Roach, C., & Wyatt, N. (1988). *Successful listening.* New York: Harper & Row.

Rodriguez, R. (1982). *The hunger of memory.* New York: Bantam.

Rogers, E. M., & Bhowmik, D. K. (1971). Homophily-heterophily. *Public Opinion Research, 34,* 523–531.

Rogers, E. M., & Shoemaker, F. (1971). *Communication of innovations* (2nd ed.). New York: Free Press.

Rogler, L. H., et al. (1980). Intergenerational change in ethnic identity in Puerto Rican family. *International Migration Review, 14,* 193–214.

Rokeach, M. (1951). A method for studying individual differences in "narrow-mindedness." *Journal of Personality, 20,* 219–233.

Rokeach, M. (1960). *The open and closed mind.* New York: Basic Books.

Rokeach, M. (1972). *Beliefs, attitudes and values.* San Francisco: Jossey-Bass.

Rokeach, M. (1973). *The nature of human values.* New York: Free Press.

Rokeach, M., Smith, P., & Evans, R. (1960). Two kinds of prejudice or one? In M. Rokeach, *The open and closed mind.* New York: Basic Books.

Roloff, M. (1987). Communication and conflict. In C. Berger & S. Chaffe (Eds.), *Handbook of communication science.* Newbury Park, CA: Sage.

Roosens, E. (1989). *Creating ethnicity.* Newbury Park, CA: Sage.

Root, M. (Ed.). (1995). *The multiracial experience.* Thousand Oaks, CA: Sage.

Rose, A. (1965). The subculture of aging. In A. Rose & W. Peterson (Eds.), *Older people and their social world.* Philadelphia: F. A. Davis.

Rose, T. (1981). Cognitive and dyadic processes in intergroup contact. In D. Hamilton (Ed.), *Cognitive processes in stereotyping and intergroup behavior.* Hillsdale, NJ: Erlbaum.

Roseman, I., Dhawan, N., Rettek, S., Naidu, R., & Thapa, K. (1995). Cultural differences and cross-cultural similarities in appraisals and emotional responses. *Journal of Cross-Cultural Psychology, 26,* 23–48.

Rosenblatt, P. C. (1964). Origins and effects of group ethnocentrism and nationalism. *Journal of Conflict Resolution, 8,* 131–146.

Rosenblatt, P., Karis, T., & Powell, R. (1995). *Multiracial couples.* Thousand Oaks, CA: Sage.

Rosenfeld, H. (1978). Conversational control functions of nonverbal behavior. In A. Siegman & S. Feldstein (Eds.), *Nonverbal behavior in communication.* Hillsdale, NJ: Lawrence Erlbaum.

Rosenthal, P. (1984). *Words and values.* Cambridge, England: Cambridge University Press.

Rosenthal, R., Hall, J., Dimatteo, M., Rogers, P., & Archer, D. (1979). *Sensitivity to nonverbal communication.* Baltimore: Johns Hopkins University Press.

Ross, L., & Ward, A. (1995). Psychological barriers to dispute resolution. In M. Zanna (Ed.), *Advances in experimental social psychology* (Vol. 27). New York: Academic Press.

Ross, L. D. (1977). The intuitive psychologist and his shortcomings: Distortions in the attribution process. In L. Berkowitz (Ed.), *Advances in experimental psychology* (Vol. 10). New York: Academic Press.

Ross, S., & Shortreed, I. (1990). Japanese foreigner talk. *Journal of Asian Pacific Communication, 1,* 134–145.

Ruben, B. D. (1975). Intrapersonal, interpersonal and mass communication process in individual and multi-person systems. In B. Ruben & J. Kim (Eds.), *General systems theory and human communication.* Rochelle Park, NJ: Hayden.

Ruben, B. D. (1976). Assessing communication competency for intercultural adaptation. *Group and Organizational Studies, 1,* 334–354.

Ruben, B. D. (1983). A system-theoretic view. In W. B. Gudykunst (Ed.), *Intercultural communication theory.* Beverly Hills, CA: Sage.

Ruben, B. D., & Kealey, D. J. (1979). Behavioral assessment of communication competency and the prediction of cross-cultural adaptation. *International Journal of Intercultural Relations, 3,* 15–48.

Rubin, D., Yang, H., & Porte, M. (2000). A comparison of self-reported self-disclosure among Chinese and North Americans. In S. Petronio (Ed.), *Balancing the secrets of private disclosures.* Mahwah, NJ: Erlbaum.

Rubin, M., & Hewstone, M. (1998). Social identity theory's elf-esteem hypothesis. *Personality and Social Psychology Review, 2,* 40–62.

Rudman, L., & Kilianski, S. (2000). Implicit and explicit attitudes toward female authority. *Personality and Social Psychology Bulletin, 26,* 1315–1328.

Ruscher, J. (2001). *Prejudiced communication.* New York: Guilford.

Ryan, E., & Carranza, M. (1977). Ingroup and outgroup reactions to Mexican-Americans language varieties. In H. Giles (Ed.), *Language, ethnicity, and intergroup relations.* London: Academic Press.

Ryan, E., Giles, H., & Sebastian, R. (1982). An integrative perspective for the study of attitudes toward language. In E. Ryan & H. Giles (Eds.), *Attitudes toward language variation.* London: Edward Arnold.

Ryan, E., Hewstone, M., & Giles, H. (1984). Language and intergroup attitudes. In J. Eiser (Ed.), *Attitudinal judgment.* New York: Springer-Verlag.

Ryu, J. S. (1976). *New-socialization function of mass media working among foreign students.* Paper presented at the Western States Speech Communication Association convention.

Saarinen, E. (1948). *The search for form.* New York: Reinhold.

Sachdev, I, & Bourhis, R. (1990). Bilinguality and multilinguality. In H. Giles & P. Robinson (Eds.), *Handbook of language and social psychology.* London: Wiley.

Sacks, H., Schegloff, E., & Jefferson, G. (1974). A systematics for the organization of turn-taking in conversations. *Language, 50,* 696–735.

Safilios-Rothchild, C. (1982). Social and psychological parameters of friendship and intimacy for disabled people. In M. Eisenberg, C. Giggins, & R. Duval (Eds.), *Disabled people as second class citizens.* New York: Springer.

Saleh, S., & Gufwoli, P. (1982). The transfer of management techniques and practices. In R. Rath, H. Aschana, D. Sinha, & J. Sinha (Eds.), *Diversity and unity in cross-cultural psychology.* Lisse, Netherlands: Swets & Zeitlinger.

Salamon, S. (1977). Family bonds and friendship bonds. *Journal of Marriage and the Family, 39,* 807–820.

San Antonio, P. (1987). Social mobility and language usage in an American company in Japan. *Journal of Language and Social Psychology, 6,* 191–200.

Sanders, J., & Wiseman, R. (1991). *Uncertainty reduction among ethnicities in the United States.* Paper presented at the International Communication Association convention.

Sanders, J., Wiseman, R., & Matz, I. (1991). Uncertainty reduction in acquaintance relationships in Ghana and the United States. In S. Ting-Toomey & F. Korzenny (Eds.), *Cross-cultural interpersonal communication.* Newbury Park, CA: Sage.

Sapir, E. (1970/1925). *Culture, language and personality.* Berkeley: University of California Press.

Sarbaugh, L. (1979). *Intercultural communication.* Rochelle Park, NJ: Hayden.

Sarbin, T., & Allen, V. Role theory. (1968). In G. Lindzey & E. Aronson (Eds.), *Handbook of social psychology* (2nd ed.). Reading, MA: Addison-Wesley.

Schaefer, R. (1979). *Racial and ethnic groups.* Boston: Little, Brown.

Scheflen, A. E. (1976). *Human territories.* Englewood Cliffs, NJ: Prentice-Hall.

Scherer, K., Banse, R., & Wallbott, H. (2001). Emotion inferences from vocal expression correlates across languages. *Journal of Cross-Cultural Psychology, 32,* 76–92.

Scherer, K., & Wallbott, H. (1994). Evidence for universality and cultural variation of differential emotion response patterning. *Journal of Personality and Social Psychology, 66,* 310–328.

Schild, E. (1962). The foreign student as stranger, learning the norm of the host culture. *Journal of Social Issues, 18,* 41–54.

Schlenker, B. (1986). Self-identification. In R. Baumeister (Ed.), *Public self and private self.* New York: Springer-Verlag.

Schlesinger, A. (1992)., *The disuniting of America.* New York: Norton.

Schmidt, K. (1991). *Exit, voice, loyalty, and neglect: Responses to sexist communication in dating relationships.* Ph.D. dissertation, Arizona State University, Tempe.

Schneider, J., & Hacker, S. (1973). Sex role imagery and the use of generic "man" in introductory texts. *American Sociologist, 8,* 12–18.

Schneider, M., & Jorden, W. (1981). Perception of the communicative performance of Americans and Chinese in intercultural dyads. *International Journal of Intercultural Relations, 5,* 175–192.

Schroder, H., Driver, M., & Streufert, S. (1967). *Human information processing: Individuals and groups functioning in complex social situations.* New York: Holt, Rinehart, and Winston.

Schuetz, A. (1944). The stranger. *American Journal of Sociology, 49,* 499–507.

Schuetz, A. (1945). The homecomer. *American Journal of Sociology, 50,* 369–376.

Schwartz, J. (1980). The negotiation for meaning. In D. Larsen-Freeman (Ed.), *Discourse analysis in second language research.* Rowley, MA: Newbury House.

Schwartz, S. (1990). Individualism-collectivism. *Journal of Cross-Cultural Psychology, 21,* 139–157.

Schwartz, S. (1992). Universals in the content and structure of values. In M. Zanna (Ed.), *Advances in experimental social psychology* (Vol. 25). New York: Academic Press.

Schwartz, S. (1994a). Are there universal aspects of the structure and content of values? *Journal of Social Issues, 50*(4), 19–45.

Schwartz, S. (1994b). Beyond individualism-collectivism. In U. Kim, H. Triandis, C. Kagitcibasi, S. Choi, & G. Yoon (Eds.), *Individualism and collectivism.* Thousand Oaks, CA: Sage.

Schwartz, S., & Bardi, A. (2001). Value hierarchies across cultures: Taking a similarities perspective. *Journal of Cross-Cultural Psychology, 32,* 268–290.

Schwartz, S., & Bilsky, W. (1987). Toward a psychological structure of human values. *Journal of Personality and Social Psychology, 53,* 550–562.

Schwartz, S., & Bilsky, W. (1990). Toward a theory of the universal content and structure of values. *Journal of Personality and Social Psychology, 58,* 878–891.

Schwartz, S., & Sagiv, L. (1995). Identifying culture-specifics in the content and structure of values. *Journal of Cross-Cultural Psychology, 26,* 92–106.

Schwartz, T. (Ed.). (1976). *Socialization as cultural communication.* Berkeley: University of California Press.

Schwimmer, B., & Warren, D. (Eds.). (1993). *Anthropology and the Peace Corps.* Ames: Iowa State University Press.

Scollon, R., & Scollon, S. (1981). *Narrative, literacy, and face in interethnic communication.* Norwood, NJ: Ablex.

Scollon, R., & Wong-Scollon, S. (1990). Athabaskan-English interethnic communication. In D. Carbaugh (Ed.), *Cultural communication and intercultural contact.* Hillsdale, NJ: Erlbaum.

Scollon, R., & Wong-Scollon, S. (1994). Face parameters in east-west discourse. In S. Ting-Toomey (Ed.), *The challenge of facework.* Albany: State University of New York Press.

Scott, J. (1993, September 24). On-line, and maybe out of line. *Los Angeles Times,* pp. A1, 32–33.

Scott, W. (1965). Psychological and social correlates of international images. In H. Kelman (Ed.), *International behavior.* New York: Holt, Rinehart, and Winston.

Scotton, C. (1983). The negotiation of identities in conversation. *International Journal of the Sociology of Language, 44,* 115–136.

Scotton, C. (1990). The sociolinguistics of language switching. In R. Jacobson (Ed.), *Code-switching as a worldwide phenomenon.* New York: Peter Lang.

Searle, W., & Ward, C. (1990). The prediction of psychological and sociocultural adjustment during cross-cultural transitions. *International Journal of Intercultural Relations, 14,* 485–506.

Sears, D. (1988). Symbolic racism. In P. Katz & D. Taylor (Eds.), *Eliminating racism.* New York: Plenum.

Sechrest, L. (1969). Nonreactive assessment of attitudes. In E. Williams & H. Raush (Eds.), *Naturalistic viewpoints in psychological research.* New York: Holt, Reinhart, & Winston.

Sechrest, L., Flores, L., & Arellano, L. (1968). Language and social interaction in a bilingual setting. *Journal of Social Psychology, 76,* 155–161.

Sedikides, C., & Brewer, M. (Eds.). (2001). *Individual self, relational self, collective self.* Philadelphia: Psychology Press.

Seelye, H., & Wasilewski, J. (1981). *Social competency development in multicultural children, aged 6–13.* Washington, DC: National Institute for Education.

Selznick, P. (1992). *The moral commonwealth.* Berkeley: University of California Press.

Selltiz, C., Christ, J., Havel, J., & Cook, S. (1963). *Attitudes and social relations of foreign students in the United States.* Minneapolis: University of Minnesota Press.

Sewell, W., & Davidsen, O. (1961). *Scandinavian students on an American campus.* Minneapolis: University of Minnesota Press.

Shack, W. (1979). Open systems and closed boundaries. In W. Shack & E. Skinner (Eds.), *Strangers in African society.* Berkeley: University of California Press.

Shaffer, D., Crepaz, N., & Sun, C. (2000). Physical attractiveness stereotyping in cross-cultural perspective. *Journal of Cross-Cultural Psychology, 31,* 557–582.

Shah, H. (1991). Communication and cross-cultural adaptation patterns among Asian Indians. *International Journal of Intercultural Relations, 15,* 311–321.

Sharkey, W., & Singelis, T. (1993). *Embarrassability and relational orientation.* Paper presented at the International Network on Personal Relationships.

Shatzer, M., Burgoon, J., Burgoon, M., Korzenny, F., & Miller, M. (1988). *A cross-cultural comparison of compliance-gaining between Japanese and North Americans.* Paper presented at the Speech Communication Association convention.

Shea, C. (1997, June 20). The University of California investigates new approaches to changing behavior. *Chronicle of Higher Education,* p. A15.

Sheehy, G. (1986). *Spirit of survival.* New York: Bantam Books.

Sherif, M. (1966). *In a common predicament.* Boston: Houghton Mifflin.

Sherif, M., Harvey, O., White, B., Hood, W., & Sherif, C. (1961). *Intergroup conflict and cooperation.* Norman: University of Oklahoma Press.

Sherif, M., & Sherif, C. (1953). *Groups in harmony and tension.* New York: Harper.

Shibazaki, K., & Brennan, K. (1998). When kinds of different feathers flock together. *Journal of Social and Personal Relationships, 15,* 248–256.

Shibutani, T., & Kwan, M. (1965). *Ethnic stratification.* New York: Macmillan.

Shim, J. (1994). *Community orientations and newspaper use.* Paper presented at the International Communication Association convention.

Shinagawa, L., & Pang, G. (1996). The impact of immigration on the demography of Asian Pacific Americans. In B. Hing & R. Lee (Eds.), *Reframing the immigration debate.* Los Angeles: University of California, Los Angeles Asian American Studies Center.

Shon, S., & Ja, D. (1982). Asian families., In M. McGolfdrick, J. Pearce, & J. Giordano (Eds.), *Ethnicity and family therapy.* New York: Guilford.

Shouby, E. (1970). The influence of the Arabic language on the psychology of the Arabs. In A. Lutifiyya & C. Churchill (Eds.), *Readings in the Arab middle eastern societies and cultures.* The Hague: Mouton.

Shuter, R. (1976). Proxemics and tactility in Latin America. *Journal of Communication, 26,* 46–52.

Shuter, R. (1982). Initial interaction of American blacks and whites in interracial and intraracial dyads. *Journal of Social Psychology, 117,* 45–52.

Sigman, S. (1980). On communication rules from a social perspective. *Human Communication Research, 7,* 37–51.

Sillars, A. (1980). Attribution and communication in roommate conflicts. *Communication Monographs, 47,* 180–200.

Sillars, A., Coletti, S., Parry, D., & Rogers, M. (1982). Coding verbal conflict tactics. *Human Communication Research, 9,* 83–95.

Simard, L. M. (1981). Cross-cultural interaction: Potential invisible barriers. *Journal of Social Psychology, 113,* 171–192.

Simard, L. M., & Taylor, D. M. (1973). The potential for bicultural communication in a dyadic situation. *Canadian Journal of Behavioral Science, 5,* 211–225.

Simard, L. M., Taylor, D. M., & Giles, H. (1976). Attributional processes and interpersonal accommodation. *Language and Speech, 19,* 374–387.

Simmel, G. (1950/1908). The stranger. In K. Wolff (Trans. & Ed.), *The sociology of Georg Simmel.* New York: Free Press.

Simon, R. (1993). Old minorities, new immigrants. *Annals of the American Academy of Political and Social Science, 530,* 61–73.

Simons, H., Berkowitz, N., & Moyer, R. (1970). Similarity, credibility, and attitude change: A review and a theory. *Psychological Bulletin, 73,* 1–16.

Sinclair, S., Sidanius, J., & Levin, S. (1998). The interface between ethnic and social system attachment. *Journal of Social Issues, 54*(4), 741–758.

Singelis, T., Bond, M., Sharkey, W., & Lai, C. (1999). Unpacking culture's influence on self-esteem and embarrassability. *Journal of Cross-Cultural Psychology, 30,* 315–341.

Singelis, T., & Brown, W. (1995). Culture, self, and collectivist communication. *Human Communication Research, 21,* 354–389.

Singelis, T., & Sharkey, W. (1995). Culture, self construal, and embarrassability. *Journal of Cross-Cultural Psychology, 26,* 622–644.

Singelis, T., Triandis, H., Bhawuk, D., & Gelfand, M. (1995). Horizontal and vertical dimensions of individualism and collectivism. *Cross-Cultural Research, 29,* 240–275.

Singhal, A., & Nagao, M. (1993). Assertiveness as communication competence. *Asian Journal of Communication, 3,* 1–18.

Skevington, S. (1989). A place for emotion in social identity theory. In S. Skevington & D. Baker (Eds.), *The social identity of women.* London: Sage.

Smalley, W. (1963). Culture shock, language shock and the shock of self-discovery. *Practical Anthropology, 10,* 49–56.

Smith, D. (1987). *The everyday world as problematic.* Boston. Northeastern University Press.

Smith, E. (1994). Social identity and social emotions. In D. Mackie & D. Hamilton (Eds.), *Affect, cognition, and stereotyping.* New York: Academic Press.

Smith, H. (1976). *The Russians.* New York: Ballantine Books.

Smith, P., & Bond, M. (1993). *Social psychology across cultures.* New York: Harvester.

Smith, P., Dugan, S., Peterson, M., & Leung, K. (1998). Individualism, collectivism, and the handling of disagreements: A 23-country study. *International Journal of Intercultural Relations, 22,* 351–367.

Smith, S., & Whitehead, G. (1984). Attributions for promotions and demotions in the United States and India. *The Journal of Social Psychology, 30,* 526–537.

Smock, C. (1955). The influence of psychological stress on the intolerance of ambiguity. *Journal of Abnormal and Social Psychology, 50,* 177–182.

Smutkupt, S., & Barna, L. (1976). Impact of nonverbal communication in an intercultural setting: Thailand. In F. Casmir (Ed.), *International and intercultural communication annual* (Vol. III). Falls Church, VA: Speech Communication Association.

Smuts, J. C. (1967/1926). *Holism and evolution.* New York: Viking.

Snyder, M. (1974). Self-monitoring of expressive behavior. *Journal of Personality and Social Psychology, 30,* 526–537.

Snyder, M., & Haugen, J. (1995). Why does behavioral confirmation occur? *Personality and Social Psychology Bulletin, 21,* 963–974.

Sodetani, L. L., & Gudykunst, W. B. (1987). The effects of surprising events on intercultural relationships. *Communication Research Reports, 4*(2), 1–6.

Sommer, R. (1968). Intimacy ratings in five countries. *International Journal of Psychology, 3,* 109–114.

Sorrentino, R., & Short, J. (1986). Uncertainty orientation, motivation, and cognition. In R. Sorrentino & E. T. Higgins (Eds.), *Handbook of motivation and cognition.* New York: Guilford.

Southworth, F. (1980). Indian bilingualism. *Studies in Child Language and Multilingualism, 345,* 121–135.

Spickard, P. (1989). *Mixed blood.* Madison: University of Wisconsin Press.

Spitzberg, B., & Cupach, W. (1984). *Interpersonal communication competence.* Beverly Hills, CA: Sage.

Spradley, J. P. (Ed.). (1972). *Culture and cognition.* San Francisco: Chandler.

Sprecher, S., Aron, A., Hatfield, E., Cortesa, A., Potapova, E., & Levitskaya, A. (1994). Love: American style, Russian style, and Japanese style. *Personal Relationships, 1,* 349–369.

Sreenivasan, S. (1996, July 22). As mainstream papers struggle, the ethnic press is thriving. *New York Times,* p. C7.

Srivastava, S. (1960). Patterns of ritual friendship in tribal India. *International Journal of Comparative Sociology,* 239–247.

Stanfield, J. (Ed.). (1995). Theories of ethnicity. *American Behavioral Scientist, 38*(3) (whole issue).

Stangor, C., & Lange, J. (1994). Mental representations of social groups. In M. Zanna (Ed.), *Advances in experimental social psychology* (Vol. 26). New York: Academic Press.

Stangor, C., Sechrist, G., & Jost, J. (2001). Changing racial beliefs by providing consensus information. *Personality and Social Psychology Bulletin, 27,* 486–496.

Stanley, J. (1977). Paradigmatic women. In D. Shores & C. Hines (Eds.), *Papers in language variation.* Tuscaloosa: University of Alabama Press.

Staub, E. (1989). *The roots of evil.* New York: Cambridge University Press.

Staub, E. (1999). The roots of evil. *Personality and Social Psychology Review, 3,* 179–192.

Stephan, W. (1985). Intergroup relations. In G. Lindzey & E. Aronson (Eds.), *Handbook of Social Psychology* (3rd ed., Vol. 2). New York: Random House.

Stephan, W. (1987). The contact hypothesis in intergroup relations. In L. Hendrick (Ed.), *Group processes and intergroup relations.* Thousand Oaks, CA: Sage.

Stephan, W., & Finley, K. (1999). The role of empathy in improving intergroup relations. *Journal of Social Issues, 55*(4), 729–744.

Stephan, W., & Rosenfield, D. (1982). Racial and ethnic stereotyping. In A. Millar (Ed.), *In the eye of the beholder.* New York: Praeger.

Stephan, W., & Stephan, C. (1985). Intergroup anxiety. *Journal of Social Issues, 41,* 157–166.

Stephan, W., & Stephan, C. (1989). Antecedants of intergroup anxiety in Asian-Americans and Hispanic-Americans. *International Journal of Intercultural Relations, 13,* 203–219.

Stephan, W., & Stephan, C. (1992). Reducing intercultural anxiety through intercultural contact. *International Journal of Intercultural Relations, 16,* 89–106.

Stephan, W., & Stephan, C. (1996). Predicting prejudice: The role of threat. *International Journal of Intercultural Relations, 20,* 409–426.

Stephan, W., Stephan, C., & Gudykunst, W. B. (1999). Anxiety in intergroup relations: A comparison of AUM theory and integrated threat theory. *International Journal of Intercultural Relations, 23,* 613–628.

Stephenson, G. (1981). Intergroup bargaining and negotiation. In J. Turner & H. Giles (Eds.), *Intergroup behavior.* Chicago: University of Chicago Press.

Stevens, L., & Fiske, K. (1995). Motivation and cognition in social life. *Social Cognition, 13,* 189–214.

Stewart, E. C. (1972). *American cultural patterns: A cross-cultural perspective.* Chicago: Intercultural Network.

Strassberg, D., & Anchor, K. (1975). Rating intimacy of self-disclosure. *Psychological Reports, 37,* 562.

Stryker, S., & Stratham, A. (1985). Symbolic interactions, and role theory. In G. Lindzey & E. Aronson (Eds.), *Handbook of social psychology* (3rd ed., Vol. 1). New York: Random House.

Stuart, I., & Abt, E. (1973). *Interracial marriage.* New York: Grossman.

Stuart, R. (1980). *Helping couples change.* New York: Guilford.

Subervi-Velez, F. (1986). The mass media and ethnic assimilation and pluralism. *Communication Research, 13,* 71–86.

Sudweeks, S., Gudykunst, W. B., Ting-Toomey, S., & Nishida, T. (1990). Developmental themes in Japanese-North American relationships. *International Journal of Intercultural Relations, 14,* 207–233.

Sugimoto, N. (1997). A Japan-U.S. comparison of apology styles. *Communication Research, 24,* 349–369.

Suleiman, M. W. (1973). The Arabs and the west: Communication gap. In M. Prosser (Ed.), *Intercommunication among nations and peoples.* New York: Harper & Row.

Sumner, W. G. (1940). *Folkways.* Boston: Ginn.

Sunnafrank, M. J. (1991). Interpersonal attraction and attitude similarity. In J. Andersen (Ed.), *Communication yearbook 14.* Newbury Park, CA: Sage.

Sunnafrank, M. J., & Miller, G. R. (1981). The role of initial conversation in determining attraction to similar and dissimilar strangers. *Human Communication Research, 8,* 16–25.

Suro, R. (1998). *Strangers among us.* New York: Knopf.

Suro, R. (1999, November). Mixed doubles. *American Demographics,* pp. 58–59.

Sussman, N., & Rosenfeld, H. (1982). Influence of culture, language, and sex on conversational distance. *Journal of Personality and Social Psychology, 42,* 66–74.

Suttles, G. (1970). Friendship as a social institution. In G. McNall (Ed.), *Social relationships.* Chicago: Aldine.

Suzuki, D. T. (1968). *The essence of Buddhism.* Kyoto, Japan: Hozokan.

Suzuki, S. (1998). In-group and out-group communication patterns in international organizations. *Communication Research, 25,* 154–182.

Swann, W. (1983). Self-verification. In J. Suls & A. Greenwald (Eds.), *Psychological perspectives on the self* (Vol. 2). Hillsdale, NJ: Erlbaum.

Swimm, J., & Campbell, B. (2001). Sexism: attitudes, beliefs, and behavior. In R. Brown & S. Gaertner (Eds.), *Intergroup processes.* Oxford, UK: Blackwell.

Swimm, J., Hyers, L., Cohen, L., & Ferguson, M. (2001). Everyday sexism. *Journal of Social Issues, 57*(1), 31–54.

Szalay, L. B., & Deese, J. (1978). *Subjective meaning and culture.* Hillsdale, NJ: Erlbaum.

Szalay, L., & Inn, A. (1988). Cross-cultural adaptation and diversity. In Y. Kim & W. Gudykunst (Eds.), *Cross-cultural adaptation.* Newbury Park, CA: Sage.

Szapocznik, J., et al. (1975). *Acculturation: Theory, measurement and clinical implications.* Rockville, MD: National Institute on Drug Abuse.

Szapocznik, J., & Kurtines, W. (1980). Acculturation, biculturalism and adjustment of Cuban Americans. In A. Padilla (Ed.), *Acculturation.* Boulder, CO: Westview.

Szapocznik, J., Kurtines, W., & Fernandez, T. (1980). Bicultural involvement and adjustment of Hispanic-Americans. *International Journal of Intercultural Relations, 4,* 353–365.

Tafarodi, R., Lang, J., & Smith, A. (1999). Self-esteem and the cultural tradeoff. *Journal of Cross-Cultural Psychology, 30,* 620–640.

Tafarodi, R., & Swann, W. (1996). Individualism-collectivism and global self-esteem. *Journal of Cross-Cultural Psychology, 27,* 651–672.

Tafoya, D. (1983). Perceptions of the roots of conflict: A theory and typology. In W. Gudykunst (Ed.), *Intercultural communication theory.* Beverly Hills, CA: Sage.

Taft, R. (1966). *From stranger to citizen.* London: Tavistock.

Taft, R. (1977). Coping with unfamiliar cultures. In N. Warren (Ed.), *Studies in cross-cultural psychology* (Vol. 1). New York: Academic Press.

Taft, R. (1988). The psychological adaptation of Soviet immigrants in Australia. In Y. Kim & W. Gudykunst (Eds.), *Cross-cultural adaptation.* Newbury Park, CA: Sage.

Tagore, R. (1961). *Toward universal man.* New York: Asia Publishing House.

Tajfel, H. (1958). Second thoughts about cross-cultural research and international relations. *International Journal of Psychology, 3,* 213–219.

Tajfel, H. (1969a). Social and cultural factors in perception. In G. Lindzey & A. Aronson (Eds.), *The handbook of social psychology* (2nd ed.). Reading, MA: Addison-Wesley.

Tajfel, H. (1969b). Cognitive aspects of prejudice. *Journal of Social Issues, 25,* 79–97.

Tajfel H. (1972). Experiments in a vacuum. In J. Israel & H. Tajfel (Eds.), *The context of social psychology.* London: Academic Press.

Tajfel, H. (1974). Social identity and intergroup behavior. *Social Science Information, 13,* 65–93.

Tajfel, H. (1978). Social categorization, social identity, and social comparisons. In H. Tajfel (Ed.), *Differentiation between social groups.* London: Academic Press.

Tajfel, H. (1981). Social stereotypes and social groups. In J. Turner & H. Giles (Eds.), *Intergroup behavior.* Chicago: University of Chicago Press.

Tajfel, H. (1982). *Human groups and social categories.* Cambridge, England: Cambridge University Press.

Tajfel, H., & Turner, J. (1979). An integrative theory of intergroup conflict. In W. Austin & S. Worchel (Eds.), *The social psychology of intergroup relations.* Monterey, CA: Brooks/Cole.

Tamir, L. (1984). The older person's communicative needs. In R. Dunkle, M. Heig, & M. Rosenberg (Eds.), *Communications technology and the elderly.* New York: Springer.

Tan, D., & Singh, R. (1995). Attitudes and attraction. *Personality and Social Psychology Bulletin, 21,* 975–986.

Tanaka, Y., Takai, J., Kohyama, T., Fujihara, T., & Minami, H. (1994). Social networks of international students in Japan. *Japanese Journal of Experimental Social Psychology, 33,* 213–223.

Tannen, D. (1975). Communication mix and mixup or how linguistics can ruin a marriage. *San Jose State Occasional Papers on Linguistics,* 205–211.

Tannen, D. (1979). Ethnicity and conversational style. In *Working papers on sociolinguistics* (Number 55). Austin, TX: Southwest Educational Development Laboratory.

Tannen, D. (1990). *You just don't understand.* New York: Ballantine.

Tannen, D. (1993). Commencement address at State University of New York at Binghamton. Printed in *Chronicle of Higher Education,* June 9, 1993, p. B5.

Tata, J. (2000). Implicit theories of account-giving: Influence of culture and gender. *International Journal of Intercultural Relations, 24,* 437–454.

Tavris, C. (1982). *Anger: The misunderstood emotion.* New York: Simon & Schuster.

Taylor, C. (1991). *The ethics of authenticity.* Cambridge, MA: Harvard University Press.

Taylor, D., Wright, S., & Porter, L. (1994). Dimensions of perceived discrimination. In M. Zanna & J. Olsen (Eds.), *The psychology of prejudice.* Hillsdale, NJ: Erlbaum.

Taylor, D. M., Dube, L., & Bellerose, J. (1986). Intergroup contact in Quebec. In M. Hewstone & R. Brown (Eds.), *Contact and conflict in intergroup encounters.* Oxford, UK: Blackwell.

Taylor, D. M., & Gardner, R. C. (1970). Bicultural communication: A study of communicational efficiency and person perception. *Canadian Journal of Behavioral Science, 2,* 67–81.

Taylor, D. M., & Simard, L. M. (1975). Social interaction in a bilingual setting. *Canadian Psychological Review, 16,* 240–254.

Taylor, S. E., & Fiske, S. T. (1975). Point of view and perceptions of causality. *Journal of Personality and Social Psychology, 32,* 439–445.

Taylor, S. E., & Fiske, S. T. (1978). Salience, attention, and attribution. In L. Berkowitz (Ed.), *Advances in experimental social psychology* (Vol. 11). New York: Academic Press.

Taylor, S. E., & Koivumaki, J. H. (1976). The perception of self and others. *Journal of Personality and Social Psychology, 33,* 403–408.

Tessler, M. A., O'Ban, W. M., & Spain, D. H. (1973). *Tradition and identity in changing Africa.* New York: Harper & Row.

Thayer, L. (1968). *Communication and communication systems.* Homewood, IL: Irwin.

Thomas, A. (1999). Racism, racial identity, and racial socialization: A personal reflection. *Journal of Counseling and Development, 77,* 35–37.

Thomas, J. (1983). Cross-cultural pragmatic failure. *Applied Linguistics, 4,* 91–112.

Thomas, K. (1983). Conflict and its management. In M. Dunnette (Ed.), *Handbook of industrial and organizational psychology.* New York: Wiley.

Thompson, L. (1993). The impact of negotiation on intergroup relations. *Journal of Experimental Social Psychology, 29,* 304–325.

Thompson, T. (1982). Disclosure as a disability management strategy. *Communication Quarterly, 30,* 196–202.

Thompson, T., & Siebold, D. (1978). Stigma management in normal-stigmatized interaction. *Human Communication Research, 4,* 231–242.

Tinder, G. (1980). *Community.* Baton Rouge: Louisiana State University Press.

Ting-Toomey, S. (1980). Talk as a cultural resource in the Chinese-American speech community. *Communication, 9,* 193–203.

Ting-Toomey, S. (1981). Ethnic identity and close friendship in Chinese-American college students. *International Journal of Intercultural Relations, 5,* 383–406.

Ting-Toomey, S. (1985). Toward a theory of conflict and culture. In W. Gudykunst, L. Stewart, & S. Ting-Toomey (Eds.), *Communication, culture, and organizational processes.* Beverly Hills, CA: Sage.

Ting-Toomey, S. (1986a). Conflict styles in black and white subjective cultures. In Y. Kim (ed.), *Current research in interethnic communication.* Beverly Hills, CA: Sage.

Ting-Toomey, S. (1986b). Japanese communication patterns. *World Communication, 15,* 113–126.

Ting-Toomey, S. (1988). A face negotiation theory. In Y. Kim & W. Gudykunst (Eds.), *Theories in intercultural communication.* Newbury Park, CA: Sage.

Ting-Toomey, S. (1989). Identity and interpersonal bonding. In M. Asante & W. Gudykunst (Eds.), *Handbook of international and intercultural communication.* Newbury Park, CA: Sage.

Ting-Toomey, S. (1991). Intimacy expression in three cultures. *International Journal of Intercultural Relations, 15,* 29–46.

Ting-Toomey, S. (1993). Communicative resourcefulness: An identity negotiation theory. In R. Wiseman & J. Koester (Eds.), *Intercultural communication competence.* Thousand Oaks, CA: Sage.

Ting-Toomey, S. (1994a). Managing conflict in intimate intercultural relationships. In D. Cahn (Ed.), *Intimate conflict in personal relationships.* Hillsdale, NJ: Erlbaum.

Ting-Toomey, S. (1994b). Managing intercultural conflicts effectively. In L. Samovar & R. Porter (Eds.), *Intercultural communication: A reader* (7th ed.). Belmont, CA: Sage.

Ting-Toomey, S. (Ed.). (1994c). *The challenge of facework.* Albany: State University of New York Press.

Ting-Toomey, S. (1997). Intercultural conflict competence. In W. Cupach & D. Canary (Eds.), *Competence in interpersonal conflict.* New York: McGraw-Hill.

Ting-Toomey, S., Gao, G., Trubisky, P., Yang, Z., Kim, H., Lin, S., & Nishida, T. (1991). Culture, face maintenance, and styles of handling conflict. *International Journal of Conflict Management, 2,* 275–296.

Ting-Toomey, S., & Korzenny, F. (Eds.). (1989). *Language, communication, and culture.* Newbury Park, CA: Sage.

Ting-Toomey, S., & Oetzel, J. (2001a). Cross-cultural face concerns and conflict styles. In W. B. Gudykunst & B. Mody (Eds.), *Handbook of international and intercultural communication.* Thousand Oaks, CA: Sage.

Ting-Toomey, S., & Oetzel, J. (2001b). *Managing intercultural conflict effectively.* Thousand Oaks, CA: Sage.

Ting-Toomey, S., Trubisky, P., & Nishida, T. (1989). *An analysis of conflict styles in Japan and the United States.* Paper presented at the Speech Communication Association convention.

Ting-Toomey, S., Yee-Jung, K., Shapiro, R., Garcia, W., Wright, T., & Oetzel, J. (2000). Cultural/ethnic identity salience and conflict styles. *International Journal of Intercultural Relations, 23,* 47–81.

Tiryakian, E. A. (1973). Perspectives on the stranger. In S. TeSelle (Ed.), *The rediscovery of ethnicity.* New York: Harper & Row.

de Tocqueville, A. (1945). *Democracy in America.* New York: Knopf.

Toffler, A. (1980). *The third wave.* New York: Bantam Books.

Tominaga, J., Gudykunst, W. B., & Ota, H. (2002). Perceptions of effective communication in the United States and Japan. Manuscript submitted for publication, California State University, Fullerton.

Torbiorn, I. (1982). *Living abroad.* New York: Wiley.

Trager, G. L., & Hall, E. T. (1954). Culture and communication. *Explorations, 3,* 137–149.

Trew, K. (1986). Catholic-Protestant conflict in Northern Ireland. In M. Hewstone & R. Brown (Eds.), *Contact and conflict in intergroup encounters.* Oxford, UK: Blackwell.

Triandis, H. C. (1964). Cultural influences upon cognitive processes. In L. Berkowitz (Ed.), *Advances in experimental social psychology* (Vol. 1). New York: Academic Press.

Triandis, H. C. (1967). Interpersonal relations in international organizations. *Journal of Organizational Behavior and Human Performance, 7,* 316–328.

Triandis, H. C. (1972). *The analysis of subjective culture.* New York: Wiley.

Triandis, H. C. (1975). Culture training, cognitive complexity and interpersonal attitudes. In R. Brislin, S. Bochner, & W. Lonner (Eds.), *Cross-cultural perspectives on learning.* New York: Wiley.

Triandis, H. C. (1977). *Interpersonal behavior.* Monterey, CA: Brooks/Cole.

Triandis, H. C. (1980). Values, attitudes, and interpersonal behavior. In M. Page (Ed.), *Nebraska symposium on motivation* (Vol. 27). Lincoln: University of Nebraska Press.

Triandis, H. C. (1983). Essentials of studying culture. In D. Landis & R. Brislin (Eds.), *Handbook of intercultural training* (Vol. 1). Elmsford, NY: Pergamon.

Triandis, H. C. (1984). A theoretical framework for the more efficient construction of cultural assimilators. *International Journal of Intercultural Relations, 8,* 301–330.

Triandis, H. C. (1988). Collectivism vs. individualism. In G. Verma & C. Bagley (Eds.), *Cross-cultural studies of personality, attitudes, and cognition.* London: Macmillian.

Triandis, H. C. (1989). The self and social behavior in differing cultural contexts. *Psychological Review, 96,* 506–517.

Triandis, H. C. (1990). Cross-cultural studies of individualism-collectivism. In J. Berman (Ed.), *Nebraska symposium on motivation* (Vol. 37). Lincoln: University of Nebraska Press.

Triandis, H. C. (1994). *Culture and social behavior.* New York: McGraw-Hill.

Triandis, H. C. (1995). *Individualism-collectivism.* Boulder, CO: Westview.

Triandis, H. C., Bontempo, R., Villareal, M., Asai, M., & Lucca, N. (1988). Individualism-collectivism: Cross-cultural studies of self-ingroup relationships. *Journal of Personality and Social Psychology, 54,* 323–338.

Triandis, H. C., Brislin, R., & Hui, C. H. (1988). Cross-cultural training acrosss the individualism-collectivism divide. *International Journal of Intercultural Relations, 12,* 269–289.

Triandis, H. C., Leung, K., Villareal, M., & Clack, F. (1985). Allocentric versus idiocentric tendencies. *Journal of Research in Personality, 19,* 395–415.

Triandis, H. C., McCusker, C., & Hui, C. H. (1990). Multimethod probes of individualism and collectivism. *Journal of Personality and Social Psychology, 59,* 1006–1020.

Triandis, H. C., & Trafinow, D. (2001). Culture and its implications for intergroup behavior. In R. Brown & S. Gaertner (Eds.), *Intergroup processes.* Oxford, UK: Blackwell.

Triandis, H. C., & Vassiliou, V. (1972). Interpersonal influence and employee selection in two cultures. *Journal of Applied Psychology, 56,* 140–145.

Triandis, H. C., Vassiliou, V., & Nassiakou, M. (1968). Three cross-cultural studies of subjective culture. *Journal of Personality and Social Psychology, 8* (Monograph Supplement No. 4), 1–42.

Trifonovitch, G. (1977). Culture learning/culture teaching. *Educational Perspectives, 16,* 18–22.

Trilling, L. (1968). *Beyond culture.* New York: Viking.

Trubisky, P., Ting-Toomey, S., & Lin, S. (1991). The influence of individualism-collectivism and self-monitoring on conflict styles. *International Journal of Intercultural Relations, 15,* 65–84.

Trungpa, C. (1973). *Cutting through spiritual materialism.* Boulder: Shambhala.

Tsai, J., & Levenson, R. (1997). Cultural influences on emotional responding: Chinese American and European American dating couples during interpersonal conflict. *Journal of Cross-Cultural Psychology, 28,* 600–625.

Tsang, E. (2001). Adjustment of mainland Chinese academics and students to Singapore. *International Journal of Intercultural Relations, 25,* 347–372.

Tse, D., Francis, J., & Walls, J. (1994). Cultural differences in conducting intra- and intercultural negotiations. *Journal of International Business Studies, 25,* 537–555.

Tseng, W. (1977). Adjustment in intercultural marriage. In W. Tseng, J. McDermott, & T. Maretzki (Eds.), *Adjustment in intercultural marriage.* Honolulu: University of Hawaii Press.

Tuan, M. (1998). *Forever foreigners or honorary whites.* New Brunswick, NJ: Rutgers University Press.

Tucker, M., & Mitchell-Kernan, C. (1995). Social structure and psychological correlates of interethnic dating. *Journal of Social and Personal Relationships, 12,* 341–361.

Turnbull, C. (1961). *The forest people.* New York: Simon & Schuster.

Turner, J. C. (1982). Towards a cognitive redefinition of the social group. In H. Tajfel (Ed.), *Social identity and intergroup relations.* Cambridge, England: Cambridge University Press.

Turner, J. C. (1987). *Rediscovering the social group.* Oxford: Blackwell.

Turner, J. H. (1987). Toward a sociological theory of motivation. *American Sociological Review, 52,* 15–27.

Turner, J. H. (1988). *A theory of social interaction.* Stanford, CA: Stanford University Press.

Turner, R. H. (1987). Articulating self and social structure. In K. Yardley & T. Honess (Eds.), *Self and society.* Chichester, UK: Wiley.

Tyler, T., Boeckmann, R., Smith, H., & Huo, Y. (1997). *Social justice in a diverse society.* Boulder, CO: Westview.

Tyler, T., & Lind, E. (1992). A relational model of authority in groups. In M. Zanna (Ed.), *Advances in experimental social psychology* (Vol. 25). New York: Academic Press.

Tyler, T., Lind, E., Ohbuchi, K., Sugawara, I., & Huo, Y. (1998). Conflict with outsiders. *Personality and Social Psychology Bulletin, 24,* 137–146.

Tyrwhitt, J. (1960). The moving eye. In E. Carpenter & M. McLuhan (Eds.), *Explorations in communication.* Boston: Beacon.

Tzeng, O., & Jackson, J. (1994). Effects of contact, conflict, and social identity on intergroup hostilities. *International Journal of Intercultural Relations, 18,* 259–276.

Uehara, A. (1986). The nature of American student reentry adjustment and perceptions of sojourn experience. *International Journal of Intercultural Relations, 10,* 415–438.

Ury, W., Brett, J., & Goldberg, S. (1988). *Getting disputes resolved.* San Francisco: Jossey-Bass.

U.S. Bureau of the Census. (1992). Marital status and living arrangements: March 1991. *Current Population Reports,* Series P–20, No. 461.

U.S. Bureau of the Census. (1997). *Interracial marriages.* Washington, DC: U.S. Government Printing Office.

Van den Berghe, P. L. (1971). The benign quota. *The American Sociologist, 6,* 40–43.

Vander Zanden, J. W. (1965). *Sociology: A systematic approach.* New York: Ronald Press.

Van Dijk, T. (1984). *Prejudice in discourse.* Amsterdam: Benjamins.

Van Oudenhoven, J., & Eisses, A. (1998). Integration and assimilation of Moroccan immigrants in Israel and the Netherlands. *International Journal of Intercultural Relations, 22,* 293–307.

Varonis, E., & Gass, S. (1985). Nonnative/native conversations. *Applied Linguistics, 6,* 71–90.

Vassiliou, V., Triandis, H., Vassiliou, G., & McGuire, H. (1972). Interpersonal contact and stereotyping. In H. Triandis, *The analysis of subjective culture.* New York: Wiley.

Verbrugge, L. M. (1977). The structure of adult friendship choices. *Social Forces, 56,* 576–597.

Verkuyten, M., deJung, W., & Masson, K. (1994). Racial discourse, attitude, and rhetorical maneuvers. *Journal of Language and Social Psychology, 13,* 278–298.

Verkuyten, M., & Hagendoorn, L. (1998). Prejudice and categorization. *Personality and Social Psychology, 24,* 99–110.

Vignoles, V., Chryssouchooou, X., & Breakwell, G. (2000). The distinctiveness principle. *Personality and Social Psychology Review, 4,* 337–354.

Vlastos, G. (1991). *Socrates, ironist and moral philosopher.* Ithica, NY: Cornell University Press.

Volkan, V. (1993). Immigrants and refugees. *Mind & Human Interaction, 4,* 63–69.

VonHippel, W., Sekaquaptewa, D., & Vargas, P. (1995). On the role of the encoding process in stereotype maintenance. In M. Zanna (Ed.), *Advances in experimental social psychology* (Vol. 27). New York: Academic Press.

Vorauer, J., & Kurnhyr, S. (2001). Is this about me or you? *Personality and Social Psychology Bulletin, 27,* 706–719.

Walbott, H., & Scherer, K. (1986). How universal and specific is emotional experience? *Social Science Information, 25,* 763–796.

Waley, A. (Trans.). (1938). *The analects of Confucius.* New York: Vintage Books.

Walker, D. (1993). *The role of the mass media in the adaptation of Haitian immigrants in Miami.* Doctoral dissertation, Indiana University.

Wallace, A. (1952). Individual differences and cultural uniformities. *American Sociological Review, 17,* 747–750.

Wallach, M. A. (1959). The influence of classification requirements on gradients of response. *Psychological Monographs, 73,* 478.

Walsh, J. E. (1973). *Intercultural education in the community of man.* Honolulu: University of Hawaii Press.

Walsh, J. E. (1979). *Humanistic culture learning.* Honolulu: University of Hawaii Press.

Wang, M. (1997). Reentry and reverse culture shock. In K. Cushner & R. Brislin (Eds.), *Improving intercultural interactions: Modules for cross-cultural training programs.* Thousand Oaks, CA; Sage.

Ward, C., & Chang, W. (1997). "Cultural fit": A new perspective on personality and sojourner adjustment. *International Journal of Intercultural Relations, 21,* 525–533.

Ward, C., & Kennedy, A. (1994). Acculturation strategies, psychological adjustment, and sociocultural competence during cross-cultural transition. *International Journal of Intercultural Relations, 18,* 329–343.

Ward, C., Okura, Y., Kennedy, A., & Kojima, T. (1998). The U-curve on trial. *International Journal of Intercultural Relations, 22,* 277–291.

Waterman, A. (1984). *The psychology of individualism.* New York: Praeger.

Waters, M. (1990). *Ethnic options.* Berkeley: University of California Press.

Watson, J., & Lippitt, R. (1955). *Learning across cultures.* Ann Arbor: University of Michigan.

Watson, O. M., & Graves, T. (1966). Quantitative research in proxemic behavior. *American Anthropologist, 68,* 971–985.

Watson, O. M. (1970). *Proxemic behavior: A cross-cultural study.* The Hague: Mouton.

Watters, E. (1995, September 17). Claude Steele has scores to settle. *New York Times Magazine,* pp. 45–47.

Watts, A. (1966). *The book: On the taboo against knowing who you are.* New York: Pantheon.

Watzlawick, P., Beavin, J., & Jackson, D. (1967). *The pragmatics of human communication.* New York: Norton.

Wegner, D., & Vallacher, R. (1977). *Implicit psychology.* New York: Oxford University Press.

Wei, A. (1980). *Cultural variations in perception.* Paper presented at the 6th annual Third World Conference.

Weick, K. (1979). *The social psychology of organizing* (2nd ed.). Reading, MA: Addison-Wesley.

Weiner-Davis, M. (1992). *Divorce busting.* New York: Summit Books.

Weinstock, A. (1964). Some factors that retard or accelerate the rate of acculturation. *Human Relations, 17,* 321–340.

Weiss, W. (1970). Selective acculturation and the dating process. *Journal of Marriage and the Family, 32,* 273–278.

Weldon, E., Jehn, K., Chan, X., & Wang, Z. (1996). *Conflict management in U.S.-Chinese joint ventures.* Paper presented at the Academy of Management convention.

Welkowitz, J., Bond, R., & Feldstein, S. (1984). Conversational time patterns of Hawaiian children as a function of ethnicity and gender. *Language and Speech, 27,* 173–191.

Wellman, B. (1992). Which types of ties and networks provide what kinds of social support? *Advances in Group Processes, 17*(2), 28–45.

Wen, K. (1976). Theories of migration and mental health. *Social Science and Medicine, 10,* 297–306.

Wendt, J. (undated). Description, interpretation and evaluation. Unpublished paper, Department of Speech Communication, University of Minnesota.

Werner, H. (1957). The concept of development from a comparative and organismic point of view. In D. Harris (Ed.), *The concept of development.* Minneapolis: University of Minnesota Press.

Westin, A. (1970). *Privacy and freedom.* New York: Atheneum.

Wetherall, M. (1982). Cross-cultural studies of minimal groups. In H. Tajfel (Ed.), *Social identity and intergroup relations.* Cambridge, England: Cambridge University Press.

Wheeler, L., & Kim, Y. (1997). What is beautiful is culturally good. *Personality and Social Psychology Bulletin, 23,* 795–800.

Wheeler, L., Reis, H., & Bond, M. (1989). Collectivism-individualism in everyday social life. *Journal of Personality and Social Psychology, 57,* 79–86.

White, S. (1989). Back channels across cultures. *Language in Society, 18,* 59–76.

Whorf, B. (1952). *Collected papers on metalinguistics.* Washington, DC: Department of State Foreign Service Institute.

Whorf, B. L. (1956). *Language, thought, and reality.* New York: Wiley.

Whorf, B. L. (1968). An American Indian model of the universe. In P. Gleeson & N. Wakefield (Eds.), *Language and culture*. Columbus, OH: Charles E. Merrill.

Wiemann, J. (1985). Interpersonal control and regulation in conversation. In R. Street & J. Cappella (Eds.), *Sequence and pattern in communicative behavior*. London: Edward Arnold.

Wiemann, J., & Backlund, P. (1980). Current theory and research in communication competence. *Review of Educational Research, 50,* 185–199.

Wiemann, J., & Bradac, J. (1989). Metatheoretical issues in the study of communicative competence. In B. Dervin (Ed.), *Progress in communication science* (Vol. 9). Norwood, NJ: Ablex.

Wiemann, J., Chen, V., & Giles, H. (1986). *Beliefs about talk and silence in cultural context*. Paper presented at the Speech Communication Association convention.

Wiemann, J., & Kelly, C. (1981). Pragmatics of interpersonal competence. In C. Wilder-Mott & J. Weaklund (Eds.), *Rigor and imagination*. New York: Praeger.

Wilder, D. (1993). The role of anxiety in facilitating stereotypic judgment of outgroup behavior. In D. Mackie & D. Hamilton (Eds.), *Affect, cognition, and stereotyping*. New York: Academic Press.

Wilder, D., & Shapiro, P. (1989). Effects of anxiety on impression formation in a group context. *Journal of Experimental Social Psychology, 25,* 481–499.

Wilder, D., & Shapiro, P. (1991). Facilitation of outgroup stereotypes by enhanced ingroup identity. *Journal of Experimental Social Psychology, 27,* 431–452.

Wilder, D., & Simon, A. (1996). Incidental and integral affect as types of stereotyping. In R. Sorrentino & E. T. Higgins (Eds.), *Handbook of motivation and cognition* (Vol. 3). New York: Guilford.

Williams, A., & Nussbaum, J. (2001). *Intergenerational communication across the lifespan*. Mahwah, NJ: Erlbaum.

Williams, A., Ota, H., Giles, H., Pierson, H., Gallois, C., Ng, S., Lim, T.S., Ryan, E., Somera, L., Maher, J., Cai, D., & Harwood, J. (1997). Young people's beliefs about intergenerational communication. *Communication Research, 24,* 370–393.

Williams, C., & Westmeyer, J. (1986). Psychiatric problems among adolescent Asian refugees. *Pacific/Asian Mental Health Research Center Newsletter, 4*(3/4), 22–24.

Williams, J. (1984). Gender and intergroup behavior. *British Journal of Social Psychology, 23,* 311–316.

Williams, R. M. (1947). *The reduction of intergroup tensions*. New York: Social Science Research Council.

Williams, R. M. (1974). *Strangers next door: Ethnic relations in American communities*. Englewood Cliffs, NJ: Prentice-Hall.

Williams, T., & Sogon, S. (1984). *Nihonjin daigakusei niokeru shudankeisei to tekio kodo* (Group composition and conforming behavior in Japanese students). *Nihon Shinrigaku Kenkyu* (Japanese Psychological Research), *126,* 231–234.

Wilmont, W. (1980). *Dyadic communication* (2nd ed.), Reading, MA: Addison-Wesley.

Wilson, A. (1985). Returned exchange students. *International Journal of Intercultural Relations, 9,* 285–304.

Wilson, S., Cai, D., & Drake, L. (1995). *Culture in context*. Paper presented at the Academy of Management convention.

Wirth, L. (1945). The problem of minority groups. In R. Linton (Ed.), *The science of man in the world crisis*. New York: Columbia University Press.

Wiseman, R., & Abe, H. (1986). Cognitive complexity and intercultural effectiveness. In M. McLaughlin (Ed.), *Communication yearbook 9*. Beverly Hills, CA: Sage.

Wish, M., Deutsch, M., & Kaplan, S. (1976). Perceived dimensions of interpersonal relations. *Journal of Personality and Social Psychology, 33,* 409–421.

Witkin, H. A., & Berry, J. (1975). Psychological differentiation in cross-cultural perspective. *Journal of Cross-Cultural Psychology, 6,* 4–87.

Witkin, H. A., Dyk, R. B., Faterson, H. F., Goodenough, D. R., & Karp, S. A. (1962). *Psychological differentiation*. New York: Wiley.

Witkin, H. A., Lewis, H. B., Hertzman, M., Machover, K., Missner, P., & Wapner, S. (1954). *Personality through perception*. New York: Harper & Row.

Wolfe, A. (1998). *One nation, after all*. New York: Viking.

Wolfgang, A., & Weiss, D. (1980). Locus of control and social distance: Comparison of Canadian and West Indian-born students. *International Journal of Intercultural Relations, 4,* 295–305.

Wolken, G., Moriwaki, S., & Williams, K. (1973). Race and social class as factors in the orientation toward psychotherapy. *Journal of Counseling Psychology, 20,* 312–316.

Wong-Rieger, D. (1984). *Testing a model of emotional and coping responses to problems in adaptation*. Paper presented at Society for Intercultural Education, Training, and Research conference.

Wood, M. M. (1934). *The stranger: A study in social relationships*. New York: Columbia University Press.

Worchel, S., & Norwell, N. (1980). Effect of perceived environmental conditions during co-operation on intergroup attraction. *Journal of Personality and Social Psychology, 38,* 764–772.

Word, C., Zanna, M., & Cooper, J. (1974). The nonverbal mediation of self-fulfilling prophecies. *Journal of Experimental Social Psychology, 10,* 109–120.

Wright, P. H. (1978). Toward a theory of friendship based upon a conception of self. *Human Communication Research, 4,* 196–207.

Wrightsman, L. (1994). *Adult personality development* (Vol. 1). Thousand Oaks, CA: Sage.

Wuthnow, R. (1991). *Acts of compassion.* Princeton: Princeton University Press.

Wuthnow, R. (1994). *Sharing the journey: Support groups and America's new quest for community.* New York: Free Press.

Wuthnow, R. (1998). *Loose connections: Joining together in America's fragmented communities.* Cambridge, MA: Harvard University Press.

Yamada, A., & Singelis, T. (1999). Biculturalism and self construals. *International Journal of Intercultural Relations, 23,* 697–709.

Yamada, H. (1990). Topic management and turn distributions in business meetings. *Text, 10,* 271–295.

Yamaguchi, S. (1994). Collectivism among the Japanese. In U. Kim, H. Triandis, C. Kagitcibasi, S. Choi, & G. Yoon (Eds.), *Individualism and collectivism.* Thousand Oaks, CA: Sage.

Yamaguchi, S., Kuhlman, D., & Sugimori, S. (1995). Personality correlates of allocentric tendencies in individualistic and collectivistic cultures. *Journal of Cross-Cultural Psychology, 26,* 658–672.

Yang, S. (1988). *The role of mass media in immigrants' political socialization.* Doctoral dissertation, Stanford University, Stanford, CA.

Yankelovich, D. (1981). *New rules.* New York: Random House.

Ybarra, O., & Trafimow, D. (1998). How priming the private self or collective self affects the relative weights of attitudes and subjective norms. *Personality and Social Psychology Bulletin, 24,* 362–370.

Yeh, C., & Hwang, K. (1996). The collective nature of ethnic identity development among Asian American college students. *Adolescence, 31,* 645–661.

Yik, M., Bond, M., & Paulhus, D. (1998). Do Chinese self-enhance or self-efface? *Personality and Social Psychology Bulletin, 24,* 399–406.

Ying, Y., & Liese, L. (1991). Emotional well-being of Taiwan students in the U.S. *International Journal of Intercultural Relations, 15,* 345–366.

Yinger, M. J. (1960). Contraculture and subculture. *American Sociological Review, 25,* 625–635.

Yinger, M. J. (1994). *Ethnicity.* Albany: State University of New York Press.

Yoshikawa, M. (1978). Some Japanese and American cultural characteristics. In M. Prosser, *The cultural dialogue.* Boston: Houghton Mifflin.

Yoshikawa, M. (1988). Cross-cultural adaptation and perceptual development. In Y. Kim & W. Gudykunst (Eds.), *Cross-cultural adaptation.* Newbury Park, CA: Sage.

Young, L., Giles, H., & Pierson, H. (1986). Sociopolitical change and perceived vitality. *International Journal of Intercultural Relations, 10,* 459–469.

Yuki, M., & Brewer, M. (1999). *Japanese collectivism versus American collectivism: A comparison of group-loyalty across cultures.* Paper presented at the Asian Social Psychology Association conference.

Yum, J. O. (1982). Communication diversity and information acquisition among Korean immigrants in Hawaii. *Human Communication Research, 8,* 154–169.

Yum, J. O. (1988a). Locus of control and communication patterns of immigrants. In Y. Kim & W. Gudykunst (Eds.), *Cross-cultural adaptation.* Newbury Park, CA: Sage.

Yum, J. O. (1988b). The impact of Confucianism in interpersonal relationships and communication in East Asia. *Communication Monographs, 55,* 374–388.

Yum, J. O. (1988c). Network theory in intercultural communication. In Y. Y. Kim & W. B. Gudykunst (Eds.), *Theories of intercultural communication.* Newbury Park, CA: Sage.

Zaharna, R. (1989). Self-shock. *International Journal of Intercultural Relations, 13,* 501–525.

Zajonic, R. (1952). Aggressive attitudes of the "stranger" as a function of conformity pressures. *Human Relations, 5,* 205–216.

Zajonic, R. (1980). Feeling and thinking. *American Psychologist, 35,* 151–175.

Zavalloni, M. (1980). Values. In H. Triandis & R. Brislin (Eds.), *Handbook of cross-cultural psychology* (Vol. 5). Boston: Allyn and Bacon.

Zax, M., & Takahashi, S. (1967). Cultural influences on response style. *Journal of Social Psychology, 71,* 3–10.

Zentella, A. (1985). The fate of Spanish in the United States. In N. Wolfson & J. Manes (Eds.), *Language of inequality.* New York: Mouton.

Zerubavel, E. (1991). *The fine line.* New York: Free Press.

Zoglin, R. (1993, June 21). All you need is hate. *Time,* p. 63.

Zurcher, L. (1968). Particularism and organizational position: A cross-cultural analysis. *Journal of Applied Psychology, 52,* 139–144.

Zweigenhaft, R. L. (1979–1980). American Jews: In or out of the upper class? *Insurgent Sociologist, 9,* 24–37.

INDEX